GORBACHEV

GORBACHEV

MAN OF THE
TWENTIETH CENTURY?

MARK SANDLE

HODDER
EDUCATION
PART OF HACHETTE LIVRE UK

First published in Great Britain in 2008 by
Hodder Education, part of Hachette Livre UK,
338 Euston Road, London NW1 3BH

www.hoddereducation.com

Hachette Livre UK's policy is to use papers that are natural, renewable and
recyclable products and made from wood grown in sustainable forests.
The logging and manufacturing processes are expected to conform to the
environmental regulations of the country of origin.

The advice and information in this book are believed to be true and
accurate at the date of going to press, but neither the author nor the publisher
can accept any legal responsibility or liability for any errors or omissions.

British Library Cataloguing in Publication Data
A catalogue record for this book is available from the British Library

Library of Congress Cataloging-in-Publication Data
A catalog record for this book is available from the Library of Congress

ISBN 978 0340 76159 5

10 9 8 7 6 5 4 3 2 1

Typeset in 10.5 on 12.5 Garamond by Phoenix Photosetting, Chatham, Kent
Printed and bound in Malta

To Ben
In loving memory.

Contents

Acknowledgements

I should like to take this opportunity to thank a few people. First, I should like to thank the AHRC and the Department of History at De Montfort University who supported the writing and research for this book with time away from my normal teaching and administrative duties. I should like to thank my colleagues at DMU for their collegiality and support. I should like to thank those who read and made comments on earlier drafts, although clearly everything that remains is my own work. Thanks then to Chris and to Ed in particular. To Luke, Beth and Caleb: you may even read this one! As ever, I owe an enormous debt to Wit. Only she knows how much she means to me.

I should like to dedicate this particular book to a former student, Ben Anders Lazarus (17 December 1984–20 January 2008), who died tragically just as this book was being completed.

Introduction

The 'problem' of Gorbachev

In search of understanding

Question: What do the following have in common? Nikita Khrushchev; Vladimir Ilych Lenin; Alexander II; Martin Luther; Pope John Paul II; Sisyphus; Anwar Sadat; Moses; John F. Kennedy; F. W. de Klerk; Franklin D. Roosevelt; Otto von Bismarck and Napoleon Bonaparte?

Answer: Of themselves, nothing. Yet they have all been linked to one man: Mikhail Sergeevich Gorbachev. All of the figures above were deployed by scholars, journalists and commentators in an attempt to understand the personality, actions, intentions, likely outcomes and legacy of Mikhail Gorbachev during the period 1985–91. This dazzling array of historical figures that was used to try to explain and comprehend what Gorbachev was up to provides the first inkling that Mikhail Gorbachev was (and still is) something of a problem for analysts.

Further clues as to the nature of this problem are provided when we begin to list the different ways in which he has been appraised. At various times, he has been described as:

- the man who changed the world;
- the man who ended the Cold War;
- the 'great liberator' of Eastern Europe who brought down the Berlin Wall;
- a bungling despot;
- a confused Leninist;
- the 'crocodile that ate Russia';
- a democratic dictator;
- the Man of the Twentieth Century;
- a glorious failure;
- a flawed visionary;
- an idealist;
- a reform communist;
- a social democrat;
- a closet capitalist;
- a tragic hero.

Gorbachev has been the subject of all of these conflicting interpretations, evaluations and assessments, and more. He has attracted adoration and vitriol, respect and scorn, sympathy and indifference. Perhaps the greatest example of the deeply contested views of Gorbachev was the different receptions accorded to Gorbachev in the East and in the West. In the West, Gorbachev appeared as a quasi-messianic, heroic figure. In the East, he came, over time, to be seen as a failure and a traitor, scorned and reviled in equal measure.[1] The scale and extent of the disputes about Gorbachev are bewildering. This is not to say that Gorbachev is in some qualitative sense a more contested or disputed individual than other key historical figures, but assessing and evaluating him is a deeply problematic exercise. If we want to get to grips with who Gorbachev was, what he was doing and what he achieved, then it is essential not just to examine him and his record, but also to try and understand why he was and is such a contested figure.

To get to the heart of this requires us to explore the dimensions of the Gorbachev 'problem'. The immediate obstacle that one confronts in this regard is that Gorbachev appears to be an enigmatic, paradoxical, ambiguous figure. This is highlighted by those appraisals listed above, especially the 'Gorbachev as both Luther and Pope' epitaph. But as we delve deeper into 'Gorbachev', then more and more puzzles, ambiguities and paradoxes appear. These are of a number of different orders.

The first layer of problems relates to Gorbachev himself: his character, his background, his values. Despite everything that we have read and heard about Gorbachev, he still appears to be relatively unknown. The glimpses into his character from his time as leader, from colleagues, confidantes and rivals, only serve to muddy the waters further. What type of person was he? What type of leader was he? Was he an emotional person, or a cold person? Were his instincts democratic or dictatorial? Was he a strong character, or a weak character? Was he a man of great intellect? The mystery deepens when we consider how it was that the Soviet system could produce someone like Gorbachev. Was he a provincial politician made good? A convinced communist who expediently espoused the value of democracy? Or was he a closet social democrat who cast off his communist mask when circumstances allowed him to do so? How could someone with those views possibly emerge from within the ranks of the Communist Party? Gorbachev as a person and as a leader proved to be something of an enigma.

A second layer of problems lies in the nature of his project: *perestroika*. This was a programme riddled with ambiguities, paradoxes and tensions. It had no clearly spelt out aims, changed and evolved and was interrupted before it could run its course. Gorbachev's intentions were thus a matter of great debate. Gorbachev's leadership has also come under scrutiny. Was he a typical, if radical Soviet leader? Or was he a leader of a new type? Did he react to situations that arose, or was he a visionary leader?

This was compounded by the specific ambiguities of *perestroika* as a project. *Perestroika* sought to do the following:

- transform the communist system, while maintaining the Communist Party in power;

- proclaim a policy of openness, yet continued to restrict openness and maintain secrecy;
- combine democracy and a one-party state;
- introduce limited, socialist pluralism.[2]

The 'interruption' of *perestroika* by the August coup of 1991 meant that it remained an unfinished project, clouding the waters even further. What would have happened if it had been allowed to run its course? In what direction was the USSR moving? Was *perestroika* unravelling? Or was it moving into a new phase? *Perestroika* – the project intimately connected to Gorbachev and his leadership – was both in general and specific terms highly ambiguous.

Finally, a third layer of problems lies in the achievements and legacy of Gorbachev. On the basis of six highly charged and momentous years in power, how should Gorbachev be assessed? As he was removed from power before he could complete his project, did he fail *or* succeed? Did he fail *and* succeed? Did he succeed because he failed? Or fail because he succeeded? How will history remember him? Was he a liberator, a democrat, a reformer who freed the world from the fear of nuclear destruction, and freed the peoples of Eastern Europe, Russia, the Baltics, the Caucasus and Central Asia from communist rule? Or was he the person who destroyed communism and put nothing in its place, condemning the Russian people to years of poverty and hardship and the world to a new era of instability and ethnically driven conflict?

These aspects – enigmatic personality and background, paradoxical project and ambiguous legacy and achievements – are the raw material out of which the deeply contested interpretations and evaluations of Gorbachev have arisen. The existence of these ambiguities and tensions at the heart of Gorbachev's character, background, leadership, programme and achievements created a situation which generated a variety of interpretations. The thrust of this work is to analyse these dimensions of the Gorbachev 'problem': his background, upbringing, personality, intentions, reception, achievements and legacy. Each chapter will explore one aspect of this problem.

The 'problem' of interpreting Gorbachev, however, lies not only in the complexity, ambiguity and enigmatic nature of Gorbachev and his project, but also in the context, values and perspectives of those who set out to interpret him. The interpretative context contained a number of dimensions: ideological, national-cultural, academic, political and personal:

- *Ideological*: Gorbachev was in power at the height of the Cold War of the 1980s between the USA and the USSR. This profoundly shaped the intellectual, cultural and media climate of interpretation and evaluation.
- *National-cultural:* the geographical and cultural perspectives again had a profound influence on judgements on Gorbachev.
- *The academic aspect*: academic writing on Gorbachev was driven by the deep ideological and professional cleavages in the Sovietological community which coloured the views of Gorbachev that emerged.

- *Political factors*: the judgements in Russia on Gorbachev after 1991 have to be understood against the backdrop of the struggle for power in post-communist Russia. Although Gorbachev had left power, his legacy and achievements continued to impinge on the politics of the new Russia.
- *Personal:* the explosion of memoir material in the aftermath of the collapse of communism has also been a key factor in determining the interpretations of Gorbachev.

This book, then, is not a biography of Gorbachev, nor a detailed treatment of the policies of *perestroika*, nor an appraisal of his role in the transformation and demise of communism or his role in the ending of the Cold War. All these works, and many more, have been done, and done in many cases extremely well elsewhere.[3] This work instead will examine the different ways in which Gorbachev was described, interpreted, evaluated and assessed by different constituencies – historians, journalists, politicians, political scientists and public opinion – as well as the influence of Gorbachev himself. It will assess the way Gorbachev's reputation and interpretation changed over time, contrasting Gorbachev in power with Gorbachev out of power. It is a study of Gorbachev, and at the same time a study of the fashioning and refashioning of an historical reputation and an assessment of the way that historical figures are used, described, deployed and interpreted by different constituencies.

By adopting this approach it is possible to do two things. First, to try and answer some of the key questions about Gorbachev: what was he trying to do? What sort of leader was he? In what areas was he most successful? Why did he fail? How will history look back on him? In doing so it will seek to evaluate the place of Gorbachev in the history of the twentieth century. Second, by placing the changing reputation and interpretations of Gorbachev in their geographical, chronological, international, political and historiographical contexts this book will decipher and illustrate the ways in which historical interpretations are constructed, manipulated and used.

The structure of the book is as follows. Each chapter examines a different problem relating to Gorbachev. Chapter 1 examines the problem of Gorbachev's origins and background and seeks to answer the question: how could the Soviet system produce someone like Gorbachev? Chapter 2 explores the way Gorbachev's own thinking developed, examining his speeches and writings to construct a picture of the way that Gorbachev sought to describe himself and his programme. In a detailed examination of Gorbachev's public rhetoric, this chapter attempts to piece together Gorbachev's own unfolding view on *perestroika*, his self-image as a leader and his understanding of what he was doing. The following two chapters explore the problem of the differential reception Gorbachev was accorded in the West and the East. The media (in both East and West) will be used to try and unpack how far it is true to say that Gorbachev was fêted in the West and hated in the East, and how we might account for this differential reception. The chapter on the Western media (Chapter 3) examines a variety of different sources – British and American, dailies and weeklies – to look at the way that Gorbachev was represented and portrayed. This serves as a means of contrast with Soviet press appraisals. The chapter on Soviet perspectives (Chapter 4) contrasts the official view constructed by the Soviet propaganda apparatus with the emergence of more critical perspectives under the impact of *glasnost'*.

A key element in the understanding of Gorbachev relates to his personality, character and *modus operandi* as leader. Chapter 5 uses a variety of memoirs – Western and Russian, colleagues and enemies, foreign politicians and diplomats – to try and give some insights into Gorbachev the man. There then follows a chapter which analyses and synthesizes academic appraisals of Gorbachev, which examine the debates and disagreements on a number of key issues:

- the nature of Gorbachev's programme – reform? Revolution? Democratization? Liberalization?
- the nature of Gorbachev's leadership;
- the question of whether Gorbachev had a clear strategy;
- a balance sheet of Gorbachev's successes and failures.

The final chapter reflects on Gorbachev's own memoirs, and his attempts to shape the collective memory of *perestroika* and his life and times in office. The conclusion seeks to appraise the significance of Gorbachev in the *longue durée* of global history in the twentieth century.

Before we turn to an examination of these different problems in appraising Gorbachev, there follows a brief synopsis of Gorbachev in power, which will provide a concise summary for the chapters that follow.

Gorbachev in power: a concise overview

Gorbachev: the first phase, 1985–7

Gorbachev started his period in office with attempts to reinvigorate the economy, to overhaul personnel, reduce corruption, ill-discipline and bureaucracy, and to increase the working performance of the population. He instituted a rapid overhaul of personnel within the party-state hierarchy, aided by the 27th Congress of the Communist Party of the Soviet Union (CPSU) which allowed a substantial reshuffle of officials, enabling Gorbachev to promote his supporters and remove those who might oppose what he was doing. In the field of economics, Gorbachev set out his aim in April 1985 as 'acceleration [*uskorenie*] of socio-economic development': to restore dynamism to the Soviet economy by increasing both the quantity of output (growth rates and productivity) and the quality of output (relying on the application of science and technology to the productive process). This was to be prefigured by a series of campaigns to bring about short-term improvements; campaigns to reduce alcohol consumption, improve workplace performance, reduce bureaucratic interference and generally get people to work harder, more responsibly, more independently and so bring about some immediate improvements in the lives of the people.

After the 27th Congress, Gorbachev set out a further set of policies, broadening the scope of the programme he had embarked upon. Gradually the concept of *uskorenie* was supplanted by the concepts of *perestroika* (restructuring, reconstruction, reorganization) and *glasnost'* (openness, public disclosure, publicity). It was not all plain sailing. In particular, the nuclear explosion at Chernobyl in April 1986 and the subsequent botched handling of the affair did serious damage to Gorbachev's reputation abroad, not withstanding the appalling damage done to the health of the people who lived and worked in the surrounding region. The programme during 1986 shifted towards the generation of a more open, critical media and cultural life (partly derived from the experience of Chernobyl) alongside discussions of ways to restructure the organization and functioning of the centrally planned economy.

The radical phase, 1987–9

The point at which there was a change of gear in Gorbachev's programme came at the end of 1986/beginning of 1987. It was heralded by the release from exile of the famous dissident scientist and human rights campaigner Andrei Sakharov. His return to public life signalled a new approach on the part of the leadership, which was more tolerant (to a degree), open to the ideas of others (officially approved) and willing to countenance (some) criticism. Or it was a PR stunt, designed for Western consumption, depending upon who you read. This was followed by a stormy and controversial plenary meeting of the CPSU Central Committee (CC) in January 1987. This, Gorbachev was later to reveal, was a thrice postponed meeting, owing to the controversial nature of the subject matter. Gorbachev announced the first steps along the road of *political reform,* something that had previously been absent from Gorbachev's pronouncements. Steps were introduced to democratize the inner workings of the Communist Party (secret ballots for party posts and competitive elections) as well as multi-candidate elections for delegates to the Soviets (i.e. in a constituency with 7 posts, there could be 9, 10, 11, etc. candidates). There was no talk (at this point) of political pluralism, or a multiparty system, or even of reforms to the institutional architecture of the state. At the end of his speech, Gorbachev also announced the convocation of a special party body – the Party conference – in June 1988, which would consider further proposals to democratize the work of the party and the life of society as a whole.[4]

These political reform measures were combined with new legislation addressing the economy. The first moves were made in November 1986 when a law was introduced which legalized individual labour activity. This was a controversial step, as it seemed to be permitting private enterprise, a taboo which had been abolished in the USSR and something that smacked of capitalism. This was followed in June 1987 by the publication of the Law on the State Enterprise, which reformed the way in which all enterprises, trusts and factories in the economy operated. This included measures to democratize the running of the enterprise, including measures to elect factory directors. The following month a series of decrees – covering all aspects of the economic life of the country, finances, pricing, planning social policy, republican relationships, science and technology – were elaborated. Overall, the measures in 1987 were designed to provide more autonomy for enterprises to take decisions on an economic basis, to devolve more power to the republics rather than the centre, to streamline the economic bureaucracy at the centre to prevent the bureaucrats from strangling the reform measures in a flurry of red tape. The package was drawn together under the umbrella concept of *khozraschet*: cost accounting or profit-loss accounting. Enterprises were supposed to become independent of the state, and to be run on economic principles. Just over a year later came the Law on Co-operatives of May 1988, which allowed small groups of people to join together and provide commodities, services, etc. to the general population (again deeply unpopular).

These political and economic measures took place alongside continued cultural liberalization and experimentation. History began to be opened up to scrutiny. Films, plays and novels were published which were much more critical, hard-hitting and controversial. The media – print and visual – gradually became more outspoken and daring in its views. The first inklings of opposition began to be discerned. Within the party, radical (coalescing around Yeltsin) and conservative (coalescing around Ligachev) groupings began to organize. Within society, more critics began to speak up. In April 1988, *perestroika* was subject to a withering critique from the conservative chemistry teacher from Leningrad, Nina Andreeva.[5] Nationalists, particularly from the Baltics, began to push for greater powers for their republics. Ethnic strife broke out in Nagorno-Karabakh.[6]

This was a time of great change, culminating in the stormy 19th CPSU conference of June 1988. Amidst surprisingly open debates and discussions, plans for a new political structure emerged. The publication of the party's theses outlined plans for a new legislative structure, incorporating a new parliament (Congress of People's Deputies) elected on a nationwide, competitive franchise (although with only one party, and with guaranteed seats for selected groups and agencies: Communist Party, trade unions, Academy of Sciences, etc.). This Congress would then elect a full-time working parliament (meaning that the precise composition of the day-to-day legislature was only indirectly chosen by the people) which would continue to be called the Supreme Soviet. Alongside these institutional innovations, there were a raft of changes to the legal framework of the state, with amendments to the Constitution, a Constitutional Review Committee and moves towards establishing the rule of law. The design seemed to be moving towards a system based on checks and balances and a separation of powers, albeit within a one-party state. This system came into operation in March 1989 with the first elections to the Congress. Profound changes to the Soviet political system had arrived.

Gorbachev abroad, 1985–9

Throughout 1985 and 1986, Gorbachev instantly began to adopt a high profile in international affairs, and to inaugurate sweeping changes to the foreign, security and military affairs personnel and structures. He restructured the control of decision-making in foreign policy, shifting it to the Party Central Committee and away from the Ministry of Foreign Affairs. Gorbachev also did not have a member of the military hierarchy within the Politburo. He took to the global stage and revolutionized popular perceptions of communist leaders. He was young, 'media-friendly' and spoke in a language of conciliation, peace and cooperation. He also favoured bold initiatives, rather than an incremental cautious approach to change. This was exemplified by the announcement in January 1986 when he called for the complete elimination of nuclear arms by the year 2000, starting with an immediate 50 per cent cut in strategic offensive arms. This was followed up at the summit in Reykjavik in October 1986 when Gorbachev proposed to eliminate intercontinental and intermediate nuclear missiles within 10–15 years, provided that the USA renounced its Strategic Defense Initiative (or Star Wars) programme. This summit was one among many (Geneva, November 1985; Reykjavik, October 1986; Washington, December 1987; Moscow, May 1988; Malta, December 1989; Helsinki, September 1990; Moscow, July 1991) between Gorbachev and Reagan, and Gorbachev and Bush. This personal diplomacy between the heads of the two superpowers began with the images of the 'fireside chats' in Geneva. This was a radical break with the past. Finally, Gorbachev's first two years saw gradual shifts in Soviet regional policies. US–Soviet relations remained a priority, of course, but greater attention began to be devoted to the Asia-Pacific region, a rapprochement with China was mooted and Third World commitments began to be scaled down. Gorbachev coined a new phrase to describe the new approach he had ushered in: New Political Thinking (NPT) (*novoe politicheskoe myshlenie*).[7] The only areas where there seemed to be little indication of a change of approach in 1985 and 1986 were in Soviet–East European relations, and in Afghanistan, where Gorbachev stepped up the military pressure during 1986.[8]

Over the next three years, Gorbachev's foreign policies, and his thinking about the world, became increasingly radical. NPT came to represent a major break with previous Soviet thinking. Many cherished beliefs began to fall by the wayside. The essential changes related to the acknowledgement of interdependence – economically and in terms of security. The existence of weapons of global destruction, and the possibility of environmental catastrophe, meant that security was now only possible through mutual action. One 'camp' (capitalist or communist) could no longer triumph over the other. The other key pillar of NPT was the primacy of human values over class or national ones. In an age where the annihilation of the species was possible, any approach which placed the interests of one particular sectional group (class or nation) over the interests of the whole (humanity) was fraught with dangers.[9]

Arising out of this, the Soviet view of the world came to accept the need for tolerance and diversity, for dialogue to solve problems, for political solutions not military ones, for realism not ideology. A flurry of quite startling reassessments flowed from this. The Soviets abandoned their view of the world as being divided into two hostile camps: capitalism and socialism. No longer could the view be sustained that Soviet socialism = 'Good' and capitalism = 'bad'. Diversity in the international arena was to be respected: the relative merits of different systems had to be judged by their ability to protect the basic rights and freedoms of the individual. The implication – that states could choose their own form of government, economy and social system – underpinned Gorbachev's non-intervention in Eastern Europe in 1989, when one by one the Communist Parties were toppled. This was an explicit rejection of the Brezhnev doctrine, elaborated after the invasion of Czechoslovakia in 1968 when it was stated that countries in the socialist bloc had limited sovereignty. Now there was full recognition of the integrity and sovereignty of nation-states.[10]

In specific national security terms, the Soviets moved to a posture that emphasized defence instead of offence ('defensive defence'), that war was unwinnable and so had to be prevented, that security had to be understood mutually, and could best be ensured through political means, not military means. The proliferation of arms was to be reined in through a shift to 'reasonable' or 'defensive' sufficiency (capacity for defence, rather than military capacity for an offensive strike). In strategic and policy terms, this thinking underpinned a radical shift. 1988 saw the start of the withdrawal of troops from Afghanistan, and proposals from Gorbachev when addressing the UN to cut Soviet conventional forces by 500,000 within two years. 1989 witnessed the revolutions in Eastern Europe. 1990 saw the emergence of a unified Germany, probably the most important indication of the commitment to national self-determination and national sovereignty.[11]

Gorbachev: decline and fall, 1989–91

The period between March 1989 and August 1991 was a time of increasing problems for Gorbachev, culminating in the August coup of 1991 which led to the collapse of communist power, and ultimately by the end of the year to the end of the USSR. Opposition to him began to mount from all quarters. National protest at central rule gathered pace. Political opposition of all hues began to speak out: *perestroika* was going too fast or too slow, too left or too right, or was just going in the wrong direction. Prominent, credible alternative political figures came on to the political stage, most notably of course Boris Yeltsin, who rode a rising tide of Russian nationalism to acquire a power base for himself independent of Gorbachev and the CPSU. Economic problems – rising prices, lengthening queues, strikes, shortages – accumulated, and solutions seemed to be non-existent. Popular discontent became more vocal and more critical. In response to these problems, and others, Gorbachev moved in a number of directions. First, he began to accumulate more and more power to himself, and at the same time began to create new patterns of power and authority to enable him to rule outside of the Communist Party structures. Power became personalized in his hands. In May 1989, Gorbachev was elected as chairman of the new Supreme Soviet. This process was deepened by two decisions taken in early 1990. In February Gorbachev persuaded the CC to abandon Article 6 of the Soviet Constitution, which guaranteed the leading role of the party in the political system. This was a highly significant moment, marking the abandonment of the constitutionally enshrined monopoly on power and opening the way for the emergence of full political pluralism. In March 1990,

Gorbachev created a new position: Executive President. He was elected to this post by a vote in the Congress, rather than by popular vote. A swathe of special powers accrued to Gorbachev as a result. The culmination of this strategy to enhance his own power, while breaking the opposition of the conservatives in the party, came at the 28th Congress of the CPSU in July 1990.

Second, Gorbachev moved to counter the intellectual criticisms of *perestroika* by setting out his statement of faith, detailing the type of society he was creating. Third, Gorbachev moved to resolve the nationalist tensions through a mixture of coercion and dialogue. Finally, he began in the summer of 1990 to search for even more radical solutions to the economic problems, embracing proposals to make a rapid shift to a market economy. Gorbachev was constantly manoeuvring to maintain the centre ground. Between October 1990 and April 1991, Gorbachev appeared to move towards the conservatives and hard-liners. After April 1991, Gorbachev appeared to move back towards the radicals and democrats. In spite of these tactical adjustments, Gorbachev found the centre ground shrinking fast, until by the summer of 1991 it had virtually disappeared. The coup of August 1991 – which many had warned was coming – swept Gorbachev and the party from power and ushered in the post-communist era.

This, in a nutshell, is a summary of Gorbachev's six-year stint in power. So how can we understand what he was about and what he achieved?

1

Who was Mikhail Gorbachev and where did he come from?

The emergence of Gorbachev as leader in 1985 led many people to search Gorbachev's past for clues as to the type of person and leader he was likely to be. Although scholars and commentators disagreed over what type of leader he would be and what he would do, no-one expected him to become a leader who would profoundly and irreversibly change the course of twentieth-century history. The question this poses then is: how could the Soviet system, a state fiercely determined to maintain the monopoly rule of the CPSU and almost genetically programmed to avoid change, incubate and subsequently unleash such a person as its leader? Who was Mikhail Gorbachev, and where did he come from?

The first pieces of the puzzle

The advent of a new leader always stirs curiosity. The advent of a leader of one of the world's superpowers even more so. So it was on 12 March 1985, when *Pravda* announced the death of Konstantin Ustinovich Chernenko, and the accession of Mikhail Sergeevich Gorbachev to the position of General Secretary of the Communist Party of the Soviet Union at the age of 54. For those wanting some background information on this new leader, the Soviet authorities published the following short biographical note:

> Born on 2nd March 1931 in the village of Privolnoye, in the Krasnoyarsk region of Stavropol into a peasant family.
>
> Soon after the Great Patriotic War at age of 15 he began his working career. He worked as a machine operator at a machine tractor station.
>
> In 1952, he became a member of the CPSU.
>
> In 1955, he graduated from the legal faculty of Moscow State University, and in 1967 from the Stavropol Agricultural Institute, obtaining the specialist qualification of scientist agronomist-economist.

From 1955 M.S. Gorbachev was engaged in Komsomol and Party work. He has been working in Stavropol kray: as First Secretary of Stavropol City Komsomol Committee Deputy Head of the Department of Propaganda and Agitation, and later Second and First Secretary of the Kray Komsomol Committee.

In March 1962, Mikhail Gorbachev was nominated as party organizer of Stavropol Territorial-Production Collective and State-Farm Directorate, and in December of the same year he was confirmed as Head of the Department of Party organs of the Kray CPSU Committee.

In September 1966, he was elected First Secretary of Stavropol City Party Committee. From August 1968, Mikhail Gorbachev worked as Second Secretary, and from April 1970 as First Secretary, of Stavropol Kray Party Committee.

M.S. Gorbachev has been a member of the CPSU Central Committee since 1971. He was a delegate at the 22nd, 24th, 25th and 26th Party Congresses. In 1978, he was elected Secretary of the CPSU CC and in 1979 candidate member of the Politburo of the CPSU CC. In October 1980, M.S. Gorbachev was promoted from candidate member to member of the Politburo of the CPSU CC. He has been a Deputy of the USSR Supreme Soviet from the 8th to the 11th convocations and is Chairman of the Foreign Affairs Commission of the Soviet Union. He has been a Deputy of the RSFSR Supreme Soviet of the 10th and 11th convocations.

Mikhail Sergeevich Gorbachev is an eminent figure of the Communist Party and the Soviet state. In all the posts which the Party entrusts to him, he works with his characteristic initiative, energy and selflessness and he devotes his knowledge, rich experience and organizational talents to the implementation of the policy of the Party and selflessly serves the great cause of Lenin and the interests of the working people.

For services to the Communist Party and the Soviet state, M.S. Gorbachev has been awarded three Orders of Lenin, the Orders of the October Revolution and Red Banner of Labour, the 'Badge of Honour' and medals.[1]

Here we have in sum the career of Mikhail Sergeevich Gorbachev. For those looking for clues as to what type of leader this Gorbachev might turn out to be, this brief biography did not reveal very much. But this selection of dates and details (and of course the absence or omission of other points) did reveal some interesting things. Notably, what were the Soviet authorities trying to communicate to us about their new leader?

A few points stand out. First, his birth into a peasant family emphasized his credentials as a man who shared his roots with the mass of the Soviet people. A humble peasant or worker background was no obstacle to advancement to the highest position in the USSR. Second, he began work at the age of 15, showing his commitment to the reconstruction of the Soviet Union after the war. Third, he had acquired a university degree and a specialist vocational qualification, combining theoretical learning and practical knowledge in the sphere of agriculture. Fourth, he had a long career in the Komsomol and the party, rising up through the provincial hierarchy and the central hierarchy. Fifth, he had served in the Supreme Soviet as a deputy (concerned with the everyday affairs of the people in his constituency) but also as the chair of the Foreign Affairs Commission and so had the experience to deal with the international arena. The final few words demonstrated his personal qualities, and recognized his devotion and labour for the Soviet state by bestowing on him awards, medals and other sundry titles. All in all, the official portrait of the new Soviet leader was on display: a hard-working, experienced, devoted communist from a peasant family.

What are the interesting silences in this biography? A few things spring out immediately. Little is said of his family background. Coming from a peasant background in the 1930s when the policy of collectivization was being brutally enforced by Stalin would almost inevitably have been a story with some intriguing details. More surprisingly, nothing is said about Gorbachev during the war. Participation in the struggle to defeat the Nazis (however minor or insignificant) was an essential part of the CV of any Soviet politician; it was the passport to instant credibility. Nothing, even in spite of Gorbachev's youth, was included.

Other questions, on which the official biography was unsurprisingly silent, were also raised by this brief note. Why did he choose to study law? Why did he return to Stavropol after his degree? How did he come to the attention of the central leadership? How did he rise to the top at such a young age, in marked contrast to the rest of the leadership? Answers to these questions, and others, began to be provided by scholars, journalists and writers from outside of the Soviet Union. The official Soviet version of Gorbachev's pre-1985 activities underwent little change between March 1985 and the final days of the Soviet Union at the end of 1991. Gorbachev himself revealed one or two minor details. At the post-Geneva summit press conference in November 1985, Gorbachev outlined that he had studied international relations during his law degree, and had memorized the dictum of Lord Palmerston ("Britain has no eternal friends and no eternal enemies, only eternal interests').[2] In his public discussions with the people during 1986 and 1987 he reminisced about his time working on the land in Stavropol and his political militancy as a Komsomol activist at university. In a biographical note published in *Izvestiya TsK KPSS* in 1989 (a bulletin of information and documents about the activities of the Central Committee of the CPSU), there were only two slight amendments to the 1985 biography. The first concerned his ethnicity. The single word '*russkii*' (meaning 'Russian') was inserted. Second, there was no mention of 'after the Great Patriotic War' in connection with the onset of his working life.[3]

The only exception to this was an interview that Gorbachev himself did with *Izvestiya TsK KPSS* in 1989, in which he replied to queries from readers of the journal.[4] In this interview, Gorbachev supplied a little more detail. He related how his maternal grandfather (Pantelei Efrimovich Gopkalo) had been an organizer of the fellowships for the Joint Cultivation of the Land, and later on of the collective farms. Both his father (Sergei Andreevich) and his mother (Maria Panteleevna) worked the land, in collective farms and machine tractor stations. His father was a machine operator, and fought during the Great Patriotic War, being decorated with several military orders. Gorbachev himself began working part-time on a collective farm at the age of 13, and from the age of 15 he combined work as an assistant harvester combine-operator with his school studies. He supplied little more detail about his time at university, except to say that he met his wife Raisa Maximovna Titorenko there in 1951 when she enrolled in the philosophy faculty. They were married in 1953. On leaving for Stavropol, Gorbachev outlined that 'It so happened that I didn't work in my speciality for long. Soon I was recommended for work in the Komsomol.'[5] Aside from some details on his daughter and grandchildren, this was all that was added to the Soviet picture of their leader. As many Soviets observed, they knew far more about the American president. A meeting with members of the intelligentsia in November 1990 provided further details on the arrests of his grandfathers in the 1930s and the impact this had on the family.[6] Aside from this, we had to wait for the publication of Gorbachev's memoirs in 1995 for the first full personal account of his background.

The attempts by those outside the USSR to fill in the gaps in Gorbachev's past went through three main phases. There was an initial burst of interest in the first 12–18 months after his accession. A flurry of activity attempted to fill in the blank spots in this biography, to shed light on the dark places and to glean something about him which might hint as to the type of leader he was going to be. This included the publication of rapidly compiled biographies and interviews with those who had first-hand knowledge of him, either from his village or from his university days. The authors of these works tended either to be journalists, or Soviet émigré writers.[7] This first wave subsided as interest turned to what Gorbachev was doing – both at home and abroad – as the full impact of his policies began to take effect, transforming the global political landscape. A second wave emerged around 1989/90. This included more detailed biographies, seeking to provide insights into this person who was having such a profound impact upon the world. The authors of these works tended to be a mixture of academics and journalists.[8] The third wave came as the dust settled after the collapse of communism. New books detailing Gorbachev and his role in the end of the Cold War, the dismantling of the Berlin Wall, the overthrow of communism in Eastern Europe and the demise of the Soviet Union appeared. They also contained new material on his past, and were written primarily by academics.[9] The subsequent appearance of a raft of memoir material (including Gorbachev's own two-volume reminiscences) added colour and texture to the monotone canvas supplied by the 1985 biographical note.[10]

Unfortunately, the more details of the story that were uncovered, the less we seemed to know. A variety of different constituencies – the Western academic community, émigré Soviet scholars and writers, Western politicians, the Western media, the Russian post-communist media – have all produced a variety of different 'Gorbachevs'. But which is the 'real' Gorbachev? A significant moment in the historiography of 'Gorbachev' came with the collapse of the Soviet Union and Gorbachev's removal from power. This brought about a profound shift in the interpretive context. The works written while Gorbachev was in power were shaped by the difficulty of gaining access to the requisite sources, the silence of their subject, their perception of Gorbachev and the nature of his leadership, and by the highly politicized environment of the late Cold War. Accounts written since the collapse of communism have gained a great deal from the reduction of international tension and ideological conflict associated with the Cold War. These have provided us with a great deal more detail, enabling us to eradicate some of the blank spots. However, the reliance on memoir material has added a further layer of difficulties. The problems of self-justification, selectivity and accuracy that accompany any memoir source mean that their value to us has to be tempered with caution at all times.

By way of introduction to the study that follows, the difficulties involved in assessing and appraising the life and career of Gorbachev can best be illustrated by examining the different narratives of his career prior to 1985. Scholars writing while he was in power looked into his past in order to find evidence to substantiate their claims about him in the present. As the details were progressively filled in, the basic elements of the 'story' of Gorbachev's rise became clear. However, there were substantive disagreements among scholars about how to interpret particular episodes, about whether to trust particular sources, and about how to interpret the 'gaps' in the story. It is in the interpretation of these issues that we can find the origins of the divergent views of Gorbachev. Scholars writing since Gorbachev has fallen from power have provided a great deal more detail, but have they given us any greater degree of insight?

Gorbachev's rise: Soviet-era accounts

Broadly speaking, in accounts written during the period 1985–91 three versions of Gorbachev's past emerged: *Gorbachev the chameleon/pragmatist*; *Gorbachev the youthful smiling innovator*; and *Gorbachev the 'masked man'*. The pragmatic view looked into his past and saw a hard-working apparatchik working his way through the hierarchy and rising to the top through a combination of luck, propitious circumstances and an ability to adapt, chameleon-like, to any political situation. He would shift his stance to reflect the opinions of those around him, appearing at times to be almost a split personality: now a staunch defender of orthodoxy, now a reformer, now a political activist and upholder of party discipline.

Others saw a skilful, innovative, open-minded, charming, modern politician who was likely to herald meaningful changes to the communist system. As he rose through the system he gradually became aware of the problems and issues besetting the system, until he finally was in a position to do something about it. What sustained him and drove him onwards and upwards was his deep faith in socialism and communism. The system could be redeemed and renewed and he was the person to do it. Still others saw either a closet Stalinist, lacking in talent, but sycophantically making his way up the ladder by wearing the right mask for the right occasion, until he was in a position to seize power himself. This view sees Gorbachev as a driven, ambitious, cold, abrasive politician. Alternatively, they saw a closet reformer who disguised his true intentions behind a mask of conformity, until, having ascended the summit of power, he was able to remove the mask to reveal the reformer within, his true self.

Generally, the most critical, sceptical appraisals tended to come from Soviet émigré writers. Their perspective appeared to be dominated by the 'nothing good can come out of there' view. The West was to remain on its guard, in case it was duped. Western journalists tended to be far more positive in their appraisals. This was a Soviet leader of a new type, far removed from the traditional grey, conservative, ageing figure. For ease of analysis, we can best tell the story of Gorbachev's rise by dividing up the period into four sections: Gorbachev's family background and childhood; his university days; his provincial political career (1955–78); his central political career (1978–85).

Gorbachev and his family background

The Stavropol region of the North Caucasus was a sparsely populated, fertile agricultural region. Gorbachev was born into a peasant family, the son of Sergei Andreevich and Maria Panteleevna Gorbachev. On his mother's side, he was descended from Ukrainian Cossacks. His mother's father (Pantelei Efrimovich Gopkalo) was the chairman of a local collective farm during collectivization. His paternal ancestors were ethnic Russians. His paternal grandfather remained an independent peasant during collectivization. However, this decision cost him, as he was denounced by his neighbour, and sentenced to nine years in the gulag (forced labour camps) in 1937. He was later released. His father was a tractor driver and a combine operator based on a machine tractor station. During the war he worked as an engineer. Little was known of Gorbachev's mother, or of his siblings. With respect to his personality and character, Doder and Branson argue that his upbringing in the Soviet countryside in an era of collectivization and enemy occupation developed in Gorbachev a sense of stoicism, a fierce determination to protect and value his immediate family, and a stubborn streak as well. This was allied to a natural talent for acting, and a basic temperament which could on occasion be extremely cool, and abrasive in his dealings with others.[11]

We begin to move into disputed territory when we examine the period from 1941–50, the war years and the post-war period just prior to going to university in September 1950. The official biography related how he worked from the age of 15 (1946) as a combine operator on a machine tractor station. This raises questions about the war, his schooling and his work. Nothing is said about what he did during the war, why he graduated in 1950 (rather than 1948). The exact nature of the work he did is also somewhat obscured. The story pieced together by various early biographers ran as follows. The North Caucasus was occupied territory during the war. The German invasion, launched on 22 June 1941, struck quickly deep into the centre and south of the Soviet Union. In July 1942, the invaders reached Stavropol, the regional capital of the North Caucasus. Privolnoye, the village home of the Gorbachevs, was only about 200 miles away. The young Mikhail was still in primary school (for ages 8–12) when the Germans invaded, and the intrusion into the Caucasus caused an interruption in his schooling, which caused him to miss either one or two years of school. There was no direct occupation of Gorbachev's village, and the family was not evacuated. The Soviet counter-offensive began in January 1943, and quickly repelled the Germans, liberating the Caucasus. Privolnoye was spared the trauma of both occupation and liberation, shielding Gorbachev from the worst horrors of this terrible time. Gorbachev was able to resume his schooling in September 1943. When he moved up to high school (12–17 years), he moved to Krasnogvardeiskoye, which meant a 10-mile walk every day. He was also conscripted for work. A state decree of 1942 outlined that all children between the ages of 12 and 16 had to work a minimum of 50 days per year. All resources – human and material – were mobilized for the state in the period after 1946 in order to undertake the massive task of reconstructing the country after the devastation of the Nazi occupation. The post-war years were difficult ones. It was a time of great austerity, and the harvests were not good. In order to stimulate production, the state initiated a series of awards and honours for agricultural workers who produced more than their planned quota. In 1948, the Privolnoye agricultural workers brought in a very good harvest and were rewarded with a number of awards. According to his official biography, Gorbachev received the Order of the Red Banner of Labour. Gorbachev also put his feet on the first rungs of the political ladder. He joined the Young Communist League (the Komsomol) in 1945. In 1950, he applied to become a candidate member of the party. He graduated from high school with a silver medal, awarded to pupils who pass their final school examinations with marks of either excellent or good. Outside of school, he was said to have been interested in amateur theatre. He succeeded in his application to Moscow State University to read law, and began his degree in September 1950.

Although the record of these events seems fairly straightforward, there have been challenges to this version. Most notably, the émigré scholars Vladimir Solovyov and Elena Klepikova, writing in 1987, argue that there were substantial falsifications, embellishments and gaps.[12] They argue that the silence about the war years and after covers up the fact that Gorbachev finished high school when he was 19, not 17, because of the German occupation, not because of academic failure. This was a very serious matter. The peoples of occupied territories were regarded very suspiciously by Stalin after the war. The suspicion of collaboration, or of infection with alien propaganda, casts a shadow over anyone hoping to rise up through the hierarchy. This deliberate silence about missing school was done to cover up his experiences during the war years. Unlike his peers at the top of the party in the 1980s, who had all embellished their war records to provide a heroic past,

Gorbachev had to gloss over his past to erase a potentially troublesome record. Furthermore, they pick apart his working record as well. They assert that his work as a combine operator was nothing more than a summer holiday job, and that this award (the Red Banner of Labour) was a fiction. It was purely an invention of propagandists, and not something that would be bestowed on some young provincial peasant. As evidence to substantiate these claims, they state that the story of the Order of the Red Banner of Labour was omitted from the official biographical sketches of Gorbachev that were published in the autumn of 1985. This appeared to run directly counter to the accounts of those biographers – including, Zhores Medvedev, Gail Sheehy, Dusko Doder and Louise Branson, Donald Morrison, Thomas Butson, Robert Kaiser and others – who all cite various sources verifying the award, and detailing that Gorbachev's work was a part of the state's drive to enlist Soviet youth to bring in the harvest before starting school in the autumn.[13] Solovyov and Klepikova's account appeared to favour speculation and rumour in looking to fill in the gaps, and always looked to cast a shadow over Gorbachev's record.

Gorbachev's application to enrol in the law faculty at Moscow State University was successful, and he left Stavropol in September 1950. Some have cast doubt upon how it was that Gorbachev, a provincial boy from a peasant background and having lived in occupied territories, could possibly have made it to one of the most prestigious universities in the Soviet Union. Were there political forces at work protecting and promoting Gorbachev? Or was it just recognition of his work for the Komsomol, his Order of Red Banner and the state's policy of promoting education for the sons and daughters of workers and peasants? The attempt to hint that there were mysterious forces at work behind the scenes easing Gorbachev's way to the top was another instance of speculation and conspiracy rushing in where there were uncertainties in the story. The preference for the 'sensational' or the conspiracy led many émigré writers to interpret Gorbachev negatively, or at least to draw pessimistic conclusions. By comparison, Western journalists and commentators looking for signs of change and innovation were far more willing to interpret these silences positively or give Gorbachev the benefit of the doubt. These disputes about Gorbachev's family background, education and youth are repeated when we examine the early accounts of Gorbachev's life at Moscow University.

University life

Gorbachev was at university for five years between 1950 and 1955. Yet these five years acquired disproportionate significance in attempts to look for the 'essence' of Gorbachev, to discover the outlook and values of the new General Secretary. This was primarily a function of the availability of sources. At Moscow State University at the time were people from all over the Soviet Union, and also from the countries of Eastern Europe. In the months after March 1985 they came forth (or were sought out) to provide a series of thumbnail sketches of Gorbachev as a student. More than just a period of acquiring a formal education and vocational training, the student years were also viewed as being a key part of his political development and his intellectual evolution. These were then deployed by his early biographers to support their 'line'. What these early works revealed was a rather contradictory picture, rife with speculation, second-guessing and inference.[14]

Gorbachev's time in Moscow coincided with a period of great uncertainty and transition in the life of the Soviet political elite. Between 1950 and 1953, there were moves initiated by Stalin to begin a new round of purges, particularly against Jews. After Stalin's death, party and society struggled to come to terms with life without the dictator. Old certainties were no more, and this required rapid adjustments and a need for a sensitive attuning to the changeable political winds. Gorbachev was in the humanities faculty of Moscow State University in the legal section. He resided in the overcrowded student hostels on the outskirts of the city, necessitating a long metro trip for classes. He encountered a number of foreign students (primarily from Eastern Europe), as well as meeting students from all over the Soviet Union. Most notably he met Raisa in 1951, and got married two years later. His courses included not just law, but also philosophy, history, Marxism-Leninism, the history of the communist movement and of the CPSU. A component part of the course involved formal legal training in public speaking, debating, interrogation. Outside of the law degree, he continued to work to supplement his meagre student grant, returning to his home village to work in the fields. In 1953, he received the Kalinin stipend, given to diligent and politically active students, and Gorbachev seems to have met both criteria. Aside from his scholarly success, he was an active member of the Faculty Komsomol committee, and became a full member of the party in 1952. He graduated in 1955, and left Moscow to return to Stavropol to take up a position with the Komsomol, rather than in the juridical field.

As to what this time revealed about Gorbachev, then the picture becomes more blurred and indistinct. The first puzzle relates to the choice of law as a degree. The status of law in the USSR at the time was very low: it usually attracted careerists, who wished to work for the procuracy or to join the internal security services. So why law? Again the contemporary reading of Gorbachev thoroughly coloured the answer to this question. The sceptics (e.g. Solovyov and Klepikova) saw in this choice evidence of the conformist, careerist nature of Gorbachev. He was set on a path of climbing up the political hierarchy.[15] Those of the 'Gorbachev the pragmatist' view speculated that Gorbachev, who openly professed a fascination with science and mathematics, may have failed the entrance exams to these faculties.[16] Was the law faculty the only one that would accept him? Those of the 'Gorbachev the innovator' persuasion speculated that the choice of law, with the opportunity of studying 'bourgeois' systems and theorists other than Marx, Engels, Lenin and Stalin, reveals a penchant for unorthodox thinking, an interest in new ideas and a willingness to explore the new and the unusual. Further speculation was fuelled by whether the choice of law was derived from his personal beliefs and experiences: was he consciously modelling himself on Lenin (who had studied law)? Or was he so scarred by the arrest of his grandfather that he wished to join the procuracy in order to put right the wrongs that had been done to his family?[17]

But what type of student was Gorbachev, and what did his time at university reveal about him? The main sources for this period are memoir material from Gorbachev's contemporaries. In the reminiscences of Zdenek Mlynar, a Czech communist studying in Moscow at the time, and a long-time friend of Gorbachev, he comes across as an open-minded, critical-thinking individual with a deep interest in all things foreign, and particularly Western. He was hard-working, politically active, loyal to his friends and scathing of formalism and political conformity. The incident is cited of his open scorn for his fellow students who just read out extracts from Stalin's latest work. He was also said to have publicly defended his Jewish friend - Vladimir Lieberman - during the anti-Semitic times of 1953, when some sought to denounce and attack him.[18]

Other reminiscences are not quite so complimentary. They remembered him as a sycophantic careerist, desperate to do anything to work his way up through the hierarchy. He was also deemed to be unscrupulously ambitious in his pursuit of power. He was said to have acquired the position of Komsomol organizer at university by getting the incumbent drunk and then denouncing his behaviour at a public Komsomol meeting. Some (including one of his roommates) suspected him of being an informer for the security agencies.[19] This was the only explanation for his being able to get his placement in the Lubyanka, the headquarters of the NKVD. They also construct a picture of Gorbachev as a thorough-going Stalinist: openly in support of the anti-Semitism of the time, a ruthless, militant leader of the Komsomol in his department, and something of a puritan in his taste and manners. Stalin's death would find Gorbachev openly weeping at the loss of their leader. They cite the fact that Gorbachev was permitted to share quarters with foreigners as evidence of his close links with the political authorities and security forces. Only the most trusted communists were allowed to do this, in case they became 'infected' by alien ideas and values coming in from outside.

The 'pragmatic' picture tries to marry these quite divergent memories. One explanation put forward emphasizes a public/private split. In public, Gorbachev was staunchly orthodox, impeccably in tune with the current political line and militantly active in the service of the Young Communist league. In private, Gorbachev was critical, realistic and emotional.[20] As for being 'Stalinist', well, everyone was. There was no alternative. Stalinist patterns of thought and action were deeply ingrained within everyone within the system. The existence of links with the security services is implied, but was probably a function of his position with the Komsomol. Gorbachev had many layers to his personality, and he only allowed certain people the chance to get close to him.[21] Many, consequently, only experienced his public, officious, political activist personality. A slightly different interpretation highlights the university years as another stage in the process by which the staunch orthodoxy of Gorbachev was gradually joined in his personality by a more reformist bent, the two co-habiting uneasily within him. University awakened in Gorbachev an awareness of some of the deficiencies of the system, and dissatisfaction with some of the glib formulae of the official ideology.[22]

Finally, there is some dispute as to why Gorbachev, on graduating, did not take up a post in this profession in Moscow, but instead ended up back in the provincial backwater of Stavropol working for the Komsomol. Gorbachev mentioned this in passing in his interview in 1989, stating that,

> After graduation from the University we worked in Stavropol, my home region. It so happened that I didn't work in my speciality for long. Soon I was recommended for work in the Komsomol. And ever since I've been doing Komsomol and party work.[23]

But this does not tell us why he went to the provinces, or why he moved to the Komsomol. Was this a conscious choice on his part, turning his back on a career with the procuracy and opting instead to work in the Komsomol? Medvedev argues that this was the case.[24] Not having acquired a postgraduate place, he could not stay in Moscow. Having graduated with a distinction, he had first choice on where to go to work. He chose Stavropol for his placement, as it was his home region. However, he was unwilling to join the procuracy and become embroiled in the Sisyphean task of reviewing the lists of cases for rehabilitation, and opted instead to join the Komsomol. This move (along with joining the party apparatus) was the only way that a young graduate could avoid having to take up a compulsory appointment. Or was this move from Moscow forced upon him? Interviews with contemporaries of Gorbachev (who all remained in Moscow and began their rise up the political hierarchy) confirmed that he was desperate to remain in Moscow. Speculation and rumour suggest that either his past (occupied territory, relatives in the gulag) or possible links with the disgraced leader of the secret police under Stalin (Lavrentii Beria) meant that the opportunity to stay in Moscow was denied him, and he was sent to the provinces. Gorbachev's golden reputation had been tarnished.[25]

Solovyov and Klepikova put forward the view that Gorbachev was thwarted by having placed all his eggs in the Stalinist basket. The change of orientation led by Khrushchev and Malenkov caught Gorbachev with having made the wrong contacts. They argue that his activities at university – denouncing people, informing, working tirelessly for the Komsomol – were all rendered useless by Stalin's death. In the new conditions, he was hopelessly implicated in the 'old ways' and had no future in Moscow. The provinces beckoned. Moreover, the extent of Gorbachev's fall from grace can be gauged, according to Solovyov and Klepikova, from the fact that his position in Stavropol was Assistant Head of the Propaganda section of the Komsomol Territorial Committee. 'Never before', they postulate, 'had a graduate of Moscow University had to take such a lowly position.'[26] So how did he fare?

A provincial life, 1955–78

Gorbachev spent 23 years in the provinces, before moving back to Moscow in 1978. Appraisals of these provincial years written after 1985 aimed to answer the following questions: what do we know of his time as a provincial leader? How did he manage to make his way up the ladder? What type of provincial boss did he prove to be? Any lessons from these years could point to the type of national leader Gorbachev might become. The story is one of Gorbachev steadily working his way up through the provincial political hierarchy until he finally came to the attention of the central leadership. We can divide this period into two parts, hinging around his appointment as a Full Member of the CC of the CPSU after the 24th Congress in 1971.

As noted above, Gorbachev joined the Komsomol structures and steadily worked his way up the Komsomol ladder until 1962. In 1956, he became First Secretary of the Stavropol City Komsomol Committee. Two years later, he was appointed deputy chief of the Department of Propaganda and Agitation for the whole Stavropol province. Between 1958 and 1962, he worked his way through the hierarchy to become First Secretary of the Stavropol Provincial Committee. These were interesting times as a propagandist, having to travel around the province to explain and defend the new party line determined at the 22nd Congress in 1961. In 1962, he changed tack, and joined the CPSU structures as an organizer of the territorial production administration of collective and state farms. This was something of a backward step, but it allowed Gorbachev to put himself inside the party apparatus for the first time. The following year, he took over the running of the party organs of the CPSU for the Stavropol province. In 1966, he went on his first visits abroad, to France and to the GDR. In the same year he became First Secretary of the Stavropol City CP Committee. In 1968, he was promoted to Second Secretary of the Stavropol Provincial Committee of the CPSU (with responsibility for agriculture). Finally, in 1970, he made it to the top of the provincial ladder when he became First Secretary of the Stavropol Provincial Committee. At the same time he was made a member of the Military Council of the North Caucasian Military District, and was elected as a Deputy to the Supreme Soviet, and was a member of the Standing Commission of the Supreme Soviet on Preservation of the Environment.

How do we account for this rise through the hierarchy, from the lowest rung of the provincial ladder to the top in 15 years? Was it due to outstanding personal qualities allied to demonstrated achievement? Was it due to the 'cultivation' of personal contacts among the influential and powerful in the region, greasing the wheels with 'sycophancy, flattery, loyalty and bribery'[27]? Was it due to the protection and promotion of key individuals? Or was it due to luck and being in the right place at the right time? Common to all descriptions of Gorbachev's rise is the important role played by 'patrons': influential local political dignitaries who protected and promoted subordinates.[28] His first boss in the Komsomol was Vsevolod Murakhovsky. In the party organs he was advanced by Fedor Kulakov (who was head of the Stavropol provincial party committee between 1960 and 1964) and Leonid Efremov, who replaced Kulakov in 1964 when he was promoted to the central party leadership in Moscow. Much of Gorbachev's subsequent career was linked to Kulakov. Why, though, did Gorbachev enjoy such patronage? Many accounts stress that Gorbachev proved himself to be a reliable, safe, loyal assistant.

He was willing, energetic and enthusiastic, but lacked any initiative, originality or independence of thought. Zemtsov and Farrar argue that he always supported the majority view and his views invariably coincided with those higher up the ladder.[29] Solovyov and Klepikova assert that Gorbachev's early advance through the hierarchy was a mechanical process, filling posts as they became vacant. It then took two years for Kulakov to notice Gorbachev. Their relationship was based upon Kulakov's abundance of new ideas, and Gorbachev's lack of them.[30] Sheehy also recognizes Gorbachev's ability to adapt to the different individuals he encountered, terming him a 'brilliant chameleon'.[31] On this reading Gorbachev displayed a mixture of *pragmatism and conformity*.

But there are those who see in Gorbachev a mixture of *pragmatism and innovation*, tempering this view of an unoriginal operator of infinite flexibility. For those working within the system, an ability to adapt was essential for survival and advancement. This was the position put forward by those biographers writing in the late 1980s and early 1990s who were struggling to match the Gorbachev they knew in the present (the bold, innovative leader striding the world stage) with the Gorbachev of dull, conformist regional politics in the 1950s, 1960s and 1970s. They argued that Gorbachev skilfully adapted to his situation, keeping quiet when necessary, and speaking out only when it was prudent to do so. His ambition meant that he conducted himself in exemplary fashion, aware that the path to the top was likely to be a slow, unspectacular one.[32]

But Gorbachev was not an infinitely flexible politician, as some insisted. His support for Khrushchev was contingent, backing his stance on Stalin, but impatient with his constant policy changes and zig-zags. He was a supporter of greater decentralization within the system. His visits abroad, particularly his trip to France in 1966 (which necessitated missing the 23rd Congress), gave him experience of another world.[33] His correspondence with Mlynar continued, and was supplemented by a visit from his old university friend in 1967, just a year prior to the momentous events in Prague when the Soviet army crushed an incipient reform movement among Czech communists, led by Alexander Dubcek. This persistent exposure to non-Soviet thinking and experiences was identified as an important factor in broadening his world-view.[34] Moreover, the choices made by Gorbachev demonstrated that he was willing to take on work, learn and develop his skills rather than just taking the easy route. His switch to the party organs in 1962, encouraged by Kulakov, saw him leave the Komsomol hierarchy and take on a new and demanding role overseeing the work of the collective and state farms. In order to cope with this position, he enrolled for a correspondence course at Stavropol agricultural institute, graduating in 1967 with a diploma in agronomy. This decision to acquire specialist knowledge of agriculture was to stand him in good stead in the future and demonstrated a shrewd awareness on Gorbachev's part. He had learned from observing Kulakov that agricultural success would bring you into the gaze of the central party organs. It was not enough to say the right things at the right time. You also had to be able to show success, or at least be able to take the credit for economic achievements.

These early years of political work in the provinces were also highlighted as being significant in shaping Gorbachev's ideals and also his working style. His policy of using the press to communicate with the people, and his populist approach of getting out and about to meet the people, were cited as evidence of Gorbachev's distinctive style. But what was most noteworthy was his intelligence, energy, faith and self-confidence. Gorbachev seemed to be animated by far more than just the cynical acquisition of power and privilege. Gorbachev believed in the system. Gorbachev had faith in the capacity of the people in the system to transform it. It was this faith which sustained him in his travails in provincial Stavropol.

Gorbachev's activities between 1970 and 1978 afforded scholars and journalists the chance to assess Gorbachev as a leader. What was his working style? How did he manage his province? Was he able to demonstrate any economic achievements or success in Stavropol? Once more we come across sharply divergent appraisals of his time as First Secretary. Schmidt-Hauer insisted that Gorbachev became a down-to-earth, hard-working provincial leader, walking to his office and consciously seeking a low profile. In his dealings with officials he was exacting and intolerant of incompetence or slackness.[35] Solovyov and Klepikova conversely argue that Gorbachev turned himself into an old-style provincial boss, consciously modelling himself on Stalin. He was deemed to be arrogant and prone to bouts of 'blindness' to corruption among officials.[36] Sheehy categorized him as a popular leader: willing to listen to people, consciously seeking out the opinions of farmers, intellectuals and workers alike.[37] Medvedev also stressed that Gorbachev did not surround himself with the trappings of power, or create a cult of his personality as First Secretary, which many of his peers were wont to do.[38]

There was a greater degree of consensus when considering the reasons for Gorbachev's appointment to the central leadership in November 1978: Gorbachev's relations with his superiors and the economic achievements of his province. This was identified by everyone as crucial to Gorbachev's rise by bringing him to the attention of the central leadership. Where commentators differed was in the relative weight to give to each factor. The making of 'Gorbachev the grey apparatchik' was something engineered for him by his superiors, who desired a loyal, trustworthy subordinate. He was the beneficiary of patronage from above, and his ability to please his patrons accounts for his rise.[39] The making of 'Gorbachev the innovator' was down to his careful yet experimental management of agriculture in Stavropol. His reforms enabled huge productivity increases, and produced schemes which were subsequently adopted throughout the system. This accounts for his appointment to the CC with responsibility for agriculture in 1978.[40] The making of 'Gorbachev the pragmatist' was a result of the careful cultivation of powerful patrons alongside cautious policy initiatives.[41]

Gorbachev had important supporters high up within the hierarchy. Already firmly ensconced within Kulakov's entourage, Gorbachev benefited hugely from the geographical advantages that Stavropol offered to the Soviet leadership. The North Caucasus was used extensively as a holiday region, and also as a place for rest and recuperation because of the mineral springs in the area. This brought him regular contact with visitors from Moscow, and Gorbachev cultivated these assiduously. Most notably, he came to enjoy the protection of Mikhail Suslov and Yuri Andropov. Suslov had originated from the North Caucasus, and saw in Gorbachev someone who could counterbalance the accumulation of people loyal to Brezhnev in the CC. In other words, Gorbachev was seen as being promoted as a result of power struggles at the centre. But these contacts would not have been of any use if he had been unable to demonstrate economic success. In this, Gorbachev was also the beneficiary of geography. The North Caucasus was a highly fertile region, which made it easier to demonstrate agricultural achievement, which was traditionally the Achilles' heel of the Soviet economy. Indeed, Solovyov and Klepikova argued that the good performance of the Stavropol agricultural sector at this time was more a function of its natural fertility than any interventions on the part of Gorbachev.[42]

Others have sought a more positive appraisal of his agricultural initiatives. Gorbachev's oversight of the agriculture of the region was seen as being a curious mixture of experimentation and innovation on the one hand, and also sharp turns in policy in line with the dictates of the centre. Gorbachev advanced the link (*zveno*) or team approach to farming which stressed that teams should be paid according to results, and should be given far greater autonomy in deciding what to do, and how to do it. Small teams were set up with responsibility for ploughing, sowing, harvesting. This freed the farmers from the excessive controls of the officials, and the results seem to have been impressive: Sheehy noted a six-fold increase in productivity.[43] Yet this was abandoned in favour of a scheme known as the Ipatovsky method.

This initiative has been examined in some detail. In brief, the Ipatovsky method was developed by Fedor Kulakov. It was designed to overcome one of the main problems dogging Soviet agriculture: the need for rapid harvesting to ensure that the crop did not rot in the fields. Kulakov's solution was to develop large-scale harvesting squads which would move around an area rapidly bringing the crop in before moving on to the next farm. It was trialled in the Ipatovsky district of the Stavropol province in 1977. It was a huge success, according to Zhores Medvedev, with the harvest taking only nine days instead of the expected three to four weeks.[44] However, it ran completely counter to the thrust of Gorbachev's earlier focus on small, autonomous link teams. But was this imposed upon Gorbachev? Or was this major shift in policy a calculated move on Gorbachev's part to put his province in the national spotlight and to please his patron Fedor Kulakov? Whatever the reason, Gorbachev went ahead, and he was to enjoy national prominence as a result, appearing on the front cover of *Pravda* and writing an article for *Kommunist*, the CPSU's main theoretical journal.

The onward march of the Ipatovsky method was halted abruptly by the sudden and somewhat mysterious death of Fedor Kulakov in July 1978, in circumstances which have never been fully explained. In the months that followed, Brezhnev undertook a reshuffle of the top personnel. In November 1978, Gorbachev was appointed as Secretary of the CC with responsibility for agriculture. After 23 years, Gorbachev had made it back to Moscow at the comparatively youthful age of 47. Within seven years he was to scale the final summit. But why was Gorbachev selected by Brezhnev? Was it because he 'gave no-one cause for alarm'? Or was it because Suslov, after the death of his first choice Kulakov, was looking for a new heir to assume power when Brezhnev died? Or was it rather the result of complex political bargaining among the elite, with Brezhnev advancing his favourites – Chernenko and Tikhonov – and accepting Gorbachev as the quid pro quo from Suslov and Andropov? Or was he appointed because of his agricultural successes? Again, the answer provided by the various early commentators reflected their interpretive framework.

The final struggle: Gorbachev in Moscow, 1978–85

Between 1917 and 1978 there were four leaders of the Soviet Union: Lenin, Stalin, Khrushchev and Brezhnev. Between 1978 and 1985 there were also four leaders: Brezhnev, Andropov, Chernenko and Gorbachev himself. The seven years it took for Gorbachev to attain the summit of Soviet power were times of great upheaval in the Soviet elite. Much of this time was taken up with behind-the-scenes manoeuvring for power among the various factions. How did Gorbachev manage to emerge victorious out of this in-fighting?

The rise of Gorbachev was astonishingly quick, aided by the increased turnover among the elite as death and infirmity took its toll. Appointed to the CC secretariat in November 1978, he was made a candidate member of the Politburo in 1979 and attained full membership the following year. He was given the honour of delivering the keynote address of 22 April 1983, celebrating the anniversary of Lenin's birth. In 1983–84, he was made responsible for the economy, cadres (personnel) and agriculture. In 1984, he was made responsible for all of the above, plus world communist affairs. In 1980, he was elected as a deputy to the RSFSR Supreme Soviet. In 1984, he was appointed Chairman of the USSR Supreme Soviet Commission on foreign affairs. He also undertook a number of trips abroad in this period, including Czechoslovakia (1979), Mongolia (1981), Canada and Portugal (1983), Bulgaria, Italy and Great Britain (1984).

In seeking to explain Gorbachev's final victory in March 1985, the initial observations stressed the circumstances in which Gorbachev was operating, the machinations of the top leaders and the choices made by Gorbachev as to what sort of image to project. No-one pointed to Gorbachev's record as Secretary with responsibility for agriculture to explain his rise. The performance of the Soviet rural economy continued to be poor. The harvests of 1979, 1980 and 1981 were all very bad, partly due to bad weather but not wholly. Gorbachev survived this because he had just taken over, and so could not be held to blame for this poor performance. Indeed, Medvedev stresses that this actually assisted his rise through the hierarchy, as it was argued that he needed more authority and power if he was to materially affect what was happening.[45]

If performance in office had little to do with his success, then luck and circumstance clearly did. All commentators explore the way that Gorbachev benefited from the rapidly changing situation between 1978 and 1985. Medvedev argues that Gorbachev should have been the scapegoat for the poor harvest of 1982, but was saved by the traditions of the party which deemed that negative decisions and information are shunned in years which celebrate the anniversaries of the October 1917 Revolution. 1982 fell into this category, being the 65th anniversary, and so Gorbachev escaped.[46] Three days after the official anniversary celebration, Brezhnev died and Andropov became General Secretary. Brezhnev's death saw the election of Andropov to the position of General Secretary. The close links that had developed between Andropov and Gorbachev ensured that Gorbachev's rise would continue. He was chosen to deliver the Lenin anniversary speech in April 1983. He also benefited from the rapid deterioration in Andropov's health, as he became a reliable right-hand man for Andropov. After the demise of Andropov, the leadership elected Konstantin Chernenko in February 1984 (another elderly and infirm character). Gorbachev appeared to be the heir-apparent to Chernenko, with Grigori Romanov as his main rival. Yet again circumstances came to the aid of Gorbachev. Gorbachev's youth, his energy and his image as a Western-style leader meant that he was strongly favoured by many in the leadership, including the highly influential Gromyko. His youth and vigour would stand in great contrast to both the succession of aged, infirm Soviet leaders (Brezhnev, Andropov, Chernenko), and also the US President Ronald Reagan. In the propaganda wars with the USA, a young personable media-friendly leader could be a vital weapon.

Two related questions are begged by all these circumstantial arguments. First, how did Gorbachev come to be sponsored/promoted by a particular faction in the leadership? Did they choose him as a safe pair of hands whom they could control? Or did he attach himself to a particular group as part of his ambitious drive to accumulate personal power? Second, did he have a recognized standpoint or did he shift and change his perspective in line with the changeable winds of Kremlin politics? The question of sponsorship/ambition was clearly a relationship of mutual self-interest. The opponents of the Brezhnev–Chernenko–Romanov grouping needed as many supporters as possible. Gorbachev was identified as a loyal, dependable follower. However, it clearly aided his own political ambitions to have the patronage of others higher up. The second question of his ideological position is much more complicated. Did Gorbachev emerge as a reformer, and if he did, why?

For those commentators who saw Gorbachev as little more than a glorified apparatchik, his actions were viewed as prefiguring a reversion back to Stalinist ways (but not full Stalinism). Solovyov and Klepikova argued that he was reviving Stalinist motifs (his spring 1984 speech endorsed a return to Stakhanovism). This view also rejected the view of Andropov as a proto-reformer; on this reading he was a hard-liner destined to restore order and discipline to the Soviet system.[47] For those who saw Gorbachev as a pragmatic leader, they argued that Gorbachev was endorsing more reformist measures (in line with the reformist views of Andropov, who had advocated a mixture of moderate changes and a restoration of discipline). But why had he switched to stressing reformist ideals? Zemtsov and Farrar raised the question, without answering it: was he finally revealing his true colours, or was he adopting a new set of political clothes in line with the changing times?[48] For Sanders, the questions of ideological standpoint and political ambition were intimately linked: Gorbachev acquired a reform programme as part of his campaign to defeat his enemies and acquire personal power. Reformist credentials were a weapon in the struggle for power.[49] But for those who saw in Gorbachev a reformist in the making, this period can be seen as part of the gradual unveiling of his true nature: he was developing new ideas, exploring unorthodox ideas and discussing policies in private, while ostensibly sticking to the official line when necessary. A careful reading of his speeches in this period revealed a leader with clear leanings towards a programme of radical change.[50] The death of Chernenko would provide him with the platform to initiate this programme. The difficulties in interpreting Gorbachev are at their most acute here. No-one could work their way up through the communist hierarchy without being a loyal, obedient member of the communist apparatus who knew how to please his superiors and make the right noises. At the same time, Gorbachev clearly exhibited tendencies favouring innovation and experimentation, was open to new or unorthodox ideas, and sought out the opinions of others.

Soviet-era accounts of Gorbachev's past demonstrate a remarkable lack of agreement about the type of person he was, the reasons for his rise and the nature of his beliefs and values. This was in part due to the lack of detail: large gaps in the narrative of his life inevitably encouraged speculation and guesswork. However, there were also other factors at work, most notably a 'reading backwards' from their perception of his leadership in the hope of throwing light on how his time in office might develop and evolve. The émigré accounts – which portrayed Gorbachev as a closet Stalinist and sought to besmirch him at every opportunity – proved to be wholly unreliable and wildly inaccurate in their assessment of Gorbachev. However, the debate between those who viewed him prior to 1985 as a pragmatist working his way up through the system, and those who saw him as a consistent proponent of reform and change, remained unresolved.

The rapid and unforeseen collapse of the Soviet system in 1991 brought a new context. The aims and the intentions of authors were now very different. Works on Gorbachev now sought to assess what he had achieved, his place in history, the origins of his views and policies and to try and understand how it was that such a leader could have been produced by the Soviet system. This context was also radically altered by the emergence of a raft of memoir material from the key figures in the Soviet elite during the *perestroika* era. Gorbachev himself began to reflect publicly on his experiences through a series of interviews in the press and most significantly with the publication of his two volumes of memoirs in 1995. This material enabled scholars to fill in many of the gaps in the narrative of his past, reducing the speculation and guesswork that had marked the earlier works on Gorbachev. However, the publication of Gorbachev's memoirs (and the memoirs of others) inevitably shaped subsequent works on Gorbachev, as they came to rely heavily on this one source. Gorbachev had created his own narrative of his past. What did this add to the earlier works?

Gorbachev's past: in the shadow of memoirs

Although Gorbachev undertook a number of interviews with both Western and Russian media sources after his resignation as president in December 1991, the key moment in establishing his own version of events came with the publication of his memoirs, *Zhizn' i reformy* (Life and Reforms) in 1995.[51] Gorbachev spends the first 270 pages of his memoirs on his background: 'Who I am and where I am from'. In the Foreword to the 1997 English language edition published by Bantam Books (a piece absent from the two-volume 1995 Russian language edition), Gorbachev notes that,

> [T]his book will not so much be about myself but rather about the times and circumstances that shaped our generation, about the men and women who helped me gain insight into the mysteries of life and politics and influenced both my character and my beliefs ... [I]n these memoirs I write about myself and my efforts to explain my decisions and to describe the difficulties involved in implementing radical change during *perestroika*.[52]

The aim of the memoirs was to illuminate the factors that contributed to the making of the convictions, beliefs and values of Gorbachev which led ultimately to *perestroika*, not to describe Gorbachev's past on its own terms. Hence the memoirs do not always shed light on some of the problematic parts of Gorbachev's past identified by his early biographers. Let us see what his memoirs added to the narrative of his pre-General Secretary days.

Gorbachev, family and the war

He opened his memoirs with his appointment as CC Secretary for Agriculture in November 1978, relating the discussions with Andropov, Chernenko and Brezhnev leading up to the unanimous ratification of his nomination by Brezhnev at the plenum on 27 November 1978.[53] Two things stand out from this choice of episode to open the book. First, it provides a clear sense of the hinge around which his life revolved: Stavropol (until 1978, except for his university days) and Moscow (from 1978 onwards). Second, Gorbachev stressed something of his character: his outspokenness, his unwillingness to conform, his willingness to confront and challenge complacency.

The sections on his family life fill in some of the detail about his origins, the work of his parents and grandparents, and the experiences his family underwent during some of the most brutal periods of twentieth-century history: the Soviet countryside during collectivization and the Nazi occupation. These episodes were omitted from Gorbachev's public past during the Soviet era, although he did inform a group of intellectuals of the arrest of his grandfather in November 1990. Similarly, in an interview in 1992, he remarked on the shadow that the arrest of his grandfather cast over the rest of his political life, forcing him to declare it at every turn.[54] Gorbachev relates the contrasting lives of his grandparents. His maternal grandparents (Gopkalo) supported the revolution and his grandfather was to become chairman of a collective farm. Gorbachev lived with them until he went to school. He also notes the co-existence of communist belief (his grandfather) and religious belief (his grandmother) within the same household, remarking on the 'admirable tolerance' of his grandfather.[55] The obviously painful episode of the arrest and torture of his grandfather in 1937 (and subsequent release and restoration as chairman of the collective farm in 1939) is recounted. The story of his paternal grandparents was equally fraught. Andrei Gorbachev remained an independent peasant, refusing to join the collective farms. He too was arrested (for not fulfilling the 1934 sowing plan) and sent to a forced labour camp. He was released in 1935 and joined the local collective farm. Aside from the details of these arrests, and some minor details of his family life and studies, Gorbachev's memoirs add very little to the information contained in the early Western biographical works.[56]

Clearly the decade leading up to the war was a traumatic one and left a strong impression on the young Gorbachev. These feelings were deepened by the experience of invasion and Nazi occupation for a number of months in 1942. He remarks on the privations of war, the desperate struggle to rebuild and survive in the years after their liberation and the anxiety caused by an erroneous telegram informing them of his father's death. Sergei Gorbachev was wounded later on in Czechoslovakia and returned to the village of Privolnoye. Gorbachev noted how he had to leave school for two years to work and help his mother look after the family. Gorbachev returned to school in 1944 and had to live away when he began to attend the district secondary school 20 km away. In 1946, he joined his father to work in the summers as a combine harvest operator. In 1948, he won the first of his honours (the Order of the Red Banner of Labour) for the exceptional harvest that was gathered. This account clearly undermines the view that Gorbachev falsified his post-war experiences to present himself with an acceptable past. By 1995, there was no need to embellish his past.

What picture does Gorbachev paint of his life in those early years? The characteristics he highlights are ones of struggle, sacrifice, privation, independence, hard work and endurance. His experiences seemed to have developed a strongly moral, almost puritanical, attitude towards life and work, exemplified by his anecdote about the time he was tricked by his fellow farm workers into drinking pure alcohol, which gave him an aversion to drinking for the rest of his life. He expressed a strong admiration for his father and maternal grandfather, for their sense of duty, patriotism and their attitude towards work.[57] Two other things are worthy of note. First, the absence of any overt Marxist ideological framework for understanding his past, and second, the scattering of religious imagery and phraseology.

University life

Gorbachev's memoirs also amplify accounts of his experiences at university in a number of ways. However, little more is disclosed about how Gorbachev came to be accepted into Moscow State University, or why he chose law. On the first point, he attributes this to the state award, his worker/peasant origins and his work record. On the second point, he suggests that he chose law as he had been impressed by the position of judge or prosecutor. The rest of the chapter describes his intellectual experiences. Twin processes of intellectual awakening and the acquisition of knowledge, on the one hand, and a growing awareness of the dogmatism, conformism and constraints on thinking, on the other, were at work. He speaks glowingly of the breadth of the curriculum, and of his thirst for knowledge. He relates incidents where he stood out, or spoke out against the prevailing orthodoxy, clashed with the authorities and began to question the received wisdoms, including times which left him penalized in his exams, or facing investigations from the university authorities. He also acknowledges that as students they readily absorbed the official ideological world-view, and were devastated by the death of Stalin in 1953. Indeed, Gorbachev wrote an essay, 'Stalin – our combat glory, Stalin – the elation of our youth', which was held up by the university authorities as a model essay for years to come. The chapter closes with details of how he met and married Raisa, and of his unsuccessful attempts to join the procuracy.[58]

The brief chapter on his times at Moscow University ends with Gorbachev reflecting on the significance of this experience. Alongside the influence of his family, schoolteachers and work colleagues, he cites his university days as being decisive in the formation of 'Gorbachev the politician'.[59] For such a decisive period, this is a relatively short chapter. There is little or no mention of Gorbachev's political activities as the Komsomol organizer, something that had stirred controversy in the early biographies. Gorbachev's ability to survive investigations, to prosper in spite of the controversial past of his family, is explained away rather casually as being due to his worker/peasant origins. Most notable though was the attempt to demonstrate the beginnings of unorthodox thinking that was ultimately to lead to *perestroika*. He cites an incident in which he met a former student in December 1991 who said that during his student days he had been considered 'little short of a dissident'.[60] He also quotes Sakharov on the death of Stalin, citing the similarities in their responses to the demise of the dictator.[61] Gorbachev's memoirs portray him from his earliest days as undertaking a struggle against the system.

Gorbachev's political career: from Stavropol to Moscow

Gorbachev continues his story with his provincial political career. Against the dramatic backdrop of Khrushchev's denunciations of Stalin at the 20th Congress in February 1956, Gorbachev describes his struggles against the bureaucracy, his struggles to improve the lives of the young people of the area and his rise through the hierarchy. His is a story of growing frustration at the problems encountered in the running of the system, of the gradual onset of inertia and stagnation after the crushing of the Prague Spring in August 1968 and of the gap in living standards with the West from his travels abroad. His 23 years as a provincial political activist and leader had provided him with first-hand experience of the problems that beset the system, of the institutional, cultural, economic, social and political obstacles to implementing change and the opposition that was engendered by those who favoured change. Underlying Gorbachev's description of his provincial career is the notion that somehow he did not fit in, would not conform, was something of an upstart, a rebel and was different from many of his colleagues. This was partly due to his personality, but also to his level of education, his outlook and to his interest in Western theorists.[62]

At the centre, a similar story unfolds, but this time against the backdrop of decay and death at the top, a situation which encouraged rumours, plots, factions and political in-fighting. He wrote favourably of Andropov, and negatively of Brezhnev and Chernenko. Particularly important for Gorbachev was to establish the catalogue of problems that had accumulated under Brezhnev, as this provided the main justification for introducing the policies of *perestroika*. Gorbachev writes:

> Much has been written about the 18-year period of stagnation under Brezhnev. I suggest that this description needs analysis and an in-depth interpretation; all the more because in recent times conservative and fundamentalist forces have attempted to rehabilitate Brezhnevism. The purpose is obvious – to prove that the process of *perestroika* was needless and to shift the blame for the present crisis in the country onto its initiators.[63]

Herein lies the justification for *perestroika*, and also for Gorbachev's decision to accept the nomination to succeed Chernenko. In a conversation with his wife, Gorbachev recounts:

> It is difficult now to reproduce the details of our talk. However my last words that night stand out in my memory: 'You see, I have come here with hope and the belief that I shall be able to accomplish something, but so far there was not much I could have done. Therefore if I really want to change something I would have to accept the nomination – if it is made, of course. *We can't go on living like this.*'[64]

Gorbachev's narrative of his background and his rise to power – unsurprising for a memoir account – presents a story of one person's awakening to the problems in the system, his struggle to change, his unwillingness to conform, his inability to fit into the system, and almost a sense of destiny about his rise to the top, and of the urgent necessity for change. A coincidence of time and man flowed together in March 1985. There is little sense of ambiguity or compromise, and no sense of personal ambition. This contrasts with many of the earlier accounts which stressed his pragmatism or his infinite flexibility or indeed his 'closet' Stalinism. Let us turn briefly to examine how Gorbachev's early years and rise to the top have been treated in the accounts written since 1991 in the West.

Post-Soviet accounts

Although publications on Gorbachev and *perestroika* have been numerous since the collapse of communism, relatively few have focused on Gorbachev himself. The main exceptions are the works of Robert Kaiser, Archie Brown and Martin

McCauley, as well as lighter treatments in works by Galeotti, Breslauer and others. While Soviet-era accounts suffered from the lack and availability of sources, and the ever-changing situation, post-Soviet accounts have suffered from the perils of hindsight and the challenges of interpreting and evaluating a proliferating memoir source base. In particular, writing on Gorbachev after the chaotic swirl of momentous events which he oversaw has been inexorably shaped by the radical changes that were associated with him. This tended to eclipse those early accounts that questioned his credentials and outlook.

The one work which was not informed by the memoir literature (but was informed by the radical yet transient essence of *perestroika*) was Robert Kaiser's work *Why Gorbachev Happened: His Triumphs and Failures*, published in 1991 and thus straddling the Soviet/post-Soviet divide. Kaiser – an American journalist – drew parallels with the US political scene to argue that the only way for a radical to survive at the lower rungs of the Soviet political hierarchy was to have an entirely conventional political career, to reassure his superiors that he had a 'safe' pair of hands. His conclusion was that Gorbachev was a 'closet reformer': a political schizophrenic wherein dwelled both the reformer and the apparatchik. This left Kaiser with one question: how could Gorbachev – who on this reading was an innovative, energetic, creative and highly intellectual figure – survive over 20 years of stultifying boredom, conformism, condescension and ignorance? The answer lies in a combination of extreme ambition, self-assurance and faith, which allowed him to tolerate the toadying, dull speechifying and arcane rituals of Communist Party life, because his eyes were on a greater prize:

> Only Gorbachev's combination of ambition, self-confidence, and faith could have given him the patience to survive in Party politics. The faith seems a critically important ingredient; the obvious fact that he was not guided by crude selfishness or a lust for power suggests his faith in a greater purpose. But what was it?[65]

Kaiser does not answer his own rather intriguing question.

Brown is probably the most interesting, and has been very influential in shaping the academic debate about Gorbachev's role in the events between 1985 and 1991, and in assessing his place in the history of the twentieth century. Jack Matlock, when reviewing this book, states that 'Brown makes a better case for Gorbachev's record as a reformer than Gorbachev's own memoirs'![66] A highly sympathetic and remarkably detailed piece of work, Brown long held the view that Gorbachev would be a serious and sustained reformer of the system were he to become General Secretary. He had in fact said as much as far back as 1980, the result of conversations with Zdenek Mlynar, the dissident Czech intellectual who was a contemporary and close friend of Gorbachev during his time at Moscow State University. Brown's work *The Gorbachev Factor* was published after Gorbachev's memoirs, but was only able to make limited use of the German version in his research because the publication dates of the two works were so close.

Brown's line on Gorbachev's past is clear: he entitles his chapter 'The Making of a Reformer'.[67] He pieces together the period from the early biographies, interviews and the published memoir material to provide a picture of the making of the man who would innovate, transform and eventually destroy the system he had risen through. Here Gorbachev comes over as a determined, flexible, innovative figure, almost an alien product of the Soviet system. Although he had luck – the right patrons, the deaths of key figures at crucial moments, the fertility of the Stavropol soil, the distance from Moscow which allowed him to work relatively unfettered – Gorbachev was also talented and persistent. Brown is highly critical of the émigré works that cast aspersions on Gorbachev's record, particularly his university days. His successful application to Moscow University is attributed to his excellent work record, rather than his class origins. His university days are appraised overwhelmingly positively: he emerges from Brown's pages as a courageous, loyal friend, sticking up for Jewish colleagues facing persecution, as a flexible and undogmatic thinker, a good listener, a debater, and someone willing to criticize empty propaganda.

Crucial to Brown's viewpoint was his contention, derived again primarily although not exclusively from Mlynar, that Gorbachev placed a very high premium on the lessons of experience, of reality, in determining policy. Rather than squeezing reality into the mould created by the official ideology, Gorbachev preferred to examine theory in the light of reality. This enabled Brown to argue that there was a strongly pragmatic streak in Gorbachev. This pragmatism evidenced itself in certain ways throughout the years prior to 1985: his support for particular central initiatives, his ritualistic praise for the publication of Brezhnev's memoirs. In other words, Gorbachev was a reformer and an innovator prior to 1985, but was constrained by the circumstances of his position and the system. Gorbachev had to play by the rules of the Soviet game in order to reach the top and so this accounts for his timidity and caution before 1985. Having attained the summit of power, this enabled him to throw off the constraints and give vent to his deeply held beliefs.[68]

Brown goes on to argue that Gorbachev does not appear so cautious and conformist when compared to his colleagues, and that during his time in the Politburo he read widely, immersed himself in the high culture of Moscow, encouraged the publication of potentially contentious articles on agricultural matters and invited specialists and experts for discussions. All in all, while clearly nowhere near an overt dissident akin to Andrei Sakharov, Gorbachev was equally distant from the majority of the central leadership. He was a within-system reformer. Whereas earlier works saw his adoption of a reformist stance as a pragmatic decision in his drive for power, Brown saw Gorbachev adopting pragmatic positions in his drive to achieve enough power to institute reforms.

McCauley's work is based much more heavily on Gorbachev's own memoirs.[69] He traces Gorbachev's rise, and sees him as a risk-taker, a hard worker, a man of initiative who learned lessons from all of the political bosses he worked with. In fact, the whole period is for McCauley one of Gorbachev learning lessons: from colleagues, from experience, from visits abroad, preparing him for his time in power. Galeotti focuses on Gorbachev's mixed heritage, 'part dissident, part loyal apparatchik'.[70] Breslauer's appraisal, in a work comparing Gorbachev and Yeltsin, adopts a slightly different stance by exploring the nature of Gorbachev's personality, and the impact of this on his leadership style. Breslauer makes the case for Gorbachev being a dynamic, energetic, political leader who knew how to get along with significant figures and to avoid making enemies, willing to compromise and to ensure he was always on the winning side. He generally exhibited an optimistic mind-set. In terms of his outlook, Breslauer argues that prior to 1985 Gorbachev had come to be reformist: in favour of change to enable the communist system to fulfil its potential, and in favour of a reduction in international tensions. He was passionately committed to the system (a party man) and its improvement (a reformist). Once more the reformist/pragmatist/loyal apparatchik nexus is given a new twist.[71]

In sum, no-one was able to come up with a definitive portrayal of Gorbachev's rise to power. He appeared to combine sincere faith in, and great loyalty to, the system and its ideals, as well as being an innovative and 'modern' political figure open to new ideas and eager to change the system. He appeared to have a public face of abrasive, calculating political zeal and ambition, and a private face of friendship, loyalty and soul-searching. There were some mysterious elements in his rise – how he managed to work his way through the hierarchy with the stigma of having had a family member in the gulags and having lived in an occupied territory during the war, the choice of law, the move back to Stavropol after studying – which have eluded a satisfactory answer. The problems in appraising Gorbachev's rise are not just caused by the mysteries and gaps in his past, but also because many commentators have gone into Gorbachev's past looking for something, and have often then found it: a closet Stalinist, an apparatchik, a reformer in the making.

Conclusion: not many Gorbachevs, but one

The difficulty for analysts and commentators has not just been the gaps in the narrative and the sparsity of sources, but it has been wrestling with the apparent conundrums of pragmatism/conformity/reformism within one person. Gorbachev's career does seem to be full of paradoxes and puzzles. But how distinct is Gorbachev in this regard? It is surely unrealistic to expect a political figure to maintain the same set of beliefs, to be entirely consistent, to live without making compromises, conforming or shifting position as the broader political landscape shifts and changes. In this respect, Gorbachev is not unlike many other politicians in the USSR, the USA, the UK and elsewhere. A more fruitful approach to looking at Gorbachev's past is to look carefully at the interplay of context, personality, contingency, all within the notion of Gorbachev's journeys – both geographical and political – from the provinces to the centre and to the provinces and back to the centre, from the lower rungs to the higher, from apparatchik to leader.

Understanding the nature of Gorbachev's rise to power needs to be set within the context of the nature of the Soviet system, the process of political promotion, and the ideological and philosophical stranglehold there was on unorthodox thinking. Gorbachev was ambitious and hard-working and had to work his way up through the system. But social and political advancement in the Soviet system required high-level skills of micro-negotiation, of being able to determine which way the political winds were blowing, of pleasing your superiors, maintaining the appearance of political loyalty to party, state and ideology, and also of luck. Gorbachev had all these things. The key *modus operandi* for a provincial official was to ensure that you were able to demonstrate achievements and loyalty and trustworthiness. A successful provincial official made sure there were no high-level problems in their area, and that they took the applause for any achievements. A successful provincial official also had to be able to bend with the prevailing winds. The changes of General Secretary after 1956 meant many changes of line and approach, and the ability to be flexible, and to make the right choices of who to support and when were important if your career was not to stall. Gorbachev was an insider. He knew the rules of the game and he played them very well. Gorbachev's career in the Stavropol region was thus similar to many political officials starting out on their careers.

Gorbachev's personality thus deserves centre-stage in any account of his rise to power. He had all the attributes necessary to make his way up through the party. He was enough of a party man to work within certain parameters, but was also independent-minded enough to innovate or experiment in limited areas when it suited him. Moreover, Gorbachev's time in the provinces must be seen as a time of learning and political and personal formation. He learned techniques and approaches in the Komsomol in terms of dealing with people which he was to adopt when he was a national leader. He came to see first hand the problems in the system, to understand the frustrations of ordinary people and the complexities of the Soviet agricultural sector. He took time to learn and be educated in agronomic techniques. It was precisely Gorbachev's experiences of being at different levels of the system and rising up through it that formed in him the sense that change was increasingly necessary. This sense was amplified by Gorbachev being part of a new generation which was not shaped by the 1930s or the war, but whose formative political experiences came during the 1950s and 1960s, as one of the *shestidesyatniki*, the men of the 1960s. Less committed to the old ways, more open to other ways of doing Soviet socialism, this relative openness to change acted as a filter through which Gorbachev viewed and interpreted his experiences.

It is wrong, however, to divorce Gorbachev's rise and emergence from the system itself. There is a great temptation, given what Gorbachev went on to do, to try and divorce Gorbachev from the system, or to see him as some kind of alien force growing up within it. The system itself bred conformity. But it could not eradicate inward non-conformity and did not even manage to eliminate outright dissent, although it made very thorough attempts to do so. Gorbachev in many ways embodies the system itself, and his rise to power is an authentic expression of the nature of the Soviet system from 1956 to 1985. The system itself was riddled with tensions and contradictions and paradoxes, and its officials and leaders embodied these. As a system, it was deeply committed to maintaining the status quo and the prevailing distribution of power and wealth. It was almost pathologically resistant to change. Yet at the same time it continued to generate the desire for change. The external pressures of the Cold War and competition for hegemony in the socialist bloc compelled the Soviets to seek constant attempts at modernization and improvement. The ideological rationale of demonstrating progress towards communism also compelled either improvements at home, or textual ideological gymnastics to redefine communism or demonstrate that capitalism was still dying. Gorbachev grew up in this system. He remained deeply committed to the party, a firm believer in socialism and a convinced adherent to the Soviet project. He also wanted change, to improve it, breathe new life into it. There is no real puzzle here. Gorbachev was a representative member of the Soviet political spectrum which at one end contained dissidents and hard-line critics of many hues, and at the other conformists and stalwarts of the system. Inbetween were a varied bunch of people who melded change, openness, conformism and loyalty to the system. Gorbachev was one of these.

But there is also an inescapable contingency about Gorbachev's rise to power. First, his ability to escape his troubled childhood and earn a place at university in Moscow was crucial in his rise to power. Second, Gorbachev was a successful provincial politician. But the province was important. It enabled him to make contact with key figures like Andropov and Kulakov. It helped him to demonstrate agricultural achievements. Third, the sudden deaths of key figures accelerated his rise. Gorbachev could quite easily have remained a provincial party boss, or become a low-level national figure. Gorbachev took advantage very skilfully of opportunities that came his way, but he was not the architect of many of these opportunities.

In essence, some of the problems involved in appraising Gorbachev's rise lie in our inability/unwillingness to think creatively about individuals and the Soviet system. How could such a conformist, stultifying, crushingly oppressive system spawn someone like Gorbachev? And how could someone like Gorbachev exist for so long in the Soviet system without losing heart, giving up or becoming an open dissident? To understand Gorbachev's rise we need in some sense to 'normalize' his upbringing, to see him as an individual working his way up the ladder and experiencing the same fortunes as others in other countries at other times. We need to stop looking at Gorbachev 1985–91 and reading backwards from there to search for where this person came from, and start looking at Gorbachev in the period 1931–85 on his own terms, to historicize his past.

Let us turn to examine some of the other key problems in interpreting Gorbachev, starting with his reform programme: *perestroika*.

2

Gorbachev

The inside story

Introduction

Understanding *perestroika* is central to understanding Gorbachev. But *perestroika* was a programme with many tensions and ambiguities, a programme that changed and evolved and was cut short before it was completed. So, what did Gorbachev understand by *perestroika*, and what did he think he was doing? How did his understanding of his project change and evolve over time? This chapter will examine the speeches, articles, books, broadcasts, press conferences and interviews given by Gorbachev between March 1985 and August 1991 in order to answer these key questions. As a result, this chapter will attempt to piece together a sense of how *perestroika* unfolded and developed after 1985. This enables us to see in close-up the twists and turns in the journey, to notice any turning-points and to become aware of the multi-faceted complexity of the task Gorbachev undertook. By looking at the history of *perestroika* from Gorbachev's perspective, we see the intimate connection between Gorbachev and *his* project. It also allows us to reflect upon the type of leader Gorbachev was, at home and abroad, as radical reformer and crisis-manager. Deciphering Gorbachev's words helps us get to the heart of who Gorbachev was, what he was trying to do and how he wanted to be viewed.[1]

The analysis of Gorbachev's public utterances during this period has to be undertaken with an awareness of the distinctive contexts and audiences in which it was delivered. Gorbachev expressed his ideas in a variety of formats: press conferences, formal speeches, interviews, discussions with the people on walkabouts, debates, and so on, which profoundly affected the tone and content of his message. The language and content of his book *Perestroika* were obviously very different from his conversations with the working people during his walkabouts, or in his interviews with Western media outlets. Interpreting the words of a Soviet leader was an arcane business. It involved a combination of close textual analysis with the ability to read between the lines. It meant looking beneath the surface and being able to identify signs and symbols which, to the initiated, were like a flashing light or a blaring horn alerting the reader to a development of great interest. In addition, many of his speeches, articles and books were multi-authored (although Gorbachev worked assiduously in the processes of drafting and redrafting).

There were a number of basic rules governing the discourse of Soviet leaders which it is useful to be aware of, particularly when examining a leader who had just taken charge:

- Lenin must be cited. To establish authority and credibility, any Soviet leader had to display an impeccable Leninist pedigree, promising to return the Soviet state to the ideas of the Founding Fathers – Lenin, Marx and (to a lesser extent) Engels.
- Previous leaders must be criticized. Bolstering the authority of the new leader meant denouncing (either directly or indirectly) the previous leader in order to highlight the need to return to Lenin.
- New leaders needed to oversee new doctrines/ideas as evidence of their status as an accomplished theorist of Marxism-Leninism.
- The basic principles and institutions of the system must be immune from criticism. Problems in the system could be highlighted, but were to be attributed to external causes: vestiges from the past, the vagaries of international capitalism, or previous leaders (see above).
- At all times, progress towards a brighter future had to be demonstrated, even if the timetable for reaching the promised utopia remained vague.
- At all times, the inherent superiority of socialism over capitalism had to be demonstrated.
- At all times, the position of the Soviet Union as the leading force in the socialist bloc had to be maintained.

Gorbachev's leadership was a multi-faceted one. He was General Secretary of the CPSU. He was the Head of the Soviet Union. He was to become the Chairman of the Supreme Soviet and the Executive President of the Soviet state. He was the leader of the socialist bloc. He was the embodiment of Soviet communism on a global stage.[2] What sort of image did Gorbachev project in these different roles? By building up a differentiated view of Gorbachev, his message and his leadership, we begin to discern a picture of this highly complex, paradoxical figure who dominated the world stage for six years.

Gorbachev before 1985: innovator in waiting? Or advocate of orthodoxy?

Prior to becoming General Secretary of the Communist Party in March 1985 on the death of Konstantin Chernenko, Gorbachev wrote and spoke on a variety of topics and issues, although given his relative youth and his rapid rise through the hierarchy, the quantity of output was not massive. He had spoken and written mainly on agricultural issues as CC Secretary with responsibility for agriculture from 1978 onwards. This included addresses to the Supreme Soviet, articles in the party propaganda organ *Agitator*, articles in the party's main theoretical journal *Kommunist*, and pieces in the main party newspaper *Pravda*. Given that agriculture was traditionally the Achilles' heel of the Soviet economy, were there any intimations of the radical, critical approach which emerged after 1985 in his pre-1985 output?

The constraints on expressing critical, new or radical ideas were huge, but not insurmountable. It was possible to publish unorthodox ideas, but it was not always politically expedient to do so. Promotion through the Soviet hierarchy was dependent upon demonstrating public fealty to the party line, irrespective of one's private views. This appears to have posed no problem for Gorbachev. His agricultural writings supported limited experimentation – the semi-autonomous link system[3] – in agricultural affairs, but broke no real new ground. He delivered the key report to an All-Union conference on the agricultural economy on 26–27 March 1984. His report adopted a critical tone, and stressed that results had to improve, work must be intensified, people must work harder, and so on. The shift in tone was more noticeable than the content.

Perhaps the most important pieces before Gorbachev came to power were his address to a scientific conference on 10 December 1984,[4] his speech to the British Parliament[5] a week later and his RSFSR Supreme Soviet election address of 20 February 1985.[6] In all these pieces, there is a mixture of orthodox thinking and loyal phraseology, combined with some unorthodox ideas. The speech of 10 December was the one which contained the most innovative elements, talking of the need to develop the socialist self-government of the people, to observe the law, to improve the political system, to use publicity and to have trust in the people. Echoing themes from the Andropov years – the need for more discipline, order, organization – Gorbachev stressed the need for the participation of the people and for a heightened role to be played by the party workers or cadres. In the speech in Britain and in his election speech he also talked of Europe as 'our common home' and highlighted the common problems facing humanity: nuclear war, the arms race, environmental problems.[7]

There were also further intimations of Gorbachev's more critical approach, talking in both domestic speeches of unsolved problems or shortcomings, of the need for great efforts to be made, of the necessity of combating bureaucratism and formalism in the work of officialdom. Although much of this talk was standard fare for Soviet leaders in their efforts to exhort their population to work harder, and the officials to be more responsive, the emphasis in Gorbachev's speeches was clearly on what needed to be done, not on what had already been achieved. This reversed the usual order which was to celebrate what had been accomplished before mentioning what was still undone. But Gorbachev still had to play by the rules of the Soviet game. This meant making constant references to Lenin to support your arguments, as well as praising the current incumbent. His praise of Chernenko – 'a great contribution to the elaboration of Marxist-Leninist theory ... a leader of the Leninist type' – echoed earlier fawning of Brezhnev.[8] Gorbachev also reverted to Stalinist themes when he spoke of continuing Stakhanovite traditions. All in all, his pre-General Secretary positions seemed to be a mixture of orthodox and unorthodox ideas and themes.

Gorbachev's first year: a thoroughly modern Bolshevik?

Gorbachev's initial 14–15 months in power contained a number of key speeches, broadcasts and media appearances which saw the first signs of a distinctive Gorbachevian message emerging. It also saw the key motifs of his speeches being constantly repeated, as well as a new style of leadership: more frank, more critical, more attuned to the people. At the same time, Gorbachev reiterated some very traditional Bolshevik themes, confirming the impression that he was attempting to combine the old and the new. So just how distinctive and innovative was Gorbachev being in this period?

The most striking features of this period were the way that Gorbachev sought to portray himself as a leader in touch with his people, and to use the mass media (both in the USSR and in the West) to get his message across. Gorbachev very early on in his tenure went on a number of walkabouts – clearly carefully staged – to meet the people.[9] This served a number of purposes for Gorbachev. Shots of Gorbachev mixing with the crowds, talking and debating, were designed to communicate a radically different style of leader to the whole Soviet people, one who would be closer to the people, would appear to be listening, was more open, approachable, accessible. Gorbachev's obvious youth and vigour in comparison with the procession of decrepit leaders also communicated the sense of renewal and a fresh beginning. It also was a means of Gorbachev communicating his message directly to the people, without it being filtered and interpreted by local party figures or journalists. Indeed, a key part of what Gorbachev was attempting to do required that the Soviet people be mobilized to criticize those officials who were complacent and corrupt.

But what was his message? *The need for change.* The people had to change the way they thought, worked and acted. Everyone had to 'restructure themselves'. If qualitative changes to the system were to occur, this had to begin with each person changing themselves. But why was change required? In his diagnosis Gorbachev highlighted that problems had been accumulating and they had not been addressed. Economic problems – inefficiency, poor quality, wastefulness – were slowing down the development of the economy. Technological development was lagging behind. The system had to change, be modernized. Gorbachev's tone was far franker in criticizing shortcomings than previous leaders, and he also exhorted the people themselves to speak out against failures, malpractice and 'negative phenomena'. Certain themes and motifs were constantly repeated – the need for discipline to combat corruption and drunkenness, the need for energy and creativity to solve the problems, the need to work harder, increase productivity, master new technology to bring about economic advances. These were traditional Bolshevik ones, incorporating the mobilization of labour, campaigns to resolve specific problems – drunkenness, poor product quality – with the use of science and technology to produce economic improvements. The usual references – to Lenin and to the victory in the Great Patriotic War – were sprinkled throughout his conversations. Indeed, when asked about his more visible, populist style, Gorbachev responded:

This is the style that V.I. Lenin taught us. *It is not just my own personal style.* He constantly talked about the need to live in the midst of the masses, to listen to them, to catch their mood ... this is not a new practice for me. I behaved the same way when I was working in Stavropol territory and here, in Moscow, before I was elected to my present post.[10]

An interesting aspect of Gorbachev during his walkabouts was his ability to relate to the people. He talked very knowledgeably about the technical details and problems facing agricultural workers. He related their experiences to his own, emphasizing the similarities between his background and theirs, narrowing the mental gulf between leaders and led. For instance, in talking about the destruction caused by alcoholism, he related how his village had banded together to ban the sale of alcohol.[11] He was able to combine the usual array of quotes from Lenin with lessons drawn from his own experience.

He also skilfully used the foreign media to communicate his message, doing interviews with the Indian press, appearing on French television, doing a high-profile interview with the US magazine *Time,* and undertaking press conferences after the superpower summit at Geneva in November 1985. A similar objective to his domestic media appearances was in operation here. Gorbachev sought to project a new image of the USSR via projecting himself and his own message to the Western nations. This image was of a leader deeply concerned with the dangers facing humanity, personally and emotionally involved, spontaneous, frank and friendly: in a word, human.[12] His message was of the need for New Thinking. This embraced: cooperation not conflict, dialogue, hostility to the American SDI (Strategic Defense Initiative), global interdependence. The message in the West was far more positive, though. Gorbachev was less inclined to talk of the weaknesses and shortcomings in the Soviet system as the reason for his programme of changes, and much more willing to talk of the strengths and achievements of the USSR. He described as 'delusions' American ideas that the arms race would exhaust the economy of the USSR.[13] He stressed that the thrust of the domestic reforms was to 'improve the people's lives'.[14]

The message to foreign socialists/communists was different again. In talks with Western communists, Gorbachev reverted to traditional Marxist slogans and Cold War rhetoric.[15] In addresses to socialists in the Eastern Bloc, Gorbachev was quick to resort to a similar message to the one he delivered at home: economic slowdown had to be addressed via working harder and faster, psychological restructuring and the active participation of everyone, openness and acceleration.[16] His message of change was not just for the Soviets: it was for all those in the socialist bloc who owed allegiance to the USSR.

Gorbachev was at his most conservative (or perhaps was least innovative) in his dealings with the party and at high-profile events in the calendar of Soviet state rituals. In his first year, the key addresses to the party and the Soviet people came at the April 1985 plenum of the Central Committee,[17] the Victory Day speech, commemorating the 40th anniversary of the victory in the Great Patriotic War in May 1985,[18] the Political Report at the 27th Party Congress in February 1986.[19] Taking the Victory Day speech first, this was the only real ceremonial address of Gorbachev's first year, and it was a very high-profile event given the central place of the war in the mythology of the Soviet state. All of the themes of Gorbachev's first year were here, yet the tone was positive, celebratory, almost triumphalist. He talked of the challenges to be confronted – scientific and technical development, accelerating economic progress – and of the means to do it – mobilizing the energy of the Soviet people, just as in the war – without talking of the accumulating problems which needed to be addressed. The speech included some interesting detail. In what was surely an autobiographical allusion, he spoke of the contribution of the Komsomol youth behind the lines. Thus, although Gorbachev was unable, unlike all the previous Soviet leaders, to establish an unchallengeable legitimacy by pointing to extraordinarily heroic (if at times fictitious) deeds during the war, he did still attempt to generate some link between himself and the great Soviet victory. He also talked – in an echo of Stalin's May 1945 speech – of the Soviet people being inspired by the Russian people.[20] Sprinkled liberally with quotations from Lenin, Gorbachev also sprang a surprise by talking about the positive contribution made by Stalin to the military victory. Stalin was rarely, if ever, mentioned by name, and there was prolonged applause (lasting 22 seconds) at the mention of his name. In sum, Gorbachev's address was a mosaic of different motifs – Russia, Lenin, Stalin and military victory, his own past, the efforts of the people – skilfully assembled to establish his national authority and to associate himself with the dominant legitimizing symbols of Soviet power.

Gorbachev's addresses to the party – both the elite in Moscow and various party workers – adopted a different tone, and stressed different themes as he sought to establish his authority within the party. His tone was frank, critical, urgent and cajoling. Unlike the celebratory tone of his Victory Day speech, his speeches to the party highlighted difficulties and problems. He used the party addresses in a number of ways: as a forum to establish a reputation for himself as a doctrinal innovator, introducing new concepts and ideas; to criticize his predecessors and allocate blame for the current difficulties; as a forum for information gathering; and, finally, to communicate the key elements of his programme for change. Let us take these one at a time. In terms of conceptual innovation, at the April 1985 CC plenum, he talked at length for the first time of the need for *uskorenie* (acceleration) of socio-economic development and of the need to activate the human factor (basically the need to get people actively involved in changing the system). References to the need for openness or publicity (*glasnost'*) were made more frequently, as well. Second, he also offered criticisms of his predecessors (notably Brezhnev) for not addressing the accumulating problems consistently or in good time. The problems had been diagnosed, but action amounted to little more than talk. He was keen to absolve Andropov from any blame, arguing that improvements were made after 1983, but difficulties still remained and had to be addressed urgently. Herein lay the reason that 'acceleration' was required. Third,

Gorbachev was also keen to garner information and ideas from those with experience of working in the system at grass-roots levels.[21]

So what was the essence of Gorbachev's message? Three themes dominated. One was cadres/personnel policy. Gorbachev constantly referred to the need for cadres to work in new and different ways, and of the need to remove those cadres who were obstructive, corrupt, apathetic or incompetent. Cadres had to work 'more responsibly', to change their style of work, to master new technology. The second theme was the need for the people themselves to become actively involved, to show initiative and discipline, to work more productively and efficiently. Words like 'energy', 'creativity' and 'dynamism' were readily invoked to describe the contribution of the masses. Finally, Gorbachev stressed the need to accelerate socio-economic development. This meant increasing economic growth, but also creating a new kind of economic growth – efficient, productive, modernized, cost-conscious, intensive – in order to restore dynamism to the Soviet economy. How was this intensive growth to be achieved? By reorganizing economic management, instilling strong labour discipline, increasing the economic autonomy of enterprises, and applying science and technology to the productive process.[22] In a number of speeches to party workers and economic activists, Gorbachev stressed the importance of science and technology to future economic success.

The main set-piece address of Gorbachev's first year came at the 27th Party Congress in February 1986.[23] It was here that Gorbachev displayed his acute sense of historical awareness, and of the importance of historical symbolism. The Congress began on 25 February 1986, 30 years to the day from Khrushchev's momentous four-hour 'secret' speech to the 20th Congress of the Communist Party, the first attack on Stalin and the onset of the process of de-Stalinization.[24] The symbolism was clear: this Congress was a further step away from Stalinism; there was to be no turning back the clock as under Brezhnev.[25] Gorbachev's message drew together the strands of his first year: problems were still to be resolved, the need for acceleration, the importance of cadres, the need for mass participation, opposition to dogma and dogmatic thinking, a stress on concrete practical experience. There were also some new points, or stronger emphases placed on particular points. The problems of the past were now characterized as the onset of a time of 'stagnation' (*zastoi*). Criticism of the Brezhnev era (although not yet Brezhnev himself) was being stepped up.[26] Links between accelerated economic growth and wider socio-political changes were also beginning to be made. A great stress was placed on the need to increase democratization and socialist self-government. Gorbachev also took this opportunity to highlight that *uskorenie* was now established officially as a new concept. In a long passage, Gorbachev defined it thus:

What do we mean by acceleration? First of all, raising the rate of economic growth. But that is not all. In substance it means a new quality of growth: an all-out intensification of production on the basis of scientific and technological progress, a structural reconstruction of the economy, effective forms of management and of organizing and stimulating labour. The policy of acceleration ... envisages an active social policy ... a deepening of socialist democracy, and resolute overcoming of inertness, stagnation and conservatism ... In short, comrades, acceleration of the country's socio-economic development is the key to all our problems: immediate and long-term, economic and social, political and ideological, domestic and foreign. That is the only way a new qualitative condition of society can and must be achieved.[27]

Standing back from Gorbachev's message during his first months in power, certain aspects stand out. The first is that Gorbachev's leadership marked a clear break with traditional modes of Soviet leadership. There was a strong populist strand, meeting with the people on walkabouts, discussing their lives, hearing their concerns, exhorting them to join with him. It emphasized personal involvement. It was also a leadership style marked by increasing frankness and criticism. There was a greater willingness to talk about problems and shortcomings, although this was still a highly limited, selective and closely choreographed exercise in what remained a state built on secrecy and obfuscation. The moves towards greater frankness were evidenced most clearly in the treatment of the recent past. Gorbachev's leadership was also a multi-faceted one which depicted itself in different ways to different audiences, demonstrating a highly acute awareness of the power of the media as a political tool. Gorbachev seemed conversant with modern, Western modes of political leadership.

But Gorbachev was also in many ways an archetypal, traditional Soviet leader. His message, like a stick of rock, had 'Bolshevik' stamped all the way through it. The two dominant themes – revitalize the work and the membership of the cadres and accelerated economic growth – were archetypal Bolshevik themes, confirming that Gorbachev's thinking was saturated with the traditional mentality of the ruling party. His chosen means – campaigning, mobilizing and exhortatory – were again ones that the Soviet people would recognize all too well. Critical thinking about systemic change – that the problems might be the result of something inherent within the basic structures of the Soviet system – was inexpressible publicly. Critical thinking about the structure of power – the monopoly position of the CPSU – was equally unspeakable in public. Within these parameters, the main place to look for solutions was in the quality of the personnel running the system. Restoring dynamism could best be done (and most easily measured) by increasing growth rates: crude production figures had always been the favoured method for Soviet leaders to demonstrate both the superiority of socialism over capitalism, and the approach of the communist utopia. In this sense, Gorbachev was entirely orthodox. However, Gorbachev was also aware of the need to modernize, to bring Bolshevism up-to-date by recognizing that accelerated growth also required a new kind of growth: intensive, efficient, technological.

The initial Gorbachev style consisted of a synthesis of the old, the new, and the old updated in the new conditions. His critical, urgent tone, his emphasis upon the importance of publicity/openness, his stress on experience over ideology, and the links with greater democracy and self-government provided hints of unorthodoxy in Gorbachev's thinking. Yet there were strong strands of continuity: campaigns, mobilization, cadres policy and the like. The language used by Gorbachev revealed a leader attempting to combine the conceptual apparatus of Soviet Marxism-Leninism with his own personal concerns and experiences. This included a surprising number of biblical references and analogies for the leader of the world's first self-proclaimed atheist state.[28] The image Gorbachev sought to promote synthesized three main themes: populism (a leader able to relate to the experiences of the people); Leninism (a faithful follower and advocate for the ideas and values of the Founding Father of Bolshevism); and universalism (a leader who shared the concern of people across the globe about the possibilities of nuclear war and environmental catastrophe).

Gorbachev's leadership style and message in his first year embodied a series of paradoxes that lasted throughout his time in power. Gorbachev shifted between the elements in each paradox depending upon the context, the audience and the immediate task at hand. Understanding this is crucial to understanding the difficulties there are in interpreting what Gorbachev was about. The paradoxes can be expressed thus:

Gorbachev as true believer   *v.*   *Gorbachev as heretic*
Gorbachev combined a deep personal commitment to the essential features of Soviet socialism with a consistent tendency to unorthodox thinking and criticism. This was often expressed as Gorbachev as both Pope and Luther.

Gorbachev the pragmatist   *v.*   *Gorbachev the theorist*
Gorbachev married a strongly practical, problem-solving bent with a profound appreciation of the importance of theory.

Gorbachev the populist   *v.*   *Gorbachev the politician*
Gorbachev projected an image of a populist down-to-earth folksy leader deeply concerned with the everyday needs of the people, while simultaneously skilfully playing the political power game of building his own power-base and undermining his rivals.

Gorbachev as modernizer of   *v.*   *Gorbachev as preserver of the*
Bolshevism   *Bolshevik heritage*
Gorbachev was committed to modernizing the system, yet preserving the healthy elements from the Bolshevik past. Modernization was required in order to save the system. The system was worth saving because of everything that had been built, but more importantly because of all the sacrifices made by the people in building it.

Gorbachev as internationalist   v.   Gorbachev as patriot
Gorbachev constantly espoused a set of values which gave prominence to the interests of humanity as a whole in the face of the threats of global annihilation, yet was also deeply patriotic, valuing his ethnic Russian background and defending the interests of the Soviet Union.

Gorbachev the intimate leader   v.   Gorbachev as global superhero
Gorbachev's approach was intensely personal: he sought personal contact and encounters with people both at home and abroad, valued greatly his family life and upbringing, used illustrations from his own background to connect with the people he met and spoke to. Yet Gorbachev was also a global celebrity and a world statesman.

All political leaders are confronted with complex demands which compel them into adopting paradoxical stances at times. Gorbachev was no exception. Gorbachev was a particularly acute case, though, given the profound changes he sought to introduce – both at home and abroad – in such a short space of time in a system designed to maintain itself in power. Gorbachev's leadership evolved in a complex fashion, as the paradoxes set out above shifted to create a kaleidoscopic pattern. Gorbachev's leadership also became increasingly fragmented and complex. He found himself in the very tricky situation where he had to exercise leadership of the 'old' system in traditional ways, while at the same time having to exercise leadership of the emerging new system that he was creating, and had to learn new ways of operating as he went along.

Gorbachev's leadership evolved through a series of phases, each with its own imperatives, and each of which presented a new set of challenges to Gorbachev. In the first phase (between approximately July 1986 and c. November 1987), Gorbachev was engaged in designing his programme and seeking to persuade everyone to support him and his line. In the second phase (between c. January 1988 and February/March 1990), Gorbachev was essentially an activist leader attempting to put his programme into practice, coping with criticism and trying to make it work. The final phase (c. March 1990 to August 1991), Gorbachev was essentially a reactive leader, responding to situations and managing crises. Let us look at these in turn.

Phase I: *Gorbachev as architect and persuader: from* uskorenie *to* perestroika *(July 1986–November 1987)*

Between the end of the Party Congress in March 1986 and a busy summer of speeches, visits and walkabouts, Gorbachev made only a few public appearances.[29] Any speeches merely repeated the message of his Congress report: the need for more publicity, the need to develop democracy within the system. At the end of April, Gorbachev had to deal with the Chernobyl disaster. At first, the Soviet authorities attempted to cover this up, which dealt a huge blow to Gorbachev's attempt to show the West that *glasnost'* was for real. Gorbachev was able to turn this around skilfully though, using it to overhaul the Soviet media, replacing those editors who were resistant to the new line and installing more critical and reform-minded figures. Internationally though, Gorbachev used Chernobyl to substantiate his argument that the world was a dangerous place, and so great strides towards nuclear disarmament were vital. Even if conflict did not break out, accidents might trigger a war inadvertently.[30] It soon became clear that the process of change was stepping up a gear.

It would appear that Gorbachev was involved in taking stock of what had already been achieved.[31] This stock-taking resulted in a number of key speeches and addresses between the Central Committee plenary session on 16 June and his visit to Khabarovsk and the Far East at the start of August. Gorbachev used this to herald the onset of a more radical phase of change, highlighting the persistence of old ways of thinking and acting, stressing the need for more basic fundamental changes, and hinting at the first signs of resistance to his policies. Reflecting this gear change, the emphasis shifted from *uskorenie* to *perestroika* (restructuring, reconstruction, reorganization). The project to restructure the system was becoming both *broader* – to incorporate new areas – and *deeper* – to address the underlying causes of the problems, not just the surface symptoms.

Gorbachev's addresses to party forums again adopted a frank, critical tone, coupled with more exhortations aimed at party personnel. The 16 June 1986 plenum was devoted to a review of the five-year plan for the economy, but turned into a review of the initial lessons of *perestroika*.[32] What had been learned? First, the old approaches had led the economy into a blind alley, and were still holding back progress. *Perestroika* was progressing slowly because people were still unsure how to act. Moreover, the improvements that had already been achieved were a result of exploiting already existing reserves within the system. Further progress could not be achieved this way, but only through more basic changes. In other words, the emphasis on discipline, labour productivity, improved product quality and exhortations to work harder had brought limited gains. Now, according to Gorbachev, 'We must boldly execute sharp turns and not be afraid of decisive transformations.'[33] Gorbachev also continued to harangue and cajole party workers for their unwillingness to embrace the new style of working. This radical emphasis was deepened in his speeches at a ceremonial meeting in Vladivostok on 28 July 1986,[34] and to activists at Khabarovsk on 2 August 1986.[35] The Vladivostok speech recognized that it had not been possible to achieve *uskorenie* yet, because 'highly important economic, social, organizational, ideological and other measures have just begun to be carried out and are not able to produce an immediate effect'.[36] This seemed to presage a shift in emphasis: successful economic changes required a whole raft of measures in other fields. *Perestroika* was inexorably broadening its scope outside of cadre changes and narrowly economic policies.

A few days later in Khabarovsk, Gorbachev elaborated further. In doing so, he began to reveal the diagnostic process underpinning his project, and significantly radicalized the language of reform. Gorbachev reinforced his anti-dogmatic, pragmatic, experiential approach, saying that it was necessary to 'learn as we go along', that there were no 'ready-made recipes' and that 'the further we advance, the more the complexity of the task is revealed'.[37] Most significant was Gorbachev's description of *perestroika* as a 'revolution':

> I would equate the word *perestroika* with the word revolution. Our transformations, the reforms mapped out ... are a genuine revolution in the entire system of relations in society, in the minds and hearts of people, in the psychology and understanding of the present period and, above all, in the tasks engendered by rapid scientific and technical progress ... The farther we advance into *perestroika*, the more the complexity of the task is revealed ... It is becoming clearer to what extent many notions about the economy and management, social questions, statehood and democracy, upbringing and education and moral demands still lag behind today's requirements and tasks.[38]

The project for change had become both more radical and more comprehensive than at first thought. The party cadres had to respond by changing their style of work, in order to get closer to the people.

In the summer and autumn of 1986, Gorbachev went to the people, first, in Khabarovsk and Vladivostok, and then after his traditional August break he went to Krasnodar in September 1986.[39] Around his usual message to the people he met – work harder, embrace change, restructure yourself, show initiative, act responsibly – the pillars of Gorbachev's approach were beginning to become visible. Its themes were: pragmatism, collectivism, comprehensiveness, openness and expertise. The approach was to be practical and pragmatic, rather than driven by more abstract or general principles.[40] Problems (well, at least the ones the leadership wanted talked about) had to be discussed openly rather than glossed over or ignored. It was to be based on the individual contributing to the public good through their own hard work and self-sacrifice. For example, the plans to introduce private plots and more independent economic activity were to serve as a stimulus to greater production, not to inculcate a grasping, 'look after number one' mentality. Expertise – the ability to solve problems and deliver results – was to be valued over posturing and rhetoric.[41] It was to be a holistic, interconnected approach. Gorbachev was keen to address all aspects of the life of society, not just their working conditions. This explains his concern with the cultural amenities in towns and villages, and of the need to cater for the social requirements of families.[42] *Perestroika* was *broadening* out beyond cadres and the economy.

In support of this, Gorbachev adopted two lines. One was to be more selective in his use of quotations from Lenin to substantiate what he was doing. In his speech to the Krasnodar party *aktiv* in September 1986, he talked of Lenin and the New Economic Policy (NEP) to illustrate the problems in persuading people to adapt to a new situation which they may be uncomfortable with.[43] Increasingly, Gorbachev was to resort to quotations from the 'later' (i.e. after 1921) Lenin.[44] The second approach adopted by Gorbachev was to talk about his own experiences The conversations between Gorbachev and the people had a strongly nostalgic feel to them. Although Gorbachev talked often of the need for modernization, and how it was imperative to respond to the new conditions, his was also a retrospective message, looking back to a time when Soviet society (especially rural society) lived and worked together with pride and diligence. On a visit to the Izobilnenskiy state farm in September 1986, Gorbachev talked about the need to build cultural facilities where families could congregate together 'the way it always used to be'. Reminiscing, Gorbachev outlined how

> They get together and do things: the children show off their talents, then competitions – best kept yard, best kept homestead, a street festival ... we're all agronomy specialists, but we've forgotten this is human work. Man works and gives but if – outside his work, in his family, in the street, in the village – things are interesting then somehow he feels more at ease and he comes to work in a completely different mood.[45]

The themes of Gorbachev's conversations reflected these twin sources: the later Lenin and personal experience.

The late autumn of 1986 was taken up with the Reykjavik Summit and preparations for a key CC plenum which was to advance *perestroika* into the political sphere for the first time, clearly evolving out of this shift in thinking over the spring and summer of 1986. Although Gorbachev and Reagan were unable to reach agreement on disarmament proposals at Reykjavik, the Soviet leader embarked on a sustained public campaign to communicate his message that the failure to reach agreement was due to the intransigence of the USA over their Star Wars or SDI programme.[46] He was at pains to stress his commitment to peace and disarmament, and of the need for new thinking on the international stage. The message – at home and abroad – was one of overturning the old practices, ways of thinking and ways of acting. Abroad this meant energetic peace and disarmament initiatives to win over Western public support for his position.

1986 drew to a close with two important speeches from Gorbachev. One came at the closing session of the 69th anniversary celebrations of the October Revolution. Here Gorbachev continued to use Lenin in support of his pragmatic stance:

> Any self-deception means the start of troubles, and we know that. While holding sacred our great traditions, we do not forget, nor should we forget about a most important behest from Lenin: more attention to unsolved problems, and fewer grand phrases, raptures and exclamations.[47]

Reviewing 1986 in his New Year broadcast to the Soviet people, Gorbachev reiterated the dominant themes: profound changes were underway, *perestroika* would be an all-embracing, revolutionary affair, resistance and complacency were still apparent.[48] If the words communicated an accelerating rate and scale of change underway, the images which went with his TV broadcast – Reykjavik, walkabouts with the people, tanks pulling out of Afghanistan – spoke of Gorbachev as Man of Peace and Man of the People.

The moves to *deepen perestroika* were announced to a CC plenum of 27 January 1987.[49] Throughout February, Gorbachev then undertook a series of high-profile visits and addresses in which he attempted to elaborate upon the decisions taken at the plenum, and to mobilize support for the new line. It was a controversial meeting, having been thrice postponed in the latter stages of 1986. It is possible to see elements of the thinking behind the plenum speech in Gorbachev's interview with Indian journalists broadcast on Soviet television on 23 November 1986.[50] What did Gorbachev say to his party?

After a long preamble in which Gorbachev spoke frankly about the problems and short-comings in the system, and the essential features of *perestroika*, Gorbachev unveiled the centre-piece of the next phase of *perestroika*: democratization. Moves were announced to democratize various aspects of the Soviet system – the elections to the Soviets, inner-party democracy, workplace democratization – as a means of achieving the qualitative changes in Soviet society. The rationale for this development was a little murky. Gorbachev seemed to be saying a number of different things about why democratization was now necessary, not all of which happily co-existed. Three paradoxes can be detected. On the one hand, he argued that democratization was a logical development from the April 1985 plenum and the 27th Party Congress speech. In other words, it was a systematic, planned progression from earlier initiatives. On the other hand, though, he talked of how the problems that had emerged were more deep-rooted that they had thought at first. In the light of this, a new direction was needed, namely a greater attention to democracy and democratization. In other words, democratization was a response to what had been uncovered since March 1985.

Second, democratization was conceived of both positively and negatively. In a positive sense, it was designed to stimulate the participation of the masses in *perestroika*: 'A house can only be put in order by a person who feels that he owns this house.'[51] Democratization – particularly workplace democratization – was to promote a sense of ownership and belonging among the people. But democratization was also proposed as a response to the inertia, incompetence and corruption of party cadres. As it was proving impossible to get the cadres to change their style of work, then it became necessary to find another way to rejuvenate/replace the cadres and change the way they were working. The democratization of inner-party life then became a means of political control for the elite, to make the officials more responsive. Third, democracy was seen not as an end in itself, but as a means to promote all the elements of *perestroika*: the reform of production, science, technology, culture and social life. This inevitably imposed limits on the extent of democratization to be implemented, as it would only be pursued if it supported the goals of the leadership which were to transform the system, yet maintain the key elements of it: the leading role of the Communist Party, central planning, and state ownership of the means of production.

In conclusion, Gorbachev announced the convening of a special party conference 'to discuss questions of further democratizing the life of the party and society as a whole.'[52] The implication was clear: democratization was here to stay, and this was only the beginning. In closing the plenum, Gorbachev noted that '*perestroika* is an uphill climb, often along untrodden paths'.[53] What is unclear is how far Gorbachev had decided upon democratization – as a strategy to promote *perestroika* and overcome the resistance within the ruling party – and so needed to accentuate the scope and depth of the problems in Soviet society in order to explain away this shift in policy; or whether democratization was a response to the discovery of just how deep-rooted the problems in Soviet society had become.

The radical shift in policy proclaimed at this CC plenum – although clearly formulated in the spring and summer of 1986 – saw Gorbachev embark on a series of meetings, speeches and broadcasts in which he attempted to explain first of all the reasons why such comprehensive measures were now needed (and why it had become so urgent) and, second, the meaning of *perestroika*.[54] Gorbachev had to steer a difficult path in setting out why such radical measures were necessary, and were becoming urgent, and yet maintain that the system itself was still sound. He attempted this in a number of ways. First, the problems rested with the previous leadership, not the nature of the system. Extending the 'USSR as house' metaphor, Gorbachev said:

> We are living in what is, in general, a sturdy house, with a firm foundation and a reliable frame, but, at the same time, a lot of things in it already fail to satisfy us and have fallen behind the increased requirements and needs. Minor repairs would not suffice in this case. A complete reconstruction must be launched ... it is not the socialist system that is to blame but the errors made in the leadership, in the governing of the country.[55]

As an example of specific episodes, Gorbachev talked of a plenum on scientific and technical progress which was convened and prepared for but did not take place, illustrating the drift and inaction that prevailed in the 1970s.[56] He went on to say that the Soviet Union had lost '15 to 17 years'.[57]

Gorbachev also spoke revealingly about the process by which the policy of democratization emerged, noting that 'to prepare it proved a difficult matter'.[58] He constantly referred to the 'golden triangle' in the origins of *perestroika*: the April 1985 plenum, the 27th Congress and the January 1987 CC plenum. In his speeches and walkabouts in the Baltics in February 1987, Gorbachev was quick to stress that there was no alternative, that it was a long-term process and that it must not be allowed to fizzle out like so many other campaigns. His attempts to 'sell' *perestroika* did not paint a rosy picture: it was a very difficult job, the next two years would be crucial, and there would be no 'manna from heaven'.[59] Any benefits would have to come from blood, sweat, toil and tears. His message in Estonia was similar.[60] There were no short-cuts, no alternatives, no turning back.

Finally, Gorbachev although denying the existence of opposition to *perestroika* did acknowledge the existence of resistance, as *perestroika* had begun to be put into practice, and so was beginning to affect people directly for the first time. This he said was natural and inevitable. But it was clear from his remarks about democratization that critical voices about the new direction were beginning to make themselves felt.[61] In doing this Gorbachev clarified the reasoning behind democratization. It was clear, particularly from the speech to the 18th Congress of the Trade Unions, that for Gorbachev democracy was a crucial means of mobilizing the energy of the people to achieve the new type of Soviet society.[62] The old Bolshevik mobilizational mentality was highly tenacious.

The deepening of *perestroika* continued at another CC plenary meeting in June 1987, which set out detailed proposals for the reform of the economy. As a preface to the detailed proposals, Gorbachev again emphasised the depth of the crisis and of the urgency of the task at hand. Moving beyond general prescriptions about the problems which had accumulated in society in the 1970s and early 1980s, Gorbachev emphasized that:

> The understanding that *perestroika* was necessitated by the mounting contradictions in the development of society is deepening. These contradictions, gradually accumulating and not being solved in time, were actually acquiring pre-crisis forms ... History has not left us much time to solve this task.[63]

As the problems mounted, so Gorbachev's increasingly radical solutions had to be justified by demonstrating both the scale of the problems and the increasing sense of urgency. In this forum Gorbachev again took the opportunity to harangue party officials who failed to respond to the requirements of *perestroika* and wished to carry on regardless. Many party officials, especially in the regions, were lagging behind society and this could no longer continue. The party cadres had to learn to live and work in the conditions of openness and democracy. Gorbachev went on to set out his proposals for a radical restructuring of economic management, the operation of enterprises, and the rights of workers. This included introducing *khozraschet* (profit and loss accounting), greater autonomy for enterprises to decide what and how much to produce, more democratic management and greater rights for work collectives.[64]

Over the summer of 1987 Gorbachev compiled his book *Perestroika*, which set out for a global audience his understanding of what he was doing, summarizing what had been achieved and setting out what was still to be done. As a text it provides an excellent snapshot of Gorbachev's thinking two and a half years into his tenure, as well as providing insights into the image of leadership he was seeking to project to the world. It brought rave reviews among sections of the Western press, with *The Times* describing it as 'Gorbachev's grand design for the renewal of mankind'.[65] Central to Gorbachev's message was the attempt to universalize his experiences and interests with the interests of the rest of the world. The language was all about personal involvement, togetherness, mutual interest, the need to build trust.

> In writing this book it has been my desire to address directly the peoples of the USSR, the United States, indeed every country ... the purpose of this book is to talk without intermediaries to the citizens of the whole world about things that without exception concern us all ... I am convinced that they, like me, worry about the future of our planet ... For all the contradictions of the present-day world, for all the diversity of social and political systems in it and for all the different choices made by the nations in different times, this world is nevertheless one whole. We are all passengers aboard one ship, the Earth, and we must not allow it to be wrecked. There will be no second Noah's Ark.[66]

Gorbachev's preamble was a powerful appeal to the West to try and understand what was going on, to trust the 'new' Soviet Union, and particularly to assist in changing the international situation which was crucial if Gorbachev was to succeed in his reforms. Gorbachev was quick to note that the USSR required 'normal international conditions' for their internal reforms, but glided over this by noting that this was also an 'objective requirement' for the whole of humanity.[67] Once again a 'coincidence' of interests – the narrow ones of the USSR and the universal ones of humanity – had been identified.

Gorbachev's book sought to persuade. To persuade the West that *perestroika*, *glasnost'*, democratization and New Thinking were for real, Gorbachev had to paint a bleak picture of the problems that had accumulated. To persuade the West that the USSR was no longer a threat to Western civilization, Gorbachev had to emphasize their commitment to peace and to values common to all societies. Yet Gorbachev also had to persuade people at home that he was committed to socialism and to the Soviet system, and that *perestroika* was not some last-minute panic policy to avert collapse, but was a clearly thought through, planned strategy. Gorbachev's book was a carefully constructed text that attempted to balance the different messages he had to convey to different audiences, and in doing so came to embody all the tensions of the *perestroika* project as a whole.

A few examples. Why was *perestroika* necessary? Gorbachev was very unclear about this. One answer to this emphasized the need for modernization of the Soviet economy:

> At some stage – this became particularly clear in the latter half of the seventies – something happened that was at first sight inexplicable. The country began to lose momentum. Economic failures became more frequent ... Something strange was taking place: the huge fly-wheel of a powerful machine was revolving, while either transmission from it to work places was skidding or drive-belts were too loose.[68]

Gorbachev outlined that this economic slowdown in the USSR coincided with the revolution in science and technology in Western capitalism. Not only was the USSR slowing down, but it was also lagging further and further behind. A break with the old practices was therefore becoming an urgent requirement. In many ways, Gorbachev's appeal for change on the basis of urgent modernization echoed the sentiments expressed by Sergei Witte in 1899 – Russia must industrialize to prevent herself becoming a colony of the Western powers – and by Stalin in 1931 – who asserted that the USSR must catch up and surpass the capitalist powers within ten years or she would be buried. But why was *perestroika* necessary now? The situation had become urgent by the mid-1980s because 'the country was verging on crisis'.[69] This crisis – spreading out from the economy to engulf morality, society, attitudes to work, mass psychology – meant that the policy of *perestroika* could not be avoided. But these two explanations – lagging behind and impending crisis – were supplemented by a third: Gorbachev stated that *perestroika* was not caused by the disastrous state of the Soviet economy. Instead he argued that it was due to dissatisfaction, an awareness that the potential of socialism was being underutilized.[70] This is not the only example of the tensions in Gorbachev's thinking, as he sought to reconcile the demands of presenting a more open, self-critical image to the West with defending the essentials of the system and communicating the urgency of change to his own people.

Overall, the book reinforced the image of Gorbachev as a modern, people-oriented, Bolshevik leader. It was sprinkled with quotes from Lenin. It contained letters from ordinary people, where they aired their concerns. And it attempted to universalize his experiences, interests and ideas into the objective interests of humanity.

Gorbachev does history: looking back 70 years

The other major set-piece address of 1987 came in his address commemorating the 70th anniversary of the October Revolution in November 1987.[71] The Soviet past was always a highly controversial field. As one dissident historian wrote, in Soviet history you never know what is going to happen yesterday. History – the officially approved version – was constantly rewritten to suit the whim of the latest leader. Control of the content of the official history was also crucial to the legitimacy of the Soviet state. History was deployed to substantiate the claims that the USSR was moving towards communism, that October 1917 was a socialist revolution, and that socialism had been built by 1936, and so on. New appraisals of the past had to ensure that they did not deviate from the official hymn sheet, lest they erode the legitimacy of the regime.[72]

For Gorbachev, this posed a highly acute problem, on two grounds. First, he had to try and find the reasons for the failings of the Soviet economy. But how far back would he dare to go in looking for the source of the problems? Second, although he was proclaiming the importance of *glasnost'*, how much historical *glasnost'* would he permit? In his own speeches and writings, Gorbachev gradually extended his search for the roots of the USSR's problems backwards. At first he talked of the problems in the late 1970s and early 1980s. This then became a period of stagnation from the early 1970s onwards. Later on he talked of a braking mechanism which was slowing down economic development.[73]

By the time of his book *Perestroika*, Gorbachev had gone so far as to recognize that 'When we seek the roots of today's difficulties and problems we do this in order to comprehend their origin and to draw lessons for present-day life from *events that go deep into the 1930s*.'[74] The 1930s, the momentous decade of industrialization, collectivization, terror and transformation, was as far back as Gorbachev dared to go. Any further risked calling into question the deeds of Lenin, an unthinkable act. So when Gorbachev rose to speak on the history of the Soviet state and the significance of the October Revolution to a Joint Festive Meeting of the CC CPSU and the Supreme Soviets of the USSR and RSFSR, we already knew there would be few surprises. But how candid would he be about the 1930s?

The answer was: not very. As befitting a celebration address, the tone was mostly upbeat. The candour was selective and limited.[75] It began with a fulsome description of October – 'the living embodiment of the dreams of the world's finest minds' – and proceeded to outline a narrative of 70 years of heroism, struggle and sacrifice on the part of the Soviet people, alongside a more critical slant on the various Soviet leaders.[76] Underlying this narrative were some key themes or ideas. *Perestroika* was building upon certain periods/initiatives in Soviet history: notably the historic choice made in 1917 (socialism), NEP, de-Stalinization after 1956 and the economic reforms of 1965. By implication, this meant a rejection of Stalinism and Brezhnevism, of excessive centralization and authoritarianism. Second, it was infused with a celebration of pride in the achievements of the people and in Russia, under the leadership of the party, which was also assigned its traditional heroic role. Third, it was noticeable that the current task advanced by Gorbachev – i.e. democratization – was given a high profile in two respects. First, it was seen as a means of preventing negative things occurring. Gorbachev argued that democratization would have prevented the violations under Stalin (and so could prevent a similar reversion back to Stalinism in the present?). Second, it would have enabled previous reform efforts to succeed (i.e. under Khrushchev). The lesson for *perestroika* was clear. In sum, this was history with very much the present in mind.

We can encapsulate the progress of Soviet history Gorbachev-style in the following ways:

- *October 1917*: 'a powerful surge of millions of people which combined the vital interests of the working class, the everlasting aspirations of the peasantry, the thirst for peace of soldiers and sailors.'
- *The Civil War 1918–20*: 'Those years brought severe trials for the newly established Soviet republic ... Hungry, ill-clad and unshod, the poorly armed Red Army crushed a well-trained and well-armed counter-revolutionary host which was being generously supplied by Imperialists of East and West.'
- *NEP 1921–24*: 'the early twenties were highlighted by a spectacular surge of

popular initiative and creativity ... the measures of the NEP were directed to building socialism's material foundations.'

- *The 1920s and 1930s*: 'were years of hard work to the limits of human endurance ... that was when the world's first socialist society had its beginnings. It was an exploit on a historic scale and of historic significance.'
- *Industrialization*: 'raised the country to a fundamentally new level in one heave ... at the same time there were also some losses ... people had begun to believe in the universal effectiveness of rigid centralization.'
- *Collectivization*: 'flagrant violations of the principles of collectivization occurred everywhere ... nor were excesses avoided. But, comrades, if we assess the significance of collectivization as a whole in consolidating socialism in the countryside, it was in the final analysis a transformation of fundamental importance.'
- *The terror*: 'an atmosphere of intolerance, hostility and suspicion was created in the country ... it was the absence of a proper level of democratization in Soviet society that made possible the personality cult, the violations of legality, the wanton repressive measures of the thirties ... many thousands of people inside and outside the party were subjected to wholesale repressive measures.'
- *The Great Patriotic War*: 'the years of the Great Patriotic War are one of the most glorious and heroic pages in the history of the Party, pages inscribed by courage and valour, by the supreme dedication and self-sacrifice of millions of communists ... The war showed that the Soviet people, the party, socialism and the October Revolution are inseparable.'
- *The Khrushchev era*: 'a wind of change swept the country ... attempts were made to make socialism more dynamic, to emphasize humanitarian ideals and values, there were changes for the better ... however, no small number of subjectivist errors were committed ... the failures of the reforms undertaken were mainly due to the fact that they were not backed up by a broad development of democratization processes.'
- *Brezhnev et al.*: 'the March and September 1965 Plenary meetings formulated new approaches to economic management. In the first few years this changed the situation in the country for the better ... in the latter years of the life and activities of Leonid Brezhnev ... negative processes were gaining momentum, and had in fact created a pre-crisis situation.'[77]

The roll-call of Soviet leaders was easy to categorize. In descending order:

Heroic:	Lenin
Heroic but flawed:	Khrushchev
Mixed; started well but petered out:	Brezhnev
Complex, contradictory, mainly but not wholly negative:	Stalin

Gorbachev's history lesson was written to bolster and legitimize *perestroika* and his leadership. It made clear connections between his project, NEP, Lenin and de-Stalinization. It also marked an important moment in the progress of *pere-stroika*.

Gorbachev's message in this period was all about mobilizing and persuading people to get behind his evolving design for a renewed Soviet Union. This combined increasingly frank and critical appraisals of the problems with consistent advocacy of his solutions. This was a programme of persuasion; of doubters at home, sceptics abroad and the passive majority. It attempted to synthesize the crucial elements of Leninism, modernization, openness and the human touch. In this role, Gorbachev demonstrated great energy. He also showed an acute awareness of the importance of image and the use of the media, but at the same time the old Bolshevik mentality was still readily evident, emphasizing the sense of transition that Gorbachev embodied. Gorbachev's leadership was increasingly facing both backwards and forwards at the same time. How long could he continue to maintain this approach? Having outlined a full(ish) appraisal of the past, attention now turned to the present and the future. How could *perestroika* be implemented? And where was *perestroika* heading?

Phase II: Gorbachev the activist: putting it into practice (January 1988–February 1990)

The second phase of Gorbachev's leadership was all about trying to make it work. This meant continuing the art of persuasion, but also involved a more concerted attempt to build new institutions, develop new practices and renew the consciousness and behaviour of the Soviet people. Consequently, Gorbachev's leadership in the second phase became increasingly complex in terms of the demands being made upon him. To the roles of General Secretary of the CPSU, head of the international communist movement and Head of State was added the role of leader of the new parliamentary structure from 1989. How successful was Gorbachev in these different leadership roles?

The central event of 1988 was the 19th Party Conference in June. This was the special event announced by Gorbachev at the January 1987 CC plenum to decide how to deepen the process of democratization. But right from the start of 1988 Gorbachev was keen to stress that a new phase in *perestroika* had begun, the second phase. This was highlighted in two key addresses. The first was at a CC CPSU meeting with leaders of mass media organs, ideological establishments and creative unions on 12 January 1988.[78] The other came at a keynote address at a CC CPSU plenum devoted to ideological questions on 18 February 1988.[79] The purposes of these two meetings were in themselves highly revealing. Gorbachev's addresses to media workers were a crucial part of his strategy to win over the masses to *perestroika*, and to ensure that all newspapers and TV stations remained in tune with the message of the leadership. The plenum on ideological issues reflected Gorbachev's perception of the need to overcome the sceptics, the doubters and the doom-mongers. More work was needed to explain what had been done, where they were going and to correct erroneous opinions and objections about the nature of *perestroika*.

To encapsulate the nature of the second phase that awaited the Soviet people Gorbachev had to try and say what the first phase had been about. Looking back over 1987, Gorbachev noted two things: they now understood their past better and so understood what the problems besetting them were:

> We must have a profound knowledge of our fatherland's history, especially the post-October period. Knowledge of this history ... allows us to draw a lesson today as we seek to renew society and tap more fully the potential of socialism and its values. Indeed, we now have better knowledge of our history and the root causes of many phenomena which gave us all cause for anxiety in recent years and were the main cause of the decision on the need for social restructuring.[80]

Second, 1987 was a year of resolutions, of key decisions about the nature of the Soviet system, most notably the decisions taken at the January and June plenums of the CC CPSU. In sum, then, the first phase of *perestroika* was, to use a medical analogy, about examination, diagnosis and prescription. Having discovered the nature of the illness and decided on the cure, the next phase was to administer the medicine and carry out the surgery. The question was: would the patient survive the treatment?

In the run-up to the party conference in the summer, Gorbachev was out and about trying to persuade the people and the party that the treatment was necessary and that rest and recuperation would not do the job. During this period between February and June 1988, the first signs of organized opposition appeared. An article in *Sovetskaya Rossiya* by the Leningrad chemistry teacher Nina Andreeva, entitled 'I cannot forgo my principles', was a boisterous defence of the traditional virtues of Soviet socialism and a critique of *perestroika*. Gorbachev's attempts to persuade people of the need to support the implementation of the radical measures he intended had moved beyond attempts to mobilize the resisters and the apathetes, to countering the active opponents of what he was doing. The pluralist dog was starting to bark. Would it bite?

Gorbachev deployed three tacks to prepare the ground for the decisions of the 19th Party Conference. The first was to talk up the depth of the crisis he inherited and the continuing problems besetting the party. He began to speak in fairly apocalyptic terms about the pre-*perestroika* period. In his February address on ideological issues to the CC plenum, Gorbachev talked candidly about the scale of the economic crisis in the Soviet system:

> If we purge economic growth indicators of the influence of these factors [oil and alcohol], it turns out that, basically, for four five-year periods there was no increase in the absolute growth of the national income and, at the beginning of the 1980s, it had even begun to fall.[81]

This 'inherited' crisis was being exacerbated by two other factors: the decline in world oil prices, and the ban on sales of alcohol. A massive hole in the state budget had resulted. Gorbachev even began to admit that mistakes had been made in the early years of *perestroika*.[82] Only drastic measures would now halt this economic slide.

Later, in a speech to party and economic activists in Tashkent on 9 April 1988, Gorbachev noted:

> The situation turned out to be much more serious and profound than we had seen and than it appeared on the surface ... In short, comrades, the question arose essentially of the fate of our state, the fate of socialism and the future of our people.[83]

The second tack adopted by Gorbachev was to question why previous leaders had failed to bring about a successful reform of the system. Two answers were supplied by Gorbachev: first, the previous efforts (he mentioned September 1953 and March 1965) were partial and half-hearted and inconsistently implemented:

> So there have been attempts, real and serious attempts; but I would say that the solutions often turned out to be half-hearted, they were not integrated, they encompassed only some part of the problems without any linkage, without taking into account the whole way in which one problem is linked with other problems. And the main thing is that we were inconsistent in implementing even those resolutions that were adopted.[84]

To succeed, *perestroika* had to be carried through consistently, fully, wholeheartedly. The second answer, as mentioned above, was that they had failed because they had not included the masses. In other words, there was no escaping democratization.[85]

The final tack was to stress that *perestroika* had to address everything in order to succeed. Gorbachev found a precedent for this in the latter writings of Lenin. In an article 'On Co-Operation', Lenin stated that 'We have been forced to recognize a fundamental change in our entire view of socialism.'[86] This was to become a mantra for Gorbachev in the coming months. This reinforced the idea that *perestroika* had to be a fundamental, comprehensive project, a root-and-branch review. All the reforms were interdependent and could not be treated in isolation:

> Comrades! Our economic reform, the development of the processes of democratization and *glasnost'*, the renewal of the spiritual and moral sphere, that is, everything we associate with the concept of revolutionary restructuring are links in a single chain. They are closely interconnected and interdependent and demand that having begun restructuring in one of them, we continue it in another.[87]

The message was clear: no retreat from reform of the political system.

The address to the 19th Party Conference and the subsequent debates were noticeable for the outbreak of pluralism, and for the announcement of the broad contours of the political reforms to be introduced to support the economic reforms.[88] Gorbachev established the purpose of the conference right at the outset: to deepen *perestroika*. It was a frank, highly detailed speech, which acknowledged the problems in the system as well as the mistakes that had been made since 1985 (although these were not mentioned by name).

Gorbachev's speech was part self-defence/justification of *perestroika*, part commendation of the reforms that were already underway, and part proclamation of the necessity and indispensability of reform of the political system. In his defence, Gorbachev acknowledged that there were problems, but this was because they had underestimated how bad the crisis had become under the era of stagnation, not because the reforms were flawed and failing. The old ways – of working, thinking, acting, producing – had proved remarkably resilient and difficult to overcome. Going back to our medical analogy, Gorbachev said that the illness was to blame, not the medicine.

The majority of his address was given over to explanations of the need for, and details of, the reform of the Soviet political system:

> The existing political system proved incapable of preventing us from the build-up of manifestations of stagnation in the economic and social life of recent decades and doomed to failure the reforms that were undertaken at that time.[89]

The reforms were to embrace the whole spectrum of political practices: public opinion, rights of the individual, establishing the rule of law, reform of the electoral procedures, reform of the Soviets, reform of the party. Gorbachev's speech, and the theses on political reform, generated a good deal of debate among the party, and no little criticism.

In the months following the conference Gorbachev elaborated upon the reasons for political reform, and also began to spell out in more detail what these reforms would mean in practice. Right after the conference he made a visit to Poland and there he addressed the Polish Sejm. Speaking more frankly than he was able to at home, Gorbachev shed some interesting light on the origins of the reforms of the political system:

> I will say frankly that we did not understand its necessity, or even inevitability, immediately. We were led to it both by lessons of the past and life itself and the experience of the first stages of *perestroika*.[90]

Gorbachev also spoke with a surprising amount of personal candour, which seemed to go beyond the normal rhetoric of mutual affection. He spoke of the interest he had encountered from the Polish people in *perestroika*, and said he could detect the sincerity of their interest by the expression in their eyes.[91] It is evidence of how observant Gorbachev was in his meetings with the people, and of his ability to relate particular details to a much broader picture. It tends to reinforce the view that Gorbachev was extremely adept at relating to ordinary people.[92]

But perhaps the most significant development in shaping Gorbachev's thinking came on a tour of Siberia in September 1988. On his walkabouts, Gorbachev was confronted by crowds who were unusually frank, critical and outspoken. This was something of a shock for him. The people complained about the amenities, about food supplies, about the lack of hot water, about pollution, poor housing and of the actions of the new cooperatives who were deemed to be exploitative and corrupt.[93] This trip clearly imprinted itself on Gorbachev's mind. Later on that month, Gorbachev talked about it in a meeting with representatives of the Soviet media:

> And now I will tell you briefly about the impressions my visit to Krasnoyarsk made. A remarkable trip! I have experienced nothing like it before! The meetings with people were interesting! Straightforward frank talking. For the people have begun to talk openly ... I would say the Siberians have accepted *perestroika*, they want it to work ... But people are rightly angry that the simple matters are not being resolved.[94]

What conclusions did Gorbachev draw? First, it reinforced his view that the phase of analysis, discussion and strategy-formation was over. Now was the time for practical action, for implementation. This was echoed in his speech to the Supreme Soviet in November 1988.[95] Second, Gorbachev began to speak of the enormity of the task that faced them, and of the crystallization of opposition. He spoke of the colossal nature of the task, but also of the attacks on *perestroika* that were appearing, 'Both "left-wingers" and "right-wingers" are sowing confusion in society and attacking *perestroika*.'[96] This compelled Gorbachev into a passionate defence of *perestroika*. He reiterated again that the problems in the economy were not due to the economic reforms but were hangovers from the era of *zastoi*. He also felt it necessary to defend his strategy, for 'it is only by combining economic reform with political changes, democratization and *glasnost*' that we can fulfil both the immediate and long-term tasks we have set ourselves'.[97]

Gorbachev finished the year on a high, with his visit to the UN General Assembly in New York in December 1988 (cut tragically short by the Armenian earthquake disaster). This was a major showpiece occasion when Gorbachev was in the global spotlight and able to attempt to shape an international agenda to meet the requirements of his domestic programme and also project himself as a statesman of global repute. Gorbachev's speech was memorable because of the unilateral cuts in Soviet conventional forces that he announced.[98] He also outlined a proposal to accelerate a peace settlement in Afghanistan (long a thorn in East–West relations) by calling for a ceasefire and de-militarization. Gorbachev's speech contained all the main motifs of his approach to the international sphere: promoting cooperation, dialogue, tolerance and mutual dependence over confrontation, prejudice, conflict and mutual isolation and suspicion. He also identified what he believed were the main threats facing the international community: environmental destruction, nuclear proliferation, underdevelopment and regional tensions. Gorbachev's views were structured with one eye on the West and one eye at home.

The solutions proposed by Gorbachev – de-ideologization, de-militarization, pluralism of social structures – were all designed to reduce fear and suspicion and to enhance his reputation as a peacemaker, a democrat, and an agent of peaceful global change. But he was also at pains to establish the historic pedigree of his approach, the novelty of the situation and the clear theoretical underpinnings to his views. These were important in legitimating his ideas, and deflecting any criticism of him as being short-termist, defeatist or opportunist. In terms of historical pedigree, Gorbachev argued that the values he was espousing were part of an 'objectively conditioned process'.[99] In other words, Gorbachev had not just dreamt up his views; they were in line with the movement of history. Second, the novelty of the situation meant that the old approaches were no longer valid or acceptable. This did not mean casting off all the accumulated experience of the past. But it did provide the basis for exploring new approaches to international relations. Finally, the emphasis upon the strong theoretical foundations of his entire reform programme – domestic and foreign – was designed to undercut the criticisms of those who saw him as an opportunistic figure. Gorbachev thus portrays himself as a radical innovator, a theoretician and a global diplomat committed to peace and the future of humanity.

At the start of 1989 he was able to demonstrate tangibly his commitment to peace and disarmament by completing the Soviet withdrawal from Afghanistan. The removal of Soviet troops who had first invaded in 1979 had long been an aim of Gorbachev. The pull-out of troops began in July 1986. In November 1986, Gorbachev had spoken in a Politburo meeting of the need to end the war within one to two years, removing 50 per cent of troops in 1987, 50 per cent the year after.[100] However, the ongoing negotiations with the USA and the need to create a post-withdrawal regime that would give the appearance that the Soviets had not been defeated in Afghanistan meant the process was quite fitful and ad hoc. In April 1988, the USSR, the USA, Afghanistan and Pakistan met at Geneva to sign agreements on the withdrawal of troops. The full and final withdrawal was completed on 15 February 1989.

1989 was a momentous year. The new political structures began operating for the first time, radically changing the nature of the Soviet political system and accelerating the politicization of Soviet society. Popular protest stepped up. Strikes paralysed the country in the summer. Economic shortages got worse and worse. From the start of 1989 a definite shift can be detected in Gorbachev's appraisal of what had happened and what still remained to be done. The emphasis now fell upon managing and tweaking the system which had been so recently put in place. Between January 1989 and Gorbachev's keynote address which set out his vision of what a renewed socialist society might look like in November 1989, there were three dominant themes in Gorbachev's speeches: dealing with objections, coping with problems and spelling out where they were going to end up. Underlying everything that Gorbachev said was a bullish certainty allied to both frankness and optimism. On a number of occasions, he asserted that there was no alternative to his policy, to his strategy and to his tactics: to go slower or faster, or to the left or to the right or backwards would be a gross error. They had to keep going, at the same pace and in the same direction. If they did this, they would succeed. There were problems. There were difficulties. There had been setbacks. But there was no alternative. It was very much an approach directly from the Thatcher/Blair style of leadership: the lone voice, full of certitude, maintaining the line in the face of mounting resistance, criticism and opposition.

Coping with problems

One of the most impressive aspects of Gorbachev's leadership was his ability to adjust and adapt to the problems and issues as they arose. His was a pragmatic, highly practical leadership, although he still paid great attention to theoretical issues. But his theory was constantly reinterpreted in the light of the changing practice, rather than the theory driving the practice. In this regard, Gorbachev targeted the CC CPSU plenums (his main forum for introducing new directions/policies) of March 1989 and September 1989 at the main problems facing him: food supply and the nationalities. The failure of his economic reforms to provide instant results was causing problems in the everyday lives of the people. However, Gorbachev was keen to dilute blame for the poor performance of the economy. Repeating the old theme that they had no idea how bad things were when they came to power, he said that 'We now realize still more clearly just how serious the crisis in which the country found itself by the early 1980s was a crisis from which we have still not extricated ourselves.'[101] But Gorbachev also began to identify another culprit – luck:

> [I]t would have been fine had we been lucky, but so far this is what we've had: on the oil market the oil prices have gone down by a factor of 4 or 5; Chernobyl; Armenia; Afghanistan, our old sins; and so on. And on top of that we ourselves have set about vodka, but we are not sorry about this, although here we've also lost 40 billions.[102]

Guaranteeing a regular food supply was crucial to Gorbachev's chances of success. Indeed, Gorbachev noted that the underlying economic problems – embracing not just food supply but housing, medical care, etc. – were feeding into the socio-political problems that were besetting the system: nationalist demonstrations, ethnic conflict, worker protest and strikes. The plenum on agrarian policy sought to accelerate the reforms and so improve the situation in the Soviet shops.

The other issue was the nationalities, which Gorbachev now admitted was a highly complex problem which they had not fully taken account of when they first came to power:

> [T]he logic of *perestroika* and life itself have led us to conclude that the need for comprehensive profound changes is long overdue in ethnic rela-

tions. Let us be frank, we did not arrive at the understanding of the need for such changes immediately after April 1985. This was due to the widespread belief that things were more or less satisfactory in this sphere of social development ... Unresolved issues have surfaced one after another, errors and deformations that were accumulated over decades have now made themselves felt, and ethnic conflicts have erupted after smouldering for years.[103]

Gorbachev highlighted the historical roots of the current national crises, and set about his most difficult and ultimately fruitless task: devising a nationalities policy that maintained the union while recognizing the aspirations for autonomy and sovereignty among the non-Russian republics. On this issue Gorbachev remained, at heart, a centralist.

A third problem cropped up constantly, but was not addressed properly until February 1990: the role and place of the party in the new political system. This came about for two reasons. First, the new political system had created an incipient political pluralism. Many prominent party figures across the union had been defeated in the elections to the new Congress of People's Deputies in March 1989. Would this lead to multi-partyism? Was the guaranteed monopoly of the CPSU coming to an end? The second point which Gorbachev also had to address was the role of the party in *perestroika*. This issue was brought to the fore by Gorbachev in his review of the operation of the new political system to the CC CPSU in July 1989, in the midst of the massive miners' strike. Gorbachev noted:

[H]ere we are getting close to what I think is the heart of the matter. *Perestroika* within the party is lagging substantially behind the processes taking place in society ... In the present situation comrades, we cannot manage without rethinking the party's functions and role in society and determining its coordinates within the political system of socialism as it undergoes renewal.[104]

Gorbachev was in a difficult situation as he attempted to redefine what the 'leading role' of the party meant in the new conditions. Although this was finally spelt out in the February 1990 plenum, intimations of the shift in thinking can be detected in this period. Notably, Gorbachev in December 1989 argued that

History never gives anyone a mandate for permanent political leadership nor for absolute infallibility. On each occasion it is necessary to prove this right by knowledge of the people's needs and interests ... It is not possible to determine the party's place in the vanguard, at the cutting edge of social renewal, by decree.[105]

The implications of Gorbachev's remarks were clear: the party had to change. But Gorbachev's options were narrowing. He had tried exhortations. He had tried replacing the personnel. He had tried introducing secret ballots and elections to the life of the party. He had tried exposing the party to criticisms from the media. He had revived the Soviets and given them greater power. He had exposed the party to competitive elections. Yet still it seemed unwilling and recalcitrant. Where could Gorbachev go now?

Dealing with objections

From Gorbachev's remarks, it is clear that the scale and extent of the resistance and opposition to his policies were growing. On some occasions this took the form of specific grievances, most commonly the cooperatives which many ordinary people saw as exploitative. On his visit to Ukraine in February 1989, Gorbachev heard many grievances from ordinary Ukrainians about the cooperatives there. But in the main Gorbachev addressed the political critics of his policies: the 'conservatives' who wished to turn back the clock and who accused him of abandoning socialism, the 'ultra-leftists' who wanted to go faster and further down the road of reform, and those who were just sceptical of both his policies and the ultimate goal of *perestroika*. In all of this, Gorbachev sought to portray himself as a centrist figure, resisting the extremists and the conservatives, the rushers and the hesitaters. The overriding image Gorbachev outlined was one of pragmatism and problem-solving.

Criticisms took two forms. The first criticism was articulated by Gorbachev in the following way:

> I should like to react to another widespread opinion which I believe to be mistaken. I have in mind the assertion by some comrades that we are conducting the cause of restructuring in the country, as it were, without having devised a programme.[106]

In response Gorbachev took the opportunity at the outset of 1989 at a CPSU CC Conference to set out his most robust and detailed appraisal of the pre-history and history of *perestroika*. The intention was to establish a long historical pedigree, and to outline a logical, rational progression of the policies, demonstrating that it was an interconnected process. While pointing to the April 1985 plenum as the crucial turning-point in the attempt to overcome stagnation, Gorbachev stressed that 'the April plenum could only take place on the basis of vast preliminary work over previous years'.[107] Both Gorbachev and Ryzhkov said that they had received 110 documents which all fed into the decisions of the April plenum, documents drawn up by academics, scientists, cultural figures and the like. He then described the progress of the unfolding of reform: the June 1985 plenum on scientific and technical progress, the 27th Congress, the January and June 1987 plenums, the February 1988 plenum on ideology and the 19th Party Conference in June 1988. He went on to say that the conference was 'a landmark in the life of our country'.[108] However, *perestroika* was not just a logically thought-out process. It was also a broad-based one, drawing on the experience of the Soviet people as a whole (i.e.

not just the ideas of a few members of the Gorbachev brains trust), and an inter-connected one: economic and political reform were mutually supporting.

Where are we going?

The second criticism was: where are they going? Are we abandoning socialism? In response to this Gorbachev set out his own vision of where they were going. At the start of 1989, he noted that they did not have a complete picture of the society towards which they were moving, but they were working out what their new con-cept of socialism might look like. By November 1989, this process was complete. In his 'The socialist idea and revolutionary *perestroika*', Gorbachev set out his vision of a 'renewed' socialist society, although intimations of this can be seen in his speeches in the autumn of 1989.[109] The basis of his approach was to identify what had to be rejected, and then move on to the positive work of construction and creation. Two issues dominated his thinking. The first was a rejection of approaches to socialism based upon bureaucratization, authoritarianism, utopi-anism or command models. The second was a methodological issue: to define socialism on the basis of the realities of Soviet society, not to try and impose a ready-made model on Soviet society.

In its stead, while recognizing the Marxist-Leninist heritage of their ideology, Gorbachev stressed the need to place the individual at the centre of a renewed Sovi-et socialism. Drawing inspiration and legitimation from Lenin's call for a rethink-ing of our entire concept of socialism, Gorbachev argued for a greater stress on the individual, and a more flexible, less dogmatic approach. Included in this approach was the aspiration to incorporate the experiences of Western social democracy. This accorded with earlier statements by Gorbachev, who had referred to studies made of the experiences of cooperatives in Norway and Sweden while in Ukraine. The ultimate aim was to build a society of humane, democratic socialism:

> The socialism we want to build through *perestroika* is a society with an efficient economy, a high scientific, technological and cultural level and humanitarian social structures, a society that has democratized all aspects of social life and created the necessary conditions to encourage people's creative endeavour and activity.[110]

This was to provide the foundation for the 28th Party Congress which was due to meet in July 1990, and for a new party programme, the central ideological docu-ment of the CPSU.

The dimensions of Gorbachev's leadership: party, state and people

Gorbachev's message maintained its essential features – populism, Leninism, uni-versalism – during the period between 1988 and 1990, but the emphasis had begun to shift. The populist and universalist elements – particularly those themes which emphasized his democratic credentials and his commitments to the com-mon future of humanity – began to gain a higher profile than the Leninist ones.

And the Leninist motifs had also begun to shift towards Lenin as the arch prag-matist, innovator and flexible leader. But the leadership of Gorbachev acquired new dimensions in this time. To his roles as party leader, head of state and global statesman, there was now added the role of leader of the embryonic parliament. But this was not just another ceremonial position, for this new role was a reflec-tion of the transformations underway in the Soviet political system. Gorbachev had to learn new skills as head of the new parliament, and also had to adapt his leadership role within the party. How did Gorbachev's leadership style and approach change in this period?

The first Congress of People's Deputies met between 25 May and 9 June 1989. The second one met on 12 December 1989 and closed on the 24th. The first ses-sion was an incredibly chaotic, messy, dynamic time, like the removal of the cork from a champagne bottle which has been shaken and shaken. Gorbachev, as the Chairman, had to face a whole host of issues – procedural points, setting agendas, controlling the debates – just to get the Congress working properly. The following 12 days were a topsy-turvy time, as the participants in the Congress and the watching onlookers began to come to terms with a 'real' parliament and all of its disagreements, passions and opinions. What was noticeable when looking back over the conduct of Gorbachev at this time was his willingness to tolerate the pub-lic airing of criticisms, of both him and the party. He worked to establish plural-ism and voting as central parts of the operation of the Congress (although the need to maintain order often led to him being criticized for curtailing debate and preventing freedom of expression on critical issues, most notably the massacre in Tbilisi in April 1989, and the nationalities issue). But Gorbachev also had to respond to criticisms. The first set of criticisms surrounded his election as Chair-man of the Supreme Soviet:

> Comrades, I shall touch on yet another matter which is worrying all of us. It also worries me. By dint of historical reasons and distressing experi-ence, we are especially sensitive to the matter of excessive concentration of power in the hands of one leader. And this has been heard here at the Congress. This concern is present. Since the matter exists, I think it is necessary clearly and unambiguously to express one's attitude to it. You would probably simply not understand were I not to react to this which was present both on the eve of the Congress and at the Congress. As a communist, I categorically do not accept the hints expressed if not very plainly alleging that I am trying to concentrate all the power in my hands. This is alien to me, to my views, my outlook, and indeed my char-acter I hope that you are already somewhat familiar with my style and character. It was not for this that the sharp about-turn was made at the April plenum to the new policy. It was not for this that the party and people embarked on the hard work of democratization, *glasnost'*, cleans-ing and renewal of our society and public life. As General Secretary and Chairman of the Supreme Soviet I have no other policy than that of

restructuring, democratization and *glasnost*, and I declare once again to the Congress, to the working people, to the entire people my unwavering loyalty to that policy, for it is only on the basis of that that we shall be able to consolidate our society and resolutely accelerate movement along the path of restructuring. [applause] In this I see the meaning of my life and work. [applause] Comrades, Marx and Lenin considered a critical attitude to one's own activity to be essential for a revolutionary party. I think that we can say that in our party and society this is becoming a norm of life.[111]

Gorbachev's response was a familiar one. As a leader, it was his personal qualities that would ensure that there would be no abuse of power. *Perestroika* was his life and his work. It was a highly personalized response: *trust me*. It confirms the sense that Gorbachev's leadership of the country was becoming one based on judging his record and having faith in his motives, and one less based on his fidelity to the ideology of Marxism-Leninism. This was Gorbachev, the conviction politician. Unfortunately, though, Gorbachev's response did little to assuage the fears and to deflect the criticisms of those who argued that, while this may (or may not) have been problematic with Gorbachev at the helm, there was an inherent danger in consolidating so much power in the hands of one person. What would happen after Gorbachev?

The other issue concerned his decision to nominate Anatoly Lukyanov, a Polit-buro colleague as his First Deputy. This seemed to many to be an abuse of his position.

> I must disappoint you. You may or may not agree with the suggestions that are put forward by the Chairman of the USSR Supreme Soviet, but under subsequent articles I have the constitutional authority to put for-ward suggestions starting with the First Deputy Chairman of the Supreme Soviet. It was presumably not for nothing that this was record-ed in the Constitution, discussed on a nationwide basis, adopted and approved. You and I conceived the post of Chairman of the Supreme Soviet, believed that we need such a post, and wanted to see it in the form in which we approved it, and that was why we granted these exten-sive rights. And so, I make the suggestions. And that is how it will be on the other candidates. You can discuss them, and accept them or not accept them. But again if his suggestion is turned down it will be the job of the Chairman to think it over and put forward another suggestion. And so, the alternatives can come from me, once you fail to accept and turn down a suggestion. And so, I would ask the Congress to discuss my suggestion concerning Comrade Lukyanov. That is what I would ask.[112]

Here we see the other dimension of Gorbachev's leadership: Gorbachev as the constitutionalist. Yet again we have the tension at work. Gorbachev is adhering to the constitutional procedures, yet seems oblivious to the criticisms of appointing someone so closely associated with him and the old structure of power. This is another expression of the way that Gorbachev embodies the old and the new: the unstable combination in him of the old Bolshevik practice of appointing loyal personnel to bolster your power, and the new approach of a respect for constitutional processes, debate and accountability. In many ways Gorbachev himself expressed the ongoing contradictions and transitional nature of the Soviet political system which was neither the old system nor a new one, but a hybrid of the two.

As party leader up until 1988, Gorbachev had always combined some of the orthodox elements of a CPSU General Secretary, with a taste for the unexpected or for innovation. Gorbachev had built his power within the party in traditional Leninist style – promoting supporters and demoting opponents – and maintained respect for the rules of the Soviet political game, including exhorting the party to work harder, to maintain its links with the masses, and using the ceremonial set-pieces to convey the new path that was to be followed. However, Gorbachev's general secretaryship was also innovative from quite an early stage, particularly in his use of *glasnost'* as a means of trying to make the party accountable and thus to provide an imperative for change.

The party conference of 1988 marked the onset of a change in the nature and approach of Gorbachev in his leadership of the party. What was new in Gorbachev's approach after 1988 was, first, his attempt to bolster his authority by debating with and confronting the increasingly vocal criticisms of his leadership, and defending his line. Debate and disagreement were now brought out into the open. Gorbachev had had to respond to the criticisms of his proposals at the 19th Party Conference, a time where open criticisms of the General Secretary came to the fore in a concerted and consistent way. Perhaps the most notable example came from Yuri Bondarev, who argued that *perestroika* could be likened to an aeroplane: it had taken off, but where would it land?[113] In the face of growing political pluralism – both within and without of the party – Gorbachev had for the first time to outline a particular standpoint and defend it against other tendencies and viewpoints. The general secretaryship was becoming, under Gorbachev's tutelage, a political position, rather than an administrative one. His approach was to respond directly to the criticisms of those on the left and the right, those who wanted to go slower or faster. Gorbachev sought to build political authority not just through invoking Lenin, but also by establishing the essential correctness of his policy decisions. He was, in essence, becoming a Soviet conviction politician. At one time, like his contemporary in the UK, he asserted that 'there is no alternative' (somewhat at odds, I guess, with his constant haranguing of party members to learn to work in conditions of political pluralism!). Gradually, inexorably Gorbachev was shifting the ways in which Soviet leaders rationalized their rule and exercised power.

The second innovation was Gorbachev's approach to the inner workings of the party. No longer should the party operate on the basis of a strict hierarchical and centralist top-down model. The party had to become more flexible in its functioning, with greater room for local autonomy, and more scope for unorthodoxy. Gorbachev's approach to leadership was still quite Bolshevik in the sense of being mobilizational, but it was a modernized Bolshevism which seemed to have less fear of spontaneity and initiative from below, as long as it accorded with the overall goals of the party.

Gorbachev's message, however, had changed quite radically. By the end of 1988 and the start of 1989, it had become stark and at times apocalyptic. The party had to change or die. There was now no going back. The old ways had failed. The crisis in the party was a crisis caused by hanging on to obsolete methods in a radically new situation. This message – clearly designed to presage the major change which emerged in February 1990 – continued to be legitimated through the selective use of Lenin. Gorbachev was now the Great Persuader. As 1989 gave way to 1990, Gorbachev's powers of persuasion were stretched to their utmost, starting with the most difficult task of all: the role of the party.

Phase III: The reactive leader: Gorbachev and crisis management (February 1990–August 1991)

Gorbachev's last 18 months in power were turbulent times. Problems and difficulties continued to pile up. Opposition grew bolder. Crisis followed crisis. It culminated in the botched attempt to unseat Gorbachev and to restore 'order and discipline' in August 1991. Throughout it all Gorbachev attempted to steer a path which kept the Soviet Union together, advanced economic reform, deepened the political reforms while defending the Communist Party and advanced his foreign policy of disarmament and imperial retreat. In spite of his valiant efforts, though, it proved impossible to keep *perestroika* on track. Amidst the whirlwind of change, Gorbachev became increasingly beleaguered and isolated, reacting to rather than shaping events. In this section we will explore Gorbachev's message and leadership as a 'crisis manager'.

Problems, problems, problems

Gorbachev was faced with increasingly fraught decisions. Solutions to many of the urgent problems proved impossible to reconcile with the orthodox interpretation of Soviet Marxism-Leninism. How could Gorbachev hope to get agreement to introduce market relations? Private property? A multi-party system? A common pattern emerged in Gorbachev's justifications for radical shifts in policy. First, Gorbachev talked up the urgency of the situation. Radical thinking was required. Second, Gorbachev looked for historical and ideological precedents in Soviet history and/or in the writings of Lenin. Third, Gorbachev always placed these new developments within a *perestroika* context, arguing that they were either the next phase in the logical unfolding of a well-thought-out process (i.e. not a panic measure) or were the essential precondition for the next phase. Finally Gorbachev wove a narrative which attempted to appeal to both the radicals and the conservatives and so maintain his essentially centrist orientation. The issue of how to get the economy working bubbled away throughout the whole year, rising sporadically to the surface. The two issues which grabbed attention at the start of 1990 were those of political reforms and ethnic relations.

For me, the party is a sacred thing

> But the party itself is a part of the people. And not the worst part. I can assert that. I have been bound to the party since 1952 ... For me the party is a sacred thing. Everything has to be done to ensure that the party gets a second wind, and finds its place in this renewing country, and in this renewing atmosphere.[114]

How could democratization and political reforms be advanced in the midst of economic breakdown and national fragmentation? The further progress of political reforms was by this time deeply embroiled in, and dependent upon, debates about the future of the CPSU. During a visit to Lithuania, Gorbachev confronted the questions being raised about the Communist Party.[115] Should the CPSU abandon its constitutionally guaranteed monopoly on power and become a parliamentary party, competing for power in a multi-party system just like political parties elsewhere? And should the party retain its unitary structure? Or should it become federated into its constituent ethnic parts?

Gorbachev argued strongly for retaining the Union, on the basis of the mutual advantages for all those involved, and for a unitary CPSU, as moves towards federation would end up destroying it as a cogent political force. But the question of the role of the CPSU was more open. In a speech to Lithuanian party activists on 13 January, Gorbachev for the first time began to answer the question he first posed at the end of 1989, when he talked of having to 'rethink the party's role' because it was lagging behind developments in society, instead of leading like the vanguard it was supposed to be:

> The CPSU's strategy of renewal consists of a fundamental change in both its status and role in Soviet society on the basis of the division of functions in its relations with all the public and political groupings ... to which *perestroika* has given rise. This means ridding the party of its infallibility complex, its claims to leadership of all and everything and political monopolism ... Comrades, I will tell you frankly everything should be determined by the course of the political process. I don't see any tragedy in a multi-party system if it should arise, in reality and meet the interests of the society. I don't see anything bad in this. Incidentally we began after the revolution, a government and the All-Russian Central Executive Committee were formed by apparently at least three parties ... this multi-party system is not something we should avoid like the plague. No all I am saying is that there is no need for it to be foisted on us artificially ... Secondly, ... a multi-party system is no panacea.[116]

This was the sign that a highly significant rethink of the core structures of the Soviet political system was underway. Gorbachev had run out of ideas about how to make the party more responsive to his dictates, less resistant to change, less recalcitrant. In the constantly shifting centre ground, Gorbachev risked being left stranded as the radicals wished to go faster and further with *perestroika* within the new structures of power. The party was becoming increasingly marginalized within the Congress of People's Deputies. How could Gorbachev persuade the party to change, and how would he ensure that he would remain at the centre of the new political system?

A critical CPSU CC plenum was convened on 5 February 1990 to discuss this issue.[117] Gorbachev put forward proposals for the party to abandon its constitutionally guaranteed monopoly and to compete democratically with other political movements and parties. This was not, Gorbachev stressed, an outright shift from vanguard political party to parliamentary political party. Gorbachev instead argued that the party could only regain its credibility and authority by earning its vanguard role through its work among the people in a democratic manner. Gorbachev's justification was based on recognizing the reality that the party was 'lagging behind' and risked being marginalized. The new political system required separation of party and state bodies. In this situation, the constitutional guarantee, embodied in Article 6, had become an anachronism and had to go. But it was also a positive move designed to restore the party to a pre-eminent position.[118]

As the year unfolded, so Gorbachev's elaboration and defence of the decision to change the role of the party developed. As Gorbachev had noted in Lithuania, a multi-party system was not unknown in Soviet history. But Gorbachev was also able to find a Leninist precedent for a major shift in the role of the party. During his speech commemorating the anniversary of Lenin's birth – a traditional showcase of the Soviet ideological calendar – Gorbachev found what he was looking for: the backing of Lenin.[119] He found it in two ways. First, by arguing that Lenin operated on a practical, concrete basis. Sacred dogmas were never allowed to dictate in the face of cold, hard reality. Crucially, Gorbachev argued that the development of the party was dependent upon 'a change in the objective situation in the country and the world'.[120] Second, building on this principle, Gorbachev pointed to the 10th Party Congress of 1921, which has become infamous for two decisions: the introduction of NEP and the resolution banning factions in the party. Instead, though, Gorbachev cited a different resolution, one on party building. According to Gorbachev, this resolution

> rejected the possibility of an absolutely correct form of party organization and methods of party work, a form suitable for all stages in the revolutionary process. On the contrary, it was stated there, the form of organization and the work methods are determined exclusively by the specifics of the given historical situation and by the tasks which ensue directly from that situation.[121]

Having found good Leninist credentials for his shift in order to deflect his conservative critics, Gorbachev went on to elaborate on what the new party might look like. But Gorbachev was not always consistent. In a speech in Sverdlovsk on 26 April, he argued that the party must return to its original vanguard role as outlined by Lenin, and this did not mean it should become 'a party of the parliamentary type' which was what the Democratic Platform, a radical grouping inside the CPSU, was calling for.[122] During an address to Moscow workers on 12 May, Gorbachev reaffirmed his commitment to a party of the vanguard type, yet also asserted that the 'CPSU should also master the art of a parliamentary party'.[123] By the time of the 28th Congress in July 1990 – brought forward because of the need to discuss urgent issues about the nature of the party – Gorbachev had shifted slightly. There he argued that a vanguard role could not be foisted on society, but had to be fought for within the democratic process. In doing this 'it is acting as a parliamentary party'.[124] But Gorbachev had got his way: the party had remained intact yet had accepted the onset of multipartyism.[125]

Gorbachev's message to the party in this period between the February plenum and the critical 28th Congress of the CPSU was based on a defence of his line (centrism, unity and caution), and also spelling out how the party should (and should not) operate in the new conditions. Gorbachev's defence of his line was to create labels for all of his opponents (an archetypal Bolshevik approach, confirming how deeply the Bolshevik mind-set was embedded in Gorbachev) and to spell out the dangers for the party and the country for those who wished to go down a different road, at a different speed:

- *Adventurists*: radicals who wished to travel quickly and unthinkingly down the road of change; DANGER = too much too soon would make the process uncontrolled and leave the party weak and vulnerable.
- *Dogmatists*: those who wanted to hang on to the same old shibboleths; DANGER = risk becoming irrelevant.
- *Nostalgists*: those who wanted to rule in the same old ways; DANGER = risk becoming irrelevant.
- *Defeatists/pessimists*: those who had already thrown in the towel, saying that *perestroika* had failed; DANGER = opens the door for other groups to come in and seize control of the process of change.
- *Separatists/federalizers*: those who wish to split up the party into its constituent national-republican units; DANGER = fundamentally weakens the CPSU and accelerates the process of national disintegration.
- *Opportunists/anti-communists/anti-*perestroika *forces*: those who wished to take advantage of the current situation to push through their own agenda; DANGER = end of party rule.

The identifications created by Gorbachev were interesting. By highlighting the 'enemies within' whose position was detrimental to the future of the party, he also sought to defend his own line, a cautious centrist line, but one which was unequivocally committed to forging a new role for the party. We cannot go back. We should not split up. We dare not go too fast. We should not go too slowly. Follow me, in essence. Having managed to convince the party to accept its new role (by highlighting the Leninist credentials of the changes and that in the new conditions this was the best way to attract majority support) Gorbachev then had to respond to accusations that the party was losing prestige and was becoming politically weak. Cleverly, Gorbachev's response was to agree with his critics, but to turn it to his own advantage. Yes, he argued, the party is being squeezed by other political forces, and risks losing out. But the causes of this were not the decisions he had taken, but the unwillingness of the party to reform itself, and to learn to work in a new way, commensurate with the new situation. At the 28th Congress he tried to spell out the practical implications of this: what does it mean to learn to work in new conditions?

In his Congress report, Gorbachev spelt out what this would mean for party structures, party activists and party inner-workings and practices.[126] The most important thing highlighted by Gorbachev was a solution favoured by all Bolsheviks since Lenin: the quality of the personnel. The best way to guarantee the survival of the party was to ensure active, dynamic, pro-*perestroika* candidates were at all levels of the party. In terms of its organizational role, the party had to learn how to combine new aspects (operating as a parliamentary party) with more traditional roles (as an agency of unity and integration in a multinational state). This meant:

- ceasing to meddle in the work of other organizations (such as the Soviets or trade unions);
- concentrating upon working out new ideas and platforms attractive to the people;
- cooperating with all progressive political movements;
- broadening the social basis of party membership: becoming a party of the whole people;
- developing a more progressive attitude towards the role of women in politics;
- retaining the all-union, unified structure while allowing for the maximum independence of communist parties of union republics;
- reviving and renewing the inner-party democracy (it was unclear at this point whether 'democratic centralism' would remain);
- factions must be tolerated as long as they do not mean the fatal weakening of the party;
- reform of the party's leadership structures, including membership of the Central Committee and the appointment of a Deputy General Secretary.[127]

The party was at a crucial juncture. It was, according to Gorbachev, a straight choice: change or die.

All power to Gorbachev?

Alongside changes to the party Gorbachev also proposed the creation of the post of Executive President (and himself as the first incumbent, without popular election). The justification for this move was that it was expedient in the current climate of chaos and crisis. Centrifugal forces were gaining ground and a counterbalance to them was required. It was taking a long time to take decisions and get them implemented. Creating a new executive mechanism would enable more rapid, decisive responses to problems. Second, it was seen as a way of hastening the creation of the new restructured system. Gorbachev argued that they were in the midst of the most difficult period. The old system was being dismantled, yet the new one was not yet working. The Executive President was there to compress this transition from one to the other, and thereby hasten the onset of the new. The implication was that it would be a temporary measure. Finally, Gorbachev argued that his unwillingness to put himself forward for popular election was due solely to the need for speed. He was not setting himself up as a potential dictator. In an answer to Komsomol delegates, Gorbachev noted that if he had wanted to do this, he could have just left the system in 1985 intact:

> All that had to be done was to maintain the positions we held in 1985 and take advantage of the unlimited opportunities presented by the position of the General Secretary of the CPSU CC. Generally speaking, that was a dictatorship not limited by anything.[128]

Gorbachev also took the first steps in creating new structures to assist him in his new role and to try and find a means of sidestepping opposition to his rule. He created new structures to support him in his role: the Presidential Council (essentially an advisory body, chosen personally by Gorbachev) and a Federation Council. The former was a curious body, comprised of people who had key executive and legislative functions, but also personal advisers and people who held no political office altogether.[129] The latter was made up of the heads of the Union republics. Gorbachev also appointed some direct personal Presidential aides: Anatoly Chernyaev, Georgi Shakhnazarov and Nikolay Petrakov, who had previously been his CPSU aides. The problem for Gorbachev in this set-up was that having created these bodies to accelerate the process of political transformation, Gorbachev had not created any structures which gave these new bodies any real powers to implement change. Although this enabled Gorbachev to shift power away from the Politburo, it left the Presidency without a clear mechanism to rule. Power was beginning to slip through his fingers, to the republics.

As the crisis deepened, so Gorbachev maintained these arguments as he accrued more and more emergency powers to himself throughout the autumn and winter of 1990. Yet the accusations about Gorbachev – accumulating power unto himself, enjoying a variety of privileges – continued to dog him. In answers to the latter point put to him by Komsomol delegates in April 1990, Gorbachev recounted an incident when he had been First Secretary of the Stavropol Party Committee:

> at the end of 1973 and the start of 1974 – that is, the fourth [year] of my work as First Secretary of the [Stavropol] Kray Party Committee – such processes arose in Stavropol Kray, with criminals committing blue murder, that the people demanded a response from the First Secretary of the Kray Party Committee and from all the authorities. And things stood like this,

one could not go out into the town by night, and there was nobody in the towns. The menfolk, husbands would go to meet women working the second [evening] shift, because there were robberies, violence, murder. This assumed such an acute nature. At the same time, all the statistics for our kray internal affairs directorate were normal, good. What lay behind this? When we looked into it, we discovered most gross violations of socialist legality in the internal affairs bodies. We overturned the entire kray directorate, starting with the head of the directorate; we dispatched three commissars and most of the staff. We changed the leadership at 15 town and rayon departments, and after that we proceeded to unravel Stravropol Kray ... But this so cast a shadow on the Ministry of Internal Affairs that investigations ensued. And thereafter those clashes lasted a long time. I know that subsequently, already being in Moscow. All that was difficult. But the Procurator's Office then defended the Stavropol people. And that process developed. This was not forgiven for a long time; it was there all the time until Shchelokov went. I sensed that. They were always seeking something to compromise Gorbachev. I understood that. And they snipe at me now. I think that these are the same political aims, or people whose tails have been trodden on. Or those who sense that *perestroika* will lead everybody out into clear water, and it is doing that.[130]

The implication was clear: Gorbachev's tough stance on crime and unwarranted privilege had made him many enemies, and these elements were looking for revenge by smearing his character and conduct. But Gorbachev was also sending out another message here: trust. Although he had not been popularly elected, he could be trusted with the reins of power, and with the temptations of privilege. It was a highly personalized response to a critique that was essentially systemic in nature, and one which did little to allay the fears of those who both opposed Gorbachev, but also those who broadly supported him but were fearful of who (or what) might come after him.

To market, to market!

Gorbachev deployed a similar strategy in his advocacy of the shift to a market economy, arguing that the current crisis required radical measures to lift the performance of the Soviet economy. But again he was at pains to point out that this was not a panic measure. It had been set out at the 27th Congress as a core part of the economic reform and was part of the overall strategy for economic change, not a fallback because everything else had failed. The old ways of running the economy had exhausted themselves. If the Soviet economy was to benefit from the advances in science and technology and give people greater freedom and flexibility, then the market was the way to achieve this. In the same way that democratization was seen as a means of advancing economic reform, then so the market was seen as a way of achieving the goal of a modernized, efficient, technological economy. Underpinning Gorbachev's rationale for these major shifts in Soviet thinking were two ideas:

the need to incorporate the USSR into the mainstream of global civilization, while retaining and building on everything that had been achieved over the years of the existence of the Soviet state.

A fascinating insight into Gorbachev's outlook came on 29 November 1990 when Gorbachev addressed a meeting of cultural figures.[131] Speaking frankly and highly personally, Gorbachev reflected on his own past and on the progress made under *perestroika*. The speech was notable for the details Gorbachev revealed about the personal motivations behind his drive to restructure the system. He recalled a mosaic of incidents. On the eve of his accession in March 1985 he spoke of a conversation with Eduard Shevardnadze, his foreign minister. They agreed that it was not possible to carry on living that way, and that 'everything had gone rotten'. To illustrate this he spoke of the fate of his grandfather, who was arrested and deported to Irkutsk for having failed to fulfil the sowing plan for 1933. Movingly relating the horrors of his arrest, Gorbachev called it a 'plague house', as everyone had to shun them for fear of being deported too. Second, Gorbachev spoke of the deformities in the system, notably the absence of democratic, legal or constitutional procedures to protect the people:

> I do not need to be told what democracy was like prior to 1985. From the First Secretary's study, where I was for nine years, I could decide on everything without pausing to think whether it is in keeping with the law or the constitution. I made my decisions and that is that and it is a good job I have a conscience.[132]

This theme – of the inner qualities and the experiences of the honest, dedicated person – was a key part of Gorbachev's address. Once again Gorbachev expounded how his experiences had shaped his outlook, and allowed him to compare and thus draw conclusions about the need for change. Gorbachev was able to universalize his personal experiences. He talked in ways that made his own life a mirror of the history of the Soviet Union. His own life stood as metaphor. His experiences made him acutely aware of the contradictory nature of the history of the USSR: extraordinarily painful episodes alongside great heroism, dedication and sacrifice. Herein lies, I believe, the tenacity of Gorbachev's commitment to the system, to the party, to his beliefs. To abandon the system entirely would mean that the whole of his life and work, and the sacrifices of his relatives and their generation, would have been for nothing.

> Well, should we renounce things? What shall I do, renounce my grandfather who was dedicated to everything right till the end, and, having come back, he spent a further 17 years as a collective farm chairman? Never did I hear him have doubts ... That is why I cannot go against my grandfather. I cannot go against my father who fought in the Kursk salient, who crossed the Dnepr, flowing with blood, dealing with the crossing and bleeding as he reached his destination, but he made it ... So, while purg-

ing myself, while rejecting all the barrack-like mentality of Stalinism, should I indeed renounce my grandfather and what he did? This would mean rejecting generations and what they did. Well then did they live in vain? And we all are not simply in a mire ... we stand on firm ground, we do.[133]

We see here within Gorbachev's own past and his soul the wider struggle between what to retain and what to renounce, what to purge and what to preserve. Gorbachev's leadership still retained an extraordinary degree of personal involvement and identification with the system and with his project.

1990 ended with flux, uncertainty and bad news. He abolished the Presidential Council, and shifted more powers to the Federation Council in an attempt to find a *modus operandi* with the republican leaders. New bodies were created, including a Cabinet of Ministers and a Security Council (which included many of the political figures previously on the Presidential Council). A series of personnel changes occurred. Appointments were made, including Gennady Yanaev to the post of Vice-President, and Boris Pugo replaced Vadim Bakatin as Minster of the Interior. Both these individuals were to play key roles in the events of the following August. Conversely, Eduard Shevardnadze resigned, warning of a coming dictatorship. The problems in the economy continued to mount, and the forces pushing for independence from the Soviet Union were gathering a seemingly unstoppable momentum. 1991 threw up fresh challenges to Gorbachev from all parts of the political spectrum. Yeltsin continued to criticize Gorbachev's rule. The republics continued to push for autonomy and independence. Conservative figures wanted to call a halt to the reforms and engineered a crackdown in Lithuania in January 1991, which seemed to confirm Gorbachev had abandoned his centrist position and was indeed adopting a more hard-line stance. How did Gorbachev respond? He reaffirmed his belief in the correctness of the course he had embarked upon, defended the choices he had made, insisted ever more stridently that 'there is no alternative' and reiterated his belief in both the party and the Union. In particular, he seemed stung by Shevardnadze's criticisms, arguing that it seemed to suggest a degree of panic in the outlook of Shevardnadze, and that it was crucial to distinguish between dictatorship on the one hand, and the need for strong power on the other. He himself was the guarantee that the latter would never occur while he was still *in situ*.[134]

In his New Year address, Gorbachev outlined that the priority for the year ahead was the fate of the multi-ethnic state. Gorbachev, across the year, defended the Union on a number of grounds. On historical grounds, he argued that the Soviet peoples had been living together peacefully for centuries, and had forged a special bond in the course of the Soviet period in uniting to fight the fascists. On the grounds of mutual assistance, he argued that the economic and technological benefits of Union ensured that there were powerful arguments in favour of retaining it. On humanitarian grounds he pointed out that millions of people were the result of mixed marriages, and that 75 million people lived in a different republic to their own national group. All in all a unique civilization had been created and should be defended. His words carried little weight with the nationalists, who were set fair on a course for autonomy and independence, and those determined to retain the Union in its centralized form. In order to retain some form of Union, Gorbachev had to push for a renewed Union treaty and had to acquire some popular legitimacy for his project.

With this in mind, Gorbachev decided to push ahead with a referendum. But what would the question be? In the end, Gorbachev settled on the following choice of words:

> Do you consider necessary the preservation of the Union of Soviet Socialist Republics as a renewed federation of equal sovereign republics in which the rights and freedom of any individual of any nationality will be fully guaranteed?

This was put to the people on 17 March 1991. Six republics – Armenia, Georgia, Moldavia, Latvia, Lithuania and Estonia – did not take part as they had no intention of being part of a renewed federation. Gorbachev's gamble was to try and get popular backing for a new federation, based on democratic principles. In Russia, a further question was added on whether the president of Russia should be elected by popular vote.[135] The referendum in March 1991 saw a turnout of over 80 per cent, and 76.4 per cent of those who voted came out in favour of the design for the Union set out by Gorbachev, which was a strong endorsement of Gorbachev and his approach. The strongest levels of support came from rural areas; the lowest levels came from the big cities. But what type of Union would it be? Gorbachev signed an agreement at Novo-Ogarevo on 23 April with nine of the republics (excluding the Baltics, Georgia, Armenia and Moldova). These discussions led to a new draft being issued in June 1991. The new treaty was due to be signed on 20 August. Gorbachev was engaged in a delicate balancing act, and also in a race against time. The momentum was with the separatists and nationalists. The centre of gravity was shifting away from the centre and towards the republics. Gorbachev's defence of the Union did not go far enough to satisfy the nationalists, and went too far to satisfy the Centrists. His political position within the elite was becoming more precarious. Could he rescue the Soviet state, which seemed to be what a majority of people in the nine republics wanted?

Gorbachev also spent a good deal of time defending his own record, defending his programme of *perestroika* and attacking his opponents. He was criticized on a number of levels: he never should have begun it in the first place; he had made mistakes; he did not know where he was going; and he was destroying all the good things that had been built in the previous 74 years. The general thrust of his arguments displayed an almost astonishing level of certitude in his own judgements and choices, and in the inherently flawed nature of those who chose to criticize him. For someone who was constantly espousing the value of pluralism,

Gorbachev seemed unwilling to engage in constructive debate with his opponents, or to differentiate between his opponents. Gorbachev did a number of press conferences and interviews where he was asked questions akin to 'If you had your time all over again, would you do things differently?' The answer each time was the same: the programme was the right one, the choices were right and the strategy was correct. The only concession was that there may have been tactical errors along the way,

> Yes, the question is not simple for me. I will say this frankly. I would all the same have repeated this choice in the main ... if I found myself in this situation again, I would have made this choice again, for ... society could no longer live the way it did and develop normally, with the kind of processes that were underway in it ... As for the tactics, probably I should have first of all thought and should have been concerned about the main thing – not to renounce what is still working without having created new, more effective forms of life and mechanisms of action. This disparity in approaches, the absence of synchronization in the political, economic and inter-ethnic processes, resulted in our being often unprepared, behindhand, and in other cases, ahead and setting off processes as a result of which we would find ourselves in difficult situations.[136]

The only mistake Gorbachev would admit was the failure to devise a proper sequencing for reform. He wanted to arrive at the same place, but with fewer losses and fewer problems along the way. But even this admission of errors was tempered by the qualifications that: (1) the task was hideously complex; (2) the problems were far more serious than they first thought; and (3) the power struggle of 1989–91 had seriously hindered the ability to resolve problems.

To the charge that he never should have started *perestroika*, Gorbachev retorted that the Soviet Union could not have carried on for much longer, and anyway *perestroika* was not something dreamed up by him alone. On the first point, Gorbachev highlighted the notion of progress and backwardness to justify the radical changes he had introduced. Something had to be done to prevent the USSR from lagging behind the technologically advanced nations and to prevent internal social collapse. Disaster had only been averted by the massive hike in oil prices, by the voracious exploitation of the USSR's natural resources and by the exponential growth in vodka sales which plugged the hole in the state budget. There was a great temptation in 1985 to do nothing or to undertake cosmetic adjustments, but this was rejected. The only debate was where to begin. At the July 1991 CC plenum, Gorbachev appeared to suggest that political reform emerged only when other things had failed:

> To start with, we focused our efforts on scientific-technical progress, but the mechanisms for its introduction did not work. Then we took up reform of the economic mechanism, but it too was blocked. Then the

idea of political reform appeared and the entire party and the whole of society were included in the discussion of this, and eventually, it was adopted at the 19th party conference. In this way the process of reformation emerged in the mainstream, and became irreversible.[137]

Yet in a joint interview with Soviet and British television he argued that there was a debate about where to start: the economy or the political system?[138] On the second point, in a speech to the CC plenum which unveiled the radical new party programme, Gorbachev stated:

> I agree that the draft should be clearer about the inevitability of *perestroika*. Nobody thought it up, it came knocking at our door in 1953, 1965, 1966, in the seventies and the early eighties, when, it must be said, all society was seething.[139]

Gorbachev continued to extol the Leninist credentials of his thinking and his actions. In other words, Gorbachev was still concerned with demonstrating a long historical pedigree and the ideological credentials for what he was doing when addressing the party.

Gorbachev also went on the offensive against his critics. There was no going back. He reiterated this on a number of occasions. He also polarized the debate: you were either for him, or against him. There was no middle ground. He faced down critics at the April plenum of the CC, who were deeply critical of his proposals for renewing the Union. Further challenges followed in June from Prime Minister Valentin Pavlov, who attempted to accrue further powers to himself. In the face of all this criticism, how did Gorbachev cope? An intriguing insight into his background and mentality came in an interview on Soviet TV on 26 March 1991. In response to a question about where he drew his strength from, Gorbachev retorted:

> I am grateful first and foremost to my parents – peasants who, so to speak, laid down a certain foundation. Peasant life taught me to be cheerful, to endure, to be sensible and not lose my head. That is the first thing. The second thing I said was that I am grateful to Raisa Maksimovna, my wife, who takes great care of me, and understands what a burden and responsibility I have. Third, and this is no less important than what I have already said, is the fact that I believe in the rightness of my cause and of the choice I have made. Because if your faith is destroyed, nothing will save you. As long as a person is strong in spirit, as long as he preserves his faith in what he is doing, I think he will both carry on feeling all right, and will work efficiently and productively. I think that applies to everyone, and I am no exception to this.[140]

Once more, Gorbachev talks of his humble roots and upbringing, the importance of family, and the inner faith he had in the rightness of his cause.

Gorbachev the prize-winner

Although Gorbachev's stock was falling at home, abroad he still continued to occupy a prominent position. The rise of Yeltsin in 1990 and 1991, however, meant that there was now an alternative source of authority for Western governments to consider in their dealings with the USSR and Russia. Gorbachev's acceptance speech for the Nobel Peace Prize, and the subsequent meeting of the G7 in July sum up the transitional feel to Gorbachev's international diplomacy: he still occupied a prominent position, but his significance was waning. In the following section we will explore in depth how Gorbachev coped with the decline in his prominence and the attempts he made to shore up his significance. In retrospect, his speech to accept the Nobel Peace Prize was probably his last major set-piece international address. What was his message?

Gorbachev used the address to reflect upon his achievements, his struggles and the challenges still awaiting him and the global community as the world approached a new post-Cold War era.[141] He began by highlighting his understanding of the idea of peace. Interestingly he drew from his native Russian traditions (the Russian word for 'peace' – *mir* – also meant 'commune', a Russian peasant social institution which stood, according to Gorbachev for accord, harmony, mutual aid and cooperation), and also from a variety of different philosophies and religions in defining peace, failing in the process to mention either Marx or Engels or Lenin even once.[142] Gorbachev defined 'peace' in such a way as to align it with his own views of the shape of the international order: peace meant cooperation and joint creativity, a universal civilization, unity in diversity. In other words, peace was best guaranteed through his 'New Political Thinking'.[143] Reflecting upon *perestroika*, Gorbachev proclaimed boldly that it had been instigated not only on behalf of the Soviet people, but also on behalf of the world community. He also attempted to identify the causes of the problems currently besetting him. In addition to those outlined above, Gorbachev also noted that the prevalent political culture in the USSR was partly to blame. But this was not just the Soviet political culture, whereby *perestroika* had disrupted the patterns of living and working which people had worked to establish prior to 1985. This was also a Russian historical phenomenon which Gorbachev was battling to overcome:

> It is not easy to sustain a peaceful path in a country where for generation after generation people have grown accustomed to the idea that if you oppose or disagree with something and I have power or some other force, then you should be tossed over the side of politics or even put away in prison. For many centuries, everything in the country was ultimately settled through force, and this left an imprint that is hard to wash off.[144]

The image of Gorbachev as the heroic fighter for democracy, pluralism and world peace was accentuated by highlighting the centuries-old attitudes he was fighting to slay. In his vision of what was in store for humanity, Gorbachev noted that 'knowledge and trust' were the keys to a new world order of peace, tolerance and cooperation. The key thing was to seize the moment that history was presenting.

Gorbachev's final acts as party leader and as President before the August coup were highly significant. Gorbachev oversaw the drafting and publication of a controversial new party programme. This programme all but abandoned the traditional values and priorities of the CPSU (dilution of references to Marx, Engels and Lenin, etc.) and went a long way towards turning the party into a traditional European social-democratic party. To many traditionalists in the party it was a step too far, and seemed to confirm that Gorbachev had abandoned Marxism altogether in his rush to modernize the party and make it viable in the new conditions of political pluralism.[145] For Gorbachev, it represented the culmination of his attempts to remodel the party to ensure it could prosper in the new political system. While Gorbachev had ended up by rejecting huge chunks of Bolshevik heritage and Bolshevik values, he still remained committed to the party. Unfortunately, the feeling by this stage was not mutual. His final act as President was to go to the G7 meeting in London at the end of July 1991, and attempt to acquire the economic assistance necessary to shore up the ailing Soviet economy. But Gorbachev cut a rather forlorn figure as he sought, increasingly desperately, aid for his economy. He was drifting towards the wings on the world stage. At home he was becoming increasingly beleaguered. He went on holiday in August 1991. He came back to a different country.

The August coup: looking at things 'with different eyes'[146]

The 1991 coup was over in three days, but it marked the end of Gorbachev's time as the central figure in the Soviet system. Although he remained as President until his resignation on 25 December 1991, his star was on the wane from the moment that he returned and was publicly rebuked by Yeltsin. Gorbachev's story of how the coup happened, and his part in the events belongs to a subsequent chapter, when we will look at how Gorbachev reflected on his time in power. However, Gorbachev's actions and speeches in this period give us an interesting insight into his mentality and his world-view.

On his return, Gorbachev gave a press conference in Moscow before the world's media. He relayed his story of the ultimatum, the incarceration and the drama of the events at Foros.[147] He categorically stated his opposition to the coup, his resolute refusal to sign anything and his concerns for his family. Gorbachev went out of his way to praise the actions of the people in Moscow and Leningrad in standing up to the putschists, and in particular he reserved praise for the actions of Boris Yeltsin.[148] Gorbachev noted that it had been a hard lesson for him personally. He described how he had made a message to be circulated clandestinely by his bodyguards, which contained four points:

1. Yanaev's take-over on the grounds of ill-health was a 'deception', and so was in actual fact little more than a *coup d'état*.
2. All subsequent actions and decrees were therefore illegal.

3. Lukyanov should be informed of his demand to convene immediately the USSR Supreme Soviet and Congress of People's Deputies.
4. The actions of the State Committee for the State of Emergency should be stopped immediately.[149]

Gorbachev then responded to a barrage of questions. The first was: why did you choose such people for key positions in the first place? Gorbachev did not really answer this, save to say that his line was always to resolve everything without bloodshed and with consensus. In a follow-up question about the eight key figures, Gorbachev noted that he had made a mistake in pushing through Yanayev's appointment, and in particular had wrongly trusted Kryuchkov and Yazov. There then followed a key exchange which essentially identified Gorbachev with the old pre-coup world and way of thinking, and drove a wedge between him and Yeltsin. When asked by Terekhov of the Interfax agency about the party's failure to oppose the coup, Gorbachev responded:

> I see my duty ... to get rid of reactionary forces and drive them out of the CPSU ... I consider that there is the possibility of uniting all that is progressive, all that is the best thinking. When you talk about the party as a whole as being the reactionary force of the party, with that I do not agree ... we must therefore do everything to ensure that the party is reformed and becomes a living force for *perestroika*.[150]

Later on he talked about 'fighting to the end for the renewal of the party.'[151] In this way Gorbachev demonstrated his commitment to the institution which he had spent his whole life working in and through. Yet he clearly failed to judge the new mood, which was much more polarized and unforgiving. The party, in the eyes of most of the reformist elements, was part of the problem which prompted the State Committee, and was beyond reform. Gorbachev was still trying to straddle two worlds, still trying to be the centrist. In a rare moment of personal candour, when quizzed further about his trust of Yazov and Kryuchkov, Gorbachev noted his misjudgement, and seemed genuinely puzzled and saddened by their actions. He concluded, rather forlornly, by noting that it had been a distressing ordeal.

On 23 August, Gorbachev addressed the RSFSR Supreme Soviet alongside Boris Yeltsin.[152] Gorbachev attempted to plot a way forward, including political changes and personnel replacements. However, Yeltsin interrupted to insist that he read out a short transcript of a Council of Ministers session in which the members had announced their position with regard to supporting the coup. Gorbachev tried to press on with his statement, but was constantly interrupted by shouts from the hall of 'truth, truth'. Yeltsin and the other deputies continued to press Gorbachev, asking him to banish socialism, to disband the CPSU, the KGB, to nationalize the party property: in other words to destroy all the structures and institutions of the USSR. The final showdown occurred as Yeltsin signed a decree suspending the activities of the RCP. Gorbachev again tried to defend it, arguing that not all Russian communists participated in or supported the coup. But it was all to no avail. Again Gorbachev was seen very publicly to be attempting to defend and preserve an institution widely perceived to be implicated in the coup. The overall impression was that he was, day by day, becoming yesterday's man.

He concluded by responding to a question about the actions and words of Shevardnadze and Yakovlev, who had resigned their positions in the aftermath of the coup. He noted that

> Both Shevardnadze and Yakovlev shared my whole fate from 1985 and participated in all the difficult searches and in some of the mistakes that we made and permitted. This was, so to speak, also due to them. But I believe all the same that the main thing, all that we did, the choice, the adoption of a course, the working out of this course was all correct.[153]

Here we can see in outline the contours of Gorbachev's subsequent position. His whole policy choice had been correct. And he was not going to carry the can for some mistakes which may have been made.

The momentum of these days, though, was gaining speed, and Gorbachev quickly found himself having to react to the changing mood. First up was his position in the CPSU. On 24 August, Gorbachev went on Soviet television and announced:

> I do not consider it possible for myself to continue to perform the functions of General Secretary of the CPSU Central Committee and I surrender those powers. I believe that democratically inclined communists who have preserved their loyalty to constitutional legality and the course of the renewal of society will come out in favour of setting up a party on a new basis which is capable, along with all progressive forces, of joining actively in the continuation of radical democratic transformations in the interests of people of labour. *Mikhail Gorbachev.*[154]

His final act as General Secretary of the Communist Party was to submit a statement of his resignation. His association with the CPSU (almost 40 years of labour) had come to an end, although he still clearly had faith in the ability and willingness of a phoenix-like emergence from the ashes of all those communists who were 'democratically inclined' and who have retained their 'loyalty to constitutional legality'. The noteworthy aspect here is that in spite of all the problems with the party, and the failure to create a new mechanism (either political, economic or federal) which could work while the Communist Party retained its position, Gorbachev still adopted an approach which emphasized the importance of personnel over systems, institutions and processes. His political myopia persisted until the very end.

Mea culpa …

In the immediate aftermath of the coup, Gorbachev had to address the question of why it had happened, and what should happen now. In a clearly personally painful time, Gorbachev had to confront the reasons for the coup, and his own guilt or part in it. Although Gorbachev held up his hand and confessed to some errors, those he admitted to were all, in some senses, forgivable ones: ones caused by his human concern to keep the peace, think the best of people, take as many people with him as possible. In a speech to the Supreme Soviet on 26 August 1991, Gorbachev outlined the following ways in which he may have been responsible for the events of 18–21 August:

- He had shown too much 'liberalism and indulgence' to his critics and opponents.
- He (along with others in the Supreme Soviet – his audience! – party and government) had been indecisive and inconsistent in carrying out democratic reforms.
- The former mechanism of power was not finally dealt with.
- The democrats failed to work together.
- Delays in implementing the reforms to the party.
- Many of the people he had appointed turned out to be 'disgracefully helpless and faint-hearted'.[155]

The faults thus are ones where: (1) he failed to move quickly enough (because he was fearful of bloodshed or chaos) or (2) it was all of our faults. Very little actually comes to rest at Gorbachev's door *alone*. Moreover, the main thing which caused the failure of the coup was precisely all of his reforms![156] He did, however, give a nodding reference to the actions and the heroism of Yeltsin and the people in Moscow, Kiev, Leningrad and elsewhere who had resisted the coup forces.

His personal reflection on 27 August concerning his own role is highly revealing, as it sums up nicely how Gorbachev was able to clear himself of any blame, and (indirectly) take the credit for the defeat, while simultaneously appearing humble enough to recognize that his time in the spotlight of history might be up:

> I feel alright. My conscience is clear. For if I was mistaken in thinking something, maybe it was this. And I think that if we had not gone and taken this path of democratization of society and had not created another society, and if the party masses had not undergone all the same process – they underwent the process there and everywhere – then the putsch organizers could easily have done away with the *perestroika* people. Therefore, we had to steer our ship between Scylla and Charybdis, and to make sure it did not run ashore, etc. Probably, it was not always like that. But still the same course had to be plotted. If it is found that the wheel

has to be turned in quite different directions, then this all must be decided in the appropriate way. But I will not allow blackmail and I will not allow humiliation. And insults must also end.[157]

The lesson that Gorbachev drew was that the slate had been wiped clean. The defeat of the coup had been, for Gorbachev, a 'cleansing storm'.[158] Unfortunately, the storm also finished by blowing him away too.

What does this period of crisis management, turmoil and chaos tell us about Gorbachev? Gorbachev's time between 1989 and 1991 as a crisis-manager reveals someone struggling to keep his project alive as the system began to unravel. What is perhaps most remarkable in the midst of this whirlwind is that Gorbachev continues with many of his constant themes: no going back, centrism, trust me and trust Lenin. This is either symptomatic of someone with an enormous sense of certainty in the correctness of his own judgement, or sheer bloody-minded obstinacy in the face of mounting pressure to do things differently. It is precisely this approach which was his strength in the early days of *perestroika*, but increasingly became something of a weakness as time went on. Tough, unpopular and unpalatable decisions were constantly postponed or fudged and this merely compounded the sense of drift and marginalization. Gorbachev was not a great crisis-leader. He was irritated by criticism and refused to accept any real mistakes on his own part, and seemed unable/unwilling to understand those who thought differently to him. His leadership of the party and his time as Executive President revealed a leader who had partially embraced the new, while clinging on to the old. He persuaded the party to change its constitutional position, but still believed it could reform and renew itself from within, and shift from vanguard to parliamentary party. He espoused the cause of democracy and the creation of a new political system, yet continued to accrue power unto himself and leave large swathes of the old system intact. Perhaps, in the end, he was too much of a Bolshevik to be a democrat, and too much of a democrat to be a Bolshevik.

Conclusion

The Gorbachev complex: man, leader, theorist and statesman

What shall we say, then, to conclude this chapter? Two aspects have been addressed in the main: the nature of Gorbachev's project, and the nature of Gorbachev's leadership. Let us take these one at a time.

What does this close analysis of Gorbachev's words and speeches reveal about his project, *perestroika*? One of the benefits of undertaking an integrated narrative of *perestroika* (rather than fragmenting the story into economics, politics, foreign relations, the media, nationalities, etc.) is that it enables a holistic picture to emerge. It allows the different parts to be seen in their interconnectedness. As we examine Gorbachev's words and deeds, *perestroika* is revealed in its emerging complexity and breadth. It was an evolutionary process which started small and limited, and grew to become an all-encompassing programme of change. So it is impossible to take a snapshot of *perestroika* and say: that is what it was. Gorbachev's project looks very different in, say, July 1986 and July 1989. It went through a succession of phases, each more radical than the last, and ended up by abolishing the organization that set it in motion.

Telling the story is also a useful thing to do in itself. The narrative approach communicates most effectively the inherent drama of *perestroika*: the twists and turns, shocks, betrayals, heroes and villains. It also allows us to reflect a little on one of the key issues relating to an understanding of *perestroika*: how to periodize the years between 1985 and 1991? The initial period of March 1985–July 1986 was the period of preparation, discussion and consolidation. The key period was the time between July 1986 and February 1990. This was the period when Gorbachev was both architect and conductor: crafting policies, drumming up coalitions of support, pushing through changes, countering opposition. 1988 was in some senses the year of 'deep *perestroika*', of the inception of profound changes, of a sea-change in the system. After March 1990, Gorbachev is increasingly reacting rather than conducting, fighting fires rather than driving changes.

This narrative also highlights the inherent paradox of Gorbachev's project: it was a programme which sought to change and preserve. It was this duality which made it such a fascinating thing to observe. Gorbachev set out to reform, improve and enhance the existing system, not to abolish it. He was a party man and a socialist and he continued to believe in these things right up until the end. Gorbachev had always been a 'believer'. *Perestroika*, however, put Gorbachev in a quandary. He wanted change, but he wanted to restrict that change. He wanted to keep the party, and to maintain the socialist essence of the system, but increasingly it became clear that these things were an obstacle to change, were a drag on reform. What would Gorbachev's response be? Would he abandon his beliefs? Or would he abandon his reforms? The resolution for Gorbachev came when what he understood by 'the party' and 'socialism' underwent something of a shift in the period after 1985. The vanguard role of the party was still in place; it was just that the party had to earn it through the ballot box. Similarly, socialism was now something akin to European social democracy, and not the Soviet socialism of the Brezhnev years. The only way Gorbachev could continue to pursue change and maintain his belief in the core elements of the system was to undertake a process of constantly redefining his aims, a process which meant that Gorbachev's pronouncements became vaguer and less specific.

In general, Gorbachev's understanding of *perestroika* became increasingly vague and increasingly personal. As *perestroika* became swamped amidst the forces that he unleashed and was no longer able to control after 1989, Gorbachev was essentially reduced to saying *perestroika* = me. Unable to spell out either a coherent or a compelling vision of where he wanted to go, and seemingly unable to convince people that he could bring about lasting tangible change, people became increasingly reluctant to follow him. Although Gorbachev never lost faith in himself, others inside and outside the USSR did. By 1991, *perestroika* had become 'follow me'. By 1991, though, there were others to follow.

Second, what does *perestroika* reveal about Gorbachev as a leader? Gorbachev's leadership was a necessarily complex one, a function of the many roles he had to play, and the difficult task he set himself. Let us take these roles one by one. As the last General Secretary, what sort of party leader was he? Gorbachev proved to be both orthodox and unorthodox, innovative and traditional. He retained a fairly typical Bolshevik mentality for all of his time as General Secretary, and continued to refer and defer to Lenin in his public rhetoric. Yet he was also committed to the modernization and democratization of the party at the same time. At the outset, the combination of innovative and traditional approaches enabled Gorbachev to succeed (to a degree) in pushing, cajoling and nudging the party towards acceptance of the need for change. Problems came for Gorbachev's style of leadership when, under the pressure of the changes he had unleashed, the party began to fragment and the political system became more pluralistic and competitive. It was then that it became more difficult to maintain this centrist position of advocating a variety of modernized Bolshevism, or democratized communism, as he was too Bolshevik for the modernizers, and too modern for the Bolsheviks in the party. By 1990, Gorbachev was head of many parties, all existing under the umbrella of the CPSU. He was in effect a transitional leader who embodied in himself the wider contradictions of his own project. Unable to free himself of his attachment to the party and cause which he had served and dedicated himself to, he was, in the end, dragged down by it.

As a global statesman, Gorbachev wore two hats: leader of the communist world and global diplomat. His leadership of the communist world was revolutionary, although not in the way that many in the international communist movement might have wished! His determination to push the countries of Eastern Europe to embrace *perestroika* entailed a radical transformation of the relationship between the USSR and the communist satellites, and went an enormous way in encouraging the people to stand up and throw off communist rule. Gorbachev's message to the communist parties and their people was a message stripped of traditional ideological motifs, a message of choice: each country should be able to choose its own path of development. As a global diplomat, Gorbachev similarly offered a message of peace and hope, this time born out of a universalist internationalist message which emphasized the importance of common human values over ideologically entrenched positions, and cooperation over conflict. In the international arena, Gorbachev proved to be an innovative, charismatic figure, unconstrained by the forces which bedevilled him at home.

As a Marxist-Leninist theorist, Gorbachev was also something of an innovator. Aware of the problems of dogmatism and ossification which dogged official ideology, Gorbachev sought to breathe new life into the old ideas through a process of updating and adaptation. In this regard, Gorbachev as a leader was very open to a range of ideas from a number of different political, ideological and national-cultural traditions. Although obviously he was a diligent student of Lenin, Gorbachev also drew on the works of socialist and non-socialist thinkers to inform his ideas. In this sense also, Gorbachev was both a traditional Soviet Marxist-Leninist and also an innovative thinker, willing to experiment, and try different amalgams of ideas. Unfortunately, Gorbachev proved unable to renew Soviet Marxism-Leninism and mix it successfully with other ingredients and yet create something viable. The evolving radicalism of his programme to reform the USSR meant that his ideas were always playing 'catch-up', and he finished with a hotch-potch amalgam of European social democracy, quasi-dissidence and welfare liberalism. The Marxist elements were blown away in the whirlwind of 1989–91. Although Gorbachev remained committed to the socialist cause, he ended up by destroying the official ideology of Soviet Marxism-Leninism as bequeathed to him.

As national leader (which took a number of guises, including Chair of the Supreme Soviet and finally Executive President) Gorbachev was again something of a paradoxical figure, who faced forwards and backwards, westward and eastwards, communist and social democrat, yet who ultimately was a prisoner of his own upbringing and mentality. As a parliamentarian, Gorbachev struggled. In the latter years of his rule, he became increasingly verbose in his speeches, and increasingly impatient with opposition and criticism, as befits someone struggling to adjust to the conventions of democracy, opposition and pluralism. Yet he was still the leader who oversaw the emergence of the first genuine parliament in Soviet history. As a political communicator, Gorbachev was very good in off-the-cuff meetings and discussions with the people. He seemed to enjoy the chance to discuss and argue face-to-face. In high-profile set-piece occasions, he was not quite so adept. His speeches lacked clarity and he often tended to ramble. He also made a number of quite high-profile gaffes, notably in his dealings with the non-Russian nationalities, either referring to the USSR as 'Russia', or forgetting which republic he was in!

As Executive President, Gorbachev found it hard to grapple with the problems of nationalism and federalism, seemingly unable to comprehend the depth of feelings for separatism and autonomy among the non-Russians, and the resentment building up among the Russians. Yet he showed a willingness to create a looser federal structure. He was also very slow to act in certain situations that required speed and decisiveness, most notably in the field of economic reform. His constant delays exacerbated an already fraught situation further. Underpinning this was his inability or unwillingness to put the old system down and allow the new one to grow. His attachment to the old system, his belief that there was a reformable core to the old system which could be preserved and renewed, caused him to try and grow the new system from within the old. He ended up by killing both. Yet this gradualist approach was one born out of a desire to maintain peace and minimize confrontation and bloodshed. His lack of decisiveness in certain situations was often compounded by the fact that Gorbachev's solutions to problems, or his reactions to crises, often proved to be inadequate. In particular, his emphasis on solutions based on personnel rather than systems/institutions exacerbated the failure to both root out the old system and construct a new one. Almost all of these failings can be attributed to the vestigial pattern of Bolshevik thinking and acting, to the cultural and mental imprint of growing up, working and thinking in the closed world of the nomenklatura and Soviet apparatchiki. Although Gorbachev was an innovator and a radical thinker at times, he was still imprisoned by his past.

Finally, what does this tell us about Gorbachev the man? Well, it seems to confirm the paradoxical image painted at the start. Gorbachev's project required him to be transformer and preserver; heretic and true believer; democrat and autocrat; nationalist and internationalist; globalist and localist; populist and purist; Leninist and humanist. Yet the ambiguities were not solely drawn from his circumstances and his position. Gorbachev himself was an ambiguous character: conviction politician, yet also indecisive; a leader who placed great stock on personnel issues, yet seemed to be quite a poor judge of character. In the end, Gorbachev proved to be at his most creative when destroying, and his most destructive when creating.

3

Gorbachev and the Western media

Love in a cold climate

Introduction

One of the enduring conundrums of Gorbachev's career was the apparent disparity between his reputation and popularity at home and abroad. It became (and still remains) commonplace to remark that Gorbachev was fêted abroad and hated at home. But how accurate is this view? In the next chapter we will explore how Gorbachev was viewed within the USSR and assess the extent to which it is accurate to suggest that he was unpopular and discredited at home by 1991. In this chapter we will examine the way the Western media responded to Gorbachev, and assess the extent to which Gorbachev was depicted and celebrated in heroic terms. This chapter will also seek to explain why it was that Gorbachev received such a favourable reception in the West, both in the media and from the people.

The extent of the celebration of Gorbachev as a personality and as a political phenomenon can be garnered from almost any newspaper or magazine from this period. Hence,

> Mr. Gorbachev did not need Cher or superpigs or any other gimmicks to help him dazzle the heartland. Braving 49 degree gray, drizzling weather that people here called a 'Siberian cold front' Mikhail and Raisa Gorbachev created a sensation on their whirlwind trip to the Twin Cities. 'We were supposed to maintain our composure and not become complete babbling idiots,' apologised one excited television commentator. 'But this is really something to see.' Surrounded everywhere by screaming adoring crowds with cameras and video cameras who chanted 'Gorby, Gorby', including a man dressed as Uncle Sam and waving a Soviet flag, he accomplished exactly what he needed to.[1]

How could the leader of the Soviet Union, and the head of the communist bloc, come to be adored and celebrated in this quasi-messianic way in the heartland of

Western capitalism? Why did a kind of 'cult of personality' develop around Gorbachev, and what were its main themes? Was it a wholly uncritical perception, or had the emotions grown cold by 1991? Understanding the love affair between the Western media, the Western public and Gorbachev is a complex task. Uncovering the linguistic and visual patterns of representation in the Western print media not only reveals a great deal about the evolution of Gorbachev's reputation, but also sheds light on the values and outlook of Western society in the late twentieth century. Gorbachev, in spite of his ambiguities, his failures, his flaws and his critics, became a symbol of hope and liberation in a society marked with anxiety, fear and insecurity.

This chapter will examine the way that Gorbachev was presented, represented, interpreted, analysed, profiled, celebrated and ultimately mourned in the Western media during his six years in power. It will appraise the reaction to his accession, the triumphant procession of his diplomacy at the superpower summits, the twists and turns of his attempts to bring about domestic change, and conclude by examining his decline and fall in 1991. Due to the sheer pace of the changes in this period, journalists and media outlets were at the forefront of the attempts to describe, comment upon and interpret the Gorbachev years. Turning the pages of the newspapers from this time is to remind oneself of the wave of changes that swept the world, and helps to recapture the energy and dynamism of one of the most remarkable periods of recent history.

The output of the journalists provides a very different perspective from those academics who struggled to keep up with Gorbachev's energetic leadership. Both perspectives grew out of the same context – the Cold War, the nuclear threat, the rise of the New Right in the USA and the UK, the movement towards greater European integration – yet produced very different modes of discourse. Where academics were keen to locate Gorbachev within an overarching theoretical/conceptual framework (usually pro- or anti-totalitarianism), journalists provided a much more immediate judgement. There are obvious perils in this 'immediacy', but there are benefits too, particularly given the whirlwind of change that Gorbachev oversaw. Where academics tended to focus upon systemic issues, journalists focused far more on the interactions of personality, style and the exercise of political power. Images of Gorbachev dominated the front pages. There was a fascination with the Gorbachevs as a couple. This individualistic focus, this concentration upon Gorbachev the Man, his personality and his impact upon the world stood in marked contrast to the academic debates around Gorbachev. As a result, a very different picture of Gorbachev emerges, a narrative of success against the odds, constant surprises, risk-taking, heroic achievement, and greatness. It is a story of almost biblical grandeur.

A note on sources

This chapter draws upon a variety of print media sources.[2] Inevitably the need for selection narrowed the range of sources to be consulted. An Atlantic Anglo-Saxon perspective was chosen, alongside a concentration on broadsheet newspapers and a variety of different weekly magazines/journals. The selection was based on the requirement to balance political and geographical perspectives, while providing an appropriate breadth of coverage. Clearly, a great deal of interesting material from other sources could not be included. Of the sources consulted, the greatest degree of support for Gorbachev came from the *Guardian* and *Time.* The most pessimistic and critical coverage tended to come from *The Times,* the *Financial Times* and *Newsweek.* Of the more agnostic publications, the *New York Times* and the *Independent* tended to be slightly more positive, with *The Economist* slightly less so. But these general portrayals cannot do justice to the way that the reporting of Gorbachev shifted and changed as his period in office unfolded. In spite of the constraints imposed by the need for selection, a fascinating multi-faceted portrait of Gorbachev emerges.

A wise man from the East

Gorbachev first came to prominence in the Western media prior to his accession at the end of 1984 when he made his now famous visit to the UK as the head of the Supreme Soviet Foreign Affairs Committee. He had already made a trip to Canada in May 1983, but the rise of Gorbachev through the hierarchy in 1984 had led many to speculate that Gorbachev was the next General Secretary-in-waiting. This speculation was given added *frisson* by the obvious frailty of Konstantin Chernenko. The succession was likely to be sooner, rather than later. The trip to London thus became a moment to get a good look at the Young Pretender.

Prior to the trip Gorbachev was profiled.[3] Searching for indications of the type of leader that Gorbachev might turn out to be, a number of points were made which came to dominate thinking about Gorbachev. The overwhelming impression was of Gorbachev's youth in comparison with the aged, infirm leaders he was surrounded by. This was deemed to be of great political significance, as Gorbachev was depicted as the standard-bearer of a new generation of Soviet leaders, unencumbered by the ideological and historical baggage of the Brezhnev/Andropov/Chernenko generation who had grown up under Stalin and experienced the trauma of the Nazi invasion. In addition to Gorbachev's youthfulness, reports also stressed that he was far better educated than all previous Soviet leaders, Lenin excepted. His personal traits – informal, energetic, moderate, open to new ideas, intelligent, at ease with the people – also seemed to highlight the sense of a rupture or break with the past image of aged, grey, faceless, grim leaders. But would he be a herald of change or not? Opinion was divided, reflecting the ambiguities of Gorbachev's past. An orthodox product of the communist system? Or a man of innovation and reform? Which was the real Mikhail Gorbachev?

The coverage of the 15–22 December 1984 London visit confirmed these initial perceptions. Amidst the stereotypes of writing about Russia – talk of 'smiling bears' and warmer climates – the reports highlighted the cordiality of the visit, as well as noting that Gorbachev was likely to be a 'fresh wind of change blowing from the east'.[4] The newspapers perhaps took greatest delight in reporting the antics of the Gorbachevs as a couple. The image of Raisa proved to be a constant fascination: her clothes, her background, her high profile all marked her out from previous Kremlin wives, who had either rarely been seen or were kept out of the limelight. By contrast, the Gorbachevs appeared as a Western political couple: media-friendly, style-conscious and spontaneous. Western reports highlighted how far the Gorbachevs had departed from the stereotype of the communist leader. Raisa's shopping trip (in preference to a trip to Highgate Cemetery to visit Marx's grave), the impromptu stop to visit Downing Street, the meetings with business leaders all pointed to a new type of leader.[5] This is probably best summarized in the infamous phrase uttered by Mrs Thatcher, 'I like Mr Gorbachev – we can do business together.'[6] Overall, the reporting of the visit sought to promote the Gorbachevs as the human faces of the communist system, as representatives of something new within the Soviet Union, be it either a shift of style and image, or a more profound shift in outlook and orientation.

These themes were all reinforced in the reporting of his accession on 12 March 1985 after the announcement of the death of Konstantin Chernenko. Peering into Gorbachev's personality, journalists combined anticipation, eagerness and scepticism. Anticipation about the future rested on the notion that change was in the offing. Gorbachev embodied change at two levels. First, Gorbachev represented a break with the familiar, archetypal Soviet leader. He was young, informal, vigorous and energetic. Second, Gorbachev was also viewed in symbolic terms as the representative of a new generation: a new era had dawned in Moscow. Denis Healey MP, a leading member of the Labour Party, acknowledged that 'Gorbachev represents a complete break with the earlier generation.'[7] But the 'newness' of Gorbachev was reported in terms that stressed familiarity for a Western audience. In other words, Gorbachev was a leader like one of our leaders: he was described as being modern, westernized, urbane, intelligent, flexible, educated. A *Guardian* leader writer highlighted that

> It is above all the style of the man that is different. As his London hosts discovered, he smiles; he pumps hands and pummels shoulders in crowds (working them for all the world like a western politician running for office); and he makes jokes.[8]

Similarly, Robert Cullen writing in *Newsweek* noted that,

> On his visits to the West, Mikhail Gorbachev has worked the crowds as skilfully as any pol from South Boston – or Chicago's First Ward. He has a stevedore's grip and a who-loves-you smile. He stands 5 feet 10; he favors dark suits. And he is a good listener.[9]

His speech, demeanour, actions, dress sense and image presented a familiar picture to the Western public. His career – law graduate, rise through the bureaucracy – mirrored the careers of Western politicians. His generational experiences –

post-war rising living standards, Kennedy and Khrushchev, Sputnik and moon landings – reflected the experiences of a majority of the Western public. The portrayal of Gorbachev as a politician in the modern Western parliamentary mould subverted the traditional way in which Soviet leaders were depicted. Western coverage of Soviet leaders had previously been underpinned by two aspects of 'otherness' or difference from the West: the national/cultural aspect (Russia as an Eastern power, rather than a Western power) and the political/ideological aspect (the USSR as a communist power). Russia had always been perceived as something different: mystical, closed, mysterious, enigmatic, backward.[10] Gorbachev was depicted in ways that challenged these notions head on. Hence, in spite of being brought up in a peasant family, Gorbachev was described as an educated, intellectual figure in contrast to Chernenko, the 'Siberian peasant'.[11] He was described as a pragmatic, realistic politician; not as someone driven by ideology, fanaticism or dogma. Gorbachev seemed to be someone who would make the USSR more like the West, more like 'us' and was therefore someone to be welcomed, embraced and celebrated. He might just be the leader who would remove the decades-old threat that communism would destroy capitalism, and also demystify Russia in the eyes of the West.

Journalists, eager to highlight the novelty, modernity and cultured, Western manner of Gorbachev, used quite revealing ways to communicate this to their readership. The most potent comparison, wrought with many layers of significance, was the use of JFK, or Gorbachev as the 'Red Kennedy'.[12] A similar tack was pursued by the *Guardian* correspondent Martin Walker, who made allusions to a Soviet Camelot:

> There can be no doubting the very real excitement that Mikhail Gorbachev's elevation has provoked among a whole generation of Soviet officials. 'Youth has triumphed,' one of them said to me today, and some westernised Russians are already comparing the Gorbachev era to 'that happy time in America in 1960 when the Kennedys came to power.' It would be distinctly premature to talk of Moscow as a latter day Camelot, although his charming and elegant wife Raisa, and the youthful 54-year-old intellectual leader might try to make it look that way.[13]

The use of the Kennedys to symbolize something of the youth, hope, expectation and style of the new leader and his wife in Moscow was a highly evocative one, raising the expectations of what might happen in the USSR in the years ahead, although it also left open the potential for some tragic denouement as well.

This sense of heightened expectation was not shared by all. Scepticism still existed.[14] Some portrayed him as essentially a party man to his bones – how else could he have risen to the top? – and unlikely to rock the boat. Others stressed that however dynamic, youthful and personable he might be, the system remained impervious to change, and even to attempt it would amount to political suicide. Words of caution were expressed, particularly from academics, scholars and experts who were wheeled out to pronounce on what Gorbachev might do. Some talked of 'a lot of old wine in new bottles'.[15] Ed Hewett (from the Brookings Institution in Washington) outlined that 'he won't change the basic system'.[16] A selection of 'experts' in the *New York Times* differed in their appraisals of Gorbachev's likely impact, although most fell into the 'style = new, impact = minimal' camp.[17]

Interestingly, most of the scepticism originated in the likely constraints, or the strength of the opposition, which Gorbachev would be working with. Few were willing to express outright scepticism about Gorbachev himself. The cult of personality around Gorbachev had begun.

Blessed are the peacemakers

Gorbachev was *the* dominant figure on the news agenda of the Western media in the course of his high-profile global public diplomacy between 1985 and 1990. No other personality could rival him during his heyday. Primarily, this was during a series of superpower summits with the Presidents of the USA in this period, Ronald Reagan and George Bush. However, Gorbachev also made a series of visits – most notably to Great Britain, West Germany, France, China, Czechoslovakia – which were the subject of intense media scrutiny. Gorbachev became probably the best-known political figure in the world. As Gorbachev's appearances on the world stage increased after 1985, so the Western media became increasingly familiar with his style, his image and the aims and objectives underpinning his global diplomacy. In this case, however, familiarity did not breed contempt. Instead Gorbachev was fêted and celebrated: as Mikhail the Liberator, as a Peacenik, as the Great Persuader, as the Last Best Hope. These expressions of Gorbymania or Gorbophilia were not uniform, though. They took on a variety of forms, depending upon the local national/cultural/political context, and were profoundly shaped by the media's focus upon personality.

Gorbachev and the superpower summits: evangelist, salesman, showman, saviour?

The general political climate in US/USSR relations in 1985 was distinctly cool, if not frosty. Arms control negotiations between the USA and the USSR at Geneva were proceeding at a glacial pace. Ronald Reagan had adopted a highly belligerent, confrontational stance, and was supported by a similarly robust Margaret Thatcher in Europe. A general sense of unease and insecurity pervaded the populations of Western Europe and North America, fearful of the possible outbreak of a nuclear conflict, wittingly or unwittingly, worried the Cold War might get very hot, very quickly. Into this milieu stepped Mikhail Gorbachev.

In a medium dominated by personality, Gorbachev's decision to pursue arms control via personal summit meetings with the American president (running alongside the Geneva arms control talks) was the ideal event for the Western print and broadcast media. A high-profile series of encounters promised rich fare for journalists: between the capitalist former actor and the communist leader, the leader of the 'Free World' and the head of the 'Evil Empire' (© R. Reagan), notwithstanding the added *frisson* of the 'style wars' between the two First Ladies, Nancy and Raisa. This emphasis upon personality is crucial. The depictions and representations of Gorbachev, and the evolution of Gorbachev's reputation as a global statesman and a diplomat of peace, can only be fully understood within the context of the comparisons and contrasts with, on the one hand, previous Soviet leaders, and on the other, Ronald Reagan and George Bush Snr.

Geneva: 19–21 November 1985

Gorbachev's major debut on the world stage came at Geneva in November 1985. Little of substance was achieved, with agreement being reached on peripheral issues such as further regular summits, greater cultural contacts and an acceleration of arms control negotiations. The US Strategic Defense Initiative (SDI or Star Wars) continued to be an obstacle to arms control agreements. There was certainly a great deal of interest aroused by the one-to-one chats, without advisers, that Reagan and Gorbachev had. The reporting of the Geneva talks – which were dubbed the 'fireside summit' by Reagan because of the photos of the two chatting besides an open fire – stressed a number of points. The dominant theme was the sheer novelty value attached to Gorbachev, across two dimensions. First, in a Soviet dimension, in contrast to the Brezhnev–Andropov–Chernenko procession, Gorbachev's youthfulness, energy and vim were clearly evident. Yet it was the *performance* of Gorbachev that garnered most attention, particularly for the indications it gave of the type of leader Gorbachev was likely to be, and of the type of Soviet Union that might emerge under his leadership. Gorbachev was noted for being 'plainspeaking and articulate', and 'devoid of artifice'.[18] He was deemed to be 'superior in understanding and personality to any previous Soviet leader'.[19] Other sources stressed his candour, his charm, his civility, his geniality, his humour, his decisiveness. He appeared to be everything his predecessors were not. Amidst the details of the talks between the two leaders, what was communicated was the force of Gorbachev's personality, and the human qualities of the new communist leader:

> But in the end the Soviet media campaign was saved by Mr. Gorbachev's bravura performance after the summit yesterday morning. In his hour long speech with never an eye glazing over and then a courteous and 'packed' press conference in which straight answers were given, the Russian leader emerged from the summit as a statesman whose new world stature does not only depend on the missiles he deploys, but emanates from his personality ... Geneva deserves to go down in history as the Gorbachev debut.[20]

This sense of novelty also stretched to the comparisons between Gorbachev and Reagan. As the new kid on the block, there was a tangible sense of fascination surrounding Gorbachev and his wife. Reagan was well known already, and had had a high profile for over four years. There were also regional factors at play: in Europe, anti-Reagan forces were eager to create a new hero to counter Reagan's war-mongering rhetoric. Gorbachev's words of peace seemed to offer hope that Reagan could be tamed. Glimpses of the relationship between the two leaders also excited the Western media. Reagan – whose reputation was built upon being the Great Communicator – appeared to have met his match in Gorbachev. Even the light shed on disagreements and disputes between the two leaders (particularly the incident where Gorbachev was supposed to have jabbed his finger at Reagan and said, 'answer me, answer me, answer me') served to highlight the new atmosphere between the two states: after six years of hostility and suspicion, candour and open disagreement could be displayed. The verdict on Geneva was: cautious optimism for the future. The verdict on Gorbachev was: a forceful personality has emerged, projecting an image of youth, dynamism, goodwill, peace and accessibility.

Reykjavik: 10–11 October 1986

By the October of the following year, the West had begun to grow accustomed to Gorbachev's leadership and personality. Yet the Reykjavik Summit enhanced Gorbachev's reputation as a peacemaker further. It was here that the two leaders met again for a series of personal meetings, and although they agreed to move forward on a range of issues – human rights, regional disputes, missiles in Europe – they failed to reach agreement on historic cuts in strategic nuclear weapons. On the basis of proposals put forward by the Soviets for drastic reductions, the two sides were ultimately unable to reach agreement (the stumbling-block being SDI) and the summit broke up with recriminations from both sides, and with no new date for another meeting. But in the post-mortems that followed, the press was divided over who was to blame: the liberal press sided with Gorbachev, the conservative press with Reagan.[21]

Gorbachev emerged from the Reykjavik meeting with most of the plaudits. In his press conferences, he was candid, open and approachable. In his walkabouts, he and Raisa were treated like European royalty, with Mrs Gorbachev being openly compared to the Princess of Wales.[22] In his diplomacy, he was seen as a bold risk-taker, and had played a 'mean hand of poker'.[23] The Western media persisted in representing Gorbachev as a Western-style leader,

> There has always been something uncannily American about Mikhail Gorbachev. You see it in his background. The man graduated as a lawyer. He married a bright and lovely young academic who maintained her career after marriage as a philosophy lecturer at Moscow University. Their daughter is a medical researcher. Their son-in-law is a rising surgeon. This family could move straight into New York's Upper East Side as a classic example of the rising professional classes. The Gorbachevs are Soviet yuppies.

Washington: 7–10 December 1987

The visit to Washington in December 1987 was accompanied by a wave of popular acclaim for Gorbachev. The ceremonial signing of the INF treaty was the highpoint of the summit, eliminating an entire class of weapons, although the issue of

SDI remained unresolved. The outcome of the summit was in reality quite modest. But the images and the performances of the main protagonists captured the imagination of media, public and politicians alike. The whole summit was reported in minute detail, and Gorbachev's performance won him rave reviews. He dazzled the people, he amazed the Washington glitterati and he amused the media. He became almost a 'pop hero' in much of the US media. Gorbymania had arrived. His public appearances created an extremely favourable comparison with Reagan, with many commenting on Gorbachev's greater energy, visibility, eloquence and style. Opinion polls after the summit confirmed this.[24] Alongside many of the earlier themes in depicting Gorbachev – bold, charismatic, energetic, risk-taker – new themes began to come through. First, Gorbachev began to be described as a hybrid of salesman and evangelist.[25] Numerous references were made to Gorbachev's accomplished performances in front of the cameras, to his 'PR show'. He had 'out-Reaganed' Ronnie, adopting his homely, populist style, pressing the flesh, charming the crowds. Political consultants kept appearing on TV programmes to announce that 'I'd love to run Gorby in the Iowa caucuses'.[26] His appeal, according to Kremlinologist Robert Tucker, lay in the unscripted nature of Gorbachev's public utterances. In the land of the hard sell, Gorbachev seemed to have the crowds and the media eating out of his hand. Not everyone swallowed the hype, though. Some reports emphasized the disparity between Gorbachev the salesman, and Gorbachev the power politician. Variously he was described as forceful, combative and tough, and as a 'hard man in a great hurry'.[27] Gorbachev did receive some criticism – mainly in the pages of *Newsweek* and *The Times* – for haranguing the media and failing to answer the questions directed at him.[28]

The second theme which began hesitantly to come through was first alluded to by Henry Kissinger.[29] Kissinger was nearer the Gorbophobe end of the Gorby spectrum than the Gorbophile, and was reluctant to join in the euphoria surrounding Gorbachev. But Kissinger added an interesting angle on the reception of Gorbachev in the West:

> The euphoria sweeping Washington was inspired less by Soviet policies than by Gorbachev's personality. He was greeted as though he were the *deus ex machina* to solve all the West's dilemmas – a communist leader who will bring peace and tranquillity without any real effort on the part of the free countries. Business leaders and public figures were nearly abject in their eagerness to celebrate a new era.[30]

Kissinger had detected something almost messianic in some of the media portrayals of Gorbachev: the figure who appears from nowhere to provide comfort, security and to renew hope for the future in a world of uncertainty, fear and insecurity. Gorbachev himself reinforced this, saying that *perestroika* was the 'last chance we have' and one commentator noted that 'he believes that he is to his country what Ronald Reagan likes to say that America is to the world: the last, best hope.'[31] Had the West found a new saviour?

Moscow: 29 May–2 June 1988

The Moscow Summit was reported in slightly different ways to the others. The focus in the Moscow Summit was Reagan rather than Gorbachev. Reagan was in the heartland of the 'Evil Empire', it was his final few months in office and it was his performance that commanded most attention. Yet still in the midst of the media reporting, it was Gorbachev who managed to upstage the ex-actor. At the first domestic press conference ever given, Gorbachev provided an energetic, forceful performance which correspondents described as 'masterful'. Once more, Gorbachev was seen to have eclipsed the Great Communicator.

UN, New York: 7 December 1988

The quasi-messianic theme emerged with startling clarity in the reporting of Gorbachev's visit to the UN in December 1988, a visit cut short by the tragedy of the massive earthquake in Armenia. Gorbachev outlined startling unilateral cuts in Soviet conventional forces, opening the way for a new post-Cold War era based on cooperation not confrontation, dialogue not dogma, peace not conflict. His speech, according to the *New York Times*, outlined a new vision of the world unparalleled since Woodrow Wilson or Winston Churchill. Searching for words to summarize his performance, the leader wrote, 'Breathtaking. Risky. Bold. Naive. Diversionary. Heroic. All fit.'[32]

Describing his reception by the people in New York, Martin Walker in the *Guardian* wrote of the 'Big Red Superstar', and of the crowds (a *Gorby*-rally), traffic jams (*Gorby*-gridlock) and media frenzy surrounding him.[33] *Time* reported crowds lining 'the sidewalks as if it were New Year's Eve'.[34] Once again, the notion of Gorbachev as the most popular, commanding personality on the global stage was reinforced. *Time* spoke equally effusively of Gorbachev:

> Now comes Mikhail Gorbachev with a sweeping vision of a new world order for the 21st century. In his dramatic speech ... the Soviet president painted an alluring ghost of Christmas future ... His vision, both compelling and audacious, was suffused with the romantic dream of a swords-into-plowshares.[35]

Once again, Gorbachev had seized the initiative, aided by the timing of the US domestic political calendar. Bush (the incoming US President) was there but had not yet assumed office. Reagan (the outgoing US President) was yet to leave office. Gorbachev stood unchallenged in the centre of the world's gaze. In this hiatus stood Gorbachev bearing unexpected gifts, espousing a new vision for the world, a vision infused with hope for a better, more secure world.[36]

Malta: 2–3 December 1989

A month ahead of schedule, Gorbachev met the new US President George Bush on a ship amidst a violent Mediterranean storm. The weather provided the perfect metaphor for Gorbachev's situation at home. Since the Moscow meeting and the UN address, the USSR had begun to unravel in the face of ethnic and worker protest, and Gorbachev appeared as an increasingly beleaguered leader. The Malta Summit, coming amidst the tumult of the revolutions against communism in Eastern Europe, sought to set out the parameters for a post-Cold War world, and to supply American help for the ailing Soviet economy. Gorbachev said he would not intervene in the affairs of the Eastern Europeans. It was Bush who set the agenda, and who took the initiative in putting forward proposals. But it was Bush who needed to establish credibility on the international stage, not Gorbachev. By confirming his commitment to democracy in Eastern Europe, Malta affirmed the view of Gorbachev as the 'Liberator' (although conservative commentators were quick to point out that this did not seem to stretch to events within the USSR).

Gorbachev followed the Malta Summit with a visit to the Vatican to meet the Pope, the first Soviet leader to do so. His talk of the need for spiritual values in *perestroika* led to further speculation in the Western press about Gorbachev and religion. This was generally a dimension explored in the US media rather than the European, because of the greater attention to spiritual issues within US culture.[37] Tantalizing hints that Gorbachev might be a closet believer were dropped. This rapprochement between Kremlin and Vatican reinforced the perception that Gorbachev was wholly different from previous communist leaders, and was in fact a leader the West could trust and believe in. Gorbachev's reputation – as a history-maker, as a peacemaker, as a leader with a new vision of the future – was further enhanced.[38]

Washington: 29 May–4 June 1990

The second Washington Summit was a difficult one for Western journalists to characterize. There were the 'normal' celebrations of Gorbachev, his personality and his image. But lurking in the background was the nagging sense that Gorbachev's star was on the wane. The accumulating problems at home, and the rise and rise of Boris Yeltsin as a key domestic political figure (and possible successor?), cast a shadow over Gorbachev, and added a tragic, almost wistful *fin-de-siècle* air to the reporting. How long would Gorbachev be around? In the light of this, there seemed to be a conscious effort on the part of some to celebrate Gorbachev, his achievements and his performance, to begin to write the epitaphs for Gorbachev's period in office. Yet others began to piece together the reasons for the eclipse of Gorbachev.

The reporting of Gorbachev in Washington (as well as his visit to Minnesota) proffered three themes: Gorby the Showman, Gorby the Great Man of History, Gorby the Brilliant Failure. The adulation of the crowds in New York and Minnesota repeated the *Gorbymania* phenomenon of the earlier Washington summit.[39] Prominent US figures provided instant headline-grabbing quotes about the impact of Gorby. Walter Mondale, former US presidential candidate, called Gorbachev 'the world's most stellar celebrity'.[40] Dan Rather, prominent US news anchor, said memorably that Gorbachev could 'charm a dog off a meat wagon'.[41]

The celebrations of Gorbachev were as effusive as ever. Yet the sense that this was a man whose time had come and was going could not be escaped. Rupert Cornwell, writing in the *Independent*, said:

> Maybe history is about to devour Mr. Gorbachev and the whirlpool of the multiple revolution he has set in motion will overwhelm him ... if the world is now a better and more hopeful place, then that is largely due to him.[42]

Neale Ascherson, reflecting on Gorbachev's immense popularity abroad, and his dwindling reputation at home, likened him to others in this strange world of adulation and antipathy: Woodrow Wilson, Napoleon Bonaparte, Alexander II. For Ascherson, Gorbachev was the man who 'freed a whole generation in North America and West Europe from the fear of war' and was one of the 'Great Liberators'.[43] As recognition, he was given the title 'Man of History' from the Appeal of Conscience Foundation.[44] Yet not all the judgements were celebratory or laudatory. Gorbachev was described as a 'brilliant failure' in a *Newsweek* article which argued that his multiple failures at home were a reflection of his personal shortcomings: a lack of understanding and a lack of vision.[45] Leaving Washington, Gorbachev seemed to be moving off the historical stage.

London and Moscow: July 1991

Although we didn't know it at the time, July 1991 saw Gorbachev's last two appearances on the international stage. On 17–18 July, the G7 summit of the leading industrial nations met in London (the UK, the USA, Canada, France, Japan, Italy, Germany). Gorbachev hoped to use this as a means of acquiring economic aid to bolster his ailing domestic economy. The question that dominated Western reporting was: should we help this man? The division of opinion reflected the prevailing views of Gorbachev. One group – the 'back him' faction – argued a case based primarily upon a 'better the devil you know' line. Gorbachev should be thanked for what he has achieved, and should be backed because, well, we don't know what might happen if he is replaced. An apocalyptic, Balkan-style Yugoslav scenario was often quoted as the one to be avoided. From this perspective, Gorbachev should be assisted.[46] He was the best hope for the continued transformation of the Soviet Union, and for a long peace in Europe. A different group – the 'snub him' faction – argued that Gorbachev should not receive any assistance. His economic record was abysmal, and his commitment to continued reform was less than total, given his drift to the forces of reaction in the latter half of 1990 and the first half of 1991. As Tony Barber pithily put it, 'Mr. Gorbachev's tinkering with the economy has proved unoriginal, ham-fisted and thoroughly in the Soviet tradition.'[47] The world community was becoming increasingly polarized into believers and non-believers. His past achievements were beginning to count for less and less.

The extent of Gorbachev's fall from the leader who strode the world stage in 1988 can be gleaned from the sketches of Gorbachev's appearance at the G7 summit. The Italian organ *La Stampa* compared Gorbachev's appearance to that of Vercingetorix of the Gauls in Rome. He had been sent to Rome as a human trophy to celebrate the victories of Caesar, and was subsequently killed a few years later. With the Cold War over, and the West having 'won', Gorbachev was paraded like a trophy at the G7 summit by the Caesars of capitalism: Bush, Kohl, Major and Kaifu.[48] A more popular picture was to depict Gorbachev as a beggar, searching for scraps from the tables of the high and mighty.[49] Trophy or beggar, the message was clear: Gorbachev was a diminished hero, following not leading, travelling in hope, rather than as hope.

The final summit was held in Moscow on 30–31 July.[50] It confirmed that Gorbachev's role was shrinking and his authority dwindling. Yeltsin snubbed an invitation to attend a meeting with Bush. Although a significant arms control agreement was signed, the verdict of the Western press was clear: this was not so much the last of the superpower summits as the first of the new post-Cold War world. But would Gorbachev be a part of it? Was Gorbachev doomed to be the last hurrah of the old world?

For six years, Gorbachev stood at the centre of the global stage. During a succession of high-profile meetings with Reagan and Bush, the Western media consistently portrayed Gorbachev in glowing terms: as a global diplomat, an international statesman of high repute and a consistent advocate of peace, dialogue and disarmament. The excitement aroused during his accession – of a modern, cultured, educated, western-style leader – continued in the depictions of Gorbachev in the international arena. In contrast to previous Soviet leaders he was energetic, affable, open and popular. In contrast to Reagan and Bush he was novel, fresh and aroused both curiosity and expectation. Western socialists also joined the chorus. Martin Jacques argued that

> There is something else finally that the Gorbachev revolution can offer Western socialism: a new kind of leader. Why is Gorbachev so admired throughout our society? Because he is modern, he is about tomorrow though clearly rooted in a tradition; he is courageous, demonstrably prepared to lead from the front; he is not afraid of being in a minority, while being a master of compromise; he is not a prisoner of tradition or the status quo, having fearlessly attacked vested interests not least the very ones that have nurtured him. Unusually for a socialist, he says it straight, without pomposity or self-congratulation; he is a democrat, a humanitarian, a cosmopolitan and highly intelligent to boot. In short western socialist leaders have much to learn from the man in the Kremlin.[51]

Yet his appeal went further than offering a model to socialists, or in comparison with past or present leaders. Gorbachev came to be described in *universal terms*: although he was a communist, he was, in fact, a leader in a Western mould – his values, his demeanour, his image, his marriage – made him one of us. As a universal figure who transcended the ideological/geographical divide, it became possible for the Western press to hold Gorbachev up as a symbol of hope and liberation; hope for a future free of fear, uncertainty and insecurity. Ben Pimlott, writing in *The Times*, argued that,

> Mikhail Gorbachev has become a symbol in the West of something that cannot be caricatured: hope. Who provides the world's best chance for peace and orderly disarmament? The near-united answer is Gorbachov. Who is offering the Soviet peoples their best prospect of human rights since 1917? Gorbachov. Who would like to introduce a measure of democracy? Gorbachov. Who is determined to modernise the Soviet economy, and has an eye on some western freedoms with this in mind? Gorbachov. Who, by Western common consensus, is the best Russian leader for a century or two? Who would be an enjoyable companion at dinner? Gorbachov, Gorbachov.[52]

In its eagerness to celebrate Gorbachev, he became, for a short time, a quasi-messianic figure who promised almost single-handedly to save the world from the threat of nuclear annihilation. In sum, the symbolic representation of Gorbachev tells us much about Western society in the late twentieth century: insecure, uncertain, lacking faith in its own leaders and yearning for someone who could solve their dilemmas and bring about a hopeful bright future. Gorbachev was the right man at the right time.

Gorbachev goes abroad: Paris, Bonn, London, Beijing and Prague

The reception accorded to Gorbachev on his visits to foreign capitals as part of his global public diplomacy varied quite substantially, and the depiction of Gorbachev varied according to the local context within which he found himself. Quite distinctive pictures emerged of Gorbachev, depending upon the country he was visiting. In France, he received a very lukewarm response, whereas in Germany he was fêted and worshipped. In Eastern Europe and China, he was seen as a 'Great Liberator' by the people, and yet was viewed with suspicion by the ruling authorities as *perestroika* threatened to undermine the basis of their rule.

France proved to be the least susceptible to the Gorbachev charm offensive. Gorbachev made two visits there as General Secretary: once in October 1985 (his first major visit abroad) and later in July 1989 as part of the bicentennial celebrations of the French Revolution. His initial visit, which carried all the hallmarks of the Gorbachev approach – populist, informal, friendly, open – was still received with less than open arms by the French. His arms control proposals made stunning headlines, but there was a rumbling undercurrent of criticism aimed at Gorbachev and the human rights record of the USSR. The conservative press dubbed him *Gulagchev*.[53] The greater scepticism of the French than their British and German counterparts was confirmed by a *Newsweek* opinion poll. In response to the question 'Which leader is more serious about reaching an arms control agreement?', the answers were as shown in Table 3.1.

Table 3.1 'Which leader is more serious about reaching an arms control agreement?'

	Britain (%)	France (%)	West Germany (%)
Reagan	38	37	38
Gorbachev	24	10	18
Neither	23	31	36[54]

France's determination to maintain a relatively independent stance in the Cold War, and its own experiences with native communism (an element missing from the domestic politics of the UK and West Germany), left it more resistant to Gorbachev's charms, and more willing to criticize the Soviet leader. Michel Tatu, a leading French Kremlinologist, described his countrymen as Gorbophiles, rather than Gorbomaniacs.[55] The July 1989 visit proved to be a gross disappointment to most French journalists and commentators. Gorbachev proved to be obscure, evasive and lacked his usual polish.[56]

By way of contrast, the West Germans gave Gorbachev a dazzling reception during his visit there in June 1989. Crowds flocked to him wherever he went, shouting 'Gorby! Gorby!'[57] The steelworkers in the Ruhr decided to nominate Gorbachev for the Nobel Peace Prize.[58] Opinion polls reflected this tide of popular acclaim. *Der Spiegel* ran a poll that suggested that Gorbachev was the most popular world leader ever.[59] The underlying reasons for the popularity of Gorbachev in West Germany were not difficult to detect. It was not just a reaction to the obvious personal charisma and style of the Gorbachevs. Gorbachev (once again) represented a sense of hope, this time for the German people (hopes of peace, hopes of a new role and status in a reconstructed post-Cold War Europe, hopes even of reunification and new national pride).[60]

The visit of Gorbachev to Britain in April 1989 saw a different reception again, but one which had close parallels to the German experience later on that year.[61] It was the usual mix – walkabouts among the crowds, meetings with Thatcher, addresses to Parliament – and Gorbachev received a tumultuous welcome from the people. The British press stressed the 'chemistry' between Gorbachev and Thatcher, in spite of the combative discussions about nuclear arms and human rights between the two, and also the similarities between the two:

> Obviously they do see each other as some sort of kindred spirits. Both see themselves as radical reformers in their own societies, the scourges of an ossified bureaucracy. Both clearly revel in the cut-and-thrust of political debate, tolerate fools badly and are given to lecturing their colleagues and their people.[62]

Aside from the focus upon the relationship between the two leaders, the British press was eager to communicate the excitement generated by Gorbachev, because 'he embodies, either heroically or tragically, the next best hope of mankind which is the civilising of the communist world',[63] The expectations aroused by Gorbachev can be detected from the fact that there was slight disappointment when Gorbachev did not unveil any new disarmament proposal, although this was tempered by the invitation to the Queen to make a formal visit to Moscow.[64] Once again, Gorbachev was represented on two levels: as a Western-type leader, and as a symbol of hope for the whole of humanity.

In his visits to various communist capitals, Gorbachev was represented in the Western press as a symbol of liberation, democracy and freedom. In May 1989, he visited Beijing during the pro-democracy demonstrations in Tiananmen Square. With his face adorning posters, Gorbachev was clearly the popular hero of the democracy protesters, in stark contrast to his reputation among pro-democracy protesters at home.[65] Similar themes were expressed in reporting Gorbachev's visit to Prague in April 1987.[66] In the country that had seen its own communist liberalization movement snuffed out by Soviet tanks in August 1968, Gorbachev returned as an embodiment of hope for the Czechoslovak people. Indeed, Gorbachev's image as a modern, reforming, democratic leader was massively enhanced by his tour of Eastern Europe, where the norm for a communist leader was to be aged, grey, faceless and lacking charisma.[67] The different receptions accorded to Gorbachev on his visits abroad reinforce the idea that Gorbachev meant different things to different nations/cultures.[68]

A prophet without honour?

The adulatory, celebratory, quasi-messianic style of reporting Gorbachev during his public diplomacy was not replicated in Western reporting of Gorbachev during his domestic travails. Gorbachev's appearances on the international stage were frequent, eye-catching and prominent, but they were also episodic, punctuating his long-term day-to-day attempts to push through a restructuring of the Soviet system. Gorbachev's project to reform the Soviet system stimulated great interest in the West. But the portrayal of Gorbachev in a domestic Soviet context, rather than on the international stage, was of an altogether different quality. Whereas Gorbachev was celebrated and fêted for his global diplomacy, the image of Gorbachev at home was more complex, more colourful and more open to critical interpretation. This was partly because Gorbachev proved at home to be a leader with flaws and fallibilities: indeed the slow disillusionment of the Soviet people with Gorbachev and *perestroika* when set alongside the 'Gorbymania' in the West was an obvious point of interest for pundits, commentators and journalists alike.

But it was partly also driven by the fact that the gaze of the Western press on Gorbachev inside the USSR was looking at things from a different angle. There was a greater sense of detachment, of observing Gorbachev and his struggles with less of the immediate personal involvement of Gorbachev and his superpower diplomacy. But there was also a greater sense of unfolding drama about Gorbachev and *perestroika*. It was constructed as a narrative of one person's heroic struggle to shake up and rebuild a rotten system, to 'civilize' communism, to 'normalize' the

Soviet Union (i.e. make it like the West). It was a narrative with a flawed but noble hero (Gorbachev), saints (Sakharov), villains (Ligachev) and mavericks (Yeltsin). It was a story of heroism and ultimately tragedy. And it was a story with constant twists and turns, right up until the final dénouement. Underlying this story of a personal struggle was a deeper narrative. This was also couched in terms of a struggle, but an historical one whereby Russia struggles to throw off the shackles of her authoritarian legacy to become modern, Western, democratic, European. Out of this story of struggle Gorbachev emerged as a bold, prophetic leader, but increasingly as a prophet without honour in his own home.[69]

Gorbachev the Great, 1985–88

After the initial excitement of Gorbachev's accession had died down, the Western press turned to reporting the nuts and bolts of Gorbachev's leadership.[70] However, a great deal of the first year or so of Gorbachev's tenure was portrayed in the same terms that accompanied his accession: here was a new, young, vigorous, energetic, dynamic figure, and, according to Patrick Cockburn, 'a new type of Soviet leader'[71]: open, unwilling to encourage the usual sycophancy and flattery, deft and skilful. Gorbachev was being described as a bold, new leader, with a fresh vision and the energy to go with it. By the end of November 1985, Western journalists were beginning to paint in the details on the Gorbachev canvas:

> The new style in the Kremlin has raised Russia's standing a notch or two in the eyes of the world. By agreeing to face western pressmen, dropping the leaden cadences of Soviet-speak in face-to-face conversations, and bringing his wife along on foreign trips, Mr. Gorbachev presents himself as a leader in the western mould, who expects to be treated as an equal. The smile is a new technique of Soviet diplomacy, and it is proving to be an effective one.[72]

The point of departure was, as expected, Gorbachev in comparison with previous Soviet leaders. On all counts he came out strongly. He was *modern* (representative of a different generation), *sophisticated* (cultured, stylish, well-dressed unlike, say, the 'earthy' folksy ways of the peasant-born Khrushchev), *educated* (the best-educated Soviet leader since Lenin), *charming* (media-conscious) yet *tough* (unwilling to tolerate corruption, laxity, careerism).[73] The most repeated quote was the one apparently proffered by Andrei Gromyko when nominating Gorbachev: 'He may have a nice smile, but he has teeth of iron.'[74] These characteristics made Gorbachev, for many Western commentators, a thoroughly un-Soviet leader. Andy McSmith, writing in the *New Statesman*, offered a dissenting view, though, arguing that the rapid and ruthless way that Gorbachev had consolidated his hold on power prior to the 27th Party Congress in February 1986 had echoes in the Stalin era.[75]

Although many detected elements of the modern, Western leader in Gorbachev's speech and demeanour, others preferred to look back into Russian history for parallels to understand the essence of Gorbachev. At times, his style of leadership –

autocratic, but with a populist feel – was compared to the general pattern of Tsarist rule, whereby the benevolent autocrat descends upon his subjects to meet with them.[76] The most oft-quoted example was Peter the Great, who embarked on a process of rapid forced westernization and modernization of Russia at the start of the eighteenth century. Gorbachev appeared to be bent on the same process: dragging Russia into modern and Western ways by the scruff of its neck.[77]

Beneath the surface, a single question gnawed away at Western reports of Gorbachev. Was he for real? This was partly fuelled by the traditional scepticism towards Soviet leaders, but partly also by a sense of perplexity about what Gorbachev was saying, and what he was doing. Although his appearances on the world stage were garnering him laurels and plaudits in equal measure, the progress at home was more blurred. The source of this perplexity was the series of paradoxes which punctuated the period between March 1985 and the end of 1986. Perhaps they were inspired by the quote from Gromyko cited above: nice smile/iron teeth. This sense of paradox can be seen from articles which asked: will the real Mr Gorbachev please stand up?[78] The paradoxes covered a variety of aspects:

- *Charm and toughness*: Gorby appeared to be charming, friendly and engaging abroad; at home he was ruthless in consolidating his position and in dictating to the countries of Eastern Europe.[79]
- *Bold rhetoric/minimal impact*: Gorbachev talked radically and plainly, constantly surprised with new initiatives, yet his rule appeared to be short on actual achievement.[80]
- *Open and shut case*: Gorbachev preached the virtues of openness, yet only when it suited him. When the Chernobyl meltdown occurred, 18 days passed before Gorbachev made a public pronouncement, an obvious cover-up having been attempted.[81]
- *Western and Russian*: Gorbachev embodied both modern Western modes of leadership, with more traditional Russian approaches.[82]
- *The Pope and Martin Luther*: Gorbachev was an orthodox Marxist-Leninist to his boots, and a staunch defender of the Communist Party, yet he was also seeking serious structural reforms of the system.

There were others. Yet the doubts over the sincerity of Gorbachev's words began to recede from the end of 1986, primarily with his decision to release Dr Andrei Sakharov, the veteran human rights campaigner and dissident, who had been kept in exile in the closed town of Gorky. This move reinforced Gorbachev's growing reputation for boldness and as a springer of surprises.[83] This reputation was confirmed by the January 1987 plenum decision to introduce limited democracy into the Soviet system. As the reform programme became more radical, so the portrayals of Gorbachev began to shift. From a bold if paradoxical figure, the picture shifted to accentuate Gorbachev as a radical leader, as a dynamic revolutionary figure, as a man in a hurry.[84] As the scale and extent of Gorbachev's 'radicalism' grew, so the implicit question being asked by Western reporters shifted from 'Is he sincere?' to 'Can he succeed?'[85]

At times he was likened to a preacher, spreading his gospel of modernization.[86] Elsewhere he was described as a 'riverboat gambler'. [87] While it was relatively easy for Western commentators to encapsulate the style and approach of Gorbachev, it was much more difficult to try and capture the essence of what he was doing, of where the Soviet Union might end up. Parallels were again drawn with two leaders who provided the most consistent point of reference for Western journalists: Peter the Great and JFK.[88] Gorbachev's aura and rhetoric were considered to be Kennedyesque, a version of 'Camelot on ice', as Martin Walker put it. Yet his project was more like that of Peter the Great: forcible, rapid modernization. In fact, it was more common to say what Gorbachev was not doing: he was not a 'liberal in the western sense'.[89] Reflecting on whether he could succeed, the press adopted three different approaches. One was to ask: could and should the West help?[90] The second approach was to stress the breadth of Gorbachev's vision and the radical nature of his reforms. The final approach was to examine the magnitude of the task, and the problems and opposition he still faced.[91] *The Economist* opined that:

> It takes brains as well as guts to re-make a revolution, and Russia's Mikhail Gorbachev has both ... The gleam in Mr. Gorbachev's eye does look revolutionary. Yet it still may not be enough.[92]

However, by the end of the year it was this latter line which began to dominate. There was a subtle shift in the reporting, as the enormity of the task began to sink in, and in particular as the sense of resistance to Gorbachev – from within the party and from the people – began to be perceived. The words associated with Gorbachev were now 'gamble', 'risk', 'danger', rather than 'bold', 'radical' or 'visionary'. He was described as being on 'the edge of the abyss'.[93] Even the normally optimistic *Guardian* recognized the dangers for Gorbachev in the period from November 1987 to June 1988, when the party conference was due to meet:

> Gorbachev is now heading into the most dangerous period of his time in the Kremlin. The next 6 months will see one long political crisis, culminating in the extraordinary party conference on June 28 ... The first 1000 days have bolstered the image of Gorbachev as a Soviet JFK. But the next one hundred could still wreck it.[94]

These themes of gambling/risk-taking dominated the Western view of Gorbachev during 1988.[95] At the end of 1988, his reputation in the world reached its apotheosis with his speech to the UN outlining the cuts in conventional weapons. Yet his reputation at home was plummeting. Opinions were beginning to polarize. The hero had suddenly, surprisingly, been found to have clay feet. By the end of 1988, the question implicit in Western reporting on Gorbachev had shifted from 'Can he succeed?' to 'Can he survive?' By the end of 1988, a growing sense of ambiguity had seeped into Western portrayals of Gorbachev, reflecting the popular abroad/unpopular at home divide. For instance, *The Economist* asserted:

But note the contradiction between Mr. Gorbachev's message to the West ('Trust me because my reforms are irreversible') and the warnings he increasingly gives at home ('Battle on comrades or our reforms could fail'). Those reforms still depend to an alarming degree on one man. Alternative leaders are ready, alternative policies can be found ... Admirers of Gorbachev West would be wise to remember the lesson of Gorbachev East: *perestroika* is not yet irreversible.[96]

Yet Gorbachev still had effusive supporters. His appearances on the world stage continued to win him rave reviews: Simon Jenkins wrote paeans of praise in his honour, placing himself firmly in the Gorbachev-as-hero camp.[97] Jonathan Steele, looking back on all that Gorbachev had achieved by the end of 1988, noted:

After almost four years in power, Gorbachev's ability to appear fresh, innovative and exciting is astonishing. The world rightly senses that this is a man with unusual qualities for a contemporary politician. He learns as he goes along, which is the authentic mark of the non-dogmatist. He is not cynical. He has a vision and a set of values which go beyond the mere business of staying in power.[98]

This portrait painted Gorbachev as a leader with a difference, not just concerned with the grubby politics of personal power and aggrandizement (like Western politicians). Yet, even in this picture, it is stressed that 'this man is still very fallible at home'.[99] Reviews of 1988 posited that it would probably go down in history as the 'Year of Gorbachev'. But prognostications about 1989 were hedged in with qualifications.[100] The accumulating weight of evidence now pointed to problems, perils and dangers all around, rather than his triumphs. The task now looked enormous, and the prospects of success seemed to be growing dim. Crucially, other figures had now appeared on the political scene, raising the possibility – still remote at this stage – of an alternative leader. Gorbachev now began to look both fallible and vulnerable for the first time. The heroic phase of the Gorbachev story was coming to an end. A tragic denouement awaited.

Gorbachev: the tragic failure of the noble hero, 1989–91

The paradoxes kept appearing. 1989 broadened the disparity between reputation abroad and reputation at home. The paradox was at its most acute in the area of nationalism and the moves for national autonomy and independence in Eastern Europe and the Soviet Union. In Eastern Europe Gorbachev's replacement of the Brezhnev doctrine with the Sinatra doctrine saw him proclaimed as *Mikhail the Liberator* in Prague, Warsaw, Berlin and Budapest. Within the Soviet Union, Gorbachev's treatment of the Soviet nationalities – including the massacre of demonstrators in Tbilisi in April – seemed to suggest that a more appropriate description might be *Mikhail the Terrible*. But there were other paradoxes. In leadership terms, he went from being *Mikhail the Dynamic Leader* to *Mikhail the Footdragger.*

following rather than leading, reacting rather than taking the initiative. As a politician, was he *Mikhail the General Secretary* or *Mikhail the President?* In the face of all these issues, it is unsurprising to learn that Gorbachev was portrayed as a man whose political career lay in the balance. To the question 'Can he survive?', the answers started to sound more negative than ever before.[101]

The emphasis now was on struggle, difficulty, challenge. The hero was under siege. Gorbachev was in the midst of a precarious balancing act, and his project was being undermined by economic failures, national protest, social unrest and conservative party opposition. Suddenly, as radical voices began to be heard, the perspective on Gorbachev changed. Now he began to appear as a moderate, centrist, authority, establishment figure. He was no longer viewed in the context of the grey conformism of the Brezhnev years, but against the dazzling colours of *perestroika* and *glasnost'*.[102] By the end of 1989, he was increasingly being viewed as a conservative figure.[103] In this context, different 'versions' of Gorbachev can be discerned in the Western press: Gorbachev the tightrope walker; Gorbachev on the wane; and Gorbachev as yesterday's man.

Those who described Gorbachev as tightrope walker/gambler focused on the constant ability of Gorbachev to manoeuvre, manipulate and operate in a tight corner. Although it might appear that Gorbachev was being overwhelmed by circumstances, his renowned political skills and his ability to maintain the centre ground meant that all was not lost. But even some of these pictures were underpinned by a growing pessimism about Gorbachev. The tightrope analogy often talked about 'the abyss' below him. Vladimir Voinovich argued that Gorbachev, even if he survived in power, would ultimately fail, because he could no longer take the USSR to the place he wanted to:

> Mr. Gorbachev wants to cross a tightrope from bad socialism to good. On the other side of the abyss, he expected to see a sign reading 'Good socialism' but found one that reads 'capitalism'. He doesn't have the strength to go back. His choice is simple: mark time until he falls into the abyss. Or step to the other side; no matter what 'ism' it's marked with.[104]

The gambling analogy now stressed that Gorbachev was playing, albeit skilfully, a bad hand.[105]

Pessimism became the dominant perspective, though. He now seemed to be a waning power, a leader on the defensive, a politician with flaws. What was the cause of this? Undoubtedly the pictures of Gorbachev transmitted during the miners' strike in July 1989 played a great role in this. Gorbachev looked physically shaken and affected by this outburst of popular protest:

> He always seemed the master tactician. The architect of *perestroika* and *glasnost'*, the man we could do business with. Above all the man who was never lost for words. Now, for the first time, Mikhail Gorbachev is

beginning to falter ... the Soviet leader is in a more difficult position – and more visibly harassed – than ever before.[106]

Having unleashed freedom, criticism and democracy, Gorbachev now seemed as though he would be engulfed by these very forces. This sense of Gorbachev as the heroic victim of the good he had done was tempered by other opinions which stressed that the flaws and failures were his: his faulty policies, his incoherent vision, his leadership.[107] He was suffering from the 'evolution of declining expectations'.[108]

By the end of 1989, an even more pessimistic strand of reporting had emerged: Gorbachev as yesterday's man. Doubts began to be expressed about whether or not Gorbachev would last, and how his downfall might come about.[109] This speculation was in part inspired by the commemoration in October 1989 of the 25th anniversary of the removal of Nikita Khrushchev by a palace coup in the Kremlin.[110] The conclusion was that Gorbachev was not in the same danger as Khrushchev, as his position in the party was more secure, but there were far greater dangers to Gorbachev from outside of the party. However, the unthinkable now began to be expressed: would the Soviet Union be better off without Gorbachev in power?

> But just as British voters decided in 1945 that Winston Churchill, brilliant though he had been as a war leader, was not the man to run the peace so the West should be prepared for the possibility that Mr. Gorbachev, brilliant though he has been as a smasher of Stalinism, is not the man to introduce democracy. Let the West remember that keeping its Soviet hero in power is a means not an end. The aim should be for the Soviet Union to become a true democracy.[111]

Looking back over 1989, Rupert Cornwell, writing in the *Independent*, also speculated that Gorbachev might find himself swept away by the tide of history. But his conclusion was that in the immediate future the fate of the USSR and Eastern Europe 'still depends on the will of one man'.[112] Looking forward at the start of 1990, Jonathan Steele argued that Gorbachev would become renowned as the 'Great Facilitator'. He went on to say:

> But it still seems likely that he will end up in history as a transitional figure, the Moses who set the Soviet Union on the long path away from Stalinist bondage, but who was removed along with his party before reaching the Promised Land of a fully functioning civil society.[113]

But how long did this man have? And who would be the Joshua figure, leading the Soviet Union to the Promised Land?

1990 was marked by the onset of sustained questioning of Gorbachev's overall intentions. Although there were episodes across this year that seemed to confirm his continuing commitment to reform, and further evidence – if it were needed – of his political adroitness, it began and ended badly. It began with repression in Azerbaijan; it ended with the resignation of his Foreign Minister Eduard Shevardnadze, who warned of a 'coming dictatorship'. Why did these doubts begin to emerge? Essentially, Gorbachev came to be viewed as a 'sinking hero'.[114] A succession of episodes undermined his standing and the whole project of *perestroika* appeared to be unravelling. Gorbachev came to be seen as being interested in self-preservation, not in the nobler values of liberation, reform, freedom. Gorby had truly become, in the eyes of the media, a politician in the Western mould.

This ambiguity over Gorbachev was reflected in the reporting of the fifth anniversary of his time in power in March 1990. Balancing a desire to celebrate his achievements with the need to temper this with the growing doubts about his leadership, Western commentators came up with an ambiguous appraisal. The *Independent on Sunday* listed the five steps forward and the five steps back of the Gorbachev tenure.

The five steps forward were:

> *PEACE*: the Cold War was over;
> *FREE*: free to speak, free to protest, free from fear;
> *LAW*: creation of a state based on the rule of law for the first time;
> *PURGE*: removal of old-style Soviet political figures;
> *TRUTH*: revelations about History.

The five steps back were:

> *LOSS*: loss of territory, loss of power, loss of prestige;
> *CRISIS*: economic failures, shortages, strikes;
> *UNREST*: national tensions, ethnic violence;
> *BREAK*: the Baltic states prepared to secede form the union and break up the USSR;
> *ATOM*: the Chernobyl nuclear disaster.[115]

Profiles of Gorbachev also revealed ambiguities. *Perestroika* was threatening to turn into *katastroika*.[116] In spite of all the talk of democracy, pluralism and civil rights, Gorbachev as Executive President had accumulated almost as much power as Stalin.[117] Pessimism about the magnitude of the task facing Gorbachev was growing. Yet garlands were still being prepared. Hugo Young reflected on Gorbachev in the light of the most prominent Western political contemporaries of Gorbachev and dubbed him 'the unflinching and inexhaustible symbol of the most important revolution most of us will ever live to see'.[118] Even winning the Nobel Peace Prize in October 1990 only briefly halted the turn of the tide, as his problems at home seemed to make a mockery of the international adulation he was receiving.[119] But the emphasis now was upon *remembering* what he had already wrought in the world; his future was now deeply uncertain.

Further episodes confirmed that Gorbachev was now sinking. Policy failures – particularly with regard to nationalities and the economy – mounted up. His ability to deliver miracles had dried up. Indeed, the onset of winter was marked by genuine fears of a catastrophic food shortage. In the face of the accelerating pace of change, Gorbachev seemed to be following not leading. He had 'reached the limit of his imagination'.[120] In the face of the momentous scale of change, Gorbachev appeared, Canute-like, to be palpably unable to hold back the tide. The metaphors used to describe his situation – unable to control the genie he had unleashed, being devoured by his revolution, being swamped by the tidal wave of popular protest – all communicated a desperate figure, out of control, the victim of circumstance, helpless.[121] Looking for parallels to encapsulate his position as the head of a crumbling Empire, two suggestions were put forward: the Queen (nominal head of the Commonwealth) or the Holy Roman Emperor (titular head of a confederation of loosely linked states and statelets).[122] Gorbachev also now appeared to be being rapidly eclipsed by Boris Yeltsin.[123] During the 28th Party Congress in July 1990, it appeared that Gorbachev had won a major victory in steering the party away from the conservative groupings. Yet even here, Yeltsin managed to steal Gorbachev's thunder by resigning his party membership and storming out of the Congress with other radicals.[124] Consequently Yeltsin looked to be the politician whose time had arrived: popular, outspoken, credible, not tainted by the failures of office. Moreover, Gorbachev was now, clearly and publicly, deeply unpopular. Popular protests against Gorbachev at the May Day parade in Red Square – normally the apotheosis of Kremlin self-congratulation and adulatory propaganda – shocked the world. How had it come to this?[125] Gorbachev was running out of greatness. The attempts to increase his own power now appeared grubby and self-serving, rather than part of a grand strategy to impose democracy from above. In the light of all the above evidence, the doubts were being raised more frequently. Is he still good news? Is he still a liberator, or another tyrant?[126] Was he going to become another 'Russian reformer-turned-reactionary autocrat'?[127] Was he now 'Mikhail Sergeevich Pinochet'?[128] Melor Sturua had two words of advice for Gorbachev: 'Say goodnight'.[129]

Autopsies

The verdict was a severe one: 'The man who has brought hope and freedom to millions abroad is bringing despair and chaos to millions at home.'[130] *Perestroika* was at a dead end. But why had it all gone wrong? Earlier criticisms were repeated, most notably the lack of vision and the failure to deliver policy success in the key areas: the economy and the Union. However, new sources for failure began to be detected, sources which derive in part from the underlying approach of the Western media: 'personality' and 'Russianness'. The first related to flaws in Gorbachev's personality. Gorbachev was said to be short-tempered, intolerant and highly emotional in response to criticism. This, according to Mary Dejevsky, was the reason for the depth of the problems he faced:

With hindsight, Gorbachov's temperament can be blamed for some of the most acute problems he currently faces ... whether the issue is Boris Yeltsin or the Armenians, the law on the presidency or Lithuanian independence, Gorbachov seems to feel personally betrayed. He treats each not as a challenging problem to be solved, but as a personal insult calculated to sabotage his mission to improve the Soviet Union.[131]

A similar conclusion was reached by Julian Nundy in the *Independent*, who pointed out his impatience and his impulsiveness, arguing that there was

A facet of Mr. Gorbachev's personality that is little appreciated in the West. He has a lecturing, know-all, even bullying style that sits ill with radical Soviet intellectuals and the millions of people who see no material benefits from *perestroika*.[132]

The media had always had a fascination with personality.[133] From March 1990 this took on extra political significance because of the extraordinary powers that Gorbachev now wielded as Executive President. The personality of the president would leave an indelible stamp on the nature of the regime. Despite being seen as a positive force on his trips abroad, doubts about Gorbachev's personality compounded the growing suspicion about Gorbachev's motives in accumulating power unto himself.

The other theme that began to seep into Western reporting on Gorbachev was the reversion to age-old perceptions of Russian leaders and the Russian people. The Soviet/communist motif had almost totally disappeared as Gorbachev abandoned the party and made himself Executive President. This was brought in to try and explain why Gorbachev appeared to be moving inexorably towards a regime of personal (i.e. his) power, and why Russians appeared so resistant and impervious to changes which might make them more like 'us'. Russia's culture of leadership was based on autocracy, absolutism, the strong hand dragging Russia towards modernity and westernization. Unsurprisingly, the Western headlines in March 1990 were full of references to 'tsars': 'Gorbachev, super-tsar', ran one headline.[134] In the face of mounting problems, Gorbachev was doing little more than revert to type, as 'authoritarianism and strong leaders are in its blood',[135] and 'Russia's history is stuffed with tsars who began their careers as reformers and turned into reactionary autocrats in their old age. Peter the Great, Catherine the Great ... now Mikhail the Great.'[136] Western writing was strongly conditioned by its reading of the culture of Russian leadership in its attempts to explain Gorbachev's shift from liberator to potential dictator.

This sense of the burden of Russian history weighing down on Gorbachev and pressing him into its mould of the ruthless leader was accentuated by the views of the Russian masses which ran throughout much Western reporting. Analyses centred around the notion of the basic incompatibility between the Russian people and the norms of democracy and civic pluralism. This, it was implied, might help to account for the change in Gorbachev's approach, and for the failure of his reforms. In other words, Gorbachev could to some extent be vindicated: there was something in the Russian national character which stood as an almost insuperable obstacle in the way of Russia joining the rest of the world. This can be seen in a number of reports. In the section commemorating his five years in office, the report was entitled: 'He has changed the world, but can he ever change the Russians?'[137] Recalling the words of the eighteenth-century Russian Ivan Pososhkov, Julian Nundy applied them to Gorbachev: 'The Tsar pulls uphill with the strength of 10 men, but millions pull downhill.'[138] On this view the weight of Russian history compelled Gorbachev to adopt the strongman persona:

> The problem is as much with the people as with their leaders. They complain at length yet, always seeking grandiose answers, they refuse to make the small changes in their own lives which, taken together, would change their world. Moscow airport offers the perfect example of this. Foreigners are not allowed to bring roubles into the country yet the woman who hires out baggage trolleys does so only for roubles and will not change currency. When you politely suggest to her that this is not rational, her answer is immediate and fierce: 'What has it got to do with me?' To ask such a question is to invite the traditional 'firm hand' of Russian history, the kind of leadership that takes all the decisions for a passive people.[139]

As *perestroika* appeared to be heading towards the iceberg at the end of 1990, and Gorbachev seemed to have turned his back on reform, some early (albeit premature) epitaphs began to appear. Much of this was inspired by his Nobel Peace Prize, emphasizing his role in the ending of the Cold War and the general reduction in international tensions. In spite of the criticism of him, the Western press argued that his legacy would outweigh the voice of sceptics and critics at home.[140] But the overwhelming sense being communicated was of the tragic hero, of the moderate engulfed by history:

> Whatever his fate, Gorbachev will have a place in my pantheon of the centre, the temple where the moderate is tragic hero ... Brinton shares the liberal historian's affection for the good men devoured by revolutions but comments that, in revolutionary situations, 'the wisdom and common sense of the moderate are not wisdom and common sense, but folly.' That may yet come to be the epitaph for Mikhail Gorbachev.[141]

The sense of tragedy was summarized in a way that resonated with the messianic echoes of Gorbachev's forays abroad: 'He saved others, but he could not save himself.'[142]

1991 began badly for Gorbachev. Violence in Lithuania resulted in bloodshed on the streets and Soviet tanks in the capital. Jonathan Eyal urged the West to end its love affair with Gorbachev, seeing him as 'a leader whose historic mission is over'.[143] This was now a common refrain: *perestroika* was finished, democratization a sham, Gorbachev 'the new Saddam Hussein'.[144] The attention of the Western media began to turn increasingly to Boris Yeltsin as the best hope for progressive policies. The West had fallen out of love with Gorbachev.[145]

Yet Gorbachev had not finished surprising his admirers and detractors. Suddenly he seemed to turn back towards the path of reform. He held a referendum on 17 March on the vexed question of the Union.[146] Gorbachev won backing for a 'renewed federation' (although many were still sceptical about what that would really mean). Then, in April, he concluded an agreement from the leaders of nine of the Union republics for a plan for radical power-sharing between the centre and the republics. This was due to be formally signed in August. Then, in July, he oversaw the drafting of a new party programme which abandoned most of the treasured beliefs of the Communist Party, and in essence converted the CPSU into a European social-democratic party. These moves – as well as his ability to confront and defeat challenges to his leadership from the hard-line communists, striking miners, Boris Yeltsin and his own Prime Minister – seemed to confirm that Gorbachev had rejoined the path of reform.[147] The path, however, continued to be a perilous one, strewn with hazards and unseen dangers.

Three days that shook the world, 19–21 August 1991

Death ...

The coup launched by the representatives of the 'old guard' – communists, military, KGB, heavy industry, the power ministries – on Monday 19 August came totally out of the blue, although it had been whispered about for many months. It still came as a shock, but it was not really a surprise. The media coverage of Gorbachev in the coup was a roller-coaster affair: praise at one moment, brickbats the next; proclaiming his historic significance followed swiftly by a long litany of his failures and mistakes. All in all, the media coverage of these three days reflected the ambiguous status of Gorbachev as seen through the eyes of the West: by turns heroic, tragic, villainous, yet always a man of historic significance.

Reporting of Gorbachev on Day One of the coup (Monday 19 August) oscillated violently between differing perspectives: commemorating his achievements, mourning his passing and speculation on his role in, and responsibility for, the coup itself. As news filtered out of his arrest in his government dacha in Foros in the south just before he was due to fly back to sign the new union treaty, it appeared that this was the end for Gorbachev. How then should he be remembered? Weighing up his legacy and his achievements, the verdict which emerged was a mixed one. Most were happy to celebrate what had been achieved, most notably the removal of fear from the lives of the peoples of the Soviet Union, freedom in Eastern Europe, radical nuclear and conventional disarmament, withdrawal from Afghanistan, steps towards democracy, pluralism and civil rights in the USSR. The most fulsome praise came in a *Guardian* editorial:

The most important man in the world is now under arrest in a Crimean dacha. No living political leader has so profoundly changed our lives as has Mikhail Sergeyevich Gorbachev. He transformed the Soviet Union, he freed Eastern Europe, he reunified Germany, he ended 40 years of nuclear confrontation between East and West, and he brought sanity and hope back into relations between nations. His fall is not only a disaster for Russia and the USSR. It is a tragedy of planetary proportions.[148]

His ability to walk a political tightrope was mentioned a number of times; his success in hanging on this long branded 'miraculous'.[149] Gorbachev had 'reinvented his country'.[150] His place in history was secure, and it would be looked back on favourably. But in the short term, the record was a patchy one: mistakes (especially economic ones) had undermined him; his lack of a consistent vision left him improvising increasingly desperately. The legacy of Gorbachev was deemed to be equally ambiguous. His revolution had sunk deep roots into Soviet soil, but the economic crisis was the most acute one the Soviet Union had faced since the Second World War.[151]

But why had he failed? Answers to this question divided into three main categories: his fault, our fault, and an impossible task. Some pointed the finger at Gorbachev and argued that he had been the prime contributor to his own downfall, in a number of ways:

- He lacked strategic vision, did not know where he was going and was unable to persuade the people that he was moving in the right direction.
- He was able to destroy the old system, but was not radical enough to create a new one.
- His personality was ill-suited to dealing with the problems and people he came across.
- His policy choices were flawed.
- His tactical shifts left him without a loyal constituency and without either political authority or legitimacy.[152]

Others pointed the finger at the West's failure to help him by financing him at the G7 summit. The failure of the Western governments to fund him left him looking weak at home, and provoked the decision to remove him. Western economic aid could have enabled Gorbachev to buy enough time to survive the short-term crisis.[153]

Lastly, it was argued that Gorbachev was overwhelmed by the sheer enormity and magnitude of the task. The mountain was 'too high to climb'. He had been swamped by forces he unleashed and which he did not understand and was unable to control. Underlying this view were two messages. One was the message of the essential paradox of Gorbachev the political leader: he had to be both Pope and Luther, reformer and communist. The other was that Gorbachev was not just trying to reform communism, but was also battling against centuries of Russianness,

'Ultimately perhaps the victor will be the crushing historical and psychological deadweight that is Eternal Russia.'[154]

... and Resurrection

Day Two of the coup raised barely a mention of Gorbachev. Attention turned to those, led by Yeltsin, who were resisting the coup. On the third day, Gorbachev rose again. In the midst of reporting his return and the triumphant victory of Yeltsin and his supporters, two issues came to the fore. To what extent was Gorbachev responsible for the coup? What would happen to Gorbachev now? Although murky rumours abounded, suggesting that either Gorbachev or Yeltsin had indirectly stage-managed the coup in order to bolster their own position, a more popular position was to argue that Gorbachev had to share responsibility and guilt for the coup. He had chosen the men who led it. He had refused to remove them when they had overstepped the mark. He had encouraged them through his actions at the end of 1990 and the start of 1991, and by creating an executive presidency with such sweeping powers.[155] Yet this view was countered by those who argued that Gorbachev was also responsible for the failure of the coup. His reforms had changed Soviet society and made the failure of a putsch highly likely. Indeed, by allying himself with the hard-liners, he had managed to delay a coup until its success was very unlikely.

Attention was slowly shifting away from Gorbachev and on to Yeltsin. Gorbachev appeared in the eyes of most commentators to be a diminished figure, increasingly irrelevant to the new post-coup Soviet Union. His insistence on the continued importance of the Communist Party seemed to condemn him to belong to the past. The new authority and popularity of Yeltsin, who was determined to push on with the break-up of the Soviet Union, left Gorbachev in a highly impotent position: a symbolic head of state, a lame duck.[156] He already appeared to be yesterday's man:

> A historical progression may be emerging: Gorbachev as the Father of *perestroika*, Yeltsin as the hero of the barricades, and Sobchak as the honourable and capable administrator who can clear up the mess and guide the transition.[157]

The aftermath of the coup confirmed the sense of the continued diminution of Gorbachev. The parallels with historical figures past and present shifted: now it was Alexander Kerensky or Egon Krenz.[158] As he struggled to maintain his grip on power – eloquently, passionately and with conviction – so the verdicts of the Western commentators began to concur: the Gorbachev era was over.[159] It was time to say 'thank you and goodbye'.[160]

Songs of praise and a crown of thorns

The celebration of Gorbachev in the Western media and in Western society was not just reflected in the reporting and representation of Gorbachev, but was given direct expression by the succession of awards and garlands which came Gorbachev's way. Many of these were nominations of press outlets, and ranged from the sublime to the ridiculous. A few examples:

1985: *Financial Times* 'Man of the Year'[161]
1985: *Time* 'Man of the Year'[162]
1987: *Time* 'Man of the Year'[163]
1987: *Der Spiegel* 'Man of the Year'[164]
1988: Le Parisien Liberé: 'International Man of the Year'[165]
1989: *ITN/London Weekend TV* poll 'Statesman of the Decade' and 'Hope for the Future' award[166]
1989: *Time* 'Man of the Decade'[167]
1990: Nobel Peace Prize[168]
1990: Commendation in the International Best-Dressed Poll for 'liberating the fashion sense of Soviet men(!)'.[169]

The depictions of Gorbachev at these moments of celebration reveal the extent of the adulation showered upon him. The *Time* profile of him described him as 'magician, faithful communist, charismatic politician, international celebrity and impresario of calculated disorder'.[170] He was said to symbolize 'change and hope for a stagnant system, motion, creativity, an amazing equilibrium, a gift for improvising a stylish performance as he hang-glides across an abyss. Mikhail Gorbachev: superstar ... means to accomplish the salvation of an entire society.'[171] To crown the adoration, the article concluded that

Mikhail Gorbachev is the Copernicus, Darwin and Freud of communism all wrapped in one ... Gorbachev is a sort of Zen genius of survival, a nimble performer who can dance a side step, a showman and manipulator of reality, a suave wolf tamer ... Gorbachev is a visionary enacting a range of complex and sometimes contradictory roles. He is simultaneously the communist Pope and the Soviet Martin Luther, the apparatchik as Magellan and McLuhan. The Man of the Decade is a global navigator.[172]

This was the high point of Western *Gorbymania*. In here are all the themes which suffused Western representations of Gorbachev: as messiah, pioneer, hero, historic figure, great man, man of paradoxes.

Gorbachev became a media phenomenon. Western companies tapped into his popularity and began to use him as a symbol for their advertising. Guardian Royal Exchange, a financial services company, ran a picture of Gorbachev under the caption 'Offer people Freedom and Choices and you'll make a name for yourself.'[173] American traders played on Gorbymania by producing Gorby dolls (at $250 each) to sell at Christmas in 1989.[174] A whole panoply of new words entered popular usage, including:

Gorbymania (popular public adoration)
Gorbyphilia (infatuation with Gorbachev among the chattering classes)
Gorbyphobia (antipathy towards Gorbachev from Cold warriors)
Gorbasms (see *Gorbymania* and add hysteria)
Gorbeuphoria/Gorbaphoria (as *Gorbymania*)
Gorbacharmed (effect of Gorbachev on movers and shakers)
Gorbachevery (the Gorbachev style)
Gorby-gridlock (the traffic consequences of a Gorbachev visit)
Gorbachop (a Gorbachev reshuffle)
Gorbanomics (Gorbachev and economic thinking).

The miscellany of his life proved a constant source of fascination for Western reporters. A Spanish newspaper claimed that Gorbachev's grandfather was an emigrant from Galicia in Northwest Spain, the same region from which Fidel Castro's ancestors originated. Apparently, Anton Corbacho left Spain for Eastern Europe as a child, and after the Revolution he became a collective farmer in Russia, and Russified his name to 'Gorbachev'.[175] Any insights that could be gleaned about his past, or conversations while abroad that might open a window into his life, were seized upon.[176] Of all topics though, the greatest fascination was aroused by his wife Raisa, by their relationship, and her role. The great disparity between the high-profile, glamorous Raisa and previous Soviet leaders' wives was crucial in creating the JFK comparisons, and did much to persuade the West that Gorbachev was a distinctive, Western-style figure.[177]

Although the Western press were usually ready to adorn Gorbachev with garlands of flowers, the odd crown of thorns did slip through. They usually came from two broad groupings: Western cold warriors and Soviet émigrés. Criticisms were usually inspired by three distinct viewpoints. Early on in his leadership, it was argued that Gorbachev should not be trusted just because he talked nicely. He must be judged on substantial issues.[178] Second, his underlying motives needed to be examined.[179] The Soviet dissident, Vladimir Bukovsky, argued that Gorbachev was only interested in one thing: saving the system (and with it his own skin).[180]

In the latter years, criticism centred on Gorbachev's inability to deliver on his promises, and on the gap between his reputation and the reality of life in the USSR. A good example is that of Robert Kilroy-Silk, writing in *The Times*:

> History ... will pronounce Gorbachev to have been a decent but also a
> weak man, a misguided fool, an incompetent politician, a dreamer of
> impossible dreams. We can only hope that it will not go on to conclude
> that he was also responsible for more misery, destitution, destruction and
> death than Stalin and Hitler.[181]

An equally damning verdict came from Elena Bonner, a Soviet human rights campaigner and widow of Andrei Sakharov. Gorbachev, according to Bonner, had been mythologized. The myth – that he was a campaigner for freedom and democracy – was almost unchallengeable in the West. She went on to conclude that,

> For Americans, Gorbachev is the author of *perestroika*, a democrat, the liberator of Eastern Europe, Man of the Decade. They associate his name with peace, prosperity, reduced military budgets and lower taxes. He's the good wizard from a fairy tale. Another myth! They are not interested in what will happen to the peoples of the USSR under Gorbachev. A strange replay of history – a new cult of personality, but this time in the West, not the USSR. On a Moscow street, an American tourist was arguing with a young Russian who ended the conversation with an offer, 'If you like Gorbachev so much, why don't you take him?'[182]

The critics were generally sporadic lone voices up to 1990. But during his last year in power Gorbachev had become a fallen hero, although the dominant mood in the West was still one of tragedy rather than villainy. Tatyana Tolstaya posited that the West had been completely duped by Gorbachev. He was a hard-liner in democrat's clothing who had betrayed the Russian people.[183]

Gorby ascends

> As far as my work is concerned, the main purpose of my life has already been fulfilled.

History does appear at times to have an acute sense of ironic timing. For a figure so often portrayed in messianic ways, it was surely inevitable that Gorbachev would announce that he was resigning on 25 December 1991, Christmas Day. Even more apposite was the fact that this was *only Christmas Day in the West*; the Orthodox Christmas was celebrated in early January. The constant theme of Gorbachev – messiah abroad, false prophet at home – found its most perfect expression right at the very end. The Western press were full of adulatory articles, commemorating his life and times, and looking wistfully at a future without the man who 'changed the world'.

The final verdict was complex and multi-faceted, reflecting Gorbachev's own ambiguities, as well as the uncertain legacy he was leaving behind. All of the eulogies were tempered with lingering sentiments of tragedy. All of the criticisms were softened with gratitude for what had been achieved. Those on the eulogistic wing summoned history to their cause. He had made an epochal difference and had changed the world. But only when looking back would his true greatness be recognized.[184] As a political leader of global significance he was an idealist, a pragmatist, a democrat. Even his failure to carry through his project was deemed to be his greatest achievement, as it had 'freed his country to reinvent itself'.[185]

In his retirement, he seemed to confirm the initial impression that he was a Soviet leader in the Western mould:

For the first time (and last as there will be no more) a Soviet leader has departed in the manner of a western leader – with bitterness, perhaps, and a deep feeling of rejection, but with the prospect of taking up a new career. And for that no-one can take the credit but Mr. Gorbachev himself.[186]

Yet ultimately he had failed. He was the 'architect whose plans collapsed'.[187] He was the transitional figure, but not the man for the new era.[188] As a Russian proverb put it, 'The carpenter has finished the job. It's time the carpenter went.'[189] Reversing the eulogistic appraisals which depicted him as the great personality shaping history, Tony Barber wrote that 'Gorbachev's career is proof not of the impact that one man can make on history, but of how powerful historical forces sweep aside the efforts of one man to resist them.'[190]

Gorbachev had always aroused great passions and strong opinions in his short time in office. His resignation was no exception. Two pieces illustrate this. In a highly polemical attack on the 'chorus of approval' for Gorbachev, Edward Pearce presented him as a false icon, a handsome frothbottle, a vain shallow man. All of his major achievements happened contrary to what Gorbachev had planned, earning him the epithet of a master of inadvertence. His 'greatness' could only be attributed to the American obsession with image and personality: he seemed dignified, impressive, charismatic. In reality he was a decent, gallant incompetent.[191] Conversely Martin Woollacott identified Mikhail Gorbachev as the defining figure of the twentieth century when he wrote that 'The twentieth century came to an end at 7pm Moscow time on December 1991.'[192]

Conclusion: Gorbachev and the West

The first thing to note is that the adulation of Gorbachev in the West was by no means universal. It was heavily conditioned by the context – domestic or foreign affairs – and also by the time of writing. Between 1986 and 1988 was the high watermark of Western press adoration of Gorbachev. After 1989, it began to be more critical and sceptical. On the whole, however, Gorbachev was a godsend for the Western media. This was almost literally the case, given the occasionally quasi-messianic tone that characterized reporting on Gorbachev. It was the Western media that in the main were responsible for the fêting of Gorbachev, given the academic Cold War in the ranks of the Sovietologists. Gorbachev himself never gave any grounds for any quasi-messianic interpretation of himself or his project. So why was the Western media so ready to embrace and celebrate Gorbachev? And what does a study of the Western media between 1985 and 1991 tell us, if anything, about Gorbachev, *perestroika* and all that?

The 'Gorbachev' created by the Western print media tells us much about late twentieth-century Western society, its anxieties, its neuroses, its priorities and its obsessions. For in its readiness to embrace, with fervour, a seemingly wise man from the East promising peace, security and a new era of global cooperation, the reporting revealed a society at once both deeply insecure about the prospects of global nuclear annihilation, and yet profoundly sceptical about the ability of its own political elites to bring this about. The 1980s were a decade of great socio economic uncertainty. The devastating impact of Thatcherism and Reaganomics on the industrial heartlands on the USA and the UK, coupled with their bellicose rhetoric, promised a future full of uncertainty and conflict. Abroad, the impact of the Khomeini Revolution in Iran after 1979 seemed to suggest that the West was no longer the choice as a progressive model of civilization for those who were able to choose. The European left was on the retreat, and looking for a way to revive its fortunes. Non-socialist anti-American sentiment in Europe desperately sought a counterweight to Reagan.

Into this situation Gorbachev appeared, as if by magic, to assuage the fears of Western society. On the global stage he became all things to all people. To Western socialists he seemed to promise the prospect of renewing socialism in the face of Reaganomics. To Europeans he appeared to offer a realistic obstacle to the expansion of American power, speaking of a 'Common European Home'. For those concerned about nuclear war, he came speaking words of peace. The essence of the appeal of the Gorbachevs was this: he appeared to be 'one of us'. He looked like a Western statesman. He sounded like a Western statesman. His wife looked like a Western statesman's wife. Moreover, his reforms also seemed to say something profoundly reassuring: that he wanted Soviet society to be more like ours. In this way he overcame two deeply embedded fears of the 'other': the 'mystical, cultural, eastern' otherness of all things Russian, and the 'political, ideological' otherness of communism. Suddenly there was hope.

There was also a more immediate media/journalistic context: the adoration of the individual. The late twentieth-century preoccupation with celebrity, with the minutiae of the lives of the rich and famous, found an outlet in Mikhail and Raisa, one of the first celebrity political couples. The emphasis upon personality, style, public image reflected this preference for a discourse centred on the individual rather than the system, on the personality rather than the process, on the image rather than the substance. Reporting on the superpower summits, with their photo opportunities, the one-to-one negotiations and the direct comparisons of leaders and leaders' wives created a narrative which had individuals at its centre and in this context Gorbachev was both beneficiary and victim. He benefited on the global stage because he was contrasted favourably with the existing Western leaders. But domestically he suffered. At first it was fine because he was compared to Brezhnev, Andropov, Chernenko et al. But as the reform programme deepened, the West began to fix their eyes upon more noble, interesting characters such as Sakharov or Yeltsin.

On the home front, he was less successful, but no less interesting. The twists and turns of his struggle to change the Soviet system became a drama of great intensity and intense fascination. Could he succeed? Could he really make Russia more like the West? Could he really make communism work by making it more like capitalism?? In the end he proved unequal to the task. Opinion was divided on him when he left office. There were some who were unreservedly critical of him, but these were very much in the minority. The rest either applauded his boldness or acknowledged his impact. The causes of his failures – the burden of Russian history, the flaws in his personality, the unfathomably ambitious nature of his project – in a sense proved unimportant. In fact, it could be seen as adding to the mythology surrounding him. There was something comforting in the tragic hero, the noble failure, the flawed messiah. His failure at home also confirmed deeper notions about the problematic relationship between 'Russia' and 'democracy'. Gorbachev's denouement ended up as almost the perfect story for the Western press: a rise and fall narrative set against the backdrop of international tensions and cross-cultural differences.

A careful reading of the content of Western media reporting on Gorbachev helps us to confront one of the central ambiguities of Gorbachev, which is the perception of widely diverging appraisals which exist between East and West. Although the reporting of Gorbachev did contain moments of almost messianic fervour, it was on the whole much more balanced and critical than the East/West divergence would suggest. The reasons why Gorbachev was received at times very favourably in the West are not difficult to explain. Clearly his failures at home were far less relevant to Western society than his foreign policy initiatives, which did so much to reduce tension and abolish the dividing line running throughout Europe. The generally positive reception accorded to Gorbachev can be explained by the socio-political and historico-cultural context existing in the West at this time. His appearance seemed almost able to fulfil the expectations and demands of a range of different constituencies in the West, who were all able to look at Gorbachev and interpret him in ways which suited their own circumstances.

But what, if anything, does this 'Western Gorbachev' tell us about the man himself? Can it help us, in any way, to explain the phenomenon of Gorbachev? This can be explored on a number of levels: individually, politically and historically. As a political phenomenon, the Western media representations show Gorbachev as an agent of change. They emphasize the pace and scale of the changes *inaugurated by him*. It is only by re-reading the press at that time that one is able to appreciate the sheer magnitude of what was being attempted, the ever-increasing speed of the changes and also the twists and turns involved. Gorbachev comes across as a central figure – either consciously or unconsciously – in a series of events and processes which profoundly shaped the world in the late twentieth century. It's a narrative with one central character, a character finally overwhelmed by the task he has confronted. But the whole Gorbachev project is profoundly revolutionary in its scope and in its outcomes. Second, the Western media also demonstrate the limitations on the part of individuals to effect change. Gorbachev is identified as marking a sharp break with the past, yet in the end he is thwarted by the weaknesses in his own personality and character, and also the sheer size of the task that confronted him. In the Western press Gorbachev contrasts markedly with his predecessors: Gorbachev represented a break with the past, and a shift in the mentality and outlook of the Soviet leadership. Yet he is never quite able to escape the burdens of the past, or break free of his personality and character flaws.

The Western media narrative highlighted the importance of individuals in the historical process, in effecting change. It also reinforced existing stereotypes about Russia and communism. The picture painted of Gorbachev by the Western media in the end, though, tells us far more about us than it does about him.

4

The Soviet view

The slow death of the choreographed leader

Introduction

A commonplace assertion about Gorbachev has been to note the disparity
between Gorbachev's reputation and value in the West and in the East. In the
West, as we saw in the last chapter, Gorbachev was fêted abroad: as peacemaker,
democrat, diplomat. Yet the Western verdict on him at home was more complex
and variegated. In the East he was said to have become, by the end of his time in
power, a deeply unpopular leader, hated not fêted and pilloried not praised for his
reforms and his handling of the system. But is this accurate? Did Gorbachev really move quickly from 'hero to zero'? In this chapter we will examine the shift in
the appraisals of Gorbachev in the USSR, starting with the minutely choreographed image lovingly constructed and disseminated by the Soviet propagandists
and culminating in the clash of conflicting voices in the late Gorbachev era as *glasnost'* produced a range of views and opinions of their leader. In tracing this shift
away from the official monologue, we will explore the views of certain key individuals (Nina Andreeva, Boris Yeltsin, Boris Gidaspov, Andrei Sakharov), as well
as the changing views of Gorbachev in the official Soviet set-pieces (Party Congresses, key historical anniversaries), in the *glasnost'* press (in publications like
Moskovskiye novosti, Ogonyok, Krokodil), in the debates within the Supreme Soviet
and the Congress of People's Deputies, and also the views of Gorbachev as seen
from the periphery of the USSR among the non-Russians. Like the history of *perestroika* itself, the story of Gorbachev from the Soviet perspective reflects the ways
in which the official stranglehold on society was loosened until a hundred flowers
bloomed, creating a colourful array of opinions, criticisms and judgements.

   The image constructed by the Soviet state for all General Secretaries had previously rested on demonstrating some key essentials shared by all its leaders, but also
emphasizing the ways in which the new leader was an improvement upon the outgoing leader. The fanfare of adulation and celebration of the new leader's abilities
was an incredibly important moment in establishing their political legitimacy and

credibility. In the absence of a democratic mode of legitimation, the keen theoretical mind, the unswerving loyalty to the ideals of Marx and Lenin, the dedication to the principles of October, the allegiance to socialist internationalism, and the commitment to global peace and justice were crucial in establishing the new leader's suitability for the post. These values were not just to be established at the outset, however. They were to be constantly reiterated at every opportunity, but most notably at the major set-piece situations of the Soviet state: Party Congresses, anniversaries of Lenin's birth or the victory in the Great Patriotic War, or the October Revolution.

Under Gorbachev, this was palpably downgraded, without ever disappearing. In order to create a 'break' with the leadership of Brezhnev, Gorbachev set out to construct an image which was at once both more 'populist', more realistic and less adulatory. However, the Soviet state still found it very difficult to adjust itself to 'normalizing' its treatment of its leaders, in particular with regard to its willingness to tolerate any criticism. But it is crucial to note at the outset that it was Gorbachev himself who was instrumental in initiating the process which created the environment in which he was to be criticized and pilloried. He toned down the excesses of the official monologue, and he opened the way for a pluralism of opinions.

The official view of Gorbachev: the coronation and after, 1985–88

Inside the arcane world of Kremlinology, the public signifiers attached to the death and succession of the General Secretary are replete with meaning. The content of the nominating speech, the position in the photographs of both the incoming and departed leader, the length of time for mourning tell us much of the prevailing distribution of power, the levels of support for the incoming leader and the opinion of the outgoing General Secretary.

To assess the Gorbachev accession and coronation, a comparison with Andropov is quite instructive. When Andropov died on 9 February 1984, his photo appeared on the front page of the official party newspaper *Pravda* the next day. On 12 February, details of Andropov's funeral appeared. Chernenko was elected as General Secretary the next day, and Chernenko appeared on the front page of *Pravda* the next day. It was reported that Chernenko had been elected '*edinoglasno*' or unanimously. The oration and mourning for Andropov lasted for one week. If we contrast this with the Gorbachev coronation and Chernenko mourning, then this highlights the initial image of Gorbachev as portrayed in the official literature.

Chernenko died at 7.20 p.m. on 10 March 1985. In contrast with the Chernenko coronation, Gorbachev was announced as the General Secretary of the Party on the same day as the death of Chernenko was announced (11 March). Gorbachev appeared on the front page, whereas Chernenko appeared on the inside pages, and his oration in *Pravda* lasted only two days. However, Gorbachev was announced as having been elected '*edinodushno*' rather than '*edinoglasno*', emphasizing consensus rather than unanimity, hinting at some disagreements about the election behind the scenes. Indeed, the haste with which Gorbachev's election was announced also suggested that the Gorbachev group had moved quickly before the other candidates – Romanov, Grishin – could organize their campaigns.

The front page of *Pravda* on 12 March carried the official portrait of Gorbachev (with birthmark airbrushed out) and also the official biography of Gorbachev's life and past. The biography finished by noting that

> Mikhail Sergeevich Gorbachev is an eminent figure of the Communist Party and the Soviet state. In all the posts which the Party entrusts to him, he works with his characteristic initiative, energy and selflessness and he devotes his knowledge, rich experience and organizational talents to the implementation of the policy of the party and selflessly serves the great cause of Lenin and the interests of the working people.[1]

The most significant pieces of text from this time were the nominating speech made by Andrei Gromyko, and Gorbachev's speech in commemoration of Chernenko, both delivered at the Extraordinary CPSU Central Committee plenum of 11 March and published in *Kommunist* later that month. Gorbachev's oration was brief, talking of Chernenko being a 'loyal soldier', a 'tireless worker' and 'a leader deeply devoted to Leninist ideals'.[2] Gromyko's speech was also published in *Kommunist* (the party's main theoretical journal), but did not make it into *Pravda*, or into other key party publications (for example, *partiynaya zhizn*). Gromyko's speech was remarkably fulsome and eulogistic, even by Soviet standards. But this was not the normal 'official'-type praise: it was more informal, less overtly ideological. Some of the phrases used to describe him include, 'a man of strong convictions', 'a person of profound keen intelligence', 'ability to rapidly and accurately grasp the essence of the matter', 'brilliant ability to approach problems analytically', 'great ability to find a common language with the people', 'good grasp of international issues'.[3] The choice of Gromyko – a survivor from the Stalinist era – to make this speech was highly significant. There was a handover happening from one generation to the next. The message coming across from Gromyko suggested a stark contrast with Chernenko. Whereas Gorbachev had emphasized qualities such as loyalty and commitment, Gromyko talked up Gorbachev's intelligence and analytical abilities. Perhaps responding to concerns over Gorbachev's relative youth and inexperience in international matters, Gromyko emphasized Gorbachev's grasp of the international arena, and his strength of conviction. The sentence that was omitted from the *Kommunist* version contained the rather ominous words, 'he has a pleasant smile, but he has teeth of iron'.[4]

The official biography and the ceremonial surrounding Gorbachev were noticeably more muted than the paeans of praise and sycophancy that had been the hallmark of the late Brezhnev era, a time of overweening and excessive flattery. This was to set the tone for the rest of Gorbachev's time as General Secretary. There was to be little or none of the usual adornments or adorations of the General Secretary, in line it seems with Gorbachev's own desire to reduce the obviously overblown rhetoric which described the actions and writings of previous General Secretaries. So, for example, when *Pravda* ran a report on 25 December 1985 on the publication of a new collection of Gorbachev's speeches and articles, it was no longer accompanied by descriptions of the theoretical prowess of Gorbachev, or his abilities to expound the truths of Soviet Marxism-Leninism. Instead, Academician Petr Fedoseev noted that the book reflected the enormous work that had gone into upgrading and improving the party's theoretical work to face the new challenges that lay ahead, both domestically and internationally.

In the years that followed, Gorbachev set out to portray himself as man of the people and as an international statesman, a difficult balance to maintain. But it also proved difficult on occasion for the party to rid itself of its tendency to exalt its leader. Throughout his years in power, Gorbachev was filmed on numerous occasions having frank and open exchanges with the Soviet people as he journeyed across the USSR on his mission to raise awareness of the need to/for change. This campaign for 'psychological restructuring' was reported at length on Soviet TV and in the Soviet print media too, emphasizing Gorbachev's ability and willingness to meet with and relate to the masses. This strategy for relating to the people saw Gorbachev portrayed increasingly realistically, although not critically, of course. The photographs began to show Gorbachev with his prominent birthmark, rather than the overly stylized official portraits. The Gorbachev 'charm offensive' was taken a stage further in 1989 with the publication of a new biography and also an interview in *Izvestiya TsK KPSS.*

The new biography was an update on the original 1985 version, and was published alongside minibiogs of the other members of the Politburo. In fact, what was most interesting was what was omitted: the passage cited above listing his achievements and skills had disappeared.[5] On being elected as Chairman of the new Supreme Soviet in May 1989, *Pravda* also published a short biography, which included the normal information, but finished with the following paragraph:

> Mikhail Sergeevich Gorbachev is the initiator of the revolutionary process of restructuring all aspects of the life of Soviet society. The concept of new political thinking which is increasingly being asserted in the world and the package of major initiatives in building a secure, nuclear-free world are linked with his name.[6]

This is an interesting addition, which recognized Gorbachev's role at home and abroad, linked him to positive changes and to peace initiatives, yet did not garland it with excessive personal praise.

The interview in the same publication later that year arose out of a desire for greater knowledge about the Soviet leaders. Interestingly, the preamble to the interview cited a quote from a party propaganda worker for the *Znanie Society*, who wanted more information to respond to questions from members of the public about the leaders, their background, salary levels, etc. It would appear, then, that the pursuit of *glasnost'* was beginning to create a desire to know more: the secrecy and censorship culture was breaking down. There were no great revelations. Some more details about his personal life, his early history, how he met his wife, how he spent his leisure time and details about his salary, etc. all emerged.[7] But the message was clear: the lives of the leaders were no longer to be shrouded in mystery, and the leaders were no longer to be distant, unapproachable, inaccessible. Selective openness was now the order of the day.

The references to Gorbachev during the high-profile set-pieces of the Soviet politico-ideological calendar from his supporters and advisers also carried on the rather muted tone established by Gorbachev at the outset. Gorbachev's desire to make a complete break with the Brezhnev approach produced a General Secretaryship that was remarkably light on adulation. The first major set-piece of the Gorbachev era was the 27th Party Congress, which was convened in February 1986. The praise of Gorbachev in the speeches of some of the other key party figures at this Congress tended to focus more upon the content of his address, rather than Gorbachev as a political leader. The most effusive speech came from Vitali Vorotnikov, who was Chair of the Russian Republic Council of Ministers. But even here, the praise is heaped upon the content, not the speaker. Hence Vorotnikov outlines that Gorbachev's Political Report

> could without exaggeration be called an outstanding document of creative Marxism-Leninism ... [it] provides answers to the most burning questions of our time. It is full of historical optimism and faith in the triumph of communism. Its frank constructive nature prompts profound thoughts and responsible actions.[8]

Other speakers continued this theme. Dimitri Kunaev (First Secretary of the Kazakh CP) noted that the address 'brilliantly embodies the collective wisdom and will of the Central Committee'.[9] Andrei Gromyko, in appraising the global impact of Gorbachev's first year, emphasized that 'the world is hanging on every word that comes from the Kremlin'.[10] Karen Bagirov fulsomely highlighted that 'boldness, responsibility, realism and a Leninist orientation toward the future permeate every provision and conclusion, every line of the Political Report'.[11] Perhaps the most telling statement came from Eduard Shevardnadze (Minister of Foreign Affairs), who observed that 'the past 10 months have revived people's hopes'.[12]

Old habits die hard. The tendency for political subordinates to praise the leader still prevailed, although the object of affection was displaced on to the address, not the leader *per se*. The messages about Gorbachev's Political Report (and thus about Gorbachev) coming from the 27th Party Congress were of a new beginning, of a much more frank approach to the problems facing the CPSU, and of the global significance of Gorbachev's new peace offensive. As ever, though, the direct links and associations with Lenin were also established.

A similar pattern can be seen by examining the speeches made at two of the key set-piece events of the Soviet political calendar: the October Revolution anniversary and the Lenin's birthday commemoration speeches. In the October Revolution anniversary speeches, we can detect a gradual shift. As the whole *perestroika* movement became less 'ideological', so the Soviet state spent less and less time celebrating the events of 1917. Gorbachev was rarely mentioned by name, although the fundamental link between October and *perestroika* was always maintained (and thus by association the historical legitimacy of Gorbachev's policy). Indeed, after 1989, the tone became much more defensive, as the USSR seemed to be drifting away from socialism, and the party felt the need to confirm why they should still be celebrating the October Revolution.[13] The Lenin anniversary speeches also witnessed a relatively low-key approach, which implicitly linked Gorbachev to Lenin, rather than explicitly announcing the Leninist credentials of the General Secretary. The person who did most to link Lenin with Gorbachev and to highlight his strengths was, once again, Eduard Shevardnadze, who in April 1986 said:

> This sense of direction, this mood, in the work of the congress was set by Mikhail Sergeyevich Gorbachev in the Political Report, where loyalty to our fundamental principles is united with innovative views, revolutionary optimism with the courage to criticize, precision of political vocabulary with the brilliance of an imaginative system. Every formulation of a task, every conclusion, evokes thought and equips it with a fresh insight into the problems.[14]

Gorbachev himself delivered the keynote 1990 address (the 120th anniversary of Lenin's birth). In 1989, and 1991, the tone was more defensive and sought to establish the Leninist credentials of the current party line, not as a matter of ritualistic phraseology, but as a response to growing criticisms that *perestroika* had no direction, no purpose and no theoretical underpinning. Perhaps the most significant address was the 1991 one delivered by Vladimir Ivashko, which made no reference at all to Gorbachev, and was devoted to Lenin's ability as a crisis leader, a hint perhaps for Gorbachev.[15]

All in all, the trend was clear: Gorbachev's image after 1985 was carefully cultivated to ensure that there was no return to the Brezhnev days, but was still clearly linked to Lenin and October. Personal praise was minimized, but media images were constructed to promote Gorbachev as both man of the people and global statesman. The tone was one of increasing realism. The difficulty that Gorbachev encountered was that this proved to be an impossible line to hold. Toning down the rhetoric proved to be relatively easy to achieve. But encouraging openness and at the same time trying to allow limited criticisms was an unstable mix, and turned quite rapidly into a completely new situation, whereby the General Secretary himself began to be criticized and questioned. The major shift in the tone of the reports and speeches at the set-piece moments of the Soviet state came in 1988. More precisely, the shift came at the 19th Party Conference in June 1988.

Prior to this, the set-pieces tended to be very carefully choreographed. From the 19th Party Conference, though, the possibility of open criticism being expressed started to come to the fore. This in itself helped to accelerate the process by which the General Secretary was no longer named and exalted, but was now open to criticism. So what happened at the 19th Party Conference to change things?

Before turning to explore the 19th Party Conference in some detail, it is worth backtracking a little. The growth of criticisms of *perestroika* (and so by extension of Gorbachev) can be traced to two key moments: the spat with Yeltsin in October 1987, and the publication of a critical article written by Nina Andreeva (a Leningrad chemistry teacher) entitled 'I cannot foresake my principles' in *Sovetskaya Rossiya* in March 1988. The October 1987 incident saw Yeltsin resign after a disagreement among the leadership (of which more below). Although the details were not made public until 1989, the people were aware that there was significant discontent at the very highest level. Andreeva, by comparison, was accusing *perestroika* of abandoning the deeply cherished traditions and values of the USSR. Thus, by the summer of 1988, the precedent for expression of public criticism of the leadership had been set. Moreover, the emergence of a pluralism of opinions both within the leadership and about *perestroika* meant that there were many different views ready to be expressed, and many of these were likely to be critical. There was growing disquiet and anxiety in the party.

The Conference opened on 28 June 1988 in Moscow, at which there were 4991 delegates from across the USSR. The Conference was convened as an extraordinary party forum to discuss and debate a series of proposals that Gorbachev wanted to adopt in order to promote the reform process. Gorbachev wanted to push reform through, but could not wait until the next Party Congress (which was due to meet in 1991) and so convened a party conference. The last one had met in 1941, although in the early days of the Soviet state they were fairly common. The Conference (which closed on 1 July 1988) was to discuss ten theses published by the Central Committee of the CPSU in May 1988. These ten theses covered the following issues:

- ideology, media and *glasnost'*
- economic reforms
- changes in science, technology, education and culture
- democratization
- the role of the CPSU
- the role of the Soviets
- federal reforms and the nationalities issue
- legal reforms
- the role of Soviet public organizations
- the international policy of the Soviet state.

These theses provided the framework for a wide-ranging discussion, which was kicked off by Gorbachev's opening address on 28 June. The debate ranged far and wide across the big issues – constitutional reforms, democratization, economic reforms, ecological changes – as well as contentious political debates, most notably the proposal to limit the tenures for key party posts, including the post of General Secretary, and the Yeltsin question. The tone of the conference was very different from previous set-piece political occasions, which had been heavily choreographed. In the middle of a long contribution, V. Belyaninov was heckled for straying from the point into 'boring blather'. In a report in *Pravda* (which did not figure in the stenographic reports), it was noted:

> when one of the speakers began to stray from the point, people in the audience began clapping. No, not in support of the speech, of course, it was a distinctive protest against boring blather. And since the speaker could not get back into a businesslike key, the clapping grew until he left the rostrum. Finally, the presiding officer read out a note that had come from the Presidium: don't get caught up in self-congratulation or laudatory talk – it takes up too much time to no purpose … the delegates to the 19th Party Conference will not accept twaddle and general, fine sounding phrases![16]

This was the clear evidence that the tone of official meetings had changed, that empty phrase-mongering was out and also that a growing frankness was likely to presage criticisms and open, public debate within the party itself. In the midst of these discussions, the first inklings of a growing critique of *perestroika* began to emerge, along with some veiled criticisms of Gorbachev and the leadership, *from within the ranks of the party itself,* not just from disaffected groups or outspoken individuals (i.e. Sakharov or Andreeva).

The key criticisms put forward were as follows. Yeltsin continued his attacks on privilege and also launched an attack on Gorbachev, and the attitude of the party leadership towards criticism. He noted:

> Another thing. Now, despite a clear statement from the General Secretary that there are no zones or leaders in our country, including himself, who are above criticism, in practice it turns out differently. There is a zone, a line above which the very first attempt at criticism is followed by the instantaneous warning 'Hands Off!' So it happens that even members of the Central Committee are afraid to express their personal opinion if it differs from the report, or to speak out at the leadership.[17]

This was the next step in the slowly smouldering feud between the two men which was to ignite in 1990 and continued for the next 15 years. Leonid Abalkin, a pro-reform economist, spoke of the economic crisis in the country and speculated about whether real democratization could be achieved in a one-party state.[18] Perhaps the most significant critique was put forward by Yuri Bondarev, the deputy chairman of the Writers' Union of the RSFSR, and a member of the Bureau of the

USSR Writers' Union. Bondarev, a conservative Russian nationalist figure, was deeply critical of the whole thrust and aim of *perestroika*. In a memorable phrase, Bondarev noted that, 'Can we compare our *perestroika* with an aeroplane, which, having taken off, does not know where it will land?'[19] To continue the analogy, clearly Bondarev was pointing the finger at the pilot for having no flight plan, and thus was endangering both the plane and the passengers. This was the closest that the Conference came to outright criticism of Gorbachev.

Other issues also generated some criticisms. Mikhail Ulyanov – a playwright and chairman of the board of the Russian Republic Union of Theatre Workers – argued strongly for a pluralistic press to support *perestroika*.[20] He spoke of the need to move away from the situation of a monopolistic press (both national and local) in order to encourage criticism and promote pluralism. V. I. Postnikov – the general director of a broiler-producing factory – and V. I. Melnikov – the first secretary of the Komi obkom – were both keen to see those opposed to *perestroika*, or those who were still hanging around from the Brezhnev era, rooted out and removed, witch-hunt style.[21]

The issues which generated most debate, though, were the proposals put forward to limit leadership positions to two terms (which frightened many who saw their privileges and perks suddenly disappearing) and the proposal to combine the position of party First Secretary and Chair of the Soviet at that level. For many this seemed to be an unnecessary fusion which placed too much power in the hands of one person and seemed to be going against the whole thrust of the political reforms, which were about increasing choice, devolving power, reviving the Soviets. Although there was some disquiet at these proposals, they did bring some comments which were supportive of Gorbachev.

> But we need Mikhail Sergeevich Gorbachev in the post of General Secretary for as long a time as possible. Our democratic barriers are still too weak for us not to be afraid of some disaster in the form of a 'father and teacher'. But we have faith in Gorbachev. Therefore I propose that we elect Gorbachev alone to a third term as an extraordinary decision. This is the exception not the rule, because a social revolution is underway now. In a revolution, you don't change horses in midstream ... Leaders must not be changed during a time of such extremely serious efforts.[22]

In spite of some criticisms, disquiet and frank debates, this supportive attitude was still the dominant attitude towards Gorbachev within the CPSU at this point. But the 19th Party Conference was the point at which things began to change, as a real pluralism of opinions began to emerge. After 1988 a variegated picture of Gorbachev started to appear, a colourful, kaleidoscopic view very different from the monochrome album provided by the official propaganda machine. Gorbachev was entering a different phase as Soviet leader. He was now about to experience a more 'normal' political and media environment, one of conflicting opinions, rivals' criticisms, media scrutiny and popular exposure.

Let us turn to examine some of these different views of Gorbachev, beginning with the period between the Andreeva letter (March 1988) and the election of Gorbachev as Executive President (March 1990).

The critiques of Gorbachev: March 1988–March 1990

The conservative traditionalist: Nina Andreeva on Gorbachev and perestroika

The Andreeva affair – as it became known – caused something of a storm in the CPSU when it first broke in March 1988. On 14 March, Gorbachev left for a state visit to Yugoslavia. The day before, the newspaper *Sovetskaya Rossiya* printed a letter from a Leningrad chemistry teacher Nina Andreeva. It was entitled 'I cannot forsake my principles'.[23] It quickly became seen as a kind of manifesto for anti-*perestroika* forces and forced the publication of a robust rebuttal and defence of *perestroika* in *Pravda* on 5 April, drafted by Aleksander Yakovlev.[24] Andreeva's article was the first shot in a war waged by the conservatives and the traditionalists in the party leadership against what they saw as the corrosive and damaging effects of *glasnost'*, with its attacks on the Soviet past, and its criticisms of the flawed present. At the time, the controversy was stoked because it was believed that Yegor Ligachev – Gorbachev's number two in the Kremlin – was either the 'real' author or the guiding force behind the publication of the letter.

The story behind the publication of the letter is still contested. It appears that in February 1988 Andreeva circulated three copies of her letter: to *Sovetskaya Rossiya*, *Sovetskaya Kul'tura* and *Pravda*. The original ran to more than 30 pages, and was more of an extended treatise than a letter. There were many such letters at the time, due to the growing unease that many people were feeling at the pace and depth of the changes being introduced by Gorbachev. Although Ligachev denies any part in the genesis of the letter, other accounts suggest that Valentin Chikin (the chief editor of *Sovetskaya Rossiya*) sent the letter to Ligachev, who recommended an abridged version for publication, as it seemed to accord with his own concerns about the treatment of Soviet history.[25] On publication, Gorbachev was alerted to the letter by Georgii Shakhnazarov. While Gorbachev and Yakovlev were out of the country, Ligachev chaired a meeting with the editors of the main Soviet newspapers. Here he recommended that they read and discuss the contents of the Andreeva letter. He also is said to have recommended that the letter be reprinted and distributed to papers in the Soviet provinces. On their return from Yugoslavia and Mongolia, Gorbachev and Yakovlev initiated a discussion about how best to respond, leading to the 5 April editorial in *Pravda*.

The Andreeva letter is best understood as part of the run-up to the 19th Party Conference, as the conservatives and the traditionalists sought to create some obstacles to slow the pace and scope of the changes due to be discussed. The thrust of Andreeva's ire was directed at what she called 'left-wing liberal intellectual socialism'.[26] She railed against the abandonment of a class-based view of the world, against those who had adopted a one-eyed, prejudiced stance on Stalin, against those who were deliberately undermining the Soviet past, ignoring its achievements and highlighting only its crimes and mistakes. The rationale was the need to provide clear guidance for the young people of the Soviet Union. Andreeva's *bête noire* was clearly the Yakovlev–Gorbachev axis, with their espousal of humanism and New Political Thinking:

> The first and most swollen ideological current which has already manifested itself in the course of *perestroika* … claims to offer a model of some kind of left-wing liberal intellectual socialism which allegedly expresses the most genuine humanism, 'cleansed' of class accretions. Its champions counter proletarian collectivism with the 'intrinsic value of the individual' … it is the champions of 'left-wing liberal socialism' who shape the tendency towards falsifying the history of socialism. They try to make us believe that the country's past was nothing but mistakes and crimes, keeping silent about the greatest achievements of the past and the present.[27]

Andreeva's critique was an accusation of the abandonment of 'proper' socialism, of Marxism, and a capitulation to the forces of capitalism and imperialism, to the betrayal of Russia and the sale of her assets to foreign powers. Andreeva resurfaced in 1989, this time with a more explicitly personal critique of Gorbachev and his leadership. In an interview given in September 1989 with Hungarian television, Andreeva was asked for her opinion of Gorbachev (along with others like Yeltsin, Sakharov and Ligachev). She responded by saying:

> I think that he belongs among precisely the leaders who try to sit between two stools. In the course of history, no one has ever succeeded in doing this, and he will scarcely succeed in this. I believe that he himself senses this. Yet I can trace a tendency that up to now he has been led on a lead solely by the group which tries to drive us on the road of capitalist restoration. That is clear. He was the leader, the father of slogans such as '*glasnost*', so to say 'democracy', on whose bases we find ourselves facing untamed nationalism in several regions of the country. If these trends develop further, this will naturally lead to complete collapse.[28]

At this point Gorbachev was thus being blamed for the outbreak of nationalism, and had been captured by the forces of capitalist restoration.

The Andreeva letter was the first sign of a growing discontent with the pace and direction of *perestroika*. The critique from those who wished to defend the essential institutions and practices inexorably grew, expanding to encompass those of a Marxist or neo-Bolshevik stance, those of a Russian nationalist hue (who were concerned about foreign/Western infiltration of Russia) and also defenders of the Soviet Union: its borders and institutions. The conservative critique was not alone, though: soon Gorbachev was being assailed by a variety of people and groups, from diverse perspectives. The old monologue was dying.

The enemy within: Yeltsin v. Gorbachev, October 1987–March 1990

The most high-profile argument in the Gorbachev years was the one between Gorbachev and Boris Yeltsin. The spat started in the October of 1987, and continued for the next 12 years or so, reaching its zenith in the immediate aftermath of the August 1991 coup. Yeltsin – a man with not inconsiderable political ambitions – had been promoted to the Politburo in December 1985 after being the party boss in Sverdlovsk, and at the same time was made First Secretary of the Moscow City Party Committee. He had developed a reputation for being a feisty, almost maverick-like figure who could be counted upon to oppose dogmatism and inertia and provide energy and enthusiasm for the goals of *perestroika*. These qualities which first brought him to the attention of Gorbachev and Ligachev were soon to bring him into conflict with Gorbachev.

Yeltsin's approach to managing Moscow was based on confrontation and populism: he liked to portray himself as a 'man of the people', willing to confront the dead hand of bureaucracy in the interests of the people. This carefully cultivated approach – he liked to take the trolleybus to work – began to bring him into conflict with those who were cautious, who wanted to move slowly, who feared the disruption of change. In the summer and autumn of 1987, Yeltsin was becoming increasingly unhappy, the roots of which probably lay in the deteriorating relationship between Yeltsin and Ligachev.[29] The simmering resentment Yeltsin was feeling boiled over in an unexpected intervention at the CC Plenary meeting of 21 October 1987. The full transcripts of the discussion did not emerge until 1989.[30]

The plenary session was called in the main to approve Gorbachev's keynote 70th anniversary of the October Revolution speech the following month. The meeting was about to disperse when Yeltsin indicated that he wished to speak. Ligachev tried to prevent him speaking; however, Gorbachev intervened to give him the floor. Yeltsin then proceeded to say that he fully supported the content of Gorbachev's speech. So what was on his mind? He made a number of points, including the need to restructure the work of the party as a whole, but especially the work of the party committees and the Central Committee Secretariat (headed up by Yegor Ligachev). The two things which most clearly rankled with Yeltsin were, first, that the leadership, having raised popular expectations in 1985 about the changes to come, had failed to deliver anything substantial, and, second, that there was too much eulogizing and glorification of one man (Gorbachev!), and that there was insufficient collegiality and collectivism in the way the party was being led. This absence of criticism, with its allusions to the dangers of the personality cult, was deemed to be illustrative of the failure of the leadership to create the real conditions in which democracy would flourish. He concluded by offering his resignation.[31]

Gorbachev, rather bristling at these comments, summarized Yeltsin's remarks and then called for contributions from the assembled CC members. Ligachev responded first. He took the attack back to Yeltsin, denying some of Yeltsin's earlier criticisms and arguing that Yeltsin had played a very passive role in the work of the Politburo. Sergei Manyakin was next to speak, followed by Leonid Borodin, Stepan Shalayev, Georgi Bogomyakov, Fyodor Morgun and Valentin Mesyats. They all relayed criticisms of Yeltsin's contributions and defended Ligachev. Georgi Arbatov defended Yeltsin's right to express criticisms, but had reservations about what had been expressed. Nikolai Ryzhkov (the Prime Minister and a former associate from their time in the provinces) was deeply critical, accusing Yeltsin of 'political nihilism'. A succession of other contributors repeated their misgivings, and attacked Yeltsin for his personal ambitions.[32]

Finally, Yeltsin was invited to respond and he defended his views, but was interrupted by Gorbachev, who began to take him to task. Gorbachev was particularly keen to address the question of Yeltsin's ego:

> It is not enough for you that Moscow alone revolves around your personality. You also want the CC to concentrate on you? ... Just imagine developing such excessive self-admiration and conceit as to place one's own ambitions before the party's interests and our cause! Just imagine imposing this discussion on the party's Central Committee.[33]

Categorizing his speech as irresponsible and immature in deflecting the CC from the priority of developing the reform programme, Gorbachev then responded to Yeltsin's points. Gorbachev was particularly affronted at the suggestion that nothing had been achieved in the period since March 1985, saying that disseminating negative views was Yeltsin's speciality. He went on to defend his record, and also defended the *modus operandi* of the party and the secretariat. He finished by asking both the Politburo and the Moscow City Party Committee to consider Yeltsin's request to stand down. Yeltsin remained a candidate member of the Politburo until the February 1988 CC plenum, when he was removed. On 11 November 1987, though, he was removed as head of the Moscow City Party Committee. On 14 January 1988, he became first deputy chairman of the State Committee for Construction (*Gosstroi*). Yeltsin, from this point forwards, began to plot his own career path and moved into an increasingly oppositional stance. The schism with Gorbachev was to become a yawning chasm.

The next prominent intervention by Yeltsin came at the 1988 Party Conference. He repeated many of his assertions from the October plenary meeting, adding in the implications of bribery and excessive privilege for the party elite, complaining at the 'luxurious private residences, dachas and sanatoriums on such a scale'.[34] He was also critical of all those who had been members of the Politburo (and by extension the CC, including Gorbachev) under Brezhnev, for allowing the era of stagnation to grow unchecked. At the end of his speech, Yeltsin announced his desire for political rehabilitation, but in his lifetime rather than posthumously, as had happened with Stalin's victims in the 1930s.

Yeltsin made two further incursions in the period between the 19th Party Conference and Gorbachev's election as Executive President in March 1990. The first came in a speech to the Congress of People's Deputies on 31 May 1989. Yeltsin, as a member of the reformist interregional group continued with his theme of criticisms for the lack of progress on political reform, of the need for the party to reform itself and of the lack of real benefits that had accrued to the Soviet people. Two direct criticisms of Gorbachev began to be advanced by Yeltsin. The first was that Gorbachev could no longer avoid responsibility for the current state of affairs in general, or for particular issues (such as the crackdown in Tbilisi) that had occurred.[35] The second was the growing danger of dictatorship:

> The current Congress, Constitution and Party have given the head of state extraordinarily wide powers. And here a very worrying trend can be seen against the background of the general worsening of the economic situation and the aggravation of social issues there is a growth in personal influence and personal power in the hands of the head of state. These 'scissors' might lead to temptation to solve our complicated problems by methods of force and we might find ourselves, without noticing it, captive to a new authoritarian regime, a new dictatorship.[36]

This prompted a call for constitutional mechanisms to limit the powers of Gorbachev as Chairman of the Supreme Soviet. These criticisms of Gorbachev were echoed in an interview Yeltsin gave just prior to a fact-finding visit to the USA in September 1989. Gorbachev's tactics had led to *perestroika* petering out, in the face of bureaucratic foot-dragging, and was causing great dissatisfaction among the people. The strike wave that engulfed the USSR in the summer of 1989 was caused in part, according to Yeltsin, by the unsatisfactory outcome from the Congress of People's Deputies. At the root of this, however, was Gorbachev, who, in Yeltsin's words, was 'an advocate of constant compromise'.[37] Similar sentiments were expressed on 15 December 1989, when Yeltsin reflected further on the problems that were accumulating in a speech to the Congress. He noted:

> I do not agree with the assertion of several speakers at the latest plenum of the Central Committee and here at the Congress that we are taking the wrong road. No, this is not what Comrade Gorbachev, the Politburo, and the government are guilty of. The road is the right one, the socialist one, the way of the renewal of our society. The thing is we are moving along it in the wrong way, we are moving blindly, we are marking time. Our leaders themselves had a poor idea of the ditches and the obstacles along this road and society gave no warning of them. The guilt of the initiators of *perestroika* is that *perestroika* was announced as yet another slogan, without carefully worked out tactics for its implementation.[38]

Yeltsin's criticisms of Gorbachev were growing in perfect symbiosis with the advance of his own political ambitions. In 1990, when Yeltsin was to acquire political power of his own, the sniping was to turn into direct political opposition and competition.

The democrat/dissident critique: Andrei Sakharov

One of the key signifiers of Gorbachev's intentions to push through a thorough-going reform of the Soviet system was his treatment of Andrei Sakharov. Sakharov had been instrumental in the development of the Soviet nuclear weapons pro-gramme in the 1950s, working at Sarov on the hydrogen bomb, and in the process winning a number of awards from the Soviet state, including the prestigious 'Hero of Socialist Labour' in 1953. Sakharov began to have grave misgivings about the morality of the nuclear programme in the late 1960s, when he wrote an essay, 'Reflections on Progress, Peaceful Coexistence, and Intellectual Freedom', in May 1968. He moved into the orbit of the dissidents, and became one of the founders of the Moscow Human Rights Committee. Banned from all military-related research, he moved into the field of theoretical physics, and continued to press for greater human rights in the USSR, advocating greater openness and democracy in Soviet public life.

After winning the Nobel Peace Prize in 1975, Sakharov continued his public activism, and was finally arrested in January 1980 after publicly demonstrating against the invasion of Afghanistan. He was sent into internal exile in the closed city of Gorky, where he endured constant surveillance and harassment from the police. Sakharov was one of, if not the, main symbol in the West of the unequal struggle of the individual against the power of the Soviet state. Gorbachev's atti-tude to and treatment of Sakharov were thus a highly significant indicator of the direction of Gorbachev's overall approach. Equally, Sakharov's attitude towards Gorbachev would be crucial in establishing Gorbachev's democratic credentials.

Gorbachev moved quickly to end Sakharov's exile. By 1 December 1986, he had attained the agreement of the Soviet leadership for his release, and he rang Sakharov on 16 December to discuss his return from exile. Sakharov and his wife Elena Bonner returned to Moscow on 23 December 1986. His initial impressions of Gorbachev and the reform process were quite cautious, as he had not been in Moscow long enough to judge what was happening.[39] His first face-to-face meet-ing with Gorbachev occurred on 15 January 1988, at the inaugural meeting of the International Fund for the Survival and Development of Mankind. Sakharov was asked about his impressions of Gorbachev:

> For me the meeting was very interesting. I think highly of Gorbachev both as a statesman and as a person. He impressed me as a man capable of talking candidly and of listening to the interlocutor and understand-ing him. He is a more dynamic kind of politician, one more capable of off-beat decisions. I think it is such a leader that is needed by a great country at this crucial moment in human history ... I find his position most promising.[40]

In the run-up to the June 1988 Party Conference, Sakharov conducted another interview, in which he began to voice some concerns at the problems, but contin-ued to express his personal support for Gorbachev:

Admittedly, my view is that there are many problems, but overall the present policy is very serious and deserves trust. I think that Mikhail Gorbachev is an outstanding state personality. He is one of the chief initiators, one of the main personalities, of *perestroika*. I wish him luck with all my heart, him and the cause which is linked with his name.[41]

Sakharov was, however, critical of the new electoral and constitutional set-up which emerged out of the 1988 Party Conference, believing that it had not gone far enough in establishing the basis for democracy to grow in the USSR, and contained the potential for a reactionary group to remove Gorbachev and turn back the clock. This view had appeared in an interview that Sakharov and Bonner did with the French newspaper *Le Figaro*. This prompted a response from the Soviet newspaper *Izvestiya*, which said that Sakharov had predicted the defeat of restructuring, described the nomination of deputies as undemocratic and even asserted that Gorbachev was likely to be overthrown.[42] Sakharov and Bonner felt the need to respond as they believed that both *Le Figaro* and *Izvestiya* had deliberately misrepresented their views. In their defence, Sakharov and Bonner asserted that their supportive comments about Gorbachev had not been included; in particular, the view that Gorbachev was the only leader the USSR had, and that he need not fear a direct election as he would certainly win. But the tone was starting to shift, as Sakharov became increasingly concerned about the problems and opposition, urging Gorbachev to push on further and faster with democratization and *glasnost*.[43]

Sakharov's main platform for expressing his views on Gorbachev and *perestroika* came when he was elected as a deputy to the Congress of People's Deputies in March 1989. The most famous exchange between the two came during the televised sessions of the Congress of People's Deputies in May and June 1989. The first major intervention came during the nominations for the chairmanship of the Supreme Soviet.[44] In the morning session of 25 May, Sakharov intervened to argue that the election of the Chairmanship of the Supreme Soviet should not take place before there had been a significant discussion and debate about the state of the country. In the course of his speech, he ventured the following view on Gorbachev:

> In my speeches I have on several occasions voiced support for the candidacy of Mikhail Sergeevich Gorbachev. I still maintain that position now, inasmuch as I do not see anyone else who could lead our country, I do not see it at the present time. My support is of a conditional nature ... He should speak both about the achievements and about the mistakes, speak about it self-critically, and our standpoint will also depend on that. And, most important, he should say what he intends and if there are other candidates, then they should also say what they intend to do in the near future in order to overcome the extremely difficult situation which has come about in our country, and what they will do in the longer term.[45]

Sakharov's support had now become conditional, in fact it seemed that his support was only because there was no-one else who could do the job. The debate on the chairmanship got underway in earnest on the afternoon of 25 May.

The first foray came from Chingiz Aitmatov, a Kyrgyz writer and deputy. His was a rather effusive speech endorsing Gorbachev's candidacy, describing in overly lyrical terms the advent of Gorbachev:

> a man came and disturbed the slumbering realm of stagnation … This man by the will of destiny assumed the leadership just in time … he ventured to take on what seemed to be impossible: a revolution of minds … He ventured to take on this task not through vanity, but because he had perceived the worsening sickness in society.[46]

Aitmatov went on to make a plea for support for Gorbachev as the architect of *perestroika* to be given the opportunity to lead the next phase of changes. As others got up to discuss the election, so a variety of opinions on Gorbachev began to emerge. The Ukrainian writer Yavroviskiy stated that he would vote for Gorbachev, but that he was unhappy at the lack of choice. Others queued up to put questions before Gorbachev, on a number of issues relating to the process of democratization, the use of the army to quell civilian disturbances, the number of dachas used by Gorbachev, the role of his wife. Many referred to the dangers inherent in combining the position of Chairmanship of the Supreme Soviet with General Secretary of the CPSU. Was this not too much power concentrated in one person's hands? Gorbachev was a little surprised at the extent of the questioning but saw it as a signifier that democracy and parliamentary traditions were taking hold. Gorbachev's candidature was endorsed with only four abstentions.

As for other candidates, Aleksandr Obolensky put himself forward. He was a non-party deputy from Leningrad and a self-styled 'engineer-designer' who worked at the Polar Geophysical Institute of the Kola scientific centre of the Academy of Sciences. Obolensky's platform was based on a desire for the rule of law, a crackdown on privilege, but primarily it was about setting a precedent for holding elections. The importance was symbolic, given that he would inevitably lose. In fact, it turned out worse for Obolensky than he had envisaged. In the vote as to whether his name should appear on the ballot paper, he received 689 votes, but 1415 deputies voted against his name going forward (33 abstained).[47] Yeltsin decided to withdraw his candidature. Gorbachev won the one-horse race, polling 95.6 per cent of the vote (2123 in favour, and 87 against).

The main confrontation between Gorbachev and Sakharov came during the final session of the Congress of People's Deputies. Sakharov insisted on speaking, and refused to yield when his time was up, forcing Gorbachev to intervene. The issue was the same one that he had expressed earlier: the excessive concentration of power at the top, but it soon broadened out into a series of recommendations. Sakharov noted that 'the construction of the house of state has started with the roof, which is clearly not the best way of going about things'.[48] He then proposed a 'Decree on Power' which had the following clauses:

- repeal of Article 6 of the Constitution;
- exclusive legislative authority rests with the CPD;
- Supreme Soviet is the working body of the Congress;
- [clause 4 was omitted because Sakharov did not have time to announce it];
- election and recall of the highest USSR officials (i.e. Gorbachev);
- restricted functions for the KGB.[49]

In the face of constant interruptions from Gorbachev exhorting him to finish, Sakharov ploughed on, calling for reforms to the national-federal structure and also denouncing the events in Tiananmen Square. Finally, Gorbachev was able to wrest the microphone from Sakharov, who sat down to great applause. He was able to continue his line in an interview published in *Literaturnaya Gazeta* on 21 June.[50] Gorbachev was, in Sakharov's words, 'an absolutely brilliant politician', but had allowed too much power to be concentrated in his hands, and was thus in danger of being controlled by 'forces behind the scenes'.[51]

Sakharov died on 14 December 1989. He had witnessed the faltering emergence of parliamentary democracy in the USSR, and attributed much of this to the bravery and skill of Gorbachev. However, Sakharov's endorsement of Gorbachev grew increasingly conditional and contingent after December 1986, as the flaws in the embryonic system became clear, and the diffusion of power from the centre failed to materialize. Unfortunately Sakharov died before Gorbachev made himself Executive President in March 1990, with a vast array of powers. It would have been very interesting to have heard Sakharov's opinion. Would he have voted for him then? It seems unlikely.

The view from afar: nationalist critiques of Gorbachev

One of the earliest signs of the political reawakening under Gorbachev was the growth of nationalist movements in the Baltics and elsewhere. Starting as movements of ecological protection and recovery of historical memory in 1987, the Baltic republics witnessed the rapid growth of grass-roots movements for national autonomy. These movements were generally about the periphery wishing to lessen control from the centre. Elsewhere in the USSR, nationalist tensions between different ethnic groups began to grow, especially between Azeris and Armenians in the dispute over the territory of Nagorno-Karabakh. As the reform agenda unfolded after the 1988 Party Conference, so there emerged – fitfully and gradually – a chorus of disapproval of Gorbachev's policies towards the non-Russian republics, as he appeared to be dragging his feet, propping up the centre and generally maintaining the Union in the face of their desire for a restructured (or dissolved) relationship between centre and periphery.

The main nationalist critiques came after March 1990 as the momentum for the break-up of the Union began to gather pace. In fact, what is noticeable about the period up to the end of 1988 was the degree of support and backing that

Gorbachev received from the movements for peripheral nationalism. This is fairly easy to explain. Most of these figures saw in Gorbachev a beacon of hope. They believed that *perestroika* might become the vehicle to bring about change in their own republic. They wanted to use Gorbachev against their own republican leadership, to cajole and compel their leaders towards a position of greater autonomy. This explains why many of the popular demonstrations in 1987 and 1988 were staunchly *pro*-perestroika and *pro-Gorbachev*. Rallies in Vilnius, Tallinn and Riga all expressed their support for the reform programme of Gorbachev. For instance, in a pre-1988 Conference rally in Vilnius on 28 June 1988, the crowd displayed banners saying things like, '*Perestroika* movement for all Lithuania' and 'We Support Gorbachev!' and, tellingly, 'Molotov = Ribbentrop'.[52] Many pictures of Gorbachev were also visible.

Clearly, however, the depth and level of this support were highly conditional. The support of the movements for peripheral autonomy for Gorbachev was clearly conditional on his conception of change coinciding with theirs. As 1988 drew to a close, it soon became clear that the respective understandings of *perestroika* had begun to diverge. Gorbachev's commitment to maintaining the Union led inevitably to a collision course between them. The nationalities issue was one which Gorbachev never got to grips with properly. The difficulties he was to have were clearly evidenced in the events in Tbilisi 1989 and Baku in 1990.

The background to the Tbilisi massacre of 9 April 1989 lies in the escalating national tensions within the USSR. The multi-layered nature of ethnic rivalries was graphically illustrated in Georgia. Abkhaz separatists were agitating for the right of Abkhazia to secede from Georgia. Georgian nationalists wanted independence for Georgia. Many Georgian communists wanted to remain within the Soviet Union. Protests and demonstrations began to increase in intensity during March and April 1989. Abkhazian separatists organized a mass demonstration and subsequently anti-Soviet Georgian protesters mobilized, claiming that the Union government in Moscow was intent on using Abkhaz separatism to undermine the Georgian nationalist movement. A wave of demonstrations by the Georgian nationalist movement peaked on 4 April 1989 outside the House of Government on Rustaveli Avenue in Tbilisi. The local Georgian authorities rapidly lost control of the situation, and the militia were sent in to restore order. In the ensuing mêlée, soldiers attacked the demonstrators (some reports talked of the use of toxic gas) with trenching spades.[53] Twenty people – mainly female – died and around 4000 were injured. A national strike ensued and the Soviet Georgian government resigned. Forty days of mourning were announced.

The political fall-out from the deaths in Tbilisi was almost immediate, and became one of the first tests of the new parliamentary regime that had come into being. Questions were raised about the responsibility for ordering the troops in, and about the use of force. It was first discussed in the Congress of People's Deputies in May–June 1989. The general tenor of the debate centred around finding out who was responsible as well as the broader and deeper issues of managing nationality relations, and the defence of democracy and civil rights in the newly evolving political system. The debate about Tbilisi was caught up in the wider debates about the future of the Union, but also in two other issues which directly affected Gorbachev: the debates about the Chairmanship of the Supreme Soviet, and the discussion of privileges for high-ranking officials. The Tbilisi events thus became something of a political football, kicked around by those groups who wished to criticize/defend Gorbachev, or push/obstruct the reform process.

Questioned about the response of the central leadership to the events in Tbilisi, Gorbachev was quick to set up a series of commissions to provide a full and proper investigation of the causes of the tragedy.[54] His own version of the events outlined that he had returned from his overseas trip to Cuba and the UK on Saturday 9 April. On hearing that the situation was quite tense, Shevardnadze and Razumovskiy arranged to fly out there the same day. They abandoned this course of action later that day when a subsequent communication informed them that things had become less tense. The next morning they discovered what had happened and immediately took steps to find out what had gone wrong. This version of the events clearly did not satisfy many who wished to get to the bottom of what had happened. The heart of the debate came around 30–31 May. Tamaz Gamkrelidze rose to speak on the evening of 30 May. Gamkrelidze was the Director of the Institute of Oriental Studies in the Georgian Academy of Sciences. He was particularly damning of the actions of the military and called for General Rodionov (the Commander of the Transcaucasus Military District, and so responsible for the actions of the troops on that night) to be removed from the Congress. In an astonishing retort, Rodionov got up to defend himself, and in doing so drew parallels with 1937 (the high point of the Stalinist terror), equating the criticism of the *glasnost'* media with the campaigns of denunciation unleashed in the madness of the purges![55] In the midst of the debates about the Tbilisi events, some interesting perspectives on Gorbachev and the reform process came to light.

The 'critical' voices expressed a number of concerns. Few, if any, were willing publicly to question Gorbachev's direct role in the events. A deputy from Estonia – Lauristin – questioned Gorbachev about the guarantees he could give about protecting the sovereignty of the republics, about the use of the army and about how he could ensure that this tragedy was never repeated. These questions were linked with support for Gorbachev's candidature. Others spoke of the situation and personnel surrounding Gorbachev. Some talked of a counter-revolution taking place, acknowledging the limitations on Gorbachev's freedom of action.[56] Perhaps the most revealing intervention came from Yevgeniy Kogan, a deputy from Tallinn, Estonia. Reflecting on the continued problems in the sphere of nationalities raised by the Tbilisi events, and also the proposed candidature of Gorbachev, he noted:

> But I would like to say that it is precisely in the sphere of relations
> between nationalities that there is a need for extraordinary tactfulness. I
> wish to warn you about the fact that your name is often used in the Baltic

republics to disguise decisions that are extremely unpopular among the Russian-speaking population.[57]

The most direct attack came from Yuri Vlasov, People's Deputy from the Lublyansky district of Moscow and former world weightlifting champion. Amidst a number of savage verbal attacks on the Soviet establishment (most notably the KGB), Vlasov also verbally assaulted Gorbachev. In a speech on 31 May, Vlasov noted that it was 'inadmissible' for Gorbachev not to know all the events of the Tbilisi massacre. This cleared the way for a new proposal: the constitutional right to impeach the President, and the need to have constitutional and political control of the KGB. What was clear was the explicit linkage of Tbilisi to the wider agendas of the groups and individuals within the Congress, rather than a concern with Tbilisi *per se*.

The defenders of Gorbachev moved swiftly to his side. Perhaps the most fulsome defence came from Givi Gumbaridze, the First Secretary of the CP of Georgia Central Committee. Gumbaridze (as one would probably expect from a local Communist rep) acknowledged Gorbachev's pro-active role in establishing the Commission, in discussing the events with the key parties and in facilitating the speedy response of the medical teams – both Soviet and international – to the tragedy.[58] In an interesting aside during the debates on Gorbachev's candidature, a People's Deputy from Moscow (Medvedev) argued that the dangerous times for the reform process were whenever Gorbachev was out of the country, and Tbilisi was no exception. Thus it was not just necessary to elect a new captain for the *Good Ship USSR,* but also to find a new, reliable crew too.[59]

Preliminary findings were published on 11 June 1989 in *Zarya Vostoka.*[60] The main conclusions were that General Rodionov had brought troops into the city unlawfully, because there was no decree from the Presidium of the Supreme Soviet to that effect, and that there must have been a direct decision by the USSR Minister for Internal Affairs because of the use of their troops in the actions to 'restore order'. The broader socio-political conclusions drawn were that this tragedy had been caused by the autocratic and tyrannical actions of local officials, which in turn was a function of the 'inertia of Stalinist thinking'.[61] No aspersion was ever cast upon the role of Gorbachev.

The full commission findings did not come out until much later in the year. The Commission, headed by Anatolii Sobchak, reported their findings to the Congress of People's Deputies in December 1989, although he gave an earlier interview to Georgian television on 25 October 1989.[62] The final report was delivered to the Congress and a summary was published in *Izvestiya* on 30 December 1989. The gist of the report was to blame the local Georgian communist leadership, the local leaders of the rallies and those involved in the decisions to deploy troops. Gorbachev was, of course, exonerated. But the reputation of his reform programme had been severely dented.

A similar situation emerged in Baku in January 1990. The conflict between Azeris and Armenians had been bubbling away for a number of years, and erupted on 13 January 1990 in a separatist uprising by Azerbaijani nationalists. Soviet troops and tanks were ordered into Baku in order to suppress this uprising when the local authorities, it was claimed, were unable to act. Official figures put the death toll at around 137 (including subsequent protests in February), although unofficial estimates put the figure around 300. Gorbachev went on Soviet TV on 20 January, talking about 'criminal elements', and arguing that 'the tragic events in Baku, the border areas of Azerbaijan and Armenia and the other areas of Trans-caucasia are revealing the full cost of the nationalist rampage and the speculation on sacred national feelings'.[63] A state of emergency was declared by the USSR Supreme Soviet Presidium. These events quickly became known as *Black January* in Azerbaijan. Criticisms of Gorbachev and Dimitri Yazov quickly began to be expressed. The actions of the troops were heavily criticized in an extraordinary ses-sion of the Azeri Supreme Soviet on 22 January 1990. Allahshukur Pashazada (who was a senior figure on the Spiritual Board of Muslims of the Caucasus) wrote to Gorbachev calling him a 'merciless killer'. Tehran also voiced its protest. Azeri President Elmira Kafarova broadcast on local radio that the Azeri people would never forgive those responsible for the deaths. Yeltsin too joined the cacophony of criticism, arguing that it was always a mistake to dispatch troops to try and solve ethnic problems.[64]

Taken together, these instances of crackdowns in the republics – although they were quite dissimilar in some respects – were to become symbolic of the growing disillusionment with Gorbachev among certain sections of the intelligentsia and also among the radical nationalists and separatists. Although Gorbachev sanc-tioned one intervention and not the other, the invocation of Tbilisi and Baku in demonstrations, speeches and protests were held up as examples of the preference of Gorbachev for centrism and coercion over autonomy and negotiation.[65]

Highlights from the glasnost' *press*

The progress of *glasnost'* in the Soviet media was faltering and hesitant at first. This was understandable given the years of heavy-handed control and censorship which the party had operated. Unsure of what would or wouldn't be tolerated, and uncertain over whether the reform programme would last, editors and journalists were highly cautious at first. This was very frustrating for Gorbachev. It was only from about 1988 onwards that the first shoots of pluralism could be detected in the print and broadcast media, and things only really began to blossom from 1990 onwards. The period up to March 1990 produced very little in the way of radical writings on Gorbachev from Soviet journalists. However, this is not to say that there was little of interest or note produced.

The publications which were most experimental were a series of weeklies. They were the first to embrace the new climate of *glasnost'* and new thinking, many of the daily newspapers lagging behind somewhat.[66] In publications such as *Krokodil*,[67] *Novoe Vremya*,[68] *Moskovskiye Novosti*,[69] *Argumenty i fakti* and *Sobesed-nik*,[70] a gradual momentum was developed which saw an increasing degree of frankness, resulting in 1990 and 1991 in a much more critical press. Much of the progress was due to the impact of new editors, like Yegor Yakovlev at *Moskovskiye*

Novosti. Let us take a couple of examples. *Ogonyok* in 1985 was a typical Soviet weekly: dull, conformist and lacking any spark or vim. Gradually after 1985 it began to change, although the real catalyst (as in other cases) was the appointment of a reformist, progressive and bold editor (Vitaly Korotich) in the autumn of 1986. In the early years of *perestroika*, *Ogonyok* carried on the fine tradition of transmitting and publicizing party campaigns: anti-corruption, anti-alcohol, exhortations to change. Gorbachev – as the Gensek – was prominent, particularly in the photographs of events that week. At the end of 1986, though, and with the appointment of Korotich, the focus began to change. In 1987, there was a shift towards more stories about the everyday lives of Soviet people, rather than the latest party diktat.[71] 1988 again saw less and less official party-biased material, and increasing concentration on the historical revelations of *glasnost*', of opposition to *perestroika*, as well as the international rapprochement with the USA. What became quite noticeable was the growing invisibility of Gorbachev: the traditional Soviet focus on the cult of the leader was starting to disappear. 1989 and 1990 witnessed a series of interviews with prominent foreign figures – Margaret Thatcher,[72] Strobe Talbott,[73] Milovan Djilas[74] – as well as with the key domestic political figures: Eduard Shevardnadze, Gavril Popov, Igor Klyamkin, Andrei Sakharov, Nina Andreeva. In a telling sign of the growing problems Gorbachev was facing, *Ogonyok* ran a series of articles which noted the lessons of the failure of Khrushchev which needed to be heeded – most notably that Gorbachev was vulnerable to removal from an entrenched bureaucracy opposed to change.[75]

Prior to March 1990, the *glasnost*' media tended to limit themselves to discussions of some of the problems of the implementation of *perestroika*, or the emergence of opposition to Gorbachev. Gorbachev, of course, remained generally in a 'no-criticism' zone, and was portrayed as the prime mover in the push for change, pluralism and reform.[76] The main topics for criticism centred on the lack of progress in the economy, especially queues and shortages (which clearly was an indirect criticism of *perestroika*), faltering progress in *glasnost*', and the bureaucrats who appeared to be obstructing change (which was one of Gorbachev's favourite explanations for the former problem). *Krokodil* ran a prolonged cartoon campaign, from the middle of 1989 onwards, highlighting the faltering progress of *glasnost*' in the face of the deadening wall of bureaucratic opposition.[77] In *Moskovskiye Novosti*, a few articles critical of Gorbachev did begin to emerge before March 1990. For example, Yeltsin and Gorbachev were compared in 1989, and Yeltsin came out of the comparison favourably.[78] But mostly *Moskovskiye Novosti* sought to defend Gorbachev. Vitaly Tretyakov, in an article entitled 'Gorbachev's enigma', sought to rally to the defence of Gorbachev. He justified Gorbachev's compromises as an astute tactical scheme, more offensive than defensive and designed to ensure a constant coalition in support of change. He also defended Gorbachev's *apparat* background (no other stairs existed before 1985 for Gorbachev to climb). Tretyakov, though, did acknowledge that Gorbachev had made mistakes (most notably the anti-alcoholism policy) and that it was the energy and support of the people (and also the West) that pushed *perestroika* towards political change. Tretyakov finished by commending Gorbachev's honesty and tolerance in the face of criticism and hostility, and emphasized a faith in Gorbachev's ability, like a chess grand master, to produce a stunning tactical move should it be required.

Argumenty i fakti was one of the most outspoken publications of the *glasnost'* years. The stories covered in 1989 included material on Khrushchev too, like those in *Ogonyok*.[79] There was an also an interview with Gorbachev in May 1989, in which the weekly asked Gorbachev a series of questions which were quite personal and informal, reflecting a desire among its readership for details about the personal life of their leader: information on his parents, his family, his working day, how he spends his free time.[80] As the pace of reforms gathered, so *Argumenty i fakti* began to cover the accumulating problems in the system, as well as the new initiatives. Most evident was the exposure given to the miners' strike in July 1989, although there was still nothing directly critical of Gorbachev contained within.[81] Excerpts from the foreign press about Gorbachev's visits – to Italy and to meet George Bush Snr at Malta in 1989 and Latvia in early 1990 – were also included. But these were all positive in tone. *Sobesednik* carried a copy of the interesting interview that Roi Medvedev – a dissident historian and People's Deputy – gave to Giulietto Chiesa for *L'Unità*. Medvedev talked of his conditional support for Gorbachev (describing himself as a 'loyal oppositionist') and speculating that Gorbachev may need to introduce extreme measures if the chaos deepened.[82] *Novoe vremya* tended to focus almost exclusively upon Gorbachev's foreign forays, combined with the odd foreign correspondent's reflections on Gorbachev.[83]

Just prior to the accession of Gorbachev to the position of Executive President, *Pravda* ran a short article celebrating five years of *perestroika*.[84] This was an interesting piece which summed up the progress and problems of the previous five years, but also provides a snapshot of the official view of the party leader. The best sign of the changes that Gorbachev had overseen was the almost total absence of references to Gorbachev himself. He was mentioned in the opening preamble ('the memorable extraordinary spring plenum in March 1985 which entrusted to Mikhail Sergeyevich Gorbachev the difficult and onerous duties of General Secretary of the CPSU Central Committee'[85]) and at the end where we were reminded that Gorbachev was motivated and inspired by Lenin in his plans and visions for the USSR. Not only was hagiography dead, but also the breeze of *glasnost'* had blown through Soviet reporting. *Pravda* recognized the difficulties and problems (even mentioning some by name, such as Chernobyl and the Fergana Valley) that had cropped up, but also noted that mistakes had been made. The mistakes identified were:

- economic mistakes: the switch to independence and formation of a full-blown market;
- financial mistakes: the loss of budgetary control;
- the hasty campaigns, especially anti-alcohol;
- the organization of the cooperative movement.

Quite a limited list, with one or two notable omissions. The reasons for these mistakes were also telling: lack of skill among some people, resistance, haste and indecision (although no-one was named or even hinted at). The parade of successes and achievements was similarly quite muted, seeking to justify what had been achieved, in spite of all the problems, opposition and resistance. Most interesting of all, though, was the tone. The *Pravda* article clearly felt it was necessary to justify the choice of *perestroika*. The mantra that 'we cannot go on like this' was repeated, calling it a moral imperative to search for a solution (attacking those who were questioning the need for any change). Moreover, the specifics of *perestroika* as a strategy of change was legitimized by noting that a superficial set of changes would not suffice, necessitating an increasingly radical reform programme (an answer to those who thought that *perestroika* had gone too far). The article finishes by commending the creation of the post of Executive President: 'successful progress must be aided by the creation of the institution of the Presidency and the election to the lofty post of the USSR President of a worthy candidate who will be a powerful consolidating force in our society'.[86] The concluding sentence called it a 'time of hope'! Could Gorbachev realize these hopes, though?

The increasing confidence of openly satirical publications – such as *Krokodil* – was an important indicator of the change of atmosphere that Gorbachev had inaugurated. The greater realism and relative candour of the official press depictions of Gorbachev showed the manner in which Gorbachev had managed to shift the culture of the Soviet press to strip it of its sycophancy, and yet also demonstrated the continuing limits of press criticism. As Gorbachev took up the post of Executive President, and as the problems and opposition mounted in equal measure, the press slowly began to take on a more openly critical stance not just of the reform programme, but increasingly of Gorbachev himself. The gloves were coming off. It is this period which is widely seen as the moment when Gorbachev's reputation became tarnished.

The critiques of Gorbachev: March 1990–August 1991

The decline and fall of Gorbachev began in March 1990, when he became Executive President. The system rapidly began to unravel after that point. Divisions emerged in the party, the political system began to polarize, economic problems accumulated and nationality problems intensified. In the midst of it all sat President Gorbachev, vainly struggling to hold it all together, to keep *perestroika* on course. By assuming control at a key moment, he became the target for all kinds of criticisms, and the scapegoat for all types of ills. In the 17 months between assuming position and the August coup, Gorbachev was assailed from almost all parts of the Soviet spectrum, becoming an increasingly forlorn and isolated figure. In late February 1990, Gorbachev was severely criticized by Telman Gdlyan, a radical reformer who had been expelled from the party. Gdlyan argued that Gorbachev and Ligachev were essentially hewn out of the same rock, that Gorbachev had wrecked the economy, had no intention of introducing democracy and was wasting huge sums of money building dachas for himself.[87] It was a sign of what was to come during the debates over the Executive Presidency in February and March 1990.

Gorbachev in the spotlight I: nominations for the Executive Presidency

The debates about the Executive Presidency started in the Supreme Soviet and continued in the Congress of People's Deputies (as well as a parallel discussion in the CPSU). As the debate unfolded the two issues – do we need a President, and if so, who should it be? – became increasingly intertwined. Inherent within this debate was the question of Gorbachev: could he be trusted with these powers?

The debates about the necessity of a President fell into two main camps. Those in favour argued from a number of perspectives. The 'breakdown' scenario postulated that the depth and nature of the crisis facing the USSR at this time (economic, financial, national), and the impending breakdown of law and order, necessitated a strong central power to hold the system together. The 'consolidationist' perspective argued that a central power was required to strengthen the constitutional foundations which had been created and to enable laws to be implemented in a system which was increasingly failing to recognize the authority of the centre. Vladimir Kudryavtsev introduced the draft law on the Presidency in the Supreme Soviet on 27 February 1990.[88] He noted three reasons for the introduction: the need to delimit the relative functions of party and state; the need to harmonize the activities of the different branches of government; and finally the need to stabilize the situation. He stressed that the current position occupied by Gorbachev – Chairman of the Supreme Soviet – did not allow for speedy decisions to be taken. Hence a new position, with beefed-up powers, was required.

The debate shifted into the Congress of People's Deputies. The pro-President, pro-Gorbachev camp marshalled several arguments in favour, most notably the need for order, and to fill the vacuum of power that was rapidly emerging. It was becoming increasingly urgent to stop the ethnic and national fragmentation of the USSR. In many ways, the justifications for presidential power were all quite negative; they were a means to stop a crisis becoming a catastrophe and a collapse. Many of the key heavyweights were wheeled out to speak in favour: Aleksandr Yakovlev, Nikolai Ryzhkov, Anatoly Lukyanov. Perhaps the most coherent and theorized viewpoint came from Vadim Medvedev. He repeated the above points about the need to create a centre of power to counteract centrifugal tendencies and to provide a means for taking speedy decisions. However, he also argued that the office of Presidency was the next logical step in the process of democratization which had begun in 1987. His argument was that a great deal of work had been done in dismantling the old systems of power, and that the foundations of parliamentary democracy were in place. However, the renunciation by the party of its monopoly of power meant a new power centre was required to ensure that representative democracy could be protected and be allowed to grow.[89]

The debates in the Congress roamed across a number of issues. Many were unhappy that the office of Presidency would be elected by the Congress rather than by universal suffrage. Others wanted to discuss the question of salaries.[90] The setting of an upper age limit (65) for the post of President also generated great debate, although a proposal to remove this was defeated.[91] The strongest critique came from those who saw dangers in creating a position of such power, which also allowed this person to remain as the head of the CPSU. The potential for a new Stalin to emerge, who would crush the nascent democracy, would be a retrograde step, and was to be avoided at all costs. The most withering critique was developed by Yuri Afanasyev, the Rector of the Historical Archives and a member of the Interregional Group of Deputies, a broad democratic grouping. Afanasyev believed that it was a hasty and ill-considered move, a 'very grave political mistake'.[92] In particular, introducing these changes at a time of crisis was fraught with danger, opening the possibility of the use of force as a means to solve problems. He then went on to note the historical parallels which could easily be seen:

> If our leader [*vozhd*] and founder created foundations of anything, it is the elevation of the state policy of mass coercion and terror into a principle. And besides ... he elevated lawlessness into the principle of state policy. This was carried through the whole Stalinist period and created numerous victims, this went through the Brezhnev period when in a drunken stupor the national wealth was squandered wholesale and retail. And it is proposed that the same thing is to be continued according to tradition.[93]

He was cut short as his time had run out. But the implications were clear. It was almost as if the gigantic weight of the Stalinist personality cult and regime of personalized power was girding its loins to reassert itself after a brief breeze of democracy. If Afanasyev was candid in his criticisms of the policy (and, by implication, of Gorbachev), this was nothing compared to the personal criticisms of Gorbachev which were expressed. Although two other deputies – Ryzhkov and Bakatin – were nominated by the centrist Soyuz grouping, they refused to stand, leaving Gorbachev as the only candidate. This brought forward some of the most extreme, public, personal criticisms of Gorbachev yet aired. Teymuraz Avaliani (deputy from Kemerovo) asked the people not to vote for Gorbachev under any circumstances, arguing that he had brought the country to the brink of collapse. Deputy Schelkanov (from Leningrad) accused Gorbachev of taking 'wilful and unfounded decisions'. Ukrainian deputy Nikolay Kutsenko said Gorbachev should withdraw his nomination.[94] Gorbachev was finally elected by 1329 votes to 495 and became the first Executive President.

This election marks the onset of the final phase of Gorbachev's time in power. It was a watershed in so many ways, not least for the extent and depth of personal criticism which his nomination attracted, showing how far gone were the orchestrated, choreographed sessions of the old Soviet parliament. By making himself the Executive President (albeit without a popular mandate), Gorbachev left himself in a situation very similar to that of Nicholas II in 1915: assuming overall and very public responsibility but with a rapidly diminishing ability to do much about the situation, and with enemies and problems accruing by the day. He was now fully in the line of fire. First up were those ostensibly closest to him· his own party.

Gorbachev in the spotlight II: the 28th CPSU Congress

Between the election of Gorbachev as Executive President and the 28th CPSU Congress (which opened on 2 July 1990) two major political initiatives demonstrated the growing political polarization within Soviet politics, and the growing entrenchment and institutionalization of opposition to Gorbachev. First, Yeltsin was elected chairman of the RSFSR Supreme Soviet (essentially President of the Russian Federation) on 29 May 1990. This gave Yeltsin a power-base independent of the party and a platform to challenge Gorbachev. Then on 19 -20 June 1990, a founding meeting of the Communist Party of Russia was convened, led by Ivan Polozkov. Details on these twin threats can be seen below. For Gorbachev it signified that the competition for power was heating up. This sentiment was confirmed by the events at the 28th Congress.

Gorbachev hoped to make this Congress a crucial moment in the reform of the system. The success of his new political system required the CPSU to accept the new competitive pluralist environment, and for a deeper separation of party and state bodies. Gorbachev walked into a storm, though. A group of radicals – clustered around Yeltsin and the Democratic Platform – wanted to accelerate the whole process of reform. A group of conservatives wanted to restore the party to the centre of the political system, and to remove the apostles of reform: Yakovlev, Shevardnadze *et al.* The mass of party delegates merely wanted to vent their frustration, and the Congress was a raw and, at times, bitter one. Gorbachev was faced with an increasingly vociferous and critical audience. And they were now willing openly to express themselves.[95]

Gorbachev opened the proceedings with a speech which set out his defence of *perestroika.* His attacks on the Soviet past alienated many in the audience, who were already nervous about their immediate future in a competitive political situation. After day three had finished, Gorbachev held a meeting with a group of lower-level party secretaries (the core of the party apparatus). The exchanges (reported by Angus Roxburgh) reveal the depth of antipathy towards Gorbachev inside his own party. One is reported to have said, 'If I made a speech as weak as that [at my district meetings,] I would be drummed out of the place ... Let's have less talk. You weren't much help to us in the elections.'[96] Gorbachev was stung by these criticisms and the meeting descended into chaos. At one point he ventured that 'What are you saying, then? Is our entire course wrong?' This was perhaps not the best question to ask this particular crowd at that particular moment. The secretaries retorted, 'Yes! Yes! Yes!'[97]

The conservatives became committed to giving Gorbachev a bloody nose. The Congress required each member of the Politburo to give an account of their actions. However, the conservatives wanted to replace this and to have each person personally assessed by the Congress on a scale of 1 to 5. This would have resulted in a ringing endorsement of Ligachev and the trouncing of the reformers, especially Yakovlev and Ryzhkov. Gorbachev had to harangue and cajole the party to abandon this proposal and to carry out instead a collective assessment of the Politburo.[98] A further showdown occurred over the election of the new position of Deputy General Secretary. With Gorbachev now President, he needed one of 'his' men in position to run the party. Gorbachev favoured Vladimir Ivashko. Yegor Ligachev put himself forward, in direct opposition to Gorbachev's publicly stated views. This, according to Roxburgh, was the first time Ligachev had so openly opposed Gorbachev.[99] Gorbachev tried to manipulate the election by having Ligachev removed from the ballot paper. After one vote his name was struck off, but it was replaced after protests. Eventually Gorbachev prevailed. Ivashko was elected (3109 votes to 776). But Gorbachev's authority was eroding with every day, although his ability to scrape through testifies to his skills under pressure.

Gorbachev also faced a challenge to his position as General Secretary. The challenger was Teymuraz Avaliani (who criticized Gorbachev strongly over his decision to become President). Avaliani was a populist figure and one of the key organizers of the strike in the Kuzbass. He had been an outspoken critic of the government during 1989 and 1990, calling for the resignation of Ryzhkov as Prime Minister in the strikes of 1989. In the votes, Avaliani received 501 votes for and 4026 against. Gorbachev received 3411 votes for and 1116 votes against. The final confrontation came over the elections to the CC on the final day of the Congress. Gorbachev, trying to avoid another showdown, nominated 398 people for 398 places. Delegates to the Congress added their own nominees, though (14 in total), and all these were elected, leading to 14 of Gorbachev's nominees potentially facing ejection. Gorbachev proposed that as all candidates had received over 50 per cent they should all be elected. Congress refused. Gorbachev raged, talking about the work of the Congress being wrecked, and he got his way. But the constant need for threats to get his own way merely served to reinforce the perception of a leader at war with his own party.

The speeches at the Congress reflected the growing polarization and criticism of Gorbachev. Many continued to question his decision to combine the positions of General Secretary and Executive President. Mikhail Startsev asked Gorbachev to renounce his position as General Secretary.[100] One delegate repeated the accusation that Gorbachev was leading the USSR to a restoration of capitalism.[101] Support for Gorbachev came from Kazakh and Belorussian CP delegates. Personal defences of Gorbachev came from Yakovlev, Ryzhkov, Shevardnadze and Vadim Medvedev. The Congress finished on a dramatic moment as Yeltsin, Gavril Popov and Anatoli Sobchak declared that they were leaving the party. They attacked Gorbachev for staying. It was to presage a momentous 12 months in Gorbachev's life.

Conservative critiques: the RCP, Russian nationalists, neo-Bolsheviks and the old guard

By the summer of 1990, the monologue was well and truly over and the criticisms were beginning to come thick and fast. The fragmentation of the political system was creating new opportunities for all those either alienated by how far and how fast the system had changed, or frustrated at how slow and limited the changes were. A variety of voices began to articulate an essentially conservative agenda: bemoaning the changes and looking to 'turn back the clock'. These ranged from the cautious criticisms of someone like Yegor Ligachev, to the frothing bile and vulgar Marxist invective of Nina Andreeva.

Let's start with Andreeva. In April 1990, Andreeva gave an interview for Budapest radio. She outlined that, although Gorbachev had come to power in 1985 with a vibrant, energetic programme of change, he had gone awry since 1987. She asserted that he had adopted a 'right-wing opportunist' stance and that his programme would inexorably lead to the victory of capitalism.[102] Later on that year, Andreeva issued a declaration of no-confidence in Gorbachev at the 3rd All-Union Conference of the conservative neo-Bolshevik Society 'Unity for Leninism and Communistic Ideals' which met on 28 October 1990. This no-confidence motion called for the dismissal of Gorbachev and argued that he and his associates had unleashed a 'bourgeois counter-revolution'. Andreeva's one-woman campaign against the Gorbachev clique was directed at trying to wrest control of the CPSU back from these 'right-wingers' and restoring the 'Bolshevik' heart of the party. Andreeva's group – along with other groups such as the 'Bolshevik' platform in the CPSU, and the Marxist platform – became increasingly strident in their criticisms. In July 1991, at a conference in Minsk of the supporters of the Bolshevik platform, Andreeva argued that the problems in the country were primarily down to a combination of the failures of what she termed 'Gorbostroyka' and also the rag-tag band of pseudo-democrats (Yeltsin, Sobchak, Shevardnadze *et al.*) who were guilty of 'cosmopolitanism' (often a thinly veiled term for anti-Semitism). By the summer of 1991, the critique had become a vitriolic concoction of Marxism, Russian nationalism, xenophobia (agents of 'foreign special services' were also to blame for the problems in the USSR) and personal abuse.[103]

At the other end of the conservative spectrum stood Yegor Ligachev. After 1987, Ligachev became increasingly critical of the Gorbachev programme, but this was often couched in terms of a dissatisfaction with the pace of change and the problems that were arising, rather than a deep-seated critique of either Gorbachev or *perestroika per se*.[104] In 1990, having been sidelined by Gorbachev after a number of personnel reshuffles, Ligachev became a focus for the discontented conservatives in the CPSU. He was a key player in the creation of the CP RSFSR (of which more below) and also stood for the post of Deputy General Secretary of the CPSU at the 28th Congress in July 1990. However, although Ligachev did express criticisms, he could never quite bring himself to break completely with either Gorbachev or *perestroika*. In his nomination speech, he was critical of a number of issues – the return of private ownership, the attacks on the Soviet past, the dangers of nationalism – but reiterated his commitment to change. He did talk of the differences he had with Gorbachev:

> I have worked with the comrades and with Mikhail Sergeevich and I will tell you in all frankness that yes, we have tactical differences but he and

myself have never had strategic differences. I deeply respect this man – I have perhaps the right to say this – but at the same time we have had different views on certain tactical issues. I have never been a brake on *perestroika*.[105]

Ligachev's position – rather like Gorbachev, somewhat ironically – was rapidly overtaken by events as the support for a conservative reformist position was quickly overtaken as the political system polarized into left and right. A more coherent, critical conservative platform began to coalesce around the newly formed CP RSFSR, and Ligachev became something of an irrelevance. Having lost the vote for the Deputy General Secretary to Vladimir Ivashko at the 28th Congress, Ligachev went into retirement.

The main vehicle for the articulation of the conservative platform came through the creation of the Russian Communist Party (CP RSFSR). The question of a separate organization for the Russian communists was one which had rumbled on throughout almost the entire Soviet period. However, it was brought into sharp relief by the elections to the CPD in the spring of 1989, which seemed to presage the growing power of the different republics. In the light of this, the Russian communists began to speculate on the need for their own Communist Party. Ligachev was in favour. Gorbachev was uneasy, though, fearing it might become a vehicle of conservatism and opposition to reform. In December 1989, Gorbachev created a Russian bureau of the CPSU CC, which included among others the conservative Leningrad official Boris Gidaspov. However, for the Russian communists this seemed to be wholly unsatisfactory, a half-measure, a token gesture on Gorbachev's part.

In the spring of 1990, an unstoppable momentum towards the creation of a Russian Communist Party was developing. On 21/22 April 1990, an Action Congress of conservatives debated the formation of a Russian Communist Party, led by Gidaspov. Gorbachev was invited but declined to go. The leadership – Gorbachev, Yakovlev, Shevardnadze, in particular – were strongly criticized and told to resign. This congress arranged the founding conference of the CP RSFSR for 19–23 June 1990. In many ways this turned into a dress rehearsal for the 28th CPSU Congress. Gorbachev came along and spoke in defence of his programme and his record. Many regional secretaries – especially figures like Melnikov, the first secretary of the Kemerovo *oblast'* – were critical of the leadership team. Gorbachev suffered a serious reverse when his favoured candidate for the leadership of the CP RSFSR – Valentin Kuptsov – was defeated by Ivan Polozkov. However, the CP RSFSR was not wholly dominated by conservatives. Many figures spoke in favour of Gorbachev, and the electoral victory of Polozkov was quite a narrow one.

From June 1990 to August 1991, Polozkov, Gidaspov, Melnikov and others developed a conservative platform critical of Gorbachev (but more critical of Yakovlev). Increasingly, the conservative critique became a synthesis of fears over nationalist dissent, a mourning of the loss of great power status of the USSR and also concern over the situation of the ordinary working people. Criticisms of

Gorbachev were rarely openly personal. The initial press conferences after the June 1990 founding Congress were quite muted. Gidaspov was at pains to stress the positive things Gorbachev had achieved, and the inadmissibility of personal criticism of the President.[106]

Polozkov's criticisms were more acute at the 28th Congress, calling on the CPSU leadership to be accountable for their errors.[107] The full platform of the CP RSFSR was not revealed until October 1990.[108] Although the CP RSFSR claimed to be being guided by the 28th CPSU Congress statement on 'Towards humane, democratic socialism', their programmatic statement expressed their desire to defend the Union, stabilize the economy and reform the political system. Underlying this was a strong commitment to maintain the fundamentals of the existing system, to preserve rather than to dismantle wholesale. By the start of 1991, however, Polozkov was articulating a much stronger line. In a speech in February 1991, he outlined:

> The so-called democrats have managed to supplant the aims of *perestroika* and seize the initiative from our party. The people are being robbed of their past, their present is being destroyed and no-one can yet give a convincing account of what they can expect in future.[109]

According to Polozkov, the CPSU had been hijacked by reactionaries, liberals and pseudodemocrats. Only the CP RSFSR could guarantee to uphold the principles of socialism. Polozkov also highlighted his fears for the continued existence of the USSR, and commended the Chinese model of reform. In an interview following his visit to China in June 1991, he expressed his support for the approach of the Chinese, who had combined radical economic changes with a 'respectful attitude towards history' (unlike *glasnost*'s attacks on Soviet history) and without 'sensation, hullabaloo and outcry' (nationalist dissent and anti-communist forces).[110] The final word from the conservatives on Gorbachev and the reformers came in a speech given by Polozkov to the CP RSFSR CC in August 1991, prompted by the CPSU draft programme, which had all but abandoned Marxism-Leninism and communism. Calling themselves the true supporters of *perestroika* in its efforts to improve the economy and the people's well-being, Polozkov vented his anger against the radicals:

> The liberal radicals ... aspire to a radical change of social order, destruction of our social gains ... pushing Russia into western ways they trample on our people's humanitarian traditions ... Never before have the working people suffered so severely ... the false democrats lay the blame for all the misfortunes upon socialism, upon the past 70 years, upon the older generations.[111]

By August 1991, the conservatives were now putting forward a distinct, full critique of the CPSU and the Gorbachev line. As guardians of the Soviet system and the ideological purity of Soviet Marxism-Leninism, the old order had found its defenders. Gorbachev had now become a false prophet, a heretic who had lost his way. Just two weeks later, the guardians of orthodoxy would attempt to slay the heretic.

The Yeltsin viewpoint

The spring and early summer of 1990 was a momentous time in the politics of the USSR. Not only did Gorbachev have to endorse the emergence of the CP RSFSR, but one of his main rivals – Boris Yeltsin – acquired a power-base independent of the Communist Party. When the RSFSR Congress of People's Deputies convened in May 1990, Yeltsin was elected as Chairman of the RSFSR Supreme Soviet. Yeltsin was quick to point out – in a bit of a dig at Gorbachev – that he had been elected through a democratic, open contest and that he was opposed to the combining of posts (party secretary and chairman of the local Soviet). However, he did express a willingness to work with Gorbachev, and at the founding Congress of the CP RSFSR, Gorbachev and Yeltsin had shaken hands, which seemed to herald a thawing in their relationship. Indeed, Yeltsin had taken the opportunity at the Russian Communist Party Congress to defend Gorbachev from many attacks. In retrospect, the key moment came on 12 June 1990 when the CPD RSFSR issued a declaration of sovereignty. This was to set Russia against the USSR and Yeltsin against Gorbachev, creating the context for the infamous 'War of Laws' between the two centres of authority, Soviet and Russian. The start of the breakdown in their relationship came at the 28th CPSU Congress.

In a press conference on 26 June 1990 relayed on Soviet TV, Yeltsin restated the argument advanced by Sakharov that there were grave dangers of Gorbachev trying to combine the posts of General Secretary and Executive President and that he should renounce one (specifically the GS position). Yeltsin mentioned that there were dangers of a revival of the cult of personality (shorthand for Stalin) and also that Gorbachev had in many ways neglected the CPSU. As a result of this neglect, Yeltsin stated that the party was now at a critical moment: it could either change and renew itself by throwing off the dominance of the conservative apparatchiks, or it would quite likely face a split. Yeltsin in fact called for a postponement of the 28th Congress in order to stabilize the political situation. Yeltsin was clearly fearful of a conservative backlash.[112] His position hardened at the 28th Congress. His speech was a harsh attack on the conservatives and a call for radical reform of the party's internal structures and practices and also its position within the political system. He wanted to see the party move to becoming a parliamentary-type party to reflect the new multi-party politics of Russia.[113] However, when this was not forthcoming, Yeltsin got up and walked out. Gorbachev stayed.

For a brief while in the summer, the two men joined forces to advance the cause of economic reform. Gorbachev pressed ahead with a series of radical decrees and measures at home and abroad which culminated in the plan for the 500-day transition to the market (the so-called Shatalin–Yavlinksy plan). Gorbachev and Yeltsin met for a five-hour meeting at the end of August 1990 to discuss the economic programme. Their agreement on the need for urgent measures to confront the spiralling economic crisis in the USSR seemed to presage a new era of cooperation. So what went wrong?

The package of measures it entailed included powers to give economic independence to the republics, the freeing of prices, massive amounts of privatization, the selling-off of state assets and land reform. However, Gorbachev also had another set of plans on his desk: a much more conservative cautious approach as outlined by the Prime Minister Nikolai Ryzhkov. Gorbachev hesitated, fearful of the backlash from the conservatives and the potential chaos of unleashing radical reform. He asked Aganbegyan, his economic adviser, to try and combine the Shatalin and Ryzhkov plans. On 16 October, Gorbachev presented his 'President's Programme' to the Supreme Soviet. Yeltsin felt betrayed, having commented earlier that 'you cannot cross a hedgehog and a snake'.[114] Yeltsin was convinced now that Gorbachev had thrown in his lot with the conservatives, rather than the reformers. A chasm between the two was beginning to open up, although the chasm was still bridgeable at this time, as we shall see.

Gorbachev's dalliance with the conservatives and the hard-liners seemed to have pushed him and Yeltsin in diametrically opposed directions at the start of 1991. The resignation of Shevardnadze and the crackdown in Lithuania appeared to herald a coming dictatorship. This led in February 1991 to Yeltsin demanding Gorbachev's resignation. In an interview on Soviet TV with Sergei Lomakin, Yeltsin heavily criticized both Gorbachev and his record as President:

> In the first two years after 1985, Gorbachev inspired certain hope in many of us. In fact from that moment there began his active policy – I'm sorry – his deceiving of the people ... This has particularly revealed itself in recent times when it became perfectly obvious that he wants, while preserving the word *perestroika*, not to restructure, but to preserve the system, to preserve harsh centralized authority, and not to give independence to the republics ... I think that my personal mistake was excessive trust in the President ... having carefully analysed the events of recent months, I declare I warned in 1987 that Gorbachev has in his character an aspiration to absolutization of personal power. He has already done this, eloquently terming this presidential rule. I distance myself from the position and the policy of the President and advocate his immediate resignation.[115]

Confirming his analysis of Gorbachev as having gone back on his early commitment to reform, Yeltsin, when interviewed in France, accused Gorbachev of carrying out little more than a 'cosmetic facelift of the communist and totalitarian structures'.[116] The gulf between them at this point seemed huge, but things changed quite rapidly in late April when Gorbachev began the process of dissolving the Union through the Novo-Ogarevo agreement, and creating a renewed Union of sovereign states. Yeltsin saw this as a great victory for the republics and the forces of reform. Gorbachev, according to Yeltsin, was now an ally again.[117] To assist Gorbachev, Yeltsin agreed to the preservation of the All-Union Presidency.

Gorbachev was faced with opposition from within his own party, though, and conservative forces called for his resignation prior to the April 1991 plenum. A blast of criticism from speaker after speaker was directed at Gorbachev. In an attempt to see off this criticism, Gorbachev offered his resignation. However, the party baulked at this, recognizing that this would split the party and render it even weaker. The CC decided to remove the question of Gorbachev's resignation from the agenda by 322 votes to 13 (with 14 abstentions).[118]

After Yeltsin's election as President of Russia on 12 June 1991, he and Gorbachev seemed to be quite closely aligned again. Yeltsin wished Gorbachev well on his trip to London for the G7 meeting in July, and the two began to meet in private. Yeltsin maintained that he would support Gorbachev's nomination as President of the Union. The only fly in the ointment was Yeltsin's decree of 20 July which banned political parties from state bodies in Russia, which was a key part of the working structure of the CPSU and one which Gorbachev opposed removing.[119] However, on the surface with the upcoming new Union treaty about to be signed, it looked as though a personal and political rapprochement was developing. The storm of August was to put paid to that, though.

Critical friends? Shevardnadze's resignation, December 1990

One of the most difficult times for Gorbachev came at the end of 1990. Having retreated somewhat on his commitment to the radical 500-Day Plan, Gorbachev, it seemed, had turned back towards the conservatives and was adopting a more centrist and authoritarian approach to change. In the midst of this Eduard Shevardnadze, the Foreign Affairs Minister, got up to speak in the CPD on 20 December 1990. After making some opening remarks about the Gulf War, he turned to the question of the correlation of political forces internally. Concerned at the accumulating power and confidence of people he termed 'reactionaries', Shevardnadze announced his resignation, out of the blue:

> The reformers have gone to ground. Dictatorship is coming, I state it with complete responsibility. No one knows what kind this dictatorship will be, and who will come … I am resigning, let this be my contribution … my protest against the onset of dictatorship. I express profound gratitude to Mikhail Sergeevich Gorbachev. I am his friend. I am a fellow thinker of his … But I cannot reconcile myself to the events which are taking place in our country.[120]

The fall-out from this was instant and contentious. The pro-reform journalist Aleksandr Bovin argued in *Izvestiya* that Shevardnadze was wrong to quit; the best way to resist dictatorship was to stay and fight. He also commented that the President (i.e. Gorbachev) 'should pay more attention to the feelings and the emotional mood of his closest colleagues'.[121] On the other side of the fence, Anatolii Lukyanov (the Chairman of the USSR Supreme Soviet and an increasingly conservative figure), when interviewed by Vladimir Pozner, stated that there was a growing yearning in society for greater stability and order, but that this should not be confused with a coming dictatorship, unless this could be described as a dictatorship of law, order and stability, in which case Lukyanov was in favour of it.[122] The Soviet media was also embroiled in this row with an episode of *Vzglyad*, the radical news show, being pulled.[123]

Gorbachev's response to this resignation expressed his surprise and hurt.[124] He also thoroughly condemned Shevardnadze's actions as it was tantamount to deserting the cause when *perestroika* was in its most dangerous phase. He had been part of the original group which had seen the need for wholesale change before 1985, yet he now was jumping ship, in a way that could only damage the likelihood of success.

But Gorbachev then dealt with the lingering question implicitly raised by Shevardnadze: where was the dictatorial threat coming from, and who was it likely to be? For, along with the criticisms raised previously by both Sakharov and Yeltsin, could the coming dictator be the President himself, either wittingly or cajoled into it by the forces and people around him? Gorbachev tried to make a distinction between the need for strong power in the current crisis situation, and the emergence of some kind of dictatorial junta:

> Comrades, let us not mix up and lump everything together. It is one thing that we can see that our society is in this particular state – political instability, a war of laws, a lack of effectiveness of executive authority, and breaks in this chain of executive authority ... and this requires urgent and immediate measures to impose order, to give our society stability, as without these it is impossible to move forward the transformations ... This must be done and there is here no question of any dictatorship but of a strong power and this should not be confused.[125]

The intriguing thing about this episode was not just that someone from within the inner sanctum of Gorbachev's entourage had broken rank and decided to quit, but that here we see the way in which Gorbachev was now caught clearly in the cross-fire of the polarizing political system, as both 'left' and 'right' trained their sights on him. Gorbachev was now, either directly (by concentrating more and more power in his own hands) or indirectly (by doing nothing about the rising influence of the conservative forces) crushing the democratic reform process, according to the radicals. On the other hand, Gorbachev was responsible for the spiralling crisis, the growth of poverty, crime, ethnic strife, and so on, according to the conservatives, because he was failing to take a firm hand, and was instead pandering to the demagogues. By the start of 1991, support for Gorbachev was ebbing away, and it was about to get a whole lot worse.

A dress rehearsal for August? The Lithuanian moment, January 1991

The speculation concerning Gorbachev's latest political makeover at the end of 1990 seemed to be confirmed by the events in Lithuania from 11 to 13 January

1991 (and shortly afterwards in Latvia too). The background to these events lies in the increasing belligerence of Lithuania in asserting its right to be declared an independent republic. The Lithuanians – led by Vytautas Landsbergis, an outspoken music professor – declared their independence from the USSR on 11 March 1990, highlighting the illegal and immoral way in which Lithuania and the other Baltic states had been annexed in 1940 under the protocols of the Molotov–Ribbentrop pact of 1939. Local opposition to Lithuanian independence was orchestrated by the Lithuanian communists and also by a communist-backed workers' movement, *Edinstvo* (unity). Problems and tensions developed in the first few days of 1991, as price rises and demonstrations threatened to get out of hand. Thousands of pro-Soviet demonstrators, led by the *Edinstvo* movement, tried to storm the parliament building in protest at massive price hikes. On 8/9 January, several Soviet military units were flown in to Vilnius, including troops of the Interior Ministry (the so-called black berets), ostensibly to 'maintain order' and to identify Lithuanian youths who were evading the draft.

On 10 January, Gorbachev urged the Lithuanian parliament to 'revoke anti-constitutional acts', i.e. its declaration of independence from the preceding March, and threatened to impose direct presidential rule. Was this an example of the 'strong hand' Gorbachev was talking about? Or the coming dictatorship that Shevardnadze had forewarned of? The next day Soviet military units seized the National Defence Department building in Vilnius in the first of a series of moves against key institutions. At 3pm on 11 January, Juozas Jermalavicius, the ideology secretary of the CC of the Lithuanian Communist Party, announced the formation of the National Salvation Committee of the Lithuanian SSR, and decreed itself to be the only legitimate government in Lithuania. On 12 January, the people begin to surround the key points in order to defend the key buildings: the Supreme Council, radio and TV committee and the Vilnius TV tower. In the early hours of 13 January the tanks and troops attacked the people. Thirteen were killed (and another one died of a heart attack). However, as the crowds increased, so the military eventually backed off.

Gorbachev's reputation was greatly damaged by these events. The nagging questions which dogged Gorbachev – in spite of his denials – were: how much did he know? Did he authorize the assault? If he didn't know, was he now weak and powerless to stop the reactionaries? And were these events in Lithuania little more than a dress rehearsal for the 'real' thing to be carried out later on in Moscow? Either way, Gorbachev was increasingly seen as either desperate, weak or finally revealing his true colours. Landsbergis, over the next five to six months kept up a critical approach to Gorbachev and the Soviet state as he sought to defend Lithuania from further interventions by the centre. In February, Landsbergis attacked Gorbachev for attempting to prevent the Lithuanians from holding a referendum in their republic, calling it 'impermissible interference'.[126] Later on Lithuanian Radio, Landsbergis also stated that Gorbachev's decree reflected 'an old tradition of the USSR according to which law and authority stem not from the will of the people, as expressed by a free vote, but, autocratically from orders from the rulers'.[127]

Landsbergis was particularly incensed by the USSR procurator-general's report on the events of 11–13 January which was released on 3 June that year. This refused to condemn the actions of the military, saying that the evidence pointed to the deaths being caused by Lithuanian radicals, not the military. He accused them of spreading lies, and of doing so to protect the image and reputation of Gorbachev, who was about to go to Oslo to pick up the Nobel Peace Prize for 1990. He noted that the purpose of the procurator-general's report was to 'give some sort of argument to Mikhail Gorbachev who is about to leave for Norway to deliver the award winner's speech'.[128] The following month, Landsbergis was interviewed on Lithuanian TV about the ongoing Novo-Ogarevo discussions and relations between Lithuania, Russia and the USSR. Here he stated that he believed that it was 'prejudice' on Gorbachev's part which prevented him from coming to a peaceful agreement with Lithuania.[129]

The Lithuanian events did further damage to Gorbachev's reputation, and seemed to confirm his ever-weakening position. A large rally convened in Moscow on 20 January 1991, on the first anniversary of the Baku crackdown, to demand Gorbachev's resignation. Estimates vary from 200,000 to 1 million people who took part. They held a minute's silence in memory of the victims of Tbilisi, Baku and Vilnius. They also expressed fear that the turn back towards dictatorship was now closer than ever. Before we turn to look in detail at the events which led to his unseating in August 1991, let's take a brief detour through the *glasnost'* press and their perspectives on Gorbachev in the last 18 months of his time in power.

The press

The *glasnost'* press began to grow increasingly confident in the last 18 months of Gorbachev's time in power as the growing political pluralism found a variety of different media outlets. The type of topics that came to dominate the dailies and weeklies included topics like the economic crisis (shortages, price rises, the drift to the market), the renegotiation of the Union Treaty, and also the dramatic shifts in the international sphere, including the end of the Cold War and the relations between the USSR and the USA, and also the relations between Gorbachev and Bush. There was also a rise in interviews with key foreign political figures and thinkers, providing their perspectives on the changes currently being undertaken in the USSR.[130]

In terms of the domestic politics and the perceptions and attitudes towards Gorbachev, there was a growing interest in personalities and high-profile moments and crises in Soviet politics. Most notably, these included the creation of the Executive Presidency, the clash between Gorbachev and Yeltsin, and the resignation of Shevardnadze. There was also a notable increase in the range of opinions on offer: contrasting opinions on particular events (e.g. a debate in *Argumenty i fakti* about the appointment of Gorbachev as Executive President),[131] or alternatives put forward as to how to solve particular problems.[132] There were also one or two more human touches as the press tried to get to the 'real' Gorbachev, including a profile of Raisa[133] and an interview with his daughter, Irina.[134] Overall, in this period, although there were questions asked about Gorbachev's intentions, his objectives and the nature of his tactics in the light of the oscillations in policy between September 1990 and April 1991, the *glasnost'* press on the whole remained fairly positive and supportive of Gorbachev, aware perhaps of their fate if the hardliners were to come back. So, for example, *Argumenty i fakti* ran an article where they defended Gorbachev against accusations of corruption by detailing where the royalties from the overseas sales of his book, *Perestroika: New Thinking for Our Country and the World,* had been spent.[135] There was a great deal of coverage of Gorbachev winning the Nobel Peace Prize.[136]

There were still critical voices being raised. For example, Igor Klyamkin wrote an assessment of the reform process which contrasted Gorbachev very negatively with Boris Yeltsin, arguing that Gorbachev stood as a representative of the 'old power' structures, whereas Yeltsin was a representative of the new forces growing in Soviet society.[137] Overall, the picture which comes across of Gorbachev from the *glasnost'* press was very much of an embattled leader, a leader in flux, a leader faced with many obstacles and problems and unsure which way to turn. There was also a degree of frustration at the slow pace of reform and the inability of Gorbachev to solve the accumulating problems.

A good illustration of this can be found in the visual material in *Krokodil* for the last 15 months of Gorbachev's rule. *Krokodil* itself became increasingly explicit and pessimistic about the situation in the USSR, highlighting the accumulating, unsolved problems, especially in the economy, the opposition to change and the failures to address them. So, cartoons can be found with Gorbachev trying to stitch together a map of the Soviet Union,[138] or carrying a copy of Lenin's 'What is to be done?'[139] A confused shopper is depicted looking at a road sign with arrows pointing in four different directions showing the way to a market economy.[140] Criticisms of Gorbachev were highlighted: he is seen as holding up the renegotiation of the Union Treaty by a snarling Yeltsin.[141] But it wasn't all negative. Gorbachev is depicted positively: on one occasion he is shown in a boxing ring with George Bush Snr, both victorious having knocked out their joint opponent, *The Cold War.*

Perhaps the most telling cartoon was found in *Argumenty i fakti.* Here, Gorbachev is desperately trying to get his '*Perestroika*' hot air balloon off the ground. The balloon is barely inflated and has many patches on it, and is weighed down by sandbags of 'communism' and 'CPSU' and 'USSR'. Gorbachev is all alone and surrounded by demonstrating faceless masses, and is holding on tightly to his baggage.[142] This summarizes very neatly the abiding image of Gorbachev which can be found in the pages of the *glasnost'* press in the final months of his time in power: lonely, embattled, yearning for change but clinging to the past.

The requiem for Gorbachev: August 1991–January 1992

Ever since the resignation of Shevardnadze and the events in Lithuania, rumours had abounded that there were forces in the wings waiting to pounce. As Gorbachev embraced the reformers after April 1991, he undertook two measures which were likely to provoke a response from the conservatives. First, the Novo-Ogarevo process threatened to break up the Union. Second, Gorbachev ordered a new Party Programme which all but abandoned the whole ideological edifice of the CPSU. The question was, when might this occur? The most dangerous times in Soviet politics were always when the leader was away: either out of the country, or on holiday. Gorbachev was due in London in July, and at his dacha on the Black Sea in August. If something was going to happen, these were the danger times.

It turned out, as we know, to be August. There were some intimations of things happening behind the scenes. There was a general sense of disquiet among the reformers about the behind the scenes machinations among conservatives. The impending new Union Treaty and the continuing economic crisis seemed to be creating a momentum for action, and time was running out if they were to prevent the Novo-Ogarevo agreement being signed in August. On 17 June, Valentin Pavlov, the Prime Minister, at a closed session of the Supreme Soviet, called for a range of emergency powers to be granted to the government to implement an anti-crisis programme. In the same session, Vladimir Kryuchkov alleged that Western states were using *perestroika* as a pretext for dismantling the USSR. The conservative grouping in the Supreme Soviet – *Soyuz* – began to mobilize their opposition to the proposed new treaty. One of their leaders – Viktor Alksnis – said unequivocally that Gorbachev had to go.[143] Reports on TV noted that there was a 'continuing mutiny against Gorbachev'.[144] The same report also began to name possible members of this coterie of mutineers: Kryuchkov, Dmitri Yazov (Defence Minister) and Boris Pugo (Interior Minister). In a prescient moment, TV journalist Yuri Rostov noted:

> The choice of paths that is at last drawing near, along which the economy of our country will move is at the present time approaching an acute conflict, in the course of which the right-wingers will probably tackle the task of neutralizing the Soviet president as well.[145]

Further moves seemed to confirm these fears. On 26 June, Interior Ministry troops raided a telephone centre in Vilnius. Three days later, Shevardnadze and Yakovlev were to be investigated by the CPSU Control Commission.

In July, the reformers began to mobilize too. On 2 July, a Democratic Reform Movement was formed, led by Shevardnadze, and supported by Yakovlev, Ivan Silayev, Aleksandr Rutskoi, Gavril Popov, Anatoli Sobchak, Fedor Burlatsky and Stanislav Shatalin. Gorbachev voiced his approval before he left to visit the G7 in London to request assistance. On 4 July, Shevardnadze resigned his CPSU membership. On 16 August, Yakovlev followed suit, complaining of a concerted campaign of 'blackening, fabrications, attacks' against him.[146] The clouds were gathering, but there was no real sense of the ferocity of the storm that was about to break.

On the morning of 19 August 1991, while Gorbachev was in his dacha at Foros in the Crimea on the Black Sea, an Emergency Committee was formed. The members of this committee included many who were very close to Gorbachev, who had been appointed by him and who had worked closely with him:

- O. D. Baklanov (First Deputy Chairman of USSR Defence Council);
- V. A. Kryuchkov (Chairman of KGB);
- V. S. Pavlov (Prime Minister of USSR);
- B. K. Pugo (Interior Minister of USSR);
- V. A. Starodubtsev (Chairman of USSR Peasant's Union);
- A. I. Tizyakov (President of USSR Association of State Enterprises and Industrial Construction);
- D. T. Yazov (Defence Minister of USSR);
- G. I. Yanaev (acting President of USSR).

They issued a 'Message to the Soviet People' which outlined that, as Gorbachev was incapacitated owing to illness, power was to be transferred to the State Committee. A State of Emergency, lasting six months from 19 August, was proclaimed. The opening preamble to the message noted:

> In a dark and critical hour for the destiny of our country and of our peoples, we address you. A mortal danger hangs over our great homeland. The policy of reform initiated by M. S. Gorbachev, conceived as a means to ensure the dynamic development of the country and the democratization of the life of its society, has, for a number of reasons, come to a dead end.[147]

Their programme sought to curb popular demonstrations, restore 'order', revive the economy and prevent the devolution of power to the republics. Wages and allowances were to be raised, and prices frozen or reduced. Meetings, demonstrations and strikes were banned. The activities of various political parties and public organizations were suspended. In a press conference on 19 August 1991 given by Gennadi Yanayev, he elaborated on the nature of Gorbachev's 'condition'. He outlined that:

> Mikhail Sergeevich Gorbachev is at present on holiday and undergoing treatment in the Crimea. He has indeed, grown very tired over these past years and he will need some time to put his health in order. I would like to say that we hope that when he is recovered, Mikhail Sergeevich will return to carrying out his duties and at any rate, we will continue to follow the course which [he] began in 1985.[148]

He went on to say, however, that *perestroika* 'has not produced the expected results'.[149] At the end he also defended Gorbachev against accusations from a

Kommersant journalist who argued that Gorbachev should be investigated for his part in the Tengiz oil issue. Yanaev called Gorbachev 'a man who deserves all manner of respect'.[150]

So who came out in support of this new line? The list of those who explicitly came out in support was not massive, as many people and groups opted for a tentative 'wait-and-see' attitude. However, the following groups expressed openly their support:

- Nina Andreeva;
- Alfred Rubiks (the First Secretary of the Latvian CP);
- Sokolov, the Chairman of the Nizhny Novgorod Regional Soviet;
- Terek Cossacks;
- Soyuz faction;
- the President of Tatarstan;
- a number of members of the USSR Council of Ministers – Katushov, Orlov, Sychev, Gusev, Panyukov, Stroganov, Timoshishin, Vorontsov, Tizyakov and others.[151]

The list of those who opposed the state of emergency was much longer and more diverse: the Memorial Society, the Moldovan Popular Front, Anatolii Sobchak and Ivan Silayev, the Regional Soviets in Kemerovo, Tyumen and Voronezh', trade unions in Khabarovsk, the Estonian and Latvian parliaments to name but a few.[152] Gorbachev also received broad expressions of support from Vladimir Shcherbakov (the First Deputy Prime Minister).[153] The lack of preparation, and the general incompetence on the part of the State Committee, meant that the six-month state of emergency barely lasted three days. By the end of 21 August, it had fizzled out. Attention began to turn to sorting out the post-putsch mess, and also to trying to find out why it had happened and who was to blame.

In the press conferences after his return on 21 August, a number of questions were addressed to Gorbachev from both foreign and domestic correspondents.[154] These can be reduced to: how much did he know about the impending coup? What did he do during the time of his incarceration? Why did he appoint/trust the people on the Emergency Committee? A couple of examples will suffice. In a press conference on 21 August after the collapse of the coup, Arkady Volskiy, the leader of the Soyuz faction, repeated the criticisms of the democrats against Gorbachev – for being indecisive, inconsistent, making gross mistakes in the selection of cadres – but outlined that the statement about Gorbachev's health was a fabrication and that his removal was illegal. He also refuted the accusation, voiced by Anatoly Lukyanov, that Gorbachev knew about everything that was happening and also directly sanctioned it.

A much more critical perspective was articulated by the TV programme *Vesti*. Their appraisal was that Gorbachev was very much to blame for the August days, because of his constant compromising and attempts to assuage the conservatives. He appointed the Emergency Committee members to their positions and refused to remove them when they began to agitate and criticize. In short,

The coup was prepared for in good time. The start of the plot apparently was made last autumn. At that time the communist top echelons still considered Gorbachev a duffer, but at least their own man ... Gorbachev was engaged in balancing, in seeking compromises. He did not interfere in events and always in all conflicts, supported the victors. General Rodionov, who perpetrated the carnage in Tbilisi, the feeble Ryzhkov ... he went on balancing too long and the day came when his comrades-in-arms decided that they could manage without him.[155]

The key political moment was when Gorbachev went to the Russian Parliament to address the deputies there and was confronted with a euphoric Yeltsin, basking in the new authority he had acquired as a result of his stand against the coup. Gorbachev faced a barrage of questions from the deputies, and also a series of rather humiliating interventions from Yeltsin, who was relishing the situation of putting Gorbachev on the hook, and watching him wriggle and squirm. The most symbolic moment came when Yeltsin confronted Gorbachev and forced him to read out the short account which detailed, one by one, the disloyalty and betrayal of the vast majority of the USSR Council of Ministers. Gorbachev was continually interrupted, criticized and laughed at. At one point as Gorbachev read out the response of Panyukov, the Minister for Civil Aviation, Yeltsin interjected that 'It is good you flew back from there in our airplane and not in theirs!'[156] RSFSR deputies called for the disbanding of the CPSU as a criminal organization, the banning of socialism, the nationalization of CPSU property, disbandment of the KGB. They repeated Lukyanov's assertion that the whole coup was carried out with his knowledge and tacit support. They asserted that Gorbachev had done little or nothing to resist the coup in his dacha. Towards the end Yeltsin announced the suspension of the activities of the Russian Communist Party, a move vehemently opposed by Gorbachev. In response, Gorbachev appealed for calm, wanted to adopt a measured response, to investigate things properly and also reiterated his belief in and support for many of the old structures and institutions, which he believed could be rescued.

But Gorbachev cut a forlorn figure. His authority had dwindled and virtually disappeared. He had been completely eclipsed by Yeltsin. He was being humiliated and ridiculed. He had in many ways failed to understand the new mood in Moscow, and seemed rooted in a way of thinking and acting which had been substantively swept away when the coup crumbled. He was yesterday's man. The party was over. And Gorbachev was a king without a kingdom. It all seemed a very long way from the fanfares of the choreographed coronation of March 1985.

The requiems for Gorbachev did not really begin to be written until the end of 1991 and the start of 1992, just after his resignation as Soviet President on 25 December 1991. Soviet commentators, journalists and colleagues wrote some immediate appraisals of Gorbachev and his era, although much of it was overshadowed by the ongoing investigation into the August coup events. In the interim period of September there were one or two interesting articles, some appraisals of Gorbachev and interviews with those close to Gorbachev. *Moskovskiye Novosti* published a report from the Chinese Communist Party which slated Gorbachev as the 'restorer of capitalism' and approved of the attempted coup.[157] In the same month, *Dialog* included an interview with Georgii Shakhnazarov, one of Gorbachev's closest advisers and one the 'brains trust' responsible for many of the key ideas and policies of *perestroika*. In response to questions about Gorbachev, Shakhnazarov said that he had not been particularly difficult to work with, but that working with him was 'interesting'. He also denied that he was responsible for the August events. Shakhnazarov reiterated that the dominant ideas in Gorbachev's thinking were those of legitimacy and legality.[158]

But far and away the most interesting appraisal came from Leonid Gozman.[159] Gozman wrote an overview of Gorbachev's time in power and contrasted the divergent opinions of Gorbachev. Was he an angel or a demon? A reformer or an adventurist? He identified a 'romantic' view of Gorbachev, and a 'demonic' view of Gorbachev. The 'romantic' view saw Gorbachev as a closet reformer who kept his powder dry when rising up through the hierarchy, but unleashed a war on the totalitarian system when he became General Secretary. The 'demonic' view saw him as a man dedicated to maximizing his own personal power. Gozman's view was that there was an inner conflict within Gorbachev: in political terms he was something of a reformer, but in his personality he was 'deeply authoritarian'.[160] Gozman saw Gorbachev's personality as a key problem explaining his downfall. His many mistakes – notably his dealings with Yeltsin – were derived from his character flaws. His authoritarian personality made it nigh on impossible for Gorbachev to develop constructive working relations with the independent intelligentsia. The key moment for Gozman came at the end of the summer of 1990, when Gorbachev had the opportunity to change his authoritarian standpoint, embrace the democrats and reinvent himself as something of a Perez de Cuellhar-type figure. Or he could have left the democrats and thrown in his lot with the authoritarians. In the end his dogmatism and his blindness to the people around him created the possibility for a putsch. Gozman looked forward to reading Gorbachev's account of his time in power, of the man who had overseen the end of communism.[161]

Gorbachev's resignation saw a brief flurry of verdicts on Gorbachev in the Soviet press at the end of December 1991 and the start of January 1992. Inna Muravyova, writing in *Rossiiskaya gazeta,* outlined a fairly positive, almost wistful reflection. Gorbachev's era had seen 'fear depart'. She went on to note:

> So, what has Gorbachev left us? From his adversaries' viewpoint a broken power that used to be called the Soviet Union; unchecked inflation, beggars on the streets ... but on the other hand we have the name of Andrei Sakharov and the recovery of our sight.[162]

Vitaly Tretyakov (the editor-in-chief of *Nezavisimaya gazeta*) called him the 'greatest reformer of the twentieth century'.[163] The problem for Tretyakov was that Gorbachev's triumphs were achieved at the expense of defeats and problems at home.

He concluded by saying: 'This is his chief tragedy and his chief triumph – he did not become a national hero, he became an international hero.'[164] For Vitaly Portnikov, Gorbachev was undermined by his obsession with the idea of preservation, but in the end undone by the multinational nature of the USSR, which he never understood and did not know how to handle.[165]

We will leave the last word to Fedor Burlatsky, a reformist journalist, and supportive but not uncritical commentator and adviser to Gorbachev.[166] In his 'report card', Burlatsky identified the following positive aspects:

- a talented, kind and pliable man;
- destroyed the nuclear monster that terrorized people and oppressed the peoples of the USSR;
- the first true parliamentary leader in Russian history;
- he created an opposition;
- he embraced modernity.

On the negative side, Burlatsky noted:

- He left without having completed his mission.
- He was unable to wield power when it was absolutely necessary to do so.
- He was born to be a prophet, not a leader.
- Gorbachev was essentially a creative person, but his main historic task was the destroyer of the old system.
- Gorbachev's whole programme looked like a massive improvization.[167]

Burlatsky argued that the reasons for Gorbachev's ultimate failure to see it through to the end were his ideological prejudices and his character flaws. His ideological prejudices were his unwillingness to give up socialism and the USSR and to embrace private ownership, the market and entrepreneurialism. The biggest problem, like Gozman, was Gorbachev's character. His flaws, for Burlatsky, included:

- He always moved forward while facing backward.
- He was afraid of taking risks.
- He was too soft, kind and indecisive, avoiding action when decisive measures were needed.
- He was unable to get the measure of people.
- He was unable to negotiate the labyrinth of opinions with which he was surrounded.

He concluded:

> Gorbachev can blame his downfall on no-one … A good woodcutter he methodically cut off the roots that held his power … Gorbachev is going into retirement, overwhelmed by the Scylla and Charybdis of 'right-wing' and 'left-wing' currents. But regardless of his future activity, he has already gone down in history. And he has done so as a true reformer. His mistakes will seem less and less noticeable, and the work he began will

assume greater and greater significance as the country progresses towards modern civilization.[168]

The Gorbachev era was over.

Conclusion

It was a long six years for a Soviet leader. It was an amazing journey for the Soviet people. The ideologically constructed, carefully airbrushed, minutely sculpted official image of the Soviet leader – wise, ideologically pure, internationalist, fighter for peace and justice, friend of the people, party man, slayer of oppression – yielded inch by inch to an embattled leader, besieged on all sides by a chorus of critical voices and opinions. Why did this death by a thousand cuttings occur?

The initiative for this shift clearly lies with Gorbachev himself. A bit like the Velveteen Rabbit, Gorbachev wished to become 'real', not to exist in the highly mythologized, propaganda-fuelled world of the traditional CPSU General Secretary. He wished to end the sycophancy and idolatry, to tone down the rhetoric surrounding him, to become more accessible. Unfortunately, unlike the Velveteen Rabbit who became real when he was loved, Gorbachev quickly found out that the more realistic tone of reporting and the pluralism of opinions did not always produce loving endorsements. Gorbachev was undone largely by his own initiatives in this regard, by the perils of loosening the ties that bound the system together. As the solo performance became an ensemble, so the variety of voices increased, became more confident and more intense.

If Gorbachev was the initiator of the end of the monologue, then other people were crucial in accelerating it. If we could change the analogy for a moment, Gorbachev's flight of Icarus was caught between the choppy waters of Nina Andreeva and the sunny heat of Boris Yeltsin. Embodied in these two very different individuals was the essential dilemma of trying to escape the prison of one's past. Andreeva spoke of the dangers of change. Yeltsin spoke of the need for faster, more radical change. In the end Gorbachev flew too close to the sun, and his wings fell off spectacularly, rather like Icarus, in fact. Once it had been established that other views and opinions were legitimate, the floodgates were open. The multinational nature of the Soviet Union immediately provided a cacophony of voices. The televising of the debates in the Congress of People's Deputies brought a new phenomenon into the homes of the Soviet people: public disagreements and disputes. The freer press began to hold Gorbachev more responsible and accountable. Having started it, the process developed a momentum all of its own, one Gorbachev tried, but failed, to control.

What picture emerges of Gorbachev from the East? The geography is important here. The Western celebration of Gorbachev was in the main drawn from his foreign activities. Unlike the Western press, which highlighted Gorbachev's international activities, the Soviet press concentrated on the domestic side, and so it was increasingly a story of difficulties and obstacles as 1989 gave way to 1990 and beyond. There is an interesting comparison to be drawn here with Ronald Reagan, who remained relatively popular at home but was increasingly criticized by the foreign press abroad. As we saw, Gorbachev benefited abroad because he compared favourably with the existing Western leaders. At home, though, Gorbachev had almost the diametrically opposite experience. But it is rather simplistic to suggest that Gorbachev was deeply unpopular and pilloried at home in contrast with his reception abroad. His treatment at home was an inexorable part of the normalization of Soviet politics, the unravelling of the Union and the hectic pace and scale of political change, as the monologue became a dialogue. The newly found ability to criticize their leader was an opportunity not to be missed, and the chaotic circumstances of *perestroika* gave people much to speak and grumble about. He was the establishment figure. He was the one calling the shots. It is vital to place the criticisms of Gorbachev in the contexts of both the rapid collapse of the choreographed image and the problems and perils of the new political situation that Gorbachev himself had created. On the surface it seems as though Gorbachev slipped very quickly from a beacon of hope to an embattled, unpopular, lonely figure. In reality, though, he had become something like a 'normal' politician.

But perhaps what was most distinctive about the Soviet perspectives on their leader was that for the first time they were able to see their leader close up, to view him as an individual, to perceive his character, to note his choice of advisers, to debate his decisions, to read about his mistakes, to conceive of alternatives. In the end, Gorbachev got what he wanted. He had become a 'real' leader. The irony was that he wasn't the leader they wanted.

5

Gorbachev remembered

The personality conundrum

Introduction

Ten years is a very long time in the life span of an historical reputation. In 1991, Gorbachev was departing the stage of history. His period in office was over, and Boris Yeltsin was moving into the limelight. The legacy of the coup seemed to be hanging around him, and it appeared that, like Khrushchev before him, he might well shuffle away into retirement and semi-obscurity. By March 2001, however, Russian newspapers were celebrating Gorbachev's 70th birthday with garlands of flowers and tributes, fond recollections and letters of thanks from grateful Russians. In the intervening period, Gorbachev was the focus of a series of reminiscences: from fellow political leaders, ambassadors, colleagues, assistants, advisers, rivals, journalists and the like. Out of these pages emerge many revelations, many insights, some vitriol and some praise.

The memoirs offer a means of exploring one of the central conundrums of Gorbachev: the question of his personality, character, values, beliefs and leadership style as perceived by those closest to him: rivals and supporters, colleagues and aides, friends and enemies. In any assessment of Gorbachev's time in power, his conduct and leadership are often remarked upon in explaining both his remarkable achievements, but also his failures and his eventual fall from power. It is also a frequent observation that Gorbachev was an intensely private man, who gave little clues to his inner nature. As has been noted by many commentators, given the extraordinary power wielded by any General Secretary (even given the opposition and resistance that there was to change in the Soviet system) the question of the new leader's personality and values is inevitably an important one.[1] Gorbachev's personality is crucial in understanding the way in which he exercised power, the qualities he looked for in making appointments, his reactions to criticism and his ability to act decisively, to compromise, to take advice, to learn from others. Given the close connection between Gorbachev and his reform project, the personalized way in which Gorbachev exercised power, and the enormous influence Gorbachev exerted over domestic Soviet developments and global diplomacy after 1985, insights into Gorbachev's personality are significant pieces of evidence in understanding the Gorbachev phenomenon.

Although there are many problems with memoir literature, with careful handling they can be a very useful source. Indeed, when we are looking for insights into the personality and character of a key historical figure, memoirs offer us things that cannot be gleaned elsewhere. Many of these memoir accounts are perceptive and balanced, insightful and interesting. Others are bilious, inaccurate and unreliable, telling us more about the memoirist than Gorbachev. The very nature of the memoir as a source tends to focus upon the *dramatis personae* and the personalities involved, often to the detriment of broader political and historical questions, such as the origins and course of *perestroika*, for instance. But if we narrow our focus to questions relating to Gorbachev's personality, then the memoirs do provide fertile ground. The opening section explores the Western view through selected prominent Western politicians who were contemporaries of Gorbachev, as well as the British and US ambassadors in Moscow, Rodric Braithwaite and Jack F. Matlock Jr. The second half explores the Russian/Soviet dimension, drawing on a range of perspectives, both positive and critical, reputation affirming and reputation destroying. The chapter concludes with a glimpse of the 70th birthday celebrations.

The view from the West I: how the Cold War was won

The memoirs of Gorbachev's Western contemporary political leaders – for instance, Margaret Thatcher, Ronald Reagan, John Major, Geoffrey Howe, George Shultz, James A. Baker – were primarily concerned to establish their own role in the major events of this era: the end of the Cold War and the collapse of communism in Eastern Europe and the Soviet Union. They were also bent on establishing their own reputations as fearless defenders of freedom and the market, of the individual and of capitalism. In many ways, Gorbachev appears as an historical adjunct to their own triumphs and achievements, although most recognize the positive contribution of Gorbachev to their epoch.

New insights on Gorbachev are few and far between. More often, these recollections merely confirmed existing views, or provided further evidence to substantiate what we already knew. What these memoirs most clearly communicated was some of the human qualities of Gorbachev the person and Gorbachev the leader, as well as some of the personal weaknesses and failings he displayed. Little was said of his trials and tribulations at home, except insofar as it impinged upon the superpower rivalry. The feature most often commented upon was his working style and approach, which contrasted so markedly with that of his predecessors. His openness, his eagerness to debate, his spontaneity and willingness to depart from the script and to operate without briefing notes were all seen as remarkable departures from the grey Soviet apparatchik norm. He was described variously as energetic, a good listener, humorous, frank, feisty, confident, exceptionally sensitive, charismatic and exuding optimism.[2] For Reagan, they developed something close to friendship.[3] His relative lack of dogmatism – particularly with regard to the use of Marxist-Leninist slogans – could not disguise that, for both Reagan and Thatcher, Gorbachev was a true believer in communism and a Soviet patriot. Reagan believed that the motivation behind Gorbachev's reforms was that communism was not working.[4] These remarks would seem to confirm the viewpoint that Gorbachev was a genuine believer in socialism Soviet-style, but was not the old-style dogmatist. He was willing to experiment in order to find something that would make the system work.

Aside from these positive personality traits, Gorbachev's strengths were deemed to be his hard bargaining,[5] his wily way of manipulating Western public opinion in pursuit of his wider goals, and his detailed personal grasp of complex issues. Gorbachev also had an almost unquenchable curiosity about life in the West, remarking to Geoffrey Howe about the diversity of village shops in rural England. Gorbachev often reminisced about his time growing up in the countryside in his discussions with Soviet citizens. This curiosity also reflects someone with an abiding personal interest in the way that things were done differently elsewhere, and the lessons that might be learned that could be applied in the USSR.

Margaret Thatcher drew an interesting comparison between Gorbachev and F. W. de Klerk, who oversaw the dismantling of the apartheid regime in South Africa. Both had a combination of vision and prudence in their respective attempts to change their systems. Denis Healey was particularly positive about Gorbachev, noting him to be one of the first world leaders to take the ecological issue seriously.[6] This seems to confirm those views which saw Gorbachev as a genuine convert to New Political Thinking who was concerned with the common threats to human survival: nuclear and ecological.

Recollections of incidental episodes do corroborate to a degree our understanding of Gorbachev's own values and beliefs. There is a passage in George Shultz's memoirs where Shultz describes how he himself had spoken of the social and political adaptations needed to respond to the new scientific and technological developments. Gorbachev retorted by arguing that Shultz should take over the running of Gosplan, as he had more ideas than they did! This reiterates Gorbachev's views about the inflexibility of the Soviet economy and of the importance of modernization encompassing more than just the economic structures.[7] In a similar debate with James Baker, Gorbachev is said to have been irritated by the American's constant use of the term 'western values'. Gorbachev argued that the term 'western' implied that reformers in the USSR had not embraced or subscribed to some of these values, whereas they had. This aside reaffirms that Gorbachev was indeed a convert to the primacy of universal human values over the class-based model.[8]

But weaknesses and problems in Gorbachev the person and Gorbachev the leader also came through. A common criticism was that Gorbachev appeared to have been poorly informed about life in the West, and in particular seemed to have been captive to rather outdated and stereotypical propaganda about the West, especially Western economic forms and practices. Indeed, Gorbachev's lack of economic expertise was highlighted by John Major:

Gorbachev was schooled in tales of dark satanic mills, and expounded a very Victorian image of private ownership. His understanding of privatisation was negligible: he seemed to believe it was no more than a benevolent state selling a company to a profiteering private owner who would worsen the service and increase the price.[9] He had no concept of the free market, and the merits of competition were alien to him.[10]

Other weaknesses were also identified. He was said, by more than one observer, to be exceptionally sensitive to criticism, particularly in the exchanges over human rights during superpower negotiations. He was said to have been overconfident to the point of cockiness and arrogance at times. He was susceptible to being excessively verbose.[11] Gorbachev's preoccupation with the media and his image was also remarked upon. Geoffrey Howe related that his visit to Britain in December 1984 before coming to power had been organized not 'to negotiate but to explore and to project himself (and the Soviet case) in a new light – as much to his domestic audience as to the world'.[12] James Baker noted that he avidly devoured translations of Western press reports about him, and on visits to the West expended great efforts playing to the crowds.[13] Major and Thatcher both thought that Gorbachev had shown great courage, but had been unable to throw off fully the communist mind-set, unlike his nemesis Boris Yeltsin.[14]

The overall assessment of Gorbachev was, of course, overwhelmingly positive. He had transformed Russia and the international environment. He had shown great courage. James Baker remarked, 'I felt Gorbachev was a true historic figure, perhaps responsible for transforming the world as we'd known it.'[15] But the mystery of Gorbachev still remained for Denis Healey, who posed the question, 'When Gorbachev finally flew home he left me puzzling over a mystery I still find insoluble: how could so nice a man have risen to the top in the Soviet system?'[16]

The view from the West II (in Moscow): the ambassadorial perspective

More detailed perspectives have been supplied by the US and British ambassadors in Moscow during the *perestroika* era, Jack Matlock and Rodric Braithwaite.[17] Their recollections are an interesting combination of close observation and relative detachment from the object of their remembering. In addition, as they have not been involved in the post-communist era of Russian politics, the ambassadorial perspectives have not been shaped by the political imperatives of the present as many of the Russian memoirs. But significant differences in the picture of Gorbachev emerge from the pages of the memoirs of the two ambassadors.

Matlock's Gorbachev

The story told by Matlock (who enjoyed a closer relationship to Gorbachev than Braithwaite) is a narrative dominated by the personalities of the key protagonists, most notably Gorbachev and Yeltsin. Matlock offers an insightful appraisal of

Gorbachev's leadership and legacy, which although fairly positive, identifies the source of Gorbachev's failings as lying in his character and judgement.

In terms of Gorbachev's leadership style, Matlock identified Gorbachev as an articulate and lucid figure, quick in debates but somewhat defensive in tone at times. He was an adroit manipulator of situations and flexible enough to change tack, compromise and manoeuvre. He was quick to learn from his mistakes.[18] But Gorbachev's leadership was undermined by his penchant for the pomp and ceremony of power, and by the need for adoration from the public, which increasingly came only during his visits overseas. The other problem which dogged his leadership was his inability to handle criticism. As the problems mounted, it became a 'if you're not for me, you're against me' style of leadership. He became irritated when criticized, and through 1989 and 1990 came to see criticism from the radicals as a sign of betrayal. Vacillation from one camp to the other inevitably resulted in the winter of 1990, and Gorbachev became a prisoner of events, reacting to, not shaping, circumstances.[19]

Overwhelmingly, it was the Yeltsin affair that showed the true mettle of Gorbachev's leadership. Matlock argues that envy of Yeltsin – envy of his popularity – blinded Gorbachev's judgement. He looked upon charismatic popular colleagues as rivals and competitors. This led him to ostracize Yeltsin (who should have been incorporated into the inner sanctum) and also to appoint mediocre people to positions around him, figures who could not compete with Gorbachev. Gorbachev's arrogance and lack of judgement in personnel issues were crucial for Matlock in explaining Gorbachev's failures as a leader.[20]

Matlock's major criticism was that Gorbachev had no overarching strategic vision, and no real sense of where he was going. His ultimate failure to transform the Soviet Union was partially due to the complexity of the task itself, but also due to his own character failings. First, Matlock asserts that Gorbachev was an intensely private person which 'made it difficult for him to develop effective consultative and advisory bodies'.[21] He talked to his advisers rather than listening and never used them consistently and regularly. He had no close friends – apart from his wife – and seemed more at home with foreign dignitaries than with senior Soviet figures. This seriously hindered the quality of advice he was receiving. Second, Gorbachev's preference for surrounding himself with nonentities brought weaklings and mediocrities into the government, making it an ineffective organ. Moreover his misplaced trust in the people he appointed had catastrophic consequences for Gorbachev. In Lithuania it was clear that he was being deliberately misinformed, and had lost control of the armed forces. In sum, 'I am convinced that Russia will eventually regard Mikhail Gorbachev as the person who led it out of bondage. The fact that he was unable to reach the Promised Land is secondary.'[22]

Braithwaite's Gorbachev

Braithwaite paints a different picture of Gorbachev the person, and gives a much more positive appraisal of Gorbachev the leader. Writing ten years after Gorbachev left office, Braithwaite counters many (but not all) of the criticisms directed at Gorbachev, and on balance has contributed to the ongoing rehabilitation of his reputation since 1999. Perhaps the greater distance from the events he describes, as well as the current travails of Russia, have contributed to this assessment.

Braithwaite concurs with Matlock on many points regarding Gorbachev's personality and character. He describes Gorbachev as quick-witted, ebullient, charismatic, direct and open. He had a powerful memory, was sophisticated and flexible in his approach to complex problems and loved to debate. He was an intensely private man, heavily reliant on his wife. He quotes Sobchak, who argued that 'anyone who believed they knew what Gorbachev was thinking was mistaken'.[23] His openness was a mask to disguise his essentially private nature. He was ambitious, energetic, cunning and vain (like other politicians) and became increasingly long-winded in his public utterances. This, for Braithwaite, became one of his major weaknesses. His lack of rhetorical skills irritated people and he failed in his addresses to inspire people to self-sacrifice.[24]

In appraising his leadership style, Braithwaite differs from Matlock in important respects. Braithwaite notes that Gorbachev did not surround himself with inferior figures because he could not cope with talented colleagues. He argues that he always had men of stature and talent around him.[25] Second, Braithwaite refuses to accept that Gorbachev was a vacillating weak leader who did not have the strength to take unpopular decisions. Braithwaite sees Gorbachev's unwillingness to take hard-line measures not as a sign of weakness, but as a sign of strength: he was committed to democratic change, to breaking the mould of Soviet/Russian authoritarian leadership and was willing to act in unorthodox ways. Third, Braithwaite argues it was a gross oversimplification to see Gorbachev as reactionary and Yeltsin as democrat. They both favoured reform and democracy, but differed over tactics. Gorbachev was a gradualist; Yeltsin an advocate of radical, urgent change. Gorbachev had a conscious strategy, whereas Yeltsin was much more of an instinctive politician.[26]

Overall, Braithwaite sees Gorbachev as having wrought a remarkable transformation up until 1990. From 1990, Gorbachev began to lag behind events. Although he made mistakes – too many compromises, too much talk and too little action – Gorbachev has not deserved the highly critical press he has endured in his own country. He should be remembered for destroying the Soviet system, taking the first steps in the transformation of Russia into a democratic state and for breaking the impasse in foreign relations to end the Cold War. In a poignant final sentence, Braithwaite remarks, 'The last General Secretary of the CPSU was not only a major historical figure. He was also a genuinely nice man.'[27]

What is interesting about these two views is the common ground they both share about Gorbachev's strengths and weaknesses. His overly 'wordy' political style, his private, rather 'closed' personality and his sensitivity to criticism were all remarked upon. They also remarked upon a certain arrogant air in his dealings with others. On the other hand, they both admired and liked him as a person, and were impressed by the considerable legacy of achievements he left behind him.

However, in two areas they identified some differences of opinion. The first was in the area of relationships. Did he surround himself with nonentities? Was he anxious to keep charismatic rivals at arm's length? It is rather dismissive of Matlock to label all Gorbachev's appointees as nonentities or mediocrities. Clearly there were talented people in his immediate entourage. However, Gorbachev's relationship with those around him and how this evolved is quite important. Gorbachev tended to surround himself increasingly with like-minded individuals, with people who were increasingly less likely to criticize or contest his decisions. This tendency was exacerbated by the close relationship he had with his wife and his seeming unwillingness to include many people in his inner sanctum.

In fact, this is only really a superficial difference of opinion, for both ambassadors are talking about two aspects of the same issue. Gorbachev's sense of certainty in himself, his decisions, his judgements, his policies. These two things – his intensely private nature and this deep inner conviction about himself – produced a working style which tended to be dismissive of criticism (or tended to personalize criticism). It also mitigated against producing robust structures of decision-making, consultation and discussion which clearly contributed to Gorbachev's growing isolation, as well as undermining effective working relationships.

The second element they disagreed over was Gorbachev's leadership style. One perception was that Gorbachev was a weak leader who did not have the strength to take unpopular decisions. He was not only intoxicated with trappings of power, but actively sought out the adoration of the crowd. This was contested by Braithwaite, who saw in Gorbachev's style an essential strength, in his willingness to act democratically rather than autocratically. So, in what follows we will try to examine these two questions – Gorbachev's personality and relationships, and also his leadership style – to see if we can shed any more light on the somewhat enigmatic character of Gorbachev the man. To do this we will take a selection of accounts from those who worked most closely with him.

The Russian view: Gorbachev on trial

A succession of accounts emerged in Russia in the period between 1991 and 1995 (prior to Gorbachev's own memoirs). Other accounts have subsequently been published but most appeared in the initial flurry after the collapse of communism. Most of these accounts were written about the latter years of *perestroika*, and indeed tended to focus upon the events leading to the coup and the demise of the Soviet Union. The purpose of these accounts was not merely to describe the great events of the *perestroika* years, but for each of those involved in some way to tell their story, to exonerate themselves, justify their decisions, to explain why it all went wrong/was a resounding triumph. In these accounts, Gorbachev stands tall as the main character: either as an heroic figure, or as the villain of the piece.

In the section below, the memoirs of some of Gorbachev's key contemporaries – advisers, assistants, colleagues, rivals, journalists – will be set out. Particular accounts have been selected to illustrate the diverse ways in which Gorbachev has been remembered and interpreted.[28] The divisions are not always neat and clear-cut; some were both political colleagues and personal advisers, or changed their roles. But to open up, let's begin by comparing two ends of the spectrum: Raisa and Boris.

The spouse's story: Raisa's I Hope

Raisa's book is not strictly a post-soviet, post-power set of reminiscences. It was compiled in the spring and summer of 1991. It took the form of an interview between Raisa and Georgi Pryakhin, a journalist who was known to the family and who also hailed from Stavropol. Her recollections and reflections were fairly unstructured and followed a loose chronological pattern, starting with her childhood in Siberia up to her experiences as first lady after 1985. Although an intensely personal account, Raisa was keen to make some key points to rebut criticisms of both her and her husband. At the time of writing – the summer of 1991 – Gorbachev's stock was very low and Raisa's book must be seen as a part of the attempt to restore his image both at home and abroad and so bolster his crumbling authority.

Her story confirmed many things that we already knew about Gorbachev, but also revealed some interesting snippets in passing. At the outset, Raisa repeats the story about the conversation in the garden the night before Gorbachev took over, highlighting the phrase 'we just cannot go on living like this'. She attributes her much higher profile as first lady (in comparison to previous Soviet leaders' wives) as evidence of the processes of liberalization at work after 1985. Clearly the accusations of vanity and self-promotion had had an impact. Her observations on the character of Gorbachev – intelligent, reliable, friendly, loved and respected people as individuals and a man of strong opinions who defends them vigorously – although unsurprisingly glowing, do indicate a genuine sense of closeness and admiration between the two.

Probably the most interesting sections are those dealing with their life at university and later on in Stavropol. Raisa's fundamental line was that Gorbachev's progression through the system to become the radical reformer of *perestroika, glasnost'* and New Political Thinking after 1985 were born out of the conjunction between Gorbachev's personality and character, on the one hand, and his experiences of living and working in the Soviet provinces, on the other. In other words, Gorbachev's outlook was formed out of a journey, learning first-hand what the problems in the system were and seeking solutions to them. From Raisa we learn that Gorbachev spent only about ten days in the Prosecutor's office in Stavropol, before transferring to the Komsomol, which was the beginning of his journey through the Soviet party hierarchy. In an extract from one of his letters apparently written to her while he was working in Stavropol in June 1953, Gorbachev outlines his disillusionment with the exercise of power in the Soviet provinces:

I am so depressed by the situation here ... one feels all the more keenly how disgusting my surroundings are. Especially the manner of life of the local bosses. The acceptance of convention, subordination, with everything predetermined, the open impudence of officials and the arrogance. When you look at one of the local bosses you see nothing outstanding apart from his belly. But what aplomb, what self assurance and the condescending, patronising tone![29]

This quote highlights a key theme which emerges from the pages of Raisa's book: namely that Gorbachev's personality and working style stood in marked contrast to that of your traditional Soviet apparatchik. Whereas the apparatchik stood for convention, Gorbachev was an innovator. Where the apparatchik preferred secrecy, Gorbachev wanted things in the open. Instead of patronizing the people, Gorbachev preferred discussion and genuine dialogue with the people. Gorbachev's time as party boss in Stavropol saw, in Raisa's words,

> An improvement in the moral atmosphere ... a new and more dynamic spirit ... a spirit and style characteristic of Mikhail Sergeevich – frankness, close contact with the people, the ability to listen and respect other people's opinion, and not to keep down the person working next to you, but rather to encourage and support him.[30]

The portrait of Gorbachev painted by his wife is distinguished by two key elements. Gorbachev became a radical reformer as a result of the clash between his style and personality, on the one hand, and the experience of governing and running the system, on the other. In other words, Gorbachev's personal qualities disposed him in the direction of someone who was unwilling to put up with the status quo. Gorbachev's working and living experiences sharpened these impressions and eventually gave him the opportunity to put them into practice.

In conclusion, Raisa made three very interesting observations about Mikhail. First, she tried to counter the widespread perception that Gorbachev was indecisive. She argued very strongly that Gorbachev was always willing to listen to others, tolerant of others, willing to absorb the ideas of others and consider them carefully before acting. She realized that this could be construed as a sign of weakness or indecision, but rejects this conclusion categorically. It was all part of his style of working with people. Second, she reiterated that Gorbachev had a profound sense of the importance of treating all people with dignity and respect, '[N]ever in his life has he humiliated people next to him so as to make himself taller. Never.'[31] Finally, Raisa also highlighted something that Gorbachev himself stressed: the sense that his project was as much a matter of faith as anything else. What sustained Gorbachev after 1985 was, according to Raisa, 'his faith in the correctness of the path he had chosen, and the aim he had set himself'.[32] This strong sense of inner belief and of faith in the correctness of his chosen path comes across very strongly, and adds to the impression that Gorbachev persisted in believing that it was in some sense his 'destiny' to carry out *perestroika*.

The rival's story: Boris Yeltsin

The other prominent figure in the memoir accounts of the *perestroika* years was Boris Yeltsin. Yeltsin rose to become Gorbachev's rival and nemesis, eventually ousting him from power and becoming the President of Russia until his retirement in 2000. Yeltsin's story was written in a number of stages over a period of ten years. In 1990, his book *Against the Grain*[33] (written just before he became President of Russia) was published. In 1994, in the middle of his presidency *The View from the Kremlin* was published. Finally in 2000, after his resignation, *Midnight Diaries* were brought out. What picture of Gorbachev emerges from these pages?

Yeltsin's story concentrates on highlighting the weaknesses and failings of Gorbachev, for obvious reasons. In his first volume, written while Gorbachev was still in power, Yeltsin charts Gorbachev's failings to illustrate the gulf between the two of them, and to maintain the image of Gorbachev as still essentially a communist establishment man, and Yeltsin as the outspoken, decisive, maverick man of the people. It is not entirely negative. He commends Gorbachev for having the courage to initiate change. When he began in 1985, Yeltsin says that Gorbachev was open, sincere and frank and worked with great finesse. But after 1987 (and his bust-up with Yeltsin), Gorbachev began to go awry.[34] He outlines a number of points.

First, Gorbachev became intoxicated with power and its trappings. He grew to love the privileges, the dachas, the perquisites and this disparity between his lifestyle and that of the masses destroyed the faith of the people in *perestroika* and its custodians. He also became more autocratic and domineering in his leadership: more monologues, less dialogue, less discussion. He began to lose touch with reality.[35] On his walkabouts people were bussed in to create modern-day 'Potemkin villages'. Gorbachev knew it. The people knew it. Yet everyone played the game and pretended that it was all going swimmingly. Gorbachev was very concerned with his image, and created two high-profile figures: Ligachev (the conservative villain) and Yeltsin (the bully-boy radical). Gorbachev sought to portray himself as the omniscient, wide voice of reason between these two poles. In other words, Yeltsin argued that Gorbachev needed a Yeltsin figure.[36]

Second, Gorbachev was criticized for being indecisive, and for having no idea where he was going when he embarked on *perestroika*. He entitled him the 'lover of half-measures and half-steps'. He was said to have a fear of taking decisive measures, and had not properly thought through his reforms. He had no systematic long-term plan. He did not achieve anything concrete. Essentially, he did not wish to touch the party machine and its privileges.[37]

In the second tome of his memoirs, Yeltsin reflects on the latter years of Gorbachev, on his oscillations between left and right and on his decline and fall. Gorbachev emerges in 1990 and 1991 as a very weary figure, drained of energy, unable to cope with the extremely polarized political conditions. Yeltsin argues that Gorbachev's preferred political style – all compromise, intrigue, diplomacy, cunning – was an oriental style of rule. He was entirely unsuited to the role of strong man which he was attempting to play. His double-dealing had run out of steam, as by the spring of 1991 he had to make a choice between left and right, and he always pulled back from destroying the essence of the Soviet system to which he remained committed. The final twist of Yeltsin's knife came when he disclosed that in his resignation settlement, Gorbachev's demands were almost all 'material'.[38]

The final volume of the Yeltsin memoirs, covering the period after 1994, has relatively little to say about Gorbachev, apart from a passage near the end which outlined how Yeltsin had treated Gorbachev when he resigned. Yeltsin was trying to make the point that it was his humane and enlightened treatment of Gorbachev in 1991 that enabled a 'normal' process for Presidents to retire and not fear for their safety, security or liberty. This precedent had provided the basis for his own retirement in 1999. Yeltsin also noted that, in spite of Gorbachev's continual sniping at him, he had retained his dignity, and had been able to be partially reconciled to him after the death of Raisa. The death of Raisa, says Yeltsin, has been responsible for a change of public mood towards Gorbachev. Instead of blaming him for all the problems and crises in the Russian economy, the people now viewed him with sympathy and understanding.[39]

So once again we come across this stark dichotomy of views on Gorbachev: a good listener who respected people or an autocrat who liked the sound of his own voice? An indecisive leader who was blown this way and that, or a democrat who listened and considered before acting? A man driven by material and personal gain and vanity, or a man motivated by selfless devotion and a sense of destiny for the role that history had allotted him? To answer these questions let us turn to examine the views of those who worked most closely with him, those who sit between Raisa and Boris on the spectrum of opinion.

The colleagues' view: Ligachev, Ryzhkov, Shevardnadze

The most prominent Communist Party figures who worked most closely with Gorbachev at the summit of the system were Yegor Ligachev, Nikolai Ryzhkov and Eduard Shevardnadze. All three were members of the Politburo under Gorbachev. Ligachev was the number two to Gorbachev in the early stages of *perestroika*, but after 1988 was increasingly marginalized from the political stage as he criticized the speed and direction of the reforms. He became the *éminence grise* of Soviet conservatism. Ryzhkov was Gorbachev's Prime Minister, and was responsible for the implementation of his policies, most notably his economic reforms. Shevardnadze was Gorbachev's Foreign Minister and became a member of Gorbachev's Presidential Council in 1990. He resigned very abruptly in December 1990. These three have been chosen for the variety of perspectives from which they approach Gorbachev.

Ligachev's book devoted itself to an attempt to explain why *perestroika* and Gorbachev, after a promising start, were blown off course and ended up in the demise of the Soviet Union and the collapse of the Communist Party. It was started in 1990, and completed prior to Gorbachev's final resignation in December 1991.[40] It was published the following year. It focuses almost exclusively on the leadership, and Gorbachev in particular, and describes how Gorbachev became ensnared in the grip of the radicals and radical reforms, much to the ire and dismay of Ligachev, who believed the Soviet system was reformable.

Ligachev's description of Gorbachev stresses two things. First, Gorbachev was far more concerned with the ephemeral and the intellectual aspects of the job of leader than the practical work of actually running the country. In particular, Ligachev highlights how Gorbachev became increasingly attracted to the role of an 'enlightened monarch', rather than an active, problem-solving politician dealing with the problems that were accumulating. He surrounded himself with academics and intellectuals, rather than practical workers and gradually became more divorced from the day-to-day realities of running the country. He failed to ensure that political decisions were implemented. A further aspect of the 'enlightened monarch' syndrome was an excessive concern with his image and historical reputation. He met regularly with the media – but only to harangue and bully them about their output and to make sure the Gorbachev line was followed.[41] Ligachev goes on to say:

> I remember someone once saying to me about Gorbachev, 'Mikhail Sergeevich is a President who wants to go down in history as a clean man, whom no one can accuse of dictatorship.' Perhaps this concern about his 'historical image' did sometimes keep Gorbachev from taking decisive, necessary, but unpopular measures.[42]

This concern with his image and his political reputation also, for Ligachev, fed into the style of leadership of Gorbachev. Gorbachev zig-zagged constantly because he was fearful of the Khrushchev syndrome: the fear of being removed from power by opponents within the party. This led him into alliances with different groups, compromises to keep people happy and an aversion to taking unpopular decisions. Gorbachev often manoeuvred between mutually contradictory positions instead of taking a decisive stand. In addition, Gorbachev always waited before intervening, almost until it was too late according to Ligachev. This was partly because he preferred being late to being wrong (better for your reputation), and also because stepping in at the last minute allowed him to adopt the role of saviour, emerging at the last moment to avert a catastrophe.[43]

The second theme stressed how Gorbachev was taken hostage by the radicals, and in particular Aleksander Yakovlev who emerges as the *bête noire* of Ligachev's story. Gorbachev was increasingly under the influence of Yakovlev, who installed his own people in influential positions and this led to the peripheralization of Ligachev. He argues that the radicals stepped up their influence after the 1988 Party Conference which was the start of the decline which led to the break-up of the Soviet Union and the victory of the forces of nationalism and separatism. Ligachev is clear that the radicals had captured Gorbachev.

> It sometimes seemed to me that Gorbachev was being forced to rush at breakneck speed so that all his strength would go to preventing an imminent catastrophe. Gorbachev proved himself to be a virtuoso driver of the locomotive of *perestroika*. But at the speed at which he had to tear along, he could not foresee the future with any degree of sagacity.[44]

Moderates, gradualists and 'conservatives' were excluded and vilified in the press. Ligachev, and then Ryzhkov, were removed, and Gorbachev failed to defend them. The original conception of *perestroika* was dead. Ligachev ends by saying that the historical jury on Gorbachev has not yet pronounced its verdict.

Nikolai Ryzhkov's memoir follows a similar theme. Published in 1992 and entitled *Perestroika: History of Betrayal,* he recounts his gradual estrangement from Gorbachev in the period after 1989 as the search continued for a radical solution to the economic chaos engulfing the system.[45] Ryzhkov describes how they collaborated under Andropov in searching for new ideas and in seeking out advice from experts.[46] He argues that Gorbachev had for a long time before 1985 been in a state of internal dissidence. This search for new ideas continued after 1985 in the early years of *perestroika.*

But Ryzhkov also highlighted weaknesses in Gorbachev's working style, most notably his tendency to improvise and act impulsively without any real planning or forethought. This was illustrated most clearly in the disputes surrounding the move towards a market economy in the summer of 1990. Ryzhkov favoured a more cautious approach but found himself marginalized as Gorbachev looked for a rapid radical solution to the question of how to make the transition to a market economy. But Gorbachev chose to avoid the hard decision and tried to meld the plans together and thereby fudge the differences between the various teams working on the economic reform. Ryzhkov, shortly after suffering a heart attack, was removed by Gorbachev. His memoirs also stress Gorbachev's unwillingness to take unpopular decisions, and his concern with being counted in the elite pantheon of world movers and shakers.[47]

Eduard Shevardnadze's memoir was written during 1990 and early 1991.[48] It offers a more sympathetic portrayal of Gorbachev in spite of the differences which emerged between the two after Shevardnadze's resignation. Offering fleeting glimpses of Gorbachev amid his descriptions of his activities on the world stage as Soviet Foreign Minister between 1985 and 1990, Shevardnadze seeks to defend *perestroika* and its underlying values from its critics and opponents which were growing during 1990 and 1991. Although he is willing to acknowledge that errors were committed along the way, he refuses to lay the blame solely at Gorbachev's feet. Reflecting on the failures of the reformers (and of Gorbachev himself), Shevardnadze prefers to highlight the complex circumstances facing them. Shevardnadze admits that they moved too slowly and too late at times (in contrast to Ligachev, for whom they were moving too hastily). But the reasons for this were obvious: you cannot move ahead blithely without being aware of who is trying to thwart you (a version of the Khrushchev syndrome identified above by Ligachev).[49] The constant oscillations of Gorbachev between the reformers and the conservatives are explained not as a sign of weakness, hesitancy or indecision, but as the natural response of any politician faced with competing constituencies of support.

> you cannot ignore the actions of forces trying to prevent you from reaching your goal. But you also cannot overlook the forces that want to help

you. I cannot say that Gorbachev has ignored them. He has constantly had to choose among constituencies, and if one of them turned out to be weak and unreliable, then willingly or not, he had to cast his lot with another that could guarantee him more stability.[50]

Circumstances confounded Gorbachev and the reformers. They were hindered from the outset by their upbringing. They were victims of the system of 'unfreedom' in which they grew up, which meant they operated according to misguided assumptions. They were politically illiterate, trying to introduce a new system using the old methods. They were successful in dismantling the old system, but failed to think through carefully the process of constructing the new system, and of the forms that this new system should adopt.[51] All in all Shevardnadze emphasizes the complex circumstances which confronted Gorbachev and all the reformers in their attempts to deconstruct the Stalinist system, and highlight how unprepared they were – mentally, intellectually and politically – for the process of creating something new, rather than just destroying the old.

The assistants' view: Pankin, Grachev, Palazchenko, Boldin

Of all the memoir accounts that have emerged since 1991, those of Gorbachev's assistants/aides have proven to be the most contentious and the most divergent. They range from the sympathetic and supportive to the highly critical and condemnatory, with the space in-between also occupied. Boris Pankin – Soviet ambassador to Sweden (1982–90) and Czechoslovakia (1990–91) and Soviet Foreign Minister during 1991 – was one of the few to come out in support of Gorbachev during the coup. His account covers the 100 days between the coup and the end of the USSR.[52] Andrei Grachev – a foreign affairs adviser (1985–90) and then Gorbachev's press secretary (1990–91) – also covers the final few months of the life of the Soviet Union and offers a positive appraisal of Gorbachev.[53] Pavel Palazchenko was interpreter for both Gorbachev and Shevardnadze (mainly from 1987 onwards) and accompanied Gorbachev on his trips abroad and meetings with all of the world leaders. His insights are in the main supportive, although he is not uncritical. After the resignation of Gorbachev, he went to work as a consultant in the Gorbachev Foundation.[54] Finally, we come to Valery Boldin. Boldin was an agricultural adviser to Gorbachev between 1985 and 1987, and head of the general department of the CC CPSU. In 1990, he moved into the inner circle, being appointed to Gorbachev's Chief of Staff and a member of the Presidential Council. He was, though, one of the conspirators in the August coup. He provides a deeply critical account of Gorbachev, his time in power, his leadership and his personal attributes.[55]

The accounts of Pankin and Grachev cover the same ground, but Grachev, because of his close proximity to Gorbachev, offers a far more detailed insight into the man and the era. Pankin repeats the observations of others that there was an enigma in Gorbachev's nature that made it difficult to get to know him, or to get to the 'real' Gorbachev. He also repeats the view that Gorbachev was very slow to reach a decision on a critical issue, or on something that he cared deeply about, but he was quick to act, once a decision had been made. In his summary, Pankin argues that it was right that Gorbachev went when he did because he was totally exhausted and it was time for him to leave the scene.[56]

Grachev provides some intriguing glimpses into Gorbachev's working style, and of his strengths and weaknesses. Gorbachev, according to Grachev, felt that his main strength lay in the area of oral communication: improvised speeches, conversations, arguments and debates were his *forte*. He had an unshakeable belief in his ability to persuade people of the correctness of his own standpoint. This would seem to explain the accusations of long-windedness and verbosity that were often thrown at Gorbachev as well as his obsession with drafting and redrafting speeches rather than concerning himself with policy detail and implementation.[57] This sense of inner certainty and belief in what he was doing was reflected, according to Grachev, in his determination to join the two worlds of the USSR and the West: this appeared to be the lodestar guiding his whole political life.[58]

Grachev also detected some flaws in Gorbachev's personality that contributed to his downfall: he was overly loyal in friendship, and was prone to trying to keep all factions and groups on his side. Moreover, his desire to maintain a centrist position left him vulnerable to attacks from extremists. Gorbachev also committed mistakes in his tenure that undermined his authority: he failed to denounce the intervention in Lithuania, which meant that he lost the confidence of the republican leaders and this hastened the break-up of the Union. He constantly manipulated the constitution which undermined his democratic credibility. Gorbachev also missed crucial opportunities. He did not incorporate all the progressive democratic forces into a broad reformist coalition, which left the way open for Yeltsin. Gorbachev failed to put himself forward for popular election as President.

But how far was Gorbachev responsible for the coup and the crisis that led to it? Was it down to his faintheartedness and indecision? Or was it the result of years of inaction on the part of his predecessors? Grachev argues that Gorbachev did not foresee the consequences of some of his reforms which contributed to the chaos and crisis of 1990–91. He did not appreciate the extent to which internal structures of the Soviet state had been destroyed by the totalitarian system, which rendered a rapid collapse highly likely once the foundation stones were removed. Similarly, his foreign policy in Eastern Europe gave a massive spur to the forces of nationalism and separatism in the USSR itself. Liberated from its fear of the centre, the empire 'exploded like a balloon'.

Overall, Grachev's verdict highlights the paradox that was Gorbachev. Gorbachev's role in the coup was as both victim and vanquisher. His hesitation and misplaced loyalty led to the coup. His resolve and courage caused it to fail. His actions had caused the crisis that provoked it. His reforms enabled and empowered the people who opposed it and defeated it. Summing up, Grachev notes:

> The paradox of Gorbachev is that he made mistakes not when he compromised for the sake of practicality (something that all politicians do),

but when he betrayed himself, when he chose the bureaucratic moves of an *apparatchik* over democratic procedures, secrecy over *glasnost'*, expedience over principles. No one has ever paid a higher price for his mistakes. What can be more terrible for a reformer than to see his goal fade into the distance like the receding line of the horizon?[59]

Pavel Palazchenko offers a similarly sympathetic yet balanced account of the Gorbachev years. He notes his achievements, yet repeats the criticisms and highlights Gorbachev's mistakes. Palazchenko's position is much closer to Gorbachev. He has retained a close association with his former boss in the post-Soviet period. Palazchenko clearly is a strong admirer of Gorbachev the man, describing him as a lively, dynamic person who had a genuine affection for the people and who was a politician driven by a strong sense of morality.

Appraising his political career, Palazchenko highlighted the way that Gorbachev became increasingly radical and outspoken on assuming the position of General Secretary. In his early years, Gorbachev kept to the traditional script on the whole, although his manner and language were a little livelier than those of his peers. From 1986 onwards, Gorbachev became embroiled in the perils and the drama of domestic reform and foreign diplomacy. For Palazchenko, Gorbachev's unique achievement was that, in the period between 1986 and 1990, he set the agenda for the country and the world.[60] His greatest successes and enduring achievements came in the field of foreign relations. Conversely, he was particularly scathing of the economic failures of Gorbachev, arguing that there appeared to be no direction or purpose in domestic economic policy.[61]

Palazchenko's most arresting comments relate to Gorbachev's personality, leadership style and political situation. It is possible to detect in Palazchenko's writings a number of different layers or aspects of ambiguity in Gorbachev. Reflecting on Chernobyl, Palazchenko provides an interesting insight into Gorbachev's political leadership style:

> He could not afford either to downplay the disaster or react too emotionally. So he had to engage in a kind of balancing act, not for the first time in his career, and not the last. Unfortunately he had to do it again and again, and he sometimes continued to balance even when it was time, as they say, to fish or cut bait.[62]

This hesitancy in Gorbachev's temperament was exacerbated by the duality of his political position. He had to be both the leader and driver of the reformist programme and the new political forces that were being unleashed, and also the head of the state apparatus and defender of the old political forces that were still in place. Gorbachev's strategy was to try and hold the old and the new together until the new had had time to take root, and thus avoid the need to confront the old institutions head on. He was, according to Palazchenko, by temperament and logic, a creature of the political centre. Like the traditional symbol of Tsarist

Russia – the two headed eagle – Gorbachev was forced to face two ways at once.[63] The final dimension of Gorbachev's ambiguity rested with his approach to dealing with colleagues and subordinates. Palazchenko found Gorbachev to be a mixture of a traditional boss and a political conciliator, someone who wanted the final word on some occasions, but who also sought a compromise among his team wherever possible.[64]

In his final, fairly balanced assessment of Gorbachev, Palazchenko reiterates the flaws and failures of Gorbachev but refuses to see these as crucial in the outcome. Indeed, although Gorbachev was removed, Palazchenko sees Gorbachev as somehow prevailing because his project – to bring democracy, human rights and the rule of law to the USSR – has continued. What undermined Gorbachev was his attempt to achieve revolutionary changes by evolutionary methods which foundered on the political culture and consciousness of the people. Although the people have made him a scapegoat for their problems, the fact that they are free to articulate publicly their concerns is the final, greatest legacy of Gorbachev's rule.[65]

Valery Boldin affords us a very different view of Gorbachev. Boldin paints an exceptionally intimate portrait of the leader at work and at play, in private and in public, at home and abroad, with his wife and with his colleagues. Written while awaiting trial in 1992 for his part in the 1991 putsch (and so containing very little about the coup itself), Boldin shows no loyalty or admiration for Gorbachev. Indeed, this is an important piece of context. A justification of his role in the putsch required an appraisal of Gorbachev that outlined his failings and weaknesses on a grand scale. Although he recognizes some of his positive qualities – capacity for hard work, excellent memory, genuine belief in Leninism – Boldin sets out to puncture the Western view of Gorbachev as the lone, heroic reformer bravely battling to slay the Stalinist dragon and bring freedom and light to the peoples of the USSR. Boldin has little time for his erstwhile boss, and his memoir account is very selective and not very reliable. Gorbachev was a weak, indecisive, vain, verbose, duplicitous leader more interested in power and its trappings than the welfare of the people. He is acutely scathing of Raisa's role and lays all the blame for the failures of *perestroika* firmly at the feet of Gorbachev.[66]

Boldin's thesis is that the project of *perestroika* – which had noble and lofty intentions to improve the lot of the people – created chaos and suffering because of two aspects of the character of Gorbachev: his indecisiveness and his adherence to patterns of thinking and leading developed in his rise through the hierarchy in provincial Stavropol. As a leader, Boldin views Gorbachev as a 'poor imitation' of Mikhail Suslov, and responsible for the devastation, ruin and strife engulfing Russia. His book is dedicated to this attempt to demonstrate the failings of Gorbachev's character and leadership.[67]

Boldin highlights Gorbachev's character failings which became crucial when he became the General Secretary. Gorbachev was essentially a weak indecisive person, dominated by his wife, who used manipulation and constant manoeuvring to get his way. He responded poorly to criticism, and never forgot if someone opposed him or spoke against him. He was exceptionally ambitious, vain and susceptible to flattery. He was jealous of the popularity or abilities of his colleagues, and was haughty and rude to his subordinates.

During his rise through the provincial hierarchy, Gorbachev practised and honed particular styles of working, which then subsequently became part of his *modus operandi* as General Secretary. In this respect, Boldin sees Gorbachev as a victim of his past. He was imbued with the cultural and intellectual imprint of the Soviet system and could not shake it off. Boldin sees the location of Stavropol – with its health resorts and holiday residences – as crucial in Gorbachev's rise. He had the opportunity to develop close links with a succession of high-ranking leaders, and learned how to manipulate and manoeuvre in order to get noticed and to please his superiors. This double-dealing carried on in Moscow, where he showed the same capacity for trying to please everyone, for compromise, for the avoidance of a clear-cut position.[68]

Other elements in his character were also learned while rising through the provincial hierarchy. The very fact that he rose up through the Komsomol and party structures meant that he never had to accept responsibility for failure, and never had to endure criticism. He merely had to follow the latest diktat from the centre. Although he began his career in very humble surroundings, he soon acquired a penchant for the trappings and finery of office, something which never left him. His working style also favoured speaking and writing over practical actions and decisions.[69]

The interaction of these character flaws and his upbringing holds the key to understanding the failures of Gorbachev. Boldin cites numerous instances to back up his case. His primary charge is one of indecision, prevarication, compromise and weakness. He began *perestroika* without any idea where he was going, or of how to get there. Napoleon's dictum – let battle commence and then we'll see – was said to underpin Gorbachev's basic approach.[70] Boldin admits to being baffled as to why Gorbachev – despite having assembled a very capable 'brains trust' under the control of Aleksander Yakovlev – did not elaborate an overarching theoretical framework to guide *perestroika*. Gorbachev blundered along, vaguely groping for the way forward. Whenever he came across problems or difficulties, he would change tack and focus on something else. He was unable to be resolute or take difficult decisions. He became all things to all men.

> Gorbachev, for whom manoeuvring had become a habit, was really taking two steps forward, three to the side, and one backward, and everyone found such conduct disconcerting. He would tell Marxist hardliners that he was fighting for the bright future of communism and would never swerve from that path, while assuring free marketeers that the only possible way to proceed was through the expansion of market relations, democracy and freedom in accordance with the Austrian or Swedish models. The General Secretary's pluralism of opinions was so advanced that he had everybody confused.[71]

Underneath this constant zig-zagging of his last three years in office lay one crucial thing for Boldin: Gorbachev never fully knew what *perestroika* was actually about.

Second, this fundamental confusion was compounded by his inability to handle the people around him. Gorbachev had highly fraught relationships with his colleagues.[72] He ditched Ryzhkov when he appeared to be gaining in popularity. He was said to have been resentful of Anatoly Lukyanov's popularity in the Supreme Soviet. He appeared to need servile, not independent people around him. His constant changes of policy gradually alienated the intellectuals and advisers he had around him, which led to a high turnover of personnel. He seemed unable to trust those around him, which alienated even his most loyal supporters. He was rude to his subordinates, a function, Boldin argues, of his own rise from obscure roots. He was a poor judge of character, which led him to make mediocre appointments. By the end of his tenure Gorbachev was increasingly alone, isolated and forlorn.[73]

Third, Boldin argues that Gorbachev was essentially self-absorbed and self-serving. He was highly susceptible to flattery. He used to read avidly foreign press reports which praised him, and consciously avoided visits around the Soviet Union as he became more unpopular in favour of trips abroad where he could receive the adulation he deserved. He was obsessive about his appearance and his image, and insisted on a huge send-off whenever he left the USSR on a trip abroad. He sought out close control of the media to ensure the right image was being communicated. Boldin argues that a form of personality cult was emerging. Gorbachev was obsessed with trappings of power. Huge amounts of money were spent on building newer and more opulent residences. He used to talk endlessly, drowning the people in speeches and publications, and dominated Politburo meetings, which met with less and less frequency.[74]

Boldin also noted some mysterious elements in Gorbachev's leadership. He appeared to change his mind quite drastically without any clear reason. He says that Gorbachev at first accepted the Andreeva letter with equanimity. Yet at the CC meeting a couple of days later, he was in a rage. He is also at a loss to explain Gorbachev's drift from Leninism to social democracy. He relates how Gorbachev spent a great deal of time immersing himself in the works of Lenin, yet within a couple of years had become a convert to Western social democracy and to the importation of capitalist forms into the country.

Overall, Boldin argues that Gorbachev, in spite of his good intentions, was an unmitigated disaster. He combined verbal radicalism and practical impotence. He achieved nothing, and destroyed everything, and his rule was a tragedy for millions. His rule was riddled with contradictions, duplicity and hypocrisy. Summing up, Boldin writes:

> There was no limit to his double standards ... societies cannot change direction so abruptly and on such a massive scale when guided by weak-willed vacillating and timorous leaders. They need leaders who know what they want and can carry their plans through to completion. Life is

not a stage, though, even if it were, a clown should not be cast in the role of a great commander.[75]

A final, destructive view came from Andrei Korobeinikov.[76] The author had been a speechwriter for Gorbachev from his Stavropol days, and provides a highly critical and rather jaundiced view of Gorbachev's background. Written as a counterblast to Gorbachev's memoirs, Korobeinikov sought to demolish the myths surrounding Gorbachev, to unpick his reputation and to puncture his claims to greatness. Korobeinikov was particularly quick to attack Gorbachev's personality and character, but also spoke negatively of Gorbachev's ideology and policies. In particular, Korobeinikov was keen to highlight the messianic nature of Gorbachev's self-definition in his memoirs, and of the terrible cost that the Soviet people had suffered at the hands of his 'ineffective abstractions' and his experimentation.[77] On a personal level, Gorbachev was said to deal with his provincial colleagues with patronizing condescension, had few merits as a leader, and although he had quite humble beginnings, he lost touch with his roots as he rose through the hierarchy. He moved away from the ordinary person. Gorbachev was always careful to sculpt his image, but the reality was far removed from his projected image. Gorbachev had turned out not to be a messiah, but to be a 'herald of chaos'.[78]

Before we move on to examine the views of those who worked most closely with him as aides or advisers, it is worth stopping to reflect a moment on the central issues identified earlier. One of the observations outlined by more than one memoirist was that Gorbachev was more interested in the intellectual than the practical aspects of governing, and that he was happiest talking, discussing and debating rather than in acting, resolving and implementing. This is clear from reading Gorbachev's own words. Ideas and ideology were always a central part of Gorbachev's political life, and he clearly enjoyed the cut and thrust of debate, and talking with people. Indeed, these were clearly a great strength in his dealings with people in Stavropol, and were a key part of his campaign of mobilization and persuasion when he went around the country exhorting the people to change.

The problem with many of the commentaries which stress Gorbachev's preference for the intellectual over the practical is that it is conceived, particularly by his critics, as a serious deficiency of his leadership, or almost as a conscious choice not to become involved in the nitty-gritty, as if it were somehow beneath him. This is partly explained by the preferences and outlook of the memoirists. Their diagnosis of Gorbachev's failures lies in his inability to act decisively. These critical voices link this verbosity and lack of practical activism with deeper flaws in his character and his leadership style: his indecision, vanity, arrogance and weakness. This was all part of the Gorbachev 'package' which was more concerned with his image and his reputation, and which instinctively sought popularity and self-affirmation and which had an aversion to taking difficult or unpopular decisions.

But these appraisals of Gorbachev assume that his weakness and indecision were rooted in his character flaws, rather than in his political choices or his style of leadership. Thus Gorbachev failed because he was vain and shallow, and he allowed his own interests to dominate over those of the party and state, rather than failing because his strategy was flawed. But this is a highly debatable viewpoint, not least because it does allow his critics who worked with him to pile all the blame for the failures of *perestroika* on Gorbachev the scapegoat. It is also clear that Gorbachev was a political centrist, who either occupied the centre ground as a deliberate strategy to maintain a balanced approach, or because he was by instinct and temperament a 'man of the centre'. In addition, he was also facing an incredibly complex task, and just keeping his political balance in this context was a major feat in his own right. His oscillations were part of his tactical approach or were caused by the circumstances he found himself in, not because of his vanity and weakness. This perspective also fails to take account of the fact that Gorbachev consciously toned down the rhetoric and public praise that was heaped upon Soviet leaders. This should not conceal the fact Gorbachev's preference for the intellectual side of things and for centrism did indeed cause problems and may well have contributed to his eventual failure. But to link these failures directly to Gorbachev's personality and character is problematic, and speak more of the desires of his memoirists for revenge or self-justification than they do of the cause of Gorbachev's travails.

The aides/advisers' view: Yakovlev, Chernyaev, Shakhnazarov

Within Gorbachev's inner sanctum of advisers and colleagues, three people played highly significant roles in the shaping and execution of *perestroika*. Georgii Shakhnazarov, a political scientist, became an aide to Gorbachev between 1988 and 1991, and a member of the Gorbachev Foundation after 1991. Anatoli Chernyaev was an adviser to Gorbachev on foreign affairs between 1986 and 1991, and he also moved to the Gorbachev Foundation. Finally, Aleksander Yakovlev, often cited as the architect of *perestroika,* who was second-in-command in the Politburo between 1987 and 1990, and a personal adviser to Gorbachev during 1990 and 1991, when he resigned shortly before the coup. All three were close to Gorbachev: politically, personally and intellectually. They basically shared Gorbachev's outlook and values and their intellectual journey before 1985 had some similarities to Gorbachev's own journey. All three offer a sympathetic, though not uncritical, view on Gorbachev in power.

Yakovlev wrote soon after the collapse of the Soviet Union and focused in the main on the structural and systemic issues rather than on personalities and apportioning blame, which was the usual approach for memoirists at this time.[79] Yakovlev stood on the radical wing of the reformers, and his analysis rested on the failure of the leadership to take sufficiently bold initiatives quickly enough. In other words, *perestroika* failed because his line was not pursued with sufficient consistency or speed for it to succeed. He argued that *perestroika* was started far too late: many opportunities for change had been missed in the Brezhnev years, and a great storehouse of reformist ideas had been developed but shelved. He saved his most critical remarks about Gorbachev for his prevarication. Yakovlev states that at the end of 1985 he wrote a memo recommending that the CPSU be split into two parties. This would have united the reformist elements and liberated Gorbachev from having to appease the conservative apparatus. Gorbachev refused, failed to take sides early enough. [80]

This wavering, coupled to his desire to try and keep everyone on board, created tensions and contradictions within *perestroika*. Gorbachev ended up with a programme which was trying to reconcile the irreconcilable, like trying to unite fornication and prayer or to cross a hedgehog with a snake. He also bowed to pressure from the conservatives, and for too long continued to believe in the possibility of the party as a progressive force. In spite of all the mistakes and problems that *perestroika* generated, Yakovlev argued that what people would always remember was the freedom that they won. The shortages of bread and sausage would soon be forgotten. [81]

Anatolii Chernyaev's work *Shest let c gorbachevim (My Six Years with Gorbachev)* is an idiosyncratic, highly personal piece, which combines excerpts from his journal with subsequent commentary and reflections. [82] It is a fascinating account, combining both instant and distant reflection. It also relates private insights and conversations of Gorbachev. The closeness between Gorbachev and Chernyaev was noted by Andrei Grachev, who relays the occasion when Gorbachev introduced Chernyaev to Felipe Gonzalez (the Spanish Prime Minister) as his *alter ego*. [83] Perhaps the most valuable part of Chernyaev's text is the narrative account he provides, which charts the development of Gorbachev the leader as well as the process of *perestroika*. In Chernyaev's story, Gorbachev is portrayed as an honest, passionate man whose ideas and views evolved, but who was gradually undone by his vanity, wavering and over-attention to the peripheral at the expense of the fundamental.

As a person, Chernyaev points to Gorbachev's intelligence, honesty, passion and his deep-seated desire to initiate change and to bring about improvements in the system. He also exhibited an (exceedingly rare at the time among Soviet leaders) overt distaste for flattery and sycophancy among colleagues and subordinates. But at the same time, Chernyaev also found Gorbachev to be ambitious, egotistical and to a certain degree a prisoner of his own past. Most significantly, though, Chernyaev highlights the sense of destiny that Gorbachev appeared to discern in himself and which informed everything he did:

> Whle Dobrynin was talking, I watched Gorbachev. And I was thinking that in this man vanity is overshadowed by something else. It's as if he only saw himself as an instrument of his work. This also came through in the irony, sarcasm and distrust with which he occasionally recounted the Western media's praise of him. [84]

Chernyaev is at his most interesting in recounting the details from behind-the-scenes meetings and activities. He suggests that much of the public rhetoric of Gorbachev – about New Thinking, all-human values, a multi-dimensional world – were frequently repeated in private and so could not be considered to be part of his public face.[85] He also provides an insider's account of the working style of Gorbachev, for instance, with the drafting and redrafting of Gorbachev's best-selling work *Perestroika: New Thinking for Our Country and the World*. Having been approached by an American publisher, Chernyaev had a job to persuade Gorbachev to provide something other than the standard fare of extracts from articles and keynote speeches. Gorbachev was concerned about the opinions and views of his colleagues, because it seemed as though it was a major departure from the normal practice, perhaps hinting at lingering feelings of vulnerability in the early years of his tenure. Chernyaev and his team collected the material, but it was Gorbachev himself who dictated and redictated the work (three times, according to Chernyaev in the August of 1987) and it led to him being late back from his holidays. He completed a follow-up work, *Perestroika: The Test of Life* in 1988, but this was never published.[86] Interestingly, Chernyaev maintains that Gorbachev wrote all his own speeches, but was too fond of the sound of his own voice.

As a companion and witness to the memorable events of this period, Chernyaev helps to shed light on Gorbachev, his leadership, his policies and his weaknesses. The unfolding story that Chernyaev narrates gives us snapshots of Gorbachev's progression, as well as key events or moments which propelled his thinking and policies in new directions. Chernyaev found Gorbachev at first to be a mixture of a fresh and breezy style, but still quite conservative and bound by his and the state's past. The first major 'leap' in his thinking came in the summer of 1986 and was catalysed by three developments: his meetings with foreign leaders, the tragedy at Chernobyl, and his visit to the Soviet Far East. His encounters with foreign dignitaries exposed him to new traditions, cultures, patterns of thinking and shaped him into a world leader. Chernobyl and his talks to the Soviet people opened his eyes to the depth of the problems in the system, and the slow, slow progress that had been made. By the start of 1987, Gorbachev had increasingly come to see that:

- Domestic and foreign affairs were increasingly intertwined.
- Personnel were the root of many problems.
- Success would be slow in arriving.
- Democracy could be harnessed to achieve his aims of socio-economic modernization rather than being valued in its own right.[87]

The years between 1987 and 1988 were crucial, according to Chernyaev. Gorbachev was constantly pushing the limits of the official ideology, gradually eroding the confines of the Marxist-Leninist monolith. As Gorbachev began to push further ahead with reforms at home and abroad, the relationship between the two strands underwent a dramatic change. Increasingly obstructed and frustrated at home by opposition and inertia, Gorbachev came to see the processes of disarmament and favourable relations with the West as the motor driving the domestic reform. Previously, external changes were to provide a context within which domestic reform could be enacted. The high-water mark of Gorbachev's tenure came with his UN speech in December 1988. This marked Gorbachev as a world statesman, and the global recognition he received enabled him to push ahead with bolder and bolder foreign policy initiatives, unencumbered by the dogmas of the past.[88]

At home, though, it was an entirely different matter. It was in this period that Chernyaev was able to discern the seeds of Gorbachev's downfall. First, he did not see the ethno-national consequences of a push for democratization. This was a fatal, almost unforgivable error for Chernyaev.[89] Second, Gorbachev's tactical and strategic thinking was increasingly lagging behind events. His desire to maintain unity in the leadership led to compromise, vacillation and hesitation when often decisive action was required. His continued faith in the party as an institution which could be reformed and which could function as a 'normal' democratic party was misplaced. Gorbachev's political strategy – to keep the country governable during the transition from the party-state system to a law-governed system – foundered because the party was unwilling and unable to change in this way. Gorbachev's ideas and policies were undone, because, in Chernyaev's words, 'they were rooted in a process that was now slipping increasingly out of control'.[90] Consequently, *perestroika* began to lose momentum and direction.

This home/abroad dualism was exacerbated in 1989. The changes in Soviet/Western relations, and the revolutions in Eastern Europe contrasted with the drift at home. Gorbachev continued to waver, and nobody seemed to know where the USSR was going, and how it was going to get to wherever it was going. Opposition grew from both left and right, reformers and traditionalists. Chernyaev sums this up in a fascinating passage contrasting Gorbachev during his amazingly successful trip to Washington in June 1990 with his appearance at the Congress of the Russian Communist Party two weeks later. It is worth quoting at length.

> In America he showed maximum openness in front of people who wanted to listen ... You saw a person with an independent mind and common sense talking sincerely, naturally, about his intentions and goals, without any second thoughts. Here, in his country, faced with open hostility, he acted out of an instinctive fear for the survival of his entire cause. And he looked for a way out following the principle that 'if you are to live with the wolves, then you must howl with them.' Hence the apparat-style tactics, manoeuvring, ambiguity, the appeals for compromise and unity that were already an object of ridicule, and the calls for co-operation that were actually doing increasing harm to his cause.[91]

He went on to reflect on this foreign/domestic dualism in Gorbachev:

> During this twilight hour I saw two different Gorbachevs in front of me. And that duality somehow reflected the difference between the two worlds that he inhabited at the same time, the civilised and uncivilised worlds (as defined by universal human norms). He was more and more

'accepted' there, and more and more rejected here. That's why he found it increasingly difficult to remain in this country. He had to be ever more 'untrue to himself' in his effort to bring the two worlds together, to protect and continue this country's just-begun journey toward civilisation.[92]

In 1990, Gorbachev demonstrated that his real skill lay in dismantling the old system. He was, however, unsuited to the task of creating a new one. In the end he was too committed to making peace with everyone, too obsessed with overseeing the details, too fearful of destructive social consequences and too unwilling to break with the old ways of doing things. Reflecting more recently on Gorbachev's role in ending the Cold War, Chernyaev offers a balanced appraisal, highlighting the significance of his foreign policy in creating a new era of peace and cooperation internationally, but also noting:

> Under his leadership tactical moves were not always successful and cunning. Furthermore, he sometimes neglected the CPSU tradition. In addition he made annoying mistakes in assessing partners, exhibited unwarranted optimism, exaggerated the effects of his personal charm, and made superficial forecasts, not to mention preposterous emotional outbursts.[93]

Overall Chernyaev's portrait is that of the noble hero, flawed in many ways, but decent, honest and conscientious and one whom he believes will be vindicated by history. Indeed, he believes that Gorbachev will one day be seen as the person who ushered in a new period in world history but unfortunately suffered the fate of all great reformers – that of being swept away by the forces they helped to set in motion in the first place.

The final portrait in this section is presented by Georgii Shakhnazarov, in his work *S vozhdyami i bez nikh*.[94] Shakhnazarov provides a quite unusual perspective. A reformist intellectual, he began his rise through the intellectual hierarchy in the 1960s as a journalist in Prague on the progressively minded journal *Problemy mira i sotsializma* (*Problems of Peace and Socialism*). He played a central role in the emergence of the discipline of political science in the USSR. After 1985, he became a member of Gorbachev's *perestroika* 'brains trust', and was an architect of many key documents including the revised Party Programme of July/August 1991. He returned to academic work after 1991, and maintained close links with Gorbachev through the work of the Gorbachev Foundation. He died in May 2001. Shakhnazarov's story describes Gorbachev in glowing, almost reverential tones at times, although he does hint at weaknesses and flaws in his thinking and in his leadership. Shakhnazarov also includes some intriguing insights into Gorbachev's personality, giving us a little glimpse of Gorbachev the Man, a comparative rarity in the recollections. Shakhnazarov's account occasionally lapses into the quasi-messianic rhetoric that characterized much of the Western press, but on the whole he tells a balanced, informed and thoughtful tale.

The appearance of Gorbachev on the political scene was remarkable to Shakhnazarov, not just because he stood out against the backdrop of the decrepit Soviet leadership of the early 1980s, but because he had unusual views. As a person, Gorbachev was, according to Shakhnazarov, 'lively, sympathetic, sociable and with many friends'.[95] But his friendships were political ones: he had no real close personal friends (apart from Raisa) and kept people at arm's length, which probably accounts for why Gorbachev appears to be something of an enigma to those around him. He was a smart, smiling, confident figure, full of energy, who combined intellect, benevolence and openness. He was extremely diligent and hardworking. But Gorbachev was not a one-man band. In terms of his leadership, he worked with three separate 'teams': the Politburo, a group of journalists and media chiefs, and a narrow-circle of like-minded intellectuals.[96]

The story of *perestroika* told by Shakhnazarov is summed up in one word: reformation. Gorbachev was a reformer. His 'heroic' constructive phase occurred between 1985 and the fall of the Berlin Wall in 1989.[97] His main achievements were introducing freedom of speech, creating a parliament and starting the restraint of the forces of militarism in world politics. Shakhnazarov was particularly quick to note that Gorbachev continued to maintain an adherence to *glasnost'* in spite of the fact that he increasingly became the target of press criticisms. This was attributed to his personal belief in openness as a *modus operandi*.[98] In his observations on the political reforms, Shakhnazarov noted that Gorbachev was a centrist by instinct, not a revolutionary. His plans to reform the system were undermined by his two Achilles' heels: his lack of organizational skills (a surprising thing, Shakhnazarov notes, from someone who worked his way up through the party hierarchy where organizational skills were the sine qua non for the politically ambitious) and his indifference to the institutions he had created.[99] Gorbachev always preferred to work through informal channels, to improvise, and this was one of the reasons why Gorbachev's project stumbled: the institutions of *perestroika* failed to take root. Gorbachev failed to complete the formation of a new political system, although Shakhnazarov believes that if he had not been removed, he would have finished what he had started. However, from 1989, Gorbachev was in the grip of a left–right struggle in Soviet politics, and this finally did for him. The August coup was, in Shakhnazarov's words, 'a tragedy', with disastrous consequences for the people.[100]

In summarizing the latter years of his time in power, Shakhnazarov makes passing comparisons of Gorbachev with both Alexander II and Napoleon. He saves his most thoughtful insights though, in his comparisons of Gorbachev with Yeltsin, on the one hand, and Lev Tolstoy, on the other. Yeltsin is described as a revolutionary who sought the destruction of the totalitarian regime; Gorbachev as a reformer who sought its dismantling. The parallels with Tolstoy – fêted abroad, reviled at home, betrayed by the Orthodox Church – were clear in the life and fate of Gorbachev, who suffered a similar home/abroad split and was in turn cursed by the party who accused him of betrayal and blamed him for all its ills.[101]

The second half of his memoir turns to an appraisal of Gorbachev and an attempt to understand the Gorbachev 'phenomenon'. He includes a selection of appraisals which range from those who see Gorbachev as a fearful, demonic figure (Aleksander Prokhanov) to those who see him as the embodiment of divine providence (Eduard Samoilov).[102] Shakhnazarov, in spite of his background in political science and Enlightenment rationalism, struggled to find an explanation of the Gorbachev phenomenon which did not rest on some mystical notion of divine calling or providence. At one point, during a flight to Yerevan, Shakhnazarov asked the Gorbachevs if they had ever had any thoughts about a sense of predestination or some lofty calling on Mikhail's life. They replied that in their youth, when Mikhail was under 30,

> We both had one and the same dream: a long, dark tunnel at the end of which there blazed out a powerful light and a fiery pillar was rising upwards … 'What does this mean?' asked Mikhail. Raisa replied, 'Misha, you will be a great man.'[103]

In a detailed appraisal of his personal strengths and weaknesses, Shakhnazarov highlights the following characteristics as the distinctive qualities of Gorbachev:

- *Optimism*: 'everything will be alright in the end'.
- *Ambitious*: but not a cheap, personal egocentric ambition.
- *He loved power, to a degree*: but he voluntarily relinquished much that he inherited.
- *Tolerant and obstinate*: listened to others, but 100 per cent convinced of the correctness of his stance.
- *Belief in his power to persuade*: convinced that he could conquer by the power of his own reason, logic, argument and charm rather than the use of force. This was, according to Shakhnazarov, his 'vanity'.
- *Rejected revenge:* he did not hold grudges.
- *Was neither stingy or greedy*: he eschewed decorations and medals, practised little in the way of nepotism, but did grow accustomed to comfort.
- *Had a progressive attitude to women*: which accounts for those who criticize him of being under the thumb and unable to decide anything without his wife.[104]

Overall, Shakhnazarov described them as 'the little weaknesses of a great man'.[105]

In his final section, Shakhnazarov attempted to grasp the essence and meaning of Gorbachev. He chose to align Gorbachev with history, and with Russia. He argued that Gorbachev was the expression of the centrist movement in Russian philosophy, culture and politics, and was the embodiment of the march of history: the Gorbachev phenomenon was the 'law-governed stage of development of the Russian nation'.[106] Gorbachev was also the first Russian leader who thought like a Westerner. His great failing was to vacillate and delay in taking decisions. His great merit lay in the fact that he had the courage to throw off the blinkers of dogmatic ideology and see the world and his country as they really were. In his conclusion, Shakhnazarov outlined that, '*Perestroika* was the great turning-point of the history of the twentieth century. But however huge its significance, the personal significance of Gorbachev is far greater.'[107]

Shakhnazarov's summary provides the best and most useful insights into Gorbachev's personality. In many ways, Gorbachev's personality was full of ambiguities and these fed directly into his leadership style and were crucial in shaping the process of *perestroika*, notable because as it progressed *perestroika* became increasingly his personal project. Lacking an institutional basis, Gorbachev's exercise of power was a reflection and expression of his character and personality. Gorbachev is a classic example of a person whose strengths and characteristics in one context became weaknesses and liabilities in a different context. His ambition and sense of destiny drove him to rise up through the hierarchy, but also led him to become overly concerned with his legacy and reputation. He was someone who believed in a set of ideals and remained loyal to these ideals after circumstances had changed. This inner certainty about the correctness of his own position propelled him forward in the face of opposition and criticism but quickly became perceived as dogmatism, inflexibility and arrogance. The strengths of his leadership style created the weaknesses that finally undid him. For in his desire to use persuasion, in his belief in his ability to convince others that his way was the best way, and that they should put their trust and faith in him, we see someone seeking to develop a more consensual and inclusive style of leadership. This worked admirably at the beginning, in the stage of *perestroika* when he was the evangelist and salesman, the motivator and visionary. But as the focus shifted to the need to build institutions, to develop coalitions, to force through difficult changes, this approach became a liability.

Recent reminiscences

There have been two waves of coverage of Gorbachev post-power in the Russian press. The first wave came in the immediate aftermath of his resignation in December 1991, and these have been analysed elsewhere. After Gorbachev's catastrophic showing in the 1996 Presidential election, he gradually began to slide away from the centre of public attention over the next two or three years. Since 1999 and the untimely death of his wife, Gorbachev has begun to figure more prominently in Russian public life, helped by a couple of significant moments of commemoration. Some interesting reappraisals of Gorbachev, as well as a series of very intriguing opinion polls (which asked the respondents to reflect upon Gorbachev's time in office, and the legacy of his rule), have been published, which allow us to review how Gorbachev is perceived from a distance of 17 years since power. A series of opinion polls were carried out, intermittently between March 1995 and February 2004.[108] The polls tended to divide up into three areas: comparisons of Gorbachev with other Soviet/Russian notables (past and present); an appraisal of popular opinion towards Gorbachev (as a person and as a political figure); and finally an evaluation of Gorbachev's role in the history of the country and the impact of his reforms, for good or ill. One of the most interesting polls carried out by the Public Opinion Foundation asked its respondents to list some of his negative and positive personal qualities. The list included the following.

Negative characteristics

- Mistakes he made (collapse of the state; ruined the country; united Germany; people died and he is guilty).
- Poor political leader (talentless, incompetent).
- Dependent political leader (controlled by his wife, dictated to by other countries; scared of the mafia).
- Talked a lot, achieved little (chatterbox, irresponsible dreamer).
- Lack of understanding (especially economics).
- Morally compromised (dishonest, corrupt, mercenary, a thief, ambitious, careerist, arrogant).
- Weak-willed (spineless, too gentle, grey, an empty space, a nonentity).

Positive characteristics

- Approval of Gorbachev's actions/policies (far-sighted reformer, ended war in Afghanistan; raised the Iron Curtain; fought alcoholism; politician with a human face; freedom of speech began in his time).
- Clever, educated, responsible, good communication skills.
- International statesman (diplomatic, able to compromise).
- Morally upright (decent, honest, frank, cultured, respects people).
- Purposeful, resolute, courageous, calm.

Finally, the pollsters asked people to identify the positive things that Gorbachev and his policies brought to Russia, and also the negative things (Table 5.1).

Overall, the dominant evaluation of Gorbachev in a range of polls is one of indifference or perhaps even irrelevance. Perhaps the greatest contrast is the personal evaluations (more people were either indifferent or positive about Gorbachev as a person than negative) measured against Gorbachev's policies and the impact of his time in office, where a clear majority believe that Gorbachev did more harm than good/harm and good in equal measure. There appears to be a growing divorce between Gorbachev the man and Gorbachev the politician. Partly, this can be attributed to the death of his wife and his advancing years (which have tended to evoke a greater degree of sympathy), but partly also this is due to the fact that many of the current political class are proving to be equally if not more unpopular.

A more interesting point is Gorbachev's *comparative* standing in the pantheon of world leaders. Despite all of the opprobrium for his policies, around one quarter of those polled still consider him one of the most significant figures of the twentieth century, although he regularly lags behind Lenin, Stalin, Sakharov and Gagarin in this regard. This may well change when Gorbachev dies. It is also interesting to note that the groups who are most positive about Gorbachev are the younger, urban, wealthier, more educated groups, reinforcing the notion that

Table 5.1 Positive and negative developments of Gorbachev's rule

Positive developments (%)	Negative developments (%)
Perestroika/democratic reforms (15)	Disintegration of USSR/decline of state (47)
Foreign policy (4)	Socio-economic crisis (13)
Changes in the economy (3)	*Perestroika* (6)
Recovery from stagnation/beginning of positive changes (3)	Anti-alcohol campaign/cutting down of vineyards (5)
Withdrawal from Afghanistan (3)	General negative appraisals (3)
Changing of regime/end of 1-party system (2)	Incompetent politician (2)
Anti-alcohol campaign (2)	Incomplete actions (2)
Changed life for the better (2)	Abrupt changes/destabilization (2)
Other (2)	Withdrawal of troops from Germany/reduction of army (1)
Gorbachev didn't accomplish anything (12)	Other (1)
Hard to answer, no response (57)	Gorbachev did nothing bad (2)
	Hard to answer, no response (28)

perestroika was essentially driven by, and acted in the interests of, the Westernizing intelligentsia in the USSR.

Newspaper articles or appraisals about Gorbachev have become increasingly rare as Gorbachev becomes an increasingly historical figure, and *perestroika* a distant memory. Occasionally he is interviewed – about the international scene (for instance, the Iraq War) or about Putin's regime – but on the whole he is very much a peripheral figure. The only really notable points at which he has been remembered by the Russian press have been anniversaries (Gorbachev's 70th birthday in March 2001 or ten years after the coup in August 2001) and the death of his wife in September 1999. How is Gorbachev seen on these occasions?

These pieces were written sympathetically, laced with a little nostalgia as well as respect for an elderly statesman. Yet the sense that the world had moved on and that Gorbachev was part of a different era was unmistakable. Reporting on the conference arranged at the Gorbachev Foundation to celebrate his 70th birthday, *Kommersant* noted that there were 'more toasts than speeches'.[109] Vitali Tretyakov posed the interesting question as to why, ten years after the collapse of communism, there had still been no authoritative biography of Gorbachev published.[110] Gorbachev was still provoking divergent opinions, and also the odd rather enigmatic judgement. Lilia Shevtsova – speaking at the aforementioned conference – argued that Gorbachev was the 'creator of the end of History'.[111] The TV programme *Vox Populi* which aired on 2 March 2001 tried to evaluate Gorbachev's role. Yuri Afanasyev (rector of the Russian State Humanitarian University), Aleksander Yakovlev, Vitaliy Korotich (editor of *Ogonyok* in the 1980s) and Vadim Bakatin (Interior Minister) all jumped to Gorbachev's defence, arguing that he had brought freedom of speech and *glasnost*. Oleg Shenin – one of the coup leaders – damned Gorbachev for having destroyed the Soviet state.[112] Putin also joined the ranks of the Gorbachev fan club, saying that 'a whole epoch is righteously connected with Gorbachev's name ... an epoch which started deep transformations in this country that fundamentally changed the map of the world'.[113] But the implication was clear: that epoch is fading away, and Gorbachev is destined to fade with it.

Gorbachev has slipped quite rapidly off the pages of the Western press as well, except for anniversaries, commemorations or retrospectives. Occasionally he turns up on the TV or radio (or in an advert) but these are few and far between. Apart from the time of his wife's death (which received quite significant levels of coverage), the only really sustained time for remembering Gorbachev came at the end of the millennium and in 2001 (and even then it was fairly selective). The reporting of Raisa's death reiterated the dominant themes of the press reporting of the 1980s: the Gorbachevs as a cultural phenomenon. It emphasized the distinctiveness of the Soviet leader and his wife, and the way that she in particular seemed to be the living embodiment of *perestroika*. As the Soviet Union was attempting to transform itself into something more modern, humane and more Western, there appeared a woman who translated these values into something living with which people could identify. Her demeanour, dress sense, her set of values and her celebrity-like status in the popular media seemed to cry out that the Gorbachevs were somehow 'like us'. The decades of Cold War hostility, of feeling threatened by the communist menace, and of Russian/Eastern 'otherness' were finally on the wane. In Raisa, there was somehow evidence that 'they' wanted to be like 'us'.[114]

Perhaps the final word should be left to Tatyana Tolstaya, who wrote a brilliantly provocative and intriguing piece in *Time*, as part of their series on the 100 people of the twentieth century.[115] In this piece she highlights the enigma that is Gorbachev:

> Gorbachev is such an entirely political creature, and yet so charismatic, that it's hard to come to any conclusions about him as a person. Every attempt I know of has failed miserably. The phenomenon of Gorbachev has not yet been explained, and most of what I have read on the subject reminds me of how a biologist, psychologist, lawyer or statistician might describe an angel.[116]

Gorbachev, in Tolstaya's view, was a deeply flawed leader who made many mistakes. But why was he so castigated at home, when things have so palpably deteriorated since 1991, and when, for instance, the carnage in Chechnya is of a far greater magnitude than anything Gorbachev oversaw? The answer, for Tolstaya, resides partly in the nature of Gorbachev's task, and partly in the attitudes and culture of the Russians themselves. The task he set himself – simultaneously to contain and transform the country, to destroy and construct on the spot – was something that no-one had ever successfully managed to do. In conclusion, reflecting on the 1996 Presidential election where Gorbachev polled only 1.5 million votes, she writes that

> It turns out that there were 1.5 million dreamers, people who hadn't forgotten that bright if short period of time when the chains fell off one after another, when every day brought greater freedom and hope, when life acquired meaning and prospects, when, it even seemed, people loved one another and felt that a general reconciliation was possible.[117]

The nostalgia for Gorbachev, the quasi-messianic figure in the West, still, it seems continues.

Conclusion: the politics of remembering and forgetting

The struggle to control the public memory of an era can be a deep and bitter one. Wrapped up in this process are a whole host of factors: personal vindication; self-justification, personal prominence and promotion; political power; legitimacy; bitterness; ambition and the like. It is rarely an edifying process. The struggle over the remembering and forgetting of Gorbachev and *perestroika* is an excellent example of this. It also reaffirms the problems and the value of the memoir as a source and the increasing complexity of historical writing in an age of proliferating information and immediate judgement. But these memoir accounts are incredibly valuable because they give – admittedly partial and at times flawed – insights into the personality, values and character of Gorbachev, and this in turn is highly significant in any attempt to understand the life and fate of both Gorbachev and *perestroika*.

What can we learn from these memoirs about Gorbachev? A whole host of different Gorbachevs appear in the pages of these memoirs: weak, vacillating, vain Gorbachevs. Arrogant ambitious Gorbachevs. Astute, enlightened humane Gorbachevs. Reforming Gorbachevs. Authoritarian Gorbachevs. Calculating, greedy Gorbachevs. Thoroughly decent Gorbachevs. Panning this material to search for some nuggets of insight into the life and work of Gorbachev is a laborious task, given the ways in which they often directly contradict each other. Yet if we sift these portraits carefully a distinct picture does begin to emerge, and you do on occasion get closer to understanding the man and his life's work. He was a man of strong beliefs, determination and hard work. He was more of an intellectual politician than a pragmatist, and a centrist, reformer and persuader more than a radical or dynamic leader. He was most at home when discussing and debating, but had a tendency to be rather verbose. He proved to be a rather poor judge of character, and in particular failed to compensate for his own weaknesses by developing a team of people around him to complement his own strengths, and make good the areas he was deficient in. Gorbachev's life and work illustrate the tendency for character strengths to become weaknesses in different contexts, and the incredible complexity of the task he set himself. The central, pivotal role Gorbachev played in the whole *perestroika* drama reinforces the importance of

Gorbachev's personality in understanding both the successes and failures of this era. Gorbachev's inability to develop a new institutional structure inevitably led him to exercise power in a highly personalized way, which magnified the significance of his values, beliefs and character.

Although overall he remained an essentially private man, who allowed few people to get very close to him, three aspects of his motivations, working style and personality are crucial in understanding Gorbachev. First, Gorbachev was a humanitarian. He was motivated by a desire to make the USSR, and by extension the world, a safer, better, fairer place. He always attempted to avoid the use of violence or force, and preferred dialogue and consensus to confrontation. He had a strong sense of the importance of morality in politics. This conditioned many of his choices, and also his strategy and tactics both at home and abroad. Second, Gorbachev's preferred approach was deeply unplanned in terms of details and practice. His 'ad hocism' or his adherence to the Napoleonic idea of 'on s'engage et puis on voit' (first engage in a serious battle and then see what happens) turned from a flexible non-dogmatic approach in the beginning as the leadership searched for the right road, to a serious weakness as the reform process deepened. The need for concrete practical measures, properly sequenced reforms, structures to implement decisions, went unmet. Finally, Gorbachev was a man of excessive optimism and inner certainty, who was convinced of the correctness of his own views. He also had a profound sense of destiny, that it was his mission to be a global figure of historic significance. It was this unshakeable belief in his own judgement which defined Gorbachev, which drove him to the top, inspired him to embark on his epoch-changing programme and ultimately proved to be his undoing.

6

Gorbachev assessed

The sorcerer's apprentice?

Introduction: Gorbachev without hindsight

For the academic community in the West, the accession of Gorbachev seemed to herald the onset of something new, even if it only meant the emergence of a new generation of leaders, rather than a shift in policy or orientation for the regime. It quickly became apparent, however, that Gorbachev, his words, his actions, his policies, his initiatives were going to divide the Western academic community. Initial disputes centred around his intentions: was he going to bring about wholesale structural reform of the Soviet system? Or was he going to plough the furrow set by Brezhnev, albeit with more élan and energy? As the pace of change gradually increased, the debates then shifted: did Gorbachev have a clear idea of where he was going, and how to get there? How committed was he to introducing democracy to the USSR? As Gorbachev's reform programme became more radical, and as events began to overtake Gorbachev, so the efforts to try and understand what he was doing and its significance gathered pace. Scholars grappled with what sort of programme *perestroika* was, with the nature of Gorbachev's leadership, and with the successes/failures of his time in office. The disputes and debates have lasted much longer than his time in power. This chapter will chart the evolving views of Gorbachev which emerged within the Western academic community, explore the different interpretations and assess the numerous ways in which scholars have tried to understand Gorbachev and *perestroika*.[1]

Part I: Writings on Gorbachev, 1985–91

Context, context, context!

The writings of Western academics on Gorbachev and the USSR need to be located within their proper contexts if we are to understand how the views were formed and where they originated. The Western Sovietological community was dominated by scholars operating in American, British, French and German universities and research institutes. This included a significant number of émigré scholars: academics from the Eastern Bloc who had left and were now working in the West. Within these communities, there was a clear divide between those working in the field of foreign affairs, diplomacy and foreign policy, on the one hand, and those working in domestic Soviet politics, history, economics, social policy, culture and the like. All scholarly work on the Soviet Union, though – be it domestic or foreign – was shaped by two key contexts: the competing analytical frameworks deployed, and the political/ideological context of the Cold War/Thatcherism/Reaganomics.

The political and ideological framework of the Cold War – capitalism v. communism, USA v. USSR – set the parameters of the debate. The Gorbachev era coincided with a resurgence in Cold War rhetoric and military and diplomatic activity under Ronald Reagan in the USA, as well as a revival of right-wing political and economic programmes piloted by Reagan and Margaret Thatcher. Their agenda – a set of policies and rhetoric involving monetarism, consumerism, low taxation, and ambitions to roll back the state, cut welfare and increase personal responsibility – proclaimed itself implacably opposed not only to the Keynesian demand-management and state interventionist policies, but also to all forms of socialist economic and political practice. The USSR occupied many places in Cold War propaganda. Depicted as expansionist and bent on global domination, it was a threat to the Western way of life. It was an 'evil empire'. It had to be contained, stopped, eradicated. In ideological terms, the USSR – the apotheosis of state control, planning, intervention and ownership – was held up as the antithesis of freedom, democracy, pluralism and the market. In this way the agenda of the New Right could be legitimated, and any opposition labelled 'sympathetic' to Soviet-style communism. The Soviet Union continued to figure in domestic political conflicts as well: it was the living example of 'real' socialism and was used to try and discredit all left-wing movements and criticisms of Reaganism/Thatcherism.

This bitter, acrimonious dispute between left and right meant that politicians, commentators, scholars looked at the USSR for evidence to substantiate their (already) entrenched positions: those on the right were desperate to show that a leopard could not change its spots, and that a new leader could not, and would not, change the basic expansionist, repressive, dictatorial nature of the system. Any changes were only cosmetic, and were designed to lull the gullible, the liberals and the left into believing that the USSR's intentions were benign. Those on the left were desperate either to disassociate themselves entirely from the Soviet project, or to be able to show that Stalinism and dictatorship were dead and that the USSR was becoming more democratic, tolerant and pluralistic. A new Soviet leader was a particularly important ideological and political moment in this war of words, and Gorbachev's accession was critical in this regard. Would he be the acceptable face of the old guard, or would he herald a fresh start? Scholars and academics working in the fields of Soviet politics, Soviet history, the economics of planning, international relations, Soviet foreign policy and so on were inextricably caught up in a highly politicized web of political propaganda, rhetoric and debate. Moreover, many academics were also enlisted by policy-makers and politicians in this process, acting as advisers, sitting on committees and becoming enmeshed in shaping the political and ideological stances of Western governments.[2]

Overlaying these political and ideological conflicts were the professional rivalries and disputes between scholars and academics. These included debates over how to analyse, evaluate and understand the Soviet system, but also at times developed into rather bitter personal rivalries. Many of the entrenched positions were dug with the vindictive energy of personal affront, rather than the painstaking detachment of the dedicated scholar.[3] The modes of analysis which dominated the Sovietological community – even right up until 1985 – hinged around totalitarianism.[4] Totalitarianism was developed during the Cold War. Social scientists evaluating the regimes in Italy, Germany and the USSR argued that a new concept was needed to explain the emergence of a new phenomenon: regimes which sought to control each and every aspect of the life of society and to subordinate individuals totally – spiritually, morally, culturally, economically, politically, socially – to the will of a single leader and his party through a single ideology and a terroristic secret police. The prime directive of a totalitarian regime was to swallow up society and the individual in a gigantic state apparatus. Although the term was devised to explain the nature of the system under Stalin, it continued to be used as the starting-point for analysing the system after 1953, rather ironically as this was just the point when the high-water mark of Stalinism had been reached and the flood waters were receding. Analyses which stressed totalitarian themes could be found in all the different national Sovietological networks, although a greater preponderance of adherents to the totalitarian model could be found in the USA, and especially among the émigré community. The totalitarian model continued to be influential in shaping academic analyses of the Soviet Union up to and after 1985.

Totalitarianism began to come under critical scrutiny, though, in the 1960s. Challenges to the totalitarian model as a means of understanding the Soviet system arose from a number of different sources at roughly the same time. Underlying the shifts in scholarly appraisals were the wider socio-cultural and political changes which come under the ubiquitous umbrella of 'the 1960s'. The radicalism sprang from many sources – the struggle for civil rights in the USA, the national independence movements in the developing world, the proximity of nuclear war during the Cuban Missile Crisis – although the primary one was the Vietnam War. The war prosecuted by the USA evoked a critical grass-roots response in the West. The performance of the US forces stood in contrast with traditional Cold War rhetoric which suggested that Soviet aggression was the main danger to world peace. In the light of this, if the Cold War assumptions about the USA were now open to question, then perhaps the assumptions about the USSR were also open to question? Had they got the USSR 'wrong'?

Thus emerged 'revisionism', a broad (in some senses fairly meaningless) label under the banner of which stood any scholar who attempted to 'revise' understandings of the Soviet system, past or present. The Cold War origins of the totalitarian model inevitably brought it into question from revisionist scholars. Slowly and falteringly an alternative edifice of revisionist scholarship grew up, which challenged head-on the key aspects of totalitarianism. The initial skirmishes centred on Stalin and Stalinism, but soon broadened out to include October 1917 and also the post-Stalin years (although the battlefield remained the 1930s and in particular collectivization and the terror). It was here that the debates began to get up close and personal, particularly in debates over Stalin, Stalinism and the Great Terror. Personal insults were traded. Individuals have been accused of controlling the profession, preventing appointments, only accepting students who adopt particular views, and so on.[5]

The momentum of the revisionist movement was quickened by the growing awareness of weaknesses within the totalitarian model itself. This accelerated the search for other, better ways of analysing Soviet realities. The main weaknesses of the totalitarian model were alluded to earlier. In particular the timing of the development of the full-blown totalitarian model (early to mid-1950s) coincided with the attempts of the post-Stalin leadership to move away from the excesses and arbitrariness of Stalinism. In particular, the totalitarian model had difficulties explaining change; both the *mechanism* of change, and the *direction* of change. If a totalitarian system has emerged full-blown, then where would change come from, particularly political change? Totalitarian theory also found it difficult to explain how changes which reduced the scope of state control, or which placed clear limitations upon the institutions of terror, could be implemented. The weaknesses were not just apparent in its analysis of the elite. Looking below, and in keeping with the political radicalism of the 1960s, scholars began turning their attention away from the elites, and more towards the experiences of ordinary people, the so-called 'history from below' trend. Totalitarian theory seemed to have an almost criminal neglect of society and social forces, seeing it as little more than the passive object of elite policies.[6] Western Marxists and dissident East European Marxists also began to develop their own conceptual critiques of the Soviet system, focusing upon notions of state, class and public property to try and explain the dynamics of the Soviet system of control and production.[7] In response to the new disciplinary developments and research, many totalitarians retreated slightly, conceding that in practice the Soviet system fell short of being totalitarian, primarily because it was so ineffective and inefficient in its operation. However, the concept was still applicable because it continued to aspire to envelop society in the arms of the state.

In tandem with the rise of an atmosphere conducive to challenging Cold War stereotypes and a growing awareness of the weakness of the totalitarian model, the discipline of Sovietology began to grow and develop.[8] The need to know more about the USSR generated a need for Soviet specialists. Specialization and expertise brought in its wake more nuanced and sophisticated analyses. Sub-fields of study began to appear. Kremlinologists began to examine the labyrinthine and murky world of power struggles in the Kremlin. Much could be gleaned from examining the order of names in Politburo communiqués, or who was in front of whom at gatherings to oversee parades in Red Square. Economists developed expertise in understanding the command economy and how it functioned (or not, as was generally the case). It also brought a search for new ways of trying to understand Soviet life. Sometimes this was achieved by applying concepts and ideas used in the analysis of Western societies; at other times, it was accomplished through comparative work, highlighting similarities rather than differences.[9]

What did this new scholarship produce? It was during the late 1960s and the 1970s (coinciding with the era of détente and the hegemony of Keynesian demand management and interventionist politics) that the discipline of Sovietology began to gather pace, moving away from the totalitarian model in a number of different directions. Most notably, in the field of politics, Sovietologists began to place Soviet politics within a comparative framework. Scholars emphasized the common features of all developed political systems: the high degree of bureaucratization, conflicts between the military and the civilian hierarchies, central–local conflicts, increasing tendency to be dominated by expertise-based groups. The argument was that the processes underpinning the West and the East (broadly 'modernization', involving industrialization, urbanization, rationalization of decision-making and so on) were similar, and so the responses of the two systems were in turn likely to be very similar.[10]

Others went further, and began to look at the emergence of particular phenomena in the Soviet system that directly confronted the central tenets of the totalitarian model. Scholars such as Gordon Skilling, Susan Gross Solomon and Jerry Hough argued that the Soviet system was changing and evolving.[11] The most notable changes were identified as the presence of interest groups in the Soviet elite, creating pluralistic pressures. Hough also turned his focus on the nature of political participation in the Soviet system. Valerie Bunce and John Echols argued for the application of the concept of corporatism to the Soviet system.[12] Overall, politics was becoming less ideological, less repressive, less rooted in the personal power of a dominant leader and more routinized, institutionalized and bureaucratized. In other words, more like us. Even in the fields of sociology and economics, scholars seemed to be identifying trends within the Soviet Union which were bringing it closer to the experience of the advanced industrial Western societies. Soviet society seemed to be experiencing problems common to other industrial nations: rising crime rates, alienation, alcoholism, corruption.[13] In the economy, growth rates were slowing down, bringing the Soviet economy closer to the rates of growth experienced by capitalist economies. Overall, some of those who had rejected the totalitarian model argued that, in spite of obvious and persisting differences, the Soviet system and the West appeared to be displaying increasingly similar features (some even went so far as to talk about 'convergence'). Under a broad umbrella of post-totalitarianism, scholars unearthed a variety of different phenomena: a move from totalitarianism to authoritarianism; a liberalization leading to limited pluralism or imperfect monism; modernization and convergence. Common to all of the post-totalitarian views was an acceptance of the possibility of genuine change occurring in the nature of the Soviet system. It is this concept of 'change' – its nature, scope and significance – around which most of the disputes about Gorbachev revolved.[14]

These, broadly speaking, were the dominant frameworks for analysis within the Sovietological community at the time of Gorbachev coming to power in March 1985. In the years that followed these basic positions – totalitarians, anti-totalitarians and post-totalitarians, revisionists, Marxists, and so on – produced a spectacularly colourful and varied spectrum of opinion on Gorbachev, his intentions, his policies, his results and his significance. What is notable right at the outset was the manner in which scholars attempted to squeeze Gorbachev into their framework for understanding the Soviet Union. This chapter is divided into two main sections, in order to grasp both the evolution of academic writing and also its highly contested nature. In the first section, a flavour of the differences of interpretation and of the different ways that academics attempted to solve the conundrum of Gorbachev and *perestroika* will be sampled. These include the initial assessments on his accession, the debates around a central aspect of his programme (democratization) and finally the evaluations of his rule near the end of his period in office. The second section will examine the detailed discussions and dissection of Gorbachev that has occurred since 1991 as the scholarly community has grappled retrospectively with understanding *perestroika* and also with establishing Gorbachev's legacy and significance. Let us begin by exploring attitudes to Gorbachev up to the moment of his accession in March 1985.

Part II: Gorbachev in power

The coronation

Gorbachev was the subject of debate among specialists prior to his accession in 1985.[15] The most positive assessments of Gorbachev as a potential leader came from Archie Brown.[16] Brown maintained that Gorbachev was likely to be a very different leader to his predecessors: he was representative of a different generation, had a high level of formal education and was the youngest member of the Politburo, central committee and secretariat when he became the top man (although he was not the youngest person to become General Secretary, and was only slightly younger than both Khrushchev and Brezhnev when they came to power). This in itself was not that significant. But Brown argued that his speeches and policies during the period 1978–84 revealed a leader critical of dogmatism, open to new ideas and who appeared ready to implement political and economic changes. Gorbachev was a true believer in the Soviet system; he was not about to abandon the key elements of Soviet socialism, but he was aware of the need and potential for improvement within the system, and was likely to grasp the opportunity to bring this about.

Others, such as Jerry Hough, recognized the potential for change represented by Gorbachev, yet were unsure as to whether he would have the scope or authority to do it.[17] During the period between the deaths of Brezhnev and Chernenko, Hough consistently identified Gorbachev as a potential General Secretary, and likely to herald change. But there were some reservations: his record in the agricultural sphere over which he presided under Brezhnev showed him to be a 'timid' reformer, and Hough also questioned whether the use of 'reformist' language by Gorbachev was actually a tactical device to enlist the support of middle-ranking officials in his bid for power, rather than a consistently thought-out position. Others pointed out the impeccably orthodox nature of Gorbachev's background,[18] and judged that on this basis there was little likelihood of him becoming a man to 'rock the boat'.

The most negative and critical appraisals of Gorbachev prior to power came from the émigré community. Mikhail Heller summed up the feelings of many of those convinced that no good thing could ever come out of the USSR. A new leader would not, indeed could not, change the nature of the system. The positive things being written about Mikhail Gorbachev in the West were a superficial judgement based on his youth and his image:

> Mikhail Gorbachov's visit to Great Britain in December 1984 was an eloquent demonstration of how easy it is to charm the West. All he had to do was to bring along his wife, who differed little in her outward appearance from Western women, and everything became clear: if Gorbachev does not have a fat wife, then talk of Soviet totalitarianism must be mendacious.[19]

Gorbachev was a product of the system and, as Heller argued, 'the Soviet system docs not surrender to reform'.[20]

Here we can see the basic positions writ large: the optimists (system can be reformed, and Gorbachev has the personality, the ability and the vision to bring this about); the wait-and-seers (system is not impervious to change, but is Gorbachev the man?); and the pessimists (system cannot be reformed: end of story). As Gorbachev embarked upon his reform programme, the interpretations built upon these foundations began to grow. The most dogmatic grouping of scholars were the émigrés and the pessimists. They exhibited an almost pathological unwillingness to take anything that Gorbachev did at face value, and were constantly interpreting him and his actions sceptically and negatively. By contrast, those scholars who were open about the possibilities of change, even if they were more agnostic about the direction of change or the possibility of success, were far more accurate. This can be explained by three things. First, they exhibited a greater willingness to place Gorbachev at the centre of their analysis, rather than the system. Their starting-point was Gorbachev and his likely orientation, values and priorities. Second, their familiarity with Soviet political language and rituals had already alerted them to the possibility that Gorbachev was likely to herald change. For those who in the know, Gorbachev had already displayed significant signs of innovative thinking before coming to power. Third, and most importantly, scholars such as Brown and Hough were willing to consider a range of options, rather than merely expecting the system to crush any innovation. This openness to new possibilities was the key factor which marked out the best of the academic writing from the rest.

Making sense of Gorbachev: the use of comparisons

As *perestroika* got fully under way, Western scholars began trying to make sense of what Gorbachev was doing. It was now clear that change was on the agenda, and so the pessimists retreated somewhat, sheltering now in the 'well, he won't succeed' tent. The most common approach deployed in the early years was to use the tool of comparative analysis. Almost all of the initial comparisons were derived from a communist/Soviet context, drawn either from the Soviet past or the Soviet bloc present. The reason for the use of communist/Soviet comparisons was twofold. First, one of the purposes behind these approaches was the search for precedents which may have inspired/influenced Gorbachev himself, and thus might hold the key for understanding where Gorbachev was going, and what *perestroika* might create in the USSR. Second, it attempted to communicate something of the overall pattern detected in Gorbachev: that his programme contained both old and new elements, had both continuities and changes, was both conserving and creating. By looking at the different ways in which previous Soviet leaders, or other countries in the Soviet bloc, had sought to balance bringing in changes while retaining the central pillars of the system, scholars hoped to be able to shed light on Gorbachev and his project.

As we have seen, those who detected little new or original or radical in Gorbachev and his programme compared him to Stalin or Brezhnev: Gorbachev was essentially committed to maintaining the core structures and the operating principles established by Stalin and consolidated by Brezhnev: he was a Brezhnevian figure, albeit younger and with a more vivacious wife.[21] The sentiment underlying these approaches was to downplay the significance of Gorbachev, and to emphasize that real, systemic change in the USSR was unlikely, even with a young dynamic leader.

Other comparisons were more popular. These focused particularly on Andropov, the Lenin of the NEP and, most frequently, Nikita Khrushchev.[22] These periods were generally sought out and used by scholars who viewed Gorbachev as a harbinger of change and renewal, although the degree and scope of this change were open to debate. The Andropov comparisons were drawn because of the close links between the two. The master/disciple relationship which was said to have marked their work together emerged with Gorbachev carrying on, and extending, the programme inaugurated by Andropov but cut short by his untimely death in 1984 and the subsequent accession of Chernenko. Andropov's stress on labour discipline, anti-corruption, ideological flexibility and personnel turnover were exactly the initial themes developed by Gorbachev, and so could be seen as part of a wider project that had already been developed and was to be put into practice.[23]

The use of the 'later' Lenin, or the Lenin of the post-1921 era, was invoked partly because Gorbachev himself had used Lenin's writings from this period to justify his own move away from the status quo, and partly as an inspiration for his particular mix of policies. Gorbachev saw parallels between his project and Lenin's turn to the NEP, thus the NEP (*perestroika*), by rejecting the civil war policy of war communism (*the Stalino-Brezhnevite approach*) – involving state control, coercion – proclaimed a different way to get to communism. The NEP period was used because it combined cultural liberalization, relative economic autonomy and freedom in the agricultural sphere and the consumer sector, with state control of the industrial sectors, banking, finance and foreign trade, alongside strict one-party dominance of the political system. Scholars used this analogy to explore the extent to which Gorbachev was recreating an NEP-type approach by allowing limited economic and cultural experimentation, while maintaining state control of industry and party control of the political sphere. Academics were quick to point out that, while all previous Soviet leaders invoked Lenin to give themselves legitimacy, Gorbachev had gone the furthest in resurrecting the ethos of the NEP.[24]

Khrushchev produced perhaps the most interesting set of parallels. Khrushchev was used as an analogy both by scholars wishing to demonstrate how *radical* Gorbachev was, and also of how *conservative* Gorbachev was. This was of course due to the extremely contradictory and paradoxical nature of Khrushchev's time in power. Khrushchev had inaugurated the move away from the excesses of Stalinism, had denounced the cult of personality, overseen a cultural thaw, partially restored legality to Soviet life, encouraged the Soviet people to take an active part in the running of their localities, improved the levels of welfare, attacked the privileges of the bureaucracy and reformed Soviet agriculture. His style was populist, energetic, dynamic, confrontational. All of this had earned him the epithet of 'reformer'. Simultaneously, Khrushchev had maintained the essentials of the Stalinist system, continued to use terror (selectively), maintained the one-party rule, suppressed religion and become the single dominant political figure. In other words, he had maintained the Stalinist approach, but without the excesses. Scholars then invoked whichever picture of Khrushchev they preferred and applied it to Gorbachev. Hence Seweryn Bialer and Joan Afferica's view that Gorbachev was following in the footsteps of both Brezhnev and Khrushchev, in trying to improve economic performance 'without resorting to structural change'.[25] For Reddaway, Gorbachev was *lagging behind* Khrushchev in terms of the scope and radicalism of his programme compared to Khrushchev's de-Stalinization, but had *equalled* Khrushchev in his use of publicity to expose corruption, and *surpassed* him in his radical language.[26]

Khrushchev was also used to highlight the move away from the Brezhnevite approach of Gorbachev: his style was deemed also to be populist and confrontational, and his approach – attacking the bureaucracy and mobilizing the people – was also said to have echoes in the Khrushchevite era.[27] For Archie Brown, Gorbachev's leadership style – out in front, cajoling, enthusing – was similar to Khrushchev, but his overall programme was more subtle, consistent and had a greater degree of political insight, probably because Gorbachev had learned from Khrushchev's mistakes.[28] Sidney Ploss argued that Gorbachev resembled Khrushchev in some ways – stressing the same themes of personnel turnover, popular participation, less secrecy, criticism of Stalin – yet was less impulsive and more willing to listen to the ideas of his experts than Khrushchev had been.[29]

More general comparisons focused on the nature of Gorbachev's programme. In particular, the similarities and differences with the trajectory of the policies embarked upon in the German Democratic Republic, Hungary and the People's Republic of China were highlighted. The example of the economic reforms in the GDR were deployed as a means of highlighting that the thrust of Gorbachev's economic reforms were designed to maintain the essential operating principles and central command structure of the economy, but improve their performance through greater efficiency, increased use of technology and a reduction in bureaucracy. Hungary and China, by contrast, were used to express that the thrust of Gorbachev's reforms were going beyond increased efficiency and streamlining, to embrace decentralization, flexibility and (possibly?) even the move away from total planning to a limited use of the market (or commodity-money relations as the Soviets termed it).[30]

A few scholars were willing to go beyond a communist/Soviet framework in order to understand what was happening. Here the choice of historical parallel was deeply revealing. Robert Conquest – a dedicated counter-communist and someone who was deeply pessimistic about Gorbachev – looked to the *ancien régime* France of 1780 for his inspiration. Gorbachev was akin to some of the reform statesmen of that time (Turgot, Necker) who were attempting to change a rapidly decaying system, beset with entrenched interests.[31] Conquest did stress that the parallel was not an exact one, and the outcome might well be different, but the implication of a statesman unable to reform a corrupt, degenerating system was clear. Robert Tucker and Julian Cooper preferred instead to use the Protestant Reformation as their historical parallel. Tucker noted how similar themes could be seen in the two projects:

- root out official corruption;
- return to original sources of doctrine, rather than relying upon subsequent interpretations, additions and updates (Bible/Marx and Lenin);
- a stress on the individual;
- responsibility for yourself;
- reform at work and in private life.[32]

Here the implications of the comparison were much more positive (successful outcome), and *perestroika* became rather more than tinkering with a doomed system, as in Conquest's parallel with *ancien régime* France. Here there was a root-and-branch restructuring on the way, embracing ideas, doctrines, official life and individual behaviour.

Probably the most comprehensive analysis came from Gail Lapidus who, having compared Gorbachev with both Brezhnev and Khrushchev, found both comparisons wanting.[33] Gorbachev was not a 'true believer' like Khrushchev, and nor was he a 'conservative bureaucrat' like Brezhnev. Instead Lapidus argued that Gorbachev was the first 'modern' Soviet leader: aware of the demands made by scientific and technological advances, pragmatic, rationalizing, flexible. He was keenly aware of both the basic stability of the system and of the deficiencies in its performance during the 1970s and 1980s.[34] What was novel and original in Gorbachev's programme was its awareness of the need to include society in the mechanisms for governing. *Glasnost'*, by encouraging groups in civil society to participate and contribute to the running of the system (without transcending one-party rule), had taken Gorbachev beyond Khrushchev, and into uncharted territory. Lapidus recognized that Gorbachev could quite plausibly be seen as standing in the traditions of a reforming tsar-autocrat, or as another post-totalitarian leader mobilizing and adapting the system. However, she preferred to see Gorbachev as making a distinctive break with the Russian and Soviet past, as his programme aimed at a fundamental redefinition of the state/society relationship.[35]

The comparative analysis undertaken at the time was extremely useful in illuminating different aspects of Gorbachev's programme. In particular, a great strength of comparative analysis is its ability to identify patterns and an overall shape. This is certainly the case here, as comparisons with previous Soviet leaders highlighted elements of continuity and change, and of the way in which the particular mix of approaches adopted by Gorbachev had been put together. Another intriguing element in the comparison was of course the choice of comparison. This told us much about the perspective of the analyst. The sceptics chose Stalin or Brezhnev. The optimists tended to favour Khrushchev or the later Lenin. Khrushchev was the most intriguing choice, as he was used to highlight both the radicalism and the conservatism as we have seen. The most productive and insightful comparisons were clearly those which sought to understand the paradoxical or difficult elements of Gorbachev's programme, rather than those comparisons which were deployed just to confirm the perspective of the analyst. This is the main reason that Khrushchev was such a favourite figure to use. He too had been a contradictory and complex figure, and as such his example helped scholars to grasp the complexities and tensions in Gorbachev's programme.

Creative tensions: the debates over democracy, democratization and democrat

Although academics debated and discussed all aspects of Gorbachev's reform programme at length – foreign policy, the economy, nationalities, *glasnost'*, and so on – the most interesting debate crystallized around the question of democratization and political reform. The extension of Gorbachev's political reform programme – which had begun with personnel turnover, anti-corruption campaigns and *glasnost'* – provided a further example of the divisions within the Sovietological community over Gorbachev and his programme.[36]

The position of the extremely sceptical Gorbophobes – that the reforms of Gorbachev were merely a cosmetic exercise designed for the benefit of Western public opinion – continued to dissolve as the pace and extent of the political reforms quickened and deepened. Equally, all commentators were at one in stressing that

Gorbachev was not aiming to create a Western-style constitutional multi-party democracy. However, the motivations behind the political reforms, and the underlying intentions of the programme of democratization, legal reform and institutional innovation were murkier. As the sceptics decamped from their previous positions, they took up residence in Gorbachev as 'reluctant' democratizer. Gorbachev was essentially engaged in a limited liberalization of the Soviet system – entailing measures to make the system more just, humane and participatory without addressing the question of the distribution of power – but had been forced to make concessions to limited pluralism and restricted democratizing reforms because of the depth of the crisis he had uncovered, and because of the failures of the reforms he had so far implemented.[37]

The majority position was adopted by those who saw Gorbachev embracing democratization as a means to his particular ends. Gorbachev's project – essentially modernization of the system to make it more efficient and stable – had stalled. To put it back on track, reforms embracing democratization were deemed necessary. This position was given full expression by Seweryn Bialer, writing in 1987:

> It would stretch the imagination to believe that Gorbachev and his associates now accept the intrinsic value of democracy as the west understands it – genuine grass-roots political participation, openness and governmental accountability, a free press, diversity, and the unimpeded clash of ideas. A more realistic view is that for Soviet leaders the new course with its different values, has primarily functional importance. Gorbachev and his colleagues have become 'democrats' because they have concluded that this course is required as a precondition for and a part of modernisation.[38]

But how did 'democratization' form part of the road to modernization? Democratization and political reform promoted economic reform. The close linkages between economic and political reform were highlighted most clearly by Ronald Amann.[39] He stressed four reasons for seeing political reform as a prelude to, or accompaniment to, economic reform. First, it was necessary as a means of mobilizing the population to participate in the reforms (what Gorbachev termed the 'Human Factor'). Second, it was part of the strategy to construct a coalition of support for *perestroika*, and to try to overcome opposition to it from the entrenched interests. Third, it was needed to guard against a 'creeping recentralization'. Finally, it was seen as a means of dispelling mass unrest, and to provide an alternative means of legitimation, as the usual approaches – legitimation through ideology and material consumption – were weakened by the economic changes.[40]

Others concurred that democratization was functional for Gorbachev, but detected other ends towards which it was aimed. Astrid van Borcke argued that the Soviet leadership had now recognized that democracy was the most effective and efficient means of governing a modern, complex industrial society. On this reading, political reform and democratization were functional to the goal of creating a modernized, efficient socialism in the USSR. Democracy had now come to be seen by the Soviet leadership as something that could be used to strengthen and preserve the dominance of the CPSU.[41] Democratization was also seen as a means to a different end: Gorbachev securing his own position in the teeth of growing opposition. This had a similar origin to the above view, in that political reform emerged out of Gorbachev's learning process from his first two years in office. This had convinced him that the party apparatus was deeply conservative, obstructive of change and likely to hold back or even prevent lasting change (as they had under Khrushchev, and to a lesser extent under Brezhnev). The move to create an alternative power structure was Gorbachev's strategy to break the power of the party apparatus.[42] Opinions were divided, though, over the extent to which this was a tactical device to promote change, or a cynical move on Gorbachev's part to bolster his own position. Suspicions about the latter grew when at the 19th Party Conference in June 1988, Gorbachev proposed that the chairman of the Supreme Soviet should be chosen not by a popular nationwide ballot, but by the deputies in the new Congress, and that the General Secretary of the party should run for this position. This would give this particular figure enormous powers, as both head of the (sole) party and head of the new legislature.

Those who saw democratization and political reform as functional to other goals stressed the limitations built into the democratic system that Gorbachev had created. In the early stages of democratization (1987), before the planned changes to the institutional basis of the Soviet political system had become apparent, Bialer argued that Gorbachev was moving towards the creation of an 'inverted' democracy. Unlike Western democracy, which was democratic at the macrosocietal level and non-democratic at the micro level (firms, trade unions, etc.), Gorbachev was looking for microsocietal democracy without changes to the institutions of state.[43] Even when the plans for macro-level changes were published, doubts were cast on how 'democratic' this was. It was seen as a 'guided' democracy: electoral choice would be limited by the absence of other parties, and by the requirement to maintain an ideological commitment to the 'socialist choice'. It was to be pluralistic, but this was a qualified socialist 'pluralism'. It was a legislature composed partly of deputies elected by popular vote, and partly by reserved seats for selected state organizations. The standing parliament was only indirectly elected from among the ranks of the Congress of People's Deputies, acting as a filter to prevent radical or outspoken voices from dominating. It was, according to Andrei Sakharov, 'a campaign to achieve democracy by undemocratic means'.[44]

Even those who had consistently portrayed Gorbachev as a serious reformer maintained some reservations about the type of democracy that Gorbachev was trying to construct. The most notable eloquent exception to this was John Gooding.[45] Gooding argued that Western analysts consistently underestimated the radicalism of Gorbachev, and that Gorbachev was 'committed to democracy in the genuine rather than the hitherto perverted Soviet sense of the word'.[46] Gooding's Gorbachev was a paradoxical figure: radical, yet operating within the system;

iconoclastic, yet a convinced Marxist-Leninist. Gooding argued that democracy and democratization had been a central part of Gorbachev's programme from his accession in March 1985, and was not something which began in January 1987. Although he recognized that platitudes about 'perfecting democracy' and encouraging the masses to become involved were staple parts of every party leader's rhetoric, Gorbachev was saying something qualitatively different. Between March 1985 and January 1987, the need for democratization was brought more acutely into Gorbachev's thinking, but it had always been there. Subsequently, what unfolded was the vision of democracy espoused by Gorbachev, combining a positive evaluation of a pluralism of opinions, personal freedom, justice and socialism. Gorbachev was no western liberal, and remained committed to the monopoly rule of the CPSU. Nevertheless he was dedicated to a genuine form of democratic socialism, seeking a genuine transformation of the institutions of power, and the political practices of the state, the party and the people.[47]

The attempts of Western scholars to try to understand Gorbachev and his programme in this period between 1987 and 1989 were made difficult by the pace and scale of the change. Analyses were often rendered irrelevant within a couple of months of publication as the Gorbachev project accelerated. The difficulty facing Western scholars was the growing sense of contingency. None of the old certainties about the USSR could be 100 per cent relied upon any more. Gorbachev appeared to be rewriting the rules on a monthly basis, and the best way to analyse what was happening, or how to construct an appropriate explanatory framework, was unclear. Yet even here the old divide between those who saw the system as impervious to any change and those who viewed it more agnostically or even more positively remained. Attention began to turn to the likely outcome of Gorbachev's tenure. The pessimists or counter-communists described Gorbachev as a lonely, tragic figure, struggling against 'gargantuan' odds to change the system. Those who had previously doubted the sincerity of his motives or the depth of the transformation he had in mind, now turned their attention to the accumulating opposition he faced. He would be overwhelmed by the system. He could not succeed. His was a tragic story which only served to reinforce that the communist system could not embrace meaningful reform.[48]

For the agnostics, Gorbachev was viewed as a 'transitional figure': at times, he acted like a traditional communist; at others, he was acting in new and unusual ways. He appeared to be willing and able to destroy the old economic system, but unable to put anything new and effective in its place. For instance, at the heart of the debates surrounding 'Gorbachev the democrat' lay the question of the place of the Communist Party in *perestroika* and in Gorbachev's thinking. Was Gorbachev moving away from, even abandoning, the party as the central political institution? Could Gorbachev successfully construct a one-party democracy? Would the momentum of the changes sweep away both Gorbachev and his party? Or would the party remove Gorbachev, as it had removed Khrushchev, when its powers and privileges were under threat? Gorbachev appeared to want to defend the party and transcend it at the same time.

In describing the attempt by Gorbachev to combine the old and the new, Hewett used the analogy of a jazz pianist, seeing Gorbachev as an improviser, but 'within a definite key and a definite musical structure'.[49] It is this sense of paradox that led some to see Gorbachev as a transitional figure. The agnostics recognized the profound changes that Gorbachev was aiming to introduce, but doubted whether he would be the one to oversee their final execution. He was likely to be a figure akin to Moses, leading the Soviet people to the verge of the Promised Land, but perishing before entering. No one could be sure who the Joshua figure was.[50]

For those who were open to the possibility of change and reform in the Soviet system, the appraisals of Gorbachev were much more positive. He was seen as an heroic figure. He had embarked upon a 'titanic endeavour', and had proved himself an adept, skilful and talented politician. If he succeeded, then he would go down as one of the great statesmen of the twentieth century.[51] Here the focus was upon Gorbachev's tactical and strategic skills. Hough continued to see an unfolding, consistent strategy, calling Gorbachev a 'world-class chess player'.[52] The depth of the opposition and the extent of the task were acknowledged, but Gorbachev was still at the helm and, while that was the case, success for *perestroika* could not be ruled out. Once more, the view of Gorbachev was primarily determined by the general attitude towards the USSR.

The intriguing aspects of the debate on democratization which took place were the extent to which Gorbachev had shifted the grounds of the debate and completely wrong-footed the pessimists within three short years. Although there were still many ready to adopt a sceptical position of sorts, the intellectual high ground was now held by the optimists and the agnostics. The evidence of tangible change was too great to ignore. The debate shifted more towards the direction in which Gorbachev was heading, and the likely shape of the system in the future. The verdict on Gorbachev as democrat/democratizer was inconclusive. But the very fact that Western commentators were actually debating how democratic a Soviet leader was, and what type of democracy might eventually emerge in the USSR, was testament to the remarkable changes Gorbachev had inaugurated.

Evaluating Gorbachev

Although it became impossible for Western academic writing to keep pace with *perestroika* in 1990 and 1991, it did prove possible to begin to step back from appraisals of this or that aspect of *perestroika*, and to begin to reflect on some of the wider issues. This was generated in part by the fifth anniversary of Gorbachev in power in March 1990, but also by a burgeoning desire to grasp the wider meaning and significance of what was going on in the USSR. There were two sustained scholarly debates. In the pages of the journal *Soviet Economy*, a number of articles between 1989 and 1991 debated the qualities of Gorbachev's leadership.[53] Similarly, the journal *Soviet Union/Union Soviétique* put together a scholarly symposium assessing, in the editor Joseph Wieczynski's words, the 'efficacy and successes of Gorbachev's work'.[54] Outside of these appraisals, there were also a range of individual pieces throughout 1990 and 1991, all of which sought to form a judgement on Gorbachev, his leadership and his likely prospects.

The discussion in *Soviet Economy* was opened by George Breslauer. Breslauer maintained that Gorbachev was an 'event-making man' and a transformational leader:

> During his first 5 years in power, Gorbachev has been an event-making man, exercising unique leadership skills to break his country out of the pre-existing order at home and abroad, and to begin the process of building alternative political and international orders.[55]

Gorbachev had initiated change at home and abroad, intervened to radicalize the process of *perestroika* at key moments, refused to sanction the use of violence to quell popular protest (with the tragic exception of Tbilisi in April 1989) and had articulated a vision of a new type of international order. His leadership was not without flaws. Breslauer cited his failures in economic and nationalities policy, saying that in these areas he had been more successful at destroying than creating. Overall, though, Gorbachev had proved to be a successful transformational leader, having pursued a strategy of radical centrism: playing the radicals and conservatives off against one another, maintaining the centre ground in order to destroy the old system and encourage authentic political participation among the masses. Although he acknowledged the serious challenges and problems facing Gorbachev, he refused to write off his prospects.[56]

Peter Reddaway adopted a much more pessimistic and critical tone. He asserted that Gorbachev lacked charisma and had failed to persuade the Soviet people to rally behind his vision of the future. Gorbachev (in late 1990) was shifting back towards the conservatives and had become part of the problem, not the solution. He had procrastinated and delayed, and was likely to be seen as a tragic figure in Soviet history.[57] Archie Brown adopted a more positive tone. He viewed Gorbachev as a flexible, skilful, pragmatic political leader who had overseen massive unforeseen changes in the Soviet system up to this point.[58] Both Brown and Breslauer offered a conditionally optimistic judgement on Gorbachev, and saw his shift toward the conservatives between October 1990 and April 1991 as a temporary tactical shift to maintain the centre ground. The growing volume of criticism of Gorbachev which Brown detected during 1990 was not a testament to his incompetence or his indecision, but merely due to the depth and complexity of the task at hand.[59]

The most radical interpretation came from Jerry Hough.[60] Hough outlined how Western observers had consistently been surprised by Gorbachev, had consistently got Gorbachev wrong, and had consistently failed to agree on even basic interpretations of Gorbachev's actions. Arguing, in contradiction to Breslauer, that it was impossible to evaluate Gorbachev's leadership until you could see how it had turned out, Hough turned his article into a broadside against Sovietologists, chastising them for their errors, misperceptions, inconsistencies and inability to move beyond their established theoretical and ideological positions. Central to Hough's analysis was that Gorbachev had always been a radical reformer (in the mould of a modernizing, Westernizing Tsar); that he had a clear political strategy that had been worked out in advance (and was not just reacting to events around him). He gave a number of examples of disputed actions by Gorbachev. For example, Hough was the only theorist who saw a clear rationale in Gorbachev's policy towards the nationalities. He argued that Gorbachev was allowing unrest in the republics to demonstrate to the radicals that untrammelled democratization would lead to chaos. Gorbachev's project – guided democracy – was the only possible way. Similarly, Hough argued that Gorbachev's oscillations between October and April 1991 were perfectly consistent with his project to modernize and Westernize without moving back to Stalinism, or to full-blown Western constitutional democracy and marketization. For Hough, Gorbachev had shown himself consistently to be an adroit, skilful, astute political leader. Hough was an optimist: Gorbachev was neither a transitional nor a tragic figure. He was very likely to be in a strong position by the mid-1990s.[61]

Breslauer concluded the discussion. He took issue with many of Hough's slights against the Sovietological profession, and reiterated his stance that Gorbachev was an event-making man. He left open the question of the ultimate historical judgement that would be made on Gorbachev: either tragic or transformational would be applied, dependent upon the outcome. Underlying this thoughtful and balanced debate one can detect two underlying strands. First, there was a theoretical dispute about how to evaluate a leader who was still in office. The sense of historical perspective was absent, and the final outcome was unknown. Should judgements be informed by what had already been achieved (i.e. Gorbachev between 1985 and 1990 and the amount he had managed to change)? Or should he be judged against how much he had achieved in pursuit of his own vision (i.e. how far short is he of what he set out to do) or indeed of our vision of where we think he is heading? Or should he be evaluated not just against the choices he made, but also against the opportunities he missed? The choice of framework for evaluation was often predetermined by the attitude towards Gorbachev. Positive, optimistic scholars looked at how much had been achieved. More critical, pessimistic scholars examined the gap between vision and reality, and found him wanting. A lack of agreement on the proper framework for evaluation meant that basic disagreements were unable to be resolved. Second, the fundamental divisions among Sovietologists about the nature of the Soviet system were replicated in debates about Gorbachev. The scholarly divisions continued to run very deep.[62]

The debate in *Soviet Union/Union Soviétique* was rather more eclectic in tone and content. It was not a rolling, ongoing debate in the style of *Soviet Economy*, but was a collection of pieces by scholars who had been invited to comment upon Gorbachev and his reforms. As usual a broad spectrum of opinions emerged. Rex Wade noted that although there had been benefits in certain areas – personal freedoms, less censorship, more meaningful elections, greater freedom of expression – Gorbachev had failed to inspire his own people or to move beyond the role of a reforming autocrat. For Wade, Gorbachev stood within a long line of reformist tsars, and *perestroika* was little more than a series of adjustments and tinkerings, which lagged behind public opinion.[63] Peter Juviler asserted that Gorbachev had shown a lack of trust in spontaneity and an inability to let go of the controls, which had undermined his leadership and ultimately his project. Both Wade and Juviler contrasted Gorbachev's inability to inspire with the inspiration provided by the rapid growth of nationalism and national identity.[64]

Others saw a mixed record, contrasting his brilliant, startling successes abroad with failures, chaos and disintegration at home. Theodore von Laue set out how Gorbachev had 'normalized' international relations, ended the Cold War and reduced tensions worldwide, while unleashing long-lasting internal turmoil. It was a 'heroic gamble'.[65] In a similar vein, Roger Kanet stressed the major accomplishments in arms control, reducing superpower confrontations and bringing the Cold War to an end. At home, though, it was a different story: chaos and fragmentation.[66]

An interesting sub-theme running through many of these contributions was the question of Gorbachev's 'place in history'. As we saw above, Wade believed that Gorbachev should be viewed as part of a long tradition of Russian reformers from above.[67] Millar saw him as having established his place in Soviet history, by thoroughly de-Stalinizing Soviet society.[68] But others were prepared to go much further in their appraisal of Gorbachev and history. Jane Curry noted that Gorbachev had introduced changes 'more dramatic and deeper than those of virtually any other five years in history'.[69] Treadgold noted:

> Mikhail Sergeevich started it all, single-handed ... And therefore it may be argued, Gorbachev has made more of a contribution to human freedom than any other single person in decades, perhaps in this century ... we should not forget his great service to the human race.[70]

Alfred Meyer went furthest in establishing Gorbachev's place in the pantheon of twentieth-century political leaders. Examining the ways political leaders had been bestowed with the title of 'greatness', he found a number of different examples:

- empire builders and/or consolidators (Louis XIV; Napoleon I; Alexander the Great; Bismarck);
- empire destroyers as heralds of great change (Luther; Lenin; Oliver Cromwell);
- preservers of existing systems in face of threatening changes (Metternich);
- reformers of ailing or rotten systems (Ataturk; British parliamentary leaders).[71]

Meyer went on to state:

> Gorbachev has already established himself as one of the great political leaders of this century. He has functioned as an enlightener and as a reformer. His methods have tried to avoid brutality and vindictiveness,

even though the changes he is aiming to make will inflict considerable pain to many people in the Soviet Union. If eventually he fails, he will, as George Breslauer has pointed out, be known to historians as a tragic hero of great stature. Should he succeed in modernising the Soviet Union while preserving it in some form, his eminent place in history will be assured.[72]

Other scholars began to join the debate *ad hoc* during the course of 1990 and 1991. Twin themes emerged. One sought to assess the underlying meaning and significance of *perestroika*. Richard Sakwa argued that *perestroika* went beyond a form of de-Stalinization and represented the Europeanization of the USSR: the reincorporation of the USSR into a global society based upon the basic norms of Western liberal democracy and civic freedoms.[73] Jerry Hough argued that *perestroika* marked the end of the 'Khomeini' period of Russian history: an era of self-imposed intellectual and cultural isolation and anti-Westernism.[74] Sakwa, Hough and Ernest Gellner all noted that Gorbachev's programme was leading to the emergence of a 'normal' society: stripped of utopianism, messianism and a tendency to social engineering on a massive scale, the USSR was becoming akin to a secular, Western, industrial society.[75]

The other theme took up the 'evaluating Gorbachev' line set out above. What is noticeable about this collection of pieces is the highly negative, critical picture of Gorbachev which comes through. He is constantly referred to as a 'failure', as a 'tragic' figure, as a transitional, ambiguous, irrelevant leader. There were one or two contributions which qualified this idea of failure. Derek Spring stressed that Gorbachev could best be characterized as a politician of retreat from an authoritarian system who was likely to become a victim of his own success, swept away by the reforms he initiated.[76] Robert Kaiser also qualified his verdict. Kaiser's appraisal stressed many of the positive outcomes of Gorbachev's tenure. Listing a catalogue of monumental achievements, Kaiser added that, 'These are the most astounding historical developments that any of us are likely to experience.'[77] Ultimately, though, Gorbachev would be seen as an heroic failure.

> He could begin the process of reinventing his country, but at the critical moment he could not reinvent himself. Perhaps Gorbachev will be remembered as the leader of the prologue to true *perestroika* – the real renewal of Russia. This is no small accomplishment. On the contrary his is a heroic achievement, because Machiavelli was right when he observed that nothing is more difficult than taking the lead in the introduction of a new order of things.[78]

There were a number of ideas common to the remaining appraisals of Gorbachev. First, there was the recognition that Gorbachev's main legacy was that he was a destroyer: he had removed or undermined the main elements of the edifice of Soviet totalitarianism. This by itself would be enough to guarantee his place in history. The problem was that his project had professed to replace it with some-thing, and this he had failed to do, and it was becoming increasingly unlikely that he would be able to. The reasons for his failure were explained away as a variation on the theme of Gorbachev as transitional/ambiguous/paradoxical figure. Gor-bachev, on this reading, was a party man and a revolutionary,[79] both Luther and the Pope,[80] a proponent of both old and new thinking. Gorbachev had been unable to resolve the essential dilemma which ran through his period in office: how to maintain the system *and* transform it.

Moreover, Gorbachev's failure was becoming less of an heroic one, and more of a tragic one. The developments in 1990 and 1991 – the turn towards personal dic-tatorship, the use of repression in Lithuania – threatened to sully his reputation as a reformer, a democrat, a humanist. Anders Aslund outlined how Gorbachev had become increasingly authoritarian, conservative and hesitant, as his programme began to unravel in the face of economic collapse and national disintegration. As events spiralled out of control, he seemed to have lost his sense of direction. He seemed to be determined to preserve his own position and preserve the Soviet empire at all costs. Most damagingly for a man who had dominated the world stage for five years, Gorbachev was threatening to become an irrelevance to the future of Russia/Soviet Union.[81] Allen Lynch asked the question 'Does Gorbachev matter any more?'[82] Overwhelmed by forces he had unleashed, increasingly unpopular and isolated at home, his time appeared to be up.

Conclusion: Western academics and Gorbachev, 1985–91

What does this review of the academic appraisals of Gorbachev written at the time of his reforms tell us? The complex, contradictory picture of Gorbachev that emerged can partially be explained by the fact that Gorbachev's project was itself a constantly evolving thing, which developed incredibly rapidly. Academic analysis generally does not cope very well with rapid change. It somehow goes against the grain of the steady gaze, the reflective temper and the *longue durée* of academia. The widely diverging appraisals of Gorbachev were also a function of the pro-found divisions within the academic community. The essential problem was that the Sovietological community was often more concerned with using what Gor-bachev was doing to reinforce their pre-existing interpretation of the nature of the Soviet Union/communism than with attempting to interpret Gorbachev *on his own terms*. In other words, Gorbachev and his programme were used to confirm the theoretical or conceptual world-view of Sovietologists, and to refute the views of their opponents. Gorbachev was pushed and pulled and squeezed until he and his programme fitted into the world-view of the scholar in question.

While this was perhaps understandable in the early stages of *perestroika*, what was more remarkable was that virtually all sides of the Sovietological community – totalitarians, anti-totalitarians, post-totalitarians, revisionists – reacted to the growing radicalization by adopting a revised standpoint, but one which still con-firmed their original stance. Recognition of what Gorbachev had achieved or was attempting to do or had failed to do or had omitted to do seemed to have little impact upon assessments of Gorbachev. The entrenched positions of Sovietologists remained pretty much intact. At times it seemed that Gorbachev had become little more than a pawn in the battle of the Sovietologists. This battle for hegemony in the academic sphere turned out to be a war of attrition, and it was no longer carried out solely in the obscurity of academic journals. The media coverage given to Gorbachev meant that Sovietologists were increasingly frequent contributors to daily newspapers, weekly journals and the broadcast media too. The best way to defend your viewpoint was to become a regular commentator and contributor, using each new development to defend your viewpoint. More often than not, though, Gorbachev and his programme were lost in this fight.

The reason why Gorbachev was fought over in such a frenzied way was because he was an agent of change in a time when the Cold War had become decidedly icy. While the stasis of the latter Brezhnev years prevailed, the divisions between scholars were clear-cut and there was little to provoke debate or confront scholars with the possibility that their perspective was flawed or problematic. The advent of Gorbachev changed all that. Once a political leader committed to sustained change appeared on the scene, then the entrenched positions came under threat. The possibility of real change opened the way for either the dismantling of the totalitarian model or the confirmation of the totalitarian model, or the need for a new model or no model at all. The scale and pace of the change meant that the old shibboleths would no longer do. New shibboleths had to be found, without admitting that the old ones were wrong.

The record of assessing Gorbachev among Western academics was by turns flawed and inspired. It was at its most flawed in the early years when commentators refused to take seriously the notion that Gorbachev might be an agent of sustained, progressive change. It was at its most inspired and creative when discussing the intricacies of his programme of democratization and in looking for comparative insights into his programme. In general, the appraisals of Gorbachev generated by the sub-disciplines of Sovietology – foreign affairs, the economics of the Command system, Kremlinology and Soviet politics – produced much more useful material than those which explored Gorbachev himself, the nationalities issue or the bigger picture of the underlying meaning and direction of *perestroika*. This is part of a general malaise which tends to afflict contemporary academia which tends to eschew 'big' questions in favour of the specialist, narrow study, and which prefers structures to personalities, systems to individuals.

It was only when the latter debates on aspects of Gorbachev's leadership style emerged that this began to be addressed. Many contributions and contributors produced some deeply insightful commentary, and Gorbachev as an agent of historical change began to be discussed extensively and carefully. What was missing up until this point was an analysis which considered Gorbachev *on his own terms*. The historicizing of Gorbachev was long overdue. The problem was disentangling those perspectives which were driven more by ideology or the narrow academic politics of the Sovietological community from those which genuinely differed over methodological or interpretative issues. The deeper problems of Sovietology will be explored in the second half of this chapter. As Gorbachev moved off the global stage at the end of 1991, the question of his historical legacy, achievements and remained open to debate.

Part III: writings on Gorbachev since 1991

The sudden collapse of the communist system and the dismantling of the Soviet Union took everyone by surprise. As Gorbachev shuffled quietly away into a premature retirement, so the world of academia began immediately to undertake a process of reflection, analysis and debate as to the causes and meaning of these events. Once more the figure of Gorbachev loomed large in these works. The questions asked were of different orders. What role did Gorbachev play in ending the Cold War? Was he *responsible* for the collapse of communism? Was he to *blame* for the demise of the Soviet Union? As the events became more distant, more reflective questions began to be asked: what were Gorbachev's main achievements? What is his legacy? How will history judge him? Not unexpectedly, these questions have issued forth a dazzling variety of opinions, views, perspectives and arguments which have added further layers of complexity to our understanding of Gorbachev, and have deepened the sense of paradox and enigma even further. He has been characterized as both the 'individual who had the most profound impact on world history in the second half of the twentieth century'[83] and a 'spectacular failure'[84] in all regards, as well as all points in between.[85]

In the analysis that follows, the broad explanatory frameworks advanced by Western scholars will be outlined, followed by reflections on the achievements and legacy of Gorbachev. The main points of dispute between scholars will be examined to try and identify why he has been subject to such divergent interpretations. However, if we are searching for the reasons for the myriad explanations and interpretations of Gorbachev, his achievements, successes, failures and legacy, then this takes us beyond the man himself. We will begin our search by looking at the assumptions, influences and circumstances that shaped those who undertook to evaluate Gorbachev.

The contours and paradigms of academic writing

Earlier, we saw that academic writing on Gorbachev was fundamentally shaped by the general socio-political context of the Cold War and its intellectual sidekicks, totalitarianism and Sovietology/Kremlinology. The end of the Cold War (dated variously as either 1989, 1990 or 1991 depending on your viewpoint)[86] should have brought about a paradigm shift and enabled academic writing to be, at least partially, liberated from this context. It did not. Academic writing in general continued to divide along the same old fault-lines which had emerged and ossified during the era of the Cold War. Why? Essentially, the rapidity and unexpectedness of the collapse of the Soviet Union caught everyone by surprise. Academics responded to this by rushing in to claim that their analysis had been the correct one: 'we got it right'. Hence there was a massive exercise in self-justification, defending the positions and interpretations they had adopted between

1985 and 1991. The conflicts within the Sovietological community continued after the object of its analysis – the Soviet Union – had disappeared from history. Indeed, the collapse of communism led to a sustained debate within the Sovietological community about why it had got Gorbachev, *perestroika* and the Soviet Union so wrong. Or so right.[87] Evaluations of Gorbachev and *perestroika* were still subject to the whims of professional rivalry and ideological conflict. Would the assessments of Gorbachev be developed to defend the reputation of the previous opinions of the scholars, rather than being a genuine appraisal of the man and his era?

A second factor shaping academic appraisals was the proximity of the subject at hand. This had a number of dimensions. First, after the initial flurry of analyses looking to identify the causes of the dramatic collapse of the Soviet Union, Gorbachev entered a strange academic hinterland. Having appraised the causes of the collapse – and trying to locate Gorbachev's role in that – everyone began to move on. Political scientists, economists and scholars of international relations and foreign policy began to turn their attention to the post-communist, post-Cold War world of the much-derided 'transitology' and the 'new world order'. Gorbachev was at best a peripheral figure in these fields. At the same time he was too recent to fall within the remit of historical analysis. Historians were taking the opportunity provided by the collapse of communism and the opening of the archives to revisit the murky areas of the 1930s which were still provoking fierce debate. Gorbachev had entered the academic equivalent of the twilight zone. Second, the proximity to Gorbachev meant that, although he had moved off the scene, the impact of his time in power was still being felt, and so it was difficult to assess him authoritatively because his legacy and achievements were in a state of permanent evolution. The question of what resulted from his rule was in a state of constant uncertainty. He was, in Volkogonov's words, a frontier leader existing between a defunct regime and an unknown future.[88] This proximity either left commentators struggling to grasp a moving target, or saw commentators moving on to new areas of enquiry.

The third factor which is important to understand when analysing how the academic community has interpreted and evaluated Gorbachev is the assumptions and the approach adopted by the scholars in question. Scholars have tended to focus more on impersonal issues – structural, systemic, economic, political, institutional, social, cultural, ideological, etc. – than on the individual (unless it is within the context, say, of an analysis of leadership). This created something of a resistance to analyses centred on the individual for fear of falling into a 'Great Man'-type approach. This general in-built reluctance to focus on individuals and their roles in shaping events has led many away from Gorbachev to search for the 'deeper', more 'significant' causes of what happened, leaving personalized appraisals to biographers and journalists. Iconoclasm and the proliferation of research have created pressures for an agenda of 'permanent revisionism' in academia.

Gorbachev has been approached from many different angles, and the nature of the research agenda, the type of questions to be asked and the context of the enquiry have all profoundly shaped the view of Gorbachev that emerged. In fact, a multiplicity of 'Gorbachevs' appeared. Analysts of the demise of communism, scholars of the collapse of the union, appraisers of the disintegration of the Soviet economy, experts on superpower relations and the end of the Cold War all produced a different 'Gorbachev'. This fragmentation has made it easier to reach a verdict on Gorbachev within particular fields, say, foreign relations or as a leader, but has worked against the attempts to assess his overall contribution and impact.

The assessment of Gorbachev was also heavily conditioned by the choice of when to start the story, and when to stop it, not just the perspective from which to approach it. A story which located Gorbachev within the chaos of the collapse of communism, the coup and the end of the USSR had a very different feel to a story which began in 1985 and carried on through to 2000 and the progress of Russian democracy. In the first, Gorbachev was the man who failed to achieve what he set out to do. In the second, he was the man who started Russia on its march out of the communist darkness and into the light of democracy and civic freedoms. Within a longer Soviet historical perspective, Gorbachev appeared as the radical, liberalizing reformer in the mould of Khrushchev and Lenin. In a Russian historical perspective, Gorbachev appeared as either a reformer from above (akin to Alexander II or Petr Stolypin) or a modernizing Westernizer (like Peter the Great), or as a tragic, transitional figure (like Alexander Kerensky).[89]

So, outside of the complexity and ambiguity of both Gorbachev himself, and the *perestroika* era, it is easy to see why the academic community produced such a diverse and variegated set of assessments of Gorbachev, which makes any attempt to synthesize and summarize these assessments a complex, but fascinating, task.

Explanatory frameworks

Although scholars have produced a variety of assessments, for the sake of simplifying a complex field, they can essentially be grouped into five different categories.[90] Many theorists straddle these categories, and so, although there is a conceptual neatness in what follows, it should not obscure the fact that these are not mutually exclusive.

Gorbachev: the labour of Sisyphus

At one end of the spectrum lay the view that Gorbachev was defeated because his task was an impossible one. He had engaged, like Sisyphus, on a labour that could not be finished and so was doomed to failure from the start. There were differences over the precise reasons for the impossibility. For some, the communist system was unreformable. It existed as an integral whole, and either had to be dismantled *in toto* or would have to carry on with its essential features left intact. For others, there was a socio-cultural dimension. Gorbachev was attempting to introduce Western socio-political institutions and practices into a Eurasian system. The two were incompatible, and so Gorbachev could not have succeeded. Dawisha highlights the incompatibility between the brilliance of Gorbachev's talent and the context in which he was operating. The lack of any social, political or economic capital in the USSR meant that Gorbachev could not have succeeded, no matter how much he exerted the full force of his personality.[91]

Gorbachev: the heroic liberator

At the other end of the spectrum lay the wholly positive endorsement of Gorbachev as the heroic global statesman responsible for the liberation of the peoples of the USSR and Eastern Europe from the dual tyranny of communist totalitarianism and Soviet/Russian imperialism, and the liberation of the rest of the world from the fear of nuclear annihilation. This liberation was a multifaceted one: freedom from oppression, fear, spiritual and intellectual enslavement; freedom to speak openly, move abroad; worship. Although he was unable to maintain himself in power, the programme he inaugurated achieved things which had been unimaginable in 1985.[92]

Between these two opinions, there were three views which tried to communicate the ambivalent, paradoxical nature of Gorbachev and his programme, which seemed to have been both a resounding success and a terrible failure at one and the same time. These three views emphasize different aspects in slightly different ways.

Gorbachev: the sorcerer's apprentice

This was a very popular view at the time. In the traditional tale, the sorcerer's apprentice was overwhelmed by the forces he had unleashed, not knowing the power he was getting involved with, or indeed how to control it.[93] This stands as a metaphor for Gorbachev, who by unleashing *glasnost'* and democratization (while trying to control it) had no idea how to control the elemental social and political forces, most notably nationalism, that ensued. Gorbachev – naïve, idealistic, ill-informed – was simply swept away in the torrent. Sadly, unlike the original tale, there was no sorcerer to come and put right the chaos created by the apprentice.

Gorbachev: the glorious failure

Those who recognize both the noble aspirations and the ultimate failure of Gorbachev prefer to categorize him as a 'glorious failure'. His programmes of *perestroika* and democratization freed the peoples of the Soviet Union and Eastern Europe. His global vision saw Russia reintegrated into the rest of the world. His peace offensive freed people from fear and prevented the break-up of the Soviet Union descending into a bloody, Balkan-style outcome. These were enormous achievements which stand to his credit. But they need to be set against the fact that he ultimately failed: he did not intend to oversee the dissolution of the communist system and the demise of the Soviet Union, or to end up without a role in the system. His failures derived partly from a lack of understanding of what he was doing and partly from his weak and indecisive leadership between 1989 and 1991. He was a great reformer who was unable to prevent his reforms transforming the system out of existence.

Gorbachev: the tragic failure/incompetent reformer

The most negative appraisal of Gorbachev portrays him as a tragic, incompetent figure who failed on almost every count. His reforms were ill-conceived, lacked any coherence and were implemented in an *ad hoc*, arbitrary fashion. Gorbachev had no real intention of creating a democracy in the Soviet Union, but aimed to strengthen and defend the communist system. All of his 'achievements' were inadvertent consequences, attained against the wishes and plans of Gorbachev who proved to be a Machiavellian, power-hungry, authoritarian leader. His first priority was always his own welfare, and he left his country denuded of its international status and its people facing poverty and starvation. His rule was, in short, a disaster.

The broad contours of these different positions illustrate the great disagreement there is between scholars on this question. Appraisals exist that affirm Gorbachev and his reputation, but others also destroy and undermine his reputation. The overall effect merely seems to confirm the complex, paradoxical nature of the Gorbachev phenomenon. Can we seek a way through this tangled undergrowth? Scholars differ over three points: outcomes, intentions and strategy/tactics. First, in terms of the 'outcomes' of Gorbachev while in power – for instance, the end of the Cold War, the introduction of democracy to Russia, the end of communism in Eastern Europe – to what extent was he, directly or indirectly, responsible for them? Second, in terms of his intentions, what did Gorbachev actually set out to achieve? How far short of this did he fall, and were the 'achievements' mainly inadvertent or accidental consequences of his leadership? Third, was there a clearly thought-out strategy underpinning Gorbachev's programme? If so, was it the correct one? Or were the problems and failings of *perestroika* due to circumstances beyond his control? Let us take these points in turn, before turning to the overall assessments of Gorbachev, and his place in history.

Gorbachev: assessing the record

The question of outcomes: the significance of Gorbachev?

What were the main outcomes of the Gorbachev era, and how far can they be ascribed to Gorbachev himself? Clearly Gorbachev was a key actor in this particular drama. The difficulty here is trying to specify Gorbachev's role in all this without resorting to a 'Great Man' approach, on the one hand, or denying him any role on the other. The significance of Gorbachev in this regard lies in the fact that as General Secretary of the CPSU he exerted an enormous amount of power and influence. Moreover, as a herald of change and reform his views were new and distinctive and so his emergence was likely to have a great impact on developments at home and abroad in bringing about change. On the other hand, Gorbachev clearly did not operate alone, and worked within particular constraints and contexts not of his choosing or making. In sum, Gorbachev's significance in many of these cases lies not so much in being the central or sole cause of particular outcomes, but more in shaping why things happened at a particular time, and in a particular way.

If we examine the record in terms of specific areas, then there are five main outcomes which arose during his leadership:[94]

- the end of the Cold War;
- the dismantling of the Soviet political system (encompassing the end of repression and the dissolution of the monopoly on power of the CPSU), and the introduction of political pluralism, democracy and civic freedoms to the peoples of the former Soviet Union;
- the liberation of Eastern Europe from Soviet/communist rule;
- the breakdown of the Soviet economic system;
- the end of the Soviet Union and the emergence of new states in the former Soviet Union.[95]

Let us examine Gorbachev's contribution in all of these areas, in particular, questioning how far Gorbachev can be credited for the above outcomes which are generally seen as his 'achievements', and also how far he can be held responsible for the outcomes which are generally seen as his 'failures'.

The end of the Cold War

Although this refers primarily to end of the era of superpower confrontation between the USA and the USSR and the subsequent elimination of the threat of global nuclear annihilation resulting from a conflict between the two, it also refers to the end of the division in Europe, the retreat from the rhetoric of global expansionism and the general process of de-militarization and the search for international cooperation, dialogue and constructive engagement as a means of solving global problems. Recently, some scholars have begun to argue that the developments in the late 1980s and early 1990s were not actually an end to the Cold War, but merely an hiatus. The re-emergence of Russia as a global power, and the rise of China, will inevitably herald another era of confrontation, tensions and conflict between the USA, Russia, China and Europe. Irrespective of whether or not we see this as the end or a transition to a different type and scale of conflict, it is clear that there was a significant shift at the end of the 1980s which saw a move towards de-militarization, the re-unification of Germany and a drastic reduction in the nuclear arsenals of the great powers. What was the role of Gorbachev in bringing this about? Three scholars stand as examples of those who would assign a central, strategic position to Gorbachev as the primary cause in bringing about the end of the Cold War: Raymond Garthoff (an international relations specialist), Vladislav Zubok (a Russian expert on international affairs) and Archie Brown (from the Sovietological camp).[96]

Garthoff and Brown's argument is based on the premise that Gorbachev consciously, voluntarily and deliberately set out to end the Cold War, and that it was the combination of his espousal of New Political Thinking, his unilateral military concessions and his overhaul of the foreign policy personnel in the Soviet state that brought this about. They both argue that the Western contention that it was the hard-line stance of Reagan and Thatcher, their commitment to SDI, deterrence and containment, which undermined Soviet economic performance and forced Gorbachev into a retreat, was erroneous. Gorbachev's moves were not born of desperation caused by the declining power and status of the Soviet Union, and were not cynical moves designed to mask this decline or to acquire a breathing-space before reasserting its traditional expansionist, aggressive outlook.[97]

To substantiate this argument they placed great stress on the shift in Gorbachev's thinking. They believe that Gorbachev genuinely had adopted a new view of the world – based on interdependence, mutual cooperation and the priority of universal human values – which had emerged out of the Soviet international affairs scholars and his own reading of Western works in the 1960s and 1970s. This adoption of a more liberal, idealistic and peaceful view of the world – achieved in the teeth of Western hostility and a general failure on the part of the Western leaders to reciprocate – produced a foreign policy of imperial retreat, demilitarization and an end to confrontation. In fact, Garthoff argued that *only* a Soviet leader could have ended the Cold War, because the key was abandoning the Marxist-Leninist aspiration to global revolution and to burying capitalism. This was the essential precondition for defusing the ideological conflict between East and West, capitalism and socialism, USSR and USA. Gorbachev sought – both in his domestic policies and his foreign policies – to make the USSR a 'normal' society, integrated into the mainstream of global civil society. The reform of the system at home, and the end of the Cold War, were crucial interrelated planks of this policy.[98]

For Garthoff, Gorbachev did not lose the arms race; he 'called it off'. The twin policies of the Western powers – containment and deterrence – were not the keys to ending the Cold War. They did play a role. Containment prevented the USSR from further military expansion. Deterrence was mainly about reassuring the peoples of Western Europe, and keeping the USSR in check until its own internal problems began to overwhelm it. It was at this point that Gorbachev enters the equation, and it was his contribution that was decisive.[99] Both for Volkogonov and Garthoff, the end of the Cold War would not have happened without Gorbachev. Indeed James Galbraith asserts that Gorbachev was profoundly undermined by the Western leaders who failed to show the necessary vision to respond to what he was doing. The resultant triumphalism in the West scuppered the Gorbachev project and created the current instability in the world.[100]

A variation on this theme is provided by Zubok, who argues for the primacy of Gorbachev's personality in bringing the Cold War to an end.[101] He rejects those explanations based upon the domestic weaknesses of the Soviet system, the changes in the international system or the emergence of new ideas in the Soviet elite. For Zubok, the personality of Gorbachev – self-confident, optimistic, naïve, democratic – was crucial. This personality, when combined with a deep connection with all things Western and an aversion to the use of force, profoundly affected the conduct and direction of Soviet policy. In the circumstances in which he found himself, Gorbachev's personality traits constrained him to do all he could to embrace the West and integrate the USSR into the Western community, to end the military confrontation and to allow Eastern Europe to go its own way. His optimistic, idealistic outlook found a home in the espousal of New Thinking, and this led to the abandonment of both Marxist-Leninist world revolution and Gromykoesque realpolitik statecraft. Gorbachev's personality is the key explanatory factor in both the way in which the Cold War ended and the speed of its demise.[102]

The sceptical counterpoint to explanations which assign primacy to Gorbachev have been put by Western (usually American) scholars, such as Richard Pipes and Martin Malia.[103] Pipes is extremely critical of the Garthoff position. He argues that there is no plausible explanation for the emergence of Gorbachev in Garthoff's analysis. Gorbachev changed everything. End of story. Yet Pipes is adamant that there is a fundamental inconsistency running through this interpretation. Garthoff's approach is based on the interactionist model, which sees the superpower rivalry primarily in terms of the competition and conflict between the USA and the USSR, which had a dynamic of its own. An initiative from one power evoked a similar response from the other, and so on. For Pipes, the aggressive stance of Reagan should have evoked a similar response from the USSR following the logic of Garthoff's own position. Yet it did not – entirely the opposite, in fact. Pipes argues instead that the Reagan standpoint was crucial, compelling the Soviet Union to reform at home and to retreat abroad, and this process led to the Soviet Union unravelling. Pipes sees Gorbachev as 'a typical product of the Soviet nomenklatura', nothing more.[104]

This is only a brief résumé of a highly complex set of blasts and counterblasts over who won the Cold War, and who brought it to an end. But it illustrates the difficulties of assessing Gorbachev, as he gets a little lost in the academic crossfire. Establishing the role that Gorbachev played in these events is immensely difficult. This is partly due to the fact that scholars have adopted very different positions on the notion of the personality in history. For Zubok, this was a fundamental point: individuals can and do make a difference. For Pipes, the 'Great Man' theory was an old discredited idea, whose time had long gone. It is unsurprising that the former put Gorbachev at the centre of his analysis, the latter put him in the margins (at best). This methodological selection automatically conditioned the outcome. Overlaying the methodology were the issues of ideology and politics, notably the importance of establishing the correctness or otherwise of earlier stances. The conservative scholars, many of whom had been on Reagan's staff in the 1980s, were keen to maintain that their approach had been correct and had been vindicated. Similarly liberals, keen to puncture the claims of the Right, look to Gorbachev as the hero of this particular drama to exonerate their opposition to Reagan in the 1980s.

Clearly, the story of the Cold War and its demise cannot be told without Gorbachev. Clearly, most people saw its demise as a 'good' thing. The balance of testimony tends towards Gorbachev as having exerted enormous impact in this area. Even those who opposed Gorbachev and who saw his foreign policy as a betrayal of the national interests of the USSR/Russia held that his influence was crucial in the events that led to the end of the Cold War. This can be seen in the following ways. One, it is not just the emergence of Gorbachev which is crucial. It is also the type of beliefs and values that Gorbachev held. Gorbachev's outlook about the world that he shared with many intellectuals in Moscow in the 1960s and 1970s led him to prioritize negotiations over confrontation, human survival over class-based domination and to conceive of security as a collective enterprise of states. As the Cold War was an ideological struggle (among other things), then the accession of a new leader with the boldness and the vision to rethink his own regime's ideology was obviously a deeply significant moment. Gorbachev's rethinking of Soviet ideology opened the way for the end of the Cold War.

Second, the Cold War impasse was broken at the top, and this means exploring the dynamics of the leadership relations between Gorbachev and Reagan. The role of the two leaders – Reagan and Gorbachev – was crucial. In spite of their ideological differences, they were quickly able to establish a rapport which overcame 40 years of mistrust and suspicion, and were also able to persuade sceptical groups and individuals within their respective entourages that the other side should be trusted. The Soviets were now looking to work with and learn from the West, not destroy it. In turn Reagan's willingness to support Gorbachev's moves meant that it was no longer the 'evil empire' in US eyes.

Third, although Gorbachev and Reagan were clearly the two individuals at the centre of this dramatic story, the bit-part players also need to be recognized. It was not all down to the two leaders. Their two key advisers – George Shultz and Eduard Shevardnadze – played important roles in establishing trust. François Mitterrand (the French President) and Margaret Thatcher (the British Prime Minister) helped persuade the Americans and the Soviets to work together. Pressure was exerted by the popular anti-nuclear movement and by scientists opposed to nuclear weapons. Finally, the courage of the citizens of Eastern Europe who in 1989 were willing to take to the streets must never be discounted. Finally, it is important to leave room in any historical analysis for 'accidents'. When a young German amateur pilot (Matthias Rust) flew a small plane directly from Finland to Moscow and landed in Red Square in May 1987, Gorbachev used this as a pretext to purge the military, leaving him with a free hand in negotiations.

Overall, it is clear that the Soviet's willingness to change was the key thing. But what brought about this change of heart? Was it Reagan's hard-line stance which caused the Soviet economic decline? Or was it Gorbachev's idealistic philosophy? Or was it the technological lag between East and West? The US military build-up after 1980 brought the state of the Soviet economy sharply into focus. But the primary drive for change came from within, and Gorbachev was the key factor. He broke the impasse. Counterfactuals can help us here too. If Chernenko had lived on, then undoubtedly the Soviet Union would have muddled on as before. Reagan himself recognized this in 1988 when he said that 'Mr. Gorbachev deserves most of the credit'. Gorbachev it was who put an end to the whole previous Soviet way of thinking about the international sphere, who pursued a foreign policy with a strongly idealistic and moralistic framework. This new way of thinking was conditioned by the circles Gorbachev moved in, by the ideas he absorbed from the intellectuals and politicians (both at home and abroad) that he worked with, and also by his own humanitarian instincts. His thinking was also pushed in this direction by the Chernobyl disaster which confirmed for Gorbachev the inherent danger and immorality of nuclear weapons, an outlook he shared with Ronald Reagan. But it was not just morality and idealism which caused Gorbachev to abandon the old Soviet way of thinking. He was also aware that the old way of thinking and behaving was not working in the interests of the Soviet people or the Soviet state. Change had to come if the USSR was to maintain itself as a great power.

If the willingness to change stems in the main from Gorbachev, then the ability to introduce change also rests decisively with him, although, as mentioned above, other characters were also crucial in this drama. Gorbachev had sufficient power to reframe Soviet foreign policy, and had the boldness, the vision and the luck to pursue it. He was fortunate that those who might have chosen to obstruct or thwart chose not to speak up. He was fortunate too, with the Rust incident and to have counterparts in the USA who were willing to meet him. But Gorbachev had to take advantage of these opportunities, and had to initiate many of the developments in Eastern Europe, Germany and elsewhere. This he did. If we judge Gorbachev on either his words or his deeds in this area, he stands as the significant figure.

If we pose the question 'Why did the Cold War end?', we are left with a whole host of elements in our explanations: the long-term economic decline of the USSR, the impact of Imperial overstretch, falling oil prices, unrest in Eastern Europe, the greater cohesion and effectiveness of Western socio-political and economic systems. If we rephrase the question – 'Why did the Cold War end at that time and in that way?' – then the evidence points overwhelmingly to Gorbachev: his values, his initiatives and his interventions. On this issue, Gorbachev can be seen as the decisive factor.

Ending the political monopoly and starting the journey towards democracy, pluralism and freedom

How far was Gorbachev responsible for the political transformation of the USSR? On coming to power, the system was a one-party dictatorship with a single ideology, which made extensive use of a variety of tools – censorship, repression, surveillance, patronage – to control the population and to maintain the position of the CPSU and its leaders. On leaving power in 1991, the political system had been transformed. There was now a multi-party democracy based on the rule of law, with the separation of powers, a President elected directly by the people, political pluralism, competitive elections and a raft of civic freedoms normally associated with Western-type political systems. The Russian people had never enjoyed a period of greater freedom from state control: freedom to worship, travel, discuss, listen to foreign broadcasts. The persecution of political, religious and nationalist dissidents was ended. This far-reaching transformation occurred during Gorbachev's tenure. The legacy of Gorbachev's rule was an unparalleled freedom to speak out, freedom from the fear of repression and arbitrary arrest. He had single-handedly slain the twin-headed hydra of political and ideological monopolization. But does this warrant Gorbachev being credited as the liberator of the Soviet peoples?

The case for Gorbachev as the arch-democrat derives from the initiatives he took, in the absence of any external pressures or unrest from below, to reform the Soviet political system. Between 1985 and 1989, he consciously introduced measures, without being compelled to do so, which started the process of undermining the various forms of political control that the CPSU had deployed to maintain itself in power. The introduction of *glasnost'* undercut the state control of the press and legitimized the emergence of unorthodox opinions. The introduction of competitive elections introduced the notion of choice into the political system. The new institutional set-up began the shift in the locus of power away from the Communist Party and towards the elected bodies. A new constitutional set-up introduced legal safeguards for individuals against encroachments by the state. In all these areas Gorbachev played a decisive role in dismantling the edifice of power upon which the Soviet system had rested since the 1920s, although clearly he would not have been able to implement these goals without the willingness of people to speak out, of editors to publish, of journalists to write and of people to march, protest, and demonstrate.

But what about the journey away from this system? The underlying meaning and significance of the changes are complicated by the fact that Gorbachev introduced all of these changes while maintaining his allegiance to the centrality of the CPSU within a 'reformed' or 'restructured' political system. There were limits to his political reforms that he did not wish to transgress. Hence his attempts to impose limits on the policy of openness: a number of topics remained taboo. Hence his attempts to restrict pluralism by advocating that it had to be *socialist* pluralism. Hence his attempts to limit the potential radicalism of the new institutional set-up by including reserved seats for relevant social organizations and ensuring that the legislature would be chaired by the corresponding party head at each level. Yet, after 1989, the political changes began to reach more deeply into the nature of the system, commencing with the abandonment of the CPSU's monopoly on power in February 1990, the creation of an executive Presidency and the emergence of a popularly elected Russian President in June 1990. Did Gorbachev intend to move this far? Or was he pushed into this radicalism by pressures from below, or the strength of opposition, or the failures of his earlier reforms?

The explanations for this progressive transformation differ markedly, though. The essential dividing-line hinges around those who see Gorbachev as a *democratizer,* and those who see him as a *democrat*. The argument of the '*Gorbachev as democratizer*' camp rests on the nature and extent of limits to the measures he introduced.[105] This, they argue, demonstrates that Gorbachev was not committed to democracy *per se*, but saw it in functional terms, as means to an end. But even here there is a plurality of views. One line holds that Gorbachev used democratic instruments to overcome resistance to his reforms, most notably his economic reforms, and to consolidate his own hold on power.[106] Another line maintains that democratization was a means by which to free himself of the party structures and enable him to implement his programme unfettered by the constraints of the conservative party apparatus.[107] Another view argues that Gorbachev's espousal of democratic reforms were part of his tactical struggle for the centre-ground with Yeltsin, and so was a weapon in his own personal political struggles.[108]

Whatever the motives, this line highlights the ambivalence of Gorbachev to democracy, the half-heartedness of his measures. The reasons for this ambivalence lie in Gorbachev himself: a communist and a reformer; a Leninist and a social-democrat; a Soviet patriot and a westerniser. Gorbachev was committed to trying to synthesize the essence of the Soviet system with elements borrowed from abroad and from the Soviet past to try and renew the USSR, to give the party a new sense of legitimacy, popularity and vitality. Some interpreted this as a process of liberalization.[109] Others saw it as an attempt to combine Leninism with Western democratic practices. The reason that Gorbachev during 1990 and 1991 went beyond this framework to the eventual transformation of the system was inadvertent. The changes he introduced went beyond the framework he envisaged, as society radicalized and polarized. Forced to respond in order to keep his hand on the tiller, Gorbachev ended up with a total political transformation, rather than a reform. In this sense it could be argued that Gorbachev's political reforms were a personal 'failure' for Gorbachev, but a 'success' for the people.[110]

Other criticisms have been levelled at Gorbachev's lack of understanding of the nature and basis of democracy. The political legacy bequeathed by Gorbachev to post-Soviet Russia was a poorly developed institutional basis for representative democracy partly because of the extent of the powers which accrued to the President in 1990 and 1991, and partly because of the sheer enormity and difficulty of the task itself. This left the parliament in a weak situation, and also reinforced the tendency for conflict between legislature and executive. His highly personalized style of rule and decision-making, which circumvented the official organs of power, also did little to promote and develop the norms and practices of democratic decision-making and policy-making. Further, Jerry Hough argues that Gorbachev's consistent reluctance to use force betrays not a democratic spirit, but a profound misunderstanding of the nature of democracy. This, for Hough, was naïvety in the extreme. The selective use of force would have enabled Gorbachev to have stabilized the situation in society, and given the regime time to get the economy working.[111]

For those who argue for a '*Gorbachev as democrat*' line, their argument rests on a view that Gorbachev was always firmly committed to a thorough democratization of the system, and consciously was aiming to transform the Soviet political system after 1988, gradually creating something new. Starting from his speech of December 1984 where he proposed that a democratization of all spheres of Soviet life was essential for the further progress and development of Soviet society, Gorbachev gradually sought to implement his democratic programme, the specific details and tempo of which emerged as Gorbachev proceeded. The critical moment came at the 19th Party Conference in 1988, when Gorbachev pushed ahead for a transformation of the political system (i.e. a change into something completely different) rather than settling for a reform of the system. Gorbachev's democratic credentials were not just about the institutional set-up he created. He was also a democrat by instinct, preferring consensus, dialogue and cooperation and generally eschewing force as a means of solving problems. After 1988, Gorbachev consciously and deliberately set out to pull down the political structures of the communist system, and created the basis for a pluralistic, democratic, system of government. His most important legacy is unquestionably the freedom he gave to all the peoples of the former Soviet Union, most notably the freedom to speak out without fear.[112]

If we balance up the outcomes of Gorbachev's political reforms, we can see that as a direct result of his policies, the Soviet system became more pluralistic and he gave more people more of a say in local and national politics than previously. In addition, he created new political institutions that were both more accountable and more representative than the old Soviet institutions. At the same time, the political system that began to take shape was also hedged in with limitations, still had a central role for the Communist Party in its design blueprint, and rested after 1990 on a foundation in which Gorbachev himself, as Executive President, stood as the guarantor of both the changes already in place and those still to come. The interpretative differences centre on three issues: (1) the place of the party in Gorbachev's political reforms and his vision of a reformed political system; (2) the reasons why there was a shift toward more fundamental political changes; and (3) the relative weight and significance to be assigned to his destructive/creative actions. Let us examine these in turn.

Assessing Gorbachev's impact in the political sphere is tricky for a number of reasons. Gorbachev's vision of a preferred future was subject to change and evolution after 1985, being neither fixed in stone nor infinitely negotiable. There are also problems over our understanding of 'democracy' and also Soviet understandings of democracy. But at the heart of much of the confusion is the fact that Gorbachev was trying to combine complex, at times paradoxical, elements together:

- He saw 'democracy' as both an end towards which he wanted to move, and also a means of achieving that end.
- He was a firm believer in the party, but also desired to change and revive the party at the same time.
- He was leader and architect of change, as well as head of the institution he wished to change, causing him to need to be both radical and cautious at the same time.
- He was interested in mixing and matching Western and Soviet political practices and approaches but the balance of the two was a matter of constant negotiation.

Gorbachev was embarking, initially anyway, upon a reformation. The defining elements of Gorbachev's political strategy were his attempts to consciously construct a more democratic version of Soviet socialism, a hybrid combining elements of Western-type political practice with aspects of the Soviet political system. He was in essence engaging in a process of reforming the Soviet political system and within that process the Communist Party continued to figure very prominently in his thinking right up until the final moments of its life. But the role of the party in Gorbachev's thinking changed and evolved as Gorbachev's programme unfolded. This complex amalgam of Western and Soviet forms shifted over time, with the former gradually coming to displace the latter. After 1988, reformation became transformation. But Gorbachev never fully gave up on the party, which led him into a zone of permanent revisionism, constantly revising the role of the party in the transformed political system. Gorbachev's conception of the party's role in this new set-up shifted away from the traditional vanguard role, towards a kind of 'vanguard-light' role in which the party was to maintain its leading role, only in the new multi-party conditions this was to be done via the ballot-box. Even as Gorbachev moved to create the Presidential system (which marginalized the CPSU) and sanctioned the creation of the RCP (which weakened the CPSU further), he continued to maintain in public his commitment to the party. What does Gorbachev's continued adherence to the party, his faith in its reformability in the face of requests by his supporters to split the party or abandon it altogether testify to? Primarily, that Gorbachev may have been able to abandon the one-party state and create the foundations for a multi-party Presidential republic to emerge, yet he was also a man of great loyalty and belief (and possibly wishful thinking!). His continued defence of the party, even after the coup in August 1991, is probably best explained by the importance it held in Gorbachev's life and past, rather than a considered view on the future of the Soviet political system.

The second question relates to the reasons for the radicalization of the political reforms: from controlled liberalization and limited pluralism to systematic democratization and the construction of new institutional bases for the Soviet political process. What were Gorbachev's motivations here? The process by which the political reforms became more radical suggest that Gorbachev was clear on the general shape of what he wanted to achieve, but short on the specifics of what this would look like in practice, and in particular how to get there. He knew what he didn't want: the status quo or a full-scale imitation of Western forms. He knew – in outline – where he wanted to go: reformed, popular, democratically elected Communist Party, pluralistic system, micro-societal democracy, more open discussions and debates, popular participation and the like. But the details of this system were not spelt out, and this is probably a defensible position, as he did not want to pre-judge the outcome, or prescribe the discussions too much. However, the precise reasons for the radicalization of the reform process, the sequencing of the reforms and the means Gorbachev chose to undertake this transition are key here. In essence, the radicalization was in part driven by the momentum the process itself had gathered, and was partly Gorbachev's reaction to the opposition he faced and the failures of policies elsewhere, notably the economy. The pace and direction of Gorbachev's political changes were in many ways dictated by the circumstances of the time, and by Gorbachev's preferences to retain as much power and control in his own hands in order to ensure that he could steer the ship in the direction he wished to go. Although he was the architect of the political changes that were introduced, he was also responding to pressures from below and was seeking to retain himself in power while redefining the party's role to ensure it was not completely marginalized by the changes that were occurring. This is where the ambiguities over Gorbachev's political programme come in and cloud the judgements. Gorbachev's strategy for achieving his democratic goals became increasingly personalized and undemocratic, and was handicapped by his unwillingness to rid himself of his attachment to the party. The reforms accelerated because Gorbachev had to try and stay one step ahead. They became deeper because the earlier reforms had not achieved their aims. They became more personalized because Gorbachev only really trusted himself to carry them through. To paraphrase Sakharov, Gorbachev's political reforms were a campaign to achieve democracy using rather limited democratic means, rather than undemocratic means.

The final question relates to the balance of creation and destruction in Gorbachev's political legacy, and here it is clear that Gorbachev did much to destroy the basis of the old political system, and to start to address the creation of a culture of democracy in the post-Soviet bloc, but his tangible contribution to the building of democratic institutions was limited by both the reformist nature of his programme which continued to balance change and continuity, and by his penchant for personalized decision-making which hindered the creation of a clear institutional basis for democracy. It is easy to overlook the complexity and difficulty of trying to build an institutional basis for democracy in the USSR, to change the political culture of a people, to confront opposition without resorting to excessive force or violence.[113] Yet even acknowledging this, Gorbachev's greatest success came in the field of destruction and dismantling the old system, and his transitional arrangements for building a new system, may well have undermined the long-term goal of building a new democratized political system.

Overall, Gorbachev must be credited with the boldness to conceive of the programme of democratization and to attempt to implement it. His reforms culminated in significant political and civic freedoms for the Soviet people, and to the de-monopolization of Soviet politics. But the lines of causation are hazy here: the ambiguities of Gorbachev's programme and his attempts to restrict the process of democratization meant that the struggle for political freedoms and the end of the monopoly of the CPSU were taken up by the Soviet people, the popular fronts, the key individuals (Sakharov, Yeltsin, *et al.*), the *glasnost'* editors and so on. Gorbachev set these things in motion, but at some point during 1990, it began to slip from his grasp and he never quite got it back. The momentum shifted elsewhere and he was powerless to stop it.

The Independence of Eastern Europe

This issue is far less complicated than the question of democracy and pluralism. But there are two sorts of debate here. One debate relates to the Gorbachev question: did Gorbachev consciously seek to cut adrift the states of Eastern Europe from Soviet control? The other debate derives from similar historical examples of the retreat from Empire: did the colonial power withdraw or was it overthrown by popular pressure?

There is a far greater degree of consensus here that Gorbachev was in the main responsible for the collapse of the Soviet Empire in Eastern Europe in 1988/89. Gorbachev refused to intervene militarily to prop up the East European communist parties when they came up against pressure from their own people to change. But what lay behind this refusal of Gorbachev to intervene? Here the question is more complex. Was it due to the shift in Gorbachev's thinking which now espoused the rights of all peoples to determine their own future and the absolute refusal to use force in politics? Was it driven by his wider foreign policy goals to ensure that de-militarization and nuclear disarmament could proceed more rapidly? Was it driven by the economic realities of the cost to the USSR of maintaining an unruly Empire in Eastern Europe? Or did Gorbachev just stand and watch as events in Eastern Europe took their own course?[114]

Even the critics of Gorbachev admit that Gorbachev must be credited with the liberation of Eastern Europe from communist rule, even if they prefer to describe his contribution as one of passive non-intervention driven by the economic interests of his domestic programme, rather than a principled stand derived from his own set of values and beliefs. It is evident that in the case of Eastern Europe – as with other elements of his programme – Gorbachev adopted strategies which would propel his reforms at home. The fate of Eastern Europe was always intimately bound up with Soviet interests in the area, and Gorbachev was no exception to this. The major difference by 1988/89 was that Gorbachev was willing to let the outer Empire go, and that there was a coincidence of Gorbachev's own values and world-view and the international, economic and political interests of the Soviet state. At this stage, it was in Gorbachev's interests to allow the Eastern European states to determine their own fate, hence his non-intervention. Here the outcome – the freedom of the peoples of Eastern Europe – can be seen as a direct consequence of something Gorbachev refused to do, although clearly the actions of the people of Eastern Europe themselves are also critical in this regard. The struggle for freedom in Eastern Europe was won on the streets of Budapest, Warsaw and Berlin, but the opportunity was created by Gorbachev's willingness to let go.

The breakdown of the Soviet economy

This is widely perceived to be the greatest area of failure in Gorbachev's portfolio. The legacy that he left his successors was one of chaos, poverty, inflation and unemployment.[115] He is widely seen as having successfully dismantled a (poorly) functioning economy, and replaced it with ... nothing. The destruction of the old command system may have happened with astonishing rapidity, but the almost total failure to put in place a functioning economic mechanism has been laid squarely at Gorbachev's feet. Is this fair?

Few people feel able to defend Gorbachev's economic record. Even his erstwhile supporters consistently cite this (along with the nationalities issue) as Gorbachev's Achilles' heel. An exception to this is Stephen Cohen, who argues that it was Gorbachev who laid all the foundations for the subsequent de-statization of the economy and the development of market relations and private ownership in Russia.[116] A concession of sorts, ironically, comes from those who saw the Soviet system as unreformable. The Soviet economy was an integral whole. It either existed. Or it didn't. There was no way to reform or change one sector, and hope for an overall improvement, as piecemeal changes were always swallowed up by the great monolithic economic bureaucracy and then squeezed and squeezed until they ceased to be effective and petered out. That was the experience of every reform initiative prior to 1985. Gorbachev was just another in a long line of unsuccessful attempts to reform the unreformable. Gorbachev's failure in this regard was understandable, but wholly predictable. He was attempting the impossible.[117]

Others see a successful reform of a Soviet-type economy as possible (given the examples of the GDR, Hungary and China). The failure to reform lies almost wholly in Gorbachev and his efforts after 1985. The catalogue is a long one:

- His was a search for an economic El Dorado: a mythical third way between Western capitalist market-led economies and Soviet state socialist command economies.
- The reforms to the economy had no chief architect. As a result, they were very much of the 'trial-and-error' type, *ad hoc* and reactive.
- Gorbachev did not understand economics, and when confronted with a problem or a critical decision he always went with the familiar.
- The initial reforms were essentially organizational, which undermined the system of central planning without replacing it. The existing system began to break down very quickly.
- He disregarded finance entirely, and this created a massive revenue shortfall right at the outset.
- He delayed the introduction of substantive structural changes until circumstances had deteriorated significantly.
- The sequencing of reform was deeply flawed: he should not have shifted to political reforms at a time of economic hardship, and he showed no understanding of how to cope with the dynamics of simultaneous economic and political reform.
- Gorbachev's commitment to the core elements of the communist economic system (state ownership and planning) meant that the reforms of the economy were essentially self-limiting.
- Gorbachev failed to come to a clear view on the question of the speed and method of making the transition to a market economy.[118]

Amidst the paeans of condemnation of Gorbachev's economic policies, a couple of points are regularly overlooked. First, the accidents and problems that Gorbachev was forced to confront, most notably the Chernobyl disaster and the Armenian earthquake, both of which made an even larger hole in the Soviet budget. Much of what happened was beyond Gorbachev's control. The second concerns the roles played by Gorbachev's economic advisers: what responsibility do they bear for the nature, timing and sequencing of the reforms that were introduced?

Overall, the verdict is clear: Gorbachev categorically failed in his attempts to make the Soviet economy more productive, more efficient, more modern and more consumer-responsive. If ever there was a task which approximates to a mod ern-day Sisyphean labour, then this was probably it. But the failures of economic policy displayed by Gorbachev were not just a result of the incredible difficulty of the task. It was also clearly a result of the failings and flaws in Gorbachev's thinking, diagnosis and solutions. The reasons for the failure are complex, but the majority of the explanations put forward have Gorbachev at, or very near, the centre. As Hanson has remarked, it is difficult to imagine anyone else in the Soviet leadership at the time introducing similar reforms.[119] Others may not have succeeded. Greater help from the West may have been useful. Luck did not smile on Gorbachev. But the scale and speed of the Soviet economic collapse were caused by Gorbachev and his economic policies.

The end of the Soviet Union

The dual endings of August–December 1991 were the bitterest pill for Gorbachev to swallow. In two strokes, the regime and the country he had led and served both came to an end. This, surely, was a direct result of Gorbachev's actions, and evidence of his ultimate failure? Three types of explanation have been put forward.

1. *Gorbachev: nationalism as blind spot.* The end of the Soviet Union and the subsequent transformation of this body into the Commonwealth of Independent States is constantly advanced as the greatest of Gorbachev's failures. Gorbachev is said to have had no real understanding of the potency of nationalism as a mobilizing ideology and of the passions that ethnic tensions aroused, and consequently he failed to develop any viable strategy or policy to deal with until it was far too late. His catastrophic lack of awareness of the likely ethnic/nationalist consequences of his policies of *glasnost'* and democratization meant that Gorbachev was responsible for creating his own gravediggers. It has been described as Gorbachev's 'blind spot'. His was a ham-fisted, clumsy approach. He ignored the ticking bomb he was sitting on until it was too late, and from 1989 onwards he was always reacting to events, which were spiralling out of control.[120]
2. *Gorbachev: the weaknesses of naïveté and morality.* A different perspective argues that Gorbachev failed because he refused to adopt a hard-line stance in the face of ethnic conflict and minority nationalist protest at central rule. In the face of the growing clamour for concessions for greater autonomy and

sovereignty, Gorbachev should have responded with a crackdown. Instead he engaged in a desperate search for ways to keep the Union together which ended up alienating all the parties involved.[121] Hough argues, in contradiction to the above line, that Gorbachev was only too aware of the powers of minority nationalism, but instead of fighting fire with fire he tried to accommodate them, win their trust and work to find a peaceful, consensual solution to this issue. In this way, he vastly overestimated the possibility for compromise, and also his own powers of persuasion and his own standing and authority.[122]

3. *Gorbachev: the tides of history.* The third perspective is a much more generous one. It argues that Gorbachev was the victim of forces beyond his control. There are two versions to this. In the first one, the nationalities 'problem' was insoluble. No-one could have come up with a solution to what was an impenetrably complex and conflict-ridden issue, exacerbated by its suppression for many decades. Although Gorbachev's reforms played a key part in bringing these nationalist tensions to life, they were in essence part of a wider trend in the late twentieth-century world: nationalism as a mode of resistance. The processes which dominated the world – globalization, industrialization, political centralization and bureaucratization, cultural homogenization (Coca-Colanization and Disneyfication) – brought a response from minority nationalities and ethnic groups which expressed itself in a nationalist or ethnic idiom. The rise of nationalism has to be seen as part of a wider trend, albeit with local peculiarities derived from the Soviet situation, and the failure of Gorbachev is another example of the failure of conventional politicians to deal with the rise of nationalism.[123] In the Soviet context, radical nationalism and radical nationalists proved impervious to compromise and discussion. The intervention of Yeltsin, the rise of Russian nationalism, the intransigence of Baltic claims for independence all created an insoluble set of problems which anyone would have found impossible to address. The second variant is more narrowly focused. Gorbachev had successfully managed to renegotiate a Union Treaty at Novo-Ogarevo, and it was only the ill-fated coup which blew his plan out of the water and hastened the end of the USSR. Without the coup, our perspectives on Gorbachev and the nationalities may well be quite different.[124]

It has become conventional wisdom to say that the nationalities issue was Gorbachev's greatest failure. By 1991, he had brought about the very scenario he had fought so hard to avoid: the demise of the Union. He identified very strongly with the Soviet Union. If we judge this scenario purely on outcomes, then it is justifiable to draw this conclusion. In spite (or perhaps because of) his best efforts, Gorbachev failed to keep the Union together. But the other types of criticism are more contentious. Should he really be vilified for failing to use force to keep the Union together? Can he at one and the same time be justifiably criticized for having no real understanding/policy to deal with the nationalities issue, and having a strategy which was too lenient, too consensual and too optimistic? Should our judgements on Gorbachev not be considered in the light of other leaders attempts to manage protest in large multi-ethnic states? Considering the complexities and the latent tensions, was not the relatively bloodless and peaceful disintegration of the system not something of a major triumph for Gorbachev? The verdict on the nationalities issue must take into account that Gorbachev clearly failed either to see the ethnic consequences of his reforms and to conceive of a policy to deal with it, or that he failed to understand the depth and intensity of nationalist grievances and so consistently underestimated them, or overestimated his ability to keep people on his side. This does not seem to be an inevitable collapse brought about by forces outside of his control. Although Gorbachev was steeped in partymindedness and in the Marxist-Leninist modes of thinking, this did not stop him from thinking speculatively and creatively about how to reform the Soviet system. However, he failed to apply the same levels of imagination and creativity to thinking about the nationalities, and consequently, in this area, as with the economy, he came up short. It is ironic then that the relatively peaceful way the Union finally fell apart can actually be seen as a creditable outcome for Gorbachev, even if it was not the outcome he either intended or desired.

The overall record

Attempting to disaggregate his overall record leaves us with a complex picture, then. In certain areas the 'Heroic Liberator' label clearly fits (most notably with regard to the end of the Cold War), although the contributions of others need to be foregrounded too. In the economy he failed to get to grips with the problems, and devised poorly thought-out and wrongly sequenced changes which destroyed much but created little. The everyday living conditions of the Soviet people were desperately impoverished. In this area the appropriate epitaph is probably a mixture of the 'labour of Sisyphus' and the 'incompetent reformer'. In terms of the nationalities, he is probably best seen as a combination of a noble or glorious failure, and the sorcerer's apprentice. The question of Eastern Europe is an interesting one as Gorbachev is credited with not doing something, and so the outcome in this area was at best indirectly attributable to Gorbachev. Here he was the passive liberator, or perhaps the inadvertent hero. The question of political pluralism, democracy and civic freedoms is the most contentious one to judge. Gorbachev was clearly a key player in dismantling the old system, in initiating the reforms to the political system, in setting in motion the process to democratize the Soviet power structures and in ending the monopoly rule of the Communist Party. The political system that Gorbachev started to build was unfinished when he was removed from power. The contours of the emerging system – more pluralistic, more freedoms, more civil rights – could clearly be seen. The shadow of the old system had been dispelled. Yet the transitional arrangements that Gorbachev put in place seemed to be storing up potential problems, creating the possibility for a future power-centre which would be authoritarian and personalized, hindering the development of democratic institutions. Although he left a legacy that was of a Russia freer and more democratic than before, it was by no means an unambiguous legacy. Here he can best be described as a heroic dismantler.

The overall balance-sheet is then a highly complex one, as we might expect. But what if we move away from a judgement on the outcomes of Gorbachev's time, and explore the intentions and motives behind his programme? This leads us into a further layer of problems and interpretations, namely the questions of what his intentions were: why did he do it?

The question of intent: what was he doing?

Judging the gap between what he achieved and what he intended is complicated not just by the problem of evaluating what he 'achieved', but also by the lack of agreement on what he was actually trying to do. The only thing everyone seems to agree upon is that there was no detailed blueprint in 1985. Outside of that, though, everything is contested. Opinions range from those who argue that he had a clear, if somewhat vaguely articulated, vision to those who see no clear vision at all. Others see him as embarking on a programme which was driven by either economic, political, international or ideological imperatives. Some see his vision evolving in interaction with the problems and issues that he was forced to confront. Others see him doing little more than conducting a series of *ad hoc* desperate improvizations. Further differences emerge between those who see him as a leader who sought to reform and transform the system, and others who see him as someone engaged in an essentially conservative defence of the existing order. The basic positions can be stated as: a liberal defender of orthodoxy; the vague reformer; the improvising modernizer; and finally the evolving transformer. Once again there are no clear-cut, absolute demarcations between these positions but they are useful tools for communicating the essential interpretative differences that exist.

Defender of the Faith

There were few scholars who conceived Gorbachev as embarking on what was basically a defence of the existing order, but some can be found. Most notably, Suraska has argued that the basic objectives of Gorbachev were to uphold the fundamental principles of the Soviet regime. He was committed right up until the end to the principles of central planning and nationalization, and to the ideals of Soviet communism. His policies were basically attempts to reconstruct the powers of the centre, and to concentrate more power at the centre, which had been dispersed during the Brezhnev years of leadership drift at the centre and venality, corruption and nepotism at the periphery. Gorbachev's aims were therefore primarily *political*: he was attempting reforms to reinvigorate the party and reconstitute its place at the centre of the system, alongside other measures to bolster the performance of the existing institutions of the system and so revive Soviet-style socialism by getting 'back to basics'. In this sense Gorbachev's aim was to defend the system he inherited.[125]

An improvising modernizer

A variation on the position above sees Gorbachev embarking on a process which aimed, initially, at a modernized, more efficient, more streamlined, humane and participatory version of a traditional 'Bolshevik' system, synthesizing new and old in a revived liberalized, modernized Leninism. His vision was either distinctly blurred or non-existent. All that drove him were some general, quite cautious aspirations for greater efficiency, flexibility and acceptance into the world community. He was not looking for any major transformation or root-and-branch reform of the system, merely liberalization and limited improvements. What drove him beyond these cautious parameters was the failure of his initial measures and the resistance of those opposed to him. Radicalism was thrust upon him, and this forced him to a series of desperate improvisations, resulting in the collapse of the pillars of the old system, but nothing in their place. Mark Kramer argues that Gorbachev decided to do more than just 'muddle through' which had been the preferred strategy of his immediate predecessors.[126] Gorbachev was motivated more by an acute sense that the comparative standing of the USSR in the world was slipping, rather than fears about the future viability of the state. However, he chose to talk up the crisis situation in order to justify the departure from the 'muddling through' approach. When his initial modest reforms were limited in their impact he began to introduce more radical ones.[127]

A vague reformer

A variant on the 'improvising modernizer' view, the 'vague reformer' position starts from the same basic premise: that Gorbachev was engaged in an attempt to synthesize the old and the new in some new amalgam. However, the emphasis on this view is on the extent and nature of the change envisaged by Gorbachev, rather than on the desire to maintain the essentials of the system by incorporating limited changes. The balance in this amalgam was on change, specifically on sweeping changes that would, paradoxically strengthen and improve the essential features of the system. For John Gooding, the aim was to advance gradually to a version of social democracy which would retain the socialist essence of the system.[128] Dmitri Volkogonov sees Gorbachev as aiming at a liberal programme which would not touch the foundations, but would build a structure combining the best of socialism and capitalism.[129] Gorbachev emerges from this with a vague notion of heading for a modernized, reformed social-democratic-type version of the existing system.

A(n) (evolving) system transformer

The most distinctive view is the one which views Gorbachev as engaging on a deliberate journey to transform the system, to change it from one qualitative state into another one. This view – expressed primarily by Archie Brown – detects in Gorbachev a clear aim to introduce deep-seated and consistent reforms into the Soviet system right from the outset.[130] Although he began cautiously, this was merely the prelude to more far-reaching reforms. Although there was a strong pragmatic, evolutionary current, this was always within the context of a vision to reform the system. As he learned more of the problems, resistance and opposition to his programme, so his position shifted from reform to transformation and the deliberate dismantling of the foundations of the communist system. Gorbachev thus emerges as a serious, consistent and committed reformer who became a system transformer.[131]

The existence of this extremely broad spectrum of interpretations of Gorbachev's intentions reproduces the nature of the 'problem' that is Mikhail Gorbachev. Academics continue to debate the essential nature and meaning of what he was doing, and little that has emerged subsequently has helped to clarify the picture at all. What have become clearer are the issues around which the interpretative differences have centred. They are:

- To what extent had Gorbachev worked out what he wanted to do before he came to power?
- Were Gorbachev's initial policies the limit of his ambitions, or the first step in a long journey?
- Was the shift to a more radical approach a deliberate conscious attempt to create something new, which evolved logically from his earlier initiatives?
- Was Gorbachev a closet social democrat all along, or did he adopt this position when it became clear that the old system was irredeemable?

Let us take these one at a time:

- *How far had Gorbachev worked out what he wanted to do?* There was no blueprint. But Gorbachev was aware of the problems in the system, and was aware of both the previous reform attempts that had failed, and of the developments in the rest of the world which were leaving the USSR behind. Equally, the status quo was not an option for Gorbachev. So, Gorbachev probably had a clear sense of what he did not want to happen, but a vague sense of where he wanted to end up, and of the broad brush strokes of his reformation. This encompassed measures to address the economic and technological lag, but also the general spiritual and moral malaise affecting the Soviet people. This vague focus was gradually sharpened as he uncovered the problems, and as he tried different solutions with varying degrees of success. Overall, it seems evident that Gorbachev always wished to move beyond his initial policies.
- *Why did his reform programme become more radical?* The shift towards radicalism was a function of both the vagueness of what to build and the certainty of knowing what NOT to build. This meant moving away from where they were, but was rather contingent about where this might lead. This led to a clash between an evolving strategy, accumulating problems and the growth of opposition. Gorbachev's initial reforms began to dismantle the old system which produced significant criticism and revealed entrenched opposition. The need to overcome this opposition and to generate support required

that Gorbachev embark upon the creative process of changing the system. The intention of making a break with the old way of doing things was the key factor here. Gorbachev's initial reforms had revealed the power of the old system to obstruct change, and measures had to be introduced to overcome this. Radicalization was not a sign of desperation, and neither was Gorbachev forced against his better judgement to introduce radical measures because his original policies had failed. But equally radicalization was not part of a planned process. It arose at a particular juncture in the reform process, forged out of the imperatives to push ahead, to confront opposition, to overcome inertia and to start the process of building something new to replace the old.

- *Was Gorbachev a closet social-democrat all along?* Gorbachev was not an orthodox Marxist in the mould of Mikhail Suslov. He was always a slightly unconventional Marxist-Leninist, and was open to new ideas and to piecing together new ideological amalgams. Gorbachev ended up dwelling in the social-democratic end of the political spectrum, but this was really a journey, which began in 1950 and carried on after 1991. This was not a 'Road to Damascus' moment some time in 1988, but nor was it a concealed belief which he had nurtured since his university days until he was finally able to throw off his Marxist mask to reveal his social-democratic soul. Gorbachev had been heavily influenced by dissident thought, by intellectual innovations among the intelligentsia in the 1960s and 1970s and by Western figures, thoughts and ideas. He gradually moved towards an ethical socialism as he increasingly rejected the ideological underpinnings of the old system: scientific socialism.

In sum, Gorbachev's intentions were initially quite vague, but became clearer as his rule unfolded and as the problems and the opponents were revealed. It was a journey. It became more radical, and at some point in 1989 it was a journey where he no longer was in control, despite his best efforts. The initial vagueness of his programme was significant, because it meant that many options could be explored and a number of potential solutions could be discussed. But this vagueness, this lack of a road map, this plane not knowing where to land, became a handicap after 1988, as there was little to guide him when things became difficult, and little to motivate or encourage people to support him. In the end, the gap between what he set out to do and what he achieved was great. The old system was destroyed, and the new system under his guidance failed to materialize. This leads us on to the final point of our enquiry: how have scholars tried to explain why Gorbachev's programme and his own political career came to grief in 1991?

The question of strategy: none, wrong or thwarted?

What happened to blow Gorbachev so widely off course? Was it because of the strategy he adopted? Was it because he did not have a strategy? Or was it due to factors outside of his control? It is, of course, essential to bear in mind the depth and intensity of the opposition Gorbachev faced, and also the boldness and complexity of the undertaking itself. Gorbachev himself, as we have seen, was also keen to note the significance of two things – luck and an unimaginative set of Western leaders – in his eventual downfall. On the other hand, Gorbachev knew from his own experiences and from previous attempts to reform the Soviet system that opposition would be intense, and that the job would be a difficult one. So, this throws the question of Gorbachev's choice of strategy and his tactical decision-making into the foreground. Although most scholars recognize that the defining feature of Gorbachev's approach was his occupation of a centrist position, constantly manoeuvring to prevent the radicals and the conservatives from driving the reforms off course, there is substantial disagreement over whether this was part of a conscious, planned strategy or whether it was symptomatic of a vacuum at the heart of Gorbachev's thinking.

Critics of Gorbachev's strategy fall into two camps: those who argue that he did not have one, and those who argue that he had one, but it was deeply flawed. The former argue that Gorbachev really had very little idea of where he was going, and even less idea of how to get there. This massive void at the heart of *perestroika* inevitably condemned Gorbachev to a strategy of improvisation and ad hoc policy formation and implementation. His 'centrist' policy of oscillating between reformers and conservatives actually highlighted the absence of a strategy. His centrism was his strategy, rather than occupying the centre ground in order to implement his strategy. When the centre ground began to shrink and disappear in 1990/91, the strategy was revealed as a mirage.[132]

Those who fall into the 'deeply flawed' camp argue that Gorbachev profoundly misunderstood the nature of his project and the consequences of his policies.[133] Three issues are highlighted. First, Gorbachev's belief that he could maintain control of the reform process by unleashing popular initiatives and pressure via democratization and *glasnost* (especially in a period of economic hardship) was extremely ill-conceived. It showed a lack of understanding of the dynamics of reform in a multinational state, and of the way in which the people would express their dissatisfaction with the economic situation. Second, Gorbachev took little heed of the question of the best way to combine or sequence the reforms. The excessive focus on the question of political reform after 1987 meant that the key question of successful economic reform was not given the urgent attention it required. Why did Gorbachev not give more attention to other models of communist reform which eschewed political reform? This was a flawed, naïve strategy. Finally, Gorbachev's adoption of a centrist position was quickly undermined by the radicalization and polarization of Soviet society and politics. Gorbachev's constant compromising and improvising began to look increasingly like weakness and vacillation, creating leadership drift and indecision at the top. Gorbachev's obsession with consensus prevented him from making common cause with the radical democrats and from applying force to crush the opposition to his rule. Gorbachev should have allied himself with one side or the other. By failing to do so, he created the vacuum which the conservative forces attempted to fill in August 1991.

Moreover, his general approach as a political leader – ad hocism, or engage and then see – also contributed in this regard, as it became readily perceived as drift, indecision, vacillation.

On the other hand, others see great qualities in Gorbachev's approach and strategy, until he was blown off course by forces outside of his control. The fullest articulation of this has come from Archie Brown, who saw in Gorbachev a combination of prescience, consensual leadership and quick learning and adaptation which enabled Gorbachev to maintain the momentum of reform for five years (up to 1990) and place himself in the vanguard of the movement for reform.[134] This strategy of flexible, centrist, consensual reform was instrumental in enabling Gorbachev to bring about the remarkable transformations to the system after 1988. Moreover it was achieved without significant bloodshed, which was even more remarkable given the scale and nature of the changes he introduced. His most sympathetic commentators do still highlight mistakes, though. Notably both Cohen and Brown argue quite forcibly that Gorbachev omitted to do two things that could have rescued him from his fate. First, he should have put himself forward for direct popular election in March 1990 when he became Executive President. If he had done this, he would have had a popular mandate and a weapon in his subsequent struggles with Yeltsin. Second, rather than maintaining a misplaced faith in the CPSU as being redeemable, he should have split the party into its reformist and conservative wings early on and aligned himself with all of the reformist forces. This would have meant he would not have had to spend so much time and energy balancing his political strategy and trying to keep the whole party together. This blind spot cost him dearly.[135]

The disagreements over the qualities of Gorbachev's strategy – or indeed the very existence of a strategy – reflect not just deep interpretative divisions over what Gorbachev was trying to do, but also reflect deep divisions over fundamental questions: the nature of democratic leadership, the balance of force and consensus in political leadership, the place of morality in evaluating political leaders. Unwillingness to use force has been advanced as evidence to substantiate Gorbachev's claim to greatness as a reforming leader, and also evidence of his weakness, naïveté and failure. But in line with what has been argued above, Gorbachev's overall strategic and tactical approach was appropriate and workable up to a point, but when that point was reached, his unwillingness to change eventually caused the whole programme to unravel. It was, in essence, the wrong-headed sequencing of reforms, the failure to adjust in the light of changing context, the unwillingness to make a break with the party and the continued, dogmatic, stubborn insistence on the correctness of his own judgement which eventually did for Gorbachev.

Alternative perspectives: longer, broader, closer, comparative

The difficulties involved in assessing Gorbachev's record while in power have led scholars to look at other ways to appraise him. The problems outlined above – the unfinished nature of Gorbachev's project, the lack of agreement on his successes and failures, the uncertainty over his intentions – created a vast spectrum of opinions and interpretations. These 'alternative' appraisals have taken a variety of forms, but essentially try and place Gorbachev within a broader global perspective, a longer historical perspective or a comparative perspective, or a combination of one or more of these. Have they proven any more fruitful, or less contentious?

There has been one consistent theme throughout the scholarly appraisals of Gorbachev upon which all have found agreement: he did an excellent job of dismantling and destroying the old system.[136] This 'lowest common denominator' approach sees Gorbachev's great merit in the destruction of the repressive communist regime, and the subsequent liberation of the peoples of the USSR and Eastern Europe. Gorbachev undermined both the institutional edifice of communism and the ideological legitimation of communist power and communist expansionism. As Anders Aslund, a highly critical commentator has noted, Gorbachev displayed a 'remarkable capacity for peaceful destruction'.[137] Rather less generously, Marshal Goldman pronounced his verdict as 'at least he tried'.[138] This destructive capacity was not purely seen in terms of a moral judgement on the nature of Soviet-style communism and that the world was better off without it, but was also predicated on the opportunities or possibilities that were now created for the peoples of the former Soviet Union and Eastern Europe to shape their own destiny. This has perhaps best been expressed by Valerie Bunce:

> By introducing some of the elements of liberalism and by destroying Stalinism Gorbachev made possible that which was impossible prior to these reforms. He opened up the opportunity that Russia could evolve in the future into a liberal state. This was and is no small achievement ... In this sense, it might be less important to think about what Gorbachev did than to focus on the options he created ... In tabulating the many costs of the Gorbachev reforms, then, we should not forget their main benefit. That benefit was the addition of positive, yet previously unthinkable scenarios for future developments – in Russia, in Europe and in the international system.[139]

The polar opposite of the search for the lowest common denominator has been speculation of the counter-factual-history type.[140] What if Gorbachev had not become General Secretary? Would the changes that occurred have happened without Gorbachev? Would things have turned out differently? Would anyone else have done it better? Was there anyone else around at the time who had the same potential for change of a global magnitude? It is difficult, looking around the Soviet leadership in 1985, to find anyone else who would have considered introducing reforms on the scale and at the speed and in the sequence that Gorbachev did. Alternative candidates are generally seen as representing a low-risk, essentially conservative path, continuing with the essentials of the system left intact. This approach, which is relatively agnostic on the cost/benefit issue, highlights the importance of Gorbachev to the processes which got under way after 1985, and emphasizes the point that substantive change could only come from the top in the

Soviet system, and the precise nature of this change was determined by the values and outlook of the leader. Given the complexity of the task, this approach is generally taken by those who are supportive of Gorbachev and wish to appraise him positively.

A third approach seeks a way around the problem of the complex and contested legacy of Gorbachev by focusing upon the ironies, ambiguities and paradoxes of his leadership. In other words, instead of trying to devise an explanation/evaluation of Gorbachev and *perestroika* that might encapsulate all of the puzzles and ambiguities and resolve them in one big idea or model, this approach chose instead to take the ambiguities as the means of defining Gorbachev and his project. Although this does little to extend our understanding or address the question of the broader significance of Gorbachev, it does have the merit of raising our awareness of the complex, messy, chaotic and problematic person that is Mikhail Gorbachev. Many ironies and ambiguities were mentioned:

- Gorbachev as a sophisticated foreign operator and an incompetent domestic reformer;
- Gorbachev as victim of his successes rather than his failures;
- Gorbachev as both a naïve and arrogant leader;
- Gorbachev as a transitional Janus-like figure, facing both the past and the future;
- Gorbachev as the most democratic leader Russia ever had, who was by instinct profoundly undemocratic;
- Gorbachev as the devoted Leninist who destroyed the Leninist system;
- Gorbachev as a cruel, capricious leader who was also marked with genius;
- Gorbachev as a prisoner of his Bolshevik past and as a leader of a modern, Western type;
- Gorbachev as Pope and Luther, defender of the faith and apostle of reformation.
- Gorbachev as Holy Fool: noble, but misguided.[141]

The comparative approach has also been used to evaluate Gorbachev. The comparisons have been developed along two axes: in a global context in order to place Gorbachev in the pantheon of statesmen and women for their impact and significance; and with his Russian predecessors, to see where he fits into the national traditions of Russian leaders.

In a global context, many have stressed the sheer magnitude and scope of the changes he initiated or which issued forth under his guidance. His life and leadership changed the course of history and changed the world irrevocably for everyone living on the planet. Not only was he significant because of his impact, but also because he was able to bring about massive change without widespread violence or bloodshed, choosing the path of rationality, peace, consensus and dialogue. Irrespective of his failures, these two factors should ensure Gorbachev a prominent place in the history of the twentieth century. In this sense, Gorbachev stands above comparisons, having transcended the achievements of others, and particularly his contemporaries. For example, Theodore von Laue argues that Gorbachev in fact occuples a unique place in history, as the leader of a global superpower who readily and voluntarily dismantled his country's ambitions, power and status.[142] Smith also ascribes uniqueness to Gorbachev, for he was attempting something that no-one else had ever done: building a road from dictatorship to democracy.[143]

Others have compared Gorbachev with notable twentieth-century political leaders. Hedrik Smith places him in the same bracket as other notable national leaders who in transforming their own nation had also profoundly affected the lives and experiences of peoples across the globe. He mentions figures such as Franklin D. Roosevelt, Lenin, Winston Churchill, Gandhi, Mao and Adenauer.[144] Joel Moses offers a more intriguing comparison. He looked at the similarities between Gorbachev and Martin Luther King Jr. He maintains that both leaders

- left a universal legacy;
- were flawed heroes;
- were vehicles for broader social changes;
- seemed to prove the 'cunning of history' in elevating to prominence key individuals at critical moments in human history who influenced events in a positive direction.[145]

The events of 1989 are unthinkable without Gorbachev. Yet his era was too brief to do anything more than dig the grave of communism. It is to others to build upon what he started, in the same way that the fight for civil rights had to be carried on by others after the assassination of King.

Other historical comparisons have also been deployed. One of the most interesting of these was an article by James McHugh, which compared Gorbachev and Joseph II, the Habsburg Emperor and known as an 'Enlightened Despot'.[146] McHugh, while recognizing the clear differences in terms of context and culture, highlights some essential similarities in upbringing, approach, values and eventual outcome. Most notably, a critical paradox ran at the heart of both projects: an agenda of both radical change and a reaffirmation of the existing order. But similarities operated at other levels. Both were liberals but remained unconvinced of the benefits of liberal democracy *per se*. Both believed in strong central authority. Both pursued substantial reform and ended up satisfying no-one. Both fell victim to the processes they had unleashed. Summarizing, McHugh argues that Gorbachev can be legitimately nominated for the title of 'Last of the Enlightened Despots', as his pattern of rule reflected the essence of an eighteenth-century approach to governance.[147]

The national Russian comparisons have taken two forms: historical and contemporary. The historical comparisons place Gorbachev in both Russian and Soviet contexts as one among many reforming leaders, including Khrushchev, Lenin, Stolypin, Alexander II, Catherine the Great and Peter the Great. Gorbachev can claim to be one of the greatest reformers in Russian history ever, according to Archie Brown.[148] Dmitri Volkogonov agrees, saying that, after Lenin, Gorbachev is clearly the most notable statesman of twentieth-century Russian history. Although parallels can be drawn with Aleksander Kerensky in that he left the scene prematurely, and apparently defeated, Volkogonov insists that Gorbachev is an 'epoch-making' figure of singular significance.[149]

Recent revivals of interest in the life and works of Nikita Khrushchev have brought forth interesting comparisons with Gorbachev as a means of understanding Khrushchev, rather than the other way round.[150] Georgii Shakhnazarov and Peter Reddaway contrasted Russian and American views of the two leaders.[151] Shakhnazarov argues that they were working towards the same goal: the liquidation of totalitarianism, the democratization of the USSR and the integration of the country into the mainstream of world civilization. Gorbachev extended and continued the Khrushchev approach, especially in terms of emancipating public consciousness at the outset of his rule, but went much further than Khrushchev in terms of breaking with the old order and instituting political reforms. Shakhnazarov speculates that, had he had his time again, Gorbachev would have embarked on political reform much earlier and much deeper than he did in reality. Echoing Gorbachev's own verdict on the fate of the reformer-democrat, Shakhnazarov suggests that all reformers are destined to either misunderstanding or oblivion at home. The best they can hope for is 'modest acknowledgement after 2–3 decades'.[152] Reddaway's American comparison highlights that both leaders sought to defend the communist monopoly on power, tried to mobilize the people and basically were motivated by the fear that was widespread among the communist ruling elite that their rule and privileges were threatened by stagnation and economic decline. Both Khrushchev and Gorbachev were essentially motivated by a conservative reaction to prop up the communist system.[153]

The contemporary Russian comparisons have attempted to evaluate the relative strengths and weaknesses of Gorbachev, Yeltsin and Vladimir Putin. Here the context is very different. In the journey away from communism, how have each of the leaders fared in their respective attempts to lead Russia towards democracy, prosperity, stability and to establish her in the new post-Cold War world order? The record of Gorbachev looks more positive when assessed alongside the achievements of his successors. Although both Gorbachev and Yeltsin probably had greater success in their destructive tasks, Gorbachev's relative lack of success in the fields of democratic reform and economic transformation bears comparison with Yeltsin who oversaw the rapid collapse of the Russian economy and its slow rebuilding, and who instituted a series of political changes which has created something akin to an elected monarchy in Russia, with enormous powers accruing to the President. Whereas both Gorbachev and Yeltsin were essentially transformational leaders, Putin has emerged as a more technocratic figure, attempting to manage and curb the chaos bequeathed to him by Yeltsin. All three leaders have attempted to synthesize Western/European forms of governance and economic activity with traditional Russian forms, institutions and practices, yet it was Gorbachev who made the boldest moves towards pluralism, openness and limitations on the power of the state, areas which have seen retrenchment under Yeltsin and

Putin. Overall, the path out of communism has not inexorably led to the shiny shores of Western-style democracy and economic prosperity via the free market. But Gorbachev's record looks very positive in comparison with his successors, who also have struggled to cope with the problems that entangled Gorbachev.[154]

On reflection, those appraisals that eschew a direct evaluation of his record have provided us with less contentious insights, and as ever the usefulness of the comparative approach has enabled scholars to tease out some of the peculiarities of Gorbachev's leadership, giving us a longer historical perspective on Gorbachev and his place in both Russian and global history at the end of the twentieth century.

Conclusion

Reflections on Sovietology, accidents, history, personality and imagination

The advent of Gorbachev into the staid and rather arcane world of Sovietology produced an earthquake-like reaction, shaking the discipline to its foundations, leaving no intellectual edifice untouched and causing a huge amount of demolition and rebuilding (even if some was done with the old materials and according to the old design!). As we have seen, the old Cold War divisions continued long into the era of the 'New World Order'. But the passing of time from the political demise of Gorbachev gives us the space and the scope to reflect a little more deeply on the discipline of Sovietology, and on the questions of personality, the individual and celebrity in history.

The post mortem on Sovietology could find no real agreement on its legacy, its achievements or on the reasons why it had failed to predict either the advent of Gorbachev or the very rapid demise of the object under consideration, the USSR itself. Is it possible to argue that the Sovietological community failed? If so, why? Or are we perhaps being a bit harsh on the Sovietologists and the Kremlinologists, for surely prediction is not a part of the life and work of a serious academic, is it?

The review of the work of Sovietology threw up both critics and defenders. Critics argued that Gorbachev and the subsequent collapse highlight the essential mediocrity of Sovietology as a discipline. They point to multiple failures at all levels, but the basic 'crime' or 'sin' of the Sovietological community was that in spite of decades of work, millions of words and voluminous pontificating they had failed to understand the nature of the communist system, and so had been taken completely unawares by its disintegration in 1989–91. This structural failure manifested itself in the analysis of Gorbachev. Few foresaw the possibility of a Gorbachev-type figure emerging. Many reacted very slowly to his agenda. Some believed he was bound to be overthrown. Others believed he would succeed triumphantly. Almost all got him wrong. Why?

Michael Cox believes that the fundamental problems with Sovietology were deep-seated. Partly it was a function of the flaws of the academic community: favouring empiricism over big ideas, resistant to prediction, lacking the ability to handle change and discontinuity. But primarily Cox believed that Sovietologists were gripped by a mode of thinking which prevented them from thinking the unthinkable: that the USSR was mortal. He concluded that the fate of Soviet studies should warn us that 'we ignore the unlikely, the impossible, the absurd even, at our peril'.[155] For Peter Rutland,[156] it was a failure of imagination. He rejected the notion that the failure of Soviet studies was due to excessive political bias (of either the right or the left) or methodological limpness. Indeed, the two 'scholarly communities' which had proved most prescient were the neo-Marxists (such as Hillel Ticktin) and the unreconstructed totalitarians (such as Zbigniew Brzezinski). Perhaps the lesson here is that political commitment actually provides better scholarship?[157]

For Rutland, there were two assumptions underpinning Sovietology which account for its failures. These were: (1) because the USSR existed it was bound to persist; and (2) there was a species of 'group think' which imprisoned the Sovietological community and which prevented creative or unorthodox thinking. Sovietologists had proved unable to see beyond the object of their study. As the system was operating, it was the job of the Soviet studies community to explain how it functioned, rather than questioning its viability.[158] Can we transfer these ideas into our analysis of Gorbachev?

Is the existence of deeply contradictory and highly fragmented appraisals of Gorbachev merely a reflection of a profoundly complex man undertaking a paradoxical project? Or are they perhaps evidence of a wider 'problematic' at the heart of the academic community? On one level clearly there are certain factors which help to account for the kaleidoscope of views and opinions. At the outset of this chapter we saw that the appraisals and critical evaluations of Gorbachev were conditioned by a number of factors: the proximity of the subject, the general fragmentation of academic life and the choice of methodological approach or chronological starting-point. But, in line with the views advanced by Cox and Rutland, there are also some deep-seated cultural and intellectual imprints within the Western academic community[159] which have hindered our ability to appraise Gorbachev, his project, his achievements and his place in history in a way which takes full account of the man and his times.

The first of these is the persistence of a Cold War mentality, which has overlain academic life. The advent of Gorbachev exposed the fissures and the problems inherent in the Sovietological community, by demonstrating how the Cold War had taken captive the mental frameworks of academics and had shaped their perspectives. Freeing themselves from this mental prison proved incredibly difficult, and was exacerbated by the churn of academic life: personal and professional rivalry, imperatives to publish, petty point-scoring, tenure and academic job security. Even after the end of the 'real' Cold War, the imperative for self-justification was incredibly strong. The second of these is the assumptions which tend to underpin academic analyses and academic discourses in general rather than Sovietology specifically. The preferences of academe – empiricism not big ideas; rationalism not nationalism; systems not individuals – all created an environment which was incredibly inhospitable to the type of thinking needed to understand Gorbachev and his times. It was precisely the ability to use one's imagination, to take individuals seriously as agents in the historical process, to understand the potency of nationalism, religion and other 'irrational' forces which was downplayed in academic discourse, which tended to be dominated by and large by rational, impersonal and structural analyses.[160] If we are to assess Gorbachev holistically and meaningfully, we must judge him on his own merits, must free our imagination and remember that historical thinking must always make room for accidents, the absurd, the unthinkable, the unlikely.

7

Gorbachev remembers

Constructing a reputation: from prominence to significance?

What is he? The destroyer of an empire? Or its supporter? A democrat? Or a communist? A winner of the Nobel peace prize – or a man who has destroyed peace and order on a sixth of the world's land surface? Or someone who has deprived us of basic prosperity? I think there is no more enigmatic figure in contemporary history than Mikhail Gorbachev.[1]

Introduction

How do you go about establishing, constructing and defending an historical reputation for yourself? This was the task that Gorbachev set himself almost immediately after his resignation as President of the USSR in December 1991. Having endured the enforced incarceration at Foros during the August coup, Gorbachev was to suffer a further series of humiliations and setbacks at the hands of Boris Yeltsin, culminating in the decision to dissolve the Soviet Union and create a new, looser structure – the Commonwealth of Independent States – which effectively abolished the reason for Gorbachev's political existence. From being one of the key figures on the global stage, Gorbachev had within a matter of months been shunted to the sidelines, divested of formal power and subjected to widespread criticism. What now for Mikhail Gorbachev?

Almost immediately, Gorbachev embarked on a campaign. A campaign to defend his rather bruised reputation, to establish his place in history and to defend the choices, achievements and policies of his project – *perestroika* – and his time as leader of the CPSU. A campaign to ensure that while he may no longer have the same prominence as before, his historical significance would be unchallenged. This campaign was waged on a number of fronts. Gorbachev undertook a constant round of interviews with the print and broadcast media at home and abroad. He also embarked on a programme of publications, most notably of his memoirs in 1995. Finally, Gorbachev sought to find a new role for himself, both within the domestic socio-political context, and also on the global stage, promoting his outlook and criticizing those who dared to attack him and his legacy. Gorbachev's campaign is of interest on a number of levels. First, it offers the chance to unpack how an individual seeks to construct their reputation. This process reveals the type of image, identifications, associations, leitmotifs and symbols that Gorbachev wished to project in constructing this reputation. Gorbachev deliberately and meticulously sought to establish his place in history. Second, it illustrates how the massive explosion in information dissemination has made it possible to utilize the media as a vehicle for the projection of a reputation and to attempt to shape the collective memory of society. This became an acute issue for Gorbachev as his time in power began to fade into the memory, and as has contemporaries started to bring out their own recollections, painting very different pictures of Gorbachev and *perestroika*. Third, it highlights both the problems and the value of memoir sources for the historian. Gorbachev's remembering has to be seen within the context of his other utterances and writings (both prior to and subsequent to), which demonstrates the underlying consistency of Gorbachev's message: history will vindicate me, on all counts. However, in constructing a detailed defence and justification of himself and his policies, Gorbachev subtly shifted and altered the origins, meaning and significance of *perestroika*.

Before turning to the period in the political wilderness, the rather strange twilight era of August–December 1991 needs analysing. This period – between resignations – was a slightly surreal time, as power and authority ebbed away from Gorbachev almost on a daily basis. His response was a defiant one, seeking to bolster his position in the present while defending his actions and his record in the past.

Gorbachev between resignations, August–December 1991

The first resignation occurred on 26 August 1991. The second occurred on 25 December 1991. In between, Gorbachev made a number of speeches, gave interviews and published his book *The August Coup: The Truth and the Lessons,* in which he set out his side of the story of the three days in August. Three clear themes emerged. One, Gorbachev told his own story: his motivations, his actions, the betrayals, and so on. Two, Gorbachev defended *perestroika*, its successes and failures. Three, Gorbachev began to take the first tentative steps in the direction of establishing his legacy and his reputation. Underlying all of this was the desire to vindicate himself. In doing this Gorbachev also, wittingly or unwittingly, began to reveal something about himself, his values, his priorities and his outlook which opened a little light on the inner life of Gorbachev the man.

My side of the story

Gorbachev was keen to put across his side of the story, both to silence any who thought he might have been implicated in the coup attempt, and also to portray himself as an heroic figure, a resister, a democrat, committed to the reformist path. Although he admitted to mistakes and errors, these were usually born out of idealism/naïveté or were collective errors shared by all those in leadership or in public life. In response to those who questioned the extent to which he may have been responsible for the coup, either directly or indirectly, Gorbachev provided the following explanations. He did this piecemeal via a number of interviews and speeches in the days and weeks after the August events, and then more systematically at the end of September, when he compiled his short book.

First, the coup was triggered by the widespread instability and chaos in the system by the summer of 1991. This was caused by the inconsistent and half-hearted implementation of the reforms, especially the socio-economic reforms and the programme of democratization. This instability gave the plotters the pretext for launching their putsch, on the grounds that the system was crumbling. But the responsibility for this was shared by all those in the leadership. Gorbachev also identified the lack of unity and coordination on the part of the democratic forces (of which he obviously was one), but this again was a collective failure on the part of all those in the democratic 'camp'.

Second, the coup was part of a wider struggle between the forces of reaction and darkness on one side, and the forces of democracy and light on the other. But was not Gorbachev responsible for the strong position of the reactionary forces? After all he had appointed these people, and he seemed to give them encouragement and support in the winter of 1990/91, when he adopted a far harsher, more authoritarian line. And could he not have foreseen the coup, given the increasingly hysterical proclamations being made by conservatives and right-wingers? Gorbachev's response was to stress that his intention all along had been to maintain the stability and equilibrium in the system in order not to provoke an explosion:

> From the very beginning of the crisis brought about by the radical transformation of our society I tried not to allow an explosive resolution of the contradictions to take place. I wanted to gain time by making tactical moves, so as to allow the democratic process to acquire sufficient stability to ease out the old ways and to strengthen people's attachment to the new values.[2]

Gorbachev's approach was to reduce tension by compromise. But his ultimate aim all along remained the path of democracy and reform. Indeed, Gorbachev was to repeat many times that the coup was an act of treachery on the part of those whom he had appointed. To explain these poor appointments, Gorbachev adopted two tacks. The first was 'It wasn't me!' He argued that his appointments had been endorsed by the Supreme Soviet: 'they were not just my personal appointments'.[3] The second approach was to water down the appointment process *per se*: it was too simplistic to say that he had made mistakes in appointing these people; a basic divergence over the meaning and direction of *perestroika* had emerged (once more absolving Gorbachev of blame). In addition, Gorbachev maintained that he thought the time for a coup had passed; society had changed too much for a coup to have any chance of success.

Finally, Gorbachev outlined the details of his ordeal. He described his arrest, the conversations with the plotters and the impact on his family. Throughout it all, he was keen to stress his indefatigable opposition, his staunch resistance and his unwillingness to cooperate with the plotters. Running underneath his description of the events in the government dacha on Cape Foros was the commitment of Gorbachev to democratic methods, his experience of dealing with difficult situations and his willingness to pay any price to defeat the putschists and their scheme. The effects on his family testified to the traumatic effects of this episode. Yet Gorbachev also felt it necessary to deny the rumours that were doing the rounds; that he knew about it in advance, that he was only interested in saving his own skin or that he had collapsed under the pressure of the moment.[4]

A work of historic significance has been done

But Gorbachev was also keen to draw lessons from the coup, a device that took him into the territory of reputation-construction and legacy-defending. Most notable was Gorbachev's diagnosis for the failure of the coup: Soviet society, the Soviet people and indeed the world as a whole had been irreversibly changed by *perestroika*. Gorbachev acknowledged the heroism of the popular resistance to the coup, and indeed the role of Yeltsin in leading this opposition. But the ultimate reason for its failure was the transformation wrought by the reforms. As a result of six years of *perestroika* a different country had been created. Society had 'breathed the air of freedom and no-one could now take that away from it'.[5] He went on to say:

> A tremendous path has been traversed in 6 years. A real breakthrough to a new life has taken place. Immense masses of people have become aware of themselves as citizens, for whom, despite all the burdens of everyday life, liberty has become the highest value. It was they who blocked the way for the plotters and wrecked their plan to return the country to its totalitarian past.[6]

But the effects of *perestroika* were not limited to the borders of the USSR. The world had been changed. New Thinking had changed the perception of the USSR in the eyes of the international community. It was no longer viewed as an enemy, and so the international community had refused to support the coup, and indeed viewed *perestroika* as 'necessary for the security and the progress of all humankind'.[7] These two factors – the democratic gains of *perestroika* and the new international climate – were the reasons for the defeat of the coup.

In other words, Gorbachev was not only not responsible for the coup, but it was his reforms that defeated the attempt to return to the past. But a careful analysis of the terms of discourse used by Gorbachev show that he had begun to change the underlying meaning and significance of *perestroika*. First, Gorbachev created a clear set of associations: *perestroika* all along had been about: democracy, freedom, the rights of the individual, justice and humanism. That was its essence. The earlier pronouncements of Gorbachev – about *perestroika* being the renewal of the Soviet system, about achieving economic prosperity and technological advancement and progress – had now disappeared from view. Second, by associating the policy of *perestroika* with freedom and democracy, all of his opponents were now liable to be labelled as defenders of totalitarianism and closet neo-Stalinists. Indeed, the increasing use of the term 'totalitarianism' to describe the Soviet past reveals the extent to which Gorbachev was seeking to disassociate himself from the old 'system'. His denunciations of it – 'that rotten amoral system'[8] – were constructed to enhance the reputation of *perestroika* as a force for liberation and democracy, omitting the catastrophic decline in living standards that had come in its wake. But this analysis was also designed with an eye on the present. Gorbachev was desperate to maintain the Union in order to preserve his position as President. By defending *perestroika* – which revolved around a renewed Union – not only did it defend his record, but it also sought to maintain Gorbachev's present political situation.

'I'm me and those are my convictions!'

Amidst the tumult of events Gorbachev was asked many questions about himself, his values and his priorities, his upbringing and his background. His responses revealed a great deal about Gorbachev the man, his motivations and the forces that made and shaped him. Underlying these insights, though, it is clear that Gorbachev had one eye on the future (i.e. establishing his historical legacy) and also one eye on his present political needs.

In terms of his own past, some interesting detail emerged. Gorbachev revealed in an interview simultaneously broadcast on Russian television and Ukrainian radio that he had both Russian and Ukrainian ancestry. It just so happened that this 'revelation' came at an acute time in the discussions about the new Union, as the threat of Ukraine breaking away from Russia became more imminent.[9] He spoke once more of the impact the arrest of his grandfather in 1937 had upon him, of how it was his 'inner revolt' against the cruel arbitrary aspects of the system that turned him into a reformer. He also described the ambiguities of his generation, the men of the 1960s, the *shestidesyatniki*. This generation were reared under Stalin but grew up during the thaw. They had to reject the excesses of Stalinism while still holding dear the achievements and sacrifices of their fathers, their grandfathers and their generation.[10] Another time he affirmed that he had always been a convinced democrat: even in his student days he had been considered by some to be something of a dissident.[11] This collection of random insights and revelations all helped to portray Gorbachev as having been a consistent opponent of the oppression of Stalinism, of being in a state of constant internal revolt against the 'system' of having a long democratic pedigree and heritage.

Gorbachev continued to assert that the choice of policy in 1985 was the correct one. There was in fact no choice: the system could not have continued like that. In an interview with Giulieto Chiesa and Enrico Singer, Gorbachev stated: 'Our country was pregnant with *perestroika* and it just needed someone – and that someone was found – who had the strength to start this process off.'[12] Gorbachev continued to admit that mistakes had been committed. But it was the usual litany of errors – too fast here, too slow there, too few willing to compromise, too much destruction, too little construction – that he had outlined earlier. He stuck doggedly to the line that he regretted nothing and if he had his time over again, he would do exactly the same, 'But none of this alters my fundamental choice, which I defend and I am basically proud of, and that is my decision to begin the process of reform in 1985.'[13]

In terms of his values, Gorbachev confirmed that he was in essence an ethical socialist. He believed in the socialist idea, in socialist values, but was not interested in the application of abstract models to everyday life. In particular, he was keen to stress the importance of spiritual values (as distinct from the highly deterministic, materialistic philosophy of Soviet Marxism-Leninism), and of the Christian roots of socialism and its yearning for a fairer, more just life. The two thinkers he cited – Thomas More and Tommaso Campanella – were both sixteenth-century political philosophers and neither would automatically appear on a list of influential socialist thinkers. Interestingly, Gorbachev argued that it is the quest, the search for a fairer more just society, that motivated him. It was socialism which best embodied this search.

In the interviews and speeches, Gorbachev portrayed himself as a man of deep personal convictions. More than this, though, Gorbachev increasingly described himself as a man of destiny.[14] He referred to his 'mission',[15] and 'I shall bear my burden to the end',[16] and 'the main goal in my life has already been accomplished'.[17] Gorbachev appears to have perceived the hand of history upon his life, rendering an almost mystical otherness to his time as a leader. *Perestroika* was not just the choice of Gorbachev. Gorbachev had been chosen to carry out *perestroika*.

Gorbachev's resignation speech

All of the themes outlined above can be found in Gorbachev's last address as Soviet President, which he gave on 25 December 1991, having resigned when it was clear that the USSR would exist no longer. The speech in its entirety is set out below. Gorbachev reviews his achievements and sets out the basis by which he believes he should be remembered.

> Dear compatriots, fellow citizens. Because of the situation which has developed with the formation of the Commonwealth of Independent States, I am ceasing my activity in the post of USSR President.
>
> I adopt this decision on principle. I have been firmly in favour of the independence and self-determination of peoples and the sovereignty of republics but, at the same time, in favour of preserving the Union state and the country's integrity. Events took a different course. A policy of splitting up the country and disassembling the state – something with which I cannot agree – has prevailed. Since the Alma-Ata meeting and the decisions adopted there, my position on that account has not

changed. Besides, I am convinced that decisions of such a magnitude should have been adopted on the basis of show of will by the people. Nevertheless, I will do all within my powers in order that the accords signed there lead to real concord in society and make easier a way out of the crisis and the process of reforms.

Addressing you for the last time in my capacity as USSR President I believe that it is necessary to give my appreciation of the way that has been passed since 1985, especially as there are quite a few contradictory, superficial and subjective views on this account.

Destiny saw to it that even when I took charge of the state it was clear that all was not well with the country. There was lots of everything – land, oil and gas, other natural wealth, to say nothing of the brains and talent with which it was endowed by God – but still we were living so much worse than the developed countries, and were slipping farther and farther behind them. The reason was clear even then society was being throttled in the jaws of the command and bureaucratic system. Doomed to serve ideology and to bear the terrible burden of the arms race, it was stretched to the limit of the possible. All the attempts at partial reform – and there were any number of them – suffered failure one after the other. The country lost its vision of the future. It was impossible to live like that any longer. What was needed was a radical change.

That is why I have never ever regretted not taking advantage of the post of General Secretary merely to reign for a number of years. I would have viewed that as irresponsible and amoral. I realized that it was an extremely difficult and even risky business to begin reforms on that sort of scale and in our sort of society. And even today I am convinced of the historical correctness of the democratic reforms begun in the spring of 1985. The process of renovating the country and key changes in the world community has turned out to be far more difficult than could have been predicted. However, what has been done should be assessed on merit. Society has acquired freedom and liberated itself politically and socially and this is the main achievement which we have not yet fully realized since we have not yet learned how to use freedom.

Nevertheless, work of historic significance has been done. A totalitarian system, which has deprived the country of an opportunity to become wealthy and prosper a long time ago, has been liquidated. A breakthrough on the way to democratic transformations has been accomplished. Free elections, free press, religious freedoms, representative power bodies and multiparty system have become a reality and human rights have been recognized as the highest principle. A movement towards a mixed economy has started. Equality of all forms of property is being established. Within the framework of a land reform, peasantry started to revive. Farmers have appeared. Millions of hectares of land are given to rural inhabitants and city dwellers. The economic freedom of the producer has been legalized and enterprising, joint-stock companies and privatization have started to gain force. While switching the economy to the market, it is important to remember that all this is done for the sake of an individual. During this difficult time everything should be done for his social protection, especially, with regard to old people and children. We are living in a new world. The Cold War is over. The arms race, the insane militarization of the country which has disfigured our economy, public consciousness and morality, has been halted. The threat of world war has been taken off the agenda.

I would like to underline again that during the transition period everything has been done on my side to retain reliable control of nuclear arms. We have opened to the world, renounced intervention in other people's business and the use of troops beyond the borders of our country. And in return we were shown trust, solidarity and respect. We have become one of the main strongholds for the transformation of modern civilization by peaceful democratic principles.

Peoples and nations have received real freedom of choice in seeking their way of self-determination. The search for the democratic reform of our multinational state brought us to the threshold of the conclusion of a new Union treaty. All these changes have demanded a great amount of effort. They were conducted in a fierce fight with the increasing resistance of forces representing that which is old, obsolete and reactionary, of the old party and state structures, the economic apparatus as well as with our habits, ideological prejudices and the philosophy of levelling down and of dependence. They came up against our intolerance, low level of political culture and fear of changes. This is why we have lost so much time. The old system collapsed before the new one could start working. The crisis in society became even more acute.

I know about the dissatisfaction with the present hard situation, the sharp criticism of the authorities at all levels, as well as my own activities. But I would like to stress once again radical changes in such an enormous country, particularly, with such a heritage, cannot go painlessly, without difficulties and shake-ups. The August coup stretched the general crisis to its utmost limit. The most destructive element in this crisis was the collapse of statehood. Today too, I am alarmed by our people's loss of their citizenship of a great country. The consequences might be very severe for everybody.

I feel that it is vitally important to preserve the democratic gains of recent years. They have been achieved through the suffering of our whole history and of our tragic experience. We must not renounce them in any circumstances or under any pretext. Otherwise, all hopes for better things will be buried. I speak about all this honestly and frankly. This is my ethical duty. I would like to express my gratitude today to all the citizens who supported the policy of renewal of the country and joined the implementation of the democratic reforms. I am grateful to the state, political and public figures, to millions of people abroad, to those who understood our intentions and supported them, who met us half-way in sincere cooperation with us. I am leaving my post with anxiety, but also with hope; with a belief in you, in your wisdom and your spiritual strength. We are heirs to a great civilization, and it depends on all and each of us now, that it should be reborn, for a modern and worthy life.

With all my soul, I wish to thank those who during these years stood alongside me for a right and good cause. Some mistakes could probably have been avoided, much be done better, but I am sure that sooner or later our shared efforts will achieve results. Our peoples will live in a flourishing and democratic society. I wish every one of you all the best.

Now what?

Having resigned as USSR President, Gorbachev was now embarking on uncharted waters. What would he do? One of the tasks facing him was to try and carve out a public role for himself to carry on his life's work and to cement his place in history and to defend and enhance his reputation. This inevitably meant that he would be engaging in debate over the state of Russia. The Russian leaders were likely to blame Gorbachev and *perestroika* for all their ills. Gorbachev would have to establish that any problems were because the new leadership had departed from the *perestroika* line, and were thus endangering all that had been achieved between 1985 and 1991.

Interviewed just after his resignation speech, Gorbachev was asked how he would like to be remembered by historians. His answer ran like this:

> I should like people to assess what has been done during these years, and I think they will do so. The difficulties and the disorder of life now prevent them from even sitting down and having a proper think and chat together about what has happened and is happening to us and about what sort of people we have become, for we have ourselves become different people and a different country. For this reason alone, we can expect that we shall change and become a democratic, prosperous and flourishing country. We have all the prerequisites for that. Therefore, one day they will be freed from these excessive burdens of everyday life, and I think that they will then assess it properly yes, it was hard, but we had to make a start, and it is good that we did. We have already started dozens of times, only to stop half-way. We must not stop now. We must go forwards.[18]

As he left office, Gorbachev set about ensuring that history would continue to look upon him as a figure of historical significance, even as his public prominence began to wane.

Gorbachev out of office, 1992–2007: rewriting the past, reinventing himself

Permanent reinvention

Surveying Gorbachev in the middle of 2008, it is still a surprise to recall that Gorbachev has been 17 years out of power, almost thrice as long as he was in power. Yet Gorbachev remains a strongly iconic figure, symbolic of the drastic upheavals which swept the globe in the 1980s and 1990s and brought the twentieth century to a premature end in 1991. He has had a long, at times fruitless, struggle to re-establish his position as a figure of global significance. This process of personal reinvention provides the backdrop to the following analysis that unravels Gorbachev's attempts to control the memory of *perestroika* and so define and defend his historical reputation and legacy.

Gorbachev's life after leaving office has been something of a roller-coaster affair. In the months immediately following his resignation in December 1991 he was embroiled in the legal wranglings surrounding the aftermath of the coup. This rumbled on for a number of years, involving the convocation of a Constitutional court and the trial of various participants in the coup. He published his account of the events of December 1991, and for a while termed it another 'coup'. In February 1992, Gorbachev set up his 'Gorbachev Foundation'.[19] This was designed with a wide-ranging remit: to undertake research on global problems, the environment, the spread of democratization, globalization, and so on. It was also set up to provide training for young activists to participate in democratic politics.[20] The unifying theme was the striving for a new civilization. Indeed, the motto of the Foundation was 'For a Single Civilization'. The work of the Foundation was funded by Gorbachev's publications and the lucrative American lecture circuit (although there were also more unorthodox means; see below). The activities of the Foundation gradually expanded. Mirror foundations have been set up in North America, Canada and Germany. The scope of activities has also grown. Conferences and seminars have been held. For example, on 18 April 1994, a conference on Khrushchev was held in the Gorbachev Foundation building commemorating the centenary of his birth. It was chaired by Gorbachev and included participants both East and West. In March 1995, a tenth anniversary conference on *perestroika* was held.[21] On 11 March 2005, a permanent exhibition was opened at the Gorbachev Foundation, 'Mikhail Gorbachev – Life and Reforms' (the same title as his memoirs). The following month, an international conference was held at the Russian Academy of Sciences in Moscow entitled 'Perestroika for Our Country and the World: Perspectives 20 Years After'. An array of speakers included Gorbachev himself, Georgii Arbatov, Aleksander Yakovlev, Yuri Osipov, Archie Brown, Giulieto Chiesa and others. In the USA on 21 October 2005, The Frank Foundation Child Assistance International hosted a gala event to commemorate 20 years since *perestroika* began. The high-profile guests included Bill Clinton, Ted Turner and Betty Williams.[22] Further conferences, seminars and symposia have followed: a 50th anniversary of the 20th Party Congress, an International

Conference on how the Cold War ended, a commemoration of the 20th anniversary of the Reykjavik summit, and an exhibit to mark the 75th anniversary of the birth of Raisa. In all of this activity, a key theme has been to sculpt a particular view of Gorbachev the man and his achievements, as well as establishing a role for himself in the present. In March 1993, Gorbachev became the President of the Green Cross International, an organization devoted to global ecological issues. The Foundation has also conducted conferences and seminars into global security, the environment, globalization. It is currently working on developing an archive, and a group to promote the role of women in Russian politics, the Raisa Maximovna Club.

Gorbachev has also gradually resurfaced into Russian domestic public and political life. In the immediate aftermath of his resignation there was some confusion about whether or not Gorbachev was leaving political life for good. Yeltsin in an interview said that a deal had been done whereby Gorbachev could set up his Foundation, but would never return to political life.[23] Gorbachev denied this. He said that after the details on setting up the Foundation had been agreed, Yeltsin turned and asked him, 'You won't create an opposition party on the basis of the Foundation, will you?' Gorbachev replied, 'No. Moreover I will support and defend the leadership of Russia as along as it conducts democratic transformations.'[24] In an oft quoted phrase, Gorbachev insisted that 'I'm not going off into the taiga; I'm not leaving politics and the sphere of public affairs.'[25] This participation in public affairs took two forms: speeches, interviews, etc. as well as more formal excursions into the democratic process.

In his speeches and interviews, Gorbachev continued to harangue the Yeltsin leadership for their shortcomings and their failures. Implicit in Gorbachev's critique was that all of the problems in Russia were due to the departure from the *perestroika* line, and the abandonment of democratic norms. In December 1992, Gorbachev did an interview with Jonathan Steele of the *Guardian*. Here he lambasted both Yeltsin and Gaidar for the shape and direction of the economic and political reforms, for riding roughshod over the interests of the people, and for selling Russia out to the West and the IMF.[26] His criticism of the Gaidar government incorporated a restatement of his own principles:

> I was for a process which was revolutionary in essence but evolutionary in its tempo. They've broken from the evolutionary path. It was against my principles to throw people back into poverty by trying to jump forward in fits and starts, splitting the country and leading to civil war.[27]

In other words, Gorbachev was continuing to defend his legacy through his critique of the present. This was augmented by his forays into the world of Russian politics. In 1996, he ran, devastatingly unsuccessfully, for the Russian Presidency. He was eliminated in the first round, having polled only 0.5 per cent of the vote. In 2001, he formed the Russian Social Democratic Party. He has continued to define himself as a Social Democrat, arguing that he is opposed to the 'fundamentalism' of both communism and Western neo-liberalism.[28] However, Gorbachev resigned as leader in May 2004, after a disagreement over tactics with the party chairman. Gorbachev has generally been highly critical of the Yeltsin Presidency and generally (although not uncritically) supportive of Vladimir Putin. He continues to denounce Yeltsin as an adventurist who broke up the Soviet Union and blew apart the economy, which caused devastation for the ordinary people. Putin, on the other hand, has made positive strides in creating the institutional foundations for democracy, but has at times made moves which have been anti-democratic, according to Gorbachev. On the whole, though, Gorbachev has been willing to give Putin the benefit of the doubt, saying in effect that the job of growing democracy in Russia (which he began) cannot be achieved overnight. Russia needs time.[29]

Gorbachev continued to appear in Russian public life in both comic and tragic ways. In December 1997, he appeared, to no little irony and ridicule, in an advert for Pizza Hut.[30] The dialogue in the 30-second advert summed up quite neatly the enduring controversy over Gorbachev and his place in history. As Gorbachev sits sharing a slice of pizza with his granddaughter Anastasia, a row breaks out:

First Man: *It's Gorbachev ... because of him we're on the edge of economic ruin ...*
Second Man: *Because of him we have freedom ...*
First Man: *Because of him we're on the edge of chaos ...*
Old Woman: *Because of him ... we're even free to go to the edge of our pizza!*
All: *Hail Gorbachev!*

Not exactly Chekhov in his prime. Deaths have also stalked Gorbachev. Tragically, in September 1999, Raisa died of leukaemia. This was a terrible time for Gorbachev, who had been devoted to his family and who had an extremely close personal and working relationship with his wife. In spite of the scorn that had been heaped on Raisa during her time as 'First Lady', the media were generally sympathetic to Gorbachev, and public attitudes to him in Russia began to soften from this time onwards. He represented Russia at the funeral of his great rival and sparring partner Ronald Reagan in June 2004, and commended him for his willingness to push for dialogue and compromise, and reflected that 'it is peacemakers who earn a place in history'.[31] The most recent funeral he attended was that of Boris Yeltsin, who died on 23 April 2007. In a rather ambivalent phrase, Gorbachev noted that 'I offer my deepest condolences to the family of a man on whose shoulders rested many great deeds for the good of the country and serious mistakes – a tragic fate'.[32]

Gorbachev has published books, articles and pamphlets consistently across this period.[33] During 1993–94, he undertook a series of taped conversations and dialogues with his long-standing friend, confidant and fellow reformer the Czech thinker Zdenek Mlynar. In these conversations they reflected upon their lives, their background, their values and their legacy. Mlynar died in 1997, and the conversations were published in 2002.[34] In 1995, his two-volume memoirs were published, entitled *Life and Reforms*. The timing of this publication – on the eve of the campaign for the 1996 presidential elections – makes these more than just the memoirs of a retired politician. They were, in many respects, an extended electoral manifesto, setting out his ideals, defending his record, and hoping to provoke comparisons with the record of the Yeltsin government. Further reflections on his life and his achievements came in the book *On My Country and the World,* published in 2000. In 2005, he published with Daisaku Ifeda, *Moral Lessons of the Twentieth Century,*[35] and in 2006 he published a further collection of thoughts and reflections on *perestroika.*[36] He has also made numerous media appearances, and been interviewed in a variety of far-flung places, including the massive Crystal Cathedral in Florida, where he was quizzed about his religious beliefs.

The past and the present have been inextricably linked in Gorbachev's thinking, writing, speaking and actions. In defending his decision to do the advert for Pizza Hut, Gorbachev outlined that

> I'm in the process of creating a library and a *perestroika* archive, and this project requires certain funds ... *Perestroika* gave impetus to Russia and to the whole world. It is very important that everything that happened be preserved in these two centres.[37]

He went on to say that he only agreed to this because of the nature of pizza. It was a food that brought people together, 'It's not only consumption, it's also socialising. If I didn't see that it was beneficial for people, I wouldn't have agreed to it.'[38] Financial concerns have continued to push Gorbachev into the world of advertising. In 2000, he advertised the OBB Austrian rail network. In late 2007, he agreed to undertake an advert for Louis Vuitton luggage. Pictured in the back of a car, against a backdrop of the Berlin Wall, the text of the advert read, 'A journey brings us face to face with ourselves'.[39] This last advert provided funds for finishing the development of the Gorbachev Foundation building and also to help set up a centre for treating childhood leukaemia.[40] In choosing which conferences to host, the choice (particularly of those dealing with historical themes) has been dictated by the need to reinforce the message of *perestroika* and the reform of the Soviet system.

Overall, Gorbachev has sought to project a particular image of himself – as a reformer, a democrat, a humanist, an environmentalist – and has tried to establish an unbroken line between his values and activities in the present and his past actions. This has entailed defending *perestroika*, reaffirming his choices and criticizing his successors, 'For the past few years I have had to struggle against those who tried to consign the name of Gorbachev to oblivion, to distort the truth about my *perestroika* activities.'[41] Absolutely central to this task has been the attempt to shape the history of *perestroika* and to control the collective memory of this time. In Gorbachev's interviews, speeches, writings and memoirs we find these imperatives outlined clearly and explicitly. This is perhaps most evident in the foreword to his memoirs. There Gorbachev writes:

I do not necessarily justify all my decisions or actions. Neither do I shrink from the responsibility for the reforms I began, for I still firmly believe that they were vital for my country, with beneficial effects for the rest of the world ... the present state of the former Soviet republics is a cause of anguish to me: a crumbling economy, armed conflicts, aggression, crime and a patent violation of citizens' and minorities' rights. This is the price to be paid for the reckless policy of ambitious politicians who drove society and the state from the course of reforms to the road of 'great upheavals'. Time is a merciless judge. Eventually things will be seen in their proper perspective ... I am still firmly convinced that the reforms conceived and initiated in 1985 were generated by historic necessity. Once the period of trials and tribulations is over, our countrymen will learn to make proper use of the main achievements of *perestroika* – liberty, democracy and civil rights.[42]

Here we see all the themes of Gorbachev's post-power discourse: the denigration of the successors for departing from *perestroika*, the defence of *perestroika's* achievements, the global impact of his years in power, the certainty of historical vindication and the notion of *perestroika* as an historic necessity. Let us begin our analysis of Gorbachev's public remembering by looking at how he described his rise to power.

Revisiting the past I: Gorbachev and the making of a reformer

Gorbachev looks at his own background and roots from a very particular perspective. His explicit intention is to describe the forces and people that shaped him, that made him into a reformer. In other words, Gorbachev constructs a specific narrative of his past which sets out to demonstrate how he became the reformer, democrat, humanist and a global proponent of peace, environmental protection and nuclear disarmament. It is, in essence, a 'whiggish' personal story, describing the triumphant progress of Gorbachev from baby to General Secretary, from impoverished rural peasant cradle to Kremlin hot seat via Moscow University. It is a remarkable story. But it is a story, like most memoirs, shorn of ambiguities, tensions and critical appreciation. In doing this, Gorbachev makes a number of interesting associations and identifications from his past, which gives us an insight into the type of image of himself he wished to project.

Gorbachev's own review of his early years, background and formative influences seemed implicitly to be addressing a question that many Western commentators and journalists had asked of Gorbachev after 1985: how could the Soviet system produce a person of such radical views and temperament? How could someone of such views have risen to the top? Gorbachev's narrative attempts to describe the complex play of factors that created this paradoxical situation: a strong believer in the system's values while being in a state of constant inner revolt against the system. His thinking was profoundly shaped by the system, yet he was constantly having rebellious thoughts. In doing this, he reveals how he came to the conclusion of the need for reform, and also identifies the reasons for some of his early errors as leader.

The first cluster of factors Gorbachev identifies are land and family. Gorbachev describes the effects of the history of his region in Stavropol in the Northern Caucasus; its ethnic complexity bred tolerance and respect for others, and its links with the Decembrists (a nineteenth-century movement for reform in autocratic Russia) highlighted a native tradition of reform, which Gorbachev said that he felt 'within him'.[43] In terms of his family upbringing, it was again a complex affair. He was brought up in wretched poverty, typical of the Soviet countryside in the 1930s in the grip of collectivization. The basic struggle of people to improve their lives was a constant refrain in Gorbachev's writings, and seems to stem from the privations of his upbringing. Whereas in the Soviet times, Gorbachev's humble beginnings were stressed to demonstrate that he was a 'man of the people', now it was highlighted to show that Gorbachev's passion for social justice on a national (and indeed a global scale) had its roots in his own upbringing. Interestingly, in recent years as he reflected back on his upbringing, Gorbachev began to talk up the significance of his Stavropol years for his conversion into an eco-warrior. He saw for the first time the damage that dust storms could do to a region in the Caucasus in 1948, and recognized the importance of living in harmony with nature.[44]

The question of Gorbachev's values and ideals was more complicated. The peasant culture of work and belief (particularly of his father and his maternal grandfather) had a big influence on Gorbachev's character: hard work, duty, sacrifice and a curiosity about the world were all highlighted as values that he acquired from his family.[45] In 2006, he noted that he was still a peasant at heart.[46] This family environment was an interesting mix of the old and the new, the modern and the traditional. His peasant home included religious icons alongside ideological icons (Marx, Lenin and Stalin).[47] He was called Viktor, but had his name changed to Mikhail when he was baptised.[48] In spite of this strong attachment to religious belief and ritual, the family was also devoted to communism and the communist ideal. This devotion became part of the oral history of his family: the revolution gave our family land.[49] This commitment to communism survived the arrest of his grandfathers in the 1930s in spite of the obvious traumas it inflicted upon the young Gorbachev. When they returned from arrest and exile, they refused to denounce the government. The ideals of communism remained intact. The system was taken as a given. This is one of the things that Gorbachev chose to highlight on a number of occasions. But in practice things were not always as they should have been. Gorbachev, looking back, sees this as a key moment in creating a sense of inner revolt against aspects of the system. However, it was not until later on in the 1950s that Gorbachev made connections between his own experience and the wider experiences of the USSR under Stalin.

The period between 1941 and 1950 encompassed the horrors of the war, and the sacrifice of the rebuilding programme. The trauma and tragedy of the war were clearly another formative experience for Gorbachev. The war meant that he stepped straight into the adult world, being forced to leave school and go to work on the land. The camaraderie of the work teams and the harsh labour conditions forced him to grow up quickly.[50] In the post-war period he had to travel to go to school, while in the summer he worked on the land with his father. He described himself as a zealous student, eager to learn, inquisitive, keen on physics, maths, history and amateur dramatics. He was awarded the Order of the Red Banner of Labour in 1948, which was a great honour for him.

In sum, Gorbachev's early years describe how his character and values were developed while growing up in the midst of the very difficult years of the terror and the Nazi occupation. He emerges as someone with a deep sense of justice, of love for his country, of respect for the values of his family and a belief in the ideals of communism. In spite of his subsequent period at university, these years gave him an insight into the lives and values of working people. Throughout this period it was hope of a better life that inspired him to work, a hope instilled him by his relatives, his work colleagues and his peers. Gorbachev's striving for a better life led him to Moscow State University in 1950.

Gorbachev identifies his time at university as the crucial period in the making of 'Gorbachev the politician'.[51] This period – between 1950 and 1955 – can probably be subtitled Gorbachev's 'awakening'. The description of his university years communicates the sense of a burgeoning feeling of revolt against aspects of the Soviet system. He relates stories of how he was critical of the teaching methods that seemed to want to crush the curious, critical spirits of the students. He includes incidents where he criticized lecturers, or defended his fellow students. Little is told of his political activities for the Komsomol, or of his application to join the CPSU in 1952, except that he had to be investigated because members of his family had been arrested in the 1930s. This is quite a striking illustration of the selective nature of Gorbachev's remembering. Joining the Communist Party was a move for the orthodox, the careerist, or those ambitious to get on within the system. It was not an obvious move for those of a critical outlook, or those in 'inner revolt' against the system. Yet Gorbachev chooses to highlight the one thing that made him something of an 'outsider' within the CPSU: his chequered past. But Gorbachev also stresses the paradoxical nature of his situation, which reinforces the idea that underpins his early years: the *gradual* nature of the awakening that turned him into a reformer and a democrat. He talks of how he was a sincere believer in the ideology (reinforcing the view of Gorbachev as an idealist) and of how moved he was by Stalin's death.

> The overwhelming majority of the students were, however, deeply and sincerely moved by Stalin's death, perceiving it as a tragedy for the country. A similar feeling, and I won't deny it, welled up in me then. The essay subject for my final school examination had been 'Stalin – our combat glory, Stalin – the elation of our youth'. I got the highest mark and my essay was held up to school graduates for some years as an example to be followed. Yet did I not know the reality of Stalin's rule? ... In those days nothing seemed more important than paying our last respects to Stalin.[52]

Most significantly, we see for the first time, that Gorbachev begins to use the term 'dissident', a term applied to those who stood out against the repression of the regime in the 1960s and 1970s.

> Many years later, during the difficult days of December 1991, I had an encounter with one of my fellow students at Moscow State University – the writer Belyaev ... He said that in those days Gorbachev was considered, to use a contemporary phrase, to be something of a dissident because of his radicalism. But of course I was not a dissident, though a critical attitude to what was happening had already begun to grow in me.[53]

The dissidents were often seen in the West as heroic, moral, idealistic figures who refused to kow-tow to the diktats of the repressive state machinery of the KGB. Gorbachev begins to align *his* past with this movement. He also identifies himself with Andrei Sakharov, the most prominent and respected of the dissidents, who espoused a liberal, democratic critique of the Soviet system. Trying to describe his reactions to Stalin's death, Gorbachev remarks that

> Some time ago, I read a letter by Academician Andrei Dimitrievich Sakharov, written in March 1953: 'I am deeply affected by the death of the Great Man. I ponder over his humanitarianism ...' Apparently I was not unique in my feelings.[54]

Gorbachev's conscious attempts to identify with Sakharov, to equate the similarity in their experiences, is clearly aimed at constructing an image of himself as having made a similar journey to Sakharov, ending up as a democrat, reformer and humanist.[55] Overall his university days reflect the view of Gorbachev as both an (idealistic) product of the system, as well as someone who was gradually awakening to the 'real' nature of the system and so to its ultimate rejection. Incidentally, Gorbachev also sheds some light on why he was turned down by the Public Prosecutor's office and returned to Stavropol on graduating. According to his memoirs, he was turned down because they were concerned at the prospect of having too many inexperienced people working there, which was said to have been one of the causes in the breakdown of legality in the 1930s.[56] It was nothing to do with Gorbachev's allegedly murky associations with Stalinism prior to 1953.

Gorbachev's pre-Kremlin working experiences are described in great detail, and continue the story of external conformity/internal revolt. Gorbachev's description of his journey up through the hierarchy continually proclaims two themes: his concern to improve the everyday lives of the people under his aegis, and his growing frustration with the stifling, bureaucratic, unyielding nature of the system. The inner awakening of his spirit and his intellect that began at university gradually came into conflict with the cold hard world of Soviet officialdom. Gorbachev provides plenty of anecdotal evidence to illustrate the nature of his activities as he gradually progressed from his earliest position as an agitprop worker for the Komsomol in 1956 until he reached the pinnacle of regional politics when he was made First Secretary of the Stavropol region in 1970. Interestingly, Gorbachev notes that he almost left Soviet politics (on three separate occasions, in fact) to go into academia, but decided against it when he was elected First Secretary.[57] The most instructive lesson, according to Gorbachev, was the clash between his style of work and that of the immense Soviet bureaucracy. He was 'always drawn to radicalism and democracy'.[58] He went on to say:

> From my own experience I could see how difficult it was, and most often how impossible it was, to change either the forms or the principles of economic activity either in industry or in agriculture. All eyes were fixed on the centre, and it rejected any kind of innovation, or else it drained the energy and vitality out of any kind of initiative. My first doubts about the effectiveness of the system were born at this time.[59]

In his memoirs Gorbachev outlined that 'Other rebellious thoughts crossed my mind. But I was much too busy to give them serious consideration.'[60] This dawning realization of the problems in the system was exacerbated by trips abroad, and by reading the works of Western socialists and theorists on the nature of the Soviet system and Marxist theory. In particular, he notes the works of Louis Aragon, Giuseppe Boffa, Roger Garaudy, Antonio Gramsci. From these sources, Gorbachev said that he began to question why the Soviet system had failed to provide a standard of living comparable with the capitalist West. These views were deepened and given substance by particular incidents, most notably the crushing of the Prague Spring in 1968 which heralded an icy wind of re-Stalinization. However, it was not just busyness which hindered the development of a critical perspective. Gorbachev also cites how officials below Politburo level rarely received full information or briefings on policy. He received very little information about the decision to intervene in Prague. Indeed, in spite of joining the Politburo in 1979, he only heard about the decision to invade Afghanistan that year on the radio, as he was not deemed to be a trusted member of Brezhnev's inner sanctum.[61]

In his memoirs, Gorbachev reflected on the different leaders under whom he served, and their significance in Soviet history, most notably in relation to the pre-history of *perestroika*. It is noticeable how Gorbachev uses the history of this time to defend himself, and to attack those who were critical of *perestroika*. So, with regard to Khrushchev, Gorbachev argued that he had begun the reformist movement, but his forays were half-hearted, limited and contradictory and so doomed to failure. In a swipe at those who had accused him of something similar, Gorbachev noted that 'I cannot accept the view that he [Khrushchev] acted as a reformer only to defeat the Stalinist guard and thus reinforce his own position before carrying out his arbitrary and subjective views.'[62]

But Khrushchev's rash decision-making and his utopian declarations about catching up and surpassing the USA and reaching communism soon became an embarrassment for the party and he had to be removed. Brezhnev presided over an era of drift and missed opportunities. Scientific, technological and industrial advances required massive changes in the socio-political and economic infrastructures, but the Soviet system was unwilling and/or unable to respond. Brezhnev's priorities were bread and defence. Gorbachev paints a picture of a besetting stagnation in the economy and society accompanied by leadership drift, political court games in the elite and growing corruption. A key part of Gorbachev's remembering Brezhnev in this way was to counter moves by Russian nationalists and neo-communist in the mid-1990s who wished to revive and rehabilitate Brezhnev and his era as an era of Soviet superpowerdom, full employment and socio-economic stability. For Gorbachev the agenda behind the moves to rehabilitate Brezhnevism was clear: to demonstrate the *perestroika* had been unnecessary, and that the problems in the system stemmed from *perestroika*, not Brezhnev. Equally, though, Gorbachev can be accused of talking up the crisis to justify the radicalism of his policies.[63]

In an interesting passage in his exchanges with Zdenek Mlynar, Gorbachev identifies the limitations of his thinking. Although it gradually began to dawn on him that something was wrong within the system itself, the only prescription he had was to change the people. Better people staffing the system were the proper cure. At this point, he still could not contemplate rejecting the system. Gorbachev, even in the early years of *perestroika,* was in the grip of 'orthodox' thinking. Although a process of inner revolt was under way, and was accelerated by his move to Moscow to become part of the central leadership in 1978, Gorbachev still had the cultural imprint of Stalinism running through him. This is a significant admission on the part of Gorbachev. It helps to explain the paradox of Gorbachev's pre-1985 career in terms of the internal revolt/external conformity paradigm. For, while he was having 'rebellious thoughts', these were not system-rejecting and enabled him to continue to be a loyal, hard-working yet ambitious figure within the system. But this admission enables Gorbachev to maintain the image of a dissident critic/democrat in the making while helping to absolve him of blame for the early mistakes in the first years of *perestroika*. If he was in the grip of orthodox thinking, it was because he could not but be a product of the system.

The turning-point came between 1983 and 1985. In 1983, Gorbachev was chosen by Andropov to deliver the Lenin anniversary speech.

> For a long time I thought over what the central conception of this report would be, and I decided to reread Lenin's last articles ... What was the meaning of his admission that after October we took a wrong path, made a mistake and had to fundamentally revise our point of view regarding socialism ... Lenin consistently stressed the idea that socialism equals the vital creative activity of the masses ... the idea that the groundwork for socialism is prepared by the development of democracy and that socialism becomes a reality through democracy. The drama surrounding this

man was revealed to me. Here was a revolutionary giant, a man of great culture, who ended up a captive of his own ideological constructs. At the end he was trying to break out of the closed circle of dogma encompassing him.[64]

It is not difficult to detect the parallel Gorbachev is attempting to draw here between himself and Lenin's change to the NEP in 1921: both had become imprisoned by the ideology they had espoused, both were attempting to break the stranglehold of dogma, both were advocating democracy as the path to socialism. Indeed, Gorbachev was at pains to stress that, even in this period, he was committed to democracy as the solution to the ills of the system. The main problem with this analysis is that he was continuing to plead that he was imprisoned by the systemic thinking which did not enable him to see beyond cadre replacement as the panacea, while espousing that democracy was needed to reinvigorate socialism.

Revisiting the past II: Gorbachev and the origins and course of perestroika

Gorbachev, obviously, wrote extensively in his recollections about the origins, aims and course of *perestroika*. Gorbachev's account of the *perestroika* years, its course, achievements and failures obviously account for the vast majority of his two-volume memoirs. There is a great deal of interesting detail about the decisions, the personalities and the problems. Space precludes a detailed exposition of these recollections. But Gorbachev has also constantly revisited *perestroika* in conferences, books, speeches and interviews too. As his life's work and achievement, Gorbachev continues to defend himself and his project from criticism. If we take an overview of his memoirs and other writings since 1995, then the following questions are the most significant ones as we try and unpick Gorbachev's attempts to construct his reputation: why did *perestroika* happen? What were its aims? How did it evolve? What mistakes did Gorbachev make? How was he criticized?

Why did *perestroika* happen?

On the eve of his accession, Gorbachev uttered the memorable phrase, 'we cannot go on living like this'.[65] Reform had been put off, according to Gorbachev, for at least 15–20 years.[66] But the precise nature of the crisis which Gorbachev described as being like 'the ground slipping away from under our feet'[67] was complex and multi-faceted. At different times, Gorbachev tended to highlight one or more of the following five factors:

- *The modernization thesis*: Gorbachev stressed the age-old question of Russian/Soviet backwardness: there was a gap emerging between the advanced industrial nations of the West and the Soviet system. The Soviet system was stagnant, inflexible, corrupt and unresponsive to change. Unless the system was modernized, the USSR would be unable to embrace scientific and technological change and adapt to the new forces at large in the world.

- *The consumer deficit thesis*: *perestroika* was generated by the need to meet the basic living requirements of the Soviet people.[68] Gorbachev also described this as 'relieving social and economic tensions'.[69] He went on to say that he felt it personally embarrassing and humiliating to govern a country that could send people into space, but could not supply toothpaste, soap and pantyhose to its people.

- *The international sphere*: at other times, Gorbachev stressed international factors, either the need to defuse tensions, or the need to cooperate to resolve problems, and indeed ensure the survival of mankind. This also took the form of influence from outside, which caused those within the USSR to reflect upon their own experience. Gorbachev cites the Prague Spring of 1968, Eurocommunism and also the OstEuropa policy of Willy Brandt.[70]

- *The pregnant system thesis*: the reforms of the 1950s and 1960s had created an alternative view of the world within the system itself, which was exacerbated by the dissident phenomenon. Intellectuals and theorists were generating new ideas and policies to reform the system, and these pressures from 'within' were building up.

- *The liberty/democratic deficit thesis*: a cultural rejection of the system was happening within each person. They had become more educated, critical, sophisticated and felt constricted by the stifling, bureaucratic nature of the system: 'our system developed educated people who were the gravediggers of the communist system. The utopian model of communist totalitarian dogma was rejected at the cultural level, and cultural rejection is the strongest form of rejection.'[71]

The last point was not mentioned at all in Gorbachev's early writings, and reflects the shift in Gorbachev's discourse: just as *perestroika* became increasingly about democracy and freedom, and less about economic and technological modernization, so Gorbachev began to posit the democratic deficit as the underlying cause of *perestroika*, rather than the threat of economic collapse or the scientific and technological lag with the West. Gorbachev never suggested that it was the only, or even the primary, cause of the crisis, but it was a significant addition to Gorbachev's analysis and reflects the general drift in Gorbachev's appraisals of the *perestroika* era.

What were its aims?

At times, Gorbachev talked quite contingently and vaguely about his reforms. In an interview with Louise Branson in April 2006 he outlined that 'Past attempts at change had turned into a dead-end … we have to start and have to take a risk.'[72] At other points in Gorbachev's remembering, democracy and freedom were the words that he constantly projected as synonyms for *perestroika*. Looking back, Gorbachev was quite clear about this: 'the starting-point for *perestroika* was the recognition of the need to let democracy unfold'.[73] Or 'the conception of *perestroika* was aimed at a profound qualitative change in society by linking socialism with democracy'.[74] Or, 'all this was present in *perestroika*: a profound democratization of public life and a guarantee of freedom of social and political choice'.[75] In spite of the complex variety of factors that had given rise to *perestroika*, Gorbachev asserts quite firmly that the original aim of *perestroika* had democracy at its heart. At a deeper level, Gorbachev explained that the philosophical and moral roots of *perestroika* aimed at rejecting the notion that the end justifies the means, and the need to replace a doctrinaire, dogmatic ideology which stressed uniformity, with an approach based on a recognition of diversity and multiple values.[76]

How did it evolve?

Gorbachev describes the evolution of *perestroika* in terms of the sequence of reforms. The ideas were said to have been generated between December 1984 and April 1985.[77] Gorbachev continues to assert that, although the process changed and adapted, they always remained true to their original aims. The problem with his analysis is that, in recollecting how *perestroika* unfolded after 1985, it rather undermines the earlier point about how originally *perestroika* was intimately linked to democracy.

In his description of the sequence of reforms, it begins with economic measures aimed at overturning economic stagnation and starting the process of modernization. The reasons why the economy was chosen first seems a little unclear. At some points Gorbachev seems to suggest that it was a matter of political expediency: it would have been unthinkable for the General Secretary to have come out talking about political pluralism in 1985. Yet at other times, he seems to be saying that the discourse on pluralism only emerged after the initial reforms had got bogged down. In 2006, he argued that,

> Initially, we were under illusions that we could make the system work. But as early as the fall of 1986, all of us had to start shedding those illusions. We had talked of *perestroika* but nothing was changing ... By 1988 we decided we needed political reform.[78]

The transition to structural reform – both political and economic – occurred in 1987, when the initial momentum of reforms had dissipated. It was at this point that Gorbachev came to reject the view that replacing cadres would suffice. Political reform required measures to address the structures of power. The key moment for Gorbachev was the 19th Party Conference of June 1988.

> [it] was a personal landmark for me. It was a watershed, a clear line between 'before' and 'after'. In the 'before' I left behind the wavering, the fear of being torn from ideological propositions that had outlived their time but still had not lost their halo ... the fear of sailing further with the danger of 'mutiny'. We had to put all our efforts in the 'after' so as to utilise fully the unique chance for real reform offered by the conference.[79]

From Gorbachev's analysis, the moves towards democracy were an evolving process, with critical moments that advanced his thinking. As political reform got under way, Gorbachev reflected that, 'At first we had to accept pluralism of opinions. My reasoning then was that a multiparty system was neither an inevitable symptom nor a proof of democracy.'[80] As circumstances changed, Gorbachev admitted that a multi-party system was not only inevitable but also might be beneficial in his struggle with conservative elements in the party. In the autumn of 1988, Gorbachev was beginning to reflect, in private, that the party had become an obstacle to change. This compelled the decision to abandon the party's monopoly on power, and shift power to the Soviets. Circumstances in 1990 dictated a further change of tack, leading to the emergence of an Executive Presidency. But Gorbachev's description of the evolution seemed to be far more of a reactive process than an unfolding plan to implement democracy.

An interesting discussion latterly has been Gorbachev's reflections on Chernobyl, and its impact upon the evolution and outcome of *perestroika*.[81] Reflecting 20 years after, Gorbachev noted that in many ways Chernobyl was an historic turning-point, and that subsequently he viewed the world as being divided into pre- and post-Chernobyl eras. For Gorbachev, Chernobyl gave a huge boost to the policy of *glasnost* and enabled him push through an acceleration of the moves towards greater freedom of expression which was an essential underpinning of *perestroika*. However, although Chernobyl assisted Gorbachev at first, Gorbachev now alludes to Chernobyl as eventually derailing his reforms. The massive cost of the clean-up (estimated at 14–16 billion roubles) highlighted the essential economic weakness and poverty of the state, and undermined his economic reforms.[82]

What mistakes did Gorbachev admit making?

Gorbachev is most definite that *perestroika* was not a mistake: the basic conception, strategy and aims of *perestroika* were correct in all respects. In October 2005, he continued to assert that 'Our fundamental decisions proved to be correct.'[83] The mistakes Gorbachev admits to are few and far between. But four are mentioned by him on more than one occasion. The first is that 'the reformers' (i.e. not just Gorbachev himself) acted too slowly in reforming the Communist Party. The second mistake was that they acted too late to reform the union. The third mistake was failing to do enough to stabilize the consumer market.[84] The final one was trying to change things too rapidly.[85] Where Gorbachev admitted to errors, these were essentially errors of judgement about timing, or trusting people, or unwarranted delays. For instance, one of the major failures in Gorbachev's early years as General Secretary was the anti-alcohol campaign. Here Gorbachev notes that the idea was fine, but the implementation was flawed. Gorbachev's error was his failure to oversee the people (Ligachev and Solomentsev) who were implementing it, due to overwork. Another mistake was the decision to delay the nationalities plenum from June to September 1989, by which time things had become highly combustible. Gorbachev also noted the failure to put goods in the shops, which convinced people that they were on the wrong path. This was caused by two things: first, an inability to get the economy moving early on, and, second, this opinion set in among the masses because they had unleashed 'too big a revolution of expectations'.[86] Probably the greatest admission was his failure to join with the democratic forces in the autumn of 1990. If he had united all the democratic forces early on, the outcome would have been very different.[87] Even here, though, this was explained away by his overriding desire to adopt a centrist position in order to prevent a polarization of forces and so the outbreak of social and political unrest. He did accept that it was perhaps a mistake not to allow himself to go forward for direct election to the Soviet Presidency in March 1990, although his thinking at the time was that the depth of the crisis facing the USSR meant that they could not afford the luxury of a prolonged election campaign. There were more urgent matters to attend to.[88] In his memoirs he reflected on the creation of the Executive Presidency, and regretted the absence of a mechanism of power to support the Presidency, 'we failed to think the issues through to the end ... we wavered and acted inconsistently'.[89] He also regretted the failure to create a genuinely independent judicial power centre. Yet, although he acknowledged these problems in the design of the new Presidential system, he was also clear that the main reason the new Presidential system did not work was because of the rush of the republics to grasp power as they bid for greater autonomy and independence.[90] Latterly, when Gorbachev was asked whether he was a failed leader, he responded by admitting to a 'personal defeat' in 1991, because he 'allowed the opponents of *perestroika* to exploit the existing difficulties'.[91]

The only time Gorbachev came close to an admission of a failing of a strategic nature came when he reflected upon his decisions in the early years of *perestroika*. Gorbachev admitted to having underestimated the complexity of the task facing him, which delayed the onset of serious structural reforms, probably fatally. For when the serious reforms began, the situation in the economy was already chaotic. This delay meant the optimum time for reform in 1987–88 had been missed. But this was also easily explained away: all of the leaders were prisoners of 'old thinking' and it took a long time for this notion to be undermined. Gorbachev aligns himself with all the previous reform efforts.

> I think I can say that the main mistake was as follows ... I thought we could reform the existing political, state and economic model, without even confining ourselves to cosmetic measures, but taking profound measures. But I again came up against the same problem as all previous reformers. Unless we changed the entire system we could not open the way, could not provide the opportunities for renewal to proceed confidently.[92]

Elsewhere Gorbachev admits that they needed to penetrate to the foundations of the system, not merely refine it or perfect it.[93] In 2001, Gorbachev also announced that it was the inadequate understanding of finances among the leaders that caused the economic reform problems.[94] Interestingly, Gorbachev also bemoans his luck at certain points. Chernobyl is cited in this regard, but he also talked of the low oil prices there were prevalent in the 1980s.

> [W]hen *perestroika* started, I was dealing in 1985 and 1986 with an oil price that had fallen to 10 or 12 dollars a barrel and I said, 'If only it was at least 30 dollars, not even 50, 60 or 80 ...' If oil had been 30 dollars a barrel at the time, *perestroika* would have been protected.[95]

Gorbachev's admissions of his own failings or mistakes were minor concessions, and could be explained as 'positive' failures: he was too idealistic, too overworked, too much a product of his upbringing, too concerned with the welfare of the country, too worried about provoking a confrontation.

How was he criticized?

Gorbachev took every opportunity to rebut many of the criticisms thrown at him. The most oft-repeated ones were:

- *Perestroika* should never have been started.
- Gorbachev did not know where he was going.
- He had been too cautious or too extreme.
- He sequenced his reforms in the wrong order.
- He was a success abroad and a failure at home.

In response to the first criticism, Gorbachev reiterated that there was no real choice, although the decision to embark on *perestroika* was obviously a difficult one, fraught with dangers. Gorbachev summed it up by quoting from a Soviet film from the pre-*perestroika* era. In a scene where an aeroplane was in danger at a burning airport, the captain was quoted as saying, 'It's not safe to fly, but we can't stay here. So we're going to fly.'[96] This for Gorbachev summed up the dilemma facing the reformers in 1985.

To the accusation that he did not know where he was going, or that he had no clear plan, Gorbachev was equally forthright. First, the original aim was clear (see above). Second, 'no-one can answer the question that only the historical process itself can answer'.[97] In other words, there was an underlying philosophical point here which Gorbachev wished to make:

> At times of profound, fundamental change in the foundations of social development it is not only senseless but impossible to expect some sort of previously worked out 'model' or a clear-cut outline of the transformations that will take place.[98]

In his revelations about history in his October 1987 speech, Gorbachev proclaimed that he had deliberately not set out to provide a definitive statement, as he wanted the process of historical enquiry to be an open-ended one, not pre-determined. Gorbachev was quite happy to defend his cautious, centrist stance. His centrism – neither too quick nor too slow, too radical or too conservative – reflected his underlying philosophy. In terms of caution and the speed of his reforms, Gorbachev responded to criticisms that he had proceeded too slowly in the following way:

> Professor Marceau of France once asked me whether I thought that the criticism that I was working too slowly … was valid. And I said, 'Well, I think that indeed sometimes we work too slow.' She replied, 'I believe that, in fact, you took a very rapid pace of change and society couldn't digest change so rapidly.' I agree with this … We had to bear in mind that this was a very difficult country to reform. We, I think, bore it in mind, but we did not fully know our country … and therefore we had sometimes to put a brake on developments.[99]

In terms of centrism, Gorbachev noted that his overriding aim had been to prevent the outbreak of mutiny. But this robust defence of himself and his choices was difficult to square with his admission of many small mistakes with regard to tactics and timing. As Gorbachev himself admitted with regard to the post-ponement of the nationalities plenum, a few months in a time of great instability and unrest can mean the difference between success and failure. In many ways it was the tactical errors (how to get there, and at what speed) which were crucial.

Gorbachev also responded to those who argued that he should have adopted the Chinese model: advance economic reform before embarking upon political reform. He argued that they did spend most of their time searching for economic reforms, but they were not thwarted by the introduction of *glasnost'* and democratization, but by the inertia of the totalitarian system, the disillusionment of the people with the lack of progress and the emergence of populist dema-gogues.[100]

Perhaps the most damning criticisms of him related to the events in Tbilisi, Baku and Vilnius, when force was used to put down protest, and consequently lives were lost. In Tbilisi in April 1989, troops opened fire on demonstrators, 16 of whom were killed. But who had given the orders? It was assumed by many at the time that the decision had been taken by the top leadership. But this view was hotly disputed by Gorbachev, Ryzhkov and others. They claimed that by this point actions were being taken all over the USSR, and the Politburo would only find out subsequently.[101] The intervention in Baku in January 1990 was justified on the basis that it was an unavoidable necessity. If they hadn't intervened, then more than 83 people would have been killed. Others had criticized him for acting too slowly: a state of emergency should have been announced earlier. But to this accusation Gorbachev responded that they could not just override the position of the republican authorities.[102]

The situation in Vilnius in January 1991 was more complex. In setting out the context for the struggle over Lithuanian independence, Gorbachev made an interesting observation. He argues that the seeds of a compromise solution that could have formed the basis for a renewed union had been planted in April 1990. These developments were undermined by the declaration of sovereignty made by the Russian republic in June 1990. This set Lithuania and the central authorities on a collision course. The stand-off which culminated in the loss of life in January 1991 was caused by 'extremist' elements: extremist separatists and extremist centralists. Gorbachev identifies a coordinated series of actions undertaken by forces in Vilnius and Moscow – who created the Committee for National Salvation – which led to the violation of constitutional norms and to direct, violent confrontation. When force was used and lives were lost, it was not a result of a direct order from the centre, but a result of local initiative. They all went against the policy line of the leadership: to resolve conflicts peacefully and politically. Gorbachev believes that history will vindicate him, and will reveal who exactly was responsible for the decision to open fire.[103]

The 'split decision' verdict – success abroad, failure at home – was dismissed peremptorily by Gorbachev as a media cliché. The rest of the world had clearly gained from *perestroika*: independence in Eastern Europe and global peace and security for the whole of Europe. He denied, though, that the internal reforms had been a failure, and he explained the perception of domestic failure by highlighting that of all the legacies of the end of the Cold War, Russia's was the most ambiguous. The end of the Cold War coincided with the break-up of the Soviet Union, territorial loss and economic collapse. But the cause of these problems was Yeltsin, not *perestroika*. Consequently, all the positive developments – democracy, freedom, *glasnost'* – were set in train by Gorbachev and *perestroika* and the negative features which coincided with the end of the Cold War and the coup were primarily the responsibility of Yeltsin, Gaidar *et al.*[104]

Gorbachev's biggest regret clearly was the collapse of the Soviet Union, which he saw as unnecessary and avoidable. The USSR could and should have been preserved. Agreeing with Putin that the collapse of the Soviet Union was the greatest geopolitical catastrophe of the twentieth century, Gorbachev noted:

> I warned against the destructive nature of what was happening. Things needed to change, but we did not need to destroy that which had been built by previous generations … I emphasized that the dissolution of a country that was not only powerful, but that, during *perestroika*, demonstrated that it was peaceful and that it accepted the basic principles of democracy would be a tragedy.[105]

Gorbachev's recollections about *perestroika* not only sought to defend his record, but also to emphasize that *perestroika* was, right from the outset, all about the establishment of freedom and democracy in the USSR. Almost all of the negative outcomes could be explained by factors outside of Gorbachev's control, or were inadvertent outcomes of his policies.

Revisiting the past III: Gorbachev and New Thinking

The recollections about Gorbachev's activities on the global stage while General Secretary were far less controversial. The record here was one of almost untarnished success. Gorbachev's international reputation – peace-warrior, disarmer, liberator of Eastern Europe – was firmly established by the time of his resignation in December 1991. The writings of Gorbachev on international relations, and particularly his 'new thinking' were driven by a different imperative than the attempt to justify and defend what had been achieved. Instead, the aim was to insist on the continued relevance and correctness of the values and ideas of new thinking to ensure that Gorbachev himself would continue to have a significant role to play on the global stage. As the opportunities for domestic significance receded, so Gorbachev tried to build on his international reputation. This also provided Gorbachev with the opportunity to criticize his opponents and former rivals for undermining his legacy and departing from his values, and to push forward his vision of a new world order.

Gorbachev created a history for his 'new thinking'. Although he highlighted his 1984 speech in London as the moment he unveiled the broad outlines of this shift, he identified a number of key moments on the road to 1984. Specifically, he spoke of the policy of peaceful co-existence under Khrushchev, the Peace Programme elaborated at the 24th Congress in 1971, and the ongoing research and thinking within the scientific institutes in the 1950s, 1960s and 1970s.[106] The intellectual forebears of New Political Thinking were said to be Albert Einstein, Bertrand Russell and Andrei Sakharov.[107] Gorbachev stressed that New Thinking underwent constant evolution and adaptation. Interestingly, he argued that the period between March and December 1985 – the very start of his tenure – was a crucial period in the formulation of these ideas. New Thinking went through three phases: the 27th Congress phase (February 1986 to December 1988), which was concerned with defusing the Cold War; the UN speech phase (December 1988 to 1990), which sought the establishment of the primacy of global human interests; and 1990 to 1991, which articulated the need for a new paradigm of global civilization.[108]

Extending his New Thinking values into the post-*perestroika* era, Gorbachev highlighted the need to respond to six challenges: globalization, diversity, global problems, power politics, democracy and universal human values.[109] Within his discussion of these challenges facing humanity, Gorbachev asserts two key points. First, that the whole world was changed by the new thinking that originated in the USSR. In other words, the values of Gorbachev's international policy outlook have had, and continue to have, a significance of global and historic magnitude. Second, Gorbachev's thinking and values are the expression of a new historical paradigm that will shape the nature of humanity in the new millennium. In the onward march of history Gorbachev was, to borrow a phrase from Lenin, firmly in the intellectual vanguard.[110]

Criticisms of Gorbachev's international policy were restricted, in the main, to two elements. The first was that he had either 'betrayed' his friends and colleagues in the Communist Parties of Eastern Europe by refusing to support them during the popular revolts of 1989, or that he had been too patient with them. Gorbachev denied this, arguing that he acted all the time on the basis that each nation had to determine its own future without external interference.[111] The second was developed by Russian nationalists, who argued that Gorbachev had conceded far too much to the West and in doing so had destroyed Russia's great power status. Gorbachev responded that he had not meekly submitted to the West, but had been the driving-force in the negotiations and was merely giving expression to values and ideals that had ripened in the world.[112] In his book which reflected on the unification of Germany, Gorbachev noted that the imperatives for the unification of Germany came from the logic of History, 'whose rhythms are difficult to predict'.[113] Under the influence of *perestroika* and New Political Thinking, the entire international situation was changed. Once again, Gorbachev seemed to express the view that *perestroika* was something thrown up by the objective logic of historical development, almost as part of the 'destiny' of history.

The only really reflective question that Gorbachev dwelt upon was: who won the Cold War? The triumphalism in the West obviously rankled with Gorbachev:

> It is customary for Westerners to claim that the West was victorious in the Cold War and that the East – above all the Soviet Union – was defeated ... What happened is this: In the rivalry between the two social systems ... the positions held by the Western system turned out to be superior ... the responsibility for this lies in the 'model' of social development established by the Bolsheviks and the policies pursued throughout their years in power, especially after Lenin's death ... As for who won the Cold War, the answer in my opinion lies simply in rephrasing the question. We should ask, 'who gained by the termination of that war?' Here the answer is obvious: Every country, all the peoples of the world benefited.[114]

Like all good school sports days, everybody won.

Revisiting the past IV: Gorbachev and the significance of perestroika

Reflecting generally on *perestroika*, its successes and failures Gorbachev has in the period since 1991 created a very detailed balance-sheet which identifies the enormous achievements of *perestroika*, as well as the reasons why it was 'interrupted' in late 1991. In his memoirs (and after) Gorbachev accumulated a number of quotations from leading political figures as evidence of the historic significance of *perestroika* and of his contribution to it. James Baker and John Major were both quoted saying that Gorbachev's place in history was already assured. Gorbachev quotes extensively from Chingiz Atmatov's speech nominating Gorbachev as chairman of the Supreme Soviet, describing him as the 'man who has stirred up the kingdom which is asleep'.[115] Sakharov also turns up endorsing Gorbachev, cementing the identification between the two men that Gorbachev was so keen to construct.

Gorbachev described the relationship thus: 'I held Sakharov in the highest regard. It seemed to me that this was a "new Sakharov", who was inseparably linked to Gorbachev and who together with him personified *perestroika*.'[116] Gorbachev's choice of 'heroes' – Sakharov and Leonov – is a highly revealing one. Their qualities – democrats, patriots, humanists – exactly embodied the self-image Gorbachev was seeking to construct, of himself, and of *perestroika*'s essential values.

Gorbachev's proclamation of the achievements and the significance of *perestroika* runs throughout all his works. The oft-repeated line throughout all this was that *perestroika* had created freedom and democracy for the peoples of the Soviet Union, and peace and security for the rest of the world.[117] In the conference held at the Gorbachev Foundation to mark the tenth anniversary of the start of *perestroika* (which was in many respects little more than prolonged applause for its founder), the main achievement of *perestroika* was to enable the USSR to rejoin the mainstream of human civilization.[118] But the most articulate defence of *perestroika* came in his conversations with Mlynar, and in his book *On My Country and the World*. Gorbachev asks himself the question: what specifically did we accomplish as a result of the stormy years of *perestroika*? In his answer, he cites a long list:

1. Foundations of the totalitarian system were eliminated.
2. Profound democratic changes were begun.
3. Free general elections were held.
4. Freedom of the press and a multi-party system were guaranteed.
5. Representative bodies of government were established.
6. First steps towards the separation of powers were taken.
7. Human rights now became an unassailable principle.
8. Movement began towards a mixed economy.
9. Economic freedom was made into law.
10. The spirit of enterprise began to gain strength.
11. Processes of privatization and formation of joint-stock companies got under way.
12. Peasantry was reborn.
13. First privately owned banks also came on the scene.
14. Different nationalities and peoples were given the freedom to choose their own course of development.
15. The Cold War was brought to an end.
16. The end of the Cold War brought freedom of choice to many nations in Europe and the Third World.
17. The improvement and humanization of international relations.
18. The security of the USSR was fundamentally strengthened.[119]

In the epilogue to his memoirs, Gorbachev stated, 'The promise I had made to the people when I started the process of *perestroika* was kept: I gave them freedom.'[120] But Gorbachev also felt compelled to respond to criticisms that *perestroika* had left the people impoverished and the economy in ruins:

Perestroika did not give the people prosperity, something they expected of me as head of state, based on an ingrained, traditional feeling of dependence. But I did not promise that. I urged people to use this new-found freedom to create prosperity, personal and social prosperity, with their own hands and minds according to the abilities of each.[121]

Gorbachev regretted that he had not been able to see his project through to completion, but strongly asserted that he had created the conditions for freedom, democracy and prosperity at home, and peace abroad. Fundamentally, he had 'guided *perestroika* past the point of no return'. There was to be no turning the clock back to the bad old days.[122]

So why exactly had *perestroika* been blown off course? Why had various reforms failed to take root and produce results, especially in the economic sphere? Although Gorbachev, as we saw above, had been willing to admit that mistakes had been made in the formation of economic policies – primarily the delay in introducing structural reforms and the prevalence of old thinking – the reasons for failure lay elsewhere. Specifically Gorbachev notes three things: the vindictiveness of the reactionary forces; the excessive revolutionism of the radicals and the interplay between the inertia of the existing system and the expectations of the people. The economic reforms were sabotaged in their implementation by the excessive resistance to change at lower levels in the economic system. This was just one part of the excessive inertia within the old system which proved itself highly resistant to change. This created disillusionment among the people as it proved impossible to generate any real achievements with which to satisfy the basic needs of the people. Gorbachev describes this as the failure to 'harmonize' economic and political change. The former lagged behind the latter, because the leadership were set on finding the optimum, peaceful, democratic way to make the transition to the market and so avoid chaos, instability and bloodshed as far as possible. Once more the failures of *perestroika* were down to a surfeit of principle on Gorbachev's part, the sheer scale and complexity of the tasks that faced him, and the actions of the conservatives in sabotaging the reforms and taking advantage of popular dissatisfaction for their own ends. Even the loss of life during *perestroika* was placed firmly at the door of the conservatives, who resisted his policies.

But Gorbachev also had words of criticism for his erstwhile supporters (or people who should have supported him). The intelligentsia, who should have been on his side, proved more interested in criticizing Gorbachev than providing constructive support for *perestroika*. He chastises them for 'failing to make good use of this freedom'.[123] The radicals and the democrats (of whom obviously Yeltsin was the main culprit) resorted to populist demagoguery and adopted extremist stances which further polarized the situation in society. The nationalists and the leaders of the non-Russian republics took advantage of the delay in resolving the question about the nature of the Union to undermine the centre and eventually destroy the USSR.

The final acts of *perestroika* – the August coup and the Belovezh Accord bringing the Union to an end – were bitter pills for Gorbachev to swallow. How did they come about? Gorbachev's narrative describes a process of personal betrayal: by the conspirators in the putsch, and by Yeltsin between August and December. According to Gorbachev, *perestroika* and the Union were both sacrificed on the altar of the ambition and lust for power of Yeltsin and his entourage. His reflections on these final acts were also used to reaffirm the historic significance of *perestroika*.

The decision to dissolve the Union was described as a tragedy, and a global one at that. This act changed the international situation, disrupted the global balance of power and undermined many positive processes occurring in the world. The Machiavellian manoeuvrings of Yeltsin and Kravchuk to undermine the Union were given added spice by Gorbachev's revelation that a key motivation for many in supporting the Belovezh Accord was to get rid of Gorbachev.[124] The dissolution of the Union meant a permanent interruption to *perestroika*. This interruption to *perestroika* dealt a serious blow to all the gains and advances made between 1985 and 1991. Shock therapy had brought poverty and a collapse of production. The dissolution of the Union rent asunder the provision of key services – transport, health, power, communications, information – which had previously been part of a Union-wide network. Democracy declined, and the power of the bureaucrat-nomenklatura class grew. The international climate had grown more uncertain and insecure. Russia was slipping towards authoritarian rule. Russia had been weakened. Gorbachev's damning verdict? The Belovezh Accord promised great things, delivered nothing and derailed *perestroika*. All Russia's subsequent ills could be explained by this departure from Gorbachev's path.

Conclusion

In reflecting upon *perestroika*, in campaigning for election, in writing about his values and beliefs, and on his lecture tours and in his interviews, Gorbachev has touched upon a variety of other topics and issues which help to give us an insight into his thinking.

On Soviet history: February, October, Lenin, Khrushchev and the communist model

Looking back over the Soviet era, Gorbachev had some very interesting things to say. Freed from the constraints of being party leader and chief ideological cheerleader after 1991, Gorbachev revealed some highly 'revisionist' views on Russia's past, particularly the Soviet era. Although keen not to denigrate the whole period, and in particular the sacrifices and bravery of the ordinary people, nevertheless Gorbachev outlined that the 'benefits' of Soviet rule – highly educated society, industrialization, modernization, cultural revolution – had been achieved at an impossibly, immorally high cost.

Gorbachev's most comprehensive musing on the Russian and Soviet past came in his book *On My Country and the World*, published in 2000. But intimations of revised views had appeared earlier. In an interview with the US journalist and author David Remnick in 1996, Gorbachev began discussing Lenin, agreeing that cruelty was Lenin's 'main problem', but then went on to suggest:

> Had the Russians continued along the path of the February revolution, had they continued on a path of political pluralism, it would have been a different situation. Russia at the end of the nineteenth century was developing quite dynamically, and had they gone on that way it would have been much better.[125]

This re-evaluation extended into Marx, Lenin, the October Revolution and the rest of the Soviet experience. Gorbachev's basic premise was that force, violence, repression and coercion were used to impose an artificial model, a utopian schema on the Soviet people. But a terrible cost – in lives and blood – was paid. The prime purpose of this 'rather artificial model created by Marx' was to industrialize the country. But surely, Gorbachev argues, there were other ways to industrialize at a lower cost?[126]

So how, then, did Gorbachev approach the October Revolution? In an extended passage, Gorbachev argues that the October Revolution was 'historically inevitable', but that it did not have to take such a 'destructive and apocalyptic form'.[127] October was the expression of the yearning among the masses for fundamental social change. But given the violent and apocalyptic outcome, were there alternatives? What is interesting about Gorbachev's discussion of alternatives are the parallels that Gorbachev then goes on to draw between the failure of the democratic alternative in 1917 and the slide into civil war and dictatorship, and the failure of the democrats in 1990/91 and the slide into Yeltsin's era. February was undermined by rivalry and the weakness of democracy. October led to civil war because the main socialist groupings – Bolsheviks, Mensheviks, SRs – could not come to any agreement. All were equally culpable. When asked with whom he would have sided in 1917, Gorbachev gave an intriguing answer:

> I do not negate revolution, it exerted a tremendous influence. I am a man who cannot say that Soviet power did nothing, but I negate the communist model that did not accept democracy. And thus it turns out that I would have been with Plekhanov and the Mensheviks. And my fate would have been the same as theirs.[128]

He went on to defend the Whites in the Civil War (patriots now, rather than reactionary lackeys of international capitalism) and also rejected 'revolution' as a mechanism of change in history (too costly): his preference was for 'evolutionary reform'.[129]

In terms of the rest of the Soviet period, Gorbachev amplifies some of his earlier thinking on the growth of Soviet totalitarianism, particularly concerning the role of Lenin. Gorbachev has a deep and abiding interest in Lenin, his outlook and his ideas. He spent many hours poring over Lenin during his time in power looking for precedents and approaches that could be pursued under *perestroika*. Reviewing Lenin's contribution, Gorbachev argued that Lenin made many mistakes in the pre-NEP era, particularly in adopting an overly schematic and utopian model of socialism ('war communism'), although this was corrected after 1921, when he moved to the moderation and flexibility of the NEP. Unfortunately for the USSR, Lenin's NEP model was cast aside by Stalin, and a revived War Communist model was imposed on the people. While Lenin lived, the party still maintained its democratic traditions. Under Stalin, a monstrous totalitarian system grew up. The Bolshevik model – a crudely schematic one – led to a totalitarian government which was based upon the rejection of pluralism, a one-party state and a supercentralized administration of the country (albeit with 'democratic decorations').[130] In reviewing Soviet history, Gorbachev was keen to stress that the Soviet era should not be written off as a black hole or as a cul-de-sac. The modernization of the USSR was a monumental achievement, carried out by the heroic efforts of the people. But an excessively high price was paid. It could – and should – have been done differently.

In the Gorbachev Foundation programme, the commemoration of the 50th anniversary of the 20th Congress (whereby Khrushchev had denounced the Stalinist Cult of Personality) became a moment to identify the historical origins of *perestroika* and to align the two movements. The 20th Congress was the point at which the CPSU made the first moves towards the emergence of a democratic and humanistic society in the USSR. It was not just about de-Stalinization: it was about rejecting totalitarianism and in this sense was an essential precursor of *perestroika*.[131]

On socialism and social democracy

Gorbachev continued to express his faith in socialism and the ideals of social justice, fairness, humanism, democracy and freedom. This was one of the imperatives behind his decision to create the Social Democratic Party in Russia.[132] He admitted that after 1983 he realized that the Soviet system had been totalitarian rather than socialist, and that it was necessary to abandon a deterministic, model-based approach to socialism and instead to have a value-based socialism.[133] The previous conceptions of socialism had been negations of capitalism. But present-day experience suggested that aspects of all social structures, irrespective of their label, could be used to solve the problems facing humanity. However, he did note that the experiences of those countries that called themselves socialist was invaluable in providing examples to help to refine socialist doctrines, which was far more useful than theoretical reflections or innovations. Socialism, for Gorbachev, retained its historic relevance as an attempt to build a global community dominated by freedom, equality, humanism, justice, solidarity and respect for the environment. He also reiterated his rejection of what he termed 'primordial utopian communism', arguing that it pushed people towards violence. Instead, Gorbachev affirmed his belief in ethical socialism, based on the priority of life, liberty and the individual.[134] He continues to highlight the spiritual dimensions to his socialism too:

> I think we should follow a social-democratic course, like many countries do. Social democracy stresses the importance of human and civil rights, which is very important. I think this movement is important in that it

takes into account Christian values as well as the values of freedom, democracy and justice.[135]

On Yeltsin and Putin

Implicitly and explicitly, Gorbachev's defence of *perestroika* and his record was barbed with attacks upon his successor, and the person he blamed for the demise of *perestroika*: Boris Yeltsin. In an interview, Gorbachev stated that 'the thing I hate most is betrayal. And I have been betrayed many times.'[136] Yeltsin is clearly identified as one of his chief betrayers. Indeed, the Gorbachev Foundation had satirical caricatures of Yeltsin on many of its office walls. So what exactly has Yeltsin been accused of by Gorbachev?

His complaints lie in two areas: pre-1991 (betrayer in chief) and post-1991 (destroyer of the democratic gains of *perestroika*). On all occasions, Gorbachev has attempted to draw the comparison between himself (freedom-loving democrat) and Yeltsin (power-worshipping quasi-dictator). Recounting the events of October 1987, when Yeltsin had resigned from the Politburo, Gorbachev highlighted his lack of balance, his talent for lying and his overgrown ambition and lust for power.[137] In the era of *perestroika*, Gorbachev posits that Yeltsin was acting with a covert agenda to hasten the dissolution of the USSR and the subsequent independence of Russia so as to acquire more power for themselves.[138] For Gorbachev this accounts for the failure of his attempts to renew the Union treaty: it was sabotaged by Yeltsin and his entourage for the furtherance of their own political agenda. Gorbachev was clearly rankled by the way in which Yeltsin 'expelled' him from office in December 1991, talking of the 'triumph of the plunderers', and making a dig at Yeltsin's penchant for whisky.[139] Comparing the two memoir accounts of the Gorbachev/Yeltsin relationship is faintly comical: both go out of their way to say that they kept their counsel in the face of insults, hostility, bitterness, acrimony and petty vindictive outbursts from the other for the good of the country/politics/the other person.[140]

Gorbachev then contrasts the policies of *perestroika* with the policies of the Yeltsin government:

Gorbachev on the Perestroika approach	Gorbachev on the Yeltsin approach
Preserve the Union	Break up the USSR
Gradual, evolutionary reform	'Shock therapy'
Consistent use of democratic measures	Use of force as a principle of government policy
Government based on the rule of law	Emasculation of democratic institutions

The Yeltsin regime had abandoned democracy, and in its stead a corrupt oligarchy ('the family') had captured the levers of power.[141] Gorbachev's evaluation of the Yeltsin era was not wholly negative, but interestingly he criticized Yeltsin on the same grounds that he criticized Stalin: much had been achieved, but the cost incurred was far too high. Indeed, this analysis of Yeltsin and 'Yeltsinism' echoed the historical polarities of Gorbachev's historical thinking:

NEP, Khrushchev and Gorbachev = periods of moderate, pragmatic, reform aimed at improving the lot of the people;

War Communism, Stalin, Yeltsin = radical change, yet at the cost of the lives and/or livelihood of the people.

Gorbachev's attitude to Putin is an interesting and complicated one. On becoming president, Putin reached out to Gorbachev and tried to garner his support for what he was doing, aware perhaps of the political capital this might give him in the West. Gorbachev has at times criticized President Putin, although usually indirectly, but his basic position has been to defend him. To an extent this has probably been a political calculation. He has to maintain his image abroad as being a defender of democracy and freedom of speech, yet he also needs to keep Putin on side so that his freedom of operation in Russia is not curtailed. However, there are also deeper forces at work here. Gorbachev's attitude to Putin is linked to his defence of *perestroika* and antipathy towards Yeltsin. The phrase which he repeated constantly was that Putin had 'inherited chaos', a clear dig at the Yeltsin legacy. He has also defended some of Putin's authoritarian policies, as a necessary stage on the road to democracy, policies caused by the failures of Yeltsin. In many ways interesting parallels can be drawn between Gorbachev's defence of Putin's policies and tactics and Gorbachev's own record as Executive President after March 1990. Gorbachev too had embarked on a campaign to build democracy which was at times distinctly undemocratic and authoritarian. The rationale was the need for stability if modernization, democracy and economic growth were to be achieved. By identifying the struggle Putin had with terrorism in Chechnya, Gorbachev was sympathetic, but also critical of the infringements on civil liberties and democracy. For Gorbachev, it was important always to seek a political solution, and also that what was needed to combat terrorism was *glasnost*.[142]

Finally, he has also acknowledged that under Putin things were not perfect – problems with the electoral system, constraints on the media, the selection of governors – but he has been quite robust in his defence of Putin from Western criticism. In a sense this can be interpreted as Gorbachev trying to offset the criticisms directed at him within Russia. Putin has seen Russia restored to a position of global strength and power, and Gorbachev – aware of the damage done to Russia's geopolitical situation under his tutelage – is keen to be seen defending a strong Russia from Western criticism. Very much like his time in power, Gorbachev is trying to maintain a delicate balancing act in his relationship with Putin, as critical supporter.[143]

On Raisa, environmentalism, globalization, himself and the 'capricious mistress of history'

Gorbachev also makes some interesting personal reflections which give us some insights into his character, his values, and his own sense of what he accomplished. In an unusually personal interview after the death of Raisa, Gorbachev spoke about his relationship with his wife and his daughter (Irina). He described how

> [W]e understood the world in the same way. Our backgrounds were sim-
> ilar, we both came from ordinary families, we made our way in life our-
> selves, so we always understood each other well. I think generally it is
> true that people who don't come from privileged backgrounds, often
> emerge with personality and endurance in all walks of life, not just poli-
> tics.[144]

Although he was reluctant to accept the idea that Raisa was crucial in the ultimate outcome of *perestroika*, he did acknowledge that her frankness, criticisms and ideas had been of enormous help in Gorbachev's leadership. Although close to his daughter and granddaughters, it is clear that Raisa's death has profoundly affected Gorbachev. He continues to be close to his daughter – Irina – and his grand-daughters.

We also detect some of Gorbachev's key personal priorities and values. He defines himself as the embodiment of the '*shestdesyatniki*': the men of the 1960s whose credo was 'radical reform without bloodshed'.[145] He constantly reiterates the deep inner sense of conviction of the correctness of his choices, actions and policies. He talks of the importance of dignity and compromise, but that the lat-ter should not be achieved at the expense of the former. Latterly his writings have emphasized questions of morality, spirituality and the environment as he has sought to distance himself from the modernist, Enlightenment, rationalist ideolo-gies of the twentieth century and to embrace a new type of politics for the twenty-first century.[146] He has also been critical of the demonstrations of US military power, arguing that the USA should act in a more inclusive way.[147]

He has constantly attempted to depict himself and to act, work and struggle for environmental change. In his role as head of the Green Cross International, he has tried to bring international pressure and action to bear on ecological issues. The issues of global sustainability, clean drinking water, global inequalities, poverty, deforestation are the ones that are now highest on the Gorbachev agenda. He continues to argue for the values that he prioritized as leader of the USSR – dia-logue, discussion, debate, persuasion – as the means to do this. Although *perestroi-ka* is his main achievement, he is clear that ecology is the world's number one problem. Gorbachev clearly sees environmental activism as the way to maintain an international profile and to defend and sustain his reputation as an interna-tional activist committed to making the world a better, more secure place to live.[148]

A few personal details have come out which shed some light on his character and outlook. He outlines how 'betrayal' is the thing he hates most, and also how as a leader he consciously sought to foster a team approach, a team comprised of strong individuals, and that he believed that one should not be fearful that 'one of them will become a competitor to me'.[149] Here we can perhaps see the roots of the personnel problems that Gorbachev had in the latter years of his leadership. This combination of the selection of strong-minded individuals was almost certain to create a strong clash of opinions. But when this is combined with a deep personal conviction that your way is the right way, it becomes easy to see how differences can easily become construed as opposition and ultimately betrayal.

Perhaps the most interesting personal passage comes at the end of his conversation with Zdenek Mlynar. In a chapter entitled 'The conscience of the reformer', Gorbachev and Mlynar mused a little on the 'subjective' experiences of their years of politics and reform.[150] The question of 'betrayal' loomed large in their discussions. Had Gorbachev betrayed the party? Had Gorbachev been betrayed by those closest to him? To the first charge, Gorbachev responded that all the decisions and policies had been collective ones, and that he had never said one thing in public and another in private. To the second charge, Gorbachev drew a distinction between those who carried out their protest in public, and those who used conspiratorial methods to advance their agenda. In this respect, Gorbachev noted that the actions of Ligachev and Ryzhkov were very different from those of the coup plotters. In defence of himself, Gorbachev once more cited Lenin as an example of a leader legitimately changing his mind in the pursuit of his goals.[151]

His final thoughts are rather poignant, sometimes tinged with melancholy. He has finished many interviews by noting that the verdict of history ('a capricious mistress'[152]) has yet to be pronounced. He stresses that he had dedicated himself to reforms for the sake of the people, but that this was rarely a story with a happy ending, 'Mine is the usual fate of reformers: either we get killed or our contribution is acknowledged only 50 years later.'[153] Perhaps the last word should come from his conversation with Mlynar:

> Some time ago, Zdenek, I wrote that fate willed that I be given a task of a kind that very rarely falls to the lot of a single human being. At the same time, it was a burden so heavy that only my closest friends know how hard things were for me sometimes, and still can be to this day, to the point of despair. But I accept it as fate: there are no happy reformers.[154]

Conclusion

Gorbachev, man of the twentieth century?

Introduction

Gorbachev was in power for less than six years. His project collapsed ignominiously in a few days in August 1991. He left office rather forlornly, alone and eclipsed by his main rival. His attempts at a political renaissance since 1992 have all been abject failures. He has maintained a public profile of sorts, yet this is increasingly peripheral. His attempts to construct a narrative of the significance of his life and work have been partially successful at best. Yet ... he is considered by some to be a central, almost heroic figure in any history of recent times. His bold and courageous initiatives, his peace offensive, his commitment to encouraging democracy and freedoms at home and abroad, his dignity in leaving office, his unswerving devotion to his wife and family, his espousal of environmentalism, all speak of a leader who has indelibly left his imprint on the twentieth century. In a recent interview, it was asserted that he 'has, arguably, changed the world more than any living soul'.[1]

As we have seen, he remains a deeply contested figure. So, then, what shall we say about Gorbachev? How should we assess his life, his significance, his work?

Fêted

Since leaving office, Gorbachev has received a bewildering array of awards, prizes and tributes. These include the following:

- Memorial Golden Medal of Belgrade (Yugoslavia, March 1988)
- Polish Sejm Silver Medal for outstanding contribution to international cooperation, friendship and interaction between Poland and the USSR (Poland, July 1988)
- Memorial Medal of Sorbonne (Paris, July 1989)
- Memorial Medal of Rome Municipality (November 1999)
- Vatican Memorial Medal (1 December 1989)
- Franklin D. Roosevelt Liberty Medal (Washington, DC, June 1990)
- Hero Star, Ben Gurion University (Israel, 1992)
- Gold Medal, Prometheus National Technological University of Athens (Greece, 1993)
- Gold Medal of Thessaloniki (Greece, 1993)

- Philadelphia Council for World Problems, International Statesman Award (USA, 1993)
- Gold Badge, University of Oviedo (Spain, 1994)
- Simon Bolivar Grand Cross for Unity and Liberty, Latin American Unity Association in Korea (Korea, 1994)
- St. Agatha Grand Cross (San Marino, 1994)
- Grand Cross of Freedom (Portugal, 1995)
- Memorial Medal 'Gate of Freedom' to commemorate the tenth anniversary of Jewish emigration from the former USSR (Israel Bonds Corporation, New York, 1998)
- Grand Cross, special class of the Order of Merit (Germany, November 1999)
- Order of the White Lion with a ribbon (Czech Republic, 1999)
- Induction into the International Academy of Achievement (2000)

International honours included:

- 1987 Indira Gandhi Award (conferred on 19 November 1988, India)
- Golden Dove of Peace for contribution to peace and disarmament (the pacifist organization, Italian Center of Documentation on Disarmament and the National League of Cooperatives, Rome, November 1989)
- Albert Einstein Award for contribution to peace and mutual understanding among peoples (Washington, DC, June 1990)
- Historic Leader Award by the US influential religious organization, Appeal of Conscience Foundation (Washington, DC, June 1990)
- 1991 Martin Luther King International Peace Award 'For a Non-Violent World' for contribution to world peace and human rights (Washington, DC, June 1990)
- Fiuggi International Award (Fiuggi Foundation of Italy), as 'a personality whose political and public activity sets an outstanding example of work to promote human rights' (Italy, 1990)
- Albert Schweitzer Award, Hugh O'Brian Youth Foundation (USA, 1992)
- Benjamin M. Cardoso Award 'For Democracy' (Yeshiva University of New York, USA, 1992)
- Sir Winston Churchill Award to recognize contribution to peace in the Middle East (UK, 1993)
- La Pléiade Award (Piacenza, Italy, 1993)
- International Journalist and Literary Award (Modena, Italy, 1993)
- Hero of the Year Award by the Association of Small and Medium Businesses of Bologna (Bologna, Italy, 1993)
- Golden Pegasus International Award (Toscana, Italy, 1994)
- University of Genoa Award (Italy, 1995)
- King David Award (USA, 1997)
- Enron Award by the Baker Institute for outstanding service to society (Houston, USA, 1997)
- Weha Award by *Politika* weekly (Poland, 1997)

- Budapest Club Award (Frankfurt, Germany, 1997)
- Komet Award (Germany, 1998)
- International Women's Zionist Organization (Miami, USA, 1998)
- National Liberty Award for effort against oppression (Memphis, USA, 1998)
- Terracina City Award (Institute of Russian Language and Culture, Terracina, Italy, 1999)
- Reconciliation National Award (Friends for Reconciliation, Italy, 1999)
- Giorgio La Pira Award for Culture and Peace (Italy, 1999)
- Ritualis Award (Italy, 1999)
- Marsala Association for Cultural Studies 'Piano Friends' Award (Marsala, Italy, 1999)
- Aleksandr Men' Award (2000)
- St Valentine's Award (Italy, 2001).[2]

One wonders just how many awards there are out there! Anyway the message was clear. He is one of the most decorated people in history. In 2005, Gorbachev added to his own reputation when the World Political Forum (of which he was President) held an assembly of the great and good around the theme of '1985–2005: Twenty Years that Changed the World' in Turin.

In Search of Understanding

Snakes ...

At the heart of the difficulties in appraising Gorbachev and his legacy lie a number of unavoidable ambiguities. These are of different orders but overlap to create a kaleidoscope of shifting paradoxes and uncertainties. For instance, the character and personality of Gorbachev still remain something of a mystery. Despite being such a high-profile, high-visibility figure, he was an intensely private man. His personality can be classified according to a number of dichotomies:

Great Mind	Weak Character
Collegial/Consensual	Indecisive
Emotional	Cold
Humanitarian	Nakedly Self-Interested
Democrat	Apparatchik

Moreover, there are still some mysteries, still some lacunae in our knowledge of his past, his upbringing, his rise to prominence, his motives, his actions, his decisions. We feel we should know the answers to some or all of these questions, yet we don't.

Another difficulty lies in the variety and diversity of appraisals. Some have sought to crown him and fête him. Some have sought to knock down and destroy him. Some have sought to blame him. Some have used him to justify their own views. Some have sought to dismiss him. Some have tried carefully to explain him. A whole host of different constituencies have essentially used Gorbachev for their own ends, be they personal, political, institutional or ideological. A variety of Gorbachevs have been peddled to us: a 'messianic' Gorbachev In the West. 'Academic' Gorbachevs, divided by ideology, methodology and Cold War outlook. 'Remembered' Gorbachevs. Furthermore, these views have evolved and changed over time, giving us a constantly shifting quicksand on which to try and build our appraisals.

But the problems don't just end there. His whole project was riddled with enigmas. His was the paradoxical project *par excellence*: a reformer who wanted to initiate change, and also prevent change. At times it seemed like someone setting out on a long journey without any idea where he was going. It also zig-zagged and contained some bewildering U-turns at times. A further problem lies in trying to understand his achievements: did he succeed or fail?

Finally, we also have to deal with the intentional and highly conscious interventions of Gorbachev himself, who has sought to fashion his own particular historical image. Thus we not only have to confront the elusiveness of the 'real' Gorbachev, but we also have to peer through the consciously constructed and ever-changing historical reputation Gorbachev has promoted of himself (and, by extension, of *perestroika*) in the public sphere. And what is the relationship between these two things? Is it too simplistic to posit a dichotomy between the public and the private Gorbachev? How do we disentangle the 'political' project to defend his life, work and reputation from the essence of the individual?

Like snakes in the board game, all these problems keep bringing us back to the starting-point: how can we evaluate Gorbachev fully, fairly and meaningfully?

... and ladders

To ascend we need a ladder. But what can we use? Our limited perspectives offer us a problematic to be overcome. How can we judge or evaluate Gorbachev? How on earth do we escape the contingencies of geography, culture, nationality, time and ideology? The preceding chapters have all demonstrated the complexities involved. So, in order to evaluate Gorbachev, this final chapter will do two things. First, it will highlight some key elements which might help to explain, in part, some of the enigmatic aspects of Gorbachev. Second, this conclusion will address two central questions which are pertinent when we come to draw up some kind of balance-sheet or overall appraisal of his life and work: Was Gorbachev the 'Man of the Twentieth Century'? In this we will try to eschew an evaluation of Gorbachev's actions and impact along a good/bad or success/failure type spectrum, and instead try and examine Gorbachev in terms of an assessment of his particular impact, his influence, his role as an agent of change in the pantheon of influential leaders in the twentieth century. This will essentially be a comparative exercise, assessing Gorbachev relative to other similar figures. The second question is derived from a comment by Eric Hobsbawm: is Humanity in his debt?[3] If we totted up the balance-sheet of Gorbachev's time in power, what would we find? Can we rise above our ideological, personal and political perspectives for a moment and think of how he may be appraised by subsequent generations in terms of his contribution to the ebb and flow of the tides of human history?

In one sense, these are, of course, unanswerable questions, or at least deeply subjective ones, unless one is able to occupy a God's-eye view of history. But in posing these questions, the issues that emerge may allow us to find a way through the layers of ambiguity and contingency outlined above. There are, of course, other ways. But this will do for us. In doing this it also permits some broader contextual reflections, and brings in some comparative perspectives. So, let's begin. What things can we say that might help us to understand the enigma of Gorbachev?

Gorbachev: sacred dilemmas, crises of faith

Studying the life, work, speeches, words and deeds of Gorbachev one is struck by a number of things which might help us to explain some (but by no means all) of the paradoxes and problems we have encountered along the way. The first aspect is that of faith. In essence, one of the keys to understanding Gorbachev is to recognize that Gorbachev's public life was underpinned by a series of deeply held beliefs. Gorbachev was a *believer*, or *a man of faith*. Not strictly in the sense of a religious believer, but to the extent that he formed very strong personal attachments to particular ideas and concepts which stayed with him throughout his career. He had very deeply held beliefs which profoundly influenced his actions and his projected career path. In certain respects, the way he held his beliefs was similar in its intensity and devotion to the faith and belief we find among those who are spiritually or religiously inclined.

Now this is not really a shocking or surprising revelation. Indeed, given the nature of the Soviet system – which had many features in common with theocratic type systems, with its official belief-systems, canonical texts and suspicion of all other beliefs as potential heresies to be slain and heretics to be eliminated – there was always a central role for ideas and beliefs about the world. What is significant is the nature of Gorbachev's faith. He was a believer, but he was not an *orthodox Marxist-Leninist believer*. He was not content to rigidly and dogmatically defend the Soviet articles of faith. But he was devoted to certain key elements of the Soviet system: socialism, the Party, the Union, Lenin were all central symbols in Gorbachev's political identity. All these were things he believed in strongly. At the same time, his background and upbringing instilled in him a set of values and preferences. His personal philosophy or world-view seems to have comprised an amalgam of humanism, social justice, concerns for peace and the environment. These were central elements in the way he perceived the world, and were values which helped to form his ideas and ideals about politics, economics and the international sphere.

Now why is this aspect of Gorbachev significant in understanding his life, work, rise and fall? In his public political life and rise through the system he became deeply committed to the four things to which he devoted his life and energies: the Party, the Soviet Union, Lenin and socialism. You only have to examine the type of language that Gorbachev used to describe them to realize how committed he was to them. He often talked of how these things were 'sacred' to him: something to be venerated, respected, not something to be criticized, pulled down or attacked. This religious imagery gives us some clues as to the close identification Gorbachev had to these Soviet icons. The problem which confronted Gorbachev after 1985 was that his pursuit of changes and improvements to the Soviet system caused him to move in directions which brought him into conflict with these sacred icons. He was forced to choose. But he found it incredibly difficult to renounce his beliefs. Having devoted so much of his life to the party, the Union, to Lenin and to socialism, to abandon them was akin to an act of heresy, one that would have rendered much of his earlier life almost meaningless, a sacrifice in vain.

On this reading, Gorbachev's ambivalence over change, the ambiguities of his reform programme were rooted not so much in the narrow self-interest of a member of an entrenched ruling elite, but were grounded in the personal and philosophical dilemmas raised by his attempts to renew and reform the system he had grown up in. This helps to explain Gorbachev's constant balancing acts, his attempts to synthesize the old and the new, his seeming unwillingness to let go of the past, even when circumstances had rendered this standpoint anachronistic. We see this in his constant attempts to reconcile his latest reform initiatives with his belief in socialism, leading to the permanent redefining of socialism. The constant reiteration that they were still heading towards socialism was as much a process of self-persuasion as an attempt to attack his critics who postulated that he did not know what he was doing. We see this in his unwillingness to cast the party aside, even after the coup, he could not bring himself to abandon the party altogether. We see this in his efforts to stem the separatist tide in 1990 and 1991, in the Novo-Ogarevo agreement, in the planned re-creation of a new Union in August 1991. We see this in his constant scouring of Lenin's writings to find a new approach that would not only legitimate Gorbachev's actions in the eyes of the guardians of orthodoxy, but would also maintain Lenin's relevance in the new situation. Gorbachev searched long and hard always to find a 'usable' Lenin. *Perestroika* was Gorbachev's moment to put his principles into action. Gradually, inexorably, however, the radical momentum that *perestroika* gathered after 1988 – both home and abroad – forced Gorbachev into a situation that he was deeply uncomfortable with, forcing him to confront the pillars of his public life. The need to change the system, to improve it, make it viable, efficient, stronger, fairer created a profound crisis of faith. Gorbachev's struggles were not just with opponents, and rivals and intractable problems, and the vagaries of natural disasters, accidents and deteriorating economic conditions. Gorbachev's struggle was also an internal one. Gorbachev found it difficult to let go completely of the 'old' ways of doing things, did not want to abandon totally the sacred parts of his past. But the end result was that Gorbachev's time in power saw him undergo something of a crisis of faith, which was only resolved when the Soviet system was dismantled and the Soviet state collapsed.

Gorbachev: a long political journey

As highlighted earlier, two things are notable about Gorbachev. One, Gorbachev had a profound sense of inner certainty about himself, about his project, about his ability to persuade others of the correctness of his position. Second, Gorbachev also had a strong sense of destiny about his life: that history had allotted a particular role for him, not just in the USSR, but also globally. One of the things that enabled Gorbachev to rise through the system was this strong sense of self-belief. This sense of certainty carried him from his earliest times into the portals of power. And this self-belief continues to sustain him. Having lost power in 1991, Gorbachev has spent the subsequent period engaged in a sophisticated defence of his legacy and also attempting to carve out a new global role for himself. In this way, it is important to see beyond *perestroika* in an attempt to understand Gorbachev. This is not to downplay the significance of the six years between March 1985 and December 1991. But a holistic understanding of Gorbachev requires us to look pre-1985 and post-1991, and so view him in the *longue durée*. It may be helpful in this regard to use the journey or odyssey metaphor for understanding Gorbachev.

His life and work make much more sense if we examine him from 1950 to the present. As we look back we can that Gorbachev's journey was a multi-faceted one. Politically he went from being a provincial Stavropol Komsomol official to global statesman at the centre of momentous events. Geographically he went from Stavropol to Moscow to Stavropol, back to Moscow and then to Warsaw, Beijing, London, Washington and beyond. Ideologically he went from Soviet Marxism-Leninism to become a social democrat and an advocate of environmentalism, peace and democracy. Philosophically he went from Marxism-Leninism to humanism. Personally he went from rural child to urban intellectual adult. He has journeyed from obscurity to prominence. From this perspective, the *perestroika* period stands as the era of Gorbachev's global prominence. Subsequently, he has spent the time since 1991 trying to ensure his continued significance in global affairs, defending his legacy and attempting to influence the international sphere through his Foundation and through the Green Cross International.

What is interesting about this journey is the important role played by others. This was not a solo enterprise, but one with many fellow-travellers. Obviously, the significance of Raisa is paramount in this regard. Gorbachev leaned very heavily on his wife. But Gorbachev was also someone who absorbed ideas and information. He enjoyed the cut and thrust of debating with others. He liked to travel and see how things were done differently elsewhere. He learned by discussing with others who were like-minded – Mlynar, Yakovlev, Shakhnazarov, Chernyaev, Felipe Gonzalez – and also those from the other side of the political spectrum – Reagan, Thatcher, and so on. What was remarkable about Gorbachev, something which distinguished him from many of his contemporaries at the head of the CPSU was his willingness to incorporate new ideas, to learn from others, to take on board examples from other countries, to think flexibly and unconventionally.

He was, by instinct, a learner and a reflector. In negative terms he learned of the problems caused by the non-accountable exercise of power, of secrecy and censorship, of repression and coercion, of economic progress at the expense of the natural environment and of human spirituality. More positively, he came to recognize the significance of spirituality, morality, humanism, dialogue and interdependence if humanity was to survive the threats of nuclear conflict and environmental catastrophe.

By viewing Gorbachev in terms of the multi-faceted journey he has undergone since his early years in Stavropol, it helps to place his *perestroika* years in the wider context of his life as a whole, and also helps us to make sense of some of the choices and decisions of these years and after. In particular, Gorbachev's espousal of a universal humanism, his advocacy of morality in the international sphere, his ideological preference for social democracy, his concern for the environment can all be traced back to elements in his past: his rural upbringing, the lessons he learned while working in the Soviet system, the influence of others, his reflections on *perestroika*. During his time in power he wanted to make the world a better, safer, more just, equitable place. Since 1991 he has continued to work for these ends.

Gorbachev: man of the twentieth century?

How is Gorbachev perceived in popular memory? Perhaps the most celebrated 'list' of the people who did most to shape, for good or ill, the twentieth century was published by *Time* in 1999. This was broken down into five different categories – Leaders and Revolutionaries; Artists and Entertainers; Builders and Titans; Scientists and Thinkers; Heroes and Icons. The *Time* panel voted Albert Einstein the most important individual. Gorbachev took his place in the 20 people under the 'Leaders and Revolutionaries'. These included:

> David Ben-Gurion; Ho Chi Minh; Winston Churchill; Mohandas Gandhi; Adolf Hitler; Martin Luther King; Ayatollah Ruhollah Khomeini; V. I. Lenin; Nelson Mandela; Pope John Paul II; Ronald Reagan; Eleanor Roosevelt; Franklin Delano Roosevelt; Teddy Roosevelt; Margaret Thatcher; Unknown Rebel or Tank Man; Margaret Sanger; Lech Walesa; Mao Zedong.

The problems with any list are, of course, very well-known. However, does Gorbachev belong in this exalted list? And where might he lie in this top 20? Clearly, the impact that Gorbachev had – both direct and indirect, conscious and subconscious, deliberate and inadvertent – in terms of shaping the twentieth and twenty-first centuries was enormous. He was a prime figure in the collapse of communism in Eastern Europe and the USSR. He was a central player in the drama of the end of the Cold War, and the dramatic arms cuts that accompanied it. He kick-started the process that led to the fall of the Berlin Wall. He was instrumental in the reunification of Germany. His ideas caused the collapse of one of the most extensively disseminated belief systems – Marxism-Leninism – ever seen in global history. Further down the line, Gorbachev's impact has led to a reconfiguration of the European Union, and opened up a new era of economic rivalry in the world between the USA, China, India and Russia, now exerting greater and greater economic leverage through its control of energy supplies. The economic chaos caused by the collapse of the economy opened up opportunities for dramatic enrichment by a few rich oligarchs and extensive criminal activity through organized gangs. The dissolution of the Iron Curtain has allowed greater economic migration, but the easing of restrictions on travel has accelerated sex tourism, trafficking of vulnerable females and opened the former Soviet bloc to all the cultural detritus spawned by the Western liberal democracies. In longer historical perspective Gorbachev was a key figure in destroying the cultural, political, social and ideological bases of the world which was born in 1917, the world based on the contest of socialism v. capitalism, command v. free market economies, private v. public ownership.

But his impact cannot just be measured in the intangibles of global politics. The changes which emanated from Gorbachev profoundly affected, for good and ill, millions of citizens in a variety of different states. His public walkabouts changed Western public opinion about Soviet leaders and the USSR. As a result of his reforms the public spaces of Soviet cities were dramatically changed. Street names were changed, statues were pulled down, cities were renamed. People were given greater political choice. History was rewritten. Prior censorship disappeared. Freedom of movement and belief was restored. Living standards collapsed dramatically. Fear of nuclear annihilation decreased dramatically. The fallout from the collapse of the USSR led to the changing of geographical boundaries, a revival of minority languages, a resurgence of religious activism and belief, ethnic and religious conflict.

As one of the 20 'Leaders and Revolutionaries', Gorbachev's impact was truly global, historic and affected both the Grand Narrative of twentieth-century history but also the micro-narratives of individual citizens and people in Beijing and Moscow, London and Chisinau, Reykjavik and Havana, Cape Town and Cairo. So if we remove the tricky criterion of the moral judgement – was his rule one of good or ill – then it is clear that Gorbachev deserves his place in the above pantheon. But where in the list should he fall?

Clearly his impact far outstrips most of those in the above list, as their impact can primarily be measured in national or regional terms, rather than the truly global impact of Gorbachev, although this is also partly explicable in terms of the media context of Gorbachev's time in power. In fact, a clear case can be made that Gorbachev was the leader/revolutionary who did most to shape the socio-political world in which we live. However, I think an equally compelling case can be made for Lenin. His exertions in bringing about the downfall of the Tsarist Empire created the ideological divide which so defined the twentieth century, and his blueprint for revolution materially affected the course of history on every continent. A case for Gandhi can also be made also as the antithesis of Lenin: a revolutionary who eschewed violence and yet also was instrumental in bringing about the downfall of an established Empire, and catalysing forces to overthrow colonial rule across the globe. Finally, the impact of the religious revivalism of the Ayatollah Khomeini can also be measured globally. The ripples from the Iranian revolution of 1979 continue to spread outwards, encompassing more and more societies, creating in the views of some a new 'clash of civilizations' between Islam and the West. If we compare Gorbachev with these other figures, some interesting issues arise. Most notably, Gorbachev was at his most devastatingly successful as a destructive force, albeit carried out on the whole peacefully. His greatest impact was in what he removed, rather than what he built. Moreover the denouement to his rule, his long years in the political wilderness, the catastrophic failure of his reforms to achieve the goals he wanted, give his time in power in retrospect an undoubtedly tragic feel, even if tempered with an heroic tinge too. All of the other leaders, to a greater or lesser extent, not only took part in pulling something down which they perceived to be corrupt or anachronistic or repressive, but also constructed something, or left a legacy which others copied or sought to emulate. Gandhi's pattern of non-violent resistance, Lenin's model of the vanguard party of revolution and the amoral revolutionary all inspired, for good or ill, others as means to pursue their visions. New states and social systems were constructed out of the ruins of what was pulled down. Moreover, many of the 'achievements' of Gorbachev were often inadvertently or indirectly the result of his actions, rather than something intentionally willed by Gorbachev. Gorbachev, on this view, can be classified as one of the political leaders/revolutionaries who did most to shape the twentieth century, but perhaps not quite in the top echelon. But perhaps Gorbachev, in spite of his many personal flaws and weaknesses, his undoubted policy failures and political compromises, his inability to build anything sustainable, deserves a place as one of the key figures of the twentieth century in any field, because he did more than any other individual to remove the threat of global nuclear war from humanity. He obviously did not do it alone, but he worked unfailingly for peace, and espoused a universal humanistic mission to reframe the international sphere. In doing so, he went far beyond the 'normal' concerns of a national leader, and changed history dramatically.

Gorbachev: how much do we owe him?

This leads us nicely on to the point made by Eric Hobsbawm: is humanity in his debt? Well, for his initiatives to create peace, his reductions in the nuclear and conventional arms threats, his willingness to allow things to happen (the rejection of communism, the reunification of Germany), which were previously unthinkable, it is clear that many are in his debt. The reduction in fear occasioned by his peace initiatives brought incalculable benefits to humankind.

The overall balance-sheet of Gorbachev's time in power must encompass:

- the ending of communist rule in Eastern Europe and a willingness to allow the states of Eastern Europe to determine their own political status;
- the removal of the nuclear threat;

- the withdrawal of troops from Afghanistan;
- the reduction in conventional troops in Europe;
- the reunification of Germany;
- the refusal to use force and coercion to keep the Soviet Union together;
- the recognition of universal human values and morality as the basis for international diplomacy;
- the symbolic significance of a leader willing to renounce power, free prisoners, remove censorship, restore religious belief and practice.

Yet, it is obvious that not all humanity would accept this judgement, not least those people in Russia and elsewhere in the former Soviet bloc who have seen their living standards plummet, and who destroyed the pre-eminent global status of their country. Although they might recognize what he did, they are unlikely to acknowledge his greatness or his historic significance. Perhaps time will alter their judgement.

Gorbachev: a twentieth-century man?

Finally, it is perhaps worth framing the question slightly differently. Can Gorbachev be seen as someone whose life, with its twists, turns and experiences, successes and failures, could be said to be a kind of embodiment of the twentieth century? As a representative man of the twentieth century? As each chapter has shown Gorbachev is not just a revealing, interesting and paradoxical character. He also acts as something of a mirror or a signifier, telling us about ourselves. And perhaps in this sense it is possible to view Gorbachev as a signifier of the twentieth century. Perhaps in some way he enables us to understand the last century better, embodying its twists and turns, its triumphs and disasters.

Without wishing to stretch the analogy too far, there is a sense in which Gorbachev's life tells us much about the last century, a rather dark and unhappy period in human history taken in the *longue durée*. In particular, if we adopt Hobsbawm's view (which seems to me to be a persuasive one) of a Short Twentieth Century (1914–91), then Gorbachev does stand as someone whose life falls into the rhythms of the century. Hobsbawm sees the period 1914–91 as falling into three periods. The Age of Catastrophe of 1914–47, marked by war, slump, dictatorship and more war. The Golden Age (1947–73) characterized by modernization, economic advance, increasing prosperity and the like. Finally there were the crisis decades of 1973–91, whereby the Golden Age and its institutions and practices began to break down, and humanity began to see the breakdown of the Modern World, the world that dawned in 1789. A new era was being ushered in, though what that might look like was too early to say.

Gorbachev fits quite neatly into this pattern. Born in 1931, his early years were spent under the pernicious influence of both the height of the Stalinist repressions (in which members of his own family were caught up), Soviet collectivization (an example *par excellence* of one of the abiding themes of twentieth-century history: the massive extension of state power exercised over society in order to remake it in its own image) and also the Nazi occupation. His grandmother had to conceal her religious belief in the face of the worlds most zealous secular ideology, the refined essence of the hyper-rationalism of the Enlightenment world-view. He grew up during the Second World War, and worked on the land to support the Soviet war effort. He experienced the economic hardships and political arbitrariness of the interwar years, and the fear of foreign occupation so common to so many across Europe and beyond in these decades.

Yet Gorbachev's story takes a turn for the better after the Second World War. He benefits from the educational opportunities on offer to make his way to Moscow. Like so many others in the industrialized world after 1948, he experienced economic and personal advancement, increasing prosperity and the social, cultural and psychological transformation that comes with being an educated, urban man. He devoted himself to his party and his family, and slowly at first, more rapidly later, he began to make his way up the hierarchy. The certainties upon which the life of Gorbachev, the Communist Party regional apparatchik, were based were starting to unravel, though, by the mid-1970s, as people within the system became increasingly aware of its deepening economic and socio-political problems.

His ascent to the top, however, coincided with the growing global crisis which hit the world after the OPEC episode in 1973. In a world increasingly dominated by global economic uncertainties and in which traditional patterns of authority were starting to be undermined by the growing politics of identity, and by the fragmenting impact of the rise of the consumer, Gorbachev was brought to power, and sought to adapt his country and his leadership as a new world was being made and an old world unmade. Gorbachev himself reflected the transitional nature of the world at this point. On the one hand, he clearly had a foot in the old world. Reared on the dogmatic certainties of Soviet Marxism-Leninism, schooled in the Soviet command economic system and leading via the CPSU's class-based vision of the world, Gorbachev was a modernist figure of impeccable credentials. Yet, at the same time, he had begun to embrace the contingency of New Thinking, and was abandoning some of the old stereotypes and platitudes. The gathering clouds on the Soviet economic horizon compelled a radical rethink of the way the Soviet economy was performing, and the ever-increasing technological gap with the West added a sense of urgency by calling into question the USSR's long-term security situation vis-à-vis the USA. Gorbachev also embodies something about the Soviet system too. One of the constant features of the Soviet system after 1956 was the tension between its in-built resistance to change and its desire to reform itself. Gorbachev and his project, *perestroika*, perfectly replicated this essential tension.

Gorbachev, as it turned out, came to embody the paradoxes of this era extremely well, and was in the end undone by the rise of ethnic nationalism and economic collapse. He did not quite grasp the intricacies and dangers of the ethnic challenge until it was too late, and proved incapable of building a sustainable economic system. Although he embraced many of the new ideas and forces emerging in the world, he was still too tied to the old ways of thinking to survive very long in the new waters that began to lap around his feet. In this sense his fate was almost preordained: he was the archetypal twentieth-century figure who shuffled off the stage as the Short Twentieth Century also came to an end. Gorbachev had played a central and indispensable role by dismantling and delegitimizing one of the foundational components of the twentieth-century world: the Soviet communist system. Gorbachev's life mirrored, in some indefinable sense, the twentieth century. The twenty-first century was one for others to make.

We will leave the last words on his legacy to Gorbachev himself:

> It is rightly said that every age gives birth to its own heroes. Time, and not the snap judgements of contemporaries, delivers the verdict on an individual's service to history. There is, after all, an immense distance between the actions of great people and their consequences ... Although we learned important things from the 20th century, we have not found the whole truth. In many instances, the wisdom of the future must be founded on the wisdom of the past.[4]

Although verdicts on Gorbachev's 'service to History' will rise and fall as time passes, there is no doubt that in any history of the twentieth century he will remain a central character, whether that be as victim, villain or hero.

Notes

Introduction

1 The views of Gorbachev in the Soviet period only started to become significantly negative from the mid-end of 1990 onwards. Up until this point, Gorbachev was viewed positively by the people on the whole.

2 There have been numerous works on *perestroika* which are worth looking at. The following are some of the key ones, from a variety of perspectives: R. Sakwa, *Gorbachev and His Reforms 1985–90* (London: Routledge, 1990); M. Galeotti, *Gorbachev and his Revolution* (London: Macmillan, 1997); G. Hosking, *A History of the Soviet Union* (London: Fontana, 1994); S. White, *After Gorbachev* (Cambridge: Cambridge University Press, 1992); M. Goldman, *What Went Wrong with Perestroika* (New York: Norton, 1992); J. Keep, *Last of the Empires* (Oxford: Oxford University Press, 1996); Z. Brzezinski, *The Grand Failure* (London: Charles Scribner's Sons, 1990); Rachel Walker, *Six Years That Shook the World* (Manchester: Manchester University Press, 1993) G.W. Breslauer, *Can Gorbachev's Reforms Succeed?* (Berkeley, CA: University of California Press, 1990); A. Dallin and G. Lapidus (eds), *The Soviet System: From Crisis to Collapse*, rev. edn (Boulder; CO: Westview Press, 1995); J. Hough, *Russia and the West: Gorbachev and the Politics of Reform* (New York: Simon & Schuster, 1990); J. Hallenberg, *The Demise of the Soviet Union: Analysing the Collapse of a State* (Burlington, VT: Ashgate, 2002); S. Kotkin, *Armageddon Averted: The Soviet Collapse, 1970–2000* (New York: Oxford University Press, 2001); Mark Beissinger, *Nationalist Mobilization and the Collapse of the Soviet State* (Cambridge: Cambridge University Press, 2002); Ronald Grigor Suny, *The Revenge of the Past: Nationalism, Revolution and the Collapse of the Soviet Union* (Stanford, CA: Stanford University Press, 1993); Jerry Hough, *Democratization and Revolution in the USSR* (Washington, DC: Brookings Institution, 1997); David Satter, *The Age of Delirium: The Decline and Fall of the Soviet Union* (New York: Knopf, 1996); Michael Cox (ed.), *Rethinking the Soviet Collapse: Sovietology, the Death of Communism and the New Russia* (New York: Pinter, 1998); Joseph L. Wieczynski, *The Gorbachev Reader* (Salt Lake City: Charles Schlacks, Jr, 1993); Gordon M. Hahn, *Russia's Revolution from Above, 1985–2000: Reform, Transition, and Revolution in the Fall of the Soviet Communist Regime* (New Brunswick, NJ: Transaction, 2002); S. White, *Communism and Its Collapse* (New York: Routledge, 2001); G. Gill, *The Collapse of a Single-Party System: The Disintegration of the Communist Party of the Soviet Union* (New York: Cambridge University Press, 1995); Robert T. Huber and Donald R. Kelley (eds), *Perestroika-Era Politics: The New Soviet Legislature and Gorbachev's Political Reforms* (Armonk, NY: M.E. Sharpe, 1991); Robert Strayer, *Why Did the Soviet Union Collapse? Understanding Historical Change* (Armonk, NY: M.E. Sharpe, 1998); Anne de Tinguy (ed.), *The Fall of the Soviet Empire* (Boulder, CO: Westview Press, 1997); Henry Hale, *The Strange Death of the Soviet Union* (Cambridge, MA: Harvard University Press, 1999); A. Aslund, *Gorbachev's Struggle for Economic Reform* (Ithaca, NY: Pinter, 1991).

3 The main works on Gorbachev are: A. Brown, *The Gorbachev Factor* (Oxford, Oxford University Press, 1996); C. Schmidt-Hauer, *Gorbachev: The Path to Power* (Topsfield, MA: Salem

House, 1986); M. McCauley, *Gorbachev* (London: Longman, 1998); G. Sheehy, *Gorbachev: A One-Man Revolution* (New York: HarperCollins, 1990); C. Attar, *Gorbachev: The Man and His Ideas* (Delhi: Modern Pubs Dist., 1987); R.F. Miller *et al.* (eds), *Gorbachev at the Helm: A New Era in Soviet Politics?* (London: Croom Helm, 1987). Zh. Medvedev, *Gorbachev* (Oxford: Basil Blackwell, 1986); I. Zemtsov, *Gorbachev: Between Past and Present* (Fairfax, VA: Herobooks, 1987); F. Feher and A. Arato, *Gorbachev: The Debate* (Cambridge: Polity, 1989); T. Butson, *Gorbachev: A Biography* (New York: Stein & Day, 1986); D. Doder and L. Branson, *Gorbachev: Heretic in the Kremlin* (New York: Penguin, 1991); D. Morrison *et al.* (eds), *Mikhail S. Gorbachev: An Intimate Biography* (New York: Time, 1988); S. Talbott (ed.). *M.S. Gorbachev: An Intimate Biography* (New York: Signet Books, 1988); R.F. Kaiser, *Why Gorbachev Happened: His Triumphs, His Failures and His Fall* (New York: Touchstone, 1992); G. Ruge, *Gorbachev: A Biography* (London: Chatto & Windus, 1991); D. Murarka, *Gorbachev: The Limits of Power* (London: Hutchinson, 1988); M. Tatu, *Mikhail Gorbachev: The Origins of Perestroika* (New York. Columbia University Press, 1991); J. Miller, *Mikhail Gorbachev and the End of Soviet Power* (New York: St Martin's Press, 1993); F. Thom, *The Gorbachev Phenomenon* (London: Pinter, 1989); A. D'Agostino, *Gorbachev's Revolution* (New York: New York University Press, 1998); G. Breslauer, *Gorbachev and Yeltsin As Leaders* (Cambridge: Cambridge University Press, 2002).

4 The best things to read on Soviet political reform are: Archie Brown, 'Political Change in the Soviet Union', *World Policy Journal*, 16, 3, 1989, pp. 469–501; S. White, 'Democratization in the USSR', *Soviet Studies*, 42, 1, January 1990, pp. 3–20; John Gooding, 'Gorbachev and Democracy', *Soviet Studies*, 42, 2, April 1990, pp. 195–231.

5 Nina Andreeva, *Sovetskaya Rossiya*, 13 March 1988.

6 For details on these and other nationality/ethnic problems, see Ronald Suny, 'State, Civil Society and Ethnic Cultural Consolidation', in Alexander Dallin and Gail Lapidus (eds), *The Soviet System in Crisis* (Boulder, CO: Westview Press, 1991), pp. 414–29; Gail Lapidus, 'Gorbachev's Nationalities Problem', *Foreign Affairs*, Autumn 1989, pp. 92–108.

7 NPT hereafter.

8 See Z. Khalilzad, 'Moscow's Afghan War', *Problems of Communism*, January–February 1986.

9 For a good Soviet perspective, see G. Shakhnazarov, 'East–West: The Problem of De-Ideologising Relations', *Kommunist*, 3, 1989.

10 Ibid.

11 H. Adomeit, 'Gorbachev and German Unification: Revision of Thinking, Realignment of Power', *Problems of Communism*, July–August 1990.

1 Who was Mikhail Gorbachev and where did he come from?

1 *Pravda*, 12 March 1985.

2 *Pravda*, 22 November 1985.

3 *Izvestiya TsK KPSS*, 1, 1989, p. 10.

4 *Izvestiya TsK KPSS*, 5, 1989, p. 57.

5 Ibid., p. 8.

6 *Pravda*, 30 November 1990.

7 See, for example, C. Schmidt-Hauer, *Gorbachev: The Path to Power* (Topsfield, MA: Salem House, 1986); C. Attar, *Gorbachev: The Man and His Ideas* (Delhi: Modern Pubs Dist., 1987); R.F. Miller *et al.* (eds), *Gorbachev at the Helm: A New Era in Soviet Politics?* (London: Croom Helm, 1987). Zh. Medvedev, *Gorbachev* (Oxford: Basil Blackwell, 1986); I. Zemtsov, *Gorbachev: Between Past and Present* (Fairfax, VA: Herobooks, 1987); T. Butson, *Gorbachev: A Biography* (New York: Stein & Day, 1986); V. Solovyov and E. Klepikova, *Inside the Kremlin* (London: Allen & Unwin, 1987).

8 G. Sheehy, *Gorbachev: A One-Man Revolution* (New York: HarperCollins, 1990); F. Feher and A. Arato, *Gorbachev: The Debate* (New York: Humanities Press, 1989), T. Butson, *Gorbachev: A Biography* (New York: Stein & Day, 1986); D. Doder and L. Branson, *Gorbachev: Heretic in the Kremlin* (New York: Penguin 1991); D. Morrison *et al.* (eds), *Mikhail S. Gorbachev: An Intimate Biography* (New York: Time, 1988); S. Talbott (ed.). *M.S. Gorbachev: An Intimate Biography* (New York: Signet Books, 1988); G. Ruge, *Gorbachev: A Biography* (London: Chatto & Windus, 1991); D. Murarka, *Gorbachev: The Limits of Power* (London: Hutchinson, 1988); M. Tatu, *Mikhail Gorbachev: The Origins of Perestroika* (New York: Columbia University Press, 1991); F. Thom, *The Gorbachev Phenomenon* (London: Pinter, 1989); I. Zemtsov and J. Farrar, *Gorbachev: The Man and the System* (New Brunswick, NJ: Transaction Publishers, 1989).

9 A. Brown, *The Gorbachev Factor* (Oxford: Oxford University Press, 1996); M. McCauley, *Gorbachev* (London: Longman, 1998); R.F. Kaiser, *Why Gorbachev Happened: His Triumphs, His Failures and His Fall* (New York: Touchstone, 1992); J. Miller, *Mikhail Gorbachev and the End of Soviet Power* (New York: St Martin's Press, 1993); A. D'Agostino, *Gorbachev's Revolution* (New York: New York University Press, 1998); G. Breslauer, *Gorbachev and Yeltsin As Leaders* (Cambridge: Cambridge University Press, 2002).

10 See Chapter 5 for details on these memoirs.

11 Doder and Branson, op. cit., pp. 1–27.

12 Solovyov and Klepikova, op. cit., pp. 159–61. Solovyov and Klepikova are a husband and wife team who were part of the Soviet literary establishment in the late 1970s before emigrating to the USA.

13 Ibid. For a contrasting account see, for example, Doder and Branson, op. cit, Chapter 1.

14 See, for example, Schmidt-Hauer, op. cit. (1986); Doder and Branson, op. cit. (1990); Zh. Medvedev, op. cit. (1986); Sheehy, op. cit. (1990); Solovyov and Klepikova, op. cit. (1987); Butson, op. cit. (1986); Morrison, op. cit. (1988).

15 Solovyov and Klepikova, op. cit., pp. 161–8.

16 For example, Morrison (1988) argues this point.

17 Doder and Branson, op. cit., pp. 11–18.

18 See H. Smith, *The New Russians* (New York: Random House, 1990), p. 49.

19 The main sources for reminiscences of his university days are: Zdenek Mlynar, in *L'Unita* 9, April 1985; Lev Yudovich in *Soviet Analyst*, 19 December 1984; and F. Neznanskii, *An Emigre Reports: Fridrikh Neznansky on Mikhail Gorbachev, 1950–1958* (Falls Church, VA: Delphic Associates, 1985). They are also cited in Morrison, op. cit. (1988) and Solovyov and Klepikova, op. cit. (1987). Brown notes that Yudovich left MSU before Gorbachev arrived, which casts doubt on the validity of his testimony somewhat. Brown, op. cit., p. 326, n.39.

20 Sheehy, op. cit., p. 89.

21 This point is made by both Zh. Medvedev, op. cit. (1986) and Mlynar, op. cit. (1985).

22 Doder and Branson, op. cit. (1990); Schmidt-Hauer, op. cit. (1986).

23 Interview with Mikhail Gorbachev, *Izvestiya TsK KPSS* 5, 1989.

24 Medvedev, op. cit. (1986), Chapter 3.

25 See, for example, Butson, op. cit. (1986); Sheehy, op. cit. (1990); Sol Sanders, *Living off the West: Gorbachev's Secret Agenda and Why it Will Fail* (Lanham, MD: Madison Books, 1990), p. 106.

26 Solovyov and Klepikova, op. cit., p. 170.

27 Ibid., p. 169.

28 This point is made by, among others, Solovyov and Klepikova, op. cit.; Medvedev, op. cit.; Sheehy, op. cit.

29 Zemtsov and Farrar, op. cit., p. 3.

30 Solovyov and Klepikova, op. cit., p. 170.

31 Sheehy, op. cit., p. 107.

32 See, for example, Schmidt-Hauer, op. cit., pp. 53–65; Doder and Branson, op. cit., pp. 28–48.

33 Some interesting insights into the trip to France can be gleaned from M. Tatu, op. cit., pp. 41–2.

34 Morrison, op. cit., pp. 80–105; Schmidt-Hauer, op. cit., pp. 53–65.

35 Ibid., pp. 60–5.

36 Solovyov and Klepikova, op. cit., p. 179.

37 Sheehy, op. cit., pp. 110–17.

38 Medvedev, op. cit., pp. 66–80.

39 See, for example, Sheehy, op. cit.

40 This line is advanced by Schmidt-Hauer. The best analysis of the agricultural experimentation can be found in Medvedev, op. cit., pp. 44–93.

41 See, for example, Doder and Branson, op. cit. and Sanders, op. cit.

42 Solovyov and Klepikova, op. cit., p. 176.

43 Sheehy, op. cit., pp. 121–3.

44 Medvedev, op. cit., p. 84.

45 Ibid., p. 103.

46 Ibid., p. 118.

47 Solovyov and Klepikova, op. cit., p. 198.

48 Zemtsov and Farrar, op. cit., p. 7.

49 Sanders, op. cit., p. 120.

50 See A. Brown, 'Gorbachev: New Man in the Kremlin', *Problems of Communism*, May–June 1985, pp. 1–23.

51 M. Gorbachev, *Zhizn' i reformy* (Moskva: Novosti, 1995), 2 vols. His early years are contained in Volume 1.

52 M. Gorbachev, *Memoirs* (London: Bantam Books, 1997), p. xxix.

53 Gorbachev, *Zhizn'*, op. cit., p. 15.

54 *Komsomolskaya, Pravda*, 7 November 1992.

55 Ibid., p. 38.

56 Ibid., pp. 37–42.

57 Ibid., pp. 57–8.

58 Ibid., pp. 59–76.

59 Ibid., p. 76.

60 The former student was the writer Belyaev. For full details of the incident, see ibid., p. 65.

61 Ibid., p. 66.

62 See Chapters 4 and 5 in ibid., pp. 77–120.

63 Ibid., p. 220.

64 Ibid., p. 265. Emphasis in original. The Russian phrase is *Tak dal'she zhit' nel'zya*.

65 Kaiser, op. cit., p. 48.

66 J.F. Matlock, in *New York Review of Books*, vol. 43, 20, 1996.

67 Brown, op. cit., pp. 24–52.

68 Ibid., pp. 53–88.

69 McCauley, op. cit., pp. 14–49.

70 M. Galeotti, *Gorbachev and His Revolution* (Basingstoke: Macmillan, 1997), p. 45.

71 Breslauer, op. cit., Chapters 2 and 3.

2 Gorbachev: the inside story

1 It is, of course, essential to read Gorbachev critically, given the time and attention devoted to propaganda by the Soviet state. But given that the CPSU used ideology and ideas as its prime form of legitimation, then they do have a great value as objects of analysis. We should take them seriously, but this does not mean taking them at face value.

2 There has been surprisingly little attention paid to the questions of context, audience, language, etc., in analysis of Gorbachev's speeches and writings. This has tended to lead to rather one-dimensional appraisals of his thought and ideas. This chapter will attempt to create a much more nuanced view of what Gorbachev said and wrote in order to try and understand what Gorbachev thought he was doing and the type of image of his leadership he was constructing.

3 The link system was organized to give families, groups or teams more autonomy in the way in which they farmed a piece of land. It was moderately successful, but was viewed with a hint of suspicion by fellow leaders, as it seemed to represent a move away from or a dilution of the state and collective farm structures.

4 M.S. Gorbachev, *Zhivoe tvorchestvo naroda* (Moscow: Politizdat, 1984).

5 *Pravda*, 19 December 1984, pp.4–5.

6 *Pravda*, 21 February 1985.

7 An excellent analysis and commentary on this speech can be found in Archie Brown, 'New Man in the Kremlin', *Problems of Communism* 34, 3, May–June 1985.

8 Gorbachev in a speech to the Supreme Soviet declared that 'the report of Leonid Ilych Brezhnev is a significant contribution to the treasury of Marxism-Leninism', *Pravda*, 5 October 1977, cited in 'Reconsidering Brezhnev', by Edwin Bacon, *Brezhnev Reconsidered* (Basingstoke: Palgrave, 2001), p. 3.

9 In his first year, Soviet TV and radio reported the following visits of Gorbachev: Proletarsky rayon on 16 and 17 April 1985, Leningrad on 15–16 May 1985, Kiev on 25 June 1985, the Petrovskiy Metallurgical Works in Dneprpetrovsk on 28 June 1985, oil and gas plants at Nizhnevartovsk in Tyumen, 4 September 1985, agricultural conference in Tsenilograd, 7 September 1985.

10 'An interview with Gorbachev', *Time*, 9 September 1985. Also in *Pravda*, 2 September 1985. The passage in italics was not included in the *Pravda* version.

11 Meeting with workers at a Volga motor vehicle works, reported on Soviet TV on 8 April 1986, cited in BBC SWB SU/8229/C1–16, 10 April 1986.

12 A good example of this is the post-Geneva Summit press conference. See *Pravda*, 22 November 1985. Here he spoke of how 'the letters I have received have made a deep impression upon me'.

13 Ibid.

14 *Pravda*, 2 September 1985.

15 Gorbachev's speech to Alessandro Natta, the General Secretary of the PCI, TASS in Russian for abroad, 28 January 1986.

16 See in particular Gorbachev's address to the 11th Congress of the SED (East German Socialist Party), *Pravda*, 19 April 1986.

17 BBC SWB SU/7934/C/1–16, 25 April 1985.

18 *Izvestiya*, 9 May 1985.

19 *Pravda*, 26 February 1986.

20 Gorbachev the very next month committed the unpardonable sin in a multinational state of identifying the state with the majoritarian ethnic group, something guaranteed to raise the hackles all of the non-Russians. Speaking in Kiev on 25 June 1985, he noted that, 'For all people who are striving for good, for Russia – the Soviet Union I mean, that is what we call it now and that's what it is in fact …' This betrayed a certain naïveté in Gorbachev's dealings with the nationalities issue, and reflected his lack of experience and his rapid rise through the hierarchy which restricted his experience of dealing with All Union issues. BBC SWB SU/7988/C/1–4, 27 June 1985.

21 Op. cit., BBC SWB SU/7934.

22 Ibid.

23 Op. cit., *Pravda*, 26 February.

24 Gorbachev subsequently has denied that there was any conscious decision to convene the Congress on this date. But for all those who were historically aware the symbolism was clear, even if the intentions were not.

25 Gorbachev performed another set-piece confirming his historical awareness when he announced that 6 August 1986 was the date for the expiry of the nuclear test ban, which was the date commemorating the nuclear bomb falling on Hiroshima.

26 Gorbachev's political report contained a frontal attack on Developed Socialism which was the ideological centrepiece of the Brezhnev years. It was called an era of sycophancy, flattery and fawning.

27 Op. cit. *Pravda*, 26 February 1986.

28 Gorbachev made reference to 'manna from heaven' and to Noah's Ark as well. These were not isolated incidents. Gorbachev's speeches were scattered with biblical pictures, probably highlighting the importance of his grandmother, a devout Orthodox Christian, on his early years.

29 There were two main visits in this period: to Kuibyshev in early April 1986, and then to address the 11th Congress of the SED in mid-April. Much of the period in late April to mid-May was taken up with coping with the consequences of the Chernobyl nuclear disaster.

30 *Pravda*, 15 May 1986.

31 In a subsequent address while visiting Riga in February 1987, Gorbachev stated that 'For an entire year after the April plenum we sought advice from people, from scientists, we made an analysis of the past in order to understand what was what.' Cited in BBC SWB SU/8496/C/3, 19 February 1987.

32 *Pravda*, 17 June 1986.

33 Ibid.

34 Speech in Vladivostok, *Pravda*, 27 July 1986.

35 Speech in Khabarovsk in *Pravda*, 2 August 1986.

36 Op. cit., *Pravda*, 27 July 1986, p. 1.

37 Op. cit., *Pravda*, 2 August 1986, p. 2.

38 Ibid., p. 2.

39 Speech to Krasnodar party aktiv in *Pravda*, 20 September 1986.

40 In a speech to the heads of Social Science departments, Gorbachev spoke of the need to move away from dogmatic scholasticism and mechanical rote-learning. It was essential to 'turn social science to face practical matters'. BBC SWB SU/8380/B/3, 1 October 1986.

41 Echoes of this approach can be seen in Lenin's appeals for more science, and less politics in the Soviet state once they had taken power after 1917. See Lenin's 'Report of the All-Russia Central Executive Committee to the 8th Congress of Soviets', in *Selected Works*, vol. 2 (Moscow: Progress Publishers, 1971), p. 517.

42 In his talks with workers at an Agro-Industrial Combine near Krasnodar, Gorbachev talked of the need to provide alternative leisure facilities to support the anti-alcohol campaign, including cafés, ice-cream parlours and the like. See *Pravda*, 18 September 1986.

43 Op. cit., *Pravda*, 20 September 1986. The NEP was Lenin's solution to the need to restore economic production in the USSR after the ravages of the Russian Civil War, involving the partial restoration of market relations, the profit motive and so on in the countryside, while maintaining control of the key elements of the urban industrial economy. Lenin was criticized for retreating to capitalism. He argued that it was a way of building socialism with capitalist hands.

44 In the latter years of his life, Lenin turned to consider the question of how best the USSR could build socialism, given that it was a predominantly peasant country in a hostile capitalist world. The answer, according to Lenin, was to promote a mixed economy (building socialism with capitalist hands) and also an emphasis upon cultural matters to prepare the people to live

and work under socialism. Gorbachev's combination of economic reforms and *glasnost'* seems to echo this approach.

45 Moscow Home Service, 19 September 1986, cited in BBC SWB SU/8371/C/2, 23 September 1986. Gorbachev went on to say, in a tone which many teenagers growing up in the 1970s and 1980s would remember from their own upbringing, that the generation born after the war had been 'spoilt', and that it had done him no harm to be introduced to work at an early stage.

46 The press conference in Reykjavik was published in *Pravda*, 14 October 1986. Two subsequent TV addresses on the Reykjavik Summit were also published in *Pravda*, on 15 October 1986 and 23 October 1986.

47 BBC SWB SU/8412/C/22–24, 10 November 1986.

48 BBC SWB SU/8455/C/1–1, 2 January 1987.

49 Gorbachev's Report, 'On Perestroika and the Party's Personnel Policy', can be found in M.S. Gorbachev, *Izbrannye rechii i stati*, iv (Moscow: Politizdat, 1988), pp. 299–354.

50 BBC SWB SU/8425/C1/1–10, 25 November 1986.

51 Gorbachev, op. cit., p. 314.

52 Ibid., p. 349.

53 Address on Soviet TV, 29 January 1987, reproduced in BBC SWB SU/8480/C2–2, 31 January 1987.

54 These included visits to Latvia and Estonia, addresses to the 18th Congress of the Soviet Trade Unions and the 20th Komsomol Congress and a Czech-Soviet friendship rally.

55 Speech at a Czech-Soviet friendship rally, *Pravda*, 11 April 1987.

56 This same plenum is also mentioned by Georgi Arbatov in his memoirs.

57 Op. cit., *Pravda*, 11 April 1987.

58 *Pravda*, 26 February 1987.

59 Gorbachev's address to Latvian party activists. BBC SWB SU/8499/C/1, 23 February 1987.

60 Gorbachev's message in Estonia may well have been undermined by the fact that he twice referred to 'Latvia' instead of Estonia. These were dubbed out when broadcast on Soviet TV, but again showed a tendency to costly slips of the tongue on the nationalities issue.

61 Gorbachev was asked about this directly in an interview with the Italian newspaper *L'Unita*, published in *Pravda* on 20 May 1987.

62 *Pravda*, 26 February 1987.

63 See *Moscow News* 27, 1987, p. 10.

64 Ibid.

65 From the back cover of Gorbachev's book.

66 M. Gorbachev, *Perestroika: New Thinking for Our Country and the World* (London: Collins, 1987), pp. 11–12.

67 Ibid., pp. 9–13.

68 Ibid., p. 19.

69 Ibid., p. 24.

70 Ibid., pp. 24–5.

71 M.S. Gorbachev, 'October and Perestroika: The Revolution Continues', *Moscow News*, 45, 1987.

72 Ibid.

73 The 'braking mechanism' was a concept developed by Soviet scholars. See, for example, the discussion in *Voprosy Istorii* 1 and 2, 1988.

74 Ibid., p. 43. Emphasis added.

75 Gorbachev received a great deal of criticism for what was seen at the time as a very tame cautious appraisal of Soviet history. But this criticism fails to take into account the setting for the speech. Gorbachev's most critical pieces were not normally delivered at the set-piece rituals of the Soviet state.

76 Op. cit., *Moscow News*, 1987 (45).

77 Ibid.

78 *Pravda*, 13 January 1988.

79 *Pravda*, 19 February 1988.

80 *Pravda*, 13 January 1988.

81 *Pravda*, 19 February 1988.

82 In his meeting with Willy Brandt, Gorbachev noted that 'I do not think we were wise in everything or that we decided everything as we should have done.' See BBC SWB SU/0119 A1/ 1, 7 April 1988.

83 Report from Soviet TV, 9 April 1988. Relayed in BBC SWB SU/0122 B/5, 11 April 1988.

84 Ibid., B/8.

85 In a conversation with US publishers, Gorbachev also noted that 'I think that in the times of Brezhnev the leadership under him also conceived and launched big plans. But they were not brought to fruition mostly because they were not based on the decisive force – drawing people into the modernization and restructuring of society. We've learnt a lesson from our history and this is why we are developing democratization with so much persistence.' See *Pravda*, 23 May 1988.

86 V.I. Lenin, 'On Co-operation', in *Selected Works* (Moscow: Progress Publishers, 1967), vol. 3, pp. 700–1.

87 *Pravda*, 19 February 1988.

88 *Pravda*, 29 June 1988.

89 Ibid.

90 Soviet TV, 11 July 1988. Reported in BBC SWB EE/0202 C/4, 13 July 1988.

91 Soviet TV, 14 July 1988. Reported in BBC SWB EE/0206 C1/3, 18 July 1988. This same passage about people's eyes and their sincerity was repeated by Gorbachev in his visit to a Food Supplies Conference at Orel in November 1988. See BBC SWB SU/0313/C1/2.

92 Gorbachev often demonstrated his ability to relate the personal and the general. In a speech to the CC plenum on 29 July, Gorbachev noted, 'This very day I read in '*Selskaya zhizn*' a report about the work of lease contractors in Stavropol Kray. The place in question was the Balkovskiy state farm in Georgiyevsk Rayon. I know that state farm. It is a difficult farm with a constant manpower shortage.' *Pravda*, 30 July 1988.

93 In an interesting aside, Gorbachev, when exhorted to hurry up the agrarian reforms in order to solve the food supply problems retorted that 'they hurried during 1929–33, and look what that got them'. BBC SWB SU/0258 C/1, 16 September 1988.

94 *Pravda*, 25 September 1988.

95 BBC SWB SU/0323/C/1, 1 December 1988.

96 *Pravda*, 25 September 1988.

97 BBC SWB SU/0323/C/1, 1 December 1988.

98 The full extent of the concessions were as follows: reduction of armed personnel by 500,000 over two years; removal of tank and other armoured units in Warsaw Pact countries; reorganization of existing Soviet units in Eastern Europe to a more defensive standpoint; reduction of 10,000 tanks, 8,500 artillery units and 800 combat aircraft. TASS transcript of Soviet TV broadcast, cited in BBC SWB SU/0330/C1, 9 December 1988.

99 Ibid.

100 CPSU CC Politburo minutes, 13 November 1986.

101 *Pravda*, 19 July 1989.

102 Soviet TV, 21 January 1989. Cited in BBC SWB SU/0365 C1/1, 23 January 1989. I think that not all of these can properly come under the guise of luck, especially Chernobyl, Afghanistan and the ban on alcohol!

103 Soviet TV, 19 September 1989. Cited in BBC SWB SU/0567/C/1, 21 September 1989.

104 *Pravda*, 19 July 1989.

105 TASS in Russian for abroad, 25 December 1989. Cited in BBC SWB SU/0648/C1/1, 28 December 1989.
106 Tass in Russian for abroad, 7 January 1989. Cited in BBC SWB SU/0356/C2/1, 12 January 1989.
107 Ibid., C/3.
108 CPSU CC meeting with scientific and cultural figures on 7 January 1989. In BBC SWB SU/0353/C/1.
109 M.S.Gorbachev, 'Sotsialisticheskaya ideya i revolutsionnaya perestroika', *Pravda*, 26 November 1989.
110 Ibid.
111 Cited in BBC SWB SU/0488/C/1.
112 Cited in BBC SWB SU/0472/C/1.
113 Speech by Bondarev, in *XIX vsyesoyuznaya konferentsiya kommunisticheskoi partii svetskaya soyuza: stenograficheskii otchet* (Moskva: Politizdat, 1988), p. 224.
114 Gorbachev interviewed after voting in RSFSR elections, Soviet TV 1800 GMT, 4 March 1990, cited in BBC SWB SU/0705/B/1, 6 March 1990.
115 Gorbachev's address to workers at Siauliai Television Factory, *Pravda*, 14 January 1990.
116 Cited in BBC SWB SU/0663/B/1.
117 BBC SWB SU/0682/C/1, 7 February 1990.
118 Ibid.
119 Gorbachev spent a long time immersed in Lenin during 1988 and 1989 looking for exactly this type of thing. This emphasizes how seriously the leader took the issue of ideology, investing so much effort in scouring Lenin's writings. He mentioned this in a speech at a Higher Education Meeting on 12 May 1990. The full quote ran, 'A year or two ago I set myself the task of reading right through Lenin's speeches during the first post-revolutionary period, and also everything that was said at the party congresses held during those years under Lenin. I collected all the transcripts and read them.' Cited in BBC SWB SU/0763/B/1.
120 *Pravda*, 21 April 1990.
121 Ibid.
122 BBC SWB SU/0752/C1, 1 May 1990.
123 BBC SWB SU/0764/B/1, 15 May 1990.
124 BBC SWB SU/0807/C/1, 4 July 1990.
125 Ibid.
126 Ibid.
127 Ibid.
128 Gorbachev answers Komsomol delegates questions on Soviet TV. 11 April 1990. Cited in BBC SWB SU/0739/B/1, 16 April 1990.
129 The composition of this group included Anatoly Lukyanov, Yevgeny Primakov, Nikolai Ryzhkov, Eduard Shevardnadze, Vadim Bakatin, Dmitri Yazov, Vladimir Kryuchkov, Yuri Maslyukov, Alexander Yakovlev, Valery Boldin, Valentin Rasputin, Chingiz Aitmatov, Stanislav Shatalin, Veniamin Yarin. Vadim Medvedev was added later.
130 Ibid.
131 BBC SWB SU/0936/B/1, 2 December 1990.
132 Ibid.
133 Ibid.
134 Speech by Gorbachev in the CPD, 20 December 1990, on Soviet TV. Cited in BBC SWB SU/0954/C3/1.
135 This was approved by about 70 per cent of voters.
136 Text of L.P. Kravchenko's interview with Gorbachev, Soviet television, 26 March 1991. Cited in BBC SWB, 28 March 1991, SU/1032/B/1.

137 BBC SWB SU/1135/C/1, 27 July 1991.

138 BBC SWB SU/1130/C1/1, 22 July 1991.

139 *Pravda*, 27 July 1991.

140 Interview with Kravchenko, op. cit.

141 Gorbachev's speech in Oslo, 5 June 1991. Cited in BBC SWB SU/1092/C1/1, 7 June 1991.

142 The speech was made when Gorbachev was in the throes of revising the Party Programme, and he took a similar approach there, highlighting all the different streams of thought that flowed into socialism from a variety of sources, of which Marx, etc. was only one among many.

143 Gorbachev in Oslo, op. cit.

144 Ibid.

145 Some have argued that this programme was a contributory factor in the August coup. See M. Sandle, 'The Final Word: The Draft Party Programme of July/August 1991', *Europe/Asia Studies*, 48, 1996, pp. 1131–50.

146 In his speech to the USSR Supreme Soviet, Gorbachev stated that 'People are saying that I came back to another country. I agree with this. I may add to this that a man returned from the Crimea to this different country who looks at everything – both the past, the present and the future – with different eyes.' BBC SWB SU/1162/C1/1, 28 August 1991.

147 Press conference relayed on Soviet TV on Central TV First All Union programme, 22 August 1991. Cited in BBC SWB SU/1159/B/1.

148 Ibid.

149 Ibid.

150 Ibid.

151 Ibid.

152 Address relayed on Central TV First All Union programme, 23 August 1991. Cited in BBC SWB SU/1160/C1.

153 Ibid.

154 BBC SWB SU/1160/B/1, 26 August 1991.

155 BBC SWB SU/1162/C1/1, 28 August 1991.

156 This is an oddly circular point, because, without *perestroika*, the country would not have been in a position where the old forces would have wanted to seize power, but whatever.

157 Gorbachev's speech to the USSR Supreme Soviet, 27 August 1991. Cited in BBC SWB SU/1163/C2.

158 Speech at the CSCE Human Rights Conference, 10 September 1991. Cited in BBC SWB SU/1174/C1.

3 Gorbachev and the Western media

1 'Gorbachev Passes Up Stunts But Dazzles the Heartland', *New York Times*, 4 June 1990.

2 The main sources consulted are: the *Guardian*; *The Times*; the *Sunday Times*; the *Observer*; the *Financial Times*; the *Independent*; *The Economist*; the *New Statesman and Society*; the *New York Review of Books*; *Time*; *Newsweek*; the *New York Times*. It was not possible within the time frame for publication to include the output of the broadcast media. Other interesting issues – particularly contrasting European print media perspectives – were not able to be explored in great depth, but would make a very interesting research project.

3 'Kremlin's Apostle of Change', *Observer* 11 November 1984; 'A Red Star Rises in the East', *Sunday Times*, 11 November 1984.

4 *Financial Times* 18/12/84; 22/12/84; *The Times*, 15/12; 17/12, 18/12, 19/12, 20/12, 21/12; *Sunday Times* 16/12, 23/12; *Guardian*, 15/12, 17/12, 18/12, 21/12, 22/12.

5 *The Times*, 20 December 1984.

6 *Financial Times*, 22 December 1984 p. 26.

7 'Gorbachev Face to Face', *Newsweek*, 25 March 1985, p. 15.

8 *Guardian*, 12 March 1985, p. 10.

9 'A Double Identity', *Newsweek*, 25 March 1985, p. 14.

10 This sense of 'otherness'– backward, mystical, enigmatic – with regard to Russia can be seen to a greater or lesser extent in many Western writings. See, for example, 'Europeans do not easily succumb to any emissary from *Russia, that mentally remote, still almost unknown land* [my emphasis], cited in 'Comrade Europe', *The Economist*, 12 October 1985, p. 14.

11 'The Emergence of Gorbachev', *New York Times*, 3 March 1985, section 6, p. 40 onwards.

12 This was featured in the German newspaper *Stern*, and was reported in 'Ending an Era of Drift', *Time*, 25 March 1985, p. 8.

13 'A Soviet Glimpse of Camelot', *Guardian*, 12 March 1985, p. 23.

14 Scepticism, or at least questioning agnosticism, was most prevalent in *The Times* at this time. See 'Gorbachev Faces Long Battle to Push Through New Ideas', 13 March 1985, p. 6; 'Mr. Gorbachev's Hour', 12 March 1985, p. 13.

15 Anonymous state department official, quoted in *Time*, 25 March 1985, p. 8.

16 'Changing the Guard', *Newsweek*, 25 March 1985, p. 13.

17 *New York Times*, 12 March 1985, p. A18.

18 'Plain Speaking Mr. G Takes Star Role', *Guardian*, 22 November 1985.

19 'The Sparks by the Fireside', *Guardian*, 22 November 1985.

20 'Gorbachev Strides on to the World Stage', *Guardian*, 22 November 1985.

21 'Bleak House', *The Times*, 14 October 1986; 'Why Reykjavik Failed', *Guardian*, 14 October 1986.

22 'Raisa's Delicate Touch of Diplomacy', *The Times*, 13 October 1986.

23 'How Gorbachev Left the Chips on the Table', *Guardian*, 15 October 1986.

24 A *Newsweek* poll asked the following questions:
As a result of the summit, what is your opinion of Gorbachev?
32 per cent = better than before
1 per cent = worse than before
64 per cent = about the same
Which leader do you think came out of the summit looking better?
7 per cent = Reagan
23 per cent = Gorbachev
67 per cent = Equal
For the rest of the poll, see *Newsweek*, 21 December 1987, p. 16.

25 'Folksy Gorbachev Plies His Wares', *Guardian*, 10 December 1987; 'Kremlin Evangelist Preaches to Elite', *The Times*, 10 December 1987.

26 'One-Liners and Party-Liners', *Newsweek*, 21 December 1987, p. 21.

27 'The Last Chance We Have', *Newsweek*, 21 December 1987, p. 9.

28 'Hype Fails to Sell Packaged Gorbachov', *The Times*, 12 December 1987; 'Meeting Mr. Gorbachev', *Newsweek*, 21 December 1987, p. 15.

29 'The Dangers Ahead', *Newsweek*, 21 December 1987, p. 22.

30 Ibid., p. 25.

31 'The Last Chance We Have', *Newsweek*, 21 December 1987, p. 9.

32 'Gambler, Showman, Statesman', *New York Times*, 8 December 1988.

33 'Blue Apple Pays Homage to Broadway's Red Star', *Guardian*, 8 December 1988.

34 'I'll Take Manhattan', *Time*, 19 December 1988, p. 15.

35 'The Gorbachev Challenge', *Time*, 19 December 1988, p. 6.

36 'Brave New World', *Newsweek*, 19 December 1988; 'The Kremlin Roadshow in New York', *Guardian*, 7 December 1988; 'Moscow's Velvet Gauntlet', *Guardian*, 9 December 1988.

37 'Gorbachev and God', *Time*, 21 December 1987; 'God – Or History', *Time*, 19 December 1988; 'Gorbachev, God and Socialism', *Time*, 11 December 1989.

38 The messianic theme was directly referred to by Rupert Cornwell, when he wrote that, 'Today though, Mr. Gorbachev is back at home, and inevitably the West's image of him will revert from messiah to the much more familiar one of a man struggling with difficulties which may prove insuperable.' 'Gorbachev silences remaining sceptics', *Independent*, 4 December 1989.

39 'Direct Gorbachev Style Dazzles the Minnesotans', *New York Times*, 4 June 1990; 'Looking for a Slice of the Action in Land of Spam', *Guardian*, 4 June 1990.

40 'Looking for a Slice of the Action in Land of Spam', *Guardian*, 4 June 1990.

41 'Talking of Talks', *Guardian*, 2 June 1990.

42 'Out of the USSR: The Showman Rediscovers His Lost Audience', *Independent*, 1 June 1990.

43 'Gorbachev Reaps the Whirlwind', *Independent on Sunday*, 3 June 1990.

44 'History Man Gets Award from America', *Independent on Sunday*, 3 June 1990.

45 'Why He's Failing', *Newsweek*, 4 June 1990.

46 'Last Chance for Gorbachev and the West', *Independent on Sunday*, 7 July 1991; 'Should We Do Business with This Man?', *Independent*, 12 July 1991; 'Last Tango of the Superpower Era', *Independent on Sunday*, 14 July 1991.

47 'Doomed Illusions of Soviet Reform', *Independent on Sunday*, 9 June 1991.

48 'Seven Can Wait', *Guardian*, 19 July 1991.

49 'Whose Hand Is Out?', *Time*, 3 June 1991; 'Will Gorbachev Be the Spectre at the Rich Man's Feast?', *The Times*, 12 July 1991; 'The Great Panhandler', *New York Times*, 15 July 1991; 'A Yen, a Mark, a Franc, a Pound Make Gorbachev Do the Rounds', *Guardian*, 18 July 1991.

50 'Gorbachev's Shrinking Role', *Independent*, 1 August 1991; 'Not a Great Week for Muscovites', *Independent*, 1 August 1991; 'Solidarity in Moscow', *The Times*, 1 August 1991; 'Next Step for Gorbachev', *The Economist*, 3 August 1991; 'Goodfellas', *Time*, 5 August 1991.

51 'A Little Touch of Gorbachev in Our Night', *Guardian*, 9 August 1988.

52 'Moscow Tightrope', *The Times*, 8 March 1988.

53 *Le Quotidien*, cited in *Newsweek*, 14 October 1985, p. 13.

54 'A Wish List from Moscow', *Newsweek*, 7 October 1985, p. 10.

55 'Gorbachev Fails to Woo France', *Sunday Times* 9 July 1989, A18.

56 'Gorbachev Disappoints with Obfuscation', *Independent* 7 July 1989; 'Less Than Vintage', *Time*, 17 October 1989; 'French Greet Perestroika Message with Scepticism', *Guardian*, 4 July 1989.

57 'The Land of Hope and Gorbi', *Sunday Times*, 18 June 1989.

58 'Ruhr Steelworkers Seek the Nobel Peace Prize for 'Gorby'', *The Times*, 16 June 1989.

59 Cited in 'Soviet Leader Dazzles Germans', *The Times*, 6 June 1989.

60 'Gorbachev Soars High on Steelworkers Scoreboard', *Guardian*, 16 June 1989.

61 'Gorbachov Is Seen by Britons As Making the World Safer', *The Times*, 5 April 1989.

62 'Revenge, Not Rabbits', *Financial Times*, 8 April 1989.

63 'Making Sense of President Gorbachev', *Independent*, 4 April 1989.

64 'Gorbachev Invite for Queen', *Guardian*, 6 April 1989; 'Revenge, Not Rabbits', *Financial Times*, 8 April 1989.

65 'Protests Greet Gorbachev', *Guardian*, 16 May 1989.

66 ''Saviour' Mikhail in a Country of Doubts', *Sunday Times*, 12 April 1987.

67 'Prague Awaits Kiss of Life from Russia's Prince Charming', *The Times*, 4 April 1987; 'On the Road Again', *Time*, 20 April 1987; 'The Gorbachev Factor', *Time*, 8 June 1987.

68   For a useful summary of how Gorbachev evoked different responses in the capitals of Europe, see '"Glasnost" Melts the Cold War's Ice', *Guardian*, 30 April 1987.

69   Apt biblical parallels for the story of Gorbachev can quite easily be found. The full quotation for this reference is:

> Coming to his home town, he began teaching the people in their synagogue, and they were amazed. 'Where did this man get this wisdom and these miraculous powers?' they asked. 'Isn't this the carpenter's son? Isn't his mother's name Mary, and aren't his brothers James, Joseph, Simon and Judas? Aren't all his sisters with us? Where then did this man get all these things?' and they took offence at him. But Jesus said to them, 'Only in his home town and in his own house is a prophet without honour.' And he did not do many miracles there because of their lack of faith' (Matthew 13: 54–85, *The Holy Bible: New International Version*, London: Hodder and Stoughton, 1980).

70   The importance of the press – both Soviet and Western – during *perestroika* should not be underestimated. Academics, pundits, commentators and experts struggled to keep up with the bewildering pace of change, especially after 1988. As a source of information, the press proved invaluable, in spite of its obvious shortcomings. Looking back now, the press accounts allow a recreation of the tempo and the drama of these momentous times.

71   'A New Type of Soviet Leader', *Financial Times*, 28 December 1985.

72   'Russia under Gorbachev', *The Economist*, 16 November 1985.

73   See, for example, 'Gorbachev Impresses O'Neill Delegation', *Financial Times*, 11 April 1985; 'When New Men Make the News', *Financial Times*, 9 October 1985; 'Soviet Leader As Man of the People', *Financial Times*, 1 August 1986; 'Jumping a Generation', *New Statesman*, 15 March 1985; 'Streetwise Mikhail', *The Economist*, 26 July 1986.

74   Some had them made of steel.

75   'Reformer Adopts Stalin's Style', *New Statesman*, 21 February 1986.

76   'Soviet Leader As Man of the People', *Financial Times*, 1 August 1986.

77   'Reformer Adopts Stalin's Style', *New Statesman*, 21 February 1986.

78   'In Search of the Real Gorbachev; Will the Real Mr. Gorbachev Please Stand Up?', *Guardian*, 8 January 1986.

79   'When the Charm Wears Off', *The Economist*, 16 November 1985.

80   'Delays Likely in Mr. G's Dash Down the Fast Lane', *Guardian*, 13 April 1986; 'The Not-Quite Tsar', *The Economist*, 15 February 1986; 'The Weakness in Russia', *The Economist*, 15 March 1986; 'Reconditioned Engine Still Lacks Power', *Financial Times*, 12 June 1986; 'Grandmaster's Bungle', *The Economist*, 13 September 1986; 'How Mr. Gorbachev Ventured Abroad But Went Nowhere', *Guardian*, 10 December 1986.

81   There was a great deal of Chernobyl coverage. See, for example, 'Mr. Gorbachev Sets the Test', *Guardian*, 16 May 1986; 'How the Fallout Has Tainted Gorbachov', *The Times*, 6 May 1986; 'Conspiracy of Silence a Setback for Gorbachov', *THES*, 16 May 1986. 'Chernobyl Tests Gorbachev's Openness Policy', *Financial Times*, 14 May 1986; 'The Cloud over Gorbachev', *The Economist*, 24 May 1986.

82   'Comrade Europe', *The Economist*, 12 October 1985.

83   'Gorbachev's New Broom Keeps Sweeping', *Guardian*, 20 December 1986; 'Gorbachev's Big Gamble with the Man from Gorky', *Guardian*, 24 December 1986.

84   'Gorbachev Ushers in Modern Revolution', *Guardian*, 31 January 1987; 'On the Attack: Gorbachev Aims for a Second Revolution', *Sunday Times*, 1 February 1987; 'Radicalism in the Kremlin', *The Times*, 2 June 1987; 'Gorbachev Says 'Radical Reform' and Means It', *New York Times*, 27 June 1987.

85   For example, 'Can He Bring It Off?', *Time*, 27 July 1987; 'Can Gorbachov Succeed?', *THES*, 13 February 1987; 'Gorbachev at an Historic Crossroads', *New Statesman*, 27 February 1887; 'Can Gorbachev Change Russia?', *Sunday Times*, 8 November 1987; 'The leap and the

pirouette that could end in a fall', *The Economist*, 7 March 1987; 'Gorbachev May Just Mean It', *Financial Times*, 26 January 1987; 'Gorbachev's New Look', *Financial Times*, 16 February 1987; 'The Call to Reform', *Time*, 9 February 1987.

86   'The Gorbachev Era', *Time*, 27 July 1987.

87   'Gorbachev's Gambit', *New York Times*, 8 November 1987.

88   'Gorbachev Face to Face', *Sunday Times*, 4 January 1987; 'Gorbachev as Peter the Great', *New York Times*, 8 February 1987; 'The Heat's in the Kitchen at Camelot on Ice', *Guardian*, 23 December 1987.

89   'Why Gorbachov Works for the West', *Sunday Times*, 15 February 1987.

90   'Gorbachev Is Ready to Leap: Will the West Jump with Him?', *Guardian*, 13 April 1987; 'How Thatcher Could Help Glasnost Along', *The Times*, 11 March 1987.

91   *The Economist* ran a series of articles at the start of 1987 along these lines. See, for example, 'Join the Dance', 3 January 1987; 'Biggish Step for Russia, Small One for Democracy', 31 January 1987; 'Cuddly Russia', 14 February 1987 'The Gorbachev Puzzle', 21 February 1987.

92   'It Won't Be Like That', *The Economist*, 4 July 1987.

93   'Perestroika II', *The Economist*, 10 October 1987.

94   'The Heat's in the Kitchen at Camelot on Ice', *Guardian*, 23 December 1987.

95   See, for example, 'His Year of Ruling Dangerously', *The Times*, 11 March 1988; 'Moscow Tightrope', *The Times*, 8 March 1988; 'Gorbachov's Big Gamble', *The Times*, 30 September 1988.

96   'The Other Gorbachev', *The Economist*, 10 December 1988.

97   'Praise to the King of All the Russias', *Sunday Times*, 11 December 1988.

98   'Supergorby Gets the Global Vote', *Guardian*, 21 December 1988.

99   Ibid.

100   'The Year That Shook the World', *Independent*, 21 January 1989; 'Uneasy Future for Unwieldy Empire', *Sunday Times*, 1 January 1989.

101   'In the Balance', *Guardian*, 12 October 1989; 'Yesterday's Man?', *The Economist*, 16 December 1989; 'Through *Glasnost* Darkly', *New York Times*, 11 December 1989.

102   'Gorbachev Claim to Centre Ground Grows', *Guardian*, 28 March 1989.

103   'Radical on the Defensive', *Independent*, 12 December 1989.

104   'Through *Glasnost* Darkly', *New York Times*, 11 December 1989.

105   Ibid.

106   'Showing Signs of Strain', *Independent*, 26 July 1989.

107   'His Vision Thing', *Time*, 2 October 1989.

108   Ibid.

109   'Yesterday's Man?', *The Economist*, 16 December 1988; 'The Bear Turns Bullish', *Guardian*, 20 November 1989; 'Can Gorbachov Last?', *The Times*, 21 September 1989.

110   '25 Years After Khrushchev, the Soviet Coup Is a Topic Again', *Guardian*, 14 October 1989; 'History Stalks the Kremlin', *Independent*, 14 October 1989.

111   'Yesterday's man', *The Economist*, 16 December 1989.

112   'The Year of Revolution', *Independent*, 28 December 1989.

113   'Rise and Rise of the Great Facilitator', *Guardian*, 22 January 1990.

114   'A Friend in Need?', *The Economist*, 12 May 1990.

115   'Five Years of Gorbachov: He Has Changed the World But Can He Ever Change the Russians?', *Independent on Sunday*, 4 March 1990.

116   'Soviet Fears of *Katastroika*', *Guardian*, 9 March 1990.

117   'Still Riding the Back of the Bear', *Independent on Sunday*, 4 March 1990.

118   'British Thought Is Paralysed by Man of Radical Vision', *Guardian*, 9 March 1990.

119   'Gorbachev's Nobel Prize Arrives at the Wrong Time', *Guardian*, 16 October 1990. A.M. Rosenthal, writing in the *New York Times* argued that they had chosen the wrong Russian,

preferring anyone from a list of gulag internees. See 'The Wrong Russian', *New York Times*, 16 October 1990

120 'Is the Soviet President Still a Political Grandmaster or Is He Becoming a Pawn of Conservatives in the Party?', *Guardian*, 28 December 1990.

121 'Fate v Gorbachev', *The Economist*, 29 September 1990; 'Helping Mr. Gorbachev', *Financial Times*, 1 June 1990.

122 'Helping Mr. Gorbachev', *Financial Times*, 1 June 1990; 'Beyond *Perestroika*', *The Economist*, 9 June 1990.

123 'New Darling of the People', *Independent*, 30 May 1990; 'A Blow at the Heart of the Soviet Empire', *Independent on Sunday*, 10 June 1990; 'Strong Man Boris', *Independent on Sunday*, 16 September 1990.

124 'Gorbachev's Party Trick', *The Times*, 14 July 1990; 'Gorbachev Only Bought time', *New York Times*, 15 July 1990; 'Flanked by Trouble', *Time*, 23 July 1990.

125 The extent of Gorbachev's fall from grace can be gleaned from the comparisons now deployed to illustrate his leadership. Rather than Peter the Great or JFK, he was starting to be compared to Nicolae Ceausescu, the Romanian leader who had been removed after popular protests very similar to the way the crowds turned against the Kremlin leaders on May Day 1990. See 'The retreat from Red Square', *Independent*, 2 May 1990. 'Get Rid of Communism', *Newsweek*, 14 May 1990; 'A Friend in Need?', *The Economist*, 12 May 1990.

126 'Mr. Gorbachev's Ends Hardly Justify His Means', *Independent on Sunday*, 18 March 1990; 'Liberator or Another Tyrant?', *Independent*, 26 March 1990.

127 'When the Juggling Has to Stop', *The Economist*, 24 November 1990.

128 'Order, Order', *The Economist*, 22 December 1990.

129 'Say Goodnight, Gorby', *New York Times*, 19 December 1990.

130 'Gorbachev's Choice', *The Economist*, 15 December 1990.

131 'Gorbachov's New Face', *The Times*, 4 June 1990.

132 'Still Riding the Back of the Bear', *Independent on Sunday*, 4 March 1990.

133 'More Than Ever, Personality Drives World Events', *New York Times*, 30 December 1990; 'People Make History', *New York Times*, 29 December 1990.

134 'Gorbachev, Super-Tsar', *The Economist*, 3 March 1990; 'A Tsar Is Born', *Independent*, 28 February 1990; 'In the Light of History', *The Economist*, 10 February 1990.

135 'The Retreat from Red Square', *Independent*, 2 May 1990.

136 'When the Juggling Has to Stop', *The Economist*, 24 November 1990.

137 'Five Years of Gorbachev', *Independent on Sunday*, 4 March 1990.

138 'Still Riding the Back of the Bear', *Independent on Sunday*, 4 March 1990.

139 'Gorbachev's Crisis', *Independent*, 27 May 1990.

140 'Gorbachev's Nobel Prize Arrives at the Wrong Time', *Guardian*, 16 October 1990.

141 'The Moderate As Tragic Hero', *Independent*, 11 July 1990.

142 'Gorbachev Is Moving from Greatness Towards Tragedy', *Independent*, 29 May 1990. The original quote is found in The Gospel of Mark 15: 31, op. cit.

143 'How to Deal with a Dying Empire', *Independent*, 21 January 1991.

144 'The Soviet Crackdown', *Independent*, 14 January 1991; 'Gorby's Black berets', *New York Times*, 14 January 1991; 'Blood on His Hands', *The Economist*, 19 January 1091; 'Old Habits Die Hard', *Newsweek*, 28 January 1991; 'Is the Liberation of Lithuania the Death Notice for Reform?', *New York Times*, 20 January 1991.

145 'The Gorbachev Record: The Rise and Fall of Perestroika', *The Economist*, 19 January 1991; 'The Yeltsin Factor', *The Economist*, 26 January 1991; 'The Death of Perestroika', *The Economist*, 2 February 1991; 'Dealing with Gorbachev', *The Economist*, 9 February 1991; 'Who's in Charge Here?', *Newsweek*, 8 December 1991. One of the few voices to articulate an underlying coherence to the whole of Gorbachev's tenure even at this juncture was Jerry Hough,

an American academic. Writing in the *Guardian*, he argued that an underlying consistency can be detected if he is viewed not as 'a Western democrat or another Brezhnev, but as a modernising Westernising tsar often seen in the Third World ... If we understand Gorbachev in these terms, we no longer see him following a zigzag course between democracy and dictatorship. Rather we see him combining both in a complicated manner'. (Jerry Hough 'Man of Iron', *Guardian*, 20 February 1991).

146 The question was: 'Do you consider it necessary to preserve the Union of Soviet Socialist Republics as a renewed federation of equal sovereign republics, in which human rights and the freedoms of all nationalities will be fully guaranteed?'

147 'Gorbachev Bends to Survive', *The Economist*, 27 April 1991; 'Outfoxing Boris Yeltsin', *Newsweek*, 6 May 1991; 'Rewriting Communism', *Newsweek*, 5 August 1991.

148 'The World after Mikhail Gorbachev', *Guardian*, 20 August 1991.

149 'The Soviet Coup: A Front Row Seat at the Banishment of Fear', *Independent*, 20 August 1991.

150 'What Gorbachev Did to Reinvent His Country', *New York Times*, 20 August 1991.

151 'Gorbachev: The Years of Discontent', *Guardian*, 20 August 1991;

152 'Gorbachev: the Rise and Fall', *Guardian*, 20 August 1991; 'The Soviet Coup: Taking the Historical View', *Independent*, 20 August 1991; 'The World after Mikhail Gorbachev', *Guardian*, 20 August 1991; 'Reform Unleashed the Turmoil That Engulfed Leader', *The Times*, 20 August 1991; 'Moscow's Road to Ruin', *The Times*, 20 August 1991.

153 'Gorbachev: the Years of Freedom', *Guardian*, 20 August 1991; 'Hollow Promises Revive Spectre of Cold War for Complacent West', *Guardian*, 20 August 1991.

154 'The Soviet Coup: A Front Row Seat at the Banishment of Fear', *Independent*, 20 August 1991.

155 'Sharing the Guilt and the Blame', *New York Times*, 22 August 1991;

156 'Yeltsin's Heroic Day', *The Times*, 22 August 1991; 'The Humbling of Gorbachev', *The Times*, 23 August 1991.

157 'An Unflinching Date with Destiny', *Guardian*, 22 August 1991.

158 Kerensky was the head of the Provisional Government in 1917 swept aside by the Bolsheviks after it ran out of popular support. Egon Krenz was the head of the East German Communist Party who oversaw the opening of the Berlin Wall, and expected to bask in popular acclaim as a result. Instead he was swept out of power by mass demonstrations.

159 'The End of the Gorbachev Era', *Newsweek*, 2 September 1991; 'Yesterday's Hero', *New York Times*, 24 August 1991; 'Out of the Dacha and Into the Dock', *Guardian*, 24 August 1991; 'Mr. Gorbachev's Bleak Future', *Independent*, 27 August 1991; 'Gorbachev: Larger than Life', *New York Times*, 31 August 1991.

160 'A New Russian Revolution', *The Times*, 25 August 1991.

161 'A New Type of Soviet Leader', *Financial Times*, 28 December 1985.

162 'Youth and Smiles, But Familiar Attitudes', *Time*, 6 January 1986. It was pointed out that previous winners of the *Time* 'Man of the Year' poll included Benito Mussolini and Joseph Stalin.

163 'Mikhail Gorbachev', *Time*, 4 January 1988. The eulogies for Gorbachev were by now becoming excessively effusive, e.g.

> Perhaps Gorbachev's most obvious accomplishment is that he has reinvented the idea of a Soviet leader. Virtually everything about his country and its place in world affairs seems less ponderous, less opaque than it did before he became General Secretary ... In 1987 he became ... a symbol of hope for a new kind of Soviet Union: more open, more concerned with the welfare of its citizens and less with the spread of its ideology and system abroad. For fanning that hope, Gorbachev is Time's man of the year (p. 4).

164 Cited in 'World View: Simply the Largest Human Being of Our Times', *Independent*, 23

January 1988. Timothy Garton-Ash argued that the Pope should be nominated for man of the decade.

165 Cited in the *Independent*, 28 January 1988.

166 'Gorbachov Sends Best Wishes to the British', *The Times*, 30 December 1989.

167 'Gorbachev: The Unlikely Patron of Change', *Time*, 1 January 1990.

168 'Gorbachev Wins Nobel Peace Prize', *Guardian*, 16 October 1990; 'Gorbachev Wins Peace Prize and Praise', *Financial Times*, 16 October 1990; 'Acclaimed by the World, Blamed by His People', *The Times*, 16 October 1990; 'Black Bread and Nobel Peace Prizes', *The Guardian*, 24 October 1990; 'Nobel Peace Prize Awarded to Gorbachev', 16 October 1990; 'Gorbachev's Prize', *New York Times*, 16 October 1990.

169 'Glasnost a la Mode Reaps Its Reward', *The Times*, 31 March 1990.

170 'Gorbachev: The Unlikely Patron of Change', *Time*, 1 January 1990, pp. 16–17.

171 Ibid.

172 Ibid.

173 *Financial Times*, 6 April 1989. The advert coincided with Gorbachev's visit to GB.

174 'Big Mike Still Wows America', *Independent*, 29 January 1990.

175 'Ole Mikhail', *Financial Times*, 16 May 1989.

176 'Gorbachov Tells of His Private World', *The Times*, 21 May 1987; 'The Education of Mikhail Sergeevich Gorbachev', *Time*, 4 January 1988; 'Misha Professes Leninist Faith to the Class of 1950', *Guardian*, 20 June 1990; 'Gorbachev, Ordinary Man, Homely Leader', *The Times*, 20 July 1990.

177 There were many reports of Raisa's activities in the Western media. These occurred most frequently during the superpower summits when the style wars of Raisa and Nancy Reagan generated almost as many words as the summits themselves. For other reports, see, for example, 'The Rise and Rise of Raisa', *Time*, 4 January 1988; 'My Wife Is a Very Independent Lady', *Time*, 6 June 1988.

178 'We in the US are Suckers for Style', *Time*, 22 April 1985; 'Look This Gift Horse Over First', Brian Walden, in *Sunday Times*, 5 April 1987.

179 'Gorbachev Is Just a Chip Off the Old Bloc', *Sunday Times*, 4 September 1988.

180 'Gorbachev's Glasnost', Lies', *Sunday Times*, 1 November 1987.

181 'Why History Will Say That Gorbachov Was a Fool', *The Times*, 22 March 1990. It could be argued that an equal amount of misery has been caused by the television programme *Kilroy*.

182 'The Myth of Gorbachev', *Guardian*, 28 June 1990.

183 'Blind to the Real Betrayal', *Guardian*, 5 September 1991.

184 'Russia's Democrats Will Look Back and Recall a Golden Age', *Guardian*, 27 December 1991; 'Shedding Tears Over the Turkey as the Great Communist Dismantler Said Goodbye', *Guardian*, 27 December 1991; 'Dropping the Pilot', *Independent*, 11 December 1991.

185 'Goodbye Mr. Gorbachev', *Newsweek*, 23 December 1991.

186 'Dignified but Bitter Farewell', *Guardian*, 27 December 1991.

187 'An Architect Whose Plans Collapsed', *Independent*, 24 December 1991.

188 'Shedding Tears Over the Turkey as the Great Communist Dismantler Said Goodbye', *Guardian*, 27 December 1991.

189 'Flaws of the Master Builder', *Guardian*, 12 December 1991.

190 'So Farewell then Mr. Gorbachev', *Independent*, 15 December 1991.

191 'The Demise of a False Icon', *Guardian*, 27 December 1991.

192 'Suicide of Bolshevism Brings Twentieth Century to a Climax', *Guardian*, 27 December 1991.

4 The Soviet view

1 *Pravda*, 12 March 1985.

2 *Kommunist*, 5, March 1985, p. 5.

3 Ibid., pp. 6–7.

4 M. Heller, 'Gorbachov for Beginners', *Survey*, 29, 1, 1985, p. 14.

5 *Izvestiya TsK KPSS*, 1, 1989, p. 10.

6 *Pravda*, 26 November 1989, p. 1.

7 *Izvestiya TsK KPSS*, 5, 1989, p. 3.

8 *Pravda*, 27 February 1986, p. 2.

9 Ibid., p. 4.

10 Ibid., p. 5.

11 *Pravda*, 1, March 86, p. 2.

12 *Pravda*, 2, March 86, p. 3.

13 The speeches on the anniversary were given as follows: Viktor Chebrikov, *Pravda*, 7 November 1985; Yegor Ligachev, *Pravda*, 7 November 1986; Mikhail Gorbachev, *Pravda*, 3 November 1987; Nikolai Slyunkov, *Pravda*, 7 November 1988; Vladimir Kryuchkov, *Pravda*, 6 November 1989; Anatolii Lukyanov, *Pravda*, 8 November 1990.

14 E. Shevardnadze, *Pravda*, 23 April 1986, p. 1.

15 V. Ivashko, *Pravda*, 23 April 1991, p. 1.

16 *Pravda*, 29 June 1988, p. 7.

17 *Pravda*, 2 July 1988, p. 10.

18 L. Abalkin, in *XIX vsesoyuznaya konferentsiya kommunisticheskoi partii sovetskogo soyuza: Stenograficheskii otchet* (Moscow: Politizdat, 1988), vol. 1, pp. 114–20.

19 Y. Bondarev, in ibid., p. 224.

20 M. Ulyanov, *Pravda*, 30 June 1988, pp. 7–8.

21 V. I. Postnikov in *XIX vsesoyuznaya konferentsiya*, op. cit., pp. 252 7; V.I. Melnikov in ibid., pp. 266–71.

22 M. A. Ulyanov, *Pravda*, 30 June 1988, p. 8.

23 N. Andreeva, 'Ne mogu postupat'sya printsipami', *Sovetskaya Rossiya*, 13 March 1988, p. 3.

24 The *Pravda* editorial was entitled '*Printsipi perestroiki*', 5 April 1988, p. 1.

25 Y. Ligachev, *Inside Gorbachev's Kremlin* (Boulder, CO: Westview Press, 1993), pp. 298–9; A. Roxburgh, *The Second Russian Revolution* (London: BBC Books, 1991), p. 83; K. Devlin, 'L'Unita on "Secret History" of Andreeva Letter', *Radio Liberty Research Report*, 215/88, 26 May 1988.

26 Andreeva, op. cit.

27 Ibid.

28 Interview with Nina Andreeva, cited in BBC SWB SU/0572/B/1.

29 Details can be found in, for instance, A. Brown, *The Gorbachev Factor* (Oxford: Oxford University Press, 1996), pp. 169–72.

30 *Izvestiya TsK KPSS*, 2, February 1989, pp. 209–87.

31 Ibid.

32 Ibid.

33 Ibid.

34 Speech by Yeltsin in *Pravda*, 2 July 1988, p. 10.

35 Speech on Soviet TV, 31 May 1989, cited in BBC SWB SU/0472/C/1.

36 Ibid.

37 Interview given on Moscow World Service, 9 September 1989, cited in BBC SWB SU/0559/B/1.

38 Speech cited in BBC SWB SU/0644/C/1, 20 December 1989.

39 Interview with Elizabeth Hedborg of Stockholm radio on 29 December 1986, cited in BBC SWB SU/8451/A1/1.

40 Press conference on 15 January 1988 given by Andrei Sakharov. Cited in BBC SWB SU/0051/A1/1.

41 Press conference at USSR Foreign Ministry, 3 June 1988, cited in BBC SWB SU/0171/A1/1.

42 *Izvestiya*, 2 February 1989.

43 Sakharov's letter to *Izvestiya*, 7 February 1989.

44 The Supreme Soviet was the 542–member standing parliament which was elected from the ranks of the larger 2250–member Congress of People's Deputies.

45 Soviet TV, 25 May 1989, cited in BBC SWB SU/0468/C1/1.

46 Soviet TV, 25 May 1989, in BBC SWB SU/0469/C/1, 30 May 1989.

47 Ibid.

48 Soviet TV, 9 June 1989 cited in BBC SWB SU/0489/C/1.

49 Ibid.

50 Interview published in *Literaturnaya Gazeta*, 21/6, 1989.

51 Ibid.

52 Cited in BBC SWB SU/0193/B/1, 2 July 1988.

53 A report from the group Physicians for Human Rights (PHR) published in February 1990 gave some more details on the fatalities and injuries. PHR had gone in at the request of Andrei Sakharov and Dr Irakli Menagarishvili, the Minister for Public Health in the Georgian government, finally getting visas on 17 May 1989. They stated that the troops had most probably used two types of tear gas, and also a toxic agent called chloropicrin. The report went on to say that the deaths and injuries were most likely to have been caused by suffocation or asphyxiation. The PHR could not definitively prove that symptoms evidenced after 9 April were due to exposure to toxic agents. It was equally probable that psychological reactions to trauma were the cause.

54 The commissions were as follows: a Procurator's Office Commission and a Republican Commission in Georgia, followed by a Union Commission set up by the Congress to investigate.

55 Debate in the CPD on the evening of 30 May 1989. Relayed live on Soviet TV.

56 This viewpoint was expressed by Aleksandr Korshunov in his speech on the evening session of 1 June 1989, broadcast on Soviet TV.

57 Debate in the CPD of 25 May 1989. Relayed on Soviet TV.

58 Gumbaridze's speech on 8 June 1989. Relayed on Soviet TV.

59 Debate on the morning session of 29 May 1989. Relayed on Soviet TV.

60 *Zarya Vostoka*, 11 June 1989.

61 Ibid.

62 The 'slightly abridged' transcript of this interview appeared in *Molodezh Gruzii* on 31 October 1989.

63 Moscow World Service, 20 January1990, cited in BBC SWB SU/0668/B/1.

64 Given Yeltsin's subsequent actions in Chechnya, this criticism does seem rather hypocritical.

65 An investigation into the Baku events was concluded in January 1992. It concluded that the Presidium of the Supreme Soviet decree was issued in violation of the USSR constitution. It continues to be a significant part of Azeri collective memory, with millions visiting Martyrs Avenue in Baku each year on 20 January. There is a website set up to commemorate the victims, which includes an open letter to Gorbachev. See: http://www.january20.net/ In 2003, there were demands, backed by the President Geidar Aliev, to indict Gorbachev for crimes against humanity.

66 The key daily newspapers – *Pravda*, *Izvestiya*, etc. – did also embrace the new situation but this took slightly longer.

67 *Krokodil* was a satirical magazine with an extremely interesting range of cartoons!

68 Translated as *New Times*.

69 Translated as *Moscow News*.

70 Translated as *Interlocutor*.

71 See, for a good example, the articles from *Ogonyok* 5, January 1987.

72 *Ogonyok*, 11, March 1989.

73 Ibid., 5, January 1989

74 Ibid., 9, February 1990.

75 See G. Popov in *Ogonyok*, 42, 1989.

76 See, for example, *Moscow News*, 9, 1989.

77 See, for example, *Krokodil*, 28, October 1988 p. 5; 13, May 1989, p. 5; 35, December 1989, p. 16.

78 *Moscow News*, 16, 1989, p. 10.

79 See, for example, no. 15, 1989, which included extracts from Khrushchev's Secret Speech, and also an article on the fall of Khrushchev in no. 20, 1989.

80 Ibid., 20, 1989, pp. 1–2.

81 Ibid., 30, 1989, p. 1.

82 Roi Medvedev, '....I sprava mogut byt' radikaly', in *Sobesednik*, 40, September 1989, p. 10.

83 See, for example, the reports in 23, 1988; no. 39, 1988; 41, 1988; nos 15, 16, 23, 29 and 52, 1989.

84 *Pravda*, 11 March 1990, p. 1.

85 Ibid.

86 Ibid.

87 BBC SWB SU/0702/B/1, 2 March 1990.

88 Speech on Soviet TV, 27 February 1990. Text in BBC SWB SU/0701/C/1.

89 Speech by Vadim Medvedev in CPD 12 March 1990, relayed on Soviet TV. Text in BBC SWB SU/0713/C/1, 15 March 1990.

90 It was at this point that Gorbachev revealed that he received a salary only as a member of the Politburo and refused to receive the salary of the Chairman of the Supreme Soviet. See BBC SWB SU/0720/C/1, 23 March 1990.

91 Interestingly, the case of Ronald Reagan was cited as an argument in favour of lifting the age limit. In this case maybe it wasn't such a surprise that the proposal was defeated.

92 Speech in CPD, 12 March 1990, relayed on Soviet TV. Text can be found in BBC SWB SU/0712/C/1.

93 Ibid.

94 Debate in CPD on 14 and 15 March 1990 in BBC SWB SU/0714/C/1.

95 The best account of the opposition to Gorbachev at this Congress can be found in Angus Roxburgh, *The Second Russian Revolution* (London: BBC Books, 1991), pp. 186–92.

96 Ibid., p. 189.

97 Ibid.

98 Ibid., p. 190.

99 Ibid., p. 191.

100 BBC SWB SU/0814/C1/1, 12 July 1990.

101 Ibid.

102 Interview with Hungarian TV, cited in BBC SWB SU/074/I, 1990.

103 Cited in BBC SWB SU/1124, 15 July 1991.

104 See Luke March, *Egor Ligachev: A Conservative Reformer in the Gorbachev Period*, Research Paper in Russian and East European Studies, 1997.

105 Soviet TV 8.30 a.m. 11 July 1990. Cited in BBC SWB SU/0821/C1, 20 July 1991.

106 Boris Gidaspov, press conference, cited in BBC SWB SU/0798/C1.

107 *Pravda*, 9 July 1990, p. 2.

108 Published in *Sovetskaya Rossiya*, 19 October 1990.

109 *Sovetskaya Rossiya*, 2 February 1991.

110 Interview cited in TASS, 1 July 1991.

111 TASS, 5 August 1991.

112 Press conference, Soviet TV, 14.30 GMT, 26 June 1990.

113 Speech by Yeltsin on 6 July 1990, in BBC SWB SU/0813/C1, 11 July 1990.

114 Yeltsin's press conference, 1 September 1990, relayed on Soviet TV.

115 Interview on Soviet TVm 15.50 GMT, 19 February 1991.

116 Yeltsin interview on Antenne 2 TV in Paris, 15 April 1991, cited in BBC SWB SU/1048/A1.

117 *Izvestiya*, 23 May 1991.

118 Press conference on Party Plenum, in BBC SWB SU/1057/C1, 27 April 1991.

119 Leon Aron, *Boris Yeltsin: A Revolutionary Life* (London: HarperCollins, 2000), pp. 435–6.

120 Cited in BBC SWB SU/0953/C3, 21 December 1990.

121 *Izvestiya*, 22 December 1990.

122 Interview on Soviet TV, 6 January 1991, cited in BBC SWB SU/0964/B/1.

123 BBC SWB SU/0964/B/1.

124 Speech at the Congress on 20 December 1990 relayed on Soviet TV. He went on to say that he had been 'wounded' by Shevardnadze's actions.

125 Ibid.

126 TASS, 5 February 1991.

127 BBC SWB SU/0990/B/1, 7 February 1991.

128 BBC SWB SU/1090/B/1, 5 June 1991.

129 BBC SWB SU/1122/B/1, 12 July 1991.

130 See, for example, the interview with Milovan Djilas 'Vozmutitel' snokoictviya', in *Ogonyok*, 9, February 1990, pp. 25–7; interview with Gail Sheehy in *Novoe Vremya*, 19, May 1991, pp. 14–15.

131 V. Khalipov, 'Sem' raz otmer" and B. Kurshvili, 'Da spaset nas prezidentstvo' in *Argumenti i fakti*, 9, 2–9 March 1990.

132 *Novoe Vremya*, 7, 1990, pp. 5–12.

133 *Sobesednik*, 10 March 1990.

134 *Argumenty i fakti* 1, 1991.

135 'Kuda idyut gonorari M S Gorbacheva?' *Argumenty i fakti*, 25, 23–29 June 1990.

136 *Sobesednik*, 42, October 1990; *Novoe Vremya*, 26, June 1991.

137 'Oktyabrskii vyibor prezidenta', *Ogonyok*, 47, November 1990, pp. 4–7.

138 *Krokodil*, 9, March 1990.

139 Ibid., 4, February 1991.

140 Ibid., p. 32, October 1990.

141 Ibid., September 1991.

142 *Argumenty i fakti*, 32, 1990, p. 5.

143 Soviet TV, 25 June 1991.

144 Ibid.

145 Ibid.

146 Interview with Yakovlev on 16 August 1991, relayed in BBC SWB SU/1154/B/1, 19 August 1991.

147 TASS, 19 August 1991.

148 BBC SWB SU/1156/C1/1, 21 August 1991.

149 Ibid.

150 Ibid.

151 Details can be found in *Putsch: The Diary* (New York: Mosaic Press, 1991).

152 Ibid.

153 BBC SWB SU/1158/C1/1, 23 August 1991.

154 Gorbachev's own defence of his actions during this time can be found in the chapter on Gorbachev and his own writings.

155 *Vesti*, Russian TV, 19.30 GMT, 22 August 1991.

156 RSFSR Supreme Soviet meeting, 23 August 1991. Relayed in BBC SWB SU/1160/C1/1, 26 August 1991.

157 *Moscow News* 45, 10–17 November 1991, p. 12.

158 'Vyigrannaya partiya', *Dialog*, 17, November 1991, pp. 39–44.

159 'Chelovek desyatiletiya', *Ogonyok*, 49, 1991, pp. 17–18.

160 Ibid., p. 18.

161 Ibid.

162 *Rossiiskaya gazeta*, 27 December 1991, p. 1.

163 *Nezavisimaya gazeta*, 27 December 1991, p. 1.

164 Ibid.

165 Ibid., p. 2.

166 *Megapolis-Express*, 1 January 1992, pp. 20–1.

167 Ibid., p. 20.

168 Ibid., p. 21.

5 Gorbachev remembered

1 See Archie Brown, *Seven Years That Changed the World* (Oxford: Oxford University Press, 2007), Chapter 10.

2 These observations came from a variety of sources: D. Healey, *The Time of My Life* (London: Michael Joseph, 1989); R. Reagan, *An American Life* (London: Hutchinson, 1990); G. Howe, *Conflict of Loyalty* (London: Macmillan, 1994); George P. Shultz, *Turmoil and Triumph* (New York: Charles Scribner's Sons, 1993); Margaret Thatcher, *The Downing Street Years* (London: HarperCollins, 1995); James A. Baker, *The Politics of Diplomacy* (New York: G.P. Putnam's Sons, 1995).

3 R. Reagan, *An American Life*, p. 707.

4 This would fit in with Reagan's overall thesis about how it was his hard-line stance that had bankrupted the Soviet economy and forced them to introduce changes.

5 The positive traits of Gorbachev must always be measured against the extent to which they were identified in order to bolster the reputation of the memoirist. Having a gifted opponent in negotiations obviously served to emphasize their own skills in this regard.

6 D. Healey, op. cit., p. 530. This might also explain Gorbachev's work with the Green Cross International after the collapse of the USSR.

7 Shultz, op. cit., p. 591.

8 Baker, op. cit., p. 171.

9 Perhaps this was a case where Gorbachev had a much better grasp of economic realities than his capitalist teachers!

10 John Major, *John Major: The Autobiography* (London: HarperCollins, 1999) p. 499–500.

11 Baker noted that he 'loved a metaphor' and often began with a long soliloquy.

12 G. Howe, *Conflict of Loyalty* (London: Macmillan, 1994), p. 359.

13 Baker, op. cit., p. 475.

14 Major, op. cit., p.499; Thatcher, op. cit., p.804.

15 Ibid., p. 562.

16 Healey, op. cit., p. 524.

17 Jack F. Matlock, *Autopsy on an Empire* (New York: Random House, 1995); Rodric Braithwaite, *Across the Moscow River* (New Haven, CT: Yale University Press, 2002).

18 Matlock, op. cit., pp. 50–1, 288–93.

19 Ibid., p. 152,

20 Ibid., pp.122–35.

21 Ibid., p. 661.

22 Ibid., p. 663.

23 Braithwaite, op. cit., p. 71.

24 Ibid., pp. 71–2.

25 Ibid., p. 71.

26 Ibid., pp. 54–5.

27 Ibid., p. 280.

28 Numerous memoir accounts have come out since the collapse of communism. A selection only is referred to here because of the confines of space, but key texts have been chosen as illustrations of the range of perspectives and views of Gorbachev that exist. In sum, they in many ways confirm Ligachev's title: *The Enigma of Gorbachev* (*zagadka gorbacheva*).

29 Raisa Gorbachev, *I Hope* (London: HarperCollins, 1991), p. 66.

30 Ibid., pp. 113–14.

31 Ibid., p. 191.

32 Ibid.

33 B. Yeltsin, *Against the Grain* (London: Jonathan Cape, 1990); *The View from the Kremlin* (London: HarperCollins, 1994); *Midnight Diaries* (New York: Public Affairs, 2000). Yeltsin's memoirs have generally taken the form of the publication of his journals alongside some commentary.

34 Yeltsin, op. cit. (1990), p. 58.

35 Ibid., pp. 113–26.

36 Ibid., p. 156.

37 Ibid., p. 204.

38 Yeltsin, op. cit. (1994), Chapter 4.

39 Yeltsin, op. cit. (2000), pp. 359–64.

40 Y. Ligachev, *Inside Gorbachev's Kremlin* (Boulder, CO: Westview Press, 1990).

41 Ibid., Chapter 2.

42 Ibid., p. 129.

43 Ibid., p. 130.

44 Ibid., p. 349.

45 Nikolai Ryzhkov, *Perestroika: istoriya predatel'stv* (Moscow: Novosti, 1992).

46 Ibid., pp. 46–9.

47 Nikolai Ryzhkov, *Desyat' let velikikh potryasenii* (Moscow: Assotsiatsiya 'Kniga. Prosveshchenie. Miloseride', 1995), p. 543.

48 E. Shevardnadze, *The Future Belongs to Freedom* (London: Sinclair-Stevenson, 1991).

49 Ibid., p xix.

50 Ibid., p. xix.

51 Ibid., pp. 188–92.

52 Boris Pankin, *The Last Hundred Days of the USSR* (London: Tauris, 1996).

53 Andrei Grachev, *The Inside Story of the Collapse of the Soviet Union* (Boulder, CO: Westview Press, 1995). See also his later biography, *Gorbachev* (Moskva: Vagrius, 2001).

54 P. Palazchenko, *My Years with Gorbachev and Shevardnadze* (Pennsylvania: Penn State University Press, 1997).

55 Valery Boldin, *Ten Years That Shook the World* (New York: Basic Books, 1994).

56 Pankin, op. cit., p. 271.

57 Ibid., p. 13.

58 Ibid., p. 25.

59 Ibid., p. 200.
60 Palazchenko. op. cit., p. 47.
61 Ibid., pp. 69–78.
62 Ibid., p. 49.
63 Ibid., p.162.
64 Ibid., p. 190.
65 Ibid., pp. 367–78.
66 Boldin, op. cit., pp. 22–3.
67 Ibid., pp. 59–97.
68 Ibid., pp. 79–93.
69 Ibid., pp. 76–8.
70 Ibid., p. 112.
71 Ibid., p. 234.
72 Ibid., pp. 168–74.
73 Ibid., pp. 256–66.
74 Ibid., pp. 200–1.
75 Ibid., p. 299.
76 A.A. Korobeinikov, *Gorbachev: drugoe litso* (Moskva: Respublika, 1996).
77 Ibid., p. 5.
78 Ibid., p. 196.
79 A.N. Yakovlev, *Predislovie, Obval, Posleslovie* (Moscow: Novosti, 1992). A later volume of memoirs was also published, *Gor'kaya chasha* (Yaroslavl', Verkhne-Volzshkoe knizhnoe izdatelstvo, 1994).
80 Yakovlev op. cit. (1992), pp. 127–8.
81 Ibid. See the concluding section for a detailed appraisal.
82 A. Chernyaev, *My 6 Years with Gorbachev* (Pennsylvania, PA: Penn State University Press, 2000).
83 Cited in Archie Brown, *The Gorbachev Factor* (Oxford: Oxford University Press, 1997), p. 98.
84 Ibid., p. 122.
85 Ibid., pp. 23–47. Although this obviously poses problems with regard to corroboration, the picture being built up from a variety of sources would seem to confirm this point.
86 Ibid., pp. 126–7.
87 Ibid., pp. 92–101.
88 Ibid., p. 201.
89 Ibid., p. 108.
90 Ibid., p. 232.
91 Ibid., p. 275.
92 Ibid., p. 277.
93 Anatoly Chernyaev, 'Gorbachev's Foreign Policy: The Concept', in Kiron K. Skinner (ed.), *Turning Points in Ending the Cold War* (Stanford, CA: Hoover Instituion Press, 2008), p. 140.
94 Georgii Shakhnazarov, *S vozhdyami i bez nikh* (With Leaders and Without Them) (Moscow: Vagrius, 2001). The first part of this volume, *Tsena svobodu* (The Price of Freedom), was published in 1993.
95 Ibid. (2001), p. 283.
96 Ibid., p. 285.
97 Ibid., p. 386.
98 Ibid., p. 309.
99 Ibid., pp. 357–9.
100 Ibid., p. 437.
101 Ibid., p. 488.

102 Ibid., pp. 488–9.

103 Ibid., p. 493.

104 Ibid., pp. 493–6.

105 Ibid., p. 498.

106 Ibid.

107 Ibid., p. 509.

108 Since 1992, the Public Opinion Foundation has conducted weekly nationwide representative polls of the urban and rural populations through the extensive network of its regional branches and partner organizations situated in almost all areas of Russia. The full details of all the polls on Gorbachev can be found at http://bd.english.fom.ru/cat/policy/rating/ross_politiki/gorbachev_m_s_

109 'Mikhail Gorbachev kak tvorets kontsa istorii', in *Kommersant*, 38, 2 March 2001, p. 9.

110 'Rabliezanstvo gorbacheva', in *Nezavisimaya gazeta*, 2 March 2001, p. 8.

111 *Kommersant*, op. cit., p. 9.

112 *Vox Populi* shown on NTV International, 2 March 2001.

113 Interfax News Agency, 2 March 2001.

114 *The Times*, 21 September 1999; Jonathan Steele, 'Revolutionary First Lady Dies of Leukaemia at 67,' *Guardian*, 21 September 1999, p. 2; Rupert Cornwell, 'Obituary: Raisa Gorbachev', *The Times*, 21 September 1999, p. 6.

115 Tolstaya, op. cit.

116 Ibid., p. 106.

117 Ibid., p. 108.

6 Gorbachev assessed

1 This chapter will explore a range of material mainly from the UK and the USA, although there will be some material included from French scholars too.

2 On both sides of the Atlantic, academics were called in as permanent advisers or as ad hoc advisers to committees. For instance, in the USA Richard Pipes served in the National Security Council under Ronald Reagan, and Zbigniew Brzezinski worked in the Chemical Warfare Commission after 1985, in the NSC Defense Department commission, and was also a member of the President's Foreign Intelligence Advisory Board.

3 The acrimony within the Sovietological community is almost legendary. It has long roots. The spat between E. H. Carr and Alexander Gerschenkron in the 1960s carried on into the 1970s and 1980s and engulfed, in particular, the Stalinist terror in the 1930s.

4 For an excellent history of totalitarianism, see Abbott Gleason, *Totalitarianism: The Inner History of the Cold War* (New York: Oxford University Press, 1995).

5 A good example of this are the exchanges between Robert Conquest, Robert Thurston, J. Arch Getty and the like in the pages of the *NYRB, TLS, Slavic Review* and elsewhere, during the 1990s and the early years of this century.

6 The debates within *Slavic Review* in 1985 and 1986 were an important moment in the development of this debate.

7 There are a number of different groups including the Yugoslav praxis movement, and the Budapest School (set up by the famous Hungarian Marxist Gyorgy Lukács). See, for example, Milovan Djilas, *The New Class* (New York: Praeger, 1957); Andreas Hegedus *et al.*, *The Humanization of Socialism* (London: Allison and Busby, 1976); Herbert Marcuse, *Soviet Marxism* (London: Routledge and Kegan Paul, 1958); M. Rakovski, *Towards an East European Marxism* (London: Allison and Busby, 1978).

8 For a retrospective on the origins, growth and demise of Sovietology as a discipline, see Michael Cox, *Rethinking the Soviet Collapse: Sovietology and the Death of Communism and the New Russia* (London: Pinter, 1998).

9 The 1970s spawned a barrage of literature drawn from the social sciences – sociology and modernization theory in particular – which sought to apply key concepts drawn from the Western experience to the Soviet case. See, for example, Chalmers Johnson, *Change in Communist Systems* (Stanford, CA: Stanford University Press, 1970); H. Gordon Skilling and Franklyn Griffiths (eds), *Interest Groups in Soviet Politics* (Princeton, NJ: Princeton University Press, 1971); Roger E. Kanet (ed.), *The Behavioral Revolution and Communist Studies: Behaviorally-Oriented Political Research on the Soviet Union and Eastern Europe* (New York: The Free Press, 1971); Jerry Hough, *The Soviet Union and Social Science Theory* (Cambridge, MA: Harvard University Press, 1977); Frederic J. Fleron, Jr., *Technology and the Communist Future* (New York: Praeger, 1977).

10 See above, but also Donald R. Kelley, *Soviet Politics in the Brezhnev Era* (New York: Praeger, 1980); Ronald J. Hill, *Soviet Politics, Political Science and Reform* (New York: M.E. Sharpe, 1980).

11 See above and also Susan Gross Solomon (ed.), *Pluralism in the Soviet Union: Essays in Honour of H. Gordon Skilling* (London: Macmillan, 1983).

12 Valerie Bunce and John Echols, 'Soviet Politics in the Brezhnev Era: "Pluralism" or "Corporatism"?' in Kelley, op. cit. (1980).

13 See David Lane, *Soviet Economy and Society* (New York: New York University Press, 1985); Christel Lane, *The Rites of Rulers* (Cambridge: Cambridge University Press, 1981).

14 An excellent summary of the growth and development of the post-totalitarian literature can be found in Ron Amann, 'Searching for an Appropriate Concept of Soviet Politics: The Politics of Hesitant Modernization', *British Journal of Political Science*, 16, 1986, pp. 475–94.

15 See, for example, Jerry Hough, 'Changes in Soviet Elite Composition', in Seweryn Bialer and Thane Gustafson (eds), *Russia at the Crossroads: The 26 Congress of the CPSU* (London: Allen and Unwin, 1982); A. Brown and M. Kaser (eds), *Soviet Policy for the 1980s* (London: Macmillan, 1982).

16 See A. Brown, 'Gorbachev: New Man in the Kremlin', *Problems of Communism*, May–June 1985, pp. 1–23.

17 Jerry Hough, 'Soviet Succession: Issues and Personalities', *Problems of Communism*, September–October 1982, pp. 20–40; 'Andropov's First Year', *Problems of Communism*, November–December 1983, pp. 49–64.

18 See, for example, B. Meissner, 'Transition in the Kremlin', *Problems of Communism*, January–February 1983, pp. 8–17.

19 Mikhail Heller, 'Gorbachev for Beginners', *Survey*, 1, vol. 29, 1985, p. 14.

20 Ibid., p. 16.

21 See, for example, Alec Nove in *The National Interest*, no. 8, summer 1987, pp. 13–18.

22 A number of contributors made this point. See, for example, Zhores Medvedev in *New Left Review*, no. 157, 1986; S. Bialer and J. Afferica, 'The Genesis of Gorbachev's World', *Foreign Affairs*, 3, vol. 64, 1986; P. Hauslohner, 'Gorbachev's Social Contract', *Soviet Economy*, 1, vol. 3, 1987; T. Draper, 'Soviet Reformers From Lenin to Gorbachev', in *A Present of Things Past* (New York: Hill and Wang, 1990); Peter Reddaway in *The National Interest*, op. cit.

23 Bialer and Afferica were strong advocates of this position.

24 See, for example, van Borcke, 'Gorbachev's *Perestroika*: Can the Soviet System be Reformed?', in S. Clark, *Gorbachev's Agenda: Changes in Soviet Domestic and Foreign Policy* (Boulder: Westview Press, 1989); Draper, op. cit.

25 Bialer and Afferica, op. cit., p. 616.

26 Reddaway, *The National Interest*, no. 8, summer 1987, p. 24.

27 Gail Lapidus, among others, made this point about the similarity in styles between Khrushchev and Gorbachev. See G. Lapidus, 'Gorbachev and Reform of the Soviet System', *Daedalus*, 2, vol. 16, spring 1987.

28 Archie Brown, in *The National Interest*, op. cit.

29 Sidney Ploss, 'A New Soviet Era?', *Foreign Policy*, 62, 1986, pp. 46–60.

30 See E. Hewett, 'Gorbachev's Economic Strategy: A Preliminary Assessment' and P. Hanson, 'Gorbachev's Economic Strategy', *Soviet Economy*, 4, vol. 1, 1985; E. Hewett, 'Gorbachev at Two Years: Perspectives on Economic Reform', G. Schroeder, 'Gorbachev: Radically Implementing Brezhnev's Reform', J. Hough, 'The Gorbachev Reform: A Maximal Case' and P. Hanson, 'The Shape of Gorbachev's Economic Reform', *Soviet Economy*, 4, vol. 2, 1986.

31 Conquest, in *The National Interest*, op. cit.

32 Julian Cooper, 'Construction ... Reconstruction ... Deconstruction' in C. Ward and C. Merridale (eds), *Perestroika: The Historical Perspective* (London: Edward Arnold, 1991). Robert Tucker, *Political Culture and Leadership in Soviet Russia* (Brighton: Wheatsheaf Books, 1987), p. 156.

33 Lapidus, op. cit., 1987.

34 Ibid., pp. 1–15.

35 Ibid., pp. 15–24.

36 The best things to read on Soviet political reform are: Archie Brown, 'Political Change in the Soviet Union', *World Policy Journal*, 3, vol. 16, 1989, pp. 469–501; S. White, 'Democratisation in the USSR', *Soviet Studies*, 1, vol. 42, January 1990, pp. 3–20; John Gooding, 'Gorbachev and Democracy', *Soviet Studies*, 2, vol. 42, April 1990, pp. 195–231. Writings on this were extensive. Aside from the above, see also: Alexander Dallin and Gail Lapidus (eds), *The Soviet System in Crisis* (Boulder: Westview Press, 1991); Basile Kerblay, *Gorbachev's Russia* (New York: Pantheon Books, 1989); Zbigniew Brzezinski, *The Grand Failure* (London: Macdonald, 1989); Sol Sanders, *Living Off the West: Gorbachev's Secret Agenda and Why It Will Fail* (London: Madison Books, 1990); Jerry Hough, *Russia and the West* (New York: Simon and Schuster, 1990, 2nd edn); Mary McAuley, 'Soviet Political Reform in a Comparative Context', *Harriman Institute Forum*, 10, vol. 2, October 1989; A. Brown, 'The Soviet Leadership and the Struggle for Political Reform', *Harriman Institute Forum*, 4, vol. 1, April 1988; Jeffrey Hahn, 'Power to the Soviets', *Problems of Communism*, January–February 1989; E. Hewett and V. Winston (eds), *Milestones in Glasnost and Perestroika: Politics and People* (Washington, DC: Brookings Institution, 1991); Susan L. Clark, op. cit.; Michel Tatu, 'The 19 Party Conference', *Problems of Communism*, May–August 1988; E. Teague and Dawn Mann, 'Gorbachev's Dual Role', *Problems of Communism*, January–February 1990; R. Hill and J. Dellenbrant, *Gorbachev and Perestroika: Towards a New Socialism?* (Aldershot: Edward Elgar, 1989); M. L. Sondhi, *Beyond Perestroika: Choices and Challenges Facing Gorbachev* (New Delhi: Abhiner Publications, 1989); G. Hosking, *The Awakening of the Soviet Union* (London: Heinemann, 1990); Richard Sakwa, *Soviet Politics* (London: Routledge, 1989); S. White, *Gorbachev in Power* (Cambridge: Cambridge University Press, 1990); Z. Gitelman, A. Pravda and S. White (eds), *Developments in Soviet Politics* (London: Macmillan, 1990); John M. Battle, 'Uskorenie, Glasnost' and Perestroika: The Pattern of Reform Under Gorbachev,' *Soviet Studies*, vol. 40, 3, July 1988, pp. 367–84; Joel C. Moses, 'Democratic Reform in the Gorbachev Era: Dimensions of Reform in the Soviet Union 1986–89', *Russian Review*, vol. 48, 1989, pp. 235–69; Thomas Remington, 'A Socialist Pluralism of Opinions: Glasnost' and Policy-Making under Gorbachev', in ibid.; Federal Institute for Soviet and International Studies, *The Soviet Union 1987–89: Perestroika in Crisis* (London: Longman, 1990); G. Urban, *Can the Revolution be Remade?* (London: Institute for European Defence and Strategic Studies, 1988); E.P. Hoffmann, 'Technology and Political Change in Gorbachev's and Brezhnev's Ideologies', *Journal of Soviet and East European Studies*, 3–4, vol. 5, 1988, pp. 265–86; B. Jensen and B. Weil, 'Utopia and Development in the Building of Socialism from Lenin to Gorbachev', *Journal of Soviet and East European Studies*, vol. 5, 3–4, 1988, pp. 179–91; H. Dahm, 'What Restoring Leninism Means', *Studies in Soviet Thought*, vol. 39, 1990, pp. 55–76; P. Juviler and H. Kimura (eds), *Gorbachev's Reforms: US and Japanese Assessments* (New York: Aldine de Gruyter, 1988); A. Yanov, '*Perestroika* and its American Critics',

Slavic Review, winter 1988; W. Joyce, H. Ticktin and S. White (eds), *Gorbachev and Gorbachevism* (London: Frank Cass, 1988); F. Feher and A. Arato, *Gorbachev: The Debate* (Oxford: Polity, 1989); Ron Amann, 'Soviet Politics in the Gorbachev Era: The End of Hesitant Modernization', *British Journal of Political Science*, vol. 20, 3, July 1990, pp. 289–310; D. Bahry and B. Silver, 'Public Perceptions and the Dilemmas of Party Reform in the USSR', *Comparative Political Studies*, vol. 23, 2, July 1990, pp. 171–209; R.D. Grey, L.A. Jennisch and A.S. Tyler, 'Soviet Public Opinion and the Gorbachev Reforms', *Slavic Review*, vol. 49, 2, Summer 1990, pp. 261–71; L. Lerner and Donald Treadgold (eds), *Gorbachev and the Soviet Future* (Boulder, CO: Westview Press, 1988); C. Smart, 'Gorbachev's Lenin: The Myth in Service to *Perestroika*', *Studies in Comparative Communism*, vol. 23, 1, Spring 1990, pp. 5–21; Ottorino Cappelli, 'Comparative Communism's Fall: The First Phase: The Intelligentsia Revolution of 1989–90', *Harriman Institute Forum*, 6, June 1990, pp. 1–8.

37 See Amann, op. cit.

38 S. Bialer, 'Gorbachev's Move', *Foreign Policy*, vol. 68, Fall 1987, p. 62.

39 Amann, op. cit.

40 Ibid., pp. 289–306.

41 Van Borcke, op. cit.

42 See, for example, Battle, op. cit.; Remington, op. cit.

43 Bialer, op. cit. (1987), p. 64.

44 See *New York Times*, 15 November 1988.

45 Gooding, op. cit.

46 Ibid., p. 196.

47 Ibid.

48 A great selection of 'mid-term' appraisals of Gorbachev can be found in a symposium in *Soviet Union/Union Soviétique* 2–3, vol. 16. The pieces were composed and written in the summer of 1990, but did not appear until early 1991. See the contributions of T. von Laue, 'Gorbachev in Historic Perspective', pp. 163–72; J. Keep, 'Gorbachev and the Rediscovery of Russia's Past', pp. 173–82; J. Curry, 'Gorbachev's Revolution: Another Look at the Potemkin Village of Communism', pp. 183–92; R.E. Kanet, 'Mikhail Gorbachev and the End of the Cold War', pp. 193–200; J.R. Millar, 'The Conversion of the Communists: Gorbachev's Legacy', pp. 201–10; D.W. Treadgold, 'Mikhail Sergeevich and the World of 1990', pp. 211–20; A. Meyer, 'Leadership: An Appraisal of M.S. Gorbachev', pp. 221–32; R.A. Wade, 'The Russian Reform Tradition, Gorbachev and the Vision of the Soviet Future', pp. 233–44; P. Juviler, 'Presidential Power and Presidential Character', pp. 245–56. See also the article 'To the Stalin Mausoleum', written by Martin Malia but published under the pseudonym 'Z' in *Daedalus*, January 1990. V. Shlapentokh, 'Alexander II and Mikhail Gorbachev: Two Reformers in Historical Perspective', in *Russian History/Histoire Russe*, vol. 17, 4, Winter 1990, pp. 395–408. A. Braun and R.B. Day, 'Gorbachevian Contradictions', in *Problems of Communism*, May–June 1990, pp. 36–50. The pessimist school is best represented by those like Conquest, Braun and Day, Malia, Zemtsov and Farrar, Sanders.

49 Ed Hewett and V. Winston (eds), *Milestones in Glasnost and Perestroika: Politics and People* (Washington: Brookings Institution, 1991), p. 128.

50 A good example of this type of thinking can be found in Martha Brill Olcott's article on Gorbachev's Nationalities policy, 'The Soviet (Dis)Union', *Foreign Policy*, 82, Spring 1991, pp. 135–6. See also D. Spring, *The Impact of Gorbachev* (London: Pinter, 1991); H. D. Balzer, *5 Years That Shook the World* (Boulder, CO: Westview Press, 1991).

51 The positive or optimistic appraisals can be found in scholars like Brown, van Borcke, Hough, Treadgold and J. W. Parker, *The Kremlin in Transition* (Boston: Unwin Hyman, 1991).

52 Hough set out his view of Gorbachev's strategic and tactical brilliance in a number of articles and works: op. cit. (1985) and (1990). See also 'Gorbachev's Politics', *Foreign Affairs*, 68, 1990.

53 See, for example, G.W. Breslauer, 'Evaluating Gorbachev as Leader', 4, vol. 5, October–December 1989; A. Brown, 'Gorbachev's Leadership: Another View', 2, vol. 6, April–June 1990; J.F. Hough, 'Understanding Gorbachev: The Importance of Politics', 2, vol. 7, April–June 1991; A. Migranyan, 'Gorbachev's Leadership: A Soviet View', 2, vol. 6, April–June 1990; P. Reddaway, 'The Quality of Gorbachev's Leadership', 2, vol. 6, April–June 1990; G.W. Breslauer, 'Understanding Gorbachev: Diverse Perspectives', 2, vol. 7, April–June 1991.

54 See *Soviet Union/Union Soviétique*, 2–3, vol. 16, 1989, p. 163.

55 Breslauer, op. cit. (1991), p. 118.

56 Ibid.

57 Reddaway, op. cit. (1990).

58 Brown, op. cit. (1990).

59 Ibid.

60 Hough, op. cit. (1991).

61 Ibid.

62 Breslauer, op. cit. (1991).

63 Wade, op. cit. (1991).

64 Juviler, op. cit. (1991).

65 Von Laue, op. cit. (1991).

66 Kanet, op. cit. (1991).

67 Wade, op. cit. (1991).

68 Millar, op. cit. (1991).

69 Curry, op. cit. (1991), p. 183.

70 Treadgold, op. cit. (1991), p. 219.

71 A.G. Meyer, op. cit. (1991), pp. 221–32.

72 Ibid., pp. 230–1.

73 Sakwa, op. cit.

74 Hough, *Russia and the West*, op. cit.

75 See E. Gellner, '*Perestroika* Observed', *Government and Opposition*, 7, vol. 25 (1990).

76 Spring, op. cit. (1991).

77 R. Kaiser, 'Gorbachev: Triumph and Failure', *Foreign Affairs*, vol. 70, 2 (1991), p. 160.

78 Ibid., p. 174.

79 Ibid., pp. 160–1.

80 Malia, op. cit. *Daedalus* (1990).

81 A. Aslund, *Gorbachev's Struggle for Economic Reform* (London: Pinter, 1991), pp. 1–2.

82 Allen Lynch, 'Does Gorbachev Matter Anymore?' *Foreign Affairs*, 3, vol. 69, Winter 1990.

83 A. Brown, *The Gorbachev Factor* (Oxford: Oxford University Press, 1996), p. 317.

84 J. Bushnell, 'Making History out of Current Events: the Gorbachev Era', *Slavic Review*, 51, 3, Fall 1992, p. 557.

85 The main works include the following, Brown, op. cit.; G. Breslauer, *Gorbachev and Yeltsin as Leaders* (Cambridge: Cambridge University Press, 2002); A. Brown and L. Shevtsova (eds), *Gorbachev, Yeltsin and Putin: Political Leadership in Russia's Transition* (Washington, DC: Carnegie Endowment for International Peace, 2001); G. Gill and R. Markwick, *Russia's Still-born Democracy? From Gorbachev to Yeltsin* (Oxford: Oxford University Press, 2000); S. Sternthal, *Gorbachev's Reforms: De-Stalinization Through De-Militarization* (Westport, CT: Praeger, 1997); R. Garthoff, *The Great Transition* (Washington, DC: Brookings Institute, 1994); D.R. Kelley and S. Davis (eds), *The Sons of Sergei: Khrushchev and Gorbachev as Reformers* (Westport, CT: Praeger, 1992); W. Taubman, S. Khrushchev and A. Gleason (eds), *Nikita Khrushchev* (New Haven, CT: Yale University Press, 2000); S. White, *Gorbachev and After* (Cambridge: Cambridge University Press, 1991); M. McCauley, *Gorbachev* (London: Longman, 1998); D. Volkogonov, *Autopsy of an Empire: The 7 Leaders Who Built the Soviet Regime* (New York: Free

Press, 1998); A. Aslund, *How Russia Became a Market Economy* (Washington, DC: Brookings Institution, 1995); V. Mau and I. Starodubrovskaya, *The Challenge of Revolution* (Oxford: Oxford University Press, 2001); V. Tismaneanu, *The Revolutions of 1989* (London: Routledge, 1999); R. Walker, *6 Years That Shook the World* (Manchester: Manchester University Press, 1993); D. Remnick, *Lenin's Tomb* (London: Penguin, 1994); J. Hough, *Democratization and Revolution in the USSR* (Washington, DC: Brookings Institution, 1997); P. Hanson, *The Rise and Fall of the Soviet Economy* (London: Pearson, 2003); M. Cox (ed.), *Rethinking the Soviet Collapse* (London: Pinter, 1998); J. Steele, *Eternal Russia* (London: Faber and Faber, 1994); M. Goldman, *What Went Wrong with Perestroika* (New York: Norton, 1991); M. McFaul, *Russia's Unfinished Revolution: Political Change from Gorbachev to Putin* (Ithaca and London: Cornell University Press, 2001); S. White, R. di Leo and O. Cappelli, *The Soviet Transition from Gorbachev to Yeltsin* (London: Frank Cass, 1993); T. von Laue, *Why Lenin? Why Stalin? Why Gorbachev?* (London: Longman, 3rd edn, 1992); G. Hahn, *Russia's Revolution from Above* (London: New Brunswick, 2002); A. de Luca, *Politics, Diplomacy and the Media: Gorbachev's Legacy in the West* (Westport, CT: Praeger, 1998); W. Suraska, *How The Soviet Union Disappeared* (Durham, NC: Duke University Press, 1998); S. Kotkin, *Armageddon Averted: The Soviet Collapse, 1970–2000* (Oxford: Oxford University Press, 2001); R. Strayer, *Why Did the Soviet Union Collapse?* (New York: M.E. Sharpe, 1998); M. Galeotti, *Gorbachev and His Revolution* (London: Macmillan, 1997); R.G. Suny, *The Soviet Experiment* (New York: Oxford University Press, 1998); M. Malia, *The Soviet Tragedy* (New York: Free Press, 1994); C. Young, 'The Strategy of Political Liberalization: A Comparative View of Gorbachev's Reforms', *World Politics* vol. 45, 1, 1992; R. Hellie, 'An Historian's Formulation of Gorbachev's Real Problems', in *Russian History*, 1, vol. 16, 1989; J. Gooding, 'Perestroika and the Russian Revolution of 1991', *Slavonic and East European Review*, vol. 71, 2, 1993, pp. 234–56; S. White, 'Communists and their Party in the Late Soviet Period', *Slavonic and East European Review*, vol. 72, 4, 1994, pp. 544–63; S. White, 'The Failure of CPSU Democratization', *Slavonic and East European Review*, 4, vol. 75, 1997, pp. 681–97; M. McCauley, 'The Gorbachev Phenomenon', *Slavonic and East European Review*, 2, vol. 76, 1998, pp. 308–14; H. Adomeit, 'Gorbachev, German Unification and the Collapse of Empire', *Post-Soviet Affairs*, vol. 10, 3, July–September 1994, pp. 197–230; D. Shumaker, 'Understanding Gorbachev's Foreign Policy', *Communist and Post-Communist Studies*, 3, vol. 27, 1994; R. Judson Mitchell and R.S. Arrington, 'Gorbachev, Ideology and the Fate of Soviet Communism', *Communist and Post-Communist Studies*, vol. 33, 4, 2000, pp. 457–74; 'Mikhail S. Gorbachev: A Scholarly Symposium on His Years in Power', *The Soviet and Post-Soviet Review*, vol. 19, 1–3, 1992; G. Lundestad, 'Imperial Overstretch: Mikhail Gorbachev and the End of the Cold War', *Cold War History*, vol. 1, 1, 2000, pp. 1–20; V. Zubok, 'Gorbachev and the End of the Cold War: Perspectives on History and Personality', *Cold War History*, vol. 2, 2, 2002, pp. 61–100; H. J. Kusters, 'The Kohl-Gorbachev Meetings in Moscow and the Caucasus, 1990', *Cold War History*, vol. 2, 2, 2002, pp. 195–235; J. G. Stein, 'Political Learning By Doing: Gorbachev as Uncommitted Thinker and Motivated Learner', *International Organization*, vol. 48, 2, 1994, pp. 155–83; James T. McHugh, 'Last of the Enlightened Despots: A Comparison of President Mikhail Gorbachev and Emperor Joseph II', *Social Science Journal*, vol. 32, Issue 1, 1995, pp. 69–85; R. Strayer, 'Decolonization, Democratization and Communist Reform: The Soviet Collapse in Comparative Perspective', *Journal of World History*, vol. 12, 2, 2001, pp. 375–406; R. Pipes, 'Misinterpreting the Cold War', *Foreign Affairs*, vol. 74, 1, January–February 1995, pp. 154–60; D. Rowley, 'Interpretations of the End of the Soviet Union: Three Paradigms', *Kritika*, vol. 2, 2, 2001, pp. 395–426; special issue: 'The Collapse of the Soviet Union', *Journal of Cold War Studies*, vol. 5, 1, 2003; vol. 5, 4, 2003; and vol. 6. 1, 2004; J. F. Matlock Jr, 'Gorbachev: Lingering Mysteries', *NYRB*, 19 December 1996; T. Draper, 'Who Killed Soviet Communism?', *NYRB*, 11 June 1992; W. J. Tompson, 'Khrushchev and Gorbachev as Reformers', *British Jour-*

nal of Political Science, vol. 23, 1, 1993, pp. 77–105; J. Gooding, 'Perestroika As Revolution from Within', *Russian Review*, vol. 51, 1992, pp. 36–57; J. Surovell, 'Gorbachev's Last Year. Leftist or Rightist?', *Europe-Asia Studies*, vol. 46, 3, 1994, pp. 465–87; A. Shub, 'The Fourth Russian Revolution: Historical Perspectives', *Problems of Communism*, November–December 1991, pp. 20–6; S. N. Kalyvas, 'The Decay and Breakdown of Communist One-Party Systems', *Annual Review of Political Science*, vol. 2, 1999, pp. 323–43; R. Collins, 'Predictions in Macrosociology: The Case of the Soviet Collapse', *American Journal of Sociology*, vol. 100, 6, 1995, pp. 1552–93; special issue: 'Was the Soviet System Reformable?' *Slavic Review*, vol. 63, 4, 2004.

86 1989 is generally deployed by those who assign primary significance to the fall of the Berlin Wall and the end of division of Europe. 1990 relates to the agreements between Bush and Gorbachev at Malta. 1991 is obviously the demise of the communist system.

87 The most obvious example is Michael Cox (ed.), *Rethinking the Soviet Collapse* (London: Pinter 1998). See also Walter Laqueur, *The Dream That Failed* (Oxford: Oxford University Press, 1994).

88 Volkogonov, op. cit., p. 432.

89 A good example of the *longue durée* of reform in Russian history is T. Taranovski and P. McInerny (eds), *Reform in Modern Russian History: Progress or Cycle?* (New York: Cambridge University Press, 1995). See also R.V. Daniels, *The End of the Communist Revolution* (London: Routledge, 1993).

90 These frameworks are generalized types and do not conform exactly to the views of particular theorists.

91 K. Dawisha, *Slavic Review*, op. cit. (2004), pp. 513–26.

92 The best and most eloquent example of this viewpoint is Archie Brown, *Seven Years That Changed the World* (Oxford: Oxford University Press, 2007).

93 This is the story of a boy who learns magic. He goes to the castle and asks the sorcerer to help his village get food. The boy becomes the sorcerer's apprentice and the sorcerer teaches the boy magic. One day the apprentice tries to use magic to make the pail and brush fetch water. But the apprentice knows only part of the magic and does not know how to stop the brush. The castle fills with water. The sorcerer returns and puts it right and teaches the apprentice more magic and then leaves the castle, as a toad. The boy is now the sorcerer and he can give lots of food to the villagers.

94 As with any list, things could be added or taken away according to the taste or predilection of the scholar. These have been chosen because they seem to represent the main outcomes. Archie Brown, for instance, highlights 10 major achievements of Gorbachev and two strategic failures. See Brown, op. cit. (2007), pp. 328–30.

95 These outcomes are generally accepted by most scholars, and are used here irrespective of whether we think they are a 'good' thing or a 'bad' thing. Obviously for some the collapse of the USSR was a moment for celebration a moment of liberation. For others, it was an unmitigated disaster, and a catastrophe.

96 See Garthoff, op. cit., Zubok, op. cit. and Brown, op. cit. (1996) and (2007). See also the selection of pieces in Kiron K. Skinner (ed.), *Turning Points in Ending the Cold War* (Stanford, CA: Hoover Institution Press, 2008), especially chapters by Holloway, Chernyaev, Zubok.

97 Ibid.

98 Garthoff, op. cit., p. 754.

99 Ibid., p. 775.

100 James K. Galbraith, 'Gorbachev and History: An Interpretation', in V. Tolstykh (ed.), *A Millennium Salute to Mikhail Gorbachev on his Seventieth Birthday* (Moscow: R. Valent, 2001), pp. 167–74.

101 Zubok, op. cit.

102 Ibid., pp. 69–76.

103 See Malia, op. cit. (1994) and Pipes, op. cit. (1995). In general, within the 'realist' camp of International Relations scholars, the emphasis is very much upon material conditions, power, resources and prevailing military and economic conditions in bringing about change, rather than ideas, individuals and the like.

104 Pipes, op. cit., pp. 154–9.

105 Scholars like Suraska, Malia and McFaul all tend to see Gorbachev's political reforms as limited and functional to his wider goals.

106 See, for example, Gooding, op. cit. (1993); McFaul, op. cit.

107 Hough, op. cit. (1997).

108 See Suraska, op. cit.

109 Malia, op. cit.; Gill and Markwick, op. cit.

110 See, for example, Walker, op. cit. (1993); Draper, op. cit.

111 Hough, op. cit. (1997), especially pp. 140–74 and 490–525.

112 Archie Brown is the scholar who has most consistently outlined this interpretation. See also W.J. Tompson, 'Kruschev and Gorbachev as Reformers', *British Journal of Political Science*, vol. 23, 1, 1993; Hough was also positive on the whole, although qualified slightly more than Brown.

113 Brown, op. cit. (2007), pp. 298–304.

114 Many people can be cited. See, for example, Aslund, op. cit. who, although on the whole quite sceptical and critical, still sees the dissolution of the Soviet Empire in Eastern Europe as one of Gorbachev's main achievements.

115 Hanson, op. cit. has provided an excellent overview of the Gorbachev period and after.

116 Cohen, op. cit. *Slavic Review* (2004). Of course, the question of whether any of these things are in themselves 'good' things is of course a entirely different question!

117 The debate in *Slavic Review* (2004) is the best source for examining this question.

118 These ideas are derived from a variety of works. See, for example, Balzer, op. cit; Kotkin, op. cit.; Hanson, op. cit.; Galeotti, op. cit.; Hough, op. cit.; Goldman, op. cit.; Aslund, op. cit.; Steele, op. cit.

119 Hanson, op. cit., p. 177.

120 See, for example, D.R. Kelley and S. Davis (eds), *The Sons of Sergei: Krushchev and Gorbachev as Reformers* (Westport: Praeger, 1992).

121 See, for example, Joel C. Moses, 'The Legacy of Mikhail S. Gorbachev', *Soviet and Post-Soviet Review*, vol. 19, 1–3, 1992, pp. 253–63.

122 Hough, op. cit., pp. 371–9.

123 The views of Hedrik Smith, *The New Russians* (New York: Random House, 1990), are relevant in this regard. Ernest Gellner has written extensively on the nature of the challenge posed by late twentieth-century nationalism. See, for example, E. Gellner, *Encounters with Nationalism* (Oxford: Oxford University Press, 1994).

124 See Brown, op. cit., Chapter 8.

125 Suraska, op. cit.

126 Interestingly Kramer posits that if Viktor Grishin an archetypal 'muddler through' had been elected in 1985 instead of Gorbachev, then the USSR would almost certainly have lasted a lot longer, and might still be around now. See M. Kramer, 'The Reform of the Soviet System and the Demise of the Soviet State', *Slavic Review*, vol. 63, 3, 2004, p. 511.

127 Ibid.

128 J. Gooding, *Socialism in Russia* (Basingstoke: Palgrave, 2002); and also op. cit. (1992).

129 D. Volkogonov, *Autopsy of an Empire: The 7 Leaders Who Built the Soviet Regime* (New York: Free Press, 1998).

130 Brown, op. cit. (1996).

131 Ibid. See also A. Brown, *Seven Years That Changed the World* (Oxford: Oxford University Press, 2007),

132 See, for example, A. de Luca, *Politics, Diplomacy and the Media: Gorbachev's Legacy in the West* (Westport: Praeger, 1998); Hough, op. cit.; Malia, op. cit.; Volkogonov, op. cit.

133 See, for example, McCauley, op. cit; Gooding, op. cit. (2004); Von Laue, op. cit.; M. Galeotti, *Gorbachev and his Revolution* (London: Macmillan, 1997); Gill and Markwick, op. cit.

134 Brown, op. cit. (1996).

135 This point was made to Gorbachev early on in his tenure by Aleksandr Yakovlev. Brown notes that Gorbachev believed it was premature. See Brown. op. cit. (1996), p. 105 and n. 67. Presumably Machiavelli (it is best to do something unpopular quickly!) would have agreed! See also Cohen. op. cit. (2004).

136 There has not been universal agreement on this issue, though. Malia argues that Gorbachev critically undermined the pillars of communism, but did not finish them off, and this led to the August 1991 coup.

137 Aslund, op. cit. (1995), p. 36.

138 Goldman. op. cit., p. 236.

139 V. Bunce, 'Domestic Reform and International Change: The Gorbachev Reforms in Historical Perspective', *International Organization*, vol. 47, 1, winter 1993, p. 206.

140 See, for example, Hanson, op. cit. (2003); Moses, op. cit.

141 Many contributors note these paradoxes. See, for example, Suraska, op. cit.; McCauley, op. cit.; Moses, op. cit.; Steele, op. cit.; J. Thompson, *A Vision Unfulfilled* (Lexington, MA: D.C. Heath, 1996); Volkogonov, op. cit.; Walker, op. cit.

142 Von Laue, op. cit.

143 Smith, op. cit., p. 678.

144 Ibid., p. 662.

145 Moses, op. cit.

146 James T. McHugh, 'Last of the Enlightened Despots: A Comparison of President Mikhail Gorbachev and Emperor Joseph II', *Social Science Journal*, vol. 32, 1, 1995, pp. 69–85.

147 Ibid.

148 Brown, op. cit. (1996), p. 317.

149 Volkogonov, op. cit.

150 See, for example, Tompson, op. cit.; Kelley and Davis (eds), op. cit.; Taubman *et al.* (eds), op. cit.

151 G. Shakhnazarov, 'Khrushchev and Gorbachev: A Russian View', pp. 301–20; P. Reddaway, 'Khrushchev and Gorbachev: An American View', pp. 321–33. Both in Taubman *et al.*, op. cit.

152 Ibid., p. 303.

153 Ibid., pp. 324–32.

154 See, for example, Brown and Shevtsova (2001), op. cit.; Breslauer, op. cit. (2002); McFaul, op. cit. (2001).

155 Michael Cox, 'Whatever Happened to the USSR? Critical Reflections on Soviet Studies', in M. Cox (ed.), *Rethinking the Soviet Collapse* (London: Pinter, 1998), p. 27.

156 Peter Rutland identified seven arguments put forward to explain the failures of Sovietology: political bias; methodological feebleness; lack of specialist language/historical knowledge; hurdles to research inside the USSR; estrangement of émigré scholars from mainstream community; academics seduced into becoming media pundits; excessive dependence on government funding. In P. Rutland, 'Sovietology: Who Got it Right and Who Got it Wrong, and Why?' in ibid., p. 37.

157 See the introduction to the Cox volume, ibid., pp. 1–11; the chapter by Rutland and also the chapters by McNeill and Ticktin.

158 Rutland, op. cit., pp. 39–48.

159 Before anyone jumps to any conclusions, I count myself in this analysis, being both a product of traditional Soviet studies training, and also inexorably, depressingly producing students with similar mind-sets and assumptions!

160 See Rutland, op. cit., p. 33.

7 Gorbachev remembers

1 Preamble to interview with Gorbachev by Yuriy Shchekochikin in *Literaturnaya Gazeta*, 4 December 1991.

2 M. Gorbachev, *The August Coup* (New York: HarperCollins, 1991), p. 13.

3 TV interview with Gorbachev, transcribed in BBC SWB SU/1182/B/2, 20 September 1991.

4 Gorbachev, *The August Coup*, pp. 17–29.

5 Ibid., p. 32.

6 TV speech by Gorbachev at the CSCE conference in Moscow, 10 September 1991, reported in BBC SWB SU/1174/C1/2, 11 September 1991.

7 Ibid.

8 TV interview of Gorbachev with Yegor Yakovlev, the head of the All-Union State Television and Broadcasting Company on 12 October 1991. Transcribed in BBC SWB SU/1203/B/3, 15 October 1991.

9 TV interview on 8 December 1991. Transcribed in BBC SWB SU/1252/B/2, 11 December 1991.

10 Interview in *Literaturnaya gazeta*, 4 December 1991.

11 CBS interview with Gorbachev on Russian TV, 22 December 1991. Transcribed in BBC SWB SU/1263/B/3, 24 December 1991.

12 Interview in *La Stampa*, 28 December 1991. English language version in the *Guardian*, 28 December 1991.

13 Ibid.

14 Gorbachev's last address to the nation on Soviet TV, 25 December 1991. Transcribed in BBC SWB SU/1264/C/1, 28 December 1991.

15 Interview in *Literaturnaya gazeta*, op. cit.

16 Interview in *Moskovskie Novosti* no. 44, 3 November 1991.

17 Interview with Gorbachev on Soviet TV, 12 December 1991. Transcribed in BBC SWB SU/1255/B/2, 14 December 1991.

18 Interview with CNN, 25 December 1991.

19 To find out more about its current and past activities, its ethos, its publications, etc., check out the website at http://www.gorby.ru.

20 *Pravda*, 21 February 1992.

21 *Kommersant-Daily*, 2 March 1995.

22 The details can be found at: http://www.frankfoundationcai.org/?id=5492 (accessed on 19 June 2007).

23 Interview with Yeltsin in *Komsomolskaya Pravda*, 27 May 1992.

24 Interview with Gorbachev in *Komsomolskaya Pravda*, 29 May 1992.

25 Ibid.

26 Interview with Gorbachev, 'My annus horribiliski', *Guardian*, 24 December 1992, p. 19.

27 Ibid.

28 See a recent interview (2006), which can be viewed at http://www.youtube.com/watch?v=efWS8YHk8X8

29 Ibid.

30 To view this advert, go to http://www.wellesley.edu/Russian/video/gorbypizza.mov. Ironically, Gorbachev said that he was not keen on pizza!

31 News archives of the Gorbachev Foundation accessed at http://www.gorby.ru/en/rubrs.asp?art_id=23541&rubr_id=307&page=1 (19 June 2007).

32 Accessed at http://news.bbc.co.uk/1/hi/world/europe/6584785.stm (19 June 2007).

33 Gorbachev's main publications include.

- *Dekabr' 91. Moya pozitsiya (*Moscow: Novosti, 1992)
- *Gody trudnykh reshenii* (Moscow: Alfa-print, 1993)
- *Zhizn'i reformy: V2kh knigakh* (Moscow: Novosti, 1995)
- *The State of the World: Revisioning Global Priorities* (San Francisco: Harper, 1995)
- *The Search for a New Beginning: Developing a New Civilization* (San Francisco: Harper, 1995)
- *Memoirs* (NewYork: Doubleday, 1996; London: Bantam Books, 1997)
- *Kak eto bylo* (Moscow: Vagrius, 1999)
- *On My Country and the World* (New York: Columbia University Press, 2000)
- *Conversations with Gorbachev: On Perestroika, the Prague Spring and the Crossroads of Socialism* (New York: Columbia University Press, 2002)
- M.S. Gorbachev and D. Ikeda, *Moral Lessons of the Twentieth Century* (London: I.B. Tauris, 2005)
- *Ponyat' perestroyku..pochemu eto vazhno seychas* (Moscow: Al'pina Biznes Buks, 2006)

For a full, up-to-date rundown on his publications, go to the Gorbachev Foundation.

34 Mikhail Gorbachev and Zdenelk Mlynar, *Conversations with Gorbachev: On Perestroika, the Prague Spring and the Crossroads of Socialism* (New York: Columbia University Press, 2002). Translated by George Shriver.

35 Published by I.B. Tauris. The Gorbachev Foundation has also begun to publish collections of documents from the archives of the Gorbachev Foundation, designed to tell the 'real' story of *perestroika* and to defend Gorbachev's record. Interestingly one of the first volumes was about the nationalities issue and the collapse of the USSR, widely seen as one of Gorbachev's 'failures'. See *The Union Could Have Been Preserved* (Moscow: AST, 2007).

36 *Ponyat' perestroyku..pochemu eto vazhno seychas* (Moscow: Al'pina Biznes Buks, 2006).

37 http://www.cnn.com/WORLD/9712/23/gorby.pizza/ (accessed on 15 May 2003).

38 Ibid.

39 There is an interesting and rather unexplained mystery surrounding this advert. In the back of the car, Gorbachev is pictured sitting with his bag open. There is a book or magazine open which has the text 'Litvinenko's Murder — They Wanted to Give Up a Suspect for $7,000.' Litvinenko was the ex-Russian secret service agent murdered in the UK under very suspicious circumstances. No explanation has yet been forthcoming.

40 Gorbachev also paid tribute to the generosity of Ted Turner. See the interview between Mikhail Gorbachev and Ulysse Gosset, which can be found in *International Herald Tribune* (*IHT*) (Europe), 9 November 2007.

41 Gorbachev (1996), op. cit., p. 876.

42 M. Gorbachev, *Zhizn' i reformy* (Moscow: Novosti, 1995), vol. 1, pp. 11–12.

43 Ibid., pp. 33–4.

44 Interview with Quentin Peel, *Financial Times*, 17 April 2006.

45 Gorbachev (1995), *Zhizn'*, op. cit., pp. 53–8.

46 *FT* interview, op. cit.

47 Gorbachev (1995), *Zhizn'*, op. cit., vol. 1, p. 38.

48 Gorbachev (1995), *Zhizn'*, op. cit., vol. 1, p. 34.

49 Gorbachev and Mlynar, op. cit., p. 14.

50 Things did not always go swimmingly for Gorbachev. He relates the story of how his workmates played a prank on him, tricking him into drinking a large quantity of alcohol, which put him off drinking. See Gorbachev (1995), *Zhizn'*, op. cit., pp. 54–5.

51 Ibid., p. 77.

52 Ibid., p. 66.

53 Ibid., p. 65.

54 Ibid., p. 66.

55 Gorbachev's book published in 2002, *On My Country and the World*, carried the same title as one of Sakharov's dissident texts from the 1970s.

56 Gorbachev (1995), *Zhizn'*, op. cit., vol. 1, pp. 73–6.

57 'Mikhail Gorbachev: Looking Back on *perestroika*', *Harvard University Gazette*, 14 November 2002.

58 Gorbachev and Mlynar, op. cit., p. 47.

59 Ibid., p. 47.

60 Gorbachev (1995), *Zhizn'*, op. cit., p. 135.

61 'My annus horribiliski', op. cit., 1992, p. 19.

62 Ibid., p. 97.

63 Ibid., p. 220.

64 Gorbachev and Mlynar, op. cit., p. 51.

65 Gorbachev (1995), *Zhizn'*, op. cit., vol. 1, p. 265. The Russian reads *tak dal'she zhit' nel'zya*.

66 Russian TV interview with Gorbachev, 7 February 1992. Cited in BBC SWB SU/1300/ B/2.

67 Ibid.

68 In an interview in February 2002, Gorbachev highlighted how seriously the leadership considered the problem of consumer deficits. A commission was set up, under the control of Ivan Kapitonov, to solve the 'problem' of women's pantyhose.

69 Gorbachev and Mlynar, op. cit., p. 67.

70 Gorbachev (2000), op. cit., p. 55. Gorbachev also noted that 'the Eastern European nations exerted a far greater influence on the moral and political situation in the USSR than Western nations did'. See M.S. Gorbachev and D. Ikeda, *Moral Lessons of the Twentieth Century* (London: I.B. Tauris, 2005).

71 Interview with Gorbachev in *The Nation*, 2–9 February 1998. These themes are also evident in Gorbachev's latest work, *Ponyat' perestroiku…*, where he talks about 'bureaucratic super-centralization', p. 19, and also in an interview in *Kansas City Star*, 29 October 2005, where he said that 'our country had been stifled because of the absence of freedom'.

72 *USA Today*, 5 April 2006.

73 Gorbachev and Mlynar, op. cit., p. 115.

74 Ibid., p. 101.

75 Gorbachev (2002), op. cit., p. 59.

76 Gorbachev and Ikeda, op. cit., pp. 55, 93.

77 Ibid., p. 51.

78 *USA Today*, 5 April 2006.

79 Gorbachev (1995), *Zhizn'*, op. cit., vol. 1, p. 396.

80 Gorbachev and Mlynar, op. cit., p. 115.

81 Interview in *Daily Times*, 17 April 2006.

82 *IHT*, 9 November 2007.

83 *Kansas City Star*, 29 October 2005.

84 Gorbachev in the *Harvard University Gazette*, op. cit. (2002); Gorbachev on *Vox Populi*, NTV, 2 March 2001.

85 *USA Today*, 5 April 2006.

86 Interview with Gorbachev on his 65th birthday on NTV, 2 March 1996. Cited in BBC SWB EE/D2551/B, 3 March 1996. The problem of lack of consumer goods was also noted in his interview with CNN for the series on the Cold War. See http://www.cnn.com/SPECIALS/cold.war/episodes/22/interviews/gorbachev/ (accessed 28 April 2005).

87 Interview with Gorbachev on Channel 1 TV Moscow, 7 February 1992. Cited in BBC SWB SU/1300/B/1.

88 Interview with the *Guardian*, op. cit. (1992). He repeated this comment in an interview on NTV on 7 March 2004.

89 Gorbachev (1995), *Zhizn'*, op. cit., vol. 1, p. 490.

90 Ibid., pp. 490–1.

91 See a recent interview (2006), which can be viewed at http://www.youtube.com/watch?v=efWS8YHk8X8

92 Russian TV interview with Gorbachev, 7 February 1992. Cited in BBC SWB SU/1300/B/1.

93 Gorbachev (2000), op. cit., p. 57.

94 Gorbachev on *Vox Populi*, NTV, 2 March 2001.

95 *IHT*, 9 November 2007.

96 Gorbachev and Mlynar, op. cit., p. 92.

97 Ibid., p. 101.

98 Gorbachev (2000), op. cit., p. 59.

99 Gorbachev in the *Harvard University Gazette*, op. cit. (2002).

100 Gorbachev (2000), op. cit., p. 62.

101 Ibid, p. 96.

102 Ibid., p. 97.

103 Ibid., pp. 102–4.

104 'Gorbachev Reflects on the Legacy of the Coup', interview with RFE/RL, 18 August 2006.

105 *RFE/RL Bulletin*, 18 August 2006.

106 Gorbachev (1995), *Zhizn'*, op. cit., vol. 1, see Chapters 16–18.

107 Gorbachev and Ikeda (2005), op. cit., p. 51.

108 Gorbachev (2000), op. cit., p. 187.

109 Ibid., p. 222.

110 Ibid., Chapter 28.

111 Gorbachev, *Zhizn'* (1995), op. cit., vol. 2. Chapters 30 to 37 deal with relations with the socialist countries.

112 Gorbachev interview with Jonathan Steele in the *Guardian*, 24 December 1992.

113 M.S. Gorbachev, *Kak eto bylo* (Moscow: Vagrius, 1999), p. 171.

114 Gorbachev, (2000), op. cit., p. 53.

115 Gorbachev, *Zhizn'* (1995), op. cit., vol. 1, p. 439.

116 Ibid., p. 448.

117 Gorbachev interview in *Newsweek*, 7 May 2001. Gorbachev said here that *perestroika* had enabled democracy to 'take root', and that he had pulled his country out of totalitarianism and moved it towards democracy.

118 *Kommersant-Daily*, 2 March 1995.

119 Gorbachev (2000), op. cit., pp. 57–8, 205.

120 Mikhail Gorbachev (1996), op. cit., p. 673.

121 Ibid., p. 673.

122 See a recent interview (2006), which can be viewed at http://www.youtube.com/watch?v=efWS8YHk8X8

123 Gorbachev, *Zhizn'* (1995), op. cit., p. 330.

124 Gorbachev (2000), op. cit., p. 159.

125 'It was all his fault', *New Yorker*, 18 November 1996.

126 Ibid.

127 Gorbachev (2000), op. cit., p. 3.

128 Press conference with Mikhail Gorbachev, 6 November 2003. Cited in http://www.cdi.org/russia/johnson/7412–1.cfm

129 Gorbachev (2000), op. cit., pp. 11–12.

130 Ibid., pp. 20–2.

131 *RFE/RL Bulletin*, 1 March 2006.

132 The Founding Congress was in November 2001. Gorbachev was elected head of the party. Konstantin Titov was elected as Chairman. Gorbachev resigned on 22 May 2004 after falling out with Titov.

133 Gorbachev, (2002), op. cit., p. 78.

134 Gorbachev and Ikeda (2005), op. cit., p. 116.

135 *RFE/RL Bulletin*, 1 March 2006.

136 Gorbachev, 'Looking Back on *Perestroika*', *Harvard University Gazette*, op. cit.

137 Gorbachev, *Zhizn'* (1995), op. cit., vol. 1, pp. 369–75.

138 Gorbachev (2000), op. cit., p. 110.

139 Gorbachev, *Zhizn'* (1995) op. cit., vol. 2, pp. 621–2.

140 Gorbachev, *Zhizn'* (1995), op. cit., vol. 1, pp. 374–5; See also B. Yeltsin, *Midnight Diaries* (London: Phoenix, 2000), pp. 359–66.

141 'Gorbachev on his Legacy', *Newsweek International*, 7 May 2001, p. 74.

142 Interview with Gorbachev on BBC *Newsnight*, 23 September 2004.

143 *Wall Street Journal*, 1 December 2007.

144 'After Raisa', *Mail on Sunday*, 5 May 1999.

145 Interview with Gorbachev, *The Nation*, 9 February 1998.

146 Gorbachev and Ikeda, op. cit. (2005), p. 126.

147 *Kansas City Star*, 29 October 2005.

148 *IHT*, 9 November 2007.

149 'Looking Back on *Perestroika*', op. cit.

150 Gorbachev and Mlynar, op. cit. (2002), pp. 197–213.

151 Ibid., pp. 204–9.

152 'After Raisa', op. cit.

153 Interview with CRISIS, 1 February 2002.

154 Gorbachev and Mlynar, op. cit. (2002), pp. 212–13.

Conclusion

1 *Sunday Times*, 5 June 2005.

2 All these awards are courtesy of the Gorbachev Foundation website and have not been independently corroborated. In addition, he has been awarded the following honorary degrees: University of Virginia, PhD (USA, 1993), The Jepson School of Leadership (PhD, Leadership) (Richmond, 1993), Autonomous University of Madrid (Madrid, Spain, October 1990), Complutence University (Madrid, Spain, October 1990), University of Buenos Aires (Argentina, 1992), University of Cuyo (Mendoza, Argentina, 1992), C. Mendes University (Brazil, 1992), University of Chile (Chile, 1992), University of Anahuac (Mexico, 1992), Bar Illan University (Israel, 1992), Ben Gurion University (Israel, 1992), Emory University (Atlanta, USA, 1992), Pandyon University (Piraeus, Greece, 1993), Institute of International Law and International Relations, Aristotelian University (Thessaloniki, Greece, 1993), School of Law, Aristotelian University (Thessaloniki, Greece, 1993), University of Bristol (UK, 1993), University of Calgary (Canada, 1993), Carlton University (Canada, 1993), Soka Gakkai International (President Ikeda) (Japan, 1993), Kung Khi University (Korea, 1995), University of Durham (UK, 1995), Modern University of Lisbon (Portugal, 1995), Soka University (Japan, 1997), University of Tromso (Norway, 1998). He has also been given 'Honour of the City Awards' by the following cities: Berlin (FRG, 1992), Aberdeen (UK, 1993), Piraeus (Greece, 1993), Florence (Italy, 1994), Sesto San Giovanni (Italy, 1995), Kardamyla (island of Chios, Greece, 1995), El Paso (Key of the City) (USA, 1998), Terni (Italy, 2001).

3 Eric Hobsbawm, 'An Assembly of Ghosts', *London Review of Books*, vol. 27, 8, April 2005.

4 M.S. Gorbachev and D. Ikeda, *Moral Lessons of the Twentieth Century* (London: I. B. Tauris, 2005), pp. 8, 18

Bibliography

Non-Russian/Soviet sources

Adomeit, H., 'Gorbachev and German Unification: Revision of Thinking, Realignment of Power', *Problems of Communism*, July–August 1990

Amann, R., 'Searching for an Appropriate Concept of Soviet Politics: The Politics of Hesitant Modernisation', *British Journal of Political Science*, 16, 1986

Amann, R., 'Soviet Politics in the Gorbachev Era: The End of Hesitant Modernization', *British Journal of Political Science*, 3, 20, July 1990

Aron, L., *Boris Yeltsin: A Revolutionary Life*, (London: HarperCollins, 2000)

Aslund, A., 'Gorbachev's Economic Advisers', *Soviet Economy*, 3, 3, 1987

Aslund, A., 'Gorbachev, Perestroika and Economic Crisis', *Problems of Communism*, January–April 1991

Aslund, A., *Gorbachev's Struggle for Economic Reform* (Ithaca: Cornell University Press, 1991)

Aslund, A., *How Russia Became a Market Economy* (Washington: Brookings Institution, 1995)

Attar, C., *Gorbachev: The Man and His Ideas* (Delhi: Modern Pubs Dist., 1987)

Bahry, D. and Silver, B., 'Public Perceptions and the Dilemmas of Party Reform in the USSR', *Comparative Political Studies*, 2, 23, July 1990

Baker, J. A., *The Politics of Diplomacy* (New York: G.P. Putnam's Sons 1995)

Balzer, H. D., *5 Years That Shook the World* (Boulder: Westview Press, 1991)

Battle, J. M., 'Uskorenie, Glasnost and Perestroika: The Pattern of Reform under Gorbachev', *Soviet Studies*, 3, 40, July 1988

Beissinger, M., *Nationalist Mobilization and the Collapse of the Soviet State* (New York: Cambridge University Press, 2002)

Bialer, S., 'Gorbachev's Move', *Foreign Policy*, 68, Fall 1987

Bialer, S., 'The Death of Soviet Communism', *Foreign Affairs*, 5, 70, 1991

Bialer, S. and Afferica, J., 'The Genesis of Gorbachev's World', *Foreign Affairs*, 3, 64, 1986

Bialer, S. and Gustafson, T. (eds), *Russia at the Crossroads: The 26th Congress of the CPSU* (London: Allen and Unwin, 1982)

Bialer, S. and Mandelbaum, M. (eds), *Gorbachev's Russia and American Foreign Policy* (Boulder: Westview Press, 1988)

Borcke, A. van, 'Gorbachev's *Perestroika*: Can the Soviet System be Reformed?' in S. Clark, *Gorbachev's Agenda: Changes in Soviet Domestic and Foreign Policy* (Boulder: Westview Press, 1989)

Braithwaite, R., *Across the Moscow River* (New Haven and London: Yale University Press, 2002)

Braun, A. and Day, R. B. 'Gorbachevian Contradictions', *Problems of Communism*, May–June 1990

Breslauer, G. W., 'Evaluating Gorbachev as Leader', *Soviet Economy*, 4, 5, October–December 1989

Breslauer, G. W., *Can Gorbachev's Reforms Succeed?* (Berkeley: Berkeley-Stanford Program in Soviet Studies, 1990)

Breslauer, G. W., 'Understanding Gorbachev: Diverse Perspectives', *Soviet Economy*, 2, 7, April–June 1991

Breslauer, G. W., *Gorbachev and Yeltsin As Leaders* (Cambridge: Cambridge University Press, 2002)

Brown, A., 'Gorbachev: New Man in the Kremlin', *Problems of Communism*, May–June 1985

Brown, A., 'The Soviet Leadership and the Struggle for Political Reform', *Harriman Institute Forum*, 4, 1, April 1988

Brown, A., 'Political Change in the Soviet Union', *World Policy Journal*, 3, 16, 1989

Brown, A., 'Gorbachev's Leadership: Another View', *Soviet Economy*, 2, 6, April–June 1990

Brown, A., *The Gorbachev Factor* (Oxford: Oxford University Press, 1996)

Brown, A., *Seven Years That Changed the World* (Oxford: Oxford University Press, 2007)

Brown, A. and Kaser, M. (eds), *Soviet Policy for the 1980s* (London: Macmillan, 1982)

Brown, A. and Shevtsova, L. (eds), *Gorbachev, Yeltsin and Putin: Political Leadership in Russia's Transition* (Washington: Carnegie Endowment for International Peace, 2001)

Brzezinski, Z., *The Grand Failure* (London: Macdonald, 1990)

Bushnell, J., 'Making History out of Current Events: The Gorbachev Era,' *Slavic Review*, 51, 3, Fall 1992

Butson, T., *Gorbachev: A Biography* (New York: Stein and Day, 1986)

Cappelli, O., 'Comparative Communism's Fall: The First Phase: The Intelligentsia Revolution of 1989-90', *Harriman Institute Forum*, 6, 3, June 1990

Chiesa, G., 'The 28th Congress of the CPSU', *Problems of Communism*, July–August 1990

Clark, S., *Gorbachev's Agenda: Changes in Soviet Domestic and Foreign Policy* (Boulder: Westview Press, 1989)

Collins, R., 'Predictions in Macrosociology: The Case of the Soviet Collapse', *American Journal of Sociology*, 100, 6, 1995

Connor, W., 'Social Policy under Gorbachev', *Problems of Communism*, July–August 1986

Cooper, J., 'Construction… Reconstruction… Deconstruction', in C. Ward and C. Merridale (eds), *Perestroika: The Historical Perspective* (London: Edward Arnold, 1991)

Cox, M. (ed.), *Rethinking the Soviet Collapse: Sovietology, the Death of Communism and the New Russia* (New York: Cassell, 1998)

D'Agostino, A., *Gorbachev's Revolution* (New York: New York University Press, 1998)

Dahm, H., 'What Restoring Leninism Means', *Studies in Soviet Thought*, 39, 1990

Dallin, A., 'Gorbachev's Foreign Policy and "New Political Thinking" in the USSR', in P. Juviler and H. Kimura (eds), *Gorbachev's Reforms: US and Japanese Assessments* (New York: Aldine de Gruyter, 1988)

Dallin, A. and Lapidus, G. (eds), *The Soviet System: From Crisis to Collapse*, rev. edn (Boulder: Westview Press, 1995)

Daniels, R. V., *The End of the Communist Revolution* (London: Routledge, 1993)

Dawisha, K., *Eastern Europe, Gorbachev and Reform* (New York: Cambridge University Press, 1988)

Devlin, K., 'L'Unita on "Secret History" of Andreeva Letter', *Radio Liberty Research Report*, 215/88, 26 May 1988

Djilas, M., *The New Class* (New York: Praeger, 1957)

Doder, D. and Branson, L., *Gorbachev: Heretic in the Kremlin* (New York: Penguin, 1991)

Elliott, I., 'The Great Reformer', *Survey*, 1, 29, 1985

Federal Institute for Soviet and International Studies, *The Soviet Union 1987–89: Perestroika in Crisis* (London: Longman, 1990)

Feher, F. and Arato, A., *Gorbachev: The Debate* (Oxford: Polity, 1989)

Fleron, F. J., Jr, and Hoffmann, F. P., 'Sovietology and Perestroika: Methodology and Lessons from the Past', *Harriman Institute Forum*, 1, 5, September 1991

Frank, P., 'The End of Perestroika', *The World Today*, 5, 46, May 1990

Galeotti, M., *Gorbachev and His Revolution* (London: Macmillan, 1997)

Garthoff, R., *The Great Transition* (Washington: Brookings Institute, 1994)

Gati, C., 'Gorbachev and Eastern Europe', *Foreign Affairs*, 5, 65, Summer 1987

Gellner, E., '*Perestroika* Observed', *Government and Opposition*, 7, 25, 1990

Gill, G., *The Collapse of a Single-Party System: The Disintegration of the Communist Party of the Soviet Union* (New York: Cambridge University Press, 1995)

Gill, G. and Markwick, R., *Russia's Stillborn Democracy? From Gorbachev to Yeltsin* (Oxford: Oxford University Press, 2000)

Gitelman, Z., Pravda, A. and White, S. (eds), *Developments in Soviet Politics* (London: Macmillan, 1990)

Gleason, A., *Totalitarianism: The Inner History of the Cold War* (New York: Oxford University Press, 1995)

Goldman, M., *What Went Wrong With Perestroika* (New York: Norton, 1992)

Gooding, J., 'Gorbachev and Democracy', *Soviet Studies*, 2, 42, April 1990

Gooding, J., 'The XXVIII Congress of the CPSU in Perspective', *Soviet Studies*, 2, 43, 1991

Gooding, J., 'Perestroika As Revolution from Within', *Russian Review*, 51, 1992

Gooding, J., 'Perestroika and the Russian Revolution of 1991', *Slavonic and East European Review*, 71, 2, 1993

Gooding, J., *Socialism in Russia* (Basingstoke: Palgrave, 2002)

Goodman, E., 'Gorbachev Takes Charge', *Survey*, 2, 29, 1985

Grey, R. D., Jennisch, L. A. and Tyler, A. S., 'Soviet Public Opinion and the Gorbachev Reforms', *Slavic Review*, 2, 49, Summer 1990

Gustafson, T. and Mann, D., 'Gorbachev's First Year: Building Power and Authority', *Problems of Communism*, May–June 1986

Gustafson, T. and Mann, D., 'Gorbachev's Next Gamble', *Problems of Communism*, 4, 36, July–August 1987

Gunlicks, A. B. and Treadaway, J., *The Soviet Union Under Gorbachev: Assessing the First Year* (New York: Praeger, 1987)

Hahn, G. M., *Russia's Revolution from Above, 1985–2000: Reform, Transition, and Revolution in the Fall of the Soviet Communist Regime* (New Brunswick: Transaction, 2002)

Hahn, J., 'Power to the Soviets', *Problems of Communism*, January–February 1989

Hale, H., *The Strange Death of the Soviet Union* (Cambridge: Davis Center for Russian Studies, 1999)

Hallenberg, J., *The Demise of the Soviet Union: Analysing the Collapse of a State* (Burlington: Ashgate, 2002)

Hamann, H., 'Soviet Defector on Origins of "the New Thinking"', *RFE/RL Report on the USSR*, 20 October 1989

Hanson, P., 'Gorbachev's Economic Strategy', *Soviet Economy*, 4, 1, 1985

Hanson, P., 'The Shape of Gorbachev's Economic Reform', *Soviet Economy*, 4, 2, 1986

Hanson, P., *The Rise and Fall of the Soviet Economy* (London: Pearson, 2003)

Hasegawa, T., 'Gorbachev, the New Thinking of Soviet Foreign Security Policy and the Military: Recent Trends and Implications', in P. Juviler and H. Kimura (eds), *Gorbachev's Reforms: US and Japanese Assessments* (New York: Aldine de Gruyter, 1988)

Hasegawa, T. and Pravda, A. (eds), *Perestroika: Soviet Domestic and Foreign Policies* (London: Sage, 1990)

Hauslohner, P., 'Gorbachev's Social Contract', *Soviet Economy*, 1, 3, 1987

Healey, D., *The Time of My Life* (London: Michael Joseph, 1989)

Hegedus, A., *et al.*, *The Humanisation of Socialism* (London: Allison and Busby, 1976)

Heller, M., 'Gorbachev for Beginners', *Survey*, 29, 1, 1985

Hellie, R., 'An Historian's Formulation of Gorbachev's Real Problems', *Russian History*, 1, 16, 1989

Hewett, E., 'Gorbachev's Economic Strategy: A Preliminary Assessment', *Soviet Economy*, 4, 1, 1985

Hewett, E., 'Gorbachev at Two Years: Perspectives on Economic Reform', *Soviet Economy*, 4, 2, 1986

Hewett, E. and Winston, V. (eds), *Milestones in Glasnost and Perestroika: Politics and People* (Washington: Brookings Institution, 1991)

Hill, R. and Dellenbrant, J., *Gorbachev and Perestroika: Towards a New Socialism?* (Aldershot: Edward Elgar, 1989)

Hill, R. J., 'The CPSU: Decline and Collapse', *Irish Slavonic Studies*, 12, 1991

Hill, R. J., 'The CPSU: From Monolith to Pluralist?', *Soviet Studies*, 2, 43, 1991

Hill, R. J. and Frank, P., 'Gorbachev's Cabinet Building', *Journal of Communist Studies*, 2, 19, 1986

Hoffmann, E. P., 'Technology and Political Change in Gorbachev's and Brezhnev's Ideologies', *Journal of Soviet and East European Studies*, 3–4, 5, 1988

Holfheinz, P., 'Innovation and Conservatism in the New Soviet Leadership', *New Left Review*, 157, 1986

Holfheinz, P., 'Piecing Together the Gorbachev Puzzle', *Journal of Communist Studies*, 3, 20, 1987

Holloway, D., 'Gorbachev's New Thinking', *Foreign Affairs*, 1, 68, 1988/89

Hosking, G., *The Awakening of the Soviet Union* (London: Heinemann, 1990)

Hosking, G., *A History of the Soviet Union* (London: Fontana, 1994)

Hough, J., 'Soviet Succession: Issues and Personalities', *Problems of Communism*, September–October 1982

Hough, J., 'Andropov's First Year', *Problems of Communism*, November–December 1983

Hough, J., 'The Gorbachev Reform: A Maximal Case', *Soviet Economy*, 4, 2, 1986

Hough, J., 'Gorbachev Consolidating Power', *Problems of Communism*, 4, 36, July–August 1987

Hough, J., 'Gorbachev's Politics', *Foreign Affairs*, 68, 1990

Hough, J., *Russia and the West: Gorbachev and the Politics of Reform* (New York: Touchstone, 1990)

Hough, J., 'Understanding Gorbachev: The Importance of Politics', *Soviet Economy*, 2, 7, April–June 1991

Hough, J., *Democratization and Revolution in the USSR* (Washington, DC: Brookings Institution, 1997)

Howe, G., *Conflict of Loyalty* (London: Macmillan, 1995)

Huber, R. T. and Kelley, D. R. (eds), *Perestroika-Era Politics: The New Soviet Legislature and Gorbachev's Political Reforms* (Armonk: M. E. Sharpe, 1991)

Hyland, W. G., 'Reagan-Gorbachev III', *Foreign Affairs*, 1, 66, 1988

Ionescu, G., *Leadership In an Interdependent World* (Harlow: Longman, 1991)

Jensen, B. and Weil, B., 'Utopia and Development in the Building of Socialism from Lenin to Gorbachev', *Journal of Soviet and East European Studies*, 3–4, 5, 1988

Joyce, W., Ticktin, H. and White, S. (eds), *Gorbachev and Gorbachevism* (London: Frank Cass, 1988)

Judson Mitchell, R. and Arrington, R. S., 'Gorbachev, Ideology and the Fate of Soviet Communism', *Communist and Post-Communist Studies*, 33, 4, 2000

Juviler, P. and Kimura, H. (eds), *Gorbachev's Reforms: US and Japanese Assessments* (New York: Aldine de Gruyter, 1988)

Kaiser, R., 'Gorbachev: Triumph and Failure', *Foreign Affairs*, 2, 70, 1991

Kaiser, R. F, *Why Gorbachev Happened. His Triumphs, His Failures and His Fall* (New York: Touchstone, 1992)

Kalyvas, S. N., 'The Decay and Breakdown of Communist One-Party Systems', *Annual Review of Political Science*, 2, 1999

Keep, J., *Last of the Empires* (Oxford: Oxford University Press, 1996)

Kelley, D. R. and Davis, S. (eds), *The Sons of Sergei: Khrushchev and Gorbachev as Reformers* (Westport: Praeger, 1992)

Khalilzad, Z., 'Moscow's Afghan War', *Problems of Communism*, January–February 1986

Kotkin, S., *Armageddon Averted: The Soviet Collapse 1970–2000* (New York: Oxford University Press, 2001)

Kusin, V., 'Gorbachev and Eastern Europe', *Problems of Communism*, January–February 1986

Kusters, H. J., 'The Kohl–Gorbachev Meetings in Moscow and the Caucasus, 1990', *Cold War History*, 2, 2, 2002

Lapidus, G., 'Gorbachev and Reform of the Soviet System', *Daedalus*, 2, 16, Spring 1987

Lapidus, G., 'Gorbachev's Nationalities Problem', *Foreign Affairs*, Fall 1989

Larrabee, F. S. and Lynch, A., 'Gorbachev: The Road to Reykjavik', *Foreign Policy*, 65, Winter 1986/87

Laue, T. von, *Why Lenin? Why Stalin? Why Gorbachev?* 3rd edn (London: Longman, 1992)

Laqueur, W., *The Dream That Failed* (Oxford: Oxford University Press, 1994)

Legvold, R., 'Revolution in Soviet Foreign Policy', *Foreign Affairs*, 1, 68, 1988/89

Lendvai, P., 'Who is afraid of Mikhail Gorbachev?', *Survey*, 2, 29, 1985

Lerner, L. and Treadgold, D. (eds), *Gorbachev and the Soviet Future* (Boulder: Westview Press, 1988)

Light, M., 'New Thinking in Soviet Foreign Policy', *Coexistence*, 24, 1987

Luca, A. de, *Politics, Diplomacy and the Media: Gorbachev's Legacy in the West* (Westport: Praeger, 1998)

Lundestad, G., 'Imperial Overstretch: Mikhail Gorbachev and the End of the Cold War', *Cold War History*, 1, 1, 2000

Lynch, A., 'Does Gorbachev Matter Anymore?', *Foreign Affairs*, 3, 69, Winter 1990

Lyne, R., 'Gorbachev's Public Diplomacy', in R. F. Laird (ed.), *Soviet Foreign Policy* (New York: Proceedings of Academy of Political Science, 1987)

McAuley, M., 'Soviet Political Reform in a Comparative Context', *Harriman Institute Forum*, 10, 2, October 1989

McCauley, M., *Gorbachev* (London: Longman, 1998)

McCauley, M., 'The Gorbachev Phenomenon', *Slavonic and East European Review*, 2, 76, 1998

McFaul, M., *Russia's Unfinished Revolution: Political Change from Gorbachev to Putin* (Ithaca and London: Cambridge University Press, 2001)

McHugh, J. T., 'Last of the Enlightened Despots: A Comparison of President Mikhail Gorbachev and Emperor Joseph II', *Social Science Journal*, 32, 1, 1995

Major, J., *John Major: The Autobiography* (London: HarperCollins, 2000)

Malia, M., *The Soviet Tragedy* (New York: Free Press, 1994)

Malcolm, N., 'De-Stalinisation and Soviet Foreign Policy: The Roots of New Thinking', in T. Hasegawa and A. Pravda (eds), *Perestroika: Soviet Domestic and Foreign Policies* (London: Sage, 1990)

March, L., *Egor Ligachev: A Conservative Reformer in the Gorbachev Period*, Research Paper in Russian and East European Studies, University of Birmingham, 1997

Marcuse, H., *Soviet Marxism* (London: Routledge and Kegan Paul, 1958)

Matlock, J. F., *Autopsy on an Empire* (New York: Random House, 1995)

Mau, V. and Starodubrovskaya, I., *The Challenge of Revolution* (Oxford: Oxford University Press, 2001)

Medvedev, Z., *Gorbachev* (Oxford: Basil Blackwell, 1986)

Mendras, M., 'Soviet Foreign Policy: In Search of Critical Thinking', in T. Hasegawa and A. Pravda (eds), *Perestroika: Soviet Domestic and Foreign Policies* (London: Sage, 1990)

Meissner, B., 'Transition in the Kremlin', *Problems of Communism*, January–February 1983

Meyer, S. M., 'Sources and Prospects of Gorbachev's New Thinking on Security', *International Security*, 2, vol. 13, Fall 1988

Migranyan, A., 'Gorbachev's Leadership: A Soviet View', *Soviet Economy*, 2, 6, April–June 1990

Miller, J., *Mikhail Gorbachev and the End of Soviet Power* (Basingstoke: Palgrave Macmillan, 1993)

Miller, R. F. *et al.* (eds), *Gorbachev at the Helm: A New Era in Soviet Politics?* (London: Croom Helm, 1987)

Morrison, D. *et al.* (eds), *Mikhail S. Gorbachev: An Intimate Biography* (New York: Time, 1988)

Moses, J. C., 'Democratic Reform in the Gorbachev Era: Dimensions of Reform in the Soviet Union 1986–89', *Russian Review*, 48, 1989

Murarka, D., *Gorbachev: The Limits of Power* (London: Hutchinson, 1988)

Narkiewicz, O., *Soviet Leaders* (Brighton: Wheatsheaf Books, 1986)

Nevers, R. de, *The Soviet Union and Eastern Europe: The End of an Era* (New York: Adelphi Papers, 1990)

Olcott, M. B., 'The Soviet (Dis)Union', *Foreign Policy*, 82, Spring 1991

Parker, J. W., *The Kremlin in Transition* (Boston: Unwin Hyman, 1991)

Parrott, B., 'Soviet National Security under Gorbachev', *Problems of Communism*, November–December 1988

Pipes, R., 'The Soviet Union Adrift', *Foreign Affairs*, 1, 70, 1991

Pipes, R., 'Misinterpreting the Cold War', *Foreign Affairs*, 74, 1, January–February 1995

Ploss, S., 'A New Soviet Era?', *Foreign Policy*, 62, 1986

Pravda, A., 'Is There a Gorbachev Foreign Policy?', in W. Joyce, H. Ticktin and S. White (eds), *Gorbachev and Gorbachevism* (London: Frank Cass, 1988)

Rakovski, M., *Towards an East European Marxism* (London: Allison and Busby, 1978)

Read, C., *The Making and Breaking of the Soviet System* (Basingstoke: Palgrave, 2001)

Reagan, R., *An American Life* (London: Hutchinson, 1999)

Reddaway, P., 'The Quality of Gorbachev's Leadership', *Soviet Economy*, 2, 6, April–June 1990

Remington, T., 'A Socialist Pluralism of Opinions: Glasnost and Policy-making under Gorbachev', *Russian Review*, 48, 1989

Remnick, D., *Lenin's Tomb* (London: Penguin, 1994)

Rowley, D., 'Interpretations of the End of the Soviet Union: Three Paradigms', *Kritika*, 2, 2, 2001

Roxburgh, A., *The Second Russian Revolution* (London: BBC Books, 1991)

Ruge, G., *Gorbachev: A Biography* (London: Chatto and Windus, 1991)

Rumer, B., 'Realities of Gorbachev's Economic Programme', *Problems of Communism*, May–June 1986

Sakwa, R., *Soviet Politics* (London: Routledge, 1989)

Sakwa, R., *Gorbachev and His Reforms 1985–90* (London: Routledge, 1990)

Sanders, S., *Living off the West: Gorbachev's Secret Agenda and Why it Will Fail* (Lanham: Madison Books, 1990)

Sandle, M., 'The Final Word: The Draft Party Programme of July/August 1991', *Europe/Asia Studies*, 48, 1996

Sandle, M., *A Short History of Soviet Socialism* (London: University College London Press, 1999)

Satter, D., *The Age of Delirium: The Decline and Fall of the Soviet Union* (New York: Alfred A. Knopf, 1996)

Schmidt-Hauer, C., *Gorbachev: The Path to Power* (London: Pan, 1986)

Schroeder, G., 'Gorbachev: Radically Implementing Brezhnev's Reform', *Soviet Economy*, 4, 2, 1986

Schroeder, G., 'Anatomy of Gorbachev's Economic Reform', *Soviet Economy*, 3, 3, 1987

Sestanovich, S., 'Gorbachev's Foreign Policy: A Diplomacy of Decline', *Problems of Communism*, January–February 1988

Sheehy, G., *Gorbachev: A One-Man Revolution* (New York: Mandarin, 1990)

Shlapentokh, V., 'Alexander II and Mikhail Gorbachev: Two Reformers in Historical Perspective', *Russian History/Histoire Russe*, 4, 17, Winter 1990

Shub, A., 'The Fourth Russian Revolution: Historical Perspectives', *Problems of Communism*, November–December 1991

Shultz, G. P., *Turmoil and Triumph* (New York: Charles Scribner's Sons, 1993)

Shumaker, D., 'Understanding Gorbachev's Foreign Policy', *Communist and Post-Communist Studies*, 3, 27, 1994

Simes, D. K., 'Gorbachev: A New Foreign Policy', *Foreign Affairs*, 3, 65, 1986/87

Skinner, K. (ed.), *Turning Points in Ending the Cold War* (Stanford: Hoover Institution Press, 2008)

Smart, C., 'Gorbachev's Lenin: The Myth in Service to *Perestroika*', *Studies in Comparative Communism*, 1, 23, Spring 1990

Smith, H., *The New Russians* (New York: Random House, 1990)

Snyder, J., 'The Gorbachev Revolution: Waning of Soviet Expansionism?', *International Security*, 3, 12, Winter 1987/88

Solovyov, V. and Klepikova, E., *Inside the Kremlin* (London: Allen and Unwin, 1987)

Sondhi, M. L., *Beyond Perestroika: Choices and Challenges Facing Gorbachev* (New Delhi: Abhiner Publications, 1989)

Spring, D., *The Impact of Gorbachev* (London: Pinter, 1991)

Steele, J., *Eternal Russia* (London: Faber and Faber, 1994)

Stein, J. G., 'Political Learning by Doing: Gorbachev as Uncommitted Thinker and Motivated Learner', *International Organisation*, 48, 2, 1994

Sternthal, S., *Gorbachev's Reforms: De-Stalinisation Through De-Militarisation* (Westport: Praeger, 1997)

Strayer, R., *Why Did the Soviet Union Collapse? Understanding Historical Change* (Armonk: M. E. Sharpe, 1998)

Strayer, R., 'Decolonisation, Democratisation and Communist Reform: The Soviet Collapse in Comparative Perspective', *Journal of World History*, 12, 2, 2001

Suny, R., 'State, Civil Society and Ethnic Cultural Consolidation', in A. Dallin and G. Lapidus (eds), *The Soviet System in Crisis* (Boulder: Westview Press, 1991)

Suny, R. G., *The Revenge of the Past: Nationalism, Revolution and the Collapse of the Soviet Union* (Stanford: Stanford University Press, 1993)

Suraska, W., *How the Soviet Union Disappeared* (London and Durham: Duke University Press, 1998)

Surovell, J., 'Gorbachev's Last Year: Leftist or Rightist?', *Europe-Asia Studies*, 46, 3, 1994

Talbott, S. (ed.), *M. S. Gorbachev: An Intimate Biography* (New York: Signet Books, 1988)

Taranovski, T. and McInerny, P. (eds), *Reform in Modern Russian History: Progress or Cycle?* (New York: Cambridge University Press, 1995)

Tatu, M., 'The 19th Party Conference', *Problems of Communism*, May–August 1988

Tatu, M., *Mikhail Gorbachev: The Origins of Perestroika* (New York: Columbia University Press, 1991)

Taubman, W., Khrushchev, S. and Gleason, A. (eds), *Nikita Khrushchev* (New Haven and London: Yale University Press, 2000)

Teague, E. and Mann, D., 'Gorbachev's Dual Role', *Problems of Communism,* January–February 1990

Thatcher, M., *The Downing Street Years* (London: HarperCollins, 1995)

Thom, F., *The Gorbachev Phenomenon* (London: Continuum, 1989)

Thompson, J., *A Vision Unfulfilled* (Lexington: D.C. Heath, 1996)

Tinguy, A. de (ed.), *The Fall of the Soviet Empire* (Boulder: Columbia University Press, 1997)

Tismaneanu, V., *The Revolutions of 1989* (London: Routledge, 1999)

Tolstykh, V. (ed.), *A Millennium Salute to Mikhail Gorbachev on his Seventieth Birthday* (Moscow: R. Valent, 2001)

Tompson, W. J., 'Khrushchev and Gorbachev as Reformers', *British Journal of Political Science,* 23, 1, 1993

Tucker, R., *Political Culture and Leadership in Soviet Russia* (Brighton: Wheatsheaf Books, 1987)

Urban, G., *Can the Revolution be Remade?* (London: Institute for European Defence and Strategic Studies, 1988)

Various, 'Roundtable on Soviet Economic Reform', *Soviet Economy,* 1, 3, 1987

Various, 'What's Happening in Moscow?', *National Interest,* 8, Summer 1987

Various, *Soviet Union/Union Soviétique,* 2–3, 16, 1989

Various, 'Mikhail S. Gorbachev: A Scholarly Symposium on His Years in Power', *Soviet and Post-Soviet Review,* 19, 1–3, 1992

Various, 'The Collapse of the Soviet Union', *Journal of Cold War Studies,* 5, 1, 2003 and 6, 1, 2004

Various, 'Was the Soviet System Reformable?', *Slavic Review,* 63, 4, 2004

Volkogonov, D., *Autopsy of an Empire: The 7 Leaders Who Built the Soviet Regime* (New York: Free Press, 1998)

Walker, R., *Six Years That Shook the World* (Manchester: Manchester University Press, 1993)

Ward, C. and Merridale, C. (eds), *Perestroika: The Historical Perspective* (London: Edward Arnold, 1991)

White, S., 'Democratisation in the USSR', *Soviet Studies,* 1, 42, January 1990

White, S., *Gorbachev in Power* (Cambridge: Cambridge University Press, 1990)

White, S., *Gorbachev and After* (Cambridge: Cambridge University Press, 1991)

White, S., 'Rethinking the CPSU', *Soviet Studies,* 3, 43, 1991

White, S., *After Gorbachev* (Cambridge: Cambridge University Press, 1992)

White, S., 'Communists and Their Party in the Late Soviet Period', *Slavonic and East European Review,* 72, 4, 1994

White, S., 'The Failure of CPSU Democratisation', *Slavonic and East European Review,* 4, 75, 1997

White, S., *Communism and Its Collapse* (New York: Routledge, 2001)

White, S., di Leo, R. and Cappelli, O., *The Soviet Transition from Gorbachev to Yeltsin* (London: Frank Cass, 1993)

Wieczynski, J. L., *The Gorbachev Reader* (Salt Lake City: Charles Schlacks Jr, 1993)

Woodby, S. and Evans, A. B., Jr (eds), *Restructuring Soviet Ideology: Gorbachev's New Thinking* (Boulder: Westview Press, 1990)

Yanov, A., '*Perestroika* and Its American Critics', *Slavic Review,* Winter 1988

Young, C., 'The Strategy of Political Liberalisation: A Comparative View of Gorbachev's Reforms', *World Politics,* 45, 1, 1992

'Z', 'To the Stalin Mausoleum', *Daedalus,* January 1990

Zemtsov, I., *Gorbachev: Between Past and Present* (Fairfax: Herobooks, 1987)

Zemtsov, I., and Farrar, J., *Gorbachev: The Man and the System* (New Brunswick: Transaction, 1989)

Zubok, V., 'Gorbachev and the End of the Cold War: Perspectives on History and Personality', *Cold War History*, 2, 2, 2002

Russian/Soviet sources

Boldin, V., *Ten Years That Shook the World* (New York: Basic Books, 1994)

Chernyaev, A., *My 6 Years with Gorbachev* (Pennsylvania: Penn State University Press, 2000)

Gorbachev, M. S., *Zhivoe tvorchestvo naroda* (Moscow: Politizdat, 1984)

Gorbachev, M. S., *Perestroika: New Thinking for Our Country and the World* (London: Fontana Collins, 1987)

Gorbachev, M. S., *Izbrannye rechi i stati*, iv (Moscow: Politizdat, 1988)

Gorbachev, M. S., *The August Coup* (New York: HarperCollins, 1991)

Gorbachev, M. S., *Dekabr1991. Moya pozitsiya* (Moscow: Novosti, 1992)

Gorbachev, M. S., *Gody trudnykh resheniye* (Moscow: Alpha-Print, 1993)

Gorbachev, M. S., *The State of the World. Revisioning Global Priorities* (San Francisco: Harper, 1995)

Gorbachev, M. S., *The Search for a New Beginning: Developing a New Civilization* (San Francisco: Harper, 1995)

Gorbachev, M. S., *Zhizn' i reformy*, 2 vols (Moscow: Novosti, 1995)

Gorbachev, M. S., *Memoirs* (London: Bantam Books, 1997)

Gorbachev, M. S., *Kak eto bylo* (Moscow: Vagrius, 1999)

Gorbachev, M. S. and Mlynar, Z., *On My Country and the World* (New York: Columbia University Press, 2000)

Gorbachev, M. S., *Conversations with Gorbachev: On Perestroika, the Prague Spring and the Crossroads of Socialism* (New York: Columbia University Press, 2002).

Gorbachev, M. S., *Ponyat' perestroiku* (Moscow: Al'pina Biznes Buks, 2006)

Gorbachev, M. S. and Ikeda, D., *Moral Lessons of the Twentieth Century* (London: I. B. Tauris, 2005)

Gorbachev, R., *I Hope* (London: HarperCollins, 1991)

Grachev, A., *The Inside Story of the Collapse of the Soviet Union* (Boulder: Westview Press, 1995)

Grachev, A., *Gorbachev* (Moscow: Vagrius, 2001)

Korobeinikov, A. A., *Gorbachev: drugoe litso* (Moscow: Respublika, 1996)

Ligachev, Y., *Inside Gorbachev's Kremlin* (Boulder: Westview Press, 1993)

Medvedev, R., '...I sprava mogut byt' radikaly', *Sobesednik*, 40, September 1989

Palazchenko, P., *My Years with Gorbachev and Shevardnadze* (Pennsylvania: Penn State University Press, 1997)

Pankin, B., *The Last Hundred Days of the USSR* (London: Tauris, 1996)

Ryzhkov, N., *Perestroika: istoriya predatel'stv* (Moscow: Novosti, 1992)

Ryzhkov, N., *Desyat' let velikikh potryasenii* (Moscow: Assotsiatsiya Kniga. Prosveshchenie. Miloseride, 1995)

Shakhnazarov, G., 'East–West: The Problem Of De-Ideologising Relations', *Kommunist*, 3, 1989

Shakhnazarov, G., *Tsena svobodu* (Moscow: Vagrius, 1993)

Shakhnazarov, G., *S vozhdyami i bez nikh* (Moscow: Vagrius, 2001)

Shevardnadze, E., *The Future Belongs to Freedom* (London: Sinclair-Stevenson, 1991)

Various, *XIX vsyesoyuznaya konferentsiya kommunisticheskoi partii svetskaya soyuza: stenografich-eskii otchet* (Moscow: Politizdat, 1988)

Yakovlev, A. N., *Predislovie, Obval, Posleslovie* (Moscow: Novosti, 1992)

Yakovlev, A. N., *Gor'kaya chasha* (Yaroslavl': Verkhne-Volzshkoe knizhnoe izdatelstvo, 1994)
Yeltsin, B., *Against the Grain* (London: Jonathan Cape, 1990)
Yeltsin, B., *The View from the Kremlin* (London: HarperCollins, 1994)
Yeltsin, B., *Midnight Diaries* (New York: Public Affairs, 2000)

Index